Leadership

DATE DUE

MAR – – 2006		arrival Date	

DEMCO 38-296

Leadership

Succeeding in
the Private, Public, and
Not-for-Profit Sectors

Editors

Ronald R. Sims *and* Scott A. Quatro

M.E.Sharpe

Armonk, New York
London, England

Library of Congress Cataloging-in-Publication Data

Leadership : succeeding in the private, public, and not-for-profit sectors / edited by Ronald R. Sims
and Scott A. Quatro.
   p. cm.
  Includes bibliographical references and index.
   ISBN 0-7656-1429-4 (hardcover : alk. paper)—ISBN 0-7656-1430-8 (pbk. : alk. paper)
   1. Leadership. 2. Organizational change. I. Sims, Ronald, R. II. Quatro, Scott A., 1968–

HD57.7.L4355 2004
658.4'092—dc22
                                            2004009101

Printed in the United States of America

The paper used in this publication meets the minimum requirements of
American National Standard for Information Sciences
Permanence of Paper for Printed Library Materials,
ANSI Z 39.48-1984.

♾

BM (c)	10	9	8	7	6	5	4	3	2	1
BM (p)	10	9	8	7	6	5	4	3	2	

CONTENTS

Part IV: Leadership Across Multiple Organizational Contexts

Part V: Global Leadership

LIST OF TABLES AND FIGURES

TABLES

FIGURES

ACKNOWLEDGMENTS

A very special thanks to Herrington Bryce, who continues to serve as my colleague, mentor, and valued friend. The administrative support of the School of Business Administration at the College of William and Mary is also acknowledged.

Thanks and appreciation go to my wife Serbrenia and our kids, Nandi, Dangaia, Sieya, and Kani, who have supported me another time during which it seemed as if we would never complete the book. A special "keep expanding your horizons" goes out to Ronald, Jr., Marchet, Vellice, Shelley, and Sharisse.

Ronald R. Sims

A special thanks to Ron Sims, my co-editor. I have had the unique pleasure of studying under Ron as an MBA student, leveraging his wisdom as a post-MBA and pre-Ph.D. sounding board, and now working alongside him as a colleague and scholar. He has continually served as a mentor for me, and looked for opportunities to pull me into his research and writing agenda. This book and my involvement in the project are products of his personal investment in my burgeoning career as an academic.

I also wish to acknowledge David Braaten, former dean of the Ken Blanchard College of Business at Grand Canyon University, for his administrative support (including ensuring adequate course release time) and personal encouragement in regard to this project.

Sincere thanks go to my wife, Jamie, and our children McKenna, Keaton, Hallie, and Hudson. They graciously endured the long hours necessary to complete the book, and loved me through the heat of the battle, even when I left the house before daybreak and did not return until well after bedtime. Okoboji and Cornerstone Cottage, here we come!

Scott A. Quatro

* * *

We are indebted to Lynn Taylor at M.E. Sharpe Publishers, who provided a collective outlet for our ideas on leadership. A hearty round of applause and thank you to our top-notch group of contributors. Their collective wisdom as leadership theorists and practitioners becomes quite evident as one reads through the impressive content of their chapters. We believe that their work has made a significant contribution to the overall leadership dialogue, and we are indebted to them all as colleagues and friends. Without their efforts and insights, this book would not exist.

INTRODUCTION

RONALD R. SIMS AND SCOTT A. QUATRO

As we settle into the new millennium, organizations in the for-profit, government, and not-for-profit sectors are being challenged to compete against new competitors (e.g., not-for-profits are experiencing new pressures from for-profit organizations for the services they were once sole providers of) in changing domestic and global environments using diverse workforces. As the past few decades have demonstrated, leadership styles that were practical in traditional hierarchies and that relied on authoritarian controls are no longer appropriate in today's world of work. Today's organizational leaders have to practice different styles appropriate to more dynamic and complex situations. They have increasingly to inspire trust, gain credibility, and implement innovations through others while being adaptable and flexible. Moreover, leaders are increasingly challenged to balance task and relationship (people) styles and to assume not only the roles of monitors and controllers but also the roles of cheerleaders, orchestrators, conductors, coaches, mentors, and followers. As effective leaders in the new millennium, individuals at various levels of organizations must recognize that concepts like "empowerment," "workout," "quality," "life-long learning," and "excellence" are important leadership factors.

Those who can demonstrate flexibility and the ability to respond to ambiguous situations will most likely be effective in providing the leadership necessary for today's ever-changing organizational and world of work landscape. The ability to create flexible organizations that change with the demands of an increasingly complex market and environment is a leadership challenge faced by *all* organizations. How to accomplish this goal over time has been and continues to be a critical challenge to those responsible for leading and reshaping organizations.

Walk into the leadership section of any bookshop and you will be bombarded by a whole host of different ideas, strategies, and style manuals. Thus, with hundreds and hundreds of books on leadership to choose from, why another one? The answer is simple. Most other books on leadership are either too general in nature or fail to discuss both leadership and the unique challenges that confront leaders in different sectors (e.g., for-profit, not-for-profit, government, etc.) while also focusing on those leadership challenges that are generalizable to all sectors. Our look at some of the more widely read leadership books on the market reveals that, instead of providing readers with a firsthand look at leadership challenges that are sector specific and generic in nature, most books fall on one end of the continuum or the other.

BOOK CHAPTERS

Although there is a range of useful literature on leadership, until now no single reference has offered a comprehensive selection of the latest work available on leadership in various sectors (private, public, and not-for-profit). In this collection of original writing, the contributors—leaders, researchers, academics, and consultants—discuss their views on the leadership challenges confronting today's organizations. More specifically, in presenting these views, the contributors discuss what they consider to be the current and future challenges faced by those responsible for leading organizations as well as numerous methods for responding to various leadership challenges. In accomplishing their charge, the contributors provide practical recommendations that will benefit leaders at all levels of an organization regardless of the sector. The results of the collective efforts of the contributors, although written from various vantage points, provide fresh insights into the quest to improve leaders and leadership.

This book consists of five parts: (I) Leadership in For-Profit-Organizations, (II) Leadership in Not-For-Profit Organizations, (III) Leadership in Government Organizations, (IV) Leadership Across Multiple Organizational Contexts, and (V) Global Leadership.

PART I: LEADERSHIP IN FOR-PROFIT ORGANIZATIONS

Part I presents a selection of writings on leadership issues and challenges in the for-profit sector. In Chapter 1, "From Monopoly to Competition: Challenges for Leaders in the Deregulated Investor-Owned Utility Industry," R. Kevin McClean suggests that leaders in the utilities arena must drive their organizations to adopt a marketing orientation to better respond to external market forces, while concurrently addressing the very real organizational culture changes that such a shift requires.

In Chapter 2, "Reforming Wall Street: Challenges for Financial Leaders in Publicly Traded Firms," L. Keith Whitney and Michael Yonker, a researcher and a practitioner respectively, investigate the organizational population consisting of large, publicly held companies. In particular, they study the theory-to-practice implications of current attempts to better regulate U.S. equity markets. While clearly indicating philosophical support for contemporary attempts at reform and acquiescing to the need for such reforms (citing the case of Enron in support), the authors provide a balanced analysis and discussion of the mechanisms and infrastructures employed to date (specifically, the Sarbanes-Oxley Act of 2002) and of their operational impact on publicly traded firms. They propose further reforms with an eye toward the players in what they term the "corporate reporting supply chain," which includes company executives, board members, independent auditors, and even investors. Whitney and Yonker conclude that all of these players must focus increasingly on restoring the honor and integrity that once prevailed in the accounting industry and in U.S. equity markets at large.

In Chapter 3, "Beyond Wall Street: Leadership Challenges Unique to Small Private Companies and Entrepreneurial Firms," Erik Hoekstra and Scott R. Peterson (both executives at a privately held firm that is a prominent player in its industry) posit that the leadership literature at large fails to address the challenges that are unique to smaller, privately held firms. To this end, they provide a unique perspective on challenges that all leaders face (such as capital access and investor relations, recruiting, and governance), deftly outlining how each of these challenges must be uniquely addressed in small private firms as opposed to large public firms. They complement this with an analysis of the even more unique challenges facing leaders in entrepreneurial firms (such as overcoming the strong personality of the entrepreneurial founder and ensuring effective leadership succession), identifying such firms as a subset of their small private organizational typology. Hoekstra and Peterson provide a compelling chapter that significantly adds to the leadership dialogue surrounding small private companies.

In Chapter 4, the final chapter in this section, "Knowledge Management Leadership Challenges: Coping with Mental Models and Operationalizing Knowledge Management Strategy and Practice," Tom R. Eucker presents strong evidence on the growing importance of effectively managing human resources (HR) in general and intellectual and human capital in particular. According to Eucker, this begins with an understanding of the critical difference between imparting knowledge and creating knowledge, and breaking down the mental barriers that distort the significant difference between these two activities. Eucker posits that all leadership activity geared toward creating and leveraging knowledge must begin with an understanding that doing so at the deepest level, the level of tacit knowledge, is most critical to the development of a culture of learning within an organization. To illustrate several of his main points, he provides a case study of effective knowledge management leadership based on his personal experience as a longtime HR executive with Intel Corporation.

PART II: LEADERSHIP IN NOT-FOR-PROFIT ORGANIZATIONS

The chapters in Part II examine leadership issues and challenges in not-for-profit organizations. In Chapter 5, "Leadership in a Not-for-Profit World: A Mixed Toolbox," not-for-profit experts Andrea B. Bear and Michael A. Fitzgibbon, who both have extensive experience in the profit sector, posit that not-for-profit leaders must help their organizations to achieve the delicate balance between efficiency and effectiveness, and that this requires strong leadership. According to Bear and Fitzgibbon, professional leaders (i.e., paid chief executive officer, executive director, vice president, deputy directors, etc.) and volunteer leaders (i.e., board of trustees or directors, event and committee chairs) in today's not-for-profit world must ensure that business-like operations do not displace the relationship-based approach and that the mission and passion are not lost in the process. Bear and Fitzgibbon argue that the challenges, changes, and qualities of nonprofit leadership reveal a number of opportunities and lessons for success. The authors provide perspectives from several professional and volunteer nonprofit leaders interviewed for their chapter. Finally, Bear and Fitzgibbon offer a toolbox or prescription for leadership success in not-for-profit organizations.

In Chapter 6, "The Challenges of Interpersonal Relationships, Employee Discipline, and Leadership Effectiveness in Religious Nonprofit Organizations," Craig Osten shares some of the wisdom gained from operating as a leader in nonprofit religious organizations for over twenty years. Osten sensitively yet forthrightly describes some of the unique barriers to effective leadership that exist in such organizational contexts, including the "spiritualization" of employee discipline issues, unacceptable employee behavior, and unacceptable employee performance. He further addresses the unique challenge to leadership to effectively embrace spiritual plurality within religious nonprofit organizations. Osten then offers his own model for effective leadership (outlining several keys to success, including hiring compatible yet complementary co-leaders and embracing necessary change) in such organizations, providing a convincing pair of case studies demonstrating both effective and ineffective leadership relative to his proposed model.

In Chapter 7, "What the New Nonprofit Leaders Should Learn About Finance: Beyond Fund-raising and Accounting," Herrington J. Bryce begins with the premise that that there will be a net increase in the demand for leaders of nonprofit organizations, although there is no forecast of the number of new persons that must be trained to fill these slots throughout the world. Thus, Bryce suggests that in training executives as leaders of nonprofits, the issue is not how to consolidate or retrench but how to expand with some core competence that will maximize the mobility of nonprofit leaders among various types of nonprofit organizations while assuring a foundation for the successful management of any one of these organizations. Bryce goes on to suggest what he believes is the foundation knowledge—at least in finance and financial management—that must be imparted to these prospective leaders and why. The author reduces this argument to a set of core concepts, which translate into core competencies that training institutions should use to train not-for-profit leaders. Bryce argues that without certain core competencies (at least in finance) leaders may be ill prepared to lead. Bryce concludes the chapter with a discussion of an overarching ethical imperative encapsulated in the concept of due diligence.

In Chapter 8, "Team-Based Leadership and Change in the Christian Church," Rev. Michael W. Honeycutt and Rev. Clay Smith provide a unique view of the challenges faced by church leaders. They posit that post-modern society requires a fundamentally different leadership approach than the one that has been traditionally employed within church organizations, that is, a shift from an autocratic, individual-driven leadership model to a consultative, team-driven model. Honeycutt and Smith further argue that it is only via the employment of a team-based model that church organizations will achieve belonging, participation, shared ownership, and movement throughout their membership ranks. Honeycutt and Smith afford readers a glimpse into the reality of living out a team-based model, using a case study of organizational change within a church setting—in this case, a church led by Honeycutt himself. This provides a firsthand understanding of the life of a church leader in a context that clearly demonstrates the joys and pains that come with the change experience.

PART III: LEADERSHIP IN GOVERNMENT ORGANIZATIONS

Part III, "Leadership in Government Organizations," consists of four chapters that discuss leadership issues and challenges at various levels of government. In Chapter 9,

"Notes from the Belly of the Beast: Leadership Challenges in the Federal Government," Richard F. Cullins, a program manager for air traffic training for the Federal Aviation Administration in Washington, DC, who has experience working in the public and private sectors for over twenty-five years, considers the leadership challenges to agencies of the executive branch of government. Cullins defines "agencies" as cabinet-level departments and their subagencies and suggests that many of the challenges discussed in the chapter are tied, and not coincidently, to President Bush's *Management Agenda FY 2002*, which he believes has broad implications for federal civil servants. Proposing that a new model of leadership may be required if tomorrow's federal leaders are to be successful, Cullins explores the current challenges facing those leaders. He also reviews some of the literature on leadership over the past decade and compares it with the current operational environment to determine whether leadership strategies and precepts of the recent past still apply.

In Chapter 10, "The Achievements and Challenges of Military Leadership," Christopher Taylor, who spent thirteen years in the marines, presents what he refers to as a "bottom-up" view of leadership. Taylor maintains that, considering the level at which he served, a bottom-up view to understanding leadership is appropriate. With that in mind, Taylor's views on the achievements and challenges of military leadership in fact lead to the position most often found in writings on leadership, the "top-down view," he just uses a different path. Taylor argues that several true differentiators put military leadership in a class by itself. Describing character, discipline, courage, commitment, and honor as some of the traits developed in military leaders, Taylor suggests that the very nature of military service affords both junior and senior leaders the chance to develop and hone leadership skills. In addition to offering some examples of military leadership over the past six decades, Taylor concludes by offering his views on twenty-first century military challenges.

In Chapter 11, "Leadership Challenges in Education: Improving Administrative Decision Making," Serbrenia J. Sims, a teacher, and Ronald R. Sims, a graduate school business professor, who are also consultants with extensive experience in the public, private, and not-for-profit sectors, argue that educational leaders must become adept at monitoring local, state, federal, and global environments in order to accurately forecast political and social problems that will impact their schools or school systems. Sims and Sims discuss a systematic approach in the form of a balanced scorecard, which they believe will allow educators and educational leaders to make more effective administrative decisions thereby allowing them to respond best to ever-changing trends and demanding calls for accountability from a wide variety of stakeholders.

In Chapter 12, the final chapter of Part III, "Leadership Challenges in Local Government: Economic Development, Financial Management, and Ethical Leadership," William I. Sauser, Jr., Lane D. Sauser, and Joe A. Sumners contribute to our understanding of the leadership challenges confronting government officials at the local level. In an effort to help prepare local government leaders for the challenges they will face in this century, they discuss three key issues that local public officials must deal with: economic development, financial management, and ethical leadership. Addressing each of these three issues in turn, the authors recognize them as only a few of many challenges facing local government officials, but argue that they are the three most critical. The authors suggest that by working on economic development in tandem with the citizenry and business community, by following the ten steps they recommend to assure good financial management, and by adopting their suggestions for creating an ethical climate within which the local government does business, local officials can do much to improve the lives and circumstances of their citizens.

PART IV: LEADERSHIP ACROSS MULTIPLE ORGANIZATIONAL CONTEXTS

The four chapters of Part IV deal with leadership issues and challenges across multiple organizational contexts. Human resource development (HRD) experts Jerry W. Gilley and Ann Gilley provide an in-depth discussion of the need for contemporary HR leaders to embrace a new leadership model in Chapter 13, "Developmental-Servant Leadership for Human Resource Professionals." While Gilley and Gilley strongly suggest that all leaders must embrace a servant leadership model, they posit that such an approach is critical to the success of HR leaders in particular. They demonstrate that this shift is necessitated by significantly different demands made on HR professionals in the contemporary workplace (such as business consulting, change management, and organizational redesign) versus the more administrative demands traditionally expected of them. Gilley and Gilley present a model for developmental-servant leadership that is deeply rooted in the broader HR literature, emphasizing key characteristics such as a "servant first" mindset and critical principles such as the performance-oriented principles of performance partnership and organizational performance improvement; they also identify the role of business partner as the primary new function of HR professionals. Perhaps most important, Gilley and Gilley propose that embracing developmental-servant leadership will result in key benefits for both individual HR professionals and organizations that embrace the model.

In Chapter 14, "Engaging People's Passion: Leadership for the New Century," Diana Bilimoria and Lindsey Godwin argue that the job description of today's leaders has changed in comparison to the past, and that organizations and society alike are raising the bar regarding their expectations of their leaders. Therefore, given the increasing importance of leadership within today's organizational context, Bilimoria and Godwin emphasize that new frameworks must be developed to help clarify and prepare individuals for effective leadership. The authors provide an overview of what they see as five elements comprising effective leadership in this century's emerging new business paradigm. The authors discuss a model for engaging people's passion that they believe provides a coherent lens through which we can look at the factors necessary for effective leadership in the postindustrial age.

In Chapter 15, "'HR-Minded' Leadership: Five Critical Areas of Focus for Contemporary Organizational Leaders," Scott A. Quatro posits that all leaders, regardless of their functional or line responsibilities, must become increasingly "HR-minded" in their leadership approach. Doing so requires that leaders accept responsibility for developing a compelling strategic vision, designing engaging jobs, instilling a sound organizational conscience, leveraging organizational knowledge, and building change capacity. Quatro argues that only by embracing these five key areas of leadership practice will leaders demonstrate high levels of overall effectiveness and catalyze sustained organizational high performance. He provides several examples from contemporary organizational practice to substantiate the efficacy of his model and related claims, and includes a striking interpretation of how a job design change for a subteam working on the Manhattan Project contributed in a significant way to the success of the endeavor as a whole.

In Chapter 16, "Leaders Speak: Success and Failure in Their Own Words," William J. Mea and Shawn M. Carraher attempt to answer some age-old questions on leadership: What makes a leader? What elements of character make others want to follow them? In the end, what makes some leaders true successes and others failures? Mea and Carraher investigate what makes a leader good or bad. Rather than focus on theory, the authors interview accomplished leaders about leaders they have had—good and bad—and the mark these leaders have left on them. Based on these interviews Mea and Carraher present insight into some dynamic personalities of leaders who have made a difference in the interviewees' respective fields. The authors contrast those they describe as competent leaders with those who aspired to leadership but failed in some profound ways. The chapter begins with observations on leadership and a review of a limited sample of leadership theories that the authors use to frame their views on leadership.

PART V: GLOBAL LEADERSHIP

Part V deals with global leadership issues and challenges. In Chapter 17, "Worldview and Global Leadership," by John R. Visser provides a truly unique contribution to the leadership dialogue. Visser posits that leadership literature in general has failed to adequately investigate the critical role played by worldview in leadership effectiveness and provides an in-depth review of the pertinent literature to substantiate his claim. Visser argues that the only truly effective leadership is rooted in a worldview that celebrates and reinforces civil society, and he further proposes that such leadership is particularly critical at the national level. To this end, Visser proposes that nations need leaders who understand that they must nurture the development of seven different kinds of "capital" to spur real and sustainable progress: physical, economic, intellectual/emotional, spiritual/moral, environmental, governmental, and social capital. These seven forms of capital constitute a "development wheel" that, when rounded out, enables ongoing constructive economic development in a country.

In Chapter 18, "What Good Is This to Me? Managerial Implications of Global Leadership Research," Marcus W. Dickson and Deanne N. Den Hartog, who are academics as well as consultants, set forth what they view as a few rather modest goals of their contribution. Dickson and Den Hartog argue that country and culture really do matter when trying to determine what makes up that chimera called "effective leadership." They also suggest that managers and executives who deal with cultural issues relating to leadership can meaningfully apply well-designed scholarly research on cross-cultural leadership. Based on their research, Dixon and Den Hartog provide some concrete recommendations for managers and executives about the sorts of research-based information that they may find useful when wrestling with the concepts of leadership and culture, and how to go about finding that information.

In Chapter 19, "New Rules for a New Century: Help for Management and Leadership in This New Global Century," Kenneth L. Murrell builds on earlier work in which he examined changes that both managers and workers should be aware of, and, where appropriate, they should support as we move toward the twenty-first century. The common theme was "Twenty-One Rules for a New Century." Murrell takes each theme of those new rules and examines how crucial each will be to this new century. In particular, Murrell emphasizes the hope and optimism that this new century should still be able to generate. He argues that through the toughest of times the human spirit has been able to emerge and that the form of organizational life has been on a steady evolutionary path since humanity fully recognized how crucial organizations are to our very existence. Murrell posits that there is much to look forward to and also much to be cautious about and aware of in this new century. He suggests that while the rules are being rewritten daily, the observance of these "new" rules provides many opportunities for organizations to continue to evolve and develop.

In Chapter 20, "Restoring Ethics Consciousness to Organizations and the Workplace: Every Contemporary Leader's Challenge," Ronald R. Sims discusses the importance for leaders to take responsibility for restoring ethics to organizations and the workplace. He also discusses why ethics matter, in order to support his premise that leaders need to refocus their attention on "doing the right thing" in organizations. He proposes that it is important for leaders to use five mechanisms available to them, regardless of the type of organization. He stresses the significance of creating a climate for whistle-blowing and providing a forum for dialogue and moral conversation in restoring ethical consciousness to the workplace. Sims concludes with a discussion of the need for leaders to continually take advantage of opportunities to institutionalize ethical behavior in organizations.

CONCLUSION

In this book, the authors describe specific leadership challenges and present the issues and strategies confronting leaders in a variety of organizations. As such, the book represents contemporary views from a diverse group of contributors on how leaders can improve their effectiveness in leading organizations today and in the future. In so doing, the volume contributes to understanding the ethos of leadership in an ever-changing world. By highlighting a range of leadership issues, challenges, and recommendations, the authors seek to enhance our understanding of leaders and leadership.

While no single compendium of current work on a topic as complex as leaders and leadership can be complete, a timely discourse on leaders and leadership today is presented in these chapters. The role of leaders and our understanding of leadership deserve our ongoing attention. It is our hope that this book contributes to this dialogue.

Leadership

Part I

Leadership in For-Profit Organizations

CHAPTER 1

FROM MONOPOLY TO COMPETITION

Challenges for Leaders in the Deregulated Investor-Owned Utility Industry

R. KEVIN MCCLEAN

The $300 billion electric energy industry and $100 billion gas industry have been undergoing changes driven by market forces and concomitant regulatory initiatives during the past two decades. Utility managers are being challenged to redefine the regulated utility's role in the energy market, address competitive challenges where only a few years before none existed, and respond to increasing consumer demands for excellent service quality and customer service. At the same time, utilities must contain costs in an environment that is less receptive to "cost-plus" rate regulation, and motivate a workforce to meet the expectations of the various stakeholders during a period of transformational industry and organizational culture change.

The leadership challenges brought on by these changes can be viewed through prisms of a change from a production orientation to a marketing orientation and a related organization culture change:

- *Marketing Orientation.* What does a marketing orientation mean to regulated utilities? What are the implications for employees and managers? Does regulatory oversight apply, or should the market drive the level of customer satisfaction demanded of and met by the utility?
- *Culture Change.* Regulated investor-owned utilities have operated since the 1930s as quasi-governmental agencies known for job security and paternalistic management. What forces are changing this relationship and how do utility leaders cope with the change?

We will identify the issues confronting utility management and discuss how adopting a marketing orientation applies to the utility's response to external market forces and the utility's internal organization.

BACKGROUND: THE DEREGULATED ENERGY INDUSTRY

The energy marketplace has been undergoing significant change over the past twenty-five years. Regulated at both the state and federal levels, this industry is being transformed from a regulated industry to one where competition either has been introduced or is in the process of being introduced for the purchase of electricity and gas by commercial and residential consumers, as well as for direct contact business functions such as billing and call center operations. As will be discussed, other elements of the value chain remain—for now—under regulatory control. Why competition in what has been viewed as a natural monopoly? Following the trend of deregulation in other industries, such as telecommunications and airlines, it has become axiomatic that competition will result in benefits to the consumer. Societal benefits including reduced costs, innovation, and improved services are expected to accrue as a result of competition in the energy marketplace.[1]

Along with this industry restructuring, new consumer issues are being identified and addressed, principally in the area of competitive functions. Activities heretofore provided by the regulated utilities such as meter installation, meter reading, call center operations, and billing are now subject to competition (CA 1997; MA 1997; NY 1997; PA 2000; TX 2000; WI 1997).

Under the umbrella of regulation, utility leadership was primarily concerned with the safety and reliability of the systems to which they were entrusted and with achieving the allowed rate of return provided by regulators. The latter was arrived at through a regulatory rate-setting process at the state level, and this is still the case. The former, safety and reliability, is usually measured based upon agreement between regulators and utilities, oftentimes with rewards or penalties for performance (performance-based ratemaking).

There are several overriding issues that drive a desire for deregulation, including downward pressure on prices, increased customer choice, and additional services (NY PSC 1996, 4):

- Competition in the electric power industry will further the economic and environmental well-being of New York State. The basic objective of moving to a more competitive structure is to satisfy consumers' interests at minimum resource cost . . . and consumers should have a reasonable opportunity to realize savings and other benefits from competition. . . .
- Any new electric industry structure should provide: (a) increased consumer choice of service and pricing options; (b) a suitable forum for promptly resolving consumer concerns and complaints. . . .
- Pro-competitive policies should further economic development in New York State.

Cost is a significant concern in the electric and gas energy business. The generally accepted concept of increasing supply in order to decrease price via competitive forces has been a driving truism for regulators and others promoting deregulation in the energy industry. A United States Department of Energy (US DOE or DOE) study projected consumer savings on a national basis (US DOE 1999).[2]

There is wide acceptance within the industry that competition will drive down prices to the end user over the long run (Train and Selting 2000; McDermott et al. 2000; Gordon and Olson 2000; Goulding, Rufin, and Swinand 1999; Day and Moore 1998; Jovin

1998). Such acceptance is evident in the several commission opinions cited previously, and extends beyond the cost of the commodity into other customer care functions, including billing and metering (Gordon and Olson 2000; Joskow 2000). This expectation is supported by experience in other deregulated industries. According to Winston (1998) and Crandall and Ellig (1998), the airline, trucking, railroad, and telecommunications industries all realized reduced prices following deregulation.

Innovation includes *technological* innovation and *service* innovation. The advent of bill presentation and payment processing using Internet technology is one example of innovation that can affect the gas and electric industries, along with other electronic innovations (Tschamler 2000; Borenstein and Bushnell 2000; Joskow 2000).

Service innovation can be found in offerings of bundled services, such as combining electric and gas billing with cable and telephone or other accounts (Flaim 2000; Joskow 2000; Gordon and Olson 2000). Services offered may also include management of customer electric appliances and systems, such as heating, ventilation, and air-conditioning systems. Another form of service innovation is the supply of electricity produced by environmentally friendly sources of power—for example, "green" energy such as solar, wind, or hydroelectric power (Joskow 2000).

Finally, improvements in customer satisfaction and service quality are to be expected in a competitive marketplace (Gordon and Olson 2000; Joskow 2000; Tschamler 2000; Jones 1998). These terms, "customer satisfaction" and "service quality," are bedrock issues in the discipline of marketing. As with cost and innovation, the presumption is that competition will drive the players in the marketplace to provide better service than their competitors, benefiting the consumer. That service may well be tied into currently available technology (e.g., Internet-based transactions, real time pricing, or automated meter reading), improved call center operations, or simply more personalized and responsive services.

The range of issues with which the utility leadership must cope stemming from these shifts in the industry includes whether and how to compete in the production business as wellhead operators, pipeline managers, or power plant operators; whether and how to invest and maintain an adequate transmission system; how to finance adequate distribution facilities at the local level; how to address questions of organizational restructuring; and whether and how to enter competitive markets, and if so, which ones. Transcending all of these is the issue of how the utility leadership ensures that the utility is seen by the publics it serves as a valued and integral part of the energy market. To do so, it is critical that the utility understand its customers' expectations and operate in a way that will meet or exceed those expectations. We see this as the need to apply a marketing orientation, "regulated" notwithstanding, and as the probable need to change organizational culture.

THE MARKETING CHALLENGE

For over sixty years, energy utilities existed without the "invisible hand" of competition to guide the forces of its marketplace. Rather, regulation acted as a surrogate for the economic forces that exist in an open and competitive industry. Utility leaders—and some in the industry may take a contrary view of the priorities assigned—were primarily concerned first with the reliability and safety of their production and delivery systems, then with the financial performance of their companies, and finally with the satisfaction of employees and customers. The industry was largely the domain of engineers and financial managers able to design and finance an ever more complex system of production and distribution from national gas pipelines, interconnecting electric transmission systems, and larger and more efficient electric generators, to local delivery in dense urban areas, rapidly expanding suburban neighborhoods, and far-flung and remote rural areas. And, for sixty plus years, the systems worked. Reliability of gas and electric systems is simply expected, almost taken for granted by the consumer.[3]

But now, with the exigencies brought on by deregulation, utility leaders are being asked to go beyond reliability and safety and meet customers' specific wants and needs, to adopt a *customer focus*. This is a very different emphasis from the production orientation of the regulated environment—produce and deliver enough product to economically meet demand, and use average-costs methods for determining price—and calls for utility leaders first to ask what it is that customers want, and then to plan and implement actions to satisfy those wants. At the same time, regulatory strictures continue to affect pricing for the delivery systems.

THE EVOLUTION OF MARKETING

Figure 1.1 shows the evolution of production, sales, and marketing orientations over time. Energy utilities have tended to be production oriented. Gas utilities have been more sales oriented as that industry competes directly with oil for home heating in many areas of the country or as fuel for electricity production.

- *Production Orientation.* Utilities having a production orientation would view their only responsibility to the customer as ensuring that product (electricity or gas) is available to the customer when needed. Regulators set prices after public hearings and a regulatory process established within the state systems, and bills are rendered to customers based upon consumption.
- *Sales Orientation.* Utilities having excess capacity of either electricity or gas would focus efforts on enticing customers to buy more of their products without specific regard for how customers may need or use the products, making sales orientation dominant.
- *Marketing Orientation.* What is meant by a "marketing orientation?" Essentially, it calls for every employee in a firm to focus on satisfying the wants and needs of the customer; it claims that customers do not so much buy a product or service as seek to have their wants and needs satisfied and that firms exist to produce satisfied customers (Drucker 1954; Levitt 1960). Consistent with this is the construct that the *customer*, not the firm, determines value (Levitt 1960).

This thinking regarding marketing orientation has evolved from the 1950s through the 1990s and has become a dominant view in many industries (Vargo and Lusch 2004). We

Figure 1.1 **The Evolution of Marketing**

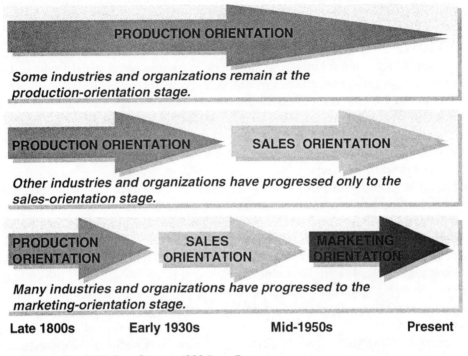

Source: Etzel, Walker, Stanton (2004), p. 7.

will further consider two views of marketing orientation in some detail, that of Slater and Narver (1992) and Frederick E. Webster, Jr. (1994, 2002), but first we ask, why a marketing orientation for utilities?

Why a Marketing Orientation for Utilities?

Rate regulation is the lifeblood of a utility. It is the way the utility obtains financial resources to operate while earning returns that would entice investors to purchase utility securities. In setting electric and gas rates, utility commissions—under whatever name a state may give to that ruling body—weigh many factors and can be influenced by a myriad of interested parties, from business organizations to consumer groups to other entries to the new competitive industry, the energy service companies.

A simplistic application of a marketing orientation is the view of electric and gas energy as satisfying basic needs such as physical (warmth or cooling, light), safety (security lighting, security systems), or even esteem (using alternative fueled vehicles that run on compressed natural gas or rechargeable batteries, contributing to societal benefits). That view would miss a critical point: that all products are packaged in services and it is the service accompanying the product that will help to meet customers' wants and needs and result in satisfied customers. The services will drive customer satisfaction. This new "dominant logic" is the thesis of Vargo and Lusch (2004) and has application in the utility industry. A customer focus and market orientation is critical to the success of the utility, if a regulated utility is to satisfy its regulators (its surrogate for competitors) and the customers it serves in a manner that will allow for the award and achievement of adequate returns to its investors and also meet targeted levels of customer satisfaction set as performance measures by regulators.

Utility customers evaluate their utility services in the context of services offered by nonutility, nonregulated entities. Customer expectations are formed by the totality of their experiences in dealing with all types of companies and service providers, with utility managers having to determine what expectations consumers have regarding the services that the utility renders.

Beyond the need for utilities to be able to justify their need for rate adjustments (increases) without encountering vocal and sometimes vociferous opposition by customer groups dissatisfied with service, pricing, or value, the newly deregulated market supports another reason for a marketing orientation. In those states where utility leaders have dealt with the introduction of competition (CAEM 2003), new corporate structures have allowed the senior management of utilities to enter the competitive energy market by establishing nonregulated and competitive energy service companies as well as subsidiaries operating in other competitive markets, such as telecommunications, investment and development companies, and power production/generation. A well-regarded utility might have a beneficial "halo" effect on affiliates in the competitive realm, while a utility that does not meet customer expectations for service could very well hurt a competitive affiliate's market entry. The former can be capitalized on by using a family branding tactic, while the latter might necessitate a distinct and different name for the competitive company or a new name for the entire enterprise.

As will be discussed, there is one other imperative for a marketing orientation: the specter of new technologies that have the potential to revolutionize the energy industry.

The question at hand, then, is what exactly is a marketing orientation and how would it apply in a utility?

A Concise View of the Marketing Orientation

Slater and Narver (1992) identified five components in the marketing concept, a customer orientation, a competitor orientation, interfunctional coordination, a long-term horizon, and a profit focus. In their model, depicted in Figure 1.2, the profit focus is viewed over a long-term period and is dependent on the first three elements:

Customer Orientation

A customer orientation takes into account the value created for and with the customer: meeting customer needs, identifying and measuring performance against sat-

Figure 1.2 **The Marketing Concept**

Source: Slater and Narver (1992).

isfaction objectives, and providing continuing (after sale) service. This can be further delineated using the dimensions developed by Zeithaml, Parasuranam, and Berry (1990), and for a utility, would call for knowing what customers expect in terms of reliability of service; responsiveness, empathy, and reassurance by employees; and tangible factors in the service experience such as communications, literature, and bill presentation.

Competitor Orientation

Competitor orientation calls for effective communications between sales (contact) employees and the leadership of the organization, who, in turn, must respond quickly to competitor strategies and look for competitive advantage. Regulated utilities themselves do not, for the moment, have direct competitors in the distribution function. Residential generation and fuel cells are the subjects of a later discussion herein, but one that Levitt (1960) had the prescience to recognize when he suggested that utilities had better be ready to one day service batteries that run households. Utility leaders need to plan how to respond to those eventual competitors if the utility is to continue to be successful—or even to survive. In the nearer term, this sensitivity to the marketplace and its players, along with the communication processes needed to stay abreast of both customer concerns and competitors, is very applicable to a utility's affiliate (competitive) companies and one that corporate leadership must inculcate throughout the organization.

Interfunctional Coordination

Interfunctional coordination connotes the idea of the left hand knowing what the right hand is doing. A means of sharing customer information among the various operations within the utility might involve rapid and detailed information between a call center and field operations in the case of service interruptions, or when field construction might interfere with customers' lifestyles, even if only temporarily. That information in the call center would permit direct and sympathetic response to customers calling about the inconvenience they are experiencing. If a gas main repair or installation will disrupt traffic in an area, advance word to local homeowners and businesses, along with an up-to-date schedule in the hands of the call center, would go a long way to allay customer concerns. Beyond that, every employee in the organization should understand how their work affects customers, not only the external customer but also internal customers—other employees. A caveat that is worth noting has to do with the restrictions in information flow about customers between the regulated utility and its competitive affiliates. Generally, regulators establish some form of affiliate transaction rules to establish a "firewall" between the regulated and nonregulated affiliates. There could be unfair advantage if the utility were to share its data on individual customers or groups of customers only with its affiliates and not with all other companies operating in the competitive energy market.

Long-term Horizon

Long-term horizon recognizes that what a company does now can and will pay dividends in the longer term, often long after the current leadership's tenure. Today, we have the immediacy of federal and state legislative and regulatory bodies pursuing competition in heretofore regulated markets (production, electric and gas pipeline transmission, customer services) but not in the local delivery systems. The question that we leave open to readers is: how confident should utility leadership be that technology will not make the existing electric systems obsolete, or at least subject to real competition? If gas is the preferred fuel for small residential generators, it represents an opportunity for that industry at the expense of the electric industry. Where does the utility fit and how will it operate in such an industry? We contend that to be a player, a serious effort at creating a market-oriented firm is now the key to success, if not to survival.

Profits

Profits are the result of a successful marketing orientation. To paraphrase Peter Drucker (1954), profits are the result of effective customer orientation: just as the human body does not exist for oxygen but needs oxygen to survive, corporations do not exist for profits—though profits are needed to survive—but for another purpose: satisfaction of the customer.

An Expanded View of the Marketing Concept

Frederick Webster (1994, 2002) offers an expanded view of what is meant by the "marketing concept" and provides a more granular view of the elements that contribute to an overall company focus on the customer. Each idea has pertinence to utilities and underscores challenges to utility leadership to effect what sometimes may be radical change in the organization culture, an item discussed further in this chapter. Webster's "key ideas in the value-delivery marketing concept . . . [and] . . . guidelines for its implementation (Webster 2002, 277), with some added ideas carried forward from Webster's earlier work (1994, 275–276) are:

1. Focus on the customer and build customer commitment throughout the organization
2. Invest in market intelligence
3. Define and nurture distinctive competence
4. Select customers carefully
5. Listen to the customer
6. Put value-capture in the business model
7. Let the customer define quality
8. Manage for profitability, not for sales volume
9. Position the firm carefully in the value chain
10. Build customer relationships and manage customer loyalty
11. Measure and manage customer expectations
12. Build and manage brand equity
13. Develop strategic partnerships with vendors and resellers, focus the network on customers, and control customer relationships
14. Innovate and improve continuously
15. Define business as a "service business
16. Create customized solutions for customers
17. Do not confuse marketing with selling
18. Destroy marketing bureaucracy
19. Manage culture along with strategy and structure

Each of these points is discussed in detail below in relating the marketing concept to the energy utility industry.

Focus on the Customer and Build Customer Commitment Throughout the Organization

Webster's conceit is simple: "the central idea is customer orientation—putting the customer first . . . to create a satisfied customer" (Webster 1994, 276). The top utility leadership must establish customer primacy throughout the organization. Too often, organizations are compartmentalized with each element of the organization well equipped and goal oriented for what that element believes to be its mission. In utilities, there is usually a "customer service" or "customer operations" element that interfaces directly with customers on billing and service issues and is too often seen as having sole "customer responsibility." The "operating end" of the business, production, and transmission and distribution—the "wires and pipes"—are typically somewhat removed from direct contact with the customer. The very well-intentioned managers of all of these organizations set performance standards—often in collaboration with the state regulators—based on their organizations' recent past performance.

For example, in customer operations, a performance standard might be to answer 90 percent of calls to its call center within forty seconds. An example in electric operations is not to exceed average customer interruption duration of one hour per customer over the course of a year. This is a widely tracked performance measure called the "customer average interruption-duration index," that focuses on both the frequency of customer interruptions and the average length of time a customer is without service. An example of a gas measure is the aim to respond to a certain percentage, for example, 90 percent, of customer emergency calls within a specified time frame, usually an hour. These all seem to the utility and regulatory leadership to be reasonable performance standards. However, if customers become irritated waiting for thirty or more seconds for a call to be answered, or if the same group of electric customers has more frequently interrupted service (although the system average remains the same), or if a gas customer has safety concerns as he or she waits up to an hour or more for a repairman, chances are the utility will encounter dissatisfied customers. The dissatisfaction occurs because the customer has expectations of performance that differ from those of utility management. Even if a utility is among the best utilities in absolute system performance, it is the utility company's customers' expectations that will define service and satisfaction.

To address this, utilities must first recognize that a gap between utility standards and customer expectations may exist; have goals that focus on customer satisfaction and incorporate customer feedback in setting those goals; maintain performance statistics at as local a level as practical to identify weaknesses in the system; identify the role each department in the organization has in providing customer satisfaction; and implement measurement and control to ensure that all parts of the organization are contributing to overall customer satisfaction.

Invest in Market Intelligence

Regulated utilities use sophisticated survey techniques to track and forecast usage by different customer classes, used for system planning/forecasting and for ratemaking (pricing) purposes. In a marketing orientation, knowing as much as possible about customers extends beyond simply tracking usage patterns. Already mentioned is the technique of using customer contact as an opportunity to gather information. In addition, knowing what technological innovations are attractive to customers, whether these are fuel cells, batteries, or individually owned generation, will help utility leadership prepare for an expansion of competition that could involve their distribution systems: electric, which may experience underutilized investment as consumers switch to alternate energy sources;

and gas, which may experience an increase in demand as customers use gas to fuel local generation. Webster (1994, 280) suggests that utility leadership and marketing management should recognize that "'knowing what we don't know' and identifying the questions that are worth asking strategically" is more important than gathering information for short-term decision making.

Define and Nurture Distinctive Competence

What is a utility's distinctive competence? For a start, customers must perceive the competence as valuable. For example, system reliability—the assurance that energy will be there when it is needed—can be a powerful competency for which some customers are willing to pay a premium. As deregulation develops nationally, utility leadership will be challenged to identify the type of company theirs should be. Some may focus on the regulated business, emphasizing their distribution capabilities (the wires and pipes business) and overall service. Others may emphasize their generation assets and capabilities, choosing to focus on the generation business. And others may move in the direction of nonregulated businesses through subsidiaries, such as energy service companies that act as brokers for the sale of electricity and gas to the business or residential consumer, along with other energy-related products. The company's distinctive competence, valued by customers, will drive strategic planning in the competitive marketplace.

Select Customers Carefully

Utilities treat customers in defined classes "on average" for ratemaking, measuring performance, and forecasting demand. Regulated rates require that no one class of customers be disadvantaged, so utilities approach customers in broad categories: large and small commercial customers, residential and residential heating (higher consumption than nonheat), with some refinement of these broad categories, and design rates (prices) based on the cost to serve these classes of customers. Utilities do not typically view customers beyond consumer type and consumption data—information that is demographic in nature. The use of psychographics, benefit and behavioral motivations, are means to better understand customers and develop an appropriate marketing mix (products, pricing, promotion, and placement or distribution). These require an investment in market research and an understanding of customer segmentation. Some utilities have experience with these refinements in customer data as they promote energy-efficiency programs, an understanding and skill-set that is essential in competing in nonregulated businesses. Others have responded to customer needs by offering "24/7" telephone service, account representatives for large customers, and other services intended to better respond to specific customers' needs. Utility leaders have recognized the need for these types of added services, but systematic and ongoing customer research may expose other, not readily apparent opportunities to develop a strong relationship with customers. To do so, to expose other opportunities, is underscored by Webster's idea to "listen to the customer."

Listen to the Customer

One thing that seems to work well in "spreading the gospel" of customer orientation is to have the managers of the various business elements listen in on call center operations involving both routine and emergency calls. Another is to have senior managers from the operating areas visit with customers to hear, firsthand, customer expectations and any dissatisfaction they have with the utility's services. These are effective means of engaging managers throughout the business with customers.

This precept, however, calls for more rigorous involvement with the customer. It means that an ongoing system for obtaining customer feedback is evaluated and acted upon. Crosby (1993), for example, identifies eight methods of obtaining customer feedback and learning customer expectations; among these methods are complaint analysis, customer surveys, problem analysis, and conjoint analysis (prioritizing alternatives). Zeithaml, Parasuraman, and Berry (1990) utilize a questionnaire survey, SERVQUAL, to understand expectations of service quality and concomitant perceptions of performance compared to those expectations.

Utilities have an excellent opportunity to gather market information through their call centers by sampling calls received at the time customers request service, when they leave the company, and during routine calls for information. The objective is to understand what is important to the customer, permitting the utility to plan to meet or exceed those expectations. If a utility does not have the systems capability to gather and aggregate such information for analysis, has not trained employees or incorporated such information-gathering techniques in their operations, or simply deems them "too expensive" or unnecessary expenses, they are missing an opportunity to stay ahead of a rapidly advancing curve, competition in their industry.

Follow-up calls and surveys of customers who have contact with other company operations (gas sales calls, energy efficiency audits, lighting surveys, and the like, as well as follow-up on emergency calls) also provide opportunities to learn about customers' expectations and perceptions of service. Systematic analysis and a commitment to rigorous attention to follow-up actions are needed for any of these data-gathering techniques to be effective.

Put Value-Capture in the Business Model

Value is something defined by the customer. Managers too often try to make that determination and miss the opportunity to cater to their customers' perceptions of value. This ties in closely with listening to your customer and making value a part of the culture of the organization. Value is a function of a customer's perceptions of price and quality, and a company-wide understanding of what customers see as value will buttress and sustain a competitive attitude among regulated utility employees. Webster (2002, 287) suggests that businesses must ask, "How can we capture a fair portion of the value that has been created for the customers we have elected to serve?" From this perspective, value creation for customers is, according to Webster (2002, 286) "the best possible use of the resources that have been committed to the business and to earn a return for the owners of those assets." For utilities, that value is a combination of price, quality, and service, with the latter two largely defined by the customer.

Let the Customer Define Quality

The customer also defines quality. Utilities typically view quality as a function of the availability and reliability of their service, but that is only part of the story. True, the engineering specifications for the frequency of electricity distributed or the thermal content of the gas sold are measurements of the quality of the product. How customer operations handles customer contacts, how flexible service personnel are in meeting customers' schedules, how all employees deal with customers they meet, all affect customer perceptions of quality. Recognize, too, that customer perceptions of quality change over time. Their experiences with other service providers help to define service and quality expectations of their utility. Continuous improvement and total quality management are methods used to move the organization toward meeting and exceeding customer quality expectations.

Manage for Profitability, Not for Sales Volume

Regulated utilities are not able to pick and choose their customers. The franchise territories that they serve determine their customer base, and all qualifying customers within the territory need to be served. However, utilities are well advised to work with municipalities and other business leaders in attracting the types of customers that will ensure the overall economic growth of the service territory and increase sales for the utility with a satisfactory profitability margin. Beyond that, a significant challenge in those jurisdictions moving to competition in the energy market is the effect on utilities as customers choose other service providers. Two problems arise: scale economies are diminished and average costs rise for the remaining utility customers (fixed costs assigned to a smaller base); and the most desirable customers are likely to be wooed by competitors, leaving the utility with low-margin or credit-risk customers. The utilities run the risk of becoming the "provider of last resort" for customers that are not attractive to the competitive energy service companies. It is beyond the scope of this chapter, but this may be one of the most critical challenges utility leaders face if retail competition is successful in their utility's service territory.

Position the Firm Carefully in the Value Chain

Positioning in this sense ties in closely to a utility firm's distinctive competence, its customer relationships, and its dealings with suppliers. Webster's view is that positioning is a key marketing management responsibility and is "guided by customer focus and market intelligence" (Webster 2002, 288). We have discussed distinctive competence, customer focus, and market intelligence. What, then, are customer relationships?

Build Customer Relationships and Manage Customer Loyalty

Customer relationship management is "attracting customers, maintaining an affiliation with them, and enhancing the bond with the customer" (McClean 2003, 40). This would not at first appear to be overly important in the context of a regulated utility, where there are no competitive delivery options. However, if we are managing for the future, relationship management may be key to the utility's long-term viability if and when alternative sources of energy become commercial (available, and at a competitive price). Research supports the notion that there is a strong relationship among satisfaction, retention, and relationship management (Churchill and Suprenant 1982; Bolton and Drew 1991; Tse and Wilton 1988). Utilities can position themselves in the minds of their customers as preferred energy providers in a competitive market by functioning as if they were in one now. Beyond a concern for relationships with customers, the utility should recognize that relationship management includes suppliers, employees, unions, government, and even competitors.

Measure and Manage Customer Expectations

Communications is a key to managing customer expectations. Through information and education, the utility can influence customer expectations of service and quality, allowing the utility to then plan to meet those expectations. What should be avoided are promises that may not be consistently met. If a service call is promised within a pre-agreed upon two-hour window, the utility's resources and processes must be capable of handling such appointments. (One company with which we are familiar pays the customer $50 if an appointment is missed!) In addition to managing customer expectations, measurement is key: the utility must know what a customer expects if it is to develop processes and assign resources to meet them, or to develop communications to better educate—and influence—those expectations.

Build and Manage Brand Equity

The overall satisfaction that customers have with their utility company can affect whether there is a "halo" effect on affiliate companies, and, in the longer view, how customers will respond to technology innovations that might open the "wires and pipes" company, the regulated distribution company, to competition.

Develop Strategic Partnerships with Vendors and Resellers, Focus the Network on Customers, and Control Customer Relationships

Regulated utilities are restricted in establishing formal business partnerships. However, the value chain in obtaining electricity or gas and delivering product to customers, including the suppliers of supporting goods and services, provides a wealth of opportunities for utilities to work with these "partners" in providing outstanding service to the utility's customers. For example, having meters, or transformers, or regulators delivered and available just when they are needed to complete service for a customer reduces the utility's inventory costs while meeting customer expectations. A close working relationship with suppliers, even sharing access to the utility's inventory system, can facilitate this relationship.

Innovate and Improve Continuously

Customers will adjust their expectations of a business based upon their experiences with all businesses they deal with. That the utility is regulated does not mean that different standards will apply. If the utility is committed to "listening to the customer," "defining marketing as market intelligence," making "customer value the guiding star," and letting " the customer define quality," then it is a logical extension that the utility will react and respond to changes in customer expectations. By incorporating a mindset of continuous improvement throughout the organization, with all company operations seeking to become more efficient at the same time they are being more responsive to the customer, the utility will build a positive relationship with the customer while meeting value expectations of the customer.

Define Business as a "Service Business"

The utility industry is a service industry. Yes, there are products (kilowatt-hours of electricity, cubic feet or thermal units of gas), but it is the service that accompanies the product that will differentiate sellers of energy. If the business is defined as a service business, a company's energies can be directed to identifying customers' service expectations and meeting them. This philosophy—that all business is a service business—has recent application in nonutility areas. IBM, clearly a manufacturer of equipment, has redefined itself as a service company, and that service in particular is what differentiates its offerings from those of its competitors (Lohr 2004).

Create Customized Solutions for Customers

Generally, deregulation will limit the regulated utility in terms of developing and marketing energy innovation. That will be left to the competitive market. However, within the context of regulation, there are opportunities for utilities to provide options that fulfill customer needs. Appointments that conform to customer schedules, bill presentation ("snail" mail versus e-mail), Internet-based information systems, automated payment systems, and even reliability of service (e.g., by offering lower "interruptible" rates to customers willing to curtail energy usage during peak demand periods) are all among the current options a utility can offer. As technology advances, more opportunities can be expected to present themselves, and utilities can respond if they have the customer focus to seek out and implement new technologies.

Do Not Confuse Marketing with Selling

While Webster (2002) makes the point that selling is short-term and tactical and marketing is long-term and strategic, with the purpose of encouraging a distinction within the organization of the firm to separate the functions, regulated utilities are somewhat con-strained in their sales function. While gas utilities do promote and sell gas service op-tions (heating and cooling) and electric utilities will promote security lighting and other electric solutions to customer problems, the sales function is also under review for its proper place in a deregulated environment. Regardless of where regulators eventually place the sales function, the distinction is appropriate in that marketing, as it is discussed in this presentation, will continue to be a critical strategic function for regulated utilities.

Destroy Marketing Bureaucracy

Webster (1994) opines that the large formal marketing organizations of the past are not sufficiently flexible or responsive to function well in today's fast-paced environment. He suggests that while marketing competence must be developed within the organization, it cannot be only the job of marketing to be focused on the customer. For a company to succeed, every one of its members must know his or her role in servicing the customer. Marketing's job is to get customer information to each organizational element within the firm. How can an organization foster such a culture? Marketing can help by working with utility leaders to understand what changes are desirable and to communicate the change throughout the organization.

Manage Culture Along with Strategy and Structure

A southwestern utility leader displayed the following on her wall: "Communicate cul-ture change; use words if necessary" (Hansen 1994, 190–191). Webster (1994) advises that there are two implications in managing culture: the entire organization must adopt customer orientation, and an entrepreneurial and responsive organization is needed to meet a changing market. A market could not be changing much more than is the electric and gas utility industry marketplace. How the organization and its employees adapt to accommodate market changes will likely determine which energy utilities thrive and prosper. Our premise that a marketing orientation is key to that success calls for one very major change: the organization's leaders must drive customer orientation and an entre-preneurial spirit, and these invariably involve organizational culture change.

THE ORGANIZATIONAL CULTURE CHANGE CHALLENGE

What do we mean by "organizational culture change?" To begin to answer that we need to define "organizational culture." Schein (1985, 494) defines culture as "a pattern of basic assumptions—invented, discovered, or developed by a given group as it learns to cope with its problems of external adaptation and internal integration—that has worked well enough to be considered valid and, therefore, to be taught to new members as the correct way to perceive, think, and feel in relation to those problems." Shafritz and Ott (1992, 481) suggest that organizational culture "is comprised of many intangible things such as values, beliefs, assumptions, perceptions, behavioral norms, artifacts, and patterns of behavior." Deshpande and Webster (1989, 4) "define organizational culture as the pattern of shared values and beliefs that help individuals understand organizational functioning and thus provide them norms for behavior in the organization." Schein (1985) further delineates culture as having levels, with *artifacts* being the most visible evidence (art, technology, visible and audible behavior). Another level, *values*, is an understanding of what ought to be. Finally, *basic assumptions* flow from repeated success with a solution such that it becomes the preferred solution.

These are some very learned definitions of culture. A perhaps more simple view is that "people who live and work in organizations know how to go along and get along" (McPherson and Jacobson 1994, 217). They have absorbed what is acceptable behavior, and know how to solve problems in a way acceptable to the organizations, and what to expect in return.

How does this affect our energy utilities, generally very mature businesses that have a very strong and ingrained culture that has developed over many decades? Utilities can be a very engineering-oriented culture, one that prides itself on its technical accomplishments and reliability and safety records or one that has great financial strength as a result of focusing on costs and efficient solutions to challenging technical problems. In any case, they will exist in a "deeply ingrained culture of regulation" (DeMichele 1994, 23), and that regulatory governance is what presents one of the more difficult obstacles for utilities to overcome. Utility leaders must effectively convey to their regulators the changes that are needed and being made by their companies and the role regulated utilities can play in a deregulated market. A proactive outreach—rather than a "hunkering-down" resistance to change—will likely leave the utility in a stronger position than it might otherwise find itself. By exemplifying a consumer, that is, a marketing, orientation, utilities will place themselves in a persuasive position at the deregulation bargaining table.

Schein (1999) offers a prescient insight about what is involved in bringing about a transformative change, as is the case with regulated utilities. Schein distills transformative culture change into three stages: creating the motivation to change, learning new concepts and new meanings for old concepts, and internalizing new concepts and meanings.

Creating the Motivation to Change

The regulated utility industry has been looking at the shadow of competition for over twenty years. There have been mixed results among the states that have instituted competition at the retail customer level. Poorly constructed deregulatory initiatives have led some states either to halt or even reverse the process. In fact, the Retail Energy Deregulation (RED) Index report, a scorecard that measures progress in energy restructuring, concluded that progress in letting consumers choose electric providers has effectively stopped in the United States. This is attributed to "California's well-publicized troubles, the ENRON collapse and the financial crisis in the energy industry" (CAEM 2003, vii).

If that is the case, what motivation do utility leaders have to drive the change we recommend? One reason is that other jurisdictions, specifically the United Kingdom and New Zealand, are having success with deregulation (CAEM 2003). And that success will likely provide the impetus for the leading states (Texas, Pennsylvania, Maine, and New York) to continue to promote and serve as models for what we expect will be a competitive market in most if not all other states.

Perhaps even more compelling is the technology under development. Fuel cells have enormous potential and, as described by the US DOE (2004):

> Using an electrochemical process discovered more than 150 years ago, fuel cells began supplying electric power for spacecraft in the 1960s. Today they are being used in more down-to-earth applications: to provide on-site power and will alter the regulated utility landsbanks, police stations, and office buildings. *In the near future, fuel cells could be propelling automobiles and allowing homeowners to generate electricity in their basements or backyards.*[Emphasis added]

Another technological development that, once commercialized, will alter the regulated utility landscape is the natural-gas-powered engine-driven electric generator. An excerpt from a Honda Corporation (Honda 2002) release describes that company's expectations:

> Honda Motor Co., Ltd. announced . . . that it has entered the final phase of development of a compact, home-use cogeneration (heat/electricity) unit. . . . The unit's compact design, which is small enough for home use, was achieved using an efficient layout combining the world's smallest natural gas engine—the GE160V—developed especially for use in the cogeneration unit, with a compact, lightweight electrical generation system . . . with a 6,000-hour (approx. 3 years) maintenance interval, a 20,000-hour (approx. 10 years) durability rating, and a redundant electrical failure detection function, the system provides carefree reliability for home use.

These two technologies have the potential to radically transform the energy industry, expanding the gas market while causing electric utilities to devise ways to salvage what could become severely underutilized distribution systems. These, more than the current deregulation initiatives, should drive the changes needed for the traditional utilities to survive in a radically different technological and competitive environment. Utility leaders need to manage their companies to provide the services that their customers want by playing an integral part in the transition to individual or localized generation.

Learning New Concepts and New Meanings for Old Concepts and Internalizing New Concepts and Meanings

Internalizing new concepts and meanings for old concepts involves, according to Schein (1999, 117), "imitation and identification with role models . . . [and] . . .

scanning for solutions and trial and error learning." In this, utility leaders as change managers can either choose to provide models and training to employees for them to learn from and adapt (a marketing orientation) to their own activities or the change manager can set goals and allow employees to seek their own solutions. This is a choice for the leaders. In doing so, the key ingredients to success involve providing a compelling vision and consistent systems and structures (Schein 1999, 124–125). Arizona Public Service's Mark DeMichele (1994) found that a new vision served not only to challenge the employees of his company but also to inspire them. DeMichele suggests that having the vision is not enough—it must be sustained. He did this through an intense training session for every employee called FOCUS, in which employees were encouraged to challenge basic assumptions about their industry and company to move the company to achievement of DeMichele's vision: to be one of the top five investor-owned utilities in the country by 1995, or "Top 5 by 95." This was a company that had, in 1988, among the highest rates and poorest customer relations in the country (Theibert 1994, 2). Did it work? Arizona Public Service won the highest honor in the electric industry, the Edison Award, in 1993. DeMichele moved his company by, among other things, setting a clear vision, providing a learning experience, consistently reinforcing the vision, and accomplishing an internalization of the vision by the employees.

CONCLUDING THOUGHTS ON THE ADOPTION OF A MARKETING ORIENTATION: THE CULTURE IS THE KEY

Utility leaders are being challenged by a myriad of demands. The competitive environment, while seemingly subdued in much of the country, is more than simply competition in production and customer operations, and is likely to move quickly as new technologies become available and regulatory agencies (having learned from past experience) establish rules to better facilitate a transition to retail access by the consumer. By recognizing these competitive challenges, articulating a clear vision for their companies, and taking steps to promote and encourage a marketing orientation among the utility workforce *now*, utility leaders can better position their companies to respond to the consumer and to competition into the increasingly competitive *future*.

As has been presented, the adoption of a marketing orientation will necessarily involve a culture change. Schein (1999) suggests that in mature organizations—and regulated utilities certainly fit that mold—culture change should not necessarily mean a radical change where the old is discarded in favor of the "new." Rather, by identifying the elements of culture through extensive interviews of groups of employees, and categorizing elements of culture as those deserving to be retained and those that require change, the culture change itself is facilitated by building upon what is good. For example, utilities generally pride themselves on reliability—an engineering-based performance criterion—which can be used to build an imperative for other forms of reliability. A case in point is keeping service appointments or other promises made to customers. As Zeithaml and colleagues point out, reliability is the most important of the service dimensions and simply means, "do what you say you are going to do" (Zeithaml, Parasuraman, and Berry, 1990, 27).

Schein (1999) also points out that mature organizations require time to test and accept new ways of doing things, and time for the new methods to become part of the basic assumptions of the organization. Changing the artifacts of culture (such as compensation, office layouts, dress codes, and other visible structures and processes) or restating values (such as vision and mission statements) are not enough. Rather, it is the basic assumptions of an organization, the collective mindset of the organization regarding what has worked in the past and resulted in success, that need to be intentionally crafted. And this will take considerable effort and time. If we believe that deregulation will progress—and reversing the momentum would be a little like trying to put the toothpaste back into the tube—and if we accept that there are technologies somewhere not just over the horizon but within view that have the potential to challenge the existing industry structure, then the time is now for leaders to assess what culture change needs to be affected over the next *decade* and begin the change process now. We believe that the essential parts of the strategy involve adopting a marketing orientation and crafting an organizational culture toward this end.

A final thought—even if technology does not usurp the existing order and deregulation does not progress, how would a utility be harmed by adopting an aggressive marketing orientation? As discussed herein, that means focusing on what the customer wants, investing in research, managing for the long term, understanding customer value, delivering on quality and service, seeking to improve continuously, *and* making all of this an integral part of a company's culture, its *psyche*. The answer, of course, is plain—it would not be detrimental in any way, and would only serve the utility by better ensuring satisfied customers who are willing to pay a fair price for the value received.

NOTES

1. Background and historical information for the deregulated energy industry are adapted from the author's dissertation (McClean 2003).

2. US DOE forecasts indicate that retail electric prices will be lower under competition. As part of the analysis for the administration's electric restructuring proposal, DOE forecasted retail electric prices in 2010 under both a competitive scenario and a cost of service or "reference" scenario. According to those forecasts, the national average price would be 6.3 cents per kilowatt-hour under the reference scenario and 5.5 cents per kilowatt-hour under the competitive scenario. By comparison, in New York, the average price would be 10.3 cents per kilowatt-hour under the reference scenario and 8.1 cents per kilowatt-hour under the competitive scenario (US DOE 1999, 9–10).

3. When there is a failure—as in the 2003 loss of electricity service to large swaths of the northeastern United States and Canada—there are reverberations at all levels of government and private industry. The efficacy of deregulation was called into question with concern that cost-cutting had left the systems vulnerable, and lack of national standards and control (of the transmission systems) had contributed to the cascading effect of neighboring systems that became overloaded when a local system failed, which in the view of some, is an assumption without merit (Malloy 2003).

REFERENCES

Bolton, R.N., and J.H. Drew. (1991). "A Longitudinal Analysis of the Impact of Service Changes on Customer Attitudes." *Journal of Marketing* 55 (1): 1–9.

Borenstein, S., and J. Bushnell. (2000). "Electricity Restructuring: Deregulation or Reregulation?" *Program on Workable Energy Regulation of the University of California Energy Institute.* Berkeley: University of California Energy Institute.

CA. (1997). Decision 97–05–040. http://162.15.7.11/wk-group/dai/dai2/36456.doc (www.cpuc.ca.gov/).

CAEM. (2003). RED Index-Center for the Advancement of Energy Management (by subscription) www.caem.org/.

Churchill, G., and C. Surprenant. (1982). "An Investigation Into the Determinants of Customer Satisfaction." *Journal of Marketing Research* 24 (11): 491–504.

Crandall, R., and J. Ellig. (1998). "Electric Restructuring and Consumer Interests: Lessons from Other Industries." *Electricity Journal* (January/February): 12–16.

Crosby, L.A. (1993). "Measuring Customer Satisfaction." In *The Service Quality Handbook*, ed. E.E. Scheuing and W.F. Christopher, 389–407. New York: AMACOM.

Day, B.R., and M. Moore. (1998). "Plugging into the Power of Leadership Teams." *Journal for Quality and Participation* 21 (3): 21–25.

DeMichele, R. (1994). "The APS Story: When Culture and Vision Make Magic." In *Lessons in Cultural Change: The Utility Industry Experience*, ed. P.R. Theibert, 1–15. Arlington, VA: Public Utilities Reports.

Deshpande, R., and F.E. Webster, Jr. (1989). "Organizational Culture and Marketing: Defining the Research Agenda." *Journal of Marketing* 53 (1): 3–15.

Drucker, P.F. (1954). *The Practice of Management.* New York: Harper and Row.

Etzel, M.J., B.J. Walker, and W.J. Stanton. (2004). *Marketing*, 13th ed. Boston: McGraw-Hill/Irwin.

Flaim, T. (2000). "The Big Retail 'Bust': What It Will Take to Get True Competition." *Electricity Journal* (March): 41–54.

Gordon, K., and W.P. Olson. (2000). "Open Entry, Choice, and the Risk of Short-Circuiting the Competitive Process." Washington, DC: Edison Electric Institute.

Goulding, A.J., C. Rufin, and G. Swinand. (1999). "The Role of Vibrant Retail Electricity Markets in Assuring that Wholesale Markets Operate Efficiently." *Electricity Journal* (December): 61–73.

Hansen, J.K. (1994). "Communicating Culture Change: A Practical Guide." In *Lessons in Cultural Change: The Utility Industry Experience*, ed. P.R. Theibert, 187–203. Arlington, VA: Public Utilities Reports.

Honda. (2002). "Honda Begins Monitor Testing." http//world.honda.com/news/2002/p020718.html.

Jones, K. (1998). "Working Smarter with Predictive Maintenance." *Electrical Apparatus* 51 (April): 23–25.

Joskow, P.L. (2000). "Why Do We Need Electric Retailers? Or Can You Get It Cheaper Wholesale?" Unpublished discussion draft.

Jovin, E. (1998). "Cal-ISO/PX Breaks the Mold: Will it Shatter the Market?" *Electrical World* 212 (May): 50–55.

Levitt, T. (1960). "Marketing Myopia." *Harvard Business Review* 38 (July–August): 26–44.

Lohr, S. (2004). "Big Blue's Big Bet—More Touch." *New York Times*, January 25, Late Edition, Section 3, p. 1, col. 1.

MA. (1997). "Legislation Restructuring the Electric Industry." www.state.ma.us/dpu/.

Malloy, K. (2003). "Nation's Energy Leaders Asleep at the Switch." www.Caem.org/internet/caem/pressrelease/blackout.html.

McClean, R.K. (2003). *Measuring Service Quality, Price and Overall Customer Satisfaction and Their Effect on Customer Retention and Referral in the Deregulated Electric Energy Industry.* New York: Pace University.

McDermott, K., K. Gordon, W.E. Taylor, and A.J. Ros. (2000). "Essential Facilities, Economic Efficiency, and a Mandate to Share: A Policy Primer." Washington, DC: Edison Electric Institute.

McPherson, C., and S.A. Jacobson. (1994). "It's the Strategy, Stupid!" In *Lessons in Cultural Change—The Utility Industry Experience*, ed. P.R. Theibert, 217–240. Arlington, VA: Public Utilities Reports.

NY. (1997). "Opinion and Order Establishing Regulatory Policies for the Provision of Retail Energy Services." Case 94–E-0952. www.dps.state.ny.us/.

NY PSC. (1996). "Vision Statement." www.dps.state.ny.us/.

PA. (2000). "Electric Choice Program." puc.paonline.com/electric/pages/asp.

Schein, E. (1985). "Defining Organization Culture." In *Classics of Organization Theory*, ed. J.M. Shafritz and S.J. Ott, 494–501. Belmont, CA: Wadsworth.

———. (1999). The *Corporate Culture Survival Guide.* San Francisco: Jossey-Bass.

Shafritz, J.M., and S.J. Ott. (1992). *Classics of Organization Theory*, 3rd ed. Belmont, CA: Wadsworth.

Slater, S., and J.C. Narver. (1992). "Superior Customer Value and Business Performance: The Strong Evidence for a Market-Driven Culture." In *Market-Driven Management*, ed. F.E. Webster, Jr., 219–224. New York: Wiley.

Theibert, P.R., ed. (1994). *Lessons in Cultural Change: The Utility Industry Experience.* Arlington, VA: Public Utilities Reports.

Train, K., and A. Selting. (2000). "The Effect of Price on Residential Customer Choice in Competitive Retail Energy Markets." Washington, DC: Edison Electric Institute.

Tschamler, T. (2000). "Designing Competitive Electric Markets: The Importance of Default Service and Its Pricing." *Electricity Journal* (March): 75–82.

Tse, D.K., and P.C. Wilton. (1988). "Models of Consumer Satisfaction Formation: An Extension." *Journal of Marketing Research* 25 (5): 204–212.

TX. (2000). "Electric Industry Restructuring, SB 7 Implementation, Project #20970." www.puc.state.tx.us/electric/projects/20970/20970.cfm (www.puc.state.tx.us/).

US DOE. (1999). "Electric Restructuring Proposal." www.energy.gov/index.html.

———. (2004). "Future Fuel Cells." http://www.fossil.energy.gov/programs.

Vargo, S.L., and R.F. Lusch. (2004). "Evolving to a New Dominant Logic for Marketing." *Journal of Marketing* 68 (1): 1–17.

Webster, F.E., Jr. (1994). *Market-Driven Management.* New York: Wiley.

———. (2002). *Market-Driven Management*, 2d ed. New York: Wiley.

WI. (1995). "Qualitative Assessment of Public Opinion on Restructuring of the Electric Utility Industry in Wisconsin." www.puc.state.tx.us/electric/arc/html.

———. (1997). "Electric Industry Restructuring." www.psc.state.wi.us/cases/elecrest (www.psc.state.wi.us/).

Winston, C. (1998). "U.S. Industry Adjustment to Economic Deregulation." *Journal of Economic Perspectives* 12 (Summer): 89–110.

Zeithaml, V.A., A. Parasuraman, and L.L. Berry. (1990). *Delivering Service Quality: Balancing Customer Perceptions and Expectations.* New York: Free Press.

Chapter 2

Reforming Wall Street

Challenges for Financial Leaders in Publicly Traded Firms

L. Keith Whitney and Michael D. Yonker

These are challenging times for the accounting profession. Through recent events, the world has learned an object lesson in the centrality of accounting and account-ability to our capital markets. This crisis brings us the opportunity to reflect and to refocus our efforts—to find new answers and make new commitments.

—"Educating for the Public Trust" (PricewaterhouseCoopers 2003)

As a result of various, well-publicized financial reporting scandals of recent years, the worldwide investing public has been reeling, questioning the integrity of the financial reporting system and the quality and usefulness of the information that system is de-signed to produce. When investor confidence in published corporate financial informa-tion is undermined, ultimately the capital markets are rendered ineffective as investors remove money from the market. Corporations are not able to raise needed capital funds for investment, and investors cannot earn adequate returns on their investments to fund retirement and other planned activities. Despite the fact that the overwhelming majority of American corporations were attempting to publish accurate financial reports, the ethi-cal and financial failures of Enron, Global Crossing, Tyco, and Adelphia Communica-tions rocked the financial world. What went wrong? How did the financial reports filed by these companies so confuse and mislead the most sophisticated investors?

THE ENRON EXAMPLE: HEDGING TECHNIQUES USED TO MISLEAD INVESTORS

Perhaps no corporate failure more dramatically eroded investor confidence in financial reporting than the failure of Enron and its high-flying stock that traded at $90 in August 2000 but dropped to less than $1 per share in 2001. In fact, Enron stock was in virtually everyone's retirement portfolio. Incredibly, precious few of the most sophisticated pro-fessional investors, many of whom have spent their entire lives reading and evaluating financial reports, understood how debt laden Enron really was. How did Enron's chief financial officer, Andrew Fastow, fool so many for so long?

In order to maintain its strong investment-grade credit rating while borrowing huge amounts of money, Enron initially followed an all-too-common approach of shifting debt off its balance sheet through another public entity. An investment-grade credit rating is reserved for the most creditworthy large corporations that, as a result of the high rating, are able to borrow at relatively low interest rates. Initially Enron used Enron Global Power and Pipelines as its counterparty entity (the entity to which an Enron asset and its associated debt would be transferred), but Fastow quickly tired of the usage of a public company, for a public company required shareholder votes and other corporate formalities. Thus, in 1997, Enron bought back the publicly traded shares of Enron Global Power and Pipelines and turned to private partnerships instead. Fastow touted the flexibility of such partnerships, but he was likely more pleased with the fact that he now had the ability to keep information private about these entities and the hedging transactions in which they engaged. Of course, Fastow and his wife were also profiting as principals in many of these partnerships. Enron profited from these transactions because the assets transferred were valued more highly than the debt transferred, and Enron recognized a gain on the transfer.

Financial Leverage Simplified

A simple illustration from fundamental corporate finance should help us understand why these transactions helped Enron earn high rates of return for holders of its equity securities. Suppose that you have two identical operating companies—A Incorporated (AI) and B Incorporated (BI). Each has total assets of $1 billion, and each has a basic earning power ratio (earnings before deducting any interest expense and taxes divided by total assets) of 10 percent. Assume a combined federal and state tax rate of 40 percent. Earnings before interest and taxes (EBIT) for each would be $100 million. AI would have no interest expense, so its taxable income would be $100 million, and its taxes would total $40 million. Thus, its net income after tax would be $60 million, and its return on equity would be $60 million divided by $1,000 million, or 6 percent.

The mirror image operating company BI would have the same EBIT, but assume that BI finances 75 percent of its assets with bond indebtedness at an investment grade bond issuer's rate of 6 percent. From its EBIT of $100 million, we first deduct interest expenses of $45 million. Taxable income is then only $55 million, and its tax expenses $22 million. BI would report net income after taxes equal to only $33 million, slightly more than one-half the amount reported by AI. However, BI's equity holders financed only 25 percent of BI's assets. So, its equity equals $250 million, and its return on equity (ROE) equals over 13 percent (13.2 percent, to be precise).

To better understand the power of leverage though, we can take our illustration one step further. Suppose that improved operations results in both AI and BI increasing their basic earning power (EBIT/Total Assets) to 15 percent. If you follow the same exercise that we followed above, then you will note that AI would increase its ROE to 9 percent; however, because BI's debt is a fixed-cost financing instrument, its interest expense will remain at $45 million. BI's taxable income will be $105 million, and its net income after taxes will be $63 million. Incredibly, BI now earns an ROE of 25.2 percent!

Recall that both AI and BI were exactly the same with regard to their business operations. The way the financial management of BI earned better ROE was through the use of *financial leverage*, the term commonly employed to describe financing some of a firm's assets with fixed-cost debt instruments. In order for Enron to grow as rapidly as it did, Fastow employed incredibly large amounts of debt—bonds and bank loans.

However, the financial markets are justifiably concerned about excessive use of debt. As a fixed-cost security, interest must be paid whether the company earns money or loses money. If either BI's basic earning power drops or its interest rates increase appreciably, the leverage effect will work in reverse. Utilization of such large percentages of debt financing greatly increases financial risk, which generally results in considerably higher interest rates. Debt loads at the levels utilized by Enron would have likely resulted in the loss of its investment-grade credit rating—thereby eliminating the positive impact of financial leverage.

What Fastow, Enron's banks, and Enron's auditors devised was a hedging scheme designed to mislead the market about the level of debt being used by Enron. In order to avoid the negative impact of issuing additional debt to finance an operation that would require more cash flow than the operation would initially produce, Enron chose to use special purpose entities to obtain off-balance-sheet financing. A special purpose entity (SPE) is a legal entity, usually a corporation, created to carry out a specific activity or series of transactions that are related. Although SPEs are common in business and have valid business purposes (for example, isolating assets or activities to protect the interest of creditors), Enron created SPEs in order to keep true economic losses off its financial statements and to hide its alarmingly high level of debt. Questionable valuation practices, which were accepted by Enron's auditor—Arthur Andersen & Company (AA & Co., the firm for which both chapter authors once worked)—allowed Enron to hedge gains that it aggressively recognized in its financial statements. Gains on Enron investments soared, but losses would be moved to the SPE.

A Specific Enron Example

In 1998, Enron acquired Rhythms Net Connections (RNC) stock for $10 million; however, a little over a year later, the stock investment had soared in value to approximately $300 million. Because Enron had signed a so-called lock-up agreement (common in initial public offerings of securities, such an agreement precludes insiders and other significant investors from selling for a certain period of time), it could not sell the investment until the end of 1999. Enron had already recognized the gain on the investment, and its management was concerned that the price of the RNC stock would drop before it could sell the investment. If that happened, Enron would have to recognize the loss, but Fastow wanted to hedge the gain (hold onto the gain, but transfer the potential for loss). Fastow, as CFO of Enron, would normally be precluded from operating an SPE created as counterparty to take the loss potential; however, the Enron board of directors specifically waived Enron's conflict-of-interest rules. Fastow and his wife made substantial profits in exchange for their willingness to manage SPEs that provided Enron with hedges that independent, commercial counterparties would never have accepted. The SPE would be substantially owned by Enron itself, but as long as other investors independent of Enron maintained at least a 3 percent equity investment in the SPE (an investment that had to be at risk throughout the transaction) and the independent owners exercised control over the SPE, the SPE financial statements did not have to be consolidated with those of Enron.

The RNC Transactions and Enron's Financial Statements

The SPE created in June 1999 to hedge the RNC investment involved a transfer of Enron's own restricted stock in exchange for a note and *put options*. An option is a contract that gives its holder the legal right to buy or sell an asset at some predetermined price within a specified period of time. An option that gives you the right to sell a stock at a specified price within some future period is called a put option. What this really means is that Enron guaranteed the value to the SPE through the value of its own stock.

So, in June 1999, Enron's accountants created assets by debiting Notes Receivable for $64 million and Put Options for $104 million. They credited Enron's Equity by $168 million. The accountants for the SPE debited Investment in Enron Stock for $168 million (the asset) and credited Revenue on the Sale of Put Options for $104 million and Notes Payable for $64 million. As long as Enron's stock increased in value over the period of the Put Option, the hedge worked perfectly to protect Enron's gain. In fact, the Enron stock did increase substantially from June 1999 to December 1999, the end of the option period and the lock-up agreement. As anticipated, the RNC stock was declining in value over the same period. To understand how the hedge worked, we need to look at how the accountants entered the next transactions on the books of Enron and the SPE.

Enron's accountants debited the loss (declined value of RNC stock) on its books and credited Investment in RNC. However, the loss was offset by the fact that Enron debited Options and recognized a Gain, the credit. While the SPE books reflected the RNC stock price decline by debiting Loss and crediting Options (a liability for the SPE), the SPE had enough asset value to cover the liability because Enron's stock increased in value over the option period. The SPE had enough asset value to cover the liability. If this had not been the case, then Enron would have had to record an impairment loss.

In early 2000, the arrangement with the SPE was concluded. The lock-up agreement had expired, and Enron sold its investment in RNC. Because the RNC stock had decreased in value, the unwinding required substantial payment from Enron to the SPE (providing substantial returns to Fastow and other investors in the SPE).

The Tumble: What Went Wrong?

This strategy of using Enron's own stock to guarantee the success of the SPE in hedging investment losses worked so well that Fastow employed the same strategy for all its investments. However, in early 2001, Enron's stock declined in value. The SPEs created to handle the hedges did not possess enough credit capacity (as a result of the declined value of the Enron stock held) to pay Enron on the hedges. As an interim fix (interim because Fastow thought Enron's stock would again increase in value), Enron employed offsetting options, using put and call options to protect the SPE's credit capacity. But the arrangement did not prevent liabilities from the swaps from increasing if Enron's hedged investments continued to slide. The scheme would have worked if either Enron's stock again increased in value substantially or if the investments themselves (stock in companies like RNC) had increased in value. But both the investments and Enron stock continued to decline. Around the time of the September 11 disaster, Enron finally terminated these hedging arrangements. The resulting pretax charge against Enron's income was $710 million. Making matters even worse, AA & Co. concluded that the RNC hedge had not really qualified either. Retroactive adjustments reduced reported net income for 1999 by $95 million and net income for 2000 by $8 million.

In summary, Enron used outside partnerships to monetize assets and move debt off its balance sheet. In the process, Enron was deeply involved in funding the partnerships. Five steps were involved in the process:

1. Enron would transfer an asset to an SPE (the partnership) to move the asset and debt off its balance sheet and to recognize a gain from the transfer.
2. Outside investors would inject at least 3 percent of the partnership's capital. Under Financial Accounting Standards Board (FASB, the independent governing body for certified public accountants) rules, a 3 percent outside investment allows Enron to avoid classifying the partnership SPE as a subsidiary.
3. At least in some cases, Enron actually helped provide some or all of the 3 percent capital injected by the purported outside investor. In addition, Fastow or his wife controlled the SPE, a violation of FASB rules.
4. Banks lent up to 97 percent of the capital needed by the partnership SPE. The SPE is expected to repay the loan from cash generated by the Enron assets it acquires or through the sale of the assets upon winding up the hedge.
5. Enron guaranteed the bank loan, in some cases also pledging Enron shares or pledging to make up any deficit.

When the Enron shares and the transferred assets declined in 2001, the deck of cards tumbled down. Great was the fall.

Who Was Culpable?

Who was to blame in the Enron collapse? Certainly, we should blame greedy corporate officials. We can blame an Enron board of directors audit committee that was asleep on the job. But we must also indict Arthur Andersen & Co., the accounting firm that was supposed to provide *independent* attestation that Enron's published financial statements accurately reflected the financial condition of Enron. Likewise, bank officers and professionally trained accountants were involved in helping Fastow devise the scheme. In addition, in 1995, lawmakers enacted legislation that shielded companies and their accountants from investor lawsuits. The law was pushed through as part of Newt Gingrich's Contract with America. The Private Securities Litigation Reform Act of 1995 emboldened securities lawyers, accountants, and corporate officers to engage in activities that they themselves likely considered questionable. After all, they were not liable for damages. Barbara Roper, director of Investor Protection at the Consumer Federation of America, indicates that the 1995 act "helped to create a culture that led to the Enron-Andersen scandal" (*New York Times on the Web*, February 3, 2002).

As finance educators, we do not escape blame either. Many commentators blame finance theory's emphasis on shareholder wealth maximization and executive compensation tied to stock price as a primary culprit. Finance professors have long argued that the best way to align the goals of professional managers and corporate shareholders is through compensation tied primarily to stock price performance, usually through stock options. Should it have surprised us that if often more than 75 percent of an executive's compensation is tied to short-term stock prices, the executive will do everything possible to manipulate the financial news that affects those stock prices?

Thus, what we have witnessed is interlocked causes of the overly hyped marketplace—imperial chief executive officers, rubber-stamping corporate boards, negligent gatekeeper auditors and other regulators, greedy bankers and institutional investors, and naive professors permitting flawed interpretations of financial theory. For reforms to be truly effective, they must touch on all these areas. Our recommendations for reform will focus on four of these key areas.

First, we will survey and evaluate the Sarbanes-Oxley Act of 2002 (Sarbanes-Oxley), the federal response to the crisis that rocked the accounting profession and the world's securities markets. The United States had what was perceived as the best-functioning and most transparent financial market in the world. Beginning with the Securities Act of 1933 that created the Securities and Exchange Commission (SEC), securities laws, regulators, and independent auditors combined to ensure dependable financial information. Suddenly, the American financial reporting system was deemed a fiction, a story told by greedy, manipulating executives out to deceive. Congress acted quickly and powerfully by enacting Sarbanes-Oxley. We survey Sarbanes-Oxley and evaluate the act and its effectiveness.

Second, we evaluate the most important players in the corporate reporting supply chain—the boards of directors, the company executives, and the independent auditors. We evaluate where American businesses stand with regard to reforming corporate governance, especially the board of directors and its audit committee. In the process, we discuss appropriate executive compensation and other changes that may more effectively focus managers on *long-term* financial success.

Third, we evaluate auditors and the auditing process. In particular, we look at Sarbanes-Oxley's impact on audit services, especially Section 404 of Sarbanes-Oxley, a provision requiring greater scrutiny over corporate internal controls.

Finally, we attempt to evaluate financial reports and reporting from the standpoint of investors. For example, should financial reports be better aligned with the information reported to senior management? Should the focus of these reports be on modern value drivers (factors that create longer-term value) rather than on backward-facing financial data?

THE CORPORATE REPORTING SUPPLY CHAIN

In their book entitled *Building Public Trust: The Future of Corporate Reporting*, Sam DiPiazza Jr. and Robert Eccles discuss what they term the "corporate reporting supply chain." It consists of virtually everyone who produces or consumes corporate reporting and analysis and is, as described by them, more extensive than the roles and parties we evaluate. The foundation of their model consists of standard setters such as the FASB, the American Institute of Certified Public Accountants (AICPA), the new Public Company Accounting Oversight Board, market regulators like the SEC, and enabling technologies. Their supply chain moves from the company executives to the boards of directors through independent auditors and information distributors to the analysts and investors, the ultimate users of the financial reports. As indicated, we intend to evaluate more fully the reform of corporate governance, including executive management and compensation, and auditing (DiPiazza and Eccles 2002).

SARBANES-OXLEY: A SUMMARY OF PROVISIONS

On July 30, 2002, President Bush signed into law a corporate reform measure commonly known as the Sarbanes-Oxley Act of 2002. The act calls for the creation of a Public Company Accounting Oversight Board (PCAOB) with the following characteristics:

- It would consist of five financially literate members, two of whom are certified public accountants.
- These full-time board members are appointed by the SEC for five-year terms.
- The PCAOB operates under SEC oversight and authority.
- The PCAOB may establish or adopt audit and other standards.
- The PCAOB conducts inspections of firms and disciplinary proceedings. It may share the results of its investigations with state boards of accountancy.

The PCAOB may recognize the FASB to set generally accepted accounting principles (GAAP).

Under Sarbanes-Oxley, public accounting firms that audit SEC-regulated clients would be required to:

- register with the PCAOB and pay fees;
- maintain audit work papers for at least seven years;
- conduct second partner review;
- evaluate internal control structure of SEC clients; and
- undergo annual inspection of more than 100 SEC clients.

Further, in order to facilitate better auditor independence, Sarbanes-Oxley prohibits auditors from offering the following nonaudit services to audit clients:

- bookkeeping or other client write-up services;
- financial information systems design or implementation;
- appraisal or valuation services, fairness opinions, or contribution-in-kind reports;
- actuarial services;
- internal audit outsourcing services;
- management function or human resources;
- broker or dealer, investment adviser, or investment banking services;
- legal or expert services unrelated to the audit;
- any other service the PCAOB determines by regulation is not permitted.

A registered public accounting firm may engage in a nonaudit service (including tax counsel) that is not described above if the activity is approved in advance by the audit committee of the company.

Mandatory audit rotation is required. The partner-in-charge of the audit must be rotated every five years. To further ensure better separation between the audit client and the CPA firm, a cooling-off period for partners and employees of the audit firm to take before they can be considered for positions like chief executive officer (CEO), chief financial officer, controller, and similar positions with the client firm is one year. Sarbanes-Oxley also requires the U.S. comptroller general to study and review the potential effects of requiring mandatory audit rotation among the firms.

Sarbanes-Oxley also sets certain corporate responsibilities. The audit committee of the board of directors is responsible for the hiring, compensation, and oversight of the auditor. Members of the audit committee must themselves be independent. They cannot accept consulting, advisory, or other compensatory fees from the company or be an affiliated person of the company or a subsidiary. Audit committees must have procedures established for complaints received about accounting, internal controls, or auditing matters. They must also have procedures for handling confidential, anonymous submission by employees of the company regarding accounting or auditing matters. Audit committees must be allowed to engage outside advisers, as they deem necessary. Companies must provide adequate funding for the audit committee and any outside advisers it deems necessary.

Under Sarbanes-Oxley the CEO and CFO must certify each annual or quarterly report, as follows:

- The signer has reviewed the report.
- Based on the officer's knowledge, the report neither contains an untrue statement of a material fact nor omits a material fact that would make the published financial statements misleading.
- Based on the officer's knowledge, the financial statements present fairly, in all material respects, the financial condition and results of operation of the company.

In addition to the above, the signing officers are responsible for establishing and maintaining the system of internal controls. In fact, the effectiveness of the internal controls must be certified as evaluated by the signer within ninety days prior to the report. The signer must also present in his or her report conclusions about the internal controls and disclose any significant deficiencies in the design or operation of the internal control system and any fraud, material or not, involving management or other employees that have a significant role in the internal control system. The signer must also indicate whether there were any significant changes in internal controls or other factors that could affect the internal control system, including any corrective actions that resulted from any significant deficiencies or material weaknesses.

Under Sarbanes-Oxley it is illegal for an officer or director of the company to fraudulently influence, coerce, manipulate, or mislead an auditor in the conduct of a financial statement audit. If a company is required to issue an accounting restatement as a result of misconduct, the CEO and CFO are required to forfeit any incentive-based or equity-based compensation from the company for the twelve-month period following the first public filing of the incorrect statements or the profits they realize from the sale of the company's securities during that same twelve-month period (Oracle 2003; PricewaterhouseCoopers 2002).

Enhanced Financial Disclosures under Sarbanes-Oxley

Corporations governed by Sarbanes-Oxley are responsible for enhanced financial disclosures. All financial statements that are filed with the SEC must also include all material correcting adjustments that were made in accordance with GAAP and SEC rules. The SEC now governs final rules on the disclosure of all material off-balance-sheet transactions, arrangements, obligations, and other relationships with unconsolidated entities or with other persons. Furthermore, the SEC determines final rules on the use of pro forma financial information in order to ensure that such information does not contain any untrue statements or omit material facts. The pro forma information must reconcile to GAAP as well.

It is also unlawful for any public corporation to arrange for the extension of credit in the form of personal loans to any director or executive of the company. This provision may have been directed at the family self-dealings of companies like Adelphia Communications. John J. Rigas, who founded Adelphia, the sixth largest cable operator in the United States, borrowed $3.1 billion from Adelphia through family-controlled entities. In addition, the company invested $3 million in *Songcatcher*, a film produced by Ellen Rigas Venetis, a daughter of the Adelphia founder. One of the most significant issues raised was why the auditor for Adelphia failed to inform the Adelphia audit committee about the inappropriate use of company funds for family purposes. Of course, part of the problem may well have been that Rigas family members served on the audit committee!

Other mandated disclosures include the fact that any person who is directly or indirectly the owner of more than 10 percent of any class of equity securities or who is a director or officer of an issuing company is required to file notification with the SEC of the purchase or sale of shares within two business days of the transaction. Of critical importance, the company is also required to disclose to the public on a rapid and current basis any information concerning material changes in the financial condition or operation of the firm. These disclosures are expected to be in plain English. Transparency is the key.

In brief, Sarbanes-Oxley mandated specific actions to improve corporate reporting. Within the framework of the provisions outlined above, each participant plays a critical part in providing investors with information on which they can reliably base investment decisions. Many of the Sarbanes-Oxley mandates were in response to the ethical failures of executives and auditors at Enron, Adelphia, Global Crossing, Tyco, WorldCom, and other entities. However, as several have noted, investor faith will be more quickly restored when participants in the corporate reporting supply chain move beyond the legal requirements and commit to the highest levels of personal integrity and transparency (openness).

CORPORATE GOVERNANCE: THE BOARD, THE AUDIT COMMITTEE, AND THE CEO

So, what are the problems that nearly destroyed faith in America's financial reporting system? We believe that most of the problems at Enron, Adelphia, Global Crossing, Tyco, WorldCom, and other problem entities can be traced to problems in corporate governance. Sound governance reinforces a culture of corporate integrity, contributes to the identification and pursuit of proper long-term strategic goals, and ensures continuity of excellent executive leadership. Boards of directors also play essential roles as watchdogs for shareholders and guardians of corporate legal and ethical compliance. However, a McKinsey survey (Felton and Watson 2002) noted that 44 percent of corporate directors failed to fully understand the key drivers of value for the organizations they governed. The tension lies in how to strengthen the role of outside directors and distance the board from CEO control without undermining management's ability to run the business (Byrne 2002; Osterland 2002).

Just What Is Corporate Governance?

Corporate governance mechanisms fall broadly into two main categories—either internal or external. External mechanisms include accounting rules and regulatory reporting requirements, as well as external audits by independent auditors and even governmental agencies. Internal corporate governance is actually what we are considering now. It includes the board of directors, subcommittees of the board (especially the audit committee, the compensation committee, and the CEO nominating committee), and compensation programs designed to align the interests of managers and shareholders.

Corporate governance has often functioned at the direction of one individual though—the CEO. After appointment to the office of CEO, many executives begin to fill the board with individuals close to them. At Adelphia, family members were even appointed to the board. Others are appointed for political correctness rather than any real expertise. In fact, several boards name the same political leaders, often to gain ethnic diversity. While diversity contributes positively to many boards of directors, we believe that no individual can serve effectively on as many as six or more boards. Yet, according to Factset, five individuals sit on six or more Standard and Poors (S & P) 500 boards. In 2003, of the top five busiest directors, three were associated with companies now plagued by problems. In fairness, the pressure for more responsible governance has helped. One year earlier, the number of individuals sitting on five or more S & P 500 boards was double what it is now. But the potential problems associated with overextended directors are clear.

The most important line of defense against fraud, abuses of power, and executive greed is a proactive, effective, and responsible board of directors. Sound corporate governance should strive to support a culture of corporate integrity, identify appropriate long-term goals of profitable growth, and diligently represent the interests of all key stakeholders, especially the long-term investors (those investing for the long haul rather than those hoping to turn a quick profit). Perhaps the Latin phrase *fides servanda est* (faith must be observed) says it best. The board, as agents of the shareholders, must not violate the confidence reposed in it.

What we are really saying is that the primary responsibility of the board is to foster the long-term success of the corporate entity while being consistent with its fiduciary responsibility to the shareholders and to outside regulators, who represent the interests of the public. We believe that the only kind of board that is likely to effectively carry out these responsibilities is a board that is independent of the executive leadership and accountable to shareholders. But there are other aspects of well-constituted and organized boards of directors that we need to evaluate. We suggest that boards should have the following attributes if we are to expect them to function well over time (Berle 1932; Dine 2000; Monks and Minow 1995).

Seven Keys to Excellent Board Governance

We outline the following as seven key areas of focus for organizational leaders intent upon building sound board governance.

1. Director Independence

The evidence for a board dominated by independent, outside directors is overwhelming. In their paper entitled "Corporate Governance and Equity Prices," Paul Gompers and Joy Ishii of Harvard University, along with Andrew Metrick of the University of Pennsylvania's Wharton School, report on their research into corporate governance and stock prices. They write, "Using performance-attribution time-series regressions from September 1990 to December 1999, we find that the Democracy Portfolio outperformed the Dictatorship Portfolio by a statistically significant 8.5 percent per year. These return differences induced large changes in firm value over the sample period" (2003, 109).

Gompers, Ishii, and Metrick (2003) posit three primary hypotheses (other than the hypothesis that the superior returns result from the governance orientation toward democratic representation) for explaining the fact that the twenty-four distinct corporate governance provisions evaluated for approximately 1,500 firms since 1990 demonstrate that firms with greater shareholder rights and lower management power outperformed the dictator firms with lesser shareholder rights and greater management power. Only one of those hypotheses tended to explain *some* of the performance differences— the hypothesis that governance provisions did not *cause* poor performance but simply happened to correlate with other unidentified characteristics that were associated with abnormal returns. However, even this hypothesis could account for only one-third of the performance differences. Therefore, the authors conclude that there is evidence strongly supportive of the hypothesis that firms that are more democratic in governance organization outperform those firms that are more dictatorial (Gompers, Ishii, and Metrick 2003).

Thus, we simply conclude from this research and from the work of various scholars and commentators that a substantial majority of the board should be comprised of independent, outside directors. More specifically, these independent, outside directors should be neither current nor former employees of the corporation. The General Motors model is a good one here: GM rules indicate that no outside board member should have a business or other relationship with the firm other than as a director and shareholder.

2. Director Qualifications

First, in order for the board to be diverse, it must be comprised of individuals with diverse business experiences. At least one director should qualify as an expert in financial issues, especially those related to financial reporting. Ideally, some outsider with audit or high level (a CFO, independent of the company and its CEO and CFO) experience should chair the audit committee. Certainly this may be much easier to suggest than to execute. Individuals who serve in the capacity of CFO are well aware of the liability issues associated with service on boards, and most of them do not have enough time to manage the financial affairs of their own companies. The ideal candidate may be a retired CFO or audit partner of a national CPA firm. Whoever the candidate is, this person should be limited to membership on one or possibly two boards.

Others qualified to sit on the board will be individuals with industry expertise. For high-tech companies, the best directors will understand the new economy and its value drivers. Some outside board members may well be chosen to represent the shareholders or even critics of the company and its policies. A board chair may be chosen for his or her expertise in mediation, as the task of managing an engaged board that maintains the proper balance between engagement and domination is difficult. The board is not chosen to manage the day-to-day affairs of the corporation; rather, it really is the watchdog for stakeholders, a check-and-balance entity. For all these reasons, some have suggested that model boards should include representation by significant customers, suppliers, financial advisers, employees, and community activists.

3. Limitations on Board Memberships

Boards should, in our judgment, be smaller. They should have no more than ten to twelve members, and, as we have indicated, outside, independent directors should outnumber inside directors by at least two to one. But we believe that there should be limits on the number of boards that any individual can serve. Chief executive officers should be limited to no more than one other board. But we should also end the professional board member, the one who earns most of his or her living by serving as the token outsider. This individual is often famous in his or her own right, perhaps even a politician. In far too many instances, these individuals are spread far too thin to be doing much more than accepting their pay.

4. Board Members Should Be Nominated by Outside Directors

Besides limiting the number of boards that CEOs and others can serve, changing the way new board members are nominated should alleviate some of the cronyism that exists (one CEO choosing another friend to serve on his board, and, in return, he will serve on her board). Ideally, outside directors should screen and recommend candidates for the board based on qualifications that have been established and written down by the board.

5. Board Alignment with Shareholders

In order to align the interests of the board with the interests of the shareholders they serve, directors should have a direct, personal and material investment in the common stock of the company. Compensation should include *restricted shares of stock* in the company rather than stock options. Just as with the top executives, the use of stock options tends to focus performance far too much on the immediate short-term period ahead. Restricted stock that cannot be sold for a considerable period of time aligns the board interests with those of the more permanent investors and lessens the tendency to manipulate information for immediate gain (Weidenbaum 1991).

6. Director Education and Commitment

Directors should attend *boarding school.* They should be required to spend some time in a preparatory workshop ideally run by some of America's best joint JD/MBA programs so that the participants learn about both the proper legal and business role each is undertaking. Directors should be required to make a specific commitment of time for each meeting. Meetings should occur monthly for a full day. In addition, the board should have one two- to three-day strategy session each year. Finally, even if the CEO is permitted to serve on the board, the outside directors should meet alone and plan the actual board meetings. The chairperson of the board should be an outside director, and this individual should have an even greater commitment of his or her time to the board (Harris 2003).

7. Boards Should Be Committed to Long-term Shareholder Value

Corporate finance has long advocated shareholder wealth maximization. We do not believe that the problem is the goal, but we do believe that a misunderstanding of that goal has adversely affected corporate management. In order to align the true interests of the firm's investors (not stock traders who are stock purchasers one day and stock sellers the next), we suggest that the board develop alternative measures of performance, such as market position, productivity, an index of employee attitudes, and other more creative measures. Even if not recognized in published financial statements, corporate boards need to define assets more broadly to include customer relations, productivity of research and development, and relative position in the market. The final goal would be to develop the board's codification of long-term shareholder value; this goal would be to articulate the factors that the board will use in judging the performance of the corporation and its management (Baysinger and Butler 1985; Blair 1995; Chew and Gillan 2005; Conger, Lawler, and Finegold 2001; Core, Holthausen, and Larcker 1999; Demsetz and Lehn 1985; Ward 2000).

A Checklist for Board Governance

In brief, as the board organizes for its duties, the board should, at the very minimum, accomplish the following:

1. Develop an agreed-upon mission statement on the board's purposes and responsibilities.
2. Boards should also articulate their chosen size, subcommittees, and policies regarding independence.
3. Boards should indicate clearly the specific criteria for choosing new board members. Although not discussed in the preceding paragraphs, the board should also develop policies regarding the maximum terms that board members may serve and indicate any mandatory retirement age. In addition, the policies of the board should include clear standards for the evaluation of directors. For example, how many meetings will a director be permitted to miss before he or she must resign?
4. The board should codify its operational rules. In this section of the board's operating rules, the board should specify who will bear the responsibility for setting the agenda of board meetings, an agenda that should always permit open discussion. The board should determine the size, composition, and the duties of specified subcommittees related to auditing and executive compensation, at a minimum.
5. Finally, the board should clearly articulate its perception of how it should interrelate with the chosen management of the corporation. This section should include an indication of how the board will evaluate the CEO and determine executive pay. Ideally the board would even have a predetermined succession policy statement that sets forth the plan for the development of a successor CEO. Tension between the CEO and the board can be avoided or lessened if these

operational guidelines also indicate clearly when and how the board should communicate with other executives (sub-CEO).

AUDITORS, AUDITING, AND THE BALANCE SHEET

In addition to the changes we believed necessary in the so-called corporate reporting supply chain and to the changes already set in motion by Sarbanes-Oxley, we now attempt to evaluate where auditing should head next, post–Sarbanes-Oxley. Certainly for larger public corporations and the financial markets, the changes mandated by Sarbanes-Oxley should greatly improve auditor independence and objectivity. We applaud the fact that this legislation requires the auditor to report directly to an audit committee of the board of directors. We also believe that eliminating the joint-venture mentality that existed at companies like Enron, where lines between Andersen employee and Enron employee were often almost impossible to detect, is an important step toward the restoration of a true auditor-client relationship. In other words, we also applaud the hiring restrictions related to auditor personnel.

However, one issue that remains is audit firm rotation, an issue that Sarbanes-Oxley referred to the U.S. comptroller general for study and eventual report back to Congress. The stated rationale for mandatory firm rotation is to ensure greater likelihood of auditor independence from company management. Presumably audit firms still have too much pressure on them to please the audit client rather than fulfill their duty to the outside user of audited financial statements, when they are permitted to audit the same firms without limit.

There are concerns about mandatory rotation that are relevant, too. First, what is there about rotation that guarantees independence? Will the next auditor be appointed by the PCAOB or some other entity, or will it be chosen by the audit committee of the board? The tendency to please the client rather than fulfill one's duty may still be great.

More important, according to most observers and in our experience, the first year or two of an audit is inefficient, or suboptimal to say the least. A five-year rotation pattern would ensure that lower quality audits were likely for 20 to 40 percent of all audits. The likelihood is that such pressures could well result in a lowering of auditing quality. Some have even suggested that the tendency may be to lessen audit quality and the resources devoted to an audit as one reaches the end of the audit cycle because the firm will have no prospects for contract renewal.

Finally, audit firms have tended to compete on two primary bases—price and industry expertise. Will mandatory rotation preclude the maintenance of real industry expertise or will it enhance the development of industry expertise across a larger group of firms? We really do not know the answer to that question, but the issue is relevant. The greater the expertise of the auditors, the greater the quality of the audits performed.

Section 404 of Sarbanes-Oxley

All that aside, it is clear that Section 404 of the Sarbanes-Oxley Act has stimulated real change in the audit itself and in audit priorities. Auditors are now demanding documentation through detailed flow charts and narrative descriptions of internal controls and control systems. Every aspect of the business, including purchasing, sales, payroll, inventory, and property, must be subject to internal controls—procedures for how the items are handled, how the documentation supports the item, and how high-level executives are regularly monitoring the transactions.

How hard is it for companies to comply with Section 404? Perhaps the best evidence that the process is daunting is the fact that the deadline for compliance has been extended more than once. The most recent deadline for compliance with Section 404 was June 15, 2004. To make matters worse, Sarbanes-Oxley undoubtedly prohibits companies from seeking the assistance of their auditors in setting up internal control systems. While *we* say "undoubtedly," Scott Taub of the Securities and Exchange Commission has said that while complete reliance on external auditors is not appropriate, independence rules do not prevent auditors from assisting management in preparing for Section 404. Most of the large accounting firms have disagreed and have refused to offer such services. They do generally realize the need to provide some guidance about what controls are necessary and appropriate. Of course, this prohibition has created another new industry—one providing Section 404 consulting for relatively high fees!

Is Sarbanes-Oxley Too Costly?

Ned Desmond, the president of Business 2.0, has written: "The Sarbanes-Oxley Act of 2002 ought to be renamed the Full-Employment Act for Lawyers, Accountants, and Insurance Executives" (2002, 75). Desmond does not argue that all the provisions of Sarbanes-Oxley are bad, but he believes that the costs of compliance will destroy some small companies. Is he correct?

Desmond is probably not correct. However, we do believe that many small public companies may be taken private. If a company is already losing money, then the prospect of spending large sums of money to develop and document better internal controls could be deemed too costly. But not all small companies will face high price tags for Section 404–compliant internal controls. Even small companies with operations in various locations, especially locations outside the United States, may face total developmental costs approaching $1 million. In addition to developmental costs, expenses related to operating more complex systems of internal control could be significant. Most of the CEOs that we have encountered want a highly qualified internal auditor and sophisticated internal controls in order to support the CEO's personal attestation of the accuracy of earnings reports and other financial statements. Finally, while not likely to be a particularly large fee for smaller companies, the PCAOB is empowered to assess fees for the PCAOB operating budget against the accounting firms and public corporations that are subject to Sarbanes-Oxley.

The good news is that some executives with whom we spoke believe that the worst is over. The most significant cost associated with Section 404 compliance is documentation, followed by detailed policy development, self-assessment, and attesting requirements. Training costs are also significant. But most observers, especially those from larger corporations, indicated that initial compliance costs were not as burdensome as feared and that ongoing costs seem to be manageable. Still, as *CFO* magazine reported in both September 2003 and February 2004, seven out of ten finance executives indicated that they believed the benefits of Sarbanes-Oxley failed to outweigh the costs.

Finally, at a recent Los Angeles meeting of the California Society of Certified Public Accountants (CPAs), most in attendance, including educators, CPAs, and American Accounting Association representatives, indicated that the burden imposed by Sarbanes-Oxley was largely a function of the size and preparedness of the publicly traded entity. The consensus was that some companies find the Sarbanes-Oxley compliance costs to be exorbitant; others have not experienced significant cost increases because they were adequately prepared, with already well-documented systems and excellent internal controls.

One of the speakers at the California Society of CPAs meeting represented a European company that was not subject to Sarbanes-Oxley. He indicated that his firm had chosen to comply anyway. As a worldwide entity, the Dutch-based firm might well decide to access the U.S. securities markets. His company had eleven people dedicated to the project full time, and he expected his firm's costs to exceed $2 million over the next twelve months.

Other small companies may need to comply, at least with Sarbanes-Oxley-like internal controls. Many start-up companies are launched in the hope that a large company will buy them out. The price that a publicly traded company is willing to pay may well depend on how difficult and costly the Section 404 compliance procedures are deemed to be. If the company has attempted to comply and has documented all processes well, then the price for the company could be higher than for the company that is deemed to possess significant weaknesses in its control systems.

There is one additional implicit cost to the smaller company related to Sarbanes-Oxley and changes in the accounting firms. For most small start-up companies, internal financial expertise is limited. These firms have often depended on their CPA firm for guidance and financial assistance. Personnel of the large CPA firm that also audits these firms have reviewed expansion plans and other important matters related to the companies' core businesses. Now, under Sarbanes-Oxley (as noted above), auditing firms are precluded from most services that would threaten independence. It is quite possible that the lack of good financial advice could lead to an increasing failure rate among these firms. As the cliché indicates—only time will tell! Of course, this is not a problem for firms that choose to go private. Most of the large CPA firms with which we spoke indicated that they were developing two tiers of practice. These services were still being offered to business entities that were not their audit clients. In addition, a preapproval waiver exists for de minimis nonaudit services, but only in extraordinarily rare circumstances.

Is Luca Pacioli Relevant Anymore?

Luca Pacioli is the Italian mathematician who developed double-entry bookkeeping in the 1400s in Venice. He offered merchants a system for keeping track of their transactions. Is this 600-year-old system still relevant? Many analysts indicate that this ancient accounting system is increasingly irrelevant in the so-called new economy. Why? What has changed?

According to Baruch Lev, the Philip Bardes Professor of Accounting and Finance at New York University's Stern School of Business and developer of a Knowledge Capital Scorecard that attempts to properly value intangible assets deemed value drivers, the fact that the market-to-book ratio of Standard and Poor's 500 (market value of the stock relative to the book value for the 500 largest companies in the United States) now routinely exceeds six means that traditional balance-sheet assets account for only 10 to 15 percent of the value of these companies. He notes that AMR Corp. sold 18 percent of its SABRE computer-reservations system and retained the remaining 82 percent. In January 2004, 50 percent of the value of AMR, one of the largest airlines in the world with numerous tangible assets, was in an intangible computer-reservation system (Webber 2000).

Intangible assets that function as value drivers are sometimes classified into four basic categories:

1. Assets associated with product innovation (research and development),
2. Assets associated with a company's brand identity, which through product differentiation facilitates higher prices for the firm's products and services,
3. Better, more efficient business systems and methods (a driver for Wal-Mart, a company that outperforms its competitors because of superior systems), and
4. Market power through intellectual property protections (patent, copyright, etc.) or through substantial sunk costs that operate as effective barriers to entry for others.

The existence of these assets, often unaccounted for under traditional accounting principles (GAAP, the rules established by the official bodies—FASB and AICPA), often explains almost the entire value of an entity. In the article noted above, Lev points out that Cisco paid $6.9 billion for Cerent Corp., a firm with six-month total sales of roughly $10 million. The point is that the cost to acquire a knowledge asset can be incredibly high; our point is that that value does not appear on a firm's financial statement until it appears in the financials of the acquiring firm.

We agree that the old accounting system really does not produce a meaningful balance sheet. Worse, many traditional performance measures that rely on balance-sheet values could be entirely misleading. For example, return on investment is determined by dividing net income after taxes by total assets. Yet, the historical cost of unamortized assets has almost nothing to do with the value of the resources under the manager's control. Even systems that improve upon traditional performance measures (such as economic value added) that charge the entity with a cost of capital employed still fail to take into account the intangible assets under management's control.

What if we had evaluated performance of IBM's management by some better performance measure that took into account the brand recognition associated with IBM, the value of its patents and other intellectual property, and its once superior systems? A rational board would not reward the managers of firms like IBM and AT&T, once dominant giants but now reduced to ordinary competitors.

Advocates of knowledge capital and valuing superior human resources believe that earnings in excess of normalized earning (a reasonable return on physical and financial assets) are created by knowledge assets, assets whose value can be determined by capitalizing these excess returns.

Our purpose is not to vouch for Lev's proposal or the numerous others that exist. Our purpose is to suggest that it is time for American accountants to seriously consider some of the innovative approaches being tried in Europe. It is time to provide investors with the same kind of information that insiders get—cost accounting and management information systems based on true cost drivers rather than ancient tradition.

Why is change so hard? First, foundational to accounting is the principle of objectivity. Fundamentally, accountants do not trust mere mortal judgment as to the value of intellectual property or superior business systems. A system built upon the principles of knowledge-based capital seems a little too fuzzy to most accountants.

Second, we think it is a little like academia. Does the current system of rank, tenure, and promotion make sense? It is probably more seriously flawed. Many in academia recognize that it is an antiquated, inefficient system. But it is a system by which those in power have succeeded. Those in control of universities became full professors because they mastered that system. They love the system because it is that system that facilitated their own recognition and rewards. Just as in academia, accountants have superior knowledge of the current system. They possess proprietary information, often privately held, that enables them to profit in the current environment. Why change?

Of course, there is another fundamental issue—why take the legal risk? To be sure, in America at least, mistakes made in valuing intangibles would be the subject of a new cottage industry—that is, lawyers suing those making the valuations and the accountants attesting to the fairness of financial reports based on those assessments. Perfecting an archaic, meaningless system subjects one to far fewer causes of legal action.

WHAT IS NEEDED TO REFORM WALL STREET?

As we consider what financial reporting system is needed, we diverge a bit. We are concerned about the way America continues to regulate its firms toward competitive disadvantage. What do we mean by this? The American CFO of a publicly traded firm must not only certify that quarterly financial reports fairly represent the position of the firm at the end of the accounting period under consideration, but he or she must also openly answer the questions of financial analysts who want to know the strategies to which the firm has committed. The American CFO must answer, and he or she must answer truthfully. Material misrepresentation can occur through intentional failure to disclose (omission) as well as through disclosure of erroneous information. Of course, this disclosure is readily available to each of the firm's competitors. These competitors listen and react.

On the other hand, these same competitors from Japan and South Korea do not face the same disclosure requirements. In some high-tech industries this disclosure is incredibly costly. If NewCo, a newly formed firm producing technological mousetraps, brings a better technology mousetrap to market first, the firm can expect to enjoy a competitive advantage for only a few months. However, if it discloses its plans months before the product launch, then that period of competitive advantage will be reduced even more. This is particularly true when a firm develops new technology that enables it to produce a product for a new market. Thus, we would advocate reducing the required public disclosures of strategies and new products.

We also believe that the financial community must address the problem by applying greater pressure for worldwide GAAP. Already the International Standards on Auditing are issued by the International Federation of Accountants, in which the United States is represented by the AICPA. These standards are being used in countries that previously lacked standards altogether. These standards will likely be adopted in the European Union and put into practice in 2005. Convergence of GAAP and auditing standards worldwide will lessen the negative impact of required disclosures here. Indeed, as foreign firms increasingly seek access to the American capital markets, differences may become even less significant.

In the final analysis, Sarbanes-Oxley has done much to restore confidence in the American financial reporting system. Development of an even better financial reporting system, one more transparent and relevant while committed to integrity and accountability, should be the goal of all responsible parties—the SEC, the FASB, the AICPA, the PCAOB, and similar international bodies. We appreciate Sarbanes-Oxley's requirements of greater auditor independence, increased depth of audit services (including internal controls and internal auditing), better corporate governance, and oversight of the auditing profession. All of us depend on sustained confidence in the accuracy and reliability of corporate reporting. Sarbanes-Oxley is a good beginning—perhaps an *excellent* beginning for large corporations. The goals should now be (1) to establish worldwide systems of financial reporting that provide timely, relevant, and transparent information to governments and investors alike, and (2) to review the unintended impact that Sarbanes-Oxley is having on smaller publicly traded companies. In all likelihood, Sarbanes-Oxley will not eliminate corporate greed and wrongdoing, but the act has eliminated some of the conflicts of interest that kept our watchdog auditors from doing their collective duty. Our hope is that the Sarbanes-Oxley mandated reorganizations of prestigious accounting firms will facilitate a similar restoration of the honor and integrity once so prevalent in the industry.

REFERENCES

Baysinger, B.D., and H.N. Butler. (1985). "Corporate Governance and the Board of Directors: Performance Effects of Changes in Board Composition." *Journal of Law, Economics, and Organization* 1: 101–124.

Berle, A.A., Jr. (1932). "For Whom Corporate Managers Are Trustees: A Note." *Harvard Law Review* 45: 1365–1372.

Blair, M.M. (1995). *Ownership and Control: Rethinking Corporate Governance for the Twenty-First Century.* Washington, DC: Brookings Institution.

Byrne, J.A. (2002). "How to Fix Corporate Governance." *Business Week* (May 6): 69–78.

Chew, D.H., Jr., and S.L. Gillan. (2005). *Corporate Governance at the Crossroads.* New York: McGraw-Hill/Irwin.

Conger, J.A., E. Lawler, and D. Finegold. (2001). *Corporate Boards: New Strategies for Adding Value at the Top.* San Francisco: Jossey-Bass.

Core, J.E., R.W. Holthausen, and D.F. Larcker. (1999). "Corporate Governance, Chief Executive Officer Compensation, and Firm Performance." *Journal of Financial Economics* LI: 371–406.

Demsetz, H., and K. Lehn. (1985). "The Structure of Corporate Ownership: Causes and Consequences." *Journal of Political Economy*, 93: 1155–1177.

Desmond, N. (2002). *Business 2.0* (December/January): 75.

Dine, J. (2000). *The Governance of Corporate Groups.* Cambridge: Cambridge University Press.

DiPiazza, S., Jr., and R. Eccles. (2002). *Building Public Trust: The Future of Corporate Reporting.* New York: Wiley.

Felton, R.F., and M. Watson. (2002). "Change Across the Board." *McKinsey Quarterly* 4: 31–45. www.mckinsey.com/practices/corporate governance/index.asp.

Gompers, P.A., J.L. Ishii, and A. Metrick. (2003). "Corporate Governance and Equity Prices." *Quarterly Journal of Economics* 118 (1): 107–155.

Harris, R. (2003). "Boarding School." *CFO.COM.* www.cfo.com.

Leibs, S. (2004). "New Terrain." *CFO* 20 (2): 40–46.

Monks, R.A.G., and N. Minow. (1995). *Corporate Governance.* Cambridge: Blackwell Business.

Nyberg, A. (2003). "Sticker Shock." *CFO* 19 (11): 50–57.

Oracle Corporation. (2003). "An Executive's Guide to Sarbanes-Oxley." www.oracle.com/solutions/corporate_governance.

Osterland, A. (2002). "Board Games: Board Reform Is Essential. Too Bad It May Backfire." *CFO. COM.* www.cfo.com.

PricewaterhouseCoopers. (2003). "Educating for the Public Trust." New York.

Ward, R.D. (2000). *Improving Corporate Boards: The Boardroom Insider Guidebook.* New York: Wiley.

Webber, A.M. (2000). "New Math for a New Economy." *Fast Company* 31: 214.

Weidenbaum, M. (1991). *The Evolving Corporate Board.* St. Louis: Washington University, Center for the Study of American Business.

CHAPTER 3

BEYOND WALL STREET

Leadership Challenges Unique to
Small Private Companies and Entrepreneurial Firms

ERIK HOEKSTRA AND SCOTT R. PETERSON

Annually, the Fortune 500 list of America's largest publicly traded companies is published to great fanfare in the corporate world, and for many this list symbolizes the very heart and soul of American capitalism. In terms of economic importance on a per-company basis, it is indisputable that these firms pack a punch unequalled by any other such group. Thus, many authors and much of the contemporary business research focus primarily on these and the roughly 7,000 other publicly traded firms as the be-all and end-all in corporate America. Equally important, although somewhat slighted in the literature, are the other 5 million or so (U.S. Census Bureau 2001) companies in America, the privately held firms. In addition to commonly traded stocks mentioned above, there are perhaps 30,000 publicly traded companies unlisted and traded via over the counter (OTC) markets (Garbade 1982). Thus, taking the market for public companies as roughly 40,000, it is clear that the securities of more than 99 percent of all companies are not traded in any organized fashion and may rightly be termed private.

While not all private companies are captured in the traditional definition of small business, Ang (1991) identifies eight characteristics for firms to qualify as small/private, the first of which is the lack of publicly traded securities. Small firms, commonly defined by the numerical designation of having fewer than 500 employees, "employ fifty-three percent of the total private non-farm workforce, contribute forty-three percent of all sales in the country, are responsible for fifty-one percent of the gross domestic product, and produce around two out of every three new jobs each year" (Megginson, Byrd, and Megginson 2000, 5). While individually small in size, it is clear that such companies collectively deliver significant economic clout.

While these closely held companies share some common characteristics with their larger public siblings, such firms also have a unique set of leadership challenges that too often go ignored in the traditional leadership literature centered on sprawling corporate mega firms. The many differences between small/private firms and their larger brethren make it inappropriate to assume that research and findings on larger firms will de facto apply to small firms (Dandridge 1979; Westhead and Cowling 1999).

Small/private firms, as a group, face many significant leadership challenges requiring distinct and specific analysis and diagnosis. While operating in the same consumer marketplace as publicly traded firms, they confront very different internal and external organizational realities. The initial portion of this chapter takes up a number of leadership challenges faced by nearly all small/private companies, namely:

1. *Capital Access and Investor Relations.* The challenge of raising capital and handling investor relationships is compared and contrasted in small/private firms with larger, publicly traded corporations.
2. *Functional Specialization.* Low numbers of staff in the small company require the hiring of functional generalists or the creation of organizational structures that allow firms to outsource specialty functions.
3. *Recruiting.* The available labor pool for small companies is unique. Human resource strategy must be crafted to deal with sometimes inadequate career development and promotional opportunities for prospective employees in the small firm.
4. *Ownership Transition.* Because ownership is most often closely held by employee-owners, it is an important and delicate matter to develop very specific and detailed succession plans for transitioning that ownership.
5. *Governance.* Company leaders must decide whether or not to have a formal board of directors and guide the board's interface with company management. Within the small firm, these decisions and interactions create unique challenges. Additionally, in the post-Enron world of Sarbanes-Oxley legislation, firms need to face the challenge of sharpening governance policy.

The second section of the chapter deals with a specific type of small/private firm, the entrepreneurial company, and the attendant challenges faced in this unique form. While confronted, to one degree or another, with all of the generic small/private company leadership challenges named above, entrepreneurial companies have additional levels of complexity best dealt with separately and distinctly.

Every company has a founding, and, consequently, also a founder or team of founding members. The term, *entrepreneurial company*, is commonly used for firms with an identifiable founding and controlling member who brings energy, vision, spark, capital, and many other assets to the company. In addition to these assets, entrepreneurs often bring the following leadership challenges to these companies as well:

1. *Personality.* Entrepreneurs are wired differently. The very personality type that serves so well during the start-up and early growth stages of the business often creates dark challenges as the business matures into adolescence.
2. *Scalability and Leadership Development.* As the business begins to grow, company operations start to get beyond the immediate reach and comfort level of the entrepreneur and start-up team. Simultaneously, training and development requirements arise, additional personnel competencies are sought, decision making demands decentralization, and an increased need for formalized policies and systems becomes evident. These realities create a variety of issues and challenges for the company.

3. *Leadership Succession.* Time ticks away and circumstances change. Inevitably, the entrepreneur must confront the brutal fact of mortality. While a pressing issue in every company, whether small or large, the replacement of a founding leader creates unusual realities in the entrepreneurial company.

LEADERSHIP CHALLENGES IN SMALL/PRIVATE COMPANIES

While all generalities run the risk of being applied too simplistically or too quickly, there are a number of common leadership challenge themes that are generally applicable to most small/private companies. Here, we identify five challenges for closer consideration and contrast these small/private company challenges with those of larger/public firms.

Capital Access and Investor Relations

Private and public companies share many of the same attributes, but they live in two very different worlds with regard to capital access, investor relations, and disclosure of information. Neither world is objectively better; however, leaders must be aware of the differences in order to position their company in the world that is best for their company over the long run.

The primary driver for entering the realm of publicly traded companies is access to capital. Secondary drivers for "going public" include a status symbol for company founders and, in some cases, a financial exit strategy. It is interesting to note that in the aftermath of the initial public offering–crazed end to the twentieth century and the ensuing Enron-type corporate scandals, many small public companies and those considering going public for less compelling reasons are rethinking their situation. Indeed, with the advent of the Sarbanes-Oxley Act of 2002, placing more controls, standards, and responsibilities on publicly traded companies, the costs, both direct and indirect, and the legal liabilities of being public have increased dramatically. In the first half of 2003, announcements of "going-private" transactions by public companies were up substantially over the previous period (Brown 2003). It will be telling over the next several years to see how many small companies mull over such objective and subjective costs and decide that staying private or returning to private status may be more advantageous.

With regard to capital market access, many companies have visions and strategic plans calling for substantial growth that cannot be funded easily through traditional financing channels. Thus, the public arena allows the current management and investors to retain control, while assisting the company in overcoming this capitalization barrier to growth through the issuance of corporate bonds and shares of stock. Companies desiring to remain private are forced to fund expansion through retained earnings and traditional financing, which may create a lid for the organization if the expansion plans are asset intensive. The traditional approach can also subject the company to increased liquidity risk, caused by the issuance of substantial debt.

Relationships between management and shareholders can be problematic in both private and public arenas; however, the causes of tension, the range of possible remedies, and the costs associated with such strain differ greatly in each context. Leaders of public

companies have to thrive in a paradoxical situation, balancing the day-to-day management issues of the firm with the multiple aims of the company shareholders. Being public, they also are required to release quarterly information to the markets, which, in
today's day-trading, market-timing frenzied world, may create an inherent tension between that activity and the maximization of long-term shareholder value. The dissemination of quarterly reports is one way that public companies compete with one another to
attract and retain investors. In recent years, the earnings estimate game has been honed
to a science within the world of publicly traded companies. Every ninety days in the
public arena, analysts, investors, and media ask the same two questions: Did the company hit, miss, or beat their earnings estimate? What are the future earnings estimates?
The trend to supply quarterly earnings estimates or other earnings guidance has dramatically increased recently. In 2003, 70 percent of public companies provided estimates or
guidance as compared to 45 percent in 1999 (Coffin 2003).

Unfortunately, the market's appetite for tasty earnings estimates has created a situation in which public companies spend thousands of hours behind the scenes, posturing
and positioning the quarterly estimates to meet and manage the market's psychological
and financial expectations. Too often, this posturing and positioning activity distracts,
disconnects, and discourages management from both running the business well from
day to day and building the business for solid results for years to come. The intensity and
insanity of estimates reached a peak in 2002 when executives began publicly questioning the practice (Fuller and Jensen 2002) and in early 2003 when McDonald's and AT&T
were among the first blue-chip companies to either suspend or alter their earnings guidance. These companies were soon joined by Gillette, Coca-Cola, and others in letting the
markets know that such preoccupation with short-term earnings was distracting management and undermining their primary responsibility to increase shareholder value over
the long run.

Private companies do not have to provide any financial information to outside individuals or companies, unless the company chooses to release such information. Thus,
management has more freedom to gravitate and focus on long-term goals and results.
This freedom allows management to focus on the critical issues of their company, running the business for today and building the business for the future, apart from the whims
and demands of earnings guidance and related short-term fixes. This flexibility enables
company leaders to make decisions that will benefit the long-term results of the company, even though such decisions may have a negative effect on the short-term results.

While such flexibility is certainly a positive, it is not entirely so. The lack of formal
disclosure requirements can also create problems. Without the urgency and external
pressure of outside monitoring, complacency and unrealistic future planning may create
performance gaps, which are harder to identify and quantify in small/private firms. The
challenge is for the company to clearly articulate performance goals, whether long run or
short term, and to enter into substantive dialogue with investors to align management's
plans with investors' aims.

While the formal requirements for communication of performance are substantially
lower in private companies, the challenges surrounding communication are possibly

more complex. While much of the government interference in the public markets is troubling, it does create a certain transparency and clarity of role for both management and investors. The situation in most small/private companies is much cloudier. Excepting firms in which one person owns 100 percent of the shares, the multiple dimensions and relationships between investors and company management create delicate and often troubling situations. Very often, employee-owners have dual citizenship as both management and investor, a fact that creates both opportunity and uncertainty.

The leadership challenge for small/private companies is to determine what level of communication is proper and appropriate for the investors. While usually informal and direct between the two groups, the need for purposeful, practical, and balanced communication is no less important than in public firms. In addition, some of the camaraderie and intimacy between investors and management in small/private companies may prevent, delay, or cause investors to avoid asking the tough questions about the direction and current performance of the company. Clarification of both investor and managerial roles for such employee-owners is a critical step in removing this tension. Further, providing regular avenues and forums allowing employee-owners to exercise the investor role and open up communication channels between investors and managers can provide additional benefit.

Functional Specialization

The Small Business Administration uses a definition of companies employing fewer than 500 people to designate a "small business." However, of the 5.6 million firms identified in this category, over 5 million of them show total employment of less than twenty. Further, of the 115 million U.S. workers more than 20 million are employed in companies of fewer than twenty people and a full 35 percent work in companies with fewer than 100 (U.S. Census Bureau 2001). Thus, the functional specialization challenge for such companies and employees is of great importance.

In large companies today, many human resource departments hail the need to cross-train employees or give emerging leaders experiences in multiple areas of the company to prepare them for a future of general management. Such is not the case in most small/private companies—every day is cross-functional day! Employees may move between functions daily or even hourly! One thirty-year-old leader we worked with in a company of forty-five performed job duties that read more like an organizational chart than a job description. These realities in smaller companies create challenges unlike those in mainstream corporate America. First, not every applicant will be a proper fit in a small company with the requirements for diverse activity. Making the corporate culture and realities of small company life very clear during the recruitment, interview, and selection process is of vital importance. Additionally, training and development efforts need to be designed to provide this flexibility, while maintaining the focus on the core value drivers for a particular position. Training must go beyond simply task-level training and focus on building the organizational capacity to deal with change, flexibility across functions, and comfort with the sometimes ambiguous nature of small company life. Finally, small companies are required to deal with the inevitable transition, as they grow, from having these flexible generalists—able to handle multiple task responsibilities in the start-up phase—to needing the expert knowledge, skills, and abilities of functional specialists later as company needs change. This may require a large investment in training and development or the expense, both financially and emotionally, of recruiting, replacement, and turnover.

Job descriptions in the small company must be carefully crafted to clearly communicate the need for employees to recognize, accept, and actively deal with the necessity to be widely available to handle multiple tasks and priorities. Including the classic, "other duties as assigned," at the end of all job descriptions is not acceptable. For job descriptions to be truly meaningful in small companies, some level of detail needs to be applied to deal with the need for flexibility across job functions without resorting to vague generalities.

Another strategy that many small companies employ to deal with the functional specialization issue is that they organize themselves as virtual companies with freelance workers (Pink 1998). These virtual entities, from professional services groups to manufacturing concerns, deliver a full value chain to the marketplace while they have much of the detailed work actually performed by any number of other small firms, most often the identities of which are completely invisible to the client. Another advent in small company life today is the rise of outsourcing. While initially done for more traditional functions of payroll or maintenance, all manner of services are available to small companies providing the specialization and expertise needed for them to compete. In fact, the rise of the Professional Employer Organization (PEO)—think temp-service on steroids—attests to this reality in a significant way. The PEO actually becomes the employer of record for all employees, from the entry-level production line to the executive-tier corner office, while the company retains control of the employees at the worksite.

Sadly, often small companies do not have the wisdom, financial resources, or humility to deal with this challenge effectively. The solution for small companies in dealing with the specialization issue is first to recognize its existence and then to address it through the employment of some combination of the various strategies presented here. No silver bullet exists and no one single strategy is right for every context. However, facing the challenge head-on and being transparent and open with employees about the challenge creates the environment for success.

Recruiting

The pool of available talent for small/private companies is much different than the pool of talent open to larger employers. This is due both to the specialization issue detailed above and to the reality that career development and advancement opportunities may be more limited in the small company environment.

While it is certainly fashionable and appropriate in today's world for all companies to be lean and to have a "flat" organizational structure, the small company has very little choice in the matter. In a company with thirty-five people, it is very unlikely to have a chain of command more than one or two layers deep. While such a structure may be ideal for company operations, it also creates a knotty leadership challenge related to few career development options and limited promotional opportunities.

While on a consulting engagement at a regional engineering firm, we heard the company president, who also served as the human resource director, mention this as a very real challenge in their efforts to both recruit and retain young engineers. While recent graduates were eager to make a start in the company, after a number of years their ability to continue advancing upward in the firm, both in terms of challenge and compensation, was severely limited. As these young engineers looked up the organizational chart they saw the next rung on the ladder occupied by either a company principal or another engineer just a few years their senior. Thus, barring any unexpected circumstances, these seats would be held for many years to come by those fortunate to have entered the firm at "just the right time." Under these circumstances, the firm was struggling to retain present employees, recruit potential hires, and provide a vibrant career picture to both of these groups.

To meet this challenge, it is important for small-firm leaders to provide job enrichment opportunities for employees when job advancement is not immediately or widely available. Further, when leadership slots do open up, small companies must carefully consider the cost and benefits of hiring from within versus bringing in outside talent. This challenge also underscores the need for continued revenue growth in small firms. While "growth for growth's sake" is certainly not healthy in the long term, sometimes the only way to keep the leadership pipeline full is to provide new and challenging options in promising market segments. Finally, it is important for developmental activities to be available to insiders, enabling them to fulfill job enrichment assignments and to prepare for both expected and unexpected leadership vacancies. It is unfortunate that in many small companies the lack of training and development efforts for internal staff often forces the need to hire outsiders when advancement positions do eventually open up.

Ownership Transition

While we take up the unique challenges of *leadership succession* in entrepreneurial companies later in the chapter, the issue of *ownership succession* is a critical, yet commonly overlooked, leadership challenge in all types of small/private companies. While chief financial officers of publicly traded companies certainly have substantial challenges, ownership transition is not among them. However, in the small/private firm perhaps only cash flow trumps ownership transition as the highest priority to ensure the continuation and bright future of the company. While ownership structures vary across firms, the majority of firms have at least one, if not all, owners also serving as employees. Thus, we focus specifically on the issue of the employee-owner as the crux of the ownership succession challenge.

In publicly traded firms, the term *agency* (Jensen and Meckling 1976) is used to define the relationship between the nonemployee shareholder and the management or leadership team within the company. Strictly speaking, the management acts as an *agent* on behalf of the shareholders, making day-to-day decisions that are, in theory, aligned with the interests of the shareholders. The literature and research is abundant on the issue of agency costs and how best to align the interests of shareholders and management to attain the best performance in public companies. In small firms, *role clarity* is of utmost importance, rather than agency, when making decisions about how and why employees of the company will be considered for ownership. The employee-owner has a responsibility to lead an almost continual "double life" and to clearly understand the roles of employee and investor as distinct, but yet function within them simultaneously every day. Only by providing clear expectations about the circumstances under which employees are allowed to become owners and the expectations of employees once they become shareholders will the proper alignment be achieved.

Stock buyout provisions should be clearly spelled out in a shareholder agreement accepted by all employee-owners. These agreements must clarify to whom, under which circumstances, and at what value the shares in a privately held company may be transferred. While it is tempting to glaze over some of the knottier issues within a shareholder agreement on the front end, our experience in working with small/private companies indicates that only with crystal-clear understanding by all parties will the relationship both start and end on a good note. Eventualities including death, disability, termination of employment, divorce, and company dissolution are never easy or comfortable to discuss. However, these are just the sorts of crises that have the potential to destroy the employee-owner paradigm unless clearly defined parameters are set up prior to the advent of these circumstances. Additionally, if any differentiation is to be made between the value of majority and minority interests in the company, these definitional issues should also be dealt with here.

Finally, life insurance or other cash-flow provisions should be considered for all significant percentage owners of company stock. To be effective, the type and maturity of such insurance and cash-flow plans must align with the provisions in the stockholder agreement. All such arrangements should be considered similarly to medical treatment; company owners should not perform "at-home" brain surgery any more than they should enter into these agreements without the assistance of legal, accounting, and insurance professionals.

Company growth is a double-edged sword as it relates to company ownership succession in small firms. On one hand, continued solid growth is important to provide the opportunity for more employees to become owners without diluting or decreasing the investment value of present ownership. However, if the growth rate of the company is too large, it may be hard for employee-owners with significant holdings to be bought out when the time comes. Too often, without a solid ownership transition plan in place, company owners or significant employee-owners find themselves nearing retirement with very few options other than to offer the company for sale to the marketplace. The size of the investment required is simply too large if the planning process is put off for too long. Related to this should be the desire of employee-owners to have a balanced representation of age groups within the ownership structure to avoid a large ownership transition within a short time period. If too much of the company needs to be transitioned within a period of a few years, the transition may be in peril as it may be impossible for new or existing employee-owners to purchase such shares quickly enough. Time can be the greatest asset or the largest liability with regard to ownership transition. Fortunately, company leaders have the choice of placing time on either side of the ledger; it all depends on how quickly they face up to and make provisions for this small company leadership challenge.

Governance

While large/public company boards of directors receive *Wall Street Journal* front-page coverage on a daily basis, nearly all small/private companies also have boards that receive far less attention. While formally, the existence, function, makeup, power, and responsibilities of small/private company boards vary widely, these entities can provide substantial value to both the management and the shareholders of such firms. A number of substantial challenges and questions face the small/private company when considering the role that the board of directors will play in the operational life of the company.

While all boards, both public and private, are typically mandated in the articles of incorporation and the members of the board are elected by the shareholders, in small/private companies the board is most often an afterthought, considered to be a nicety or something to consider later—"when we grow up." However, the decision whether or not to have a formal board is the first challenge small/private companies need to face. For clarification in this analysis, we differentiate the informal board—one consisting simply of the tight group of shareholders and meeting only annually as a perfunctory responsibility to the articles of incorporation—with the formal board—one consisting of a group of intentionally chosen members, whether shareholders or not, potentially including company outsiders, meeting at least annually with an intentional agenda and purpose.

For both entrepreneurial companies and firms with ownership entirely controlled by a single person, boards are far less common than in either more mature small/private companies or those with some level of minority ownership (Johannisson and Huse 2000). Given what is understood about the entrepreneurial firm and the psychological makeup of most company founders, this should not be a shocking finding. However, without regard to the type of small/private firm, the existence of a formal board of directors is, and must be seen as, a necessary ingredient to build an enduring company. A formal board brings guidance, accountability, structure, and direction, while forcing the need and providing the venue to "step back" from the daily grind of the operational side of the business and see the big picture. Further, a well-functioning board will demand that the management team provide performance for today and future direction for tomorrow. Some chief executive officers (CEOs) justify not establishing a formal board based on their participation with advisory boards, peer groups, or executive coaches. These types of resources certainly add value and they may even serve as stepping stones toward the formation of a board, but nothing provides the blend of formal accountability to shareholders and structural support to management that a well-run, fully functioning board of directors can (Giannini 2001).

If and when a company makes the decision to engage a formal board, the considerations of function, membership, and meeting type immediately come to mind. While boards in public companies have two main functions, fiduciary stewardship of the financial interests of the shareholders and monitoring the performance of company management (Deakins, O'Neill, and Mileham 2000), the small company board is able to perform a much wider value proposition in the life of the company. In addition to these primary stewardship and monitoring functions, responsibilities and deliverables for the private company board may include:

1. *Mentoring.* Board members may be able to play a developmental role in the life of the CEO and other leaders in the company.
2. *External Networking.* By engaging a wider membership, the company immediately gains a new set of missionaries for the company, each with its own external network of contacts and acquaintances. Such networks can provide unforeseen value to the company during different stages of growth and development and in times of need.
3. *Expertise and Experience.* By intentionally building board membership, small/private companies can make up for the small company specialization gap and "fill in" knowledge, skill, or ability gaps in the firms' management team.
4. *Discipline.* One advantage of a closely held company is the relative lack of pressure to achieve quarterly performance targets. A formal board can ensure that such lack of pressure does not spiral into procrastination resulting in expensive catch-up or missed opportunities.
5. *Voice for Minority Shareholders.* Often, minority shares are valued at a lower rate than majority shares in many private companies due to the controlling interest factor. Having a formal board of directors, particularly with outside membership, may mitigate these issues as minority shareholders gain an advocate in the boardroom. In addition, outside membership provides some accountability and a minor legal defense for the majority should minority shareholder lawsuits occur. While less frequent than in public companies, such lawsuits have been on the rise in recent years.
6. *Credibility.* For customers, banks, employees, and other investors, a formal board of directors provides both comfort and confidence. This is important day to day, but becomes particularly valuable in times of radical change or crisis. Waiting to establish a board until those times come defeats the purpose and limits the ability of the group to function well in such circumstances.
7. *Recruitment and Selection of Management Talent.* A formal board is ultimately responsible for succession planning, recruitment, and selection of the CEO. In addition, the board can provide assistance in the hiring processes for other key management slots.
8. *Voice of Reason.* Particularly in entrepreneurial and family companies, a formal board of directors with outside members can be a sounding board and mediator for interpersonal issues that may have a significant impact on the business.

9. *Venue and Ability to Ask the Hard Questions.* In small companies, various issues (i.e., the tyranny of the urgent, management familiarity or friendship, and fear of reprisal) may make it difficult for management team members to ask the tough questions of the CEO. Formal boards, particularly with outside representation, provide the context and the authority to open these issues up appropriately.

While not every board will perform all of these functions, setting clear goals on the "what" and "why" of a formal board immediately leads the company toward the appropriate answers for "who" in the membership selection process and the "how" in terms of meeting frequency and agenda. While it may seem appropriate and intuitive in a small company for every shareholder also to be a board member, such a structure very rarely works well in practice. Annual shareholder meetings are the right venue for all owners and these events should also be formalized in the process of setting up a more structured governance system in the small/private company.

As is self-evident from the list of possible board responsibilities, there are some functions of a board that a group consisting of all "insiders" simply cannot fulfill. While outside board members are not a "must have" for all companies, no company should deceive itself into thinking that having a formal board meeting as a quarterly replacement for the Monday morning management meeting will suffice. The decision whether or not to have outside membership on the board must be based on the intended function of the board. If outsiders are chosen, it is best to consider adding at least two, which avoids the frustration/fear factor for a single member and allows their contribution to be exponentially stronger.

For a board to function at this level, meetings should be more frequent than annually—to remain connected and engaged—but should not occur monthly—to avoid the danger of becoming merely operational management committees. While by title the chairman of the board may have the responsibility to call and lead meetings, the details may be delegated to other board members as the group sees fit. Establishment of a set of regularly occurring agenda items may be helpful, but care must be taken to keep the meetings fresh and interesting so that the sessions do not become perfunctory "rubber stamp" affairs.

The Sarbanes-Oxley Act of 2002 raises the bar of board structure and accountability in a number of ways. While these regulations do not strictly apply to the private company board, it is helpful to understand the intent of this legislation in building a meaningful board structure for the small firm. The new higher expectations and requirements have forced public companies to move away from the traditional "good old boy" selection process toward a formal selection procedure that evaluates potential board members on the basis of experience, abilities, and skill. Furthermore, many larger public companies are limiting the number of employee board members, thus allowing more oversight and control to pass to outside directors. Both of these features support the inclusion of outside members on the small/private company board and should encourage company owners to select outside members who have the potential to add real value to the governance process. A board consisting of "yes-men" providing nothing but "rubber stamp" governance will not increase the performance of any company.

Most public companies also have board committees that are specialty groups assigned to perform detailed work in one precise area of board responsibility. While such a committee structure may be beyond the scope of many small companies, the functions that these committees perform should be considered by any formal small company board. The Sarbanes-Oxley Act of 2002 has raised the bar for the following board committees: audit, compensation, and governance. The audit committee should be comprised entirely of outside members. This distance will allow the committee to carry out its two primary responsibilities: selecting independent auditors and monitoring the performance of the audit process. The compensation committee should be composed of all, or at least a majority of, outside members. This committee is typically responsible for reviewing and approving the compensation of the senior management and evaluating CEO and senior leader performance. Such work becomes more difficult without the objectivity of outside members. The governance committee sets policy relating to the selection, expectations, length of service, and evaluation process for directors, managers, and the CEO. Here too, having the outside perspective and distance from company management ensures a process free of partiality. While most small-firm boards are not required to have a formal board, much less the formal board committee structure outlined here, each of these areas are important to cover as a part of good governance in all companies.

Three additional notes regarding the establishment of a formal board of directors: first, outside directors should be compensated. Typically paid a per-meeting fee and reimbursed for related expenses, directors should feel as if their contribution is valued by the organization. As the old saying goes, "You get what you pay for," and when you are building a board, do not do it on the cheap. Second, both inside and outside directors should have directors and officers (D & O) insurance purchased and provided by the company. Asking someone to serve without this coverage is unacceptable; however, having directors with impeccable credentials ensures access to such coverage. Finally, directors should have a defined term of service and must clearly understand that reelection is possible, but not a given. To avoid trouble or hard feelings later, make it clear from the start what the terms of service will be.

LEADERSHIP CHALLENGES IN THE ENTREPRENEURIAL FIRM

While all small/private companies face leadership challenges, start-up or entrepreneurial companies are indeed a special case. The company is in many ways an extension of the persona of the founder, and thus these companies face unique leadership challenges that require focused analysis. We deal here specifically with the issues of personality, scalability and leadership development, and leadership succession in such firms.

Personality

One of the driving forces behind the entrepreneur's vision to start a company is the mantra, "I can do better than that!" This single-minded determination is one of the hallmarks creating the context for entrepreneurial success. In our consulting practice, we use The Highlands Ability Battery™ (Martin 2001) to assess a variety of personality preferences and core drivers of behavior. One of the assessments determines whether a person is a generalist (team player and broadly interested) or a specialist (self-sufficient, individualist, and more tightly focused). Beyond a simple work or personality preference assessment, The Highlands Ability Battery™ delves into six driving abilities and fifteen other supporting abilities. The specialist/generalist tendency is one of the driving abilities and thus must find expression in a significant life pattern. We have found that specialists are overrepresented in two particular fields, Ph.D. researchers and entrepreneurs. When one considers this finding, it provides a window into the soul of the entrepreneur. Driven to be different and stand-alone, the company founder seeks, as a Ph.D. does in many ways, to know more and more about less and less—to drill down on a particular issue and control a small part of the world. This independence and focus as well as other attributes, allow the entrepreneur to go forth boldly and create something new, different, and better, and to do so with little regard for what others think or believe.

Kets de Vries (2003) underscores the psychological dimensions of the entrepreneur's success and the related challenges. As a trained psychoanalyst, Kets de Vries approaches his leadership studies from the "inner theater" perspective of the leader and has focused much of his research on entrepreneurs. Seeing entrepreneurial organizations as fundamentally dramatic organizations in which everything seems to revolve around the leader, he has identified three organizational attributes that are in fact, he asserts, outpourings of the entrepreneurs' individual personality attributes. Each of these organizational and individual attributes serves the company and the entrepreneur well in founding the firm, but each has a dark side that must be dealt with, or at least controlled, to allow the firm to grow and flourish (Kets de Vries 1985). Centralized decision making as an organizational attribute follows from the personal characteristic of distrust of others and a need for control. Similarly, the impulsive or "opportunistic" nature of entrepreneurial companies seems to stem from the central leaders' desire for applause or validation. Finally, a start-up company's penchant for either short-interval ad hoc planning systems or the lack of any conscious planning process at all often stems from the founder's aversion to authority.

If held in check by other organizational systems, these individual and organizational personality dimensions serve the entrepreneurial company splendidly. In fact, the company would never have gotten off the ground without them. However, if allowed to go beyond the normal range, the specialist, the control, the distrust, the validation need, and the aversion to authority run amok into disruptive and truly dysfunctional behavior. Through Kets de Vries's extensive research and through our practitioner experience in working for and with entrepreneurial companies, this personality leadership challenge for such companies is too often very real indeed.

Scalability and Leader Development

When one adds a bit of corporate success to this entrepreneurial personality cocktail, the company founder has the tendency to become even more rigid and laser-like in focus as the company grows. After all, whose vision and unique idea was this burgeoning firm? As the company finds markets, customers, and profits, the entrepreneur finds validation for the vision and becomes ever more the expert, feeding and strengthening the individualist within. This increasing focus and rigidity begins to work against both the entrepreneur and the company as a whole, as operational realities move beyond the technical basics of product development or market development. Additionally, the need for new competencies and functions within the company begin to stress and tax the start-up staffers, ill-equipped to handle the new complexity. The number of decisions needing to be made in a given day exceeds the ability of the founder to make them, no matter how many hours are worked. Communication, previously informal, begins to demand precision and consistency to prevent mistakes and provide clarity to an ever-growing workforce. The entrepreneur runs harder and harder to keep up and constantly feels control slipping away. Not only the entrepreneur individually but also the start-up team collectively need to come to grips with the reality that the crazy, fun, mixed-up days and haphazard ways of the start-up are coming quickly to an end.

Mintzberg (1992) identified this need to come to grips with new organizational realities from a structural perspective as the firm grows and develops. His typology of company structure moves from a loose, informal structure during the start-up phase and identifies new more bureaucratic structures that emerge as the company finds success and matures. Adizes (1990) applies a structural life-cycle concept to the organization's development, and proposes that different structures are appropriate at different life-stages in the history of the company.

However, the entrepreneurial firm's challenge at this stage is far more than mere structure. Simultaneous with the need to build some organizational structural controls within the firm, the company finds itself needing new knowledge, skills, and abilities that are often missing on the small start-up team. The founder is faced with the reality of needing to move from the heady world of entrepreneurship to a more professionally managed firm (Flamholtz and Randle 2000), a decision that may come at a personal cost to those already in the firm.

Leader development, a key organizational attribute, is also typically missing as the foundation for scaling the company up to meet growth needs. In the name of focus and business during the heyday of company formation, the pipeline for new talent for the future has never been considered. Moreover, people hired during the start-up phase usually mirror the attributes of those already in the company, and human resource systems to effectively recruit, screen, and select a diversity of talent to deal with future growth needs are nearly always missing.

Hamm (2002) notes that both the entrepreneur and the employees of the successful start-up phase display a dedication to task, a single-mindedness of purpose, and a desire to work in isolation, attributes that are similar to the individual personality challenges discussed earlier that are so vital during company formation. However, Hamm observes an additional challenge at this stage in the company, namely, a blind loyalty to the team of people who are responsible for the success so far. Looking beyond the individual entrepreneur's personal "inner theater" to the concept of the entrepreneurial founder team (Fenn 1998; Ucbasaran et al. 2003) as a group with binding norms, values, and customs that impact the growth and development of the entrepreneurial company is a very real, yet fairly recent phenomenon. During the intense fire of start-up, members of the entrepreneurial founder team spend countless hours together, working side by side on the basics of company formation. Collectively, they dream the impossible dream and work together to make it a reality. In so doing, these people become bonded together in ways that only they can understand and appreciate. This, combined with the lack of a healthy leadership development program and weak human resource systems during start-up, adds a new social and cultural dimension to the entrepreneurs' fix.

It appears to be a no-win situation for the entrepreneur. On one hand, if the founder either waits for present staff to gain the needed competencies or promotes them blindly into positions beyond their skill zone, the company begins to crumble. On the other hand, if new staff members with the needed competencies are brought in—typically in managerial positions of authority over the present team—the entrepreneur discredits the loyalty felt so deeply within the start-up team and makes a radical culture shift, often beyond the comfort zone of the founder and company staff.

Far too often, the entrepreneur faces this prisoner's dilemma and refuses to make a choice. When this happens, the dilemma normally resolves itself as the need for company development disappears, along with the customers, markets, and future profits of the firm. The organizational structure, leadership development, incumbent loyalty, and corporate culture issues within the firm may prevent the entrepreneurial company from making the leap to the next level.

Sometimes, company founders are able to muster the courage to make difficult, and sometimes costly, short-term decisions for the long-term health of the company. Going against their grain in this regard and releasing control to others is a painful process for the entrepreneur. It is not uncommon for the company to survive while the founder either begins to check out, having lost the rush of the entrepreneurial days, or dives back in, continually finding a detail to improve or area of the business to refine while giving macro-level control of the growing enterprise to others.

One company founder with whom we worked claimed that professional managers, department heads, and standard operating procedures in his company (all of which he had put in place) had taken most of the "fun" out of running the business. Passionately in love with the details and intricacies of the product, he spent many days in his office (built for him by the professional managers to keep him away from the production floor) watching through the glass in eager anticipation of a quality problem that he could jump on and fix. Further, while he had retained every one of the first five employees he had ever hired, only one had been able to develop into a functioning member of management, a fact over which he expressed a deep sense of personal failure and regret. Additionally, throughout his attempt to give managerial roles to the other four members of the start-up team, they each created enormous dysfunction and performance gaps that he compensated for in a variety of ways, both personally and organizationally, over a fifteen-year period. As the business continued to grow and expand, he eventually made the decision, each time with a high degree of personal anguish, to remove them one by one from their respective leadership roles. Interestingly, all four continued with the company until retirement, serving in production positions while retaining their former managerial compensation to the end. Fantastically successful in business and overly active in the operation into his eighties, this entrepreneur described the process of expanding the business over a forty-year period as a continual struggle between two competing ideas in his head. While his "company growth" side knew that he needed to step back, make "business" decisions, and hire professionals who could provide control and consistency, he was always plagued by his "entrepreneurial control" side, which told him he could do every job in the place better than the people he had hired. If only there were more of him, everything would be just fine. While our work in the company was to redesign organizational systems and structures with the professional managers, more time and effort was spent helping the entrepreneur acclimate to the new systems through our conversations, many of which took on almost clinical dimensions.

Leadership Succession

Probably in no other organizational context is the issue of succession more important than in the entrepreneurial company. Clearly, during the start-up phase, but also throughout the life of the organization, such companies, more than any other type, are extensions of the personality, vision, and energy of the founder. Warren Buffet's leadership at Berkshire Hathaway is a case in point. A shareholder of the firm commented recently to us that on the day Buffet steps down, this investor fully expects the share value to dip by 25 percent. While this may be an extreme forecast, the stories and statistics of firms having difficulty moving beyond the entrepreneur are plentiful and too often destructive to the founder and to the employees, investors, customers, suppliers, and other stakeholders (Navin 1996). Several different company founders with whom we have worked continued not only to chair board meetings of their respective firms in their late seventies or early eighties, but also to run significant operational areas in the company on a day-to-day basis with very little conscious thought about what came next for them and for the company.

Three stages of entrepreneur succession are evident and instructive (Kets de Vries 1988): first, when the founder becomes aware of the necessity to step down; second, when a successor is chosen; and finally, when the new successor takes the reins and begins leading the enterprise. At each stage in the process, both the company and the entrepreneur face different leadership challenges that must be managed carefully.

Whether by reason of age, health, or complexity of operation, the inevitable moment of succession arrives at some point in every company. For the departing founder, the fear of losing power, status, and image are very real, as is the desire to deny the need for the transition at all. For the company as a whole, lack of communication about the process and uncertainties about the future can create dysfunctional behavior and losses in productivity. In extreme cases, unwanted turnover can result as employees are unable to see themselves working in an environment devoid of their long-time leader.

Once over the realization that succession is inevitable, the organization moves on to the process of selecting the new leader. Lobbying, compromise, favoritism, future strategic direction, and the fundamental question of "insider vs. outsider" all create challenges at this stage. While inside candidates often are in touch with the founder's vision and corporate history, too often the pain of singling out one person at the expense of others and politicizing the situation drives companies to focus on outside candidates. While outsiders may bring new knowledge, skills, and leadership abilities to the firm, the challenges of keeping the entrepreneurial energy and vision alive with an outside candidate—"she's not one of us,"—are very real at this stage in the succession process.

Whether insider or outsider, whether immediate or after long-term planning, one day the organization wakes up and has a new leader. This final stage in the succession process involves unique challenges and roadblocks as well. The honeymoon stage of the new successor can be of varying lengths, but what is done during this stage sends critically important messages to the organization and sets norms and boundaries for the future of the firm. Often, employees begin to romance the past, creating a false rosy picture and bigger-than-life memory of times under the old leader. Unchecked, this type of "revisionist history" behavior may sabotage the effectiveness of the new leader and create an environment in which the new leader is unable to build momentum and gain organizational credibility. In cases where the former leader remains in the organization in an intimate way during this stage, we have observed stronger sabotage behaviors with a more caustic sting. In one case, the former leader was effectively acting as the ringleader of the "romance group," thereby stoking the fires of discontent against the new leader. When the new leader failed, the entrepreneur, who was well into his seventies, was only too happy to step back in and lead, receiving a hero's welcome back to the operational throne from his loyal subjects. Such "doom loop" scenarios are far too common in entrepreneurial companies and require both careful succession planning and timely intervention to be avoided.

Managed well, succession planning for entrepreneurs need not be a somber picture or an exercise in futility. Keys to a smooth transition are an awareness of the various stages and a clear preparation process for all stakeholders—the entrepreneur, the company, and the successor—regarding what challenges the organization is likely to face at each stage. Such preparation and education about the process should ideally begin long before either the age of the founder or the circumstances of the company require the implementation of succession at too rapid a pace. With time to prepare and digest, most transitions are successful. Succession in crisis nearly always brings out the hardest edges and sharpest points of the challenges described here.

THE FUTURE FOR SMALL/PRIVATE COMPANIES

With new small/private companies starting in America every day and with more than half of all workers employed in these businesses, the unique features and leadership challenges of such firms deserve attention. Business schools, writers, and researchers have traditionally ignored this slice of commercial life and the message has too often been, "take the generic lessons from large companies and apply them as best you can."

This resounding message leads, too often, to organizational dysfunction and disappointing results for small/private company leaders as they either feel the need to apologize ("we're no General Motors"), or they find that such actions damage their firms by force-fitting inappropriate paradigms and systems (i.e., there is very little need to reengineer a small retail floral shop). The trend of overlooking the needs of small/private companies is, thankfully, changing as policy makers recognize the power and vitality of these companies in the overall economic structure and as researchers and writers become more sensitive to and interested in the peculiarities of these firms.

Our hope is that this chapter has added significantly to that dialogue, offering owners and managers of smaller, closely held companies an overview of the specific small-company challenges of financing, recruitment, specialization, ownership transition, and governance. It is our belief that with a solid understanding of these challenges, opportunities will be found to make a positive impact in small company life. Additionally, we anticipate that entrepreneurs and those working closely with them as co-workers, board members, or consultants may find insight into the entrepreneurial mindset, both personal and corporate, analyzed in this work. The unique challenges of dealing with the personality of the entrepreneur, assisting these creative pioneers in scaling their companies for growth beyond start-up, and planning for the succession of these key leaders, are very real, very demanding, and also very rewarding when breakthrough moments are reached. We offer these words as encouragement along the way.

Finally, in our work with various private companies throughout the country, we find no need for small/private firms to apologize for anything. While it is true that the likelihood of these businesses making the front page of the *Wall Street Journal* is small, the dynamic energy of these companies is substantial, and the positive impact such firms have is far-reaching for employees, customers, and the overall economy.

REFERENCES

Adizes, I. (1990). *Corporate Lifecycles: How and Why Corporations Grow and Die and What to Do About It.* Englewood Cliffs, NJ: Prentice Hall.

Ang, J. (1991). "Small Business Uniqueness and the Theory of Financial Management." *Journal of Small Business Finance* 1 (1): 1–13.

Brown, J.B. (2003). "Going-Private: Weighing Your Options." *Corporate Board* 24 (142): 16–21.

Coffin, W.F. (2003). "Is Earnings Disappearing in 2003?" *Investor Relations Strategy Series.* Sherman Oaks, CA: Coffin Communications Group.

Dandridge, T.C. (1979). "Children Are Not Little Grown-ups: Small Business Needs Its Own Organization Theory." *Journal of Small Business Management* 17: 53–57.

Deakins, D., E. O'Neill, and P. Mileham. (2000). "Insiders vs. Outsiders: Director Relationships in Small, Entrepreneurial Companies." *Enterprise & Innovation Management Studies* 1 (2): 175–186.

Fenn, D. (1998). "Hard Questions: How Do I Know I've Outgrown My Start-up Team?" *Inc.* 20 (15): 146–147.

Flamholtz, E.G., and Y. Randle. (2000). *Growing Pains: Transitioning from an Entrepreneurship to a Professionally Managed Firm.* San Francisco: Jossey-Bass.

Fuller, J., and M.C. Jensen. (2002). "Just Say No to Wall Street." *Journal of Applied Corporate Finance* 14 (4): 28–35.

Garbade, K. (1982). *Securities Markets*. Boston: McGraw-Hill.

Giannini, V. (2001). "How Do Outside Directors Add Value to Private Companies?" *Directorship* 27 (10): 8–13.

Hamm, J. (2002). "Why Entrepreneurs Don't Scale." *Harvard Business Review* 80 (12): 110–115.

Jensen, M.C., and W.H. Meckling. (1976). "Theory of the Firm: Managerial Behavior, Agency Costs and Ownership Structure." *Journal of Financial Economics* 3: 305–360.

Johannisson, B., and M. Huse. (2000). "Recruiting Outside Board Members in the Small Family Business: An Ideological Challenge." *Entrepreneurship & Regional Development* 12: 353–378.

Kets de Vries, M.F.R. (2003). "The Entrepreneur on the Couch." *INSEAD Quarterly* 5: 17–19.

———. (1988). "The Dark Side of CEO Succession." *Harvard Business Review* 66 (1): 56–61.

———. (1985). "The Dark Side of Entrepreneurship." *Harvard Business Review* 63 (6): 160–169.

Martin, L. (2001). *The Highlands Ability Battery™*. Larchmont, NY: Highlands Company.

Megginson, W., M. Byrd, and L. Megginson. (2000). *Small Business Management: An Entrepreneur's Guidebook*. Boston: McGraw-Hill.

Mintzberg, H. (1992). *Structure in Fives: Designing Effective Organizations*. Englewood Cliffs, NJ: Prentice Hall.

Navin, T.R. (1996). "Passing the Mantle: Management Succession in Industry." In *Family Business Sourcebook II*, 49–58. Marietta, GA: Business Owner Resources.

Pink, D.H. (1998). "Free Agent Nation." *Fast Company* 12: 131–138.

U.S. Census Bureau. (2001). *Statistical Abstract of the United States*.

Ucbasaran, D., A. Lockett, M. Wright, and P. Westhead. (2003). "Entrepreneurial Founder Teams: Factors Associated with Member Entry and Exit." *Entrepreneurship Theory & Practice* 28 (2): 107–127.

Westhead, P., and M. Cowling. (1999). "Family Firm Research: The Need for a Methodological Rethink." *Entrepreneurship Theory & Practice* 23 (1): 31–56.

CHAPTER 4

KNOWLEDGE MANAGEMENT
LEADERSHIP CHALLENGES

Coping with Mental Models and Operationalizing
Knowledge Management Strategy and Practice

TOM R. EUCKER

One thing all managers know is that many of the best ideas never get put into
practice. Brilliant strategies fail to get translated into action. Systemic insights
never find their way into operating policies. A pilot experiment may prove to
everyone's satisfaction that a new approach leads to better results, but widespread adoption of the approach never occurs. . . . We are coming increasingly to
believe that this "slip 'twixt cup and lip" stems, not from weak intentions, wa-
vering will, or even nonsystemic understanding, but from mental models. More
specifically, new insights fail to get put into practice because of the conflict with
deeply held internal images of how the world works, images that limit us to
familiar ways of thinking and acting.

—Peter Senge

Peter Senge in *The Fifth Discipline* (Senge 1990, 174) has captured a number of such
common insights into the challenges faced by nearly all organizations in dealing with
individual and organizational learning and change. Efforts to better manage the knowledge or "intellectual assets" of an enterprise unavoidably entail challenges that involve deeply ingrained mental models. In this chapter, I will provide the basic
background and emphasize the value that improved knowledge management can provide to the enterprise, and then highlight a few of the mental models that are commonly associated with efforts to introduce changes to knowledge management strategies
and practices. By providing some concrete examples of effective knowledge management interventions, I will highlight some basic strategies for coping with these mental
models. Note that I use the word "coping," rather than a more resolute term, to acknowledge the resiliency and pervasiveness of these "deeply held internal images of
how the world works" (Senge 1990, 174).

KNOWLEDGE AND MENTAL MODELS

Effective leadership of any enterprise requires basic understanding of the goals and objectives of the endeavor and of the resources or assets that are available to accomplish the purpose of the organization. Success, in the competitive environment of for-profit organizations, is awarded to those who produce the best results through the most productive use of the resources and assets available to them. Paul Hersey and Ken Blanchard (1982, 3), in a hallmark book on management and organizational behavior, define management as "working with and through individuals and groups to accomplish organizational goals." This straightforward model of business is a common-sense approach to management that was initially written thirty-five years ago and is still applicable today. The challenge lies in *how* to balance a focus on results and influence the "productive use" of resources, particularly human resources and most especially intellectual assets or capital. The same authors further distinguish *leadership* as "attempts to influence the behavior of an individual or group" (Hersey and Blanchard 1982, 3). The challenges of understanding the leadership and management of people has been one of the most written about topics in management literature for decades.

A comment made recently by a senior executive to an internal human resources management conference is enlightening. He admitted that to advance in the ranks of most corporations one needs to primarily have the knowledge of the technology and of the business, and that knowing how to effectively manage culture and people is seen as valuable but not necessary. As a result, people move into senior management roles without some of the essential knowledge about human resources that will enable them to develop the organization or have a positive influence on the culture. In the recent review of annual plans for the upcoming year, only one executive included information about development of the people and the organization, and that was a single slide. I am convinced that this specific example is not unique but is generally representative of boardrooms across the globe and over the history of management. While I have read about and witnessed some exceptions, this has been and continues to be the general rule. This gap, in spite of the fact that so many authors have written about the topic for decades, remains an essential challenge to those committed to improving organizations.

This chapter is not intended to address the full range of leadership challenges of historical and contemporary organizations. Rather it will highlight one obscure and unique factor for understanding people that has a profound effect upon the organizational culture and subsequently on efforts to change how people behave within that culture. In this same book, Hersey and Blanchard (1982) describe four levels of change: (1) knowledge, (2) attitudes, (3) individual behavior, and (4) group behavior. They state that, "Changes in knowledge are the easiest to make, followed by changes in attitudes. . . . Changes in behavior are significantly more difficult and time consuming than either of the two previous levels. But the implementation of group or organizational performance change is perhaps the most difficult and time consuming" (Hersey and Blanchard 1982, 2). I am convinced that the primary reason that organization performance is so difficult to affect is that we routinely underestimate this knowledge level. We mistakenly equate imparting information as creating knowledge and greatly underestimate how significant mental models are in the formation and resulting structure of knowledge, and fail to recognize that how people *think* is as important as how they feel about change. I do not agree with Hersey and Blanchard's statement that changes in knowledge are the easiest to make. While providing information and educational opportunities may be relatively easy, having an effect upon the fundamental mental models that are deeply rooted in the thinking of individuals and cultures can be extremely difficult. An essential characteristic of mental models that makes understanding and influencing them so difficult is that they are tacit. They are not observable to others. In fact, in most cases, they are not conscious to the individual whose thinking, decisions, and actions are so profoundly influenced by them. They operate as unquestioned and untested assumptions about the world.

ORGANIZATIONAL CULTURE

Schein (1988) describes the nature of culture in organizations as consisting of three levels: artifacts, values, and basic assumptions. The levels move from concrete to abstract, from surface to deep, and from visible to invisible.

Artifacts

"The most visible level of the culture is its artifacts and creations—its constructed physical and social environment. At this level one can look at physical space, the technological output of the group, its written and spoken language, artistic productions, and the overt behavior of its members" (Schein 1988, 14). This level of culture is readily observable, but dangerously superficial as a cultural insight.

Values

"In a sense all cultural learning ultimately reflects someone's original values, their sense of what 'ought' to be, as distinct from what is" (Schein 1988, 15). This level of culture defines the articulated values that can be explicitly written or evidenced by the artifacts of the organization, but their understanding does not adequately describe the deepest level of an organization's culture. "Even after we have listed and articulated the major values of an organization we still may feel that we are dealing only with a list that does not quite hang together. Often such lists of values are not patterned, sometimes they are even mutually contradictory, sometimes they are incongruent with observed behavior" (Schein 1988, 17).

Basic Assumptions

As values are tried and tested over time, they in a sense become institutionalized and automatic, in much the same way that individual behaviors can become ingrained to the point of becoming unconscious to the performer. Schein describes basic assumptions as "the implicit assumptions that actually guide behavior, that tell group members how to perceive, think about, and feel about things. . . . To relearn . . . to resurrect, reexamine, and possibly change basic assumptions . . . is intrinsically difficult because assumptions are, by definition not confrontable or debatable" (Schein 1988, 18).

An organization's culture at the deepest level is primarily the combined reflection of the character of the individuals who are part of that organization and who have shaped and internalized these basic assumptions. Gaining alignment and continuity across these levels of culture becomes essential in developing organizational health. At an individual level we would say someone who says one thing and does another lacks *integrity*. The primary challenge is that the ability of an organization to change is not so much dependent upon changing cultural artifacts or espoused values such as mission or values statements, organizational policies, or even organizational structures such as reporting relationships or decision-making processes. Rather it requires having a positive effect upon the deepest level of culture and ultimately the character of individuals who make up that community. Furthermore, it is not simply the observable actions of the people that make up their character but their attitudes and the way they *think* and ultimately who they are as people. It is at this level that mental models are most efficacious and immutable, involving the tacit and basic assumptions of an organization.

CHARACTER AND TRUST

"In the last analysis, what we are communicates far more eloquently than anything we say or do. We all know it. There are people we trust absolutely because we know their character. Whether they're eloquent or not, whether they have the human relations techniques or not, we trust them, and we work successfully with them" (Covey 1989, 22). Trust is both a huge factor in the ability to change organizations and an essential ingredient in the design of effective organizations themselves. "Trust—or the lack of it—is at the root of success or failure in relationships and in the bottom-line results of business, industry, education, and government" (Covey 1990, 31).

A key factor in managing knowledge, trust has and continues to have significant bearing on the degree to which knowledge is effectively shared. "Without trust, knowledge initiatives will fail, regardless of how thoroughly they are supported by technology and rhetoric. . . . For the knowledge market to operate in an organization, trust must be established in the following three ways: 1. trust must be visible; 2. trust must be ubiquitous; and 3. trustworthiness must start at the top" (Davenport and Prusak 1998, 34–35).

Trust, as well as other basic assumptions or principles that govern individual actions, is profoundly influenced by thought. "Our paradigms, correct or incorrect, are the sources of our attitudes and behaviors, and ultimately our relationships with others" (Covey 1989, 30). The process of changing our thinking can be described by the word favored by Peter Senge—"metanoia." Senge comments that "to grasp the meaning of 'metanoia' is to grasp the deeper meaning of 'learning,' for learning also involves a fundamental shift or movement of mind . . . through learning we re-perceive the world and our relationship to it" (Senge 2000, 13).

While organizational values statements and other explicit attempts to define the culture may have some effect, ultimately the culture is to a large extent defined by the prevailing paradigms or mental models that are tacitly held by people and underlie the values, norms, and patterns of behavior or action. Therefore, it is critical to recognize and understand the current mental models that are operating in the organization if any change is to be effectively managed or "metanoia" is to occur.

THE RISING IMPORTANCE OF KNOWLEDGE AS AN ASSET

Not only are mental models elusive and hard to change, they are also growing in importance to today's enterprise. In addition to mental models being an essential element in an organization's culture, perhaps even more important is their effect upon knowledge and knowledge creation. Mental models have a profound influence on and are an increasingly larger component of work itself. The nature of work has shifted as we have moved from an "industrial society to an information society" (Naisbitt 1982, 1). This gradual shift has had an effect on service industries as well as manufacturing. Over time, more and more companies and individuals in companies contribute to the bottom line and to the market by what they know—not just by what they do. "The most important assets companies own today are often not tangible goods, equipment, financial capital, or market share, but the intangibles: patents, the knowledge of workers, and the information about customers and channels and past experience that a company has in its institutional memory" (Stewart 1997, 1).

Karl Sveiby makes this concept concrete by using a simple ratio of market capitalization to net book value to define and quantify intangible assets. He argues that the difference between the dollar value that the market gives to a company (share price multiplied by number of shares) and the actual physical and financial assets is primarily a measure of the value of knowledge or "Intellectual Capital" (Sveiby 1997, 3).

> Shares in Microsoft, the world's largest computer software firm, changed hands at an average price of $70 per share during 1995 at a time when their so-called book value or equity was just $7 per share. In other words, for every $1 of recorded value the market saw $9 in additional value for which there was no corresponding record in Microsoft's balance sheet. What is it about Microsoft that makes it worth ten times the value of its recorded assets? What is the nature of that additional value that is perceived by the market but not recorded by the company? Or, to generalize the question, why do some companies have higher market-to-book ratios than others?

Sveiby's logic of using market-to-book ratios as a measure of the worth of its intellectual capital is compelling. While knowledge contributes more to some companies and industries than to others, the trend over time shows that the value of these intellectual assets is growing and more often a source of competitive advantage. Sveiby defines three kinds of intangible assets that contribute to this difference in market-to-book ratios: *employee competence*—education and experience, *internal structure*—patents, models, and systems, and *external structure*—customer and supplier relationships, brand names, trademarks, and so forth. Stewart uses a similar outline in describing where to look in an organization for intellectual capital: "Its people, its structures, and its customers. This is the elegant taxonomy of Hubert Saint-Onge of the Canadian Imperial Bank of Commerse, and Leif Edvinsson of Skandia. They divide intellectual capital into three parts, like Gaul: Human Capital, Structural Capital, and Customer Capital" (Stewart 1997, 75). Stewart defines human capital as "the capabilities of the individuals required to provide solutions to customers" (76). On the other hand structural capital is "the organizational capabilities of the organization to meet market requirements" (76), and customer capital is "the value of an organization's relationships with the people with whom it does business" (77). Of these three, I will focus on human capital, and particularly the competence that comes from experience, as that is where mental models are formed and most operative.

KNOWLEDGE MANAGEMENT

There are differing implications for the three kinds of intellectual capital in terms of approaches to management of that knowledge. "What leaders need to do . . . is contain and retain knowledge, so that it becomes company property. That's structural capital. Simply put, it is knowledge that doesn't go home at night" (Stewart 1997, 108). There are a couple of important distinctions within the emerging field of knowledge management that give rise to different management approaches, of primary relevance is the focus on the knowledge contained and retained by people and the knowledge that is made available to the organization in productive ways. Andrew Carnegie is quoted as saying: "The only irreplaceable capital an organization possesses is the knowledge and ability of its people. The productivity of that capital depends on how effectively people share their competence with those who can use it" (Stewart 1997, 128).

Information Is Knowledge

The first and probably most significant mental model that affects the application of knowledge management itself comes from the idea that knowledge and people are independent assets. When a senior manager who had managed manufacturing organizations for twenty years retired, he was asked to meet with some people before he left in order to "capture his knowledge." He described the process as a humiliating attempt to extract what he knew that was of value to the organization so that he, the person, could be discarded. They wanted to help him "write it all down" as if the essential value of twenty years of experience and tacit understanding of how a manufacturing system works could somehow be reduced into words or diagrams on paper in a few hours. This mental model might be best described as the "information is knowledge" paradigm or by claiming knowledge and information are synonymous. This is a very common model that is consistently addressed in the knowledge management literature (Brown and Duguid 2000; Stewart 2001). More recently, Karl Sveiby expanded upon this confusion between knowledge and information.

Knowledge and information are different. Thinking of them as similar or synony-mous distorts the entire concept of managing intangible assets. . . . When we speak or write, we use language to articulate some of our tacit knowledge in an attempt to pass it on to others. The name I give to these communications is *information.* Knowl-edge and information are often confused with each other. In the information tech-nology industry, they are even used as synonyms. Thus, the word information is usually associated with both facts and the communication of facts. Information is in many ways ideal for communicating explicit knowledge. It is fast, independent of the originator, and secure. All three of these features are of vital importance in the information technology era because the computer is designed to handle infor-mation. So it is tempting and seems commonsensical for the sender or speaker to attribute information with some sort of meaning. The trouble is that people know more than they are conscious of or can put into words. For example, try to explain in words how to drive a golf ball or serve a tennis ball. These concepts are too complex to express fully in words. Attempts to do so are often ridiculous and al-most always incomprehensible. . . . The receiver of information—not the sender—gives it meaning. Information, as such, is meaningless. Information is perfect for broadcasting articulated knowledge but is unreliable and inefficient for transfer-ring knowledge from person to person. . . . It is best not to write but to talk when we wish to transfer knowledge. (Sveiby 1997, 49–50)

Clearly such a distinction between knowledge and information is critical when discuss-ing the contemporary challenge of knowledge management. It is valuable to further de-lineate different kinds of knowledge, and, more important, to better understand the appropriate means of transferring knowledge to others.

Kinds of Knowledge

The knowledge management literature is replete with definitions and distinctions around the term "knowledge" (Brown and Duguid 2000; Stewart 1997, 2001; Sveiby 1997). One of the basic distinctions is the difference between information and knowledge and second to that is the related distinction between *explicit* and *tacit* knowledge. When we record what we know, we are making that knowledge explicit in the form of documents, graphics, or other concrete media. As Sveiby has inferred, this is converting knowledge to information. Any form of knowledge that is made explicit is no longer knowledge but information. A well-used, but nevertheless important, metaphor uses an iceberg to show the relationship between explicit and tacit knowledge (Brown 1999). *Tacit knowledge* is "knowledge that enters into the pro-duction of behaviors and/or the constitution of mental states but is not ordinarily accessible to consciousness" (Barbiero 2004) and is represented by the submerged portion of the iceberg. The part that is exposed above the water is *explicit knowledge.* The beauty of this analogy is that both the exposed and the submerged are parts of the same chunk of ice. In John Seely Brown's words, "If all you have is explicit knowledge, you can't do anything. Tacit knowl-edge makes explicit knowledge usable" (Brown 1999, 29).

Figure 4.1   **Knowledge Iceberg**

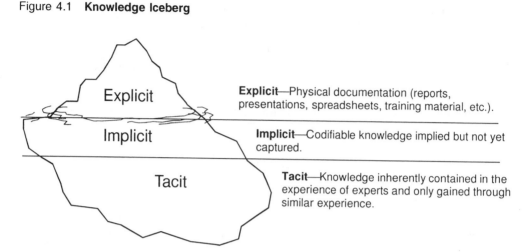

The three kinds of intellectual capital then are related to this model, with human capital represented by the submerged portion of the iceberg and structural capital by what is above the water. The management of structural knowledge involves raising the iceberg such that what was once human capital is now available to the organization in explicit form. Obviously, raising an iceberg is not an easy task and the analogy seems appropriate as the mass of tacit knowledge retained by the people in an organization will never surface. To better represent the portion of knowledge represented by the iceberg that is just below the surface of the water, I prefer to add a third distinction: implicit. Implicit knowledge is knowledge that can be codified but has not yet been made explicit (see Figure 4.1).

This model then gives clarity to three distinctly different approaches to the management of intellectual capital, and each is further addressed in the following sections.

Explicit Knowledge Management

An organization can best capitalize on the exposed explicit knowledge by providing the technology and business processes necessary to make this codified content easily accessible to those who need it within the company and to principal customers and suppliers. A significant portion of the resources and effort around knowledge management involves the design, development, and deployment of effective knowledge repositories and document management systems that organize and catalogue, thus providing easy and rapid access to the massive amounts of explicit material (paper correspondence, electronic mail, specifications, procedures, patents, training, presentations, manuals, whitepapers, etc.) that can be generated by a company. Unfortunately, many of the existing approaches to management of these explicit knowledge assets resemble the way most of us organize our attics. A colleague described the problem using the metaphor of a small used book store where the books are distributed around the room in the cardboard boxes in which they originally arrived. The process for locating what we are looking for involves an exhaustive search through every one of the boxes since no effort was made to organize the content in any meaningful way.

Implicit Knowledge Management

Assuming there is an adequate system in place for handling the explicit knowledge of an organization, a second management approach involves capturing implicit knowledge by recording it in a structured way and thus converting it into information. This can involve the straightforward documentation of core business processes, procedures, and best-known methods in document form, but can also be the collection of video recordings from key customer or management presentations and conference addresses. The development of most forms of training and education programs involves the process of translating valuable expert knowledge into information. The results can be in the form of classroom, computer-based, or on-line training, or reference material utilizing streaming audio, video, or a combination of various media.

Tacit Knowledge Management

By definition, tacit knowledge is not codifiable and remains with the individual who developed it through a combination of formal learning and experience. The means for managing this kind of knowledge are not much different from those for managing human resources in general. Competitive processes need to be designed for the effective selection of knowledgeable hires, as well as the development of all employees, plus effective compensation and benefits programs to retain the talented and knowledgeable people on whom the organization depends for innovation and decision making. Specific focus should be on mentoring and apprenticeship opportunities that are the most effective means for transfer of tacit knowledge. In addition, the norms and culture of the organization should be shaped and developed to support and encourage the sharing of knowledge and the importance of innovation and risk taking.

KNOWLEDGE AND A CULTURE OF LEARNING

These three dimensions of knowledge and the iceberg metaphor can also be related to Schein's previously referenced cultural levels. The explicit culture can be understood and at one level managed by the physical artifacts or documented mission, vision, values, operating philosophies, and policies of the organization that lie above the surface of the water. The implied culture is simply the actual culture as experienced by the people in the organization and can be made explicit through observations of the actions, espoused values, attitudes, and decisions that people make. However, at the root, and the most difficult to expose, are the tacit knowledge, basic assumptions, or mental models held by people that give rise to their felt values and ultimately observable behavior.

In an effort to create a different mental model for learning, Brown, Collins, and Duguid describe the importance of "situated" learning.

Many methods of didactic education assume a separation between knowing and doing, treating knowledge as an integral, self-sufficient substance, theoretically independent of the situations in which it is learned and used. The primary concern of schools often seems to be the transfer of this substance, which comprises abstract, decontextualized formal concepts. The activity and context in which learning takes place are thus regarded as merely ancillary to learning—pedagogically useful, of course, but fundamentally distinct and even neutral with respect to what is learned. Recent investigations of learning, however, challenge this separating of what is learned from how it is learned and used. The activity in which knowledge is developed and deployed, it is now argued, is not separable from or ancillary to learning and cognition. Nor is it neutral. Rather, it is an integral part of what is learned. Situations might be said to co-produce knowledge through activity. Learning and cognition, it is now possible to argue, are fundamentally *situated.* (Brown, Collins, and Duguid 1996, 20; emphasis added)

Brown, Collins, and Duguid (1996) present an important and essential paradox. To effectively address the challenges associated with utilizing the most valuable human capital asset, tacit knowledge and mental models, a shift in our basic assumptions about learning is required. Even more ironic, the evidence indicates that your passive reading of this chapter will do little to affect a shift in your mental model! Simply put, the most important knowledge that you possess is not gained by reading or most forms of traditional learning, but by actively *doing*. However, by describing "situations" and telling stories (even though they are in written form), we can provide a context and help make more concrete the understanding that can come from experience. "Stories have particular power to build and support social capital. For one thing, they convey the norms, values, attitudes, and behaviors that define social groups probably more fully—with more rounded context—than any other kind of communication. . . . Equally important, shared knowledge of story events—what *happened* more than the lessons taken away from what happened—draws people together" (Cohen and Prusak 2001, 112).

MENTAL MODELS THAT ARE BARRIERS TO EFFECTIVE KNOWLEDGE MANAGEMENT

Experience in attempting to put knowledge management principles into practice has brought to light some of the basic mental models about knowledge, learning, and management that impede efforts to make the necessary changes "stick." The following stories highlight two of the most prominent mental barriers.

People Get in the Way

As part of a pilot of a new "expert finder" software product, a series of interviews was conducted to define current knowledge-sharing practices and stakeholder expectations among a community of software engineers. The expert finder software being piloted was primarily designed to connect people to people as a means of transferring knowledge, and to capture knowledge shared in a question-and-answer framework. In the course of the interviews, a pattern emerged in the form of expectations expressed by several different populations of engineers. There was a significant number of individuals who strongly believed that information should be extracted from people and placed in a digital repository for easier access. One interviewee stated that the project team was going about the knowledge problem in the wrong way. In his mind, the key was to create a repository and not to rely upon people. This is reductionism applied to knowledge and human learning with the implied intent of "dehumanizing" the problem. Related to "knowledge is information," essentially this mental model values the tip of the iceberg that is visible above the surface of the water, and naively assumes that the bottom portion of the iceberg either does not exist or can somehow be separated from the explicit forms that are exposed to view.

The philosophical assumption underlying this empirical model is a dependence upon the five senses and is common in physical science-based professions like engineering. This model promotes an overemphasis on explicit knowledge management and ignores what can be the most vital knowledge required by individuals, companies, and industries in order to compete. For instance, returning to Sveiby's description of Microsoft Corporation's intangible assets, if the only competitive knowledge advantage that Microsoft has is explicit, then you can be sure that their competitors can acquire those assets quite readily. While there are certainly valuable explicit knowledge assets that are in fact sought after, having all of the explicit knowledge of the company would not be nearly as valuable as the knowledge retained in the minds of the individual Microsoft employees.

The challenge of this particular mental model is that those who think this way will look for knowledge in the repository of frequently asked questions, and if they do not find it, they will not typically ask others or be as likely to return to the repository in the future. The same model influences those assigned as experts. They will become quite impatient with repeat questions and expect that others will utilize the repository before bothering them with the question that they had already answered for someone else. If there are a sufficient number of participants who have this *tip of the knowledge iceberg* mental model, then the expert finding tool will not reach a high enough level of use to sustain itself or generate sufficient breadth and depth of information in the frequently asked questions repository to create much knowledge value. Offering incentives to use the tool will do little to overcome the effects of this mental model. Direct efforts are needed to change the culture of the organization, which will eventually create a more robust knowledge-sharing norm and challenge the idea that all valuable knowledge can be extracted. Ironically, the same people who hold so tightly to this belief will explain that they learned to be expert through personal experience and by receiving coaching from or observing others, not from reading what someone else wrote down. Returning to the quote by Sveiby: "It is best not to write but to talk when we wish to transfer knowledge" (Sveiby 1997, 50).

Not Invented Here

One of the critical elements of high-tech manufacturing is the *qualification* of the process by the customer. This is essentially measurement of key parameters (critical dimensions, performance, reliability) of the product throughout and at the end of the manufacturing process. Qualification becomes even more important to the customer when the same product is produced at more than one factory. They want to verify that the product produced at one factory is identical to the same product produced at another factory.

In the late 1980s, as Intel's microprocessor business grew to the point where the demand was greater than the capacity of an individual factory, it became essential for engineers in one state to work cooperatively with the engineers in a second state in transferring the manufacturing process. Process transfers prior to this point were primarily between the technology development organization and the factory. There were well-established indicators (data) regarding the transfer that enabled the measurement of "learning curves" relative to the ability of the receiving factory to "ramp" the process to the levels of the originating factory. The rate of learning from the first factory-to-factory process transfer was not to the level that was expected, primarily because engineers in the second factory (being in a different state at a brand new facility) felt the need to "engineer" the process that was coming from the other factory. They felt that by making changes, they would make the process better. Unfortunately, just the opposite occurred. There were literally hundreds of seemingly minor changes made without the tacit knowledge of the engineers who had done the original engineering, and the individual changes were not independent of one another. In reality, the changes interacted with other changes and the net result was a significant drop in initial process performance and resulted in longer process learning curves.

This is commonly referred to as the "not invented here" (NIH) syndrome. There was the tacit (and sometimes implicit and even explicit) belief that the engineer's job is to *engineer*. The engineer believes that if he or she did not do the engineering then it must not be good enough. A very common syndrome, particularly in engineering, this mental model was deeply entrenched in the organization. After many years and multiple process generations, this NIH mental model has been managed but not eliminated. It still creates challenges but has since been mitigated through improved process-transfer and process-matching methods (see Copy Exactly! below).

EFFECTIVE KNOWLEDGE SOLUTIONS

The following examples and situations of knowledge management efforts are effective primarily due to changes in the previous mental model and are consistent with a culture of learning.

Copy Exactly!

In addition to the challenges of overcoming NIH, the competitive market demanded that Intel continue to introduce new processes and grow manufacturing capacity while shrink-

Figure 4.2   **Process Ramp Trends at Intel from 1993 Through 2005**

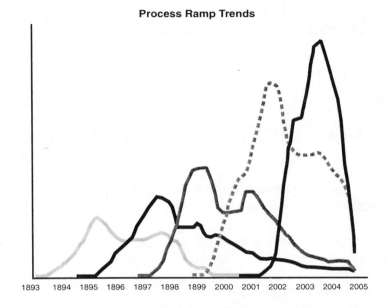

Process Ramp Trends

1893 1894 1895 1896 1897 1898 1899 2000 2001 2002 2003 2004 2005

ing product life cycles and costs. Figure 4.2 shows the process life cycles over five process generations with volume on the left margin.

To execute effectively in meeting market demand it was critical for Intel to significantly alter the methodology for transferring the process knowledge not from just one factory to another but from one factory to as many as seven other factories in a staggered but overlapping schedule. The process-matching methodology was called Copy Exactly! (CE!) with the underscore and exclamation point as essential components of the process of change that was required. There were six core strategies designed to manage the change:

1. A clear statement of management expectations
2. "Virtual factory" structure
3. Cross-factory joint change-control boards
4. Audit system to find and fix deviations
5. Cross-factory training of key technical people
6. Supplier education

Collectively, these six core strategies served to provide direction for the Copy Exactly! initiative. Each core strategy is discussed in further detail below.

A Clear Statement of Management Expectations

Early attempts to overcome the NIH syndrome with logic and a business imperative were only marginally effective. It was not until senior manufacturing management added the exclamation point to the name of the emerging process-matching methodology that the mindset began to shift. The exclamation point was added literally to the name, but also figuratively to the effort through management tenacity and in some cases resorting to language like "I want you to stamp 'Copy Exactly! Stupid' on your foreheads!" Another way of emphasizing this was through published and periodically reviewed statements such as the following signed by the highest level management at Intel:

The Assembly/Test

Virtual Factories have the goal of being identical in every respect except where there are hard barriers, e.g., floor plans, ceiling heights, etc. The best known methods and knowledge will be copied by all factories, irrespective of their source. The factory that wishes to deviate from CE! will carry the burden of elevating and justifying the change throughout the . . . structure.

Statements such as this went a long way toward clearly outlining the expectations of the senior management team.

Virtual Factory Structure

A virtual factory (VF) is comprised of all manufacturing lines at multiple sites running the same process and producing the same product. All manufacturing lines producing the same product operate as if they were a single factory, or, in other words, "virtually one factory."

This structure enables multiple factory engineers and managers to work concurrently on process transfer and improvement across the factory network by requiring process decisions to be made by the joint management teams rather than individual factories. This was not the same as centralizing decision making insofar as these teams were made up of the peers at each factory and the peer teams were empowered to make decisions for their area of responsibility. These teams and committees are examples of the "structural capital" that Stewart (1997, 75) refers to. The knowledge contained in these teams is shared through rotating leadership in such a way that they can cover for the loss of one of the team members and bring new team members up to speed very quickly through regular meetings, face-to-face visits, and sharing of documentation and reference material. The structure employed to address these important dynamics within the VF is provided in Figure 4.3.

Cross-Factory Joint Change-Control Boards

The primary means for handling improvement and changes across the VF are joint peer-led change-control boards (CCBs). To make any change to a process the engineer is required to submit a "white paper" that follows a specific template and requires standardized experiments to provide the data showing the benefits of the change and that there are no negative impacts to the change. The CCB meets weekly to review all white papers, and, less formally, to discuss common methods and best practices.

Figure 4.3   **Virtual Factory Structure at Intel**

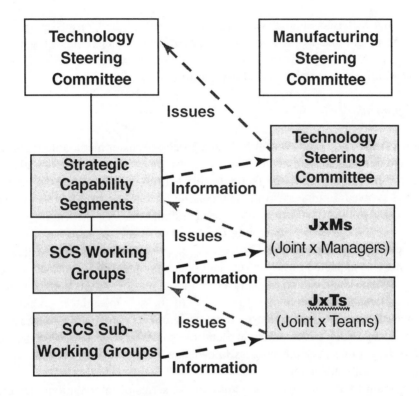

Audit System to Find and Fix Deviations

As part of the regular responsibilities of the joint management teams, audits are conducted of each of the respective factories. The CE! audit, when performed on a routine
basis (i.e., quarterly, semiannually, etc.), is a tool for the joint management teams to
measure each site's compliance to prevent drift from the virtual factory best-known method
roadmap. In addition, the cross-site face-to-face audits allow members of the respective
teams to see firsthand if the "actual" way a procedure is done really matches what the
other sites are doing as well as to become more familiar with each others' environment,
to share knowledge, and to develop camaraderie. Remember, "It is best not to write but
to talk when we wish to transfer knowledge" (Sveiby 1997, 50).

Cross-Factory Training of Key Technical People

Technician training within the virtual factory is managed through the joint training managers. Their charter is to ensure that standardized operations training based on common
operational specifications is provided that helps to ensure standard practices and procedures throughout the system.

Supplier Education

Equipment and materials suppliers are an integral part of the <u>Copy Exactly!</u> process. Suppliers are taught and worked with in regular meetings and brought together in an annual Supplier Day conference to educate them on CE! expectations. A supplier Web site provides information and knowledge regarding working with Intel.

Seed Assignments

A component of <u>Copy Exactly!</u> is a formalized process-transfer methodology that recognizes that a significant amount of tacit knowledge transfer is essential for effective manufacturing process deployment. To facilitate this learning, an extensive apprenticeship program has evolved. Engineers from the receiving factory can spend up to a year living near and working in the host factory on a "seed assignment." As seed engineers they are expected to become part of the originating factory organization contributing to that factory's volume manufacturing and process development activities. During this assignment they are also expected to stay in regular contact with their home factory in order to share the learning. There can be as many as a hundred or more engineers and their families on these seed assignments over the course of the six- to eighteen-month process transfer, and they often involve international assignments. This is a significant investment in tacit knowledge development and entirely based on the recognition that there is no shortcut to gaining in-depth process knowledge. It takes hands-on experience and interaction with knowledgeable people.

It is important to note the *systemic* nature of the series of interventions that evolved with the <u>Copy Exactly!</u> methodology. It is the combination of cultural, organizational, and procedural changes over a period of time that enabled this strategy to be effective.

Manufacturing 101

Effective manufacturing involves utilizing people, technology, materials, and processes to produce high-quality products at the lowest possible cost. To be successful, a manufacturing supervisor must learn to effectively manage each of these resources simultaneously. In response to rapid growth at Intel in the mid-1990s, a steady stream of newly hired supervisors and engineers were expected. Manufacturing executives were concerned that these new hires would lack the proper mental model that would allow them to understand the "big picture," and cause them to focus narrowly on one or two of these elements. "To train a supervisor to function effectively in Intel's manufacturing environment, a program was needed that contained more than isolated facts and how to's, or even sophisticated role plays. The essence of a supervisor's job cannot be experienced by breaking it apart and practicing each component in isolation, as is often done in traditional training programs. To experience the essence of what a supervisor does, the trainee must experience each facet of the job as an integrated whole" (Crooks and Eucker 1999, 87).

Consequently, manufacturing science experts and instructional designers at Intel designed a learning process built upon situated learning principles. This four-day factory simulation was designed to replicate the decision making and to introduce the range of experiences that would normally require a year or more of experience for a supervisor to encounter naturally. The environment was also designed to provide a rich social learning opportunity where the participants could work together and experience a variety of factory roles, and analyze realistic production schedules and reports based on their own performance in the "sim-factory." The sim-factory consists of eight individual computers each representing a process step divided into two functional areas plus inspection and reporting stations in a network to provide realistic transactions. The twelve-hour work shift is compressed into a forty-minute period such that the factory is able to process eight full production days (two shifts per day) over the four-day experience. This enabled exploring and learning about cross-shift interactions, competition, and communication challenges all in a team-learning situation with the "instructor" (actual factory shift managers) performing the factory management/coach role.

This program provided a significant alternative to previous forms of learning in that it enabled a broader more systemic understanding of manufacturing in a "situated" learning environment (Brown, Collins, and Duguid, 1996, 20).

A MODEL OF "PARADIGM PIONEERING"

Joel Barker (1985) provides an excellent summary of the "paradigm effect" and outlines how prevailing paradigms, mental models, or basic assumptions are essentially changed. The effect works gradually and succeeds not by a frontal attack on the current way of thinking, but more subtly by a focus on what gives any model or paradigm power results. The reason that people continue to think and feel as they do is because experience has taught them what works.

Thomas Kuhn's 1962 book, *The Structure of Scientific Revolutions*, has had a profound effect on the thinking about these resilient paradigms, or mental models. "Kuhn became famous for saying that the older generation has to die for a new idea to take hold. Why is there some truth in that? Because the members of the older generation have almost unconsciously built up a tremendous set of practices that govern what they do. Those practices create their frame of reference and make it impossible—or extremely difficult—for them to entertain a new idea, a new technology or a new point of view" (Brown 1999, 29). So, if it is so difficult to do, how can we hope to have an impact on knowledge management? The answer is not to sit around and wait for those who resist change to die, but to focus on resolving the problems that the current model or paradigm has not been able to solve. Barker outlines the following process that enables the paradigm effect:

1. The prevailing paradigm triggers the search for a new paradigm while it is still successful by identifying enough anomalies, "unsolvable" problems to create a critical mass;

2. Paradigm shifters are usually outsiders who come from the fringes, not the center of the prevailing paradigm community; and

3. Those who accept the new paradigm early, the pioneers, will never have enough proof to make that acceptance a rational judgment. They will choose to follow because of their trust in their intuition. (Barker 1985, 35)

Experience has shown that the key to shifting paradigms, mental models, or basic assumptions is to focus on solving problems that current thinking deems unsolvable. For the most part, people in business are practical and results oriented. Consequently, nothing is more eloquent than the bottom line in convincing an organization that there are options available for the pioneer who is willing to try new things.

CONCLUDING THOUGHTS FOR ASPIRING KNOWLEDGE MANAGERS

Any organizational change effort across the enterprise is challenging. People naturally resist ways of thinking that are different from their own. Knowledge management is itself a paradigm that requires a shift from previous ways of thinking and working. It is therefore incumbent upon those seeking to improve the way knowledge capital is utilized to understand some of these basic mental models and the changes in approach and methods necessary to cope with and mitigate their potentially limiting effects. The key to paradigm pioneering is to demonstrate improved results in some manageable domain, in order to get the attention and commitment of those who control the resources that will be essential for broader-based change to occur. The alternative posture has been described as a good definition of insanity: doing the same things you have always done and expecting different results.

REFERENCES

Barbiero, D. (2004). "Tacit Knowledge." In *Dictionary of Philosophy of Mind*, ed. C. Eliasmith. www.artsci.wustl.edu/~philos/MindDict/index.html.

Barker, J.A. (1985). *Discovering the Future: The Business of Paradigms*. St. Paul: ILI Press.

Brown, J.S. (1999). Interview in *Knowledge Directions*. IBM: Institute for Knowledge Management.

Brown, J.S., A. Collins, and P. Duguid. (1996). "Situated Cognition and the Culture of Learning." In *Situated Learning Perspectives*, ed. H. McLellaned, 19–44. Englewood Cliffs, NJ: Educational Technology Publications.

Brown, J.S., and P. Duguid. (2000). *The Social Life of Information*. Boston: Harvard Business School Press.

Cohen, D., and L. Prusak. (2001). *In Good Company: How Social Capital Makes Organizations Work*. Boston: Harvard Business School Press.

Covey, S.R. (1989). *The Seven Habits of Highly Effective People*. New York: Simon and Schuster.

———. (1990). *Principle-Centered Leadership*, New York: Simon and Schuster.

Crooks, S.M., and T.R. Eucker. (1999). "Manufacturing 101: A Simulation-Based Learning Experience." In *Implementing HRD Technology*, ed. J.J. Phillips and J. Hite, Jr., 83–94. Alexandria, VA: American Society for Training & Development Publications.

Davenport, T.H., and L. Prusak. (1998). *Working Knowledge: How Organizations Manage What They Know.* Boston: Harvard Business School Press.

Hersey, P., and K.H. Blanchard. (1982). *Management of Organizational Behavior: Utilizing Human Resources.* Englewood Cliffs, NJ: Prentice Hall.

Naisbitt, J. (1982). *Megatrends.* New York: Warner Books.

Schein, E.H. (1988). *Organizational Culture and Leadership.* San Francisco: Jossey-Bass.

Senge, M. (2000). *The Fifth Discipline: The Art & Practice of the Learning Organization.* New York: Doubleday.

Stewart, T.A. (1997). *Intellectual Capital: The New Wealth of Organizations.* New York: Doubleday.

———. (2001). *The Wealth of Knowledge: Intellectual Capital and the Twenty-first Century Organization.* New York: Doubleday.

Sveiby, K.E. (1997). *The New Organizational Wealth: Managing & Measuring Knowledge-Based Assets.* San Francisco: Berrett-Koehler.

PART II

LEADERSHIP IN NOT-FOR-PROFIT ORGANIZATIONS

CHAPTER 5

LEADERSHIP IN A NOT-FOR-PROFIT WORLD

A Mixed Toolbox

ANDREA B. BEAR AND MICHAEL A. FITZGIBBON

Great leaders often inspire their followers to high levels of achievement by showing them how their work contributes to worthwhile ends. It is an emotional appeal to some of the most fundamental of human needs—the need to be important, to make a difference, to feel useful, to be a part of a successful and worthwhile enterprise.[1]

Warren Bennis, Ph.D., founding chairman of the Leadership Institute at the University of Southern California

"Nonprofits have to start acting like for-profit organizations."
"They need to be more businesslike."
"Nonprofits need to operate more efficiently."
Experts in for-profit and nonprofit industries and businesses proclaim these mantras, and nonprofits today are paying attention. But, they are not corporations. By their nature, not-for-profit organizations follow a mission that has nothing to do with profitability, thus the not-for-profit category and attendant pitfalls. Whether environmental organizations, cultural institutions, civic associations, health care advocacy nonprofits, animal rights groups, senior centers, or even what are considered fringe cause collectives, the nonprofit mission is usually pursued with passion and zeal. Too great a focus on the emotionally driven core value of the group, however, may blind the leaders to the business needs of the organization.

A not-for-profit organization recognized by the Internal Revenue Service (IRS) must have a clearly defined mission and financial controls. The IRS identifies eight broad missions in the 501(c) section of the tax code: religious; educational; charitable; scientific; literary; testing for public safety; fostering certain national or international amateur sports competitions; and prevention of cruelty to children or animals. The IRS continues to state that if an organization wants to be tax exempt, it has to serve a purpose or mission to advance public welfare instead of a profit motive. Effective nonprofit leaders know that there are many sides to running a successful organization. First, there is clarity

Figure 5.1   **Business Details Versus Mission/Passion Continuum**

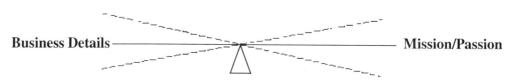

regarding the mission itself—the very reason that the nonprofit exists. Then, there are the pressures to become more professionally managed, and to articulate and achieve those bottom-line performance objectives that are pertinent to the organization. All this must be undertaken in a context of shifting demand for services, changing operating environments, and frequent financial pressures. Now, more than ever, nonprofit leaders recognize the need for a strategic management perspective for translating their missions into objectives, developing plans and programs to accomplish those objectives, and implementing those plans and programs.

Managing the balance between the mission and passion that drive not-for-profit organizations and the effective and efficient management and operations may be the single most important factor for success. Look at it as a continuum (see Figure 5.1). It is a dynamic situation, not static, and where the delicate balance lies depends in large measure on the health and viability of the not-for-profit organization. For example, if a nonprofit faces a financial crisis and runs the risk of shutting down, then there will naturally be a greater weight given to the business focus.

Former New Jersey Senator Bill Bradley, turned consultant and lead adviser with McKinsey & Company's Institute on the Nonprofit Sector, rocked the not-for-profit world in a *Harvard Business Review* article with the claim that nonprofit organizations could realize a $100 billion annual windfall "by challenging the operating practices and notions of stewardship that currently govern the sector." Bradley and his co-authors go on to say that, "Pressures to cut government spending are shifting more social burdens onto charities—a trend that will intensify when the 76 million baby boomers start retiring and the government is forced to spend an even larger share of its resources on health care and pensions. As nonprofits are increasingly asked to do more, it's important to take a hard look at how the sector operates."[2] We agree.

Achieving the delicate balance between efficiency and effectiveness requires strong leadership. Professional leaders (i.e., paid chief executive officer [CEO], executive director, vice president, deputy directors, etc.) and volunteer leaders (i.e., board of trustees or directors, event and committee chairs) in today's not-for-profit world must ensure that business-like operations do not displace the relationship-based approach and that the mission and passion are not lost in the process. "In the non-profit world balancing is important," notes Joe Widoff, president and chief executive officer of WHRO Public Broadcasting in southeastern Virginia, an $8 million a year nonprofit business. "Articulating and being faithful to the mission is key, yet you need to force accountability to meet the business requirements or you cannot deliver on the mission. One challenge in this regard is that some of the board members are not in balance and overemphasize the mission to the exclusion of the business side of the entity. At the same time, some of the business leaders on the board check their business acumen at the door, saying 'I don't have to do that here, this is a warm and fuzzy place,' when they were recruited for their business acumen in the first place" (personal interview).

In addition to balance, today's not-for-profit environment requires a good return on investment. Donors demand it. The challenges, changes, and qualities of nonprofit leadership reveal a number of opportunities and lessons for success. We examine these key issues: resources, including paid and volunteer leadership responsibilities, qualities, and challenges; changes in the nonprofit sector; planning, metrics, and evaluation. We provide perspectives from several professional and volunteer nonprofit leaders we interviewed. Finally, we offer our toolbox or prescription for leadership success in not-for-profit organizations.

RESOURCES—THE BOON AND THE BANE

The challenge of creating opportunities, enriching lives and communities, and creating fundamental change drives many leaders into the nonprofit sector. Those who get into nonprofit leadership carry an obligation to implement programs, provide services, and manage institutions effectively against a backdrop of challenging issues.

"We stand on the shoulders of those who came before us for 90 years, yet we still look forward. We need to stick to our mission, yet be adaptive to stay relevant in order to deliver on it. The messages have to be expressed differently to make sense to the community. We need to stay on the cutting edge and use our resources fully" (personal interview). Nellie Hayse has been the executive director of the Colonial Coast Conference–Girl Scouts of America since its inception in 1981. She knows how important it is to stay relevant, especially to the nearly 17,000-member nonprofit organization across a 25,000-square mile area in southeastern Virginia and northeastern North Carolina.

Financial Resources

Nonprofits range in size from the Teachers Insurance and Annuity Association to your neighborhood block party planning committee. Social investors and nonprofit stakeholders look for a return on their investment of donations to the more than 1.4 million charities in the United States, including religious organizations. In 2002 total charitable giving reached a record of nearly $241 billion, representing an estimated 2.3 percent of the U.S. gross domestic product. Yet according to the *Chronicle of Philanthropy*, total giving to the nation's 400 largest charities fell in 2002, for the first time in a dozen years, after several years of double-digit growth.[3] Overall among nonprofits of all sizes, charitable giving dropped slightly in 2002, by one-half of 1 percent when adjusted for inflation. The report of the American Association of Fundraising Counsel's Trust for Philanthropy, *Giving USA 2003*, reveals that religious organizations received the lion's share of charitable contributions (35 percent), followed by educational institutions (13.1 percent), foundations (9.1 percent), health (7.8 percent), and human services (7.7 percent). The rest of the nonprofit pie benefits public-safety, arts, culture, and humanities, the environment, animals, and international causes.[4]

Meanwhile, federal and state funding for programs and services has dropped precipitously, leaving the nonprofit sector to take on an increasingly more important role in support of so many worthwhile charitable organizations and to fill the gap left by the loss of government funds. This means that nonprofit leaders, both professional and volunteer, must become more adept at raising capital. They must become fund-raisers. Creative collaborations and mutually agreed upon shared services matter now more than ever in the not-for-profit world.

Staff Leadership

Of the nearly 1.4 million registered nonprofit organizations, less than two-thirds ever file annual IRS forms and have gross income receipts of less than $25,000. Nationally only 20 percent of all nonprofit organizations report annual budgets of more than $100,000, with less than 10 percent of million dollar budgets or more. With such small budgets by the great majority of not-for-profits, it is no small wonder that executive compensation in this sector is at a definite competitive disadvantage.

Hayse knows the challenges facing nonprofits in general and the Girl Scouts in particular. In addition to the ongoing financial strains that not-for-profits across the country are experiencing, today's Girl Scouts Council confronts drugs, teen pregnancy, and crime. "We don't pay staff members enough."

Most nonprofits are blessed with dedicated staff and volunteers. Rarely are staff members paid their worth. "The biggest issue is finding competent leadership when the pay is not very high" (personal interview), notes Paul O. Hirschbiel, a successful venture capitalist and community leader and philanthropist, who serves on the national board of the Make-A-Wish Foundation and on several local boards, including the Chrysler Museum of Art in Norfolk, Virginia. WHRO's Widoff agrees, "Nonprofits are the best bargain in America. They have quality staff, who are underpaid, yet work hard."

In nonprofit organizations today, many of the professional leaders can be heard lamenting that they did not get into their work to fund-raise or become marketing experts, or because of their people leadership skills. The community wants passion in nonprofit leaders, passion for and understanding of the mission. Angelica Light, president of the Norfolk Foundation, among the largest community foundations in the country and Virginia's first community foundation, established in 1950 says, "It's critical to lead with the heart. Nonprofit leaders must possess a keen respect for staff and be reflective in their decision-making."

The fact is that leaders of not-for-profit organizations must not only be passionate about the mission of their organizations, but must also be good leaders of people, articulate visionaries, good strategic planners, strong in organizational skills, competent in and comfortable with fund-raising, knowledgeable about financial reports and statements, and have some marketing sense (at least enough to hire strong marketing people when they can and recognize the need for marketing). Effective nonprofit executives know how to serve multiple stakeholders, balance competing demands, satisfy customers and employees, cut costs, and grow more projects. They are credible, genuine, and have the habits, values, and behaviors to engender trust and commitment. They serve as role models both inside and outside the organization. The best are tireless, innovative, inventive, observant, risk taking, and consistent supporters and enablers of management and leadership teams. It is a pretty demanding package.

In an era when nonprofit organizations have to fight harder for contributions and use their resources with greater care, many have turned to the business sector for management, and, increasingly, people with business backgrounds are becoming directors of nonprofit organizations. Mita Vail, vice president for development and government relations at the Mariner's Museum in Newport News, Virginia, notes, "Today's leaders need to possess a number of skills beyond those as the chief programmatic officer of the organization. They need not only to know the program content and mission, but also to be able to interpret that mission and the plans to fulfill it to the public and within the organization. They need to have communications skills, business and management skills, and fundraising skills." Nonprofit leaders need to know where they are going, articulate a vision, keep moving toward that vision, and inspire others to move toward it.

Nonprofits, like businesses, "must identify their markets, establish goals and devise strategic plans," notes Light of the Norfolk Foundation.[5] In 2003, the Norfolk Foundation in concert with a team from the business school at Old Dominion University (ODU) conducted focus groups and a survey with area nonprofit leaders (staff and volunteers) to learn about the leadership needs of nonprofits in the Hampton Roads region. "Clearly there is a need for training, leadership skills and the basics" (personal interview), concluded Light. Nancy Bagranoff, Dean of ODU's College of Business and Public Administration says, "The interesting thing is that this study identified so many areas of training needs for nonprofit leaders, including fund-raising, project management, finance and administration, emotional leadership, organizational management, and strategic planning."

Museum directors, for example, traditionally are trained in art history, and the love of art is why they got into the museum world. But, with declines in funding from public sources, they must get out and raise vital funds for operations and the ever-present capital campaign, as well as understand and appreciate marketing. In nonprofits today, there is the added challenge of increasingly competitive environments, competition for patrons and support, competition for good employees, competition for volunteers, awareness, and time. The "sales pitch" to raise substantial funds must include the person who knows the art—or environmental engineering, child abuse prevention, youth counseling, or religion in other not-for-profits examples. Customarily that person has been the chief executive or director, but that is changing.

WHRO CEO Widoff agrees, "Leaders who are subject-matter specialists in the arena cannot always adapt to the business side of nonprofits. Originally the leaders at WHRO were Ph.D. educators, which at the outset was fitting. Today it may be problematic."

In addition to leading with passion and business skills, today's not-for-profit leader must possess qualities of compassion, confidence, grace, competence, and a strong belief in people. Finding the right leader with the right stuff presents a challenge to most independent organizations. Compassionate nonprofit executives recognize the humanity within the organization, work to people's strengths, and guide their organizations to ride the waves of change with more heart and soul.

Volunteer Leadership

The motivations are all across the landscape on the board. They have different perspectives and objectives for being there. Every not-for-profit organization looks for three key factors in board members: *work*, *wisdom*, and *wealth*. "Wealth and wisdom are OK, but the work needs to be clearly defined," urges Light. "Seek board members with extensive business experience to benefit from that and look for people who can accept the hard questions and expect a good return on investment," Light continues (personal interview). Volunteer leaders should provide a combination of work, wisdom, and wealth, or at least two of these. Work and wisdom often come together from volunteer leaders with a zeal for the nonprofit mission. They may give generously of their time, talents, and energy, but not always of their wealth. Some leadership roles in the independent sector are so coveted that people and companies have been known to buy their way in, but financial support alone does not strengthen the relationship the volunteer has with the organization and its mission. Ideally, board members should have areas of influence in the community and provide connections to funding, services, and support—a network-maker—whom they know is important. And when appropriate, volunteer leaders should become personally involved in ensuring that the goals—financial and programmatic—are reached.

Effective boards and volunteer leadership teams or committees depend on the combined qualities and characteristics of the individual members. Volunteer leaders of not-for-profit organizations should be community people who can help with funding, set vision and direction, and oversee policy and finances. They must act as stewards of the organization and its mission. The Mariners' Museum's Vail notes, "This may mean various levels of direct involvement from helping to interpret the institution's role in the community and to the audiences served to providing financial support and securing support from others" (personal interview). Effective nonprofit leaders and board members serve as cheerleaders and ambassadors, who are clearly interested in the organization's mission and are willing to devote the time and make the commitment. They cannot be shy. They need to be knowledgeable about the organization so they can represent it well. If they do not know enough to provide answers to the community about the nonprofit mission, programs, and services, it is a missed opportunity to raise awareness of the organization's mission.

Nonprofits tend to require greater consensus building, and as a result nonprofit leaders generally have less discretion than for-profit boards. "It's not my organization, it's the community's organization. I am the temporary steward. I need to check with the

Figure 5.2 **Operations Versus Governance Balancing Continuum**

Operations   **Governance**
(Staff)   **(Board)**

stakeholders," Widoff comments on board members of WHRO (personal interview).

Diversity among boards has become increasingly important, as has the right mix of professional and technical expertise, backgrounds, talents, skills, and constituencies served. Size also matters. A board with too many people often results in multiple goals and a loss of cohesiveness.

The challenge is how to get volunteer leadership groups to stay focused on the mission and the future and not get involved in the minutia of day-to-day management or act as managers of the various departments within the organization. They have to balance governance and allow paid management to execute, and yet governance often breaks down when the lines between volunteer leadership and professional management blur. These days, with highly skilled and often highly educated executives of nonprofits, along with very busy volunteer leaders who juggle many hats, there is a tendency, for the sake of convenience either by design or by custom, to delegate to a competent executive director and staff those responsibilities that legally belong to the governing board. In these cases, a board must have adequate policies and controls in place to protect the organization in the event that management assumes too much power and misuses—or worse, abuses—authority. Without adequate board oversight and enforcement of policies, management has no accountability and the organization is at risk. This can lead to an environment where the executive director can feel invincible and can make demands and decisions that are not in the best interest of the organization. Jane Short recently resigned from a volunteer board out of concern over the actions of the executive director and cautions, "A board must be careful not to be bamboozled by its own management and must never make decisions based on fear that the executive director will quit if confronted. Even though an executive director should be given appropriate credit for the successes of the organization, the board must never forget its ultimate responsibility and must have the courage to do the required due diligence and hold the executive accountable for things that have gone wrong" (personal interview).

Again, consider this as a continuum (see Figure 5.2) with operations by staff at one end and governance by board members at the opposite end. And, again, the balance rests on the strength and effectiveness of both staff and volunteer leadership.

As executive director of the Girl Scouts chapter in southeastern Virginia, for more than twenty years Nellie Hayse has worked with hundreds of volunteer leaders and recognizes the qualities of effective board members. "They should think BIG, know the environment, have ideas on how to accomplish our mission, be willing to teach the girls, know that they are not the operating staff, and trust us to execute" (personal interview).

Leadership Relationships: Who Owns What?

"There has always been some tension between staff and board" (personal interview), notes Light, who served as a corporate attorney for twenty years before taking the helm of the Norfolk Foundation, which distributed nearly $7 million to the Hampton Roads community of more than 1.5 million in southeastern Virginia. Ownership issues contribute to the tension. When people volunteer their time, expertise, financial support, and goodwill, there is a natural sense of ownership, as there should be. Coordinated leadership on the part of the chief executive and the board becomes essential, and the board chair plays a pivotal role.

The nonprofit professional leader should be a partner with the board, and, of course, is answerable to the board. The president, CEO, or director needs to be flexible and adaptable to be able to deal with different people as the board changes. The board needs to validate the nonprofit executive, as well as recognize and respect staff at all levels. Moreover, there needs to be a high level of trust between senior management and volunteer leaders.

The board sets direction and collaborates with the chief executive to develop organizational goals. "The board should work with the executive and staff to create a strategic plan for the organization, provide a clear set of realistic expectations to the chief executive, monitor those expectations and provide guidance and counsel along the way" (personal interview), says Vail. Both paid leadership and volunteer board members must understand the connection between the things they want to see happen and the money it takes to do them. Both need to feel responsible for the financial viability of the nonprofit. Together they should do strategic planning with board members serving on committees where their expertise is relevant, such as technology or investments. And together they must also be willing to evaluate the progress toward goals. They need to be able to step back and look at the big picture, and not get overly involved with single issues, personalities, or conflicts. A financial investment adviser with a long history of volunteer leadership, Jane Short explains, "You have to be sure you recruit quality people. Don't fill a board seat just to fill a seat. We need to push board work down to committees who will present their ideas for board approval. This will keep the board from wallowing in details" (personal interview). Paul Hirschbiel agrees, "I advocate work done by board committees. Board meetings then become opportunities for the board to work on larger, more strategic issues" (personal interview).

The board should encourage professional training and development for paid leadership. At the same time, the chief executive must ensure continuous education and enlightenment of volunteer leadership, including everything from how to become a more effective board member to learning more about the organization's mission, programs, and services.

The clarification of an organization's mission and board roles and responsibilities contributes to a healthy nonprofit executive and board relationship, as does open and honest communication. Paid and volunteer leaders, however, are often reticent to engage in any confrontation. People resist stepping forward so as not to offend. Yet, one cannot overlook the fact that volunteers give of their time and usually money. Below-market compensation and fewer resources for the nonprofit executive prompt many board members to tread lightly and avoid disagreement. The key here is policy and practice. The board must ensure that policies are in place that not only protect the organization but also protect everyone involved with the organization, paid staff as well as volunteer leadership. When issues do arise, established procedures should be followed to deal with the problems at hand. The staff leader must be willing to discuss matters directly with the board, usually the board chair, making that role especially pivotal. Conflicts should be resolved quickly and there should be an established procedure to allow for the resolution of grievances in a positive manner, even if it means calling in a neutral party to mediate the situation. With so many constituents and stakeholders—including the board, annual members and donors, employees, politicians, clients served, and more—volunteer and paid nonprofit leaders must be adaptable.

Community volunteer and philanthropist Hirschbiel recommends that board members sign an annual pledge to uphold certain expectations, including expectations of financial support. The "Expectations of Board Trustees" from the 1,000-student Cape Henry Collegiate School[6] in Virginia Beach, Virginia, provides a good example and asks trustees to:

- Uphold and support the school's Mission.
- Attend six to eight full board meetings a year, including a retreat.
- Serve on at least one standing committee of the board.
- Set an example for the school's development effort by donating (contributing) to the annual campaign and capital campaign, and by supporting the solicitation efforts of the development campaign.
- Attend graduation and other special ceremonies.
- Serve as an advocate for the school in the Hampton Roads community.

Hire for Attitude and Skills, Seek to Grow, and Recruit, Recruit, Recruit

The absence of new leadership represents a major threat to the nonprofit sector. In fact, at strategic planning sessions across all types of not-for-profit organizations, leadership succession consistently emerges as a leading concern. Dwindling government support and tight budgets mean fewer not-for-profit organizations are investing in future leadership. Training and professional development of staff is considered a luxury many struggling nonprofits cannot afford. Unfortunately, recruiting and grooming the next generation of volunteer leaders in a challenging economic environment often takes a back seat to the more pressing need to raise annual operating funds. The more successful nonprofits take succession very seriously and work with nominating committees to ensure participation and consensus. The Colonial Coast Council of Girl Scouts of America "always works to improve itself by bringing in new people," notes executive director Hayse (personal interview).

Running any organization, including or perhaps *especially* not-for-profits has grown increasingly complex. More lawyers, more MBAs, and more public administrators are being hired as nonprofit CEOs. At the same time, more law schools and graduate business programs are incorporating issues of social and environmental stewardship into the fabric of their programs, presumably grooming passionate people into excellent leaders of tomorrow's nonprofit organizations.

The turnover rate among not-for-profit board members, executives, and staff has increased dramatically in recent years. Similar to the private sector, the higher the passion, the higher the risk of burnout. So whether from job stress and burnout or redirected interests and time, more change in leadership comes with good news and bad. First, the bad news: high turnover and the need to ramp up new executives and volunteers can be expensive, organizational relationships and contacts need to grow and be maintained, and institutional memory disappears. The good news is that new ideas, talents, and energy come with new people, new relationships are forged, and institutional memory disappears. Once again, the key is balance.

"Founder's Syndrome"

Like a product or person, not-for-profits (NPOs) go through life cycles, from birth to decline, sometimes death, and often rebirth. When nonprofits go out of business, it is frequently because there has been a failure to change, and because times, people, needs, and the environment all change, so must NPOs. "Founder's syndrome" represents a source of tension in many organizations and occurs when a nonprofit operates primarily according to the ideas, vision, and personality of a prominent leader within the organization, often someone who has established or shaped the charitable entity. The "way it's always been" resonates through a nonprofit suffering from founder's syndrome. Most often the syndrome is an organizational issue, not a problem with a particular person. The chief executive must be willing to lead the effort to overcome founder's syndrome. This does not mean, however, criticizing the significant contributions of those who came before, but rather ensuring continuous improvement and relevance of the nonprofit organization and its programs and services.

Phyllis Armistead, property management director for the Norfolk (Virginia) Redevelopment and Housing Authority, has seen a classic case of founder's syndrome among the not-for-profit neighborhood resident organizations (NROs) within the various public housing communities throughout the city. These nonprofits started under an initiative of the U.S. Department of Housing and Urban Development in the late 1980s. First established to provide leadership training for residents, NROs today include small businesses that provide public housing to residents, services, sometimes scholarships, and work with management serving as a liaison to the community. "The leadership of these nonprofit resident organizations typically is a single, black woman in her late fifties who has completed some high school, has grown children, often providing some support for grandchildren. The norm for them is to be protective of how things are done. They tend to be close-minded," says Armistead (personal interview). Founder's syndrome can be seen in the persistent shuffle of board positions among a select few. "The NRO president one year may serve as the vice-president the next," Armistead continues (personal interview). This is changing as more NRO participants become better trained about what it means to be a board member and better understand roles and responsibilities and what the expectations are for performance, including number of residents served, financial accountability, and increased resident involvement in the organization.

Chrysler Museum of Art has experienced two significant episodes of "founder's syndrome." For nearly forty years the museum existed as the Norfolk Museum of Arts and Sciences. Then in 1971, Walter P. Chrysler, Jr., the son of the automaker, donated his vast collection of more than 30,000 works of art to the city of Norfolk, as long as the city would provide a place to house it. The initial founders' battle was waged by a portion of the existing board of the Norfolk Museum who wanted nothing to do with Chrysler's collection and feared he would come in and take over their institution. Walter Chrysler himself had a bout of "founder's syndrome" after bringing his collection to Norfolk. For ten years, Chrysler ran the place until he was forced to hire a professional museum director in 1981 in order for the museum to become fully accredited by the American Associations of Museums.

Founders may stay focused on the original mission that fueled the organization. This can blind them to changes in the environment that can then cripple the growth and survival of the nonprofit. Good governance and policies can protect against the negative impact of "founder's syndrome."

Competition

The number of charitable organizations in the United States increased at an annual rate of more than 5 percent between 1987 and 1997, a pace twice that of the business sector over the same period. The fact that not-for-profit organizations depend on the support of charitable contributions gives one a better understanding of the fierce competition for the almighty donor. And that is just the beginning. Besides the chase for support, nonprofits compete on many levels. They compete for volunteers at all levels—from hands-on workers to quality board trustees and directors. Nonprofits, including arts organizations, zoos, historical centers, other cultural venues, and even educational institutions compete for visitors, members, ticket sales, and season subscriptions not only with each other but also with private sector attractions and publicly funded events. In-kind contributions of goods and services allow nonprofits to do some things they otherwise would do without, making them treasured gifts. In the human services, educational, and health-related areas, nonprofit organizations face increasing competition from private companies and government agencies in the delivery of programs and services, although fewer federal and state programs are providing some of these services, leaving the burden to the nonprofits.

Distinctions between nonprofits and for-profits will continue to blur as more partnerships and joint efforts occur among nonprofits, for-profits, and government agencies. The new competitive environment should not spell doom to nonprofits, but should alert their leaders to the risk of compromising the qualities that differentiate them from for-profit organizations. Consider the competitive environment for public broadcasting.

WHRO's Widoff explains, "Twenty years ago I only had to deal with three commercial networks. Today there are hundreds of stations, the Internet and other communications channels competing for viewers and time."

Marketing

Marketing is the engine that drives community awareness that the nonprofit organization exists and provides a knowledge of what it stands for. Increasing that awareness about the mission, goals, and programs does not just happen. You need salesmanship and the willingness to spend money to make money. Marketing efforts in most nonprofits today rely heavily on the free channels of public relations, and have little if any advertising dollars. Larger organizations combine the public relations efforts with some paid advertising added to the marketing mix. Take, for example, the motor-donor programs popular with many nonprofits today that ask donors for old cars to donate to charity for sale at auction. A percentage of the proceeds from the sale goes to the nonprofit, and the donor is allowed to take the documented fair market value of the vehicle for a tax deduction. In order for this kind of program to continue being successful and attracting interest, an advertising campaign is usually necessary.

Another important aspect of marketing in nonprofits today relates to the competitive forces discussed above. The programs and services provided by a nonprofit organization must be differentiated from those of its competitors through marketing and awareness campaigns. And increased awareness is important for participation and financial support.

CHANGES IN THE SECTOR

Change is an ever-present and powerful force in today's fast-paced world, and the environment in which nonprofit organizations operate today certainly has changed. Nonprofit leaders must be open-minded and prepared for change. They must not only be ready and able to adapt to change, but must also develop an organizational culture where change is used as a strategic, creative tool for growth. Institutional and individual strengths, along with important lessons from the past, help leaders break through the barriers to change.

To keep an organization clearly focused on fulfilling its mission, nonprofit leaders must develop specific strategic initiatives to meet the challenges of a constantly evolving environment. Effective nonprofit leaders as well as for-profit leaders must stay current in a dynamic environment. Hayse of the Girl Scouts succinctly notes, "The world is different today and we have to 'get with it.'"

Economic, Societal, and Technological Influences on Nonprofits

Evolving demographic, economic, technological, and lifestyle trends are changing the face of philanthropy and not-for-profit organizations. Limited compensation at the vast majority of nonprofits with small annual budgets can limit the pool of high-quality professional candidates. The pool of volunteer leaders has its own set of dichotomies. Consider, on the one hand, the growing ranks of aging baby boomers who worked—and in many cases played—at full throttle and gave generously of their time and expertise as volunteer leaders of not-for-profit organizations, as they took over from the "founders." Many of them are starting to participate less and enjoy more time for themselves, while others get energized at the opportunity to "make a difference" and contribute to worthy causes and organizations. On the other hand, economic stresses, including everything from Enron-like scandals and financial collapses, to stock market ups and downs, declining government support, increasing health care needs and costs, rising education costs, and blue- and white-collar jobs shifting overseas, have forced some people to defer retirement, take on extra jobs, and make less time and financial support available as volunteer leaders. For them volunteer leadership is not an option. Add fear of terrorist threats, attacks, and war, along with fluctuations in individual, corporate, and government retirement accounts, and reduced foundation and nonprofit assets, and it is amazing that some nonprofits stay afloat.

The succeeding generation of volunteers, now in their thirties and forties, has achieved great success and wealth; they may have "retired" once already, and they take their contributions of time and money to nonprofits very seriously. On the other hand, a good number of these up-and-coming volunteer leaders are raising families, working hard to get ahead, and simply have less time available to give. The challenge for nonprofits is to funnel enough new leaders into the pipeline to be groomed to take on increasingly more responsible volunteer leadership roles.

Technology can create operating efficiencies, improve delivery of programs and services, and enhance cultural experiences. Technology must not, however, replace the relationships that are vital in all organizations, be they for-profit or not. Technology, specifically the Internet, can be better used to raise significantly more funds for nonprofit organizations. Wider use of technology allows more meaningful outreach to more people, including information about the organization and its programs, but again, cannot replace the relationships between the chief executive and the volunteer board. Successful nonprofits find the right balance of technology and personal interaction to ensure that all arrows are properly aligned and aimed in the right direction to achieve the organization's mission and goals. Technology can facilitate personal interaction, not substitute for it.

METRICS, EVALUATION, AND PLANNING

Today, the challenges are the same in the not-for-profit as in the for-profit sector: both require the time, money, and personnel (staff and volunteer) to implement goals. A good first step is to clearly define goals and expectations, but unless there is some means of measuring and monitoring progress toward those goals, nonprofit leaders will not know success when they achieve it.

Measures and Accountability

To take on the challenges that lie ahead most effectively, "all the players in the nonprofit world will need to reevaluate how they operate. Board members, for instance, should push their organizations to establish measures of effectiveness and efficiency," notes Bradley in his May 2003 *Harvard Business Review* article.[7] All nonprofits struggle with meaningful measurements and with being able to effectively benchmark their successes and progress against similar organizations, and many contend that it is more difficult to assess success in the "touchy-feely" not-for-profit organizations than in the private sector. Volunteer and professional leaders alike dread the annual performance reviews, usually between board chair and the chief executive, and most not-for-profits are woefully lacking in this area.

Some measurements are outcome based and easy to measure, for example, dollars raised and calls made in development terms. In grant making, for example, besides the amount of funds doled out, nonprofit foundations must also consider the less quantifiable measures of the difference such support makes to nonprofit programs and services. Certainly financial performance is important, not just in terms of ensuring that income covers expenses, but also in terms of securing new resources, decreasing reliance on government support, and broadening an organization's base of financial support.

Some measurements are process based and require ongoing measurement to see whether progress toward the mission is being achieved. Is the organization feeding more people, educating more low-income children, restoring more wetlands, empowering more battered women to become independent? At the root of some of this discussion is the need to spend more time with constituents, stakeholders, and audiences to assess satisfaction in light of the mission and goals of the organizations. Perhaps more important than the measures is the process of developing those measures. Commitment and team building are developed in the process, and communications between volunteer and professional leadership becomes more open. The Mariners' Museum's Vail comments, "Of course developing a plan for measurement requires an investment of funds and a long-term commitment by the leadership of the organization to using any information. It's a way of thinking that is different from the current norm and will also require training of the CEOs and staff."

Hard-to-measure items, especially for the paid executive, are often assessed anecdotally. Are they respected in the community? Do they get along with everyone (constituents and stakeholders) or *almost* everyone? Have they solidified their position enough to make some hard (and often unpopular) choices? The Girl Scouts measure the progress toward the Council's goals. Hayse explains, "They have a goal to reach out to the Asian and Hispanic community. They also measure membership growth, take a customer service survey, and a community relations survey. The latter includes the media, members, and former board members. Measuring what people think of us is difficult."

PRESCRIPTIONS/TOOLBOX

Making a difference in the lives of others and in one's community is the ultimate measure of effective and successful leadership in not-for-profit organizations. Scottish-born

American industrialist, philanthropist Andrew Carnegie defined modern-day philanthropy by saying that those with wealth "do good" and give back to the society that helped create that wealth. Carnegie also understood the importance of humility and teamwork in effective leadership and according to him, "No man will make a great leader who wants to do it all himself, or to get all the credit for doing it."[8] This is certainly a truism in the nonprofit sector. Effective leadership among paid executives and volunteers enables charitable organizations and other independent sector organizations to fulfill their missions and to "do good." In laying out the tools for successful leadership in nonprofits, we remind you of the continuum and the importance of the right balance.

Context, Preparation, and Persuasion

Earlier we highlighted the characteristics of effective staff and volunteer leadership resources, and addressed the importance of a healthy relationship between the two. In a recent speech to group of civic leaders from Hampton Roads, former Virginia Governor Gerald L. Baliles summarized leadership in three words: *context*, *preparation*, and *persuasion*. We expand on these three attributes, as they become tools in our nonprofit leadership toolbox and present a representation of these three tools for successful nonprofit professional and volunteer leadership (see Figure 5.3).

Context

The increasingly complex environment in today's not-for-profit world presents several context issues.

- *Balance the focus on mission with efficient operations.* The higher-level context of a nonprofit is the organization's mission. It must remain relevant and current with roles and responsibilities of both paid and volunteer leaders clearly defined and articulated. A good leader understands the context of staff and volunteer leadership as it relates to fulfilling the mission and pays attention to efficient organizational operation. The late British Prime Minister Benjamin Disraeli said that a leader "must know the times in which he lives."[9] Good advice for nonprofit leaders.
- *Strive for continuous improvement in professional leadership.* Successful nonprofits hire leaders who know more than social work, civic and environmental activism, public broadcasting, Girl Scouts, religion, art history, or education, to name a few areas of expertise. Successful executives in the independent sector acquire the "nuts and bolts" of operating an organization and strengthen their skills, education, and experience across a broader set of disciplines, including financial and human resources management, marketing, public relations, technology, and fund-raising. Successful nonprofit leaders skillfully direct strategic planning efforts, ensure that goals aligned with the organization's mission are achieved, and measure performance of themselves and others, *without doing everyone else's job*—unless, of course, the nonprofit staff is only one or two persons. Again, there is a delicate balance

Figure 5.3 **Nonprofit Leadership Toolbox**

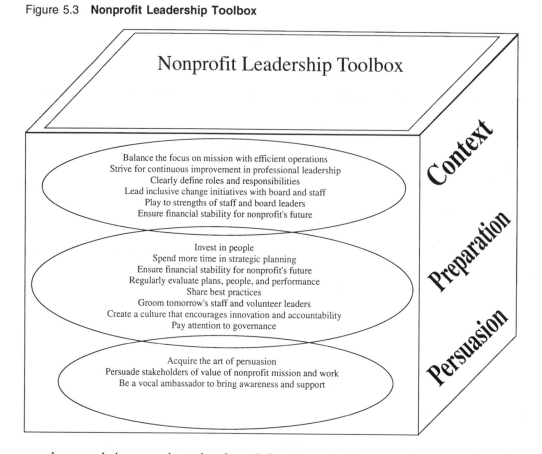

between being experienced or knowledgeable and micromanaging nonprofit staff. Allow people to do their jobs and create the atmosphere in which they reach their full potential.

- *Clearly define roles and responsibilities.* This point cannot be overemphasized and applies to professional and volunteer leaders alike. One further step we recommend is to define the relationship between volunteer and paid leaders. Understanding expectations from the outset sets the stage for greater success in achieving them.
- *Lead inclusive change initiatives with board and staff.* The context of today's environment requires nonprofit leaders who deftly and genuinely handle change within the organization and the volunteer board. This means effectively partnering with the board, involving staff, and creating a healthy environment for creativity and innovation in designing and implementing change initiatives. In the absence of the high achieving professional not-for-profit leader with all the skills outlined above, the ability to build effective management teams becomes all the more crucial.
- *Play to strengths of staff and board leaders.* Successful nonprofit chief executives play to people's strengths and seek senior staff with energy, competency, and skill sets that complement their own. The current trend to hire professionals with strong

business backgrounds and skills continues to gain momentum and is likely to continue.

- *Ensure financial stability for nonprofit's future.* Successful nonprofit leaders take a longer-term view and work to ensure a solid foundation that can be built upon.

Preparation

Good preparation is the key to readying the organization and all stakeholders to embrace and capitalize on future events and opportunities.

- *Invest in people.* Healthy nonprofit organizations invest more in people and work at growing and retaining excellent staff.
- *Spend more time in strategic planning.* Effective leaders spend more time up front in the strategic-planning processes by stakeholders, ensuring greater understanding of the organization's mission, more open communication, and better participation.
- *Regularly evaluate plans, people, and performance.* How will you know success when you get there if you do not regularly evaluate goals, plans, and staff and board performance with appropriate course correction as needed?
- *Share best practices.* Chief executives recognize the need to share best practices within their areas and across other nonprofits, and, where relevant, with the private and public sectors as well.
- *Groom tomorrow's staff and volunteer leaders.* Succession remains a challenge to not-for-profit organizations of all types. Good preparation means identifying the "next generation" of professional and volunteer leaders to guide the organization, cultivating their interest, and developing their capacity to lead.
- *Create a culture that encourages innovation and accountability.* Thriving nonprofit organizations are prepared for the changing needs of their constituencies, beneficiaries, and clients. In order to remain flexible and adaptable, effective nonprofit professional and volunteer leaders set the tone and create an environment that encourages creativity and calculated risk-taking, along with accountability.
- *Pay attention to governance.* Do not take governance for granted. Successful nonprofits prepare for changes and challenges by paying attention to how they operate, avoid conflict of interest, remain true to their mission, and, again, clearly define roles and responsibilities. Governance is the role of the board of directors and should not be delegated, or, worse, abrogated.

Persuasion

Advertising pioneer William Bernbach once said that, "Advertising is fundamentally persuasion and persuasion happens to be not a science, but an art."[10] It is an art worth developing.

- *Acquire the art of persuasion.* Effective nonprofit leaders are skillful persuaders. They influence people to listen, to act, and to follow a course of action.

- *Persuade stakeholders of value of nonprofit mission and work.* The paid executive must persuade all stakeholders, including staff, donors, and board leaders, to believe in the mission and support the organization with their time, talents, and money. Volunteer leaders want to be associated with not-for-profits that consistently fulfill their mission.
- *Be a vocal ambassador to bring awareness and support.* Effective leaders proudly boast of the good work of the not-for-profit organizations to which they volunteer their time and persuade others to join in and provide critical financial support.

Finally, Governor Baliles points out that the three leadership elements—context, preparation, and persuasion—are linked. If you do not understand the context in which you operate, you cannot be adequately prepared. If you are well prepared, you can persuade others, and it is much easier for the persuaded to execute if they too understand the context and are well prepared. So, understand the context, be prepared, and persuade others to join in. Nonprofits and the clients, causes, and constituencies they serve will benefit from adhering to these three leadership components. We add—be vigilant.

NOTES

1. Warren Bennis and Burt Nanus, *Leaders* (New York: Harper and Row, 1986), 93.
2. Bill Bradley, Paul Jansen, and Les Silverman, "The Nonprofit Sector's $100 Billion Opportunity," *Harvard Business Review* (May 2003): 2–3.
3. Aline Sullivan, "Fixing the Leak," *Barron's Online* (December 8, 2003); available at www.wsj.com/article_barrons_email/0,,SB107066381225800–H9jeoNolaV2JyoZXHb6aHm-4,00.html.
4. See www.aafrc.org/press_releases/trustreleases/charityholds.html.
5. Tom Shean, "Profit from Experience," *Virginian-Pilot*, December 7, 2003.
6. Cape Henry Collegiate School Board of Trustees Expectations of Trustees—provided to the authors by Paul Hirschbiel, a Cape Henry trustee. This one-page document is given to all school trustees.
7. Bradley, Jansen, and Silverman, "The Nonprofit Sector's $100 Billion Opportunity": 10.
8. See www.quoteworld.org/author.php?thetext=Andrew+Carnegie+%281835–1919%29.
9. See www.vba.org/mar02.htm#baliles.
10. See www.brainyquote.com/quotes/authors/w/william_bernbach.html.

CHAPTER 6

THE CHALLENGES OF INTERPERSONAL RELATIONSHIPS, EMPLOYEE DISCIPLINE, AND LEADERSHIP EFFECTIVENESS IN RELIGIOUS NONPROFIT ORGANIZATIONS

CRAIG OSTEN

UNIQUE LEADERSHIP CHALLENGES AFFORDED BY RELIGIOUS NONPROFIT ORGANIZATIONS

On the surface, one might believe that religious nonprofit organizations do not have to deal with significant workplace spirituality issues. Because the employees of a ministry share a common faith, the assumption is that conflict will be reduced, unlike in a "secular" organization that is run by "secular" rules.

However, in many cases, spirituality issues are more complex in the ministry workplace than they are in the secular business world. First, although the employees of a ministry might share a common faith, they have each developed their own set of core beliefs with regard to that faith. The result is that strongly held opinions within the same common faith framework end up clashing with each other. Second, employment issues such as tardiness, insubordination, absences, and employee conflict often take on a spiritual dimension, as employees tend to attach spiritual beliefs to these areas. Third, many religious individuals are drawn to working with ministries in the belief that the ministry workplace will greatly differ from that of the secular world. Finally, ministries have standards different from those of the secular world for termination or discipline. For instance, if a secular employee were committing adultery, it may not be grounds for dismissal unless his or her activity severely impacts either individual or organizational performance. However, in the ministry workplace, such conduct would be seen as a violation of the ministry's tenets of faith and, thus, grounds for termination. In this chapter, we will examine each of these issues as well as the positive aspects of spirituality in the ministry workplace, and the associated leadership challenges.

Related to this is the broader topic of long-term leadership effectiveness in nonprofit religious organizations. Given the intensely personal and spiritual foundations upon which ministry organizations are built, the founding leader plays a significant role in determining not only the short-term but also the long-term success of the organization, perhaps more so than in any other organizational context. Thus, the latter portion of this chapter is devoted to discussing long-term leadership effectiveness in ministry organizations, and proposes five keys to successful long-term ministry leadership.

THE POSITIVE FACTORS OF SPIRITUALITY IN THE MINISTRY WORKPLACE

One of the positive roles that spirituality plays in the ministry workplace is that employees have a common faith reference and the opportunity to express that faith openly throughout the workday. Unless their behavior becomes extreme or starts to seriously impact their effectiveness and the effectiveness of others, expression of faith is encouraged. Employees feel more secure knowing that their expression of faith will not have negative repercussions with other employees and management. Another positive aspect of spirituality in the ministry workplace is the practice that many ministries have of starting each day with a morning devotion or prayer. While it varies from employee to employee, this morning devotional time with other employees helps staff members to bond together as a team and allows a natural support group to develop. The effect of praying before the start of the workday has a calming influence on many employees and allows them to clear their minds of any distractions or burdens they feel before they have to begin their daily responsibilities. Spiritual individuals tend to be more patient and have more empathy with their peers than do secular individuals. Issues, at least initially, are dealt with in a less confrontational manner than is the case in the secular work environment. There is also an expectation that all employees will be civil toward each other and treat each other with respect. However, this desire to be patient and civil can sometimes lead to issues that should be dealt with early instead of being put off and resulting in a potentially uglier situation later on. Finally, ministry employees feel united together in a higher purpose rather than just helping the profitability of a corporation. The spiritual goal of performing work that they believe brings glory to God and ministers to others serves as a reason to put personal differences aside for the achievement of the common ministry goal, whether it is preserving families or bringing individuals to religious faith. Overall, these factors are positive elements of the ministry workplace, and are examples of how spiritual values allow for greater personal accountability of potentially harmful behaviors, and for the development of team unity and purpose.

Unfortunately, these benefits are not always realized in religious nonprofit organizations. Recognizing this reality, we turn our attention to several negative spiritual factors that can influence the ministry workplace. Each brings significant challenges that, while not altogether unique to ministry-related organizations, are certainly exacerbated in that setting.

DIFFERENCES IN BELIEF WITHIN THE MINISTRY WORKPLACE

Jack and Mark worked in the same department within a major Christian ministry.[1] While they shared the same core belief—faith in Jesus Christ—they differed greatly on issues that were not as central to that core belief. Jack liked to play cards, drink alcohol, and smoke cigars every once in a while. Mark considered these behaviors to be "sinful" and was quick to condemn anyone who engaged in them. Mark had taken his personal opinions on these behaviors and spiritualized them to the point that he considered them major moral issues. Jack, on the other hand, saw no legitimate prohibitions on his behavior, and took great offense whenever Mark confronted him about them. The result was a schism within the department, with most of the employees siding with Jack's desire to engage in behaviors that were not seen as violations of the core belief of faith in Jesus Christ and thus not in conflict with the mission of the organization.

In addition, Mark's dogmatic beliefs caused conflict in other areas. This particular ministry employed both Protestants and Catholics—as long as they professed faith in Jesus Christ. Mark had very strong opinions with regard to Roman Catholicism and made them known to whomever was willing to listen. When a Catholic employee showed a video of Pope John Paul II during a morning devotional, Mark angrily confronted her and spent the remainder of the morning engaged in theological debate with other employees, thereby hindering production and driving a spiritual wedge between employees. When confronted by management about how his beliefs were negatively impacting the workplace, Mark refused to back down and eventually the ministry was forced to terminate his employment. To this day, Mark does not see that his confrontational attitude toward his fellow employees was wrong.

Examples such as this illustrate one of the major spiritual issues that take place in the ministry workplace: the fervor of one's particular opinions or beliefs. While some employees can work beside each other for years with little or no conflict despite significant theological differences, others cannot. The result is tension, often followed by termination, for those who cannot put their theological differences aside in the interest of harmony and striving for a common goal.

In the late 1980s and early 1990s, many people with "pro-life" beliefs took part in a movement called "Operation Rescue." This movement tended to appeal to individuals who felt very strongly about the issue of abortion, and who were attracted to a cause that would bring attention to this issue. While all of the employees of the particular ministry where Mark and Jim were employed were pro-life, not all agreed with the tactics used by Operation Rescue. But for those who had jumped upon the Operation Rescue bandwagon, the refusal by their colleagues to participate or embrace the movement's practices was tantamount to siding with the "pro-choice" community. The employees who became involved in Operation Rescue held the spiritual belief that what they were doing was more important than anything else. Many of the employees who did not take part in Operation Rescue felt that these individuals were doing damage more than giving help to the pro-life cause because their activism resulted in more and more prohibitions on the ability of pro-lifers to counsel pregnant women considering abortion. The result, once again, was that schisms developed within the ministry organization—you were either one of the "true believers" (i.e., involved in Operation Rescue) or your belief in the "sanctity of human life" was perceived to be shaky at best. When the president and chief executive officer (CEO) of this ministry threw his support behind Operation Rescue, the fervor of the Operation Rescue contingent grew even stronger.

This is another instance in which fervor with respect to a particularly held belief—and one that would be considered a spiritual belief by many—caused a great deal of workplace tension. While all of the employees held to a basic core belief of faith in Jesus Christ, this difference in opinion (spiritualized by those on both sides of the issue) created a schism among co-workers who divided into two very different camps, resulting in the destruction of what had previously been a harmonious and productive workplace.

THE SPIRITUALIZATION OF EMPLOYMENT ISSUES

There is a potential among many employees of religious nonprofit organizations (particularly employees with "charismatic" denominations and backgrounds) to interpret the management of serious employment issues as a "spiritual attack" upon the employee. This can become an acute problem when a ministry has to enter into the disciplinary process with a problem employee and the employee sees the discipline as an attack on their beliefs rather than a call to personal accountability in the workplace. Such was the case with both Laura and Phillip.

The Spiritualization of Poor Task Performance

Laura was the "social butterfly" of the office. For Laura, a day at the office was like a giant party. Every day she would flit from desk to desk chatting with her fellow employees while rarely putting in more than about one to two hours of real work of her own. If there was a spare phone in a secluded area for Laura to use for personal calls, she did. This lack of productivity was not an issue for Laura. She simply felt that it was her "ministry" to be the office gadfly. When called onto the carpet for her lack of production after years of such behavior and distraction of other employees, she would go into a pout and spiritualize her subsequent insubordination as an attack upon her ability to do "ministry."

Laura had spiritualized her serious work deficiencies, and when disciplined she saw it as a spiritual attack upon her. The leaders of the ministry rightly saw her actions as resulting in a waste of organizational resources. Laura felt that the disciplinary actions taken by her supervisors meant that the ministry was more concerned about "business" than ministry. Laura then proceeded to fuel the disenchantment of other nonproductive workers and staged an "us vs. them" battle against management. When the ministry relocated to another state, Laura was told in no uncertain terms that she would not be making the move with the ministry. To this day, Laura believes that it was her "ministry" to be the social cheerleader for the department, instead of to focus her time and energies on the tasks that she was assigned to do.

The Spiritualization of Improper Attitude

Phillip was an individual whose self-esteem was based on his intelligence and theological knowledge. There was no doubt that Phillip was a brilliant individual. However, he had "spiritualized" his intellect to the point that he belittled the theological beliefs of others in the ministry. He also used his influence and intelligence to create followers of himself, rather than of the ministry. Because Phillip felt that he was spiritually superior to everyone else, he treated those he deemed intellectually and spiritually inferior with contempt. Spirituality was a weapon for Phillip, to be used to promote *himself* as opposed to promoting the larger organization.

When finally confronted about these behaviors and told why he would not be promoted to management, Phillip verbally assaulted management, resigned, and then engaged in a systematic campaign to turn his "disciples" against the ministry. Phillip could see no wrong in what he was doing because he felt that he was spiritually superior to those to whom he had reported. In a secular workplace, the behaviors he engaged in after his resignation would have been grounds for a lawsuit, but because it was a ministry, they chose not to pursue that option.

The Spiritualization of Accountability

Because the belief of both of these employees was deep-seated, they viewed any discipline or action taken by management to correct the behavior as a personal attack upon their spirituality. Thus, the critical leadership tool of workplace accountability in regard to task performance and personal attitude was rendered useless in both cases.

Unrealistic Expectations of the Ministry Work Environment—The Spiritualization of Work

Another issue that affects many ministries is the perception that working for a ministry will differ radically from working for a secular business. Many individuals believe that the ministry workplace will be less stressful and less demanding, and will be a place of constant affirmation, rather than critical appraisal, of their work. In addition, they believe that the workplace will be a source of constant affirmation of their personal spiritual beliefs.

Whenever I interview an individual for a position, the first thing I tell the prospective employee is, "Don't come in with the perception that this is going to be heaven on earth. If you do, you will become disillusioned fast." This is not said because it is a terrible place to work, but because people are people, regardless of religious faith, with the same faults as everyone else. Those employees who come in with the perception of a stress-free, perpetually harmonious workplace will become disillusioned quickly. Unrealistic expectations also play out to extreme disenchantment and subsequent bitterness against the ministry. Because the initial perception of the individual is not validated by the reality of the ministry workplace, their disillusionment slowly turns to anger.

A number of these employees had come from secular workplaces where their spirituality had not been affirmed, and in many cases, they had perceived that their spirituality was under assault. Therefore, they perceived that working for a ministry would be exactly the opposite. Obviously, a ministry workplace would be more hospitable toward, and encouraging of, religious faith. However, many successful ministries have the same work expectations and demands as the secular workplace, and in some instances, even more. Because some employees enter the ministry workplace with the expectation of a stress-free, harmonious environment, their burnout rates tend to be fairly high once they realize that the ministry workplace does not differ greatly from the secular work environment, with the exception of an overall tone of spirituality. Because these employees become disenchanted, they start to look for another ministry that might be the "heaven on earth" that they are seeking. The average burnout time I have observed for employees with unrealistic expectations of the ministry workplace is approximately eighteen months.

Thus, ministry leaders must make it clear early that the expectations of the ministry workplace will not differ greatly from those of a secular business. In addition, ministry leaders need to defuse unrealistic expectations of what the ministry workplace will be like. Dealing with these issues early should lead to less employee burnout and dissatisfaction.

The Impact of Moral Failures upon Ministries—Spiritualizing Unethical Behavior

While many ministries have had to deal with moral lapses on the part of their employees, as a whole, this tends to happen less often than in the secular workplace. On the flip side, however, when these moral lapses do occur, they generally have more serious ramifications for a ministry than they do for a secular workplace, especially when the moral lapse involves a high-profile leader.

At one major ministry with a daily radio broadcast heard by millions, two co-hosts (approximately fifteen years apart) fell into adulterous relationships with each other and resigned. In the secular workplace, and especially with the gradual removal of cultural stigmas on such behavior, the impact would not be as large. Because ministries and the public that supports them hold to a different standard, moral lapses have a much greater negative impact and often result in feelings of anger and betrayal between the ministry and the individuals involved. For a ministry, personal moral failure can be an earth-shattering event because it is seen as a violation of donor trust and, perhaps even more serious, as hypocrisy by a world that is increasingly distrustful of organized religion.

In the instance of this particular ministry, the problem was compounded when the first individual spiritually justified his affair, subsequent divorce, and remarriage. The company's president and his co-workers did not accept his behavior or actions, which in turn resulted in his "spiritualization" of the issue, and a now two-decades long attack upon the ministry and its leader. In his own mind, this person had rationalized that God would not want him to be unhappy, as he had been in his first marriage, so it was perfectly all right for him to pursue happiness, even if it was a violation of the ministry's stated beliefs.

Like secular individuals who justify ethically questionable decisions, religious individuals can do so as well. The key difference is that in the ministry workplace, some religious individuals use spiritual reasons to explain their poor personal decisions.

While spiritual arguments for morally questionable behavior will not hold water in the secular workplace, some individuals, when confronted about a moral failure, attempt to use spiritual reasons either to explain their behavior or to deflect responsibility for their actions.

All of the scenarios above describe negative spiritual issues that can occur within the ministry workplace. What they have in common is a spiritual emphasis on self, rather than on the greater goals of the ministry. Religious individuals, just as their secular counterparts, deal with trust, disappointment, insubordination, and lust, among other issues. In many cases, it is much harder for a ministry to deal with these issues because, unlike a profit-driven secular business, they are driven by a ministry mindset that advocates helping individuals to turn their lives around and become productive, happy employees. Sometimes this works and other times it does not, creating significant difficulty for ministry workplace leaders.

NAVIGATING THE COMPLEX WATERS OF SPIRITUAL PLURALITY

Because spirituality is a deeply personal issue for many people, there is a tendency to personalize issues that arise in the ministry workplace and turn them into "spiritual issues." A ministry must realize that although all of its employees share a common faith, each of them came to that faith in a different way (Conlin 1999)—and their personal practice of that faith manifests itself in their interactions with other employees. This is especially true of pluralistic or ecumenical ministries that employ mainline Protestant, charismatic or Pentecostal, reformed, evangelical, and Catholic employees. Individuals from each of these faith backgrounds are likely to perceive issues through the prism of that background. In addition, those with strong, dogmatic beliefs in one of these faith backgrounds may, as was discussed earlier, try to impose their personal beliefs upon other employees.

How does a ministry navigate these complex waters? First of all, it needs to impress upon all prospective employees at the outset that all faith backgrounds are respected in the ministry workplace. An employee who disrespects the personal spiritual beliefs of another employee needs to be disciplined as swiftly as he or she would be for sexual harassment or racial discrimination. All faith backgrounds can work together harmoniously if there is mutual respect rather than spiritual competition in the workplace.

For instance, one Christian ministry has a CEO who is Catholic and several Catholic employees. Four of the vice presidents come from a reformed background, which split from the Roman church at the time of Martin Luther. There is a great theological chasm between Roman Catholicism and reformed theology, but these individuals have set their differences aside for the sake of the common good in order to increase the size and impact of the ministry upon American culture. To the CEO's credit, he does not expect his employees to convert to Roman Catholicism, and he does not belittle those who come from a different faith background. That attitude results in respect from the rest of the staff for different theological backgrounds of other employees. If the tone is set by upper management that encourages all faith backgrounds to be embraced (given a common commitment to the mission of the organization), then many of the potential spirituality issues in the workplace can be resolved quickly, and in most cases, without conflict.

With regard to employees who "spiritualize" personal employment issues, the ministry must be careful to present their arguments in ways that do not belittle what an individual believes is a "spiritual" issue. Any remark that can potentially be seen as an invalidation of the employee's deeply held spiritual belief can make a bad situation even worse. For example, in the case of Laura discussed above, management needed to steer clear of her argument that her socialization was her form of "ministry." Instead, they had to refocus the issue on how her behavior was bad stewardship of funds voluntarily donated by supporters for a specific purpose and not for her personal form of "ministry." Management had to bring her back to the greater goal of advancing the mission of the organization.

That, of course, does not always work. Sometimes an employee is so convinced that he or she is right or spiritually superior, that there is no possible avenue for resolving the issue. In that case, a ministry needs to move swiftly either to terminate the employee or to attempt to assist the employee in finding an employer with whom he or she is more theologically compatible. If these issues are allowed to drag out, the disgruntled employee is likely to try to enlist others to his or her cause, with the result that greater damage occurs among many employees when the inevitable break occurs. Management may never be able to win a "spiritual" argument with an employee, but it can take action on the grounds that it is necessary to protect religious pluralism, harmony, and productivity in the workplace.

THE FIVE KEYS TO LONG-TERM MINISTRY LEADERSHIP SUCCESS

Given an understanding of some of the unique employment-related problems that leaders in ministry organizations face, we now turn our attention to the broader topic of ministry leadership effectiveness. The driving force behind many of today's successful ministries has been a dynamic, forceful, and visionary leader. However, in some cases, the leader's very personal and spiritual drive that made the organization great can eventually become a detriment if the ministry becomes too dependent upon his or her personality or personal beliefs. Collins (2001, 20) writes that the best leaders, what he calls "Level 5 Leaders," are not necessarily the most dynamic individuals, but individuals who have a strong combination of vision, humility, and internal drive.

What steps can a founder or leader of a ministry take to ensure the ongoing success of the ministry? I have identified five:

1. *Keep the Focus.* Do not steer off the initial course you set when you started the ministry.
2. *Hire Compatible and Complementary Co-leaders.* Hire other executives whose gifts complement, rather than compete with, your own.

3. *Let Go.* Once you have a strong executive team in place, empower them to assume leadership and personal responsibilities for decisions. Very few are effective when they feel someone is always watching over their shoulder.

4. *Keep in Touch.* As difficult as it may seem, a leader needs to spend time with the everyday workforce and not become isolated.

5. *Do Not Be Afraid to Change.* An effective leader is always looking for ways to be ahead of the curve, instead of relying on the same formula for success. If a leader does the latter, the organization is often surpassed by a younger, hungrier rival enterprise, and starts to become irrelevant.

As case studies we now take a detailed look at two different ministries (herewith referred to as Ministry A and Ministry B) through the lens of these five keys to ministry leadership success.

Ministry A—A Case of Leadership Failure

Ministry A was started by a dynamic, high-energy, and demanding president and CEO. Because of the sheer force of his personality, many others were attracted to him. This CEO also had a strong belief in excellence, which in turn led the best and the brightest in the ministry workplace world to work for him. He was also wise enough to hire strong individuals to handle areas in which he was not gifted.

This ministry experienced explosive growth for approximately twenty years. But then that growth came to a grinding halt and now the ministry finds itself in a position of financial decline and lessening influence. What happened?

1. *The leader lost focus.* As the president and CEO grew older, his primary passion and the cornerstone "cause" of the ministry—marriage and the family—became less and less important to him. Because he had gotten along on the force of his personality and charisma for so long, he had trouble understanding why people were not interested in the same things that he was. Consequently, the ministry became more and more about his personal interests at the moment and less about the ministry's core mission—to strengthen marriages and families. As Blackaby (2001, 228) writes: "By spending too much time on less significant issues, leaders invariably neglect the more important ones."

2. *The leader could not let go.* As this ministry leader got older, his grip on the ministry and on his executives grew tighter and tighter. Because this ministry had been built around his personality, his first instinct when things started to weaken was to seize even more power and to focus the ministry increasingly on himself. The result was that many of the key leaders in the organization left for other ministries where their gifts could be fully utilized.

3. *The leader could not adapt and change.* The ministry continued to recycle the same material year after year, with little or no thought toward emerging cultural trends or the creation of new material. Thus, the ministry found itself with an

aging demographic, and other younger, more in-touch rivals seized what used to be Ministry A's core audience.

With regard to spiritual issues in the workplace discussed above, the leader of Ministry A believed that he could impose his personal spiritual and moral beliefs upon his executive staff and employees. The result was tension in the workplace and eventual resentment from and loss of key staff.

Ministry B—A Case of Leadership Success

While Ministry A is descending, Ministry B is ascending. Its leader is also a dynamic visionary. So, why is this ministry growing at record pace and financially outperforming almost every other ministry, while Ministry A finds itself in retrenchment?

1. *The leader is focused.* This CEO has a goal in mind and has a plan to get there. He has never deviated from the ministry's original purpose.
2. *The leader has let go.* He has hired the best and the brightest, and makes sure as Collins (2001, 42) writes in *Good to Great*, that they are in the "right seat on the right bus." He then lets go to allow them to succeed in their core competencies. He also looks at a person's gifts and sees avenues for those gifts to blossom. He has a strong commitment to excellence.
3. *He does not want the credit.* This CEO actually shies away from the credit and wants others to receive it. This builds morale in the workplace as well as a spirit of humility among the staff.
4. *He is not afraid of change.* Rather than refusing to acknowledge that people and circumstances have changed, this leader is always looking ahead of the curve and making the proper course corrections before other ministries do.
5. *He invests in employees personally.* In addition, the president and CEO of Ministry B makes a special effort to touch base with his employees on a regular basis. The president and CEO of Ministry A rarely has any one-on-one time with his employees.

Finally, the leader of Ministry B does not believe it is his role to impose his personal spiritual and moral beliefs upon his employees. His only concern is that they passionately support the mission of the organization and they abide by the moral standards set by the company.

Other ministry organizations similar to Ministry B have lasted for the long haul and have remained strong even with periodic changes in the president and CEO. That is because they continued to be mission driven, rather than personality driven (Krames 2003). Other ministries that had become more and more dependent upon the personality of the leader did not last once that leader was gone. The bottom line is that if a ministry leader cannot adapt or change the very gifts that made him so successful initially in the launch and growth of the ministry, it will eventually lead to the ministry's decline and potential demise. The leader must also empower his employees to take responsibility and make decisions, rather than to be involved in every aspect of the organization (Biehl 1998).

LESSONS FROM THE CONTEMPORARY BUSINESS WORLD— SOME CONCLUDING THOUGHTS FOR MINISTRY LEADERS

In this chapter, we have looked at two issues involving religious nonprofit organizations: the impact of spiritual beliefs on the workplace and the leadership qualities that allow a ministry to be successful for the long haul.

Spirituality and how it manifests itself in the workplace are complex issues, and perhaps even more complex in an organization whose mission is based upon religious faith. Unlike a secular workplace, where spiritual and moral issues are often either black and white or irrelevant to the operation of the organization, the ministry workplace has to deal with several different shades of gray. Therefore, the interpersonal dynamics of confronting problematic behavior are far more difficult and complex than in a secular work environment.

For a ministry to remain successful, it must deal quickly with dysfunctional behaviors. A ministry must approach discipline in a way that corrects rather than enables the behavior. For instance, in the case of Laura discussed above, the ministry should have dealt with the problem early. Instead, the problem lingered for several years, and by the time it was addressed, Laura had spiritualized the issue. While it may seem contrary to what ministries are supposed to be about, a problem employee must be dealt with quickly because ministries have finite resources, which they cannot waste on long-term correction or enabling of the behavior.

Because ministries tend to do everything they can to be compassionate toward an individual, they may tolerate dysfunctional or harmful behaviors longer than a secular business would. Unfortunately, this need for compassion can eventually lead to a disastrous situation. For instance, because Phillip's spiritual arrogance was not dealt with early (as discussed above), it was allowed to fester and eventually the damage to the ministry was much greater than if it had been addressed immediately when it surfaced.

In addition to understanding and addressing the unique challenges associated with the "spiritualization" of employment issues, ministry leaders must also keep their focus on the bigger picture, purposefully leading the ministry forward. In short, leaders of ministries cannot rest on past laurels. As in secular businesses, if you keep cranking out the same product every year, you are eventually going to be surpassed by a hungrier, more innovative rival. A ministry leader must keep looking ahead and adapting, even if he does not like the direction he sees. A ministry that keeps pace with cultural trends, as a business does, will be successful. Those that do not will ultimately weaken and eventually fail. For example, Kmart was a huge success back in the 1970s. Kmart essentially established the big-box, discount-house retailing category. Now it is a company on the ropes, largely because it never adapted to the change in American buying habits and failed to adopt promising supply chain management technology as it emerged. Like

Kmart, Ministry A was a huge success in the 1980s but it now finds itself in retrench-ment in the year 2004 while others ascend.

Because ministries tend to be personality driven, much as the greater culture is, it is essential that they find a balance between the promotion of a personality and the percep-tion that the *ministry is the personality*. This is a tenuous balance to strike because indi-viduals tend to follow a personality rather than an organization. To use a contemporary business example, Southwest Airlines has always reflected the personality of its founder Herb Kelleher, and much of its success can be connected to *his* personal passions for customer service, operational efficiency, and fun. However, as Southwest matured as an organization, these passions became more and more connected to the mission of the organization (and hence became core competencies that Southwest continues to lever-age in the marketplace) and less and less embodied by Kelleher himself. Now that Kelleher has stepped down as CEO, people are still devotedly flying on and working for South-west because those things that make Southwest compelling (both as a service provider and employer) are intact as part of the mission of the organization. It is true that people want to identify with a personality, but if the focus of the ministry becomes more on the personality and less on the product, or if the product does not adapt to competition in the marketplace or emerging cultural trends, the ministry, just as a secular business, will face difficulties.

Thus, while leaders in nonprofit religious organizations face a number of unique is-sues, many of these are the same as those encountered in the secular workplace. The key difference is the spiritual environment of the ministry workplace, which changes the entire dynamic of interpersonal relations and employee discipline. If a ministry leader can successfully navigate the spiritual issues while keeping the organization steadfastly focused on its mission, he or she will be successful.

NOTE

1. Each of the examples in this chapter are true-life situations that the author has observed over twenty years of management in religious nonprofit organizations. The names have been changed for confidentiality reasons.

REFERENCES

Biehl, B. (1998). *30 Days to Confident Leadership*. Nashville, TN: Broadman and Holman.
Blackaby, H. (2001). *Spiritual Leadership*. Nashville, TN: Broadman and Holman.
Collins, J. (2001). *Good to Great: Why Some Companies Make the Leap . . . and Others Don't*. New York: Harper Business.
Conlin, M. (1999). "Religion in the Workplace." *Business Week*, November 1: 151–155.
Krames, J.A. (2003). *What the Best CEOs Know: 7 Exceptional Leaders and Their Lessons for Transforming Any Business*. New York: McGraw-Hill Companies.

CHAPTER 7

WHAT THE NEW NONPROFIT LEADERS SHOULD LEARN ABOUT FINANCE

Beyond Fund-raising and Accounting

HERRINGTON J. BRYCE

Unfortunately, we do not know what the annual rate of growth for new leaders of non-profit organizations will be over the next decade, and, therefore, we do not know specifically how many new leaders we must train to fill the net expected increase in leadership slots. This fact is distinguishable from two other facts. First, we do expect that the number of nonprofits in the country and the world is likely to increase and that this will increase the need for competent nonprofit leaders; and second, we do have estimates for the expected annual rate of increase in employment or jobs in the economic sectors that have a high rate of representation of nonprofit organizations—at least in the United States—and these, too, point to the rise in the number of nonprofit leaders that will be needed in the United States. The growth of nongovernmental organizations globally and the increased responsibilities thrust upon them also point to an increased demand for new nonprofit leaders.

FACTORS SHAPING THE DEMAND FOR NONPROFIT LEADERS IN THE UNITED STATES

Below, we describe two trends pointing to the upward rise in demand for nonprofit leaders. One is based on projections by the U.S. Department of Labor and the other, on Internal Revenue Service data on new nonprofit organizations.

The Expected Increase in Jobs

Table 7.1 is an extraction of figures from the U.S. Department of Labor's projections of employment growth by industry to the year 2010. The industries shown in Table 7.1 are those in which nonprofits are likely to be most represented.

The figures in Table 7.1 remind us that new nonprofit managers are not expected to perform in the same business segment and therefore all do not require identical training beyond a core. The core must be properly designed to create a universal understanding or foundation applicable across segments if the new recruits of nonprofit leaders are to

Table 7.1

Employment by Industry 1990, 2000, and Projected to 2010

| | Employment | | | | | | |
| | thousands of jobs | | | change | | average annual rate of change | |
Industry	1990	2000	2010	1990–2000	2000–2010	1990–2000	2000–2010
Health services	7,814	10,095	12,934	2,281	2,839	2.6	2.5
Offices of health practitioners	2,166	3,099	4,344	933	1,245	3.6	3.4
Nursing and personal care facilities	1,415	1,796	2,190	381	394	2.4	2.0
Hospitals	3,549	3,990	4,500	442	510	1.2	1.2
Health services*	685	1,210	1,900	525	690	5.9	4.6
Legal services	908	1,010	1,350	102	340	1.1	2.9
Educational services	1,661	2,325	2,852	664	527	3.4	2.1
Social services	1,734	2,903	4,128	1,269	1,225	5.3	3.6
Individual and miscellaneous social services	634	1,005	1,300	372	295	4.7	2.6
Job training and related services	248	380	500	131	120	4.3	2.8
Child day care services	391	712	1,010	321	298	6.2	3.6
Residential care	461	806	1,318	345	512	5.7	5.0
Museums, botanical, zoological gardens	66	106	135	40	29	4.9	2.4
Membership organizations	1,945	2,475	2,734	529	259	2.4	1.0

Source: Jay M. Berman, "Industry Output and Employment Projections to 2010," *Monthly Labor Review* 124 (November 2001), pp. 39–56.
  * Not elsewhere classified.

have maximum mobility opportunities across the nonprofit sector—given its variety in training and performance requirements.

Table 7.2 shows comparable figures of expected job growth, but specifically in the community and social services occupations. Not all of these jobs are expected to be in nonprofit organizations.

The Expected Increase in Nonprofits

The expected rise in demand for new nonprofit leaders can also be based on our assumptions about growth in the nonprofit sector itself. Between 1978 and 1997, the number of 501(c)(3)s composed of charities, educational and scientific organizations, arts and cultural agencies, and religious organizations, which together account for more than two-thirds of all tax exempt organizations, more than doubled (see Table 7.3); while during specific recession years, 1981–82, the number of nonprofits actually declined by about 1 percent (Bryce 1993).

Table 7.2

Employment by Occupation Year 2000 and Projected to 2010

| | Employment | | | | |
| | Number | | Percent distribution | | Change |
Occupation	2000	2010	2000	2010	Number
Community and social services occupations	1,869	2,398	1.3	1.4	529
Counselors	465	585	.3	.3	120
Educational, vocational, and school counselors	205	257	.1	.2	52
Marriage and family therapists	21	27	.0	.0	6
Mental health counselors	67	82	.0	.0	15
Rehabilitation counselors	110	136	.1	.1	26
Substance abuse and behavioral disorder counselors	61	82	.0	.0	21
Miscellaneous community and social service specialists	398	575	.3	.3	177
Health educators	43	53	.0	.0	10
Probation officers and correctional treatment specialists	84	105	.1	.1	20
Social and human service assistants	271	418	.2	.2	45
Religious workers	293	338	.2	.2	45
Clergy	171	197	.1	.1	26
Directors of religious activities and education	121	141	.1	.1	19
Social workers	468	609	.3	.4	141
Child, family, and school social workers	281	357	.2	.2	76
Medical and public health social workers	104	136	.1	.1	33
Mental health and substance abuse social workers	83	116	.1	.1	33
All other counselors, social, and religious workers	244	290	.2	.2	46

Source: Daniel E. Hecker, "Occupational Employment Projections to 2010," *Monthly Labor Review* 124 (November 2001), pp. 57–84.

THE RELATIONSHIP BETWEEN SECTOR GROWTH AND GROWTH IN THE DEMAND FOR NEW NONPROFIT LEADERS

The growth in nonprofits is not necessarily proportionate to growth in the numbers of new leaders who must be trained or existing leaders who need upgrading. First, many nonprofits do not have independent leadership in the sense of independent management. Private management firms manage many nonprofits.

Both the number and types of trainees that may be required will be affected to the extent that outsourcing of management increases. Clearly, a fertile area may be more training in decision-making skills for those nonprofits under contract, and more client-satisfaction skills where the client is the nonprofit being served by a management firm.

Table 7.3

Dicennial Growth of 501(c)(3)s

Year	Number	Percent change
1978	304,315	—
1989	464,138	52.5
1997	692,524	49.2

Sources of original raw data: Internal Revenue Service, Annual Report of Commissioner and Chief Consul (Washington, DC: U.S. Government Printing Office, various years up to 1989) and the United States Revenue Service, *Databook*, Washington, DC: U.S. Government Printing Office, 1997), 23 for 1997. Author's calculations.

Accordingly, a new source of demand for training may not be the nonprofit itself, but the management firms that operate the nonprofit on behalf of its clients or members.

A second trend that affects why the demand for nonprofit leaders may not be proportionate to the rise in the number of nonprofits is seen in various forms of reorganization such as mergers, consolidations, and split-ups of organizations. Whether in the for-profit or nonprofit sector, reorganization or the integration of two or more organizations usually results in a reduction (at least initially) in the number of managers. Sector growth in an environment of sector consolidation is the confrontation of two opposing forces in the determination of the demand for new nonprofit managers.

THE NEXUS BETWEEN PROJECTING THE NEED FOR LEADERS AND TRAINING THEM

It has long been recognized that the relationship between occupational forecasting and the training of individuals to fill these slots is not subject to all of the causes of disequilibria in labor markets and involves time lags between the forecast and the actual production of these people (Goldstein 1983; Freeman and Hansen 1983; Bryce 1993).

Nevertheless, the increased number of organizations requiring new management in an environment where resources may not keep up with demand means an increased need for those who prepare nonprofit managers in the skills required to make prudent decisions in a competitive environment where the global demand for their services may increase faster than the supply of resources to fulfill social needs. This is obvious from a geopolitical perspective evidenced by the global rise in the role of nongovernmental organizations (NGOs) but the dependence on roughly the same pool of country-donors even when aid is directed through a third party such as the World Bank or International Monetary Fund or the United Nations Development Programme. Organizations such as the National Council of Nonprofit Enterprise and National Arts Strategies, both in the United States, and organizations such as the Management Centre in Cyprus now complement university-based programs in providing training for nonprofit managers.

CURRENT UNIVERSITY-BASED PROGRAMS AND THE NEED FOR STANDARDIZATION

Mirabella and Wish counted 189 nonprofit management programs in U.S. universities and colleges, and they (1998a, 1998b, 1999 and 2000) have described variations in these programs and in their relationship to the attainment of a public administration degree. Bryce (2000b) calculated that only 8 percent of schools in this survey had their program connected to an MBA degree. These include MBA programs at Yale, Cornell, Columbia, Harvard, Stanford, University of Pennsylvania, Northwestern, and UCLA-Berkeley. Yet, annually, *U.S. News and World Report* magazine ranks MBA programs in several categories including a nonprofit category, and, separately, the nonprofit curricula in public affairs (public administration) or management programs.

Cyert (1988) notes the significant role that universities can play in training nonprofit managers—leaving much of the debate about content and objective to others. We do know, however, that nonprofits all have different missions and sizes, and, thus, different challenges and no need for one-fits-all training; therefore, cautions by DiMaggio (1988), Cook (1988), and Leduc and McAdam (1988) about variations in a well-designed curriculum are still valid. Indeed, as Bryce (1993) argues, there is tremendous utility in having nonprofit leaders trained not only in technical skills but also in the liberal arts.

Current university-based programs to train nonprofit managers can be placed in the following categories:

1. *General Nonprofit Management.* These are programs that give degrees or degree equivalents in nonprofit management—some allowing subspecialties. In this category, all courses (allowing for some electives or requirements) are on a nonprofit topic. Students learn various aspects of nonprofit management that may include fund-raising, marketing, managing volunteers, the history of nonprofits, the economics of nonprofits, and so on.

2. *Subspecialty Programs.* These are programs in public administration, business administration, public policy, social work administration, educational administration, and art administration that offer specific courses in nonprofit management. In this category, most courses focus on the broader area, and one or two courses on nonprofits. There are no requirements across universities regarding what those one or two courses should be or contain.

3. *Client Demand Programs.* These are programs the structure of which changes from year to year depending upon the expected demand for such programs by paying clientele. These programs play an important role in providing continuing education credits and the general advancement of existing managers.

4. *Incidentally Related Programs.* These are programs, such as hospital administration, where a manager may be well trained and successful without ever having taken a course in nonprofit management. This is because hospital administration is a highly technical enterprise and this technical phase is similar in nonprofit and for-profit hospitals.

The issue is not whether one of the four approaches is better than another. Each serves a need. The issue is, given an expected rise in the demand for nonprofit leaders, the range

of enterprises they will lead, and the need to train them: What (if any) is the core competence each form of training should provide? What is the minimum competency demanded
in a nonprofit as opposed to any other enterprise, including government service?

Core competence assures a potential nonprofit employer that the prospect has mastered, or at least had rudimentary exposure to, certain topics deemed central to nonprofit
management. A student graduating with a degree in corporate finance, for example, is
expected to know something about financial ratios, securities, the time value of money—
at the very minimum—regardless of the program the student attended. Furthermore, a
student graduating with a degree in business administration may be expected to have
some exposure to accounting even if the student is a marketing major.

These discrepancies in a rapidly growing sector call for the coordinated judgment of
educators, practitioners, and nonprofit employers, perhaps by means of an accreditation
mechanism that standardizes or at least promotes further consideration of what constitutes a suggested minimum in the training of a nonprofit leader. The remainder of this
chapter deals with such a consideration, at least as it relates to the broader picture of
finance. Why should every nonprofit senior manager know about finance and economic
decision making? What should the nonprofit manager know about these topics? The
second part of the chapter addresses how to prepare such a leader.

WHY AND WHAT SHOULD SENIOR MANAGERS KNOW
ABOUT FINANCE?

No senior executive officer can completely escape responsibility for some measurable
aspect of an organization's financial integrity, because every senior manager makes decisions that have financial impact. These decisions include hiring and firing employees,
purchasing supplies and selling inventory, using the telephone and assigning employee
duties, seeking funds to manage a program, and actually implementing the programs.

Therefore, every senior manager needs to be conscious of how his or her decisions
affect the financial integrity of the organization. But the executive officers—especially
the chief operating officers—must themselves develop certain financial competencies.
So what are the ten basic things that leadership should know in order to manage successfully in controlling the financial future, while designating certain critical micro management functions to others? What is the perspective (as opposed to the economic calculus)
that every senior manager, at minimum, should have?

1. *The management has to view the organization as an economic institution with a
welfare mission.* This means that no matter how turned off one might be by economic
realities, the organization inevitably generates costs that good managers must try to understand and control because the organization needs revenues to meet these costs, and
good managers try to maximize these revenues. The most successful managers master
the underlying techniques that this concept implies. Having a vision is not enough and
neither is love and commitment to the mission. Case studies of nonprofit organizations
in distress are effective examples that illustrate the need for management skill as well as
this basic principle: Good intentions are not enough for organizational survival.

2. *The management of the nonprofit must see the financial function as a tool—as a means to an end rather than the end itself.* This concept distinguishes the chief executive officer (CEO) from the chief financial officer (CFO) or the accountant. Whereas the latter two provide the financial information, resources, and credibility the organization needs, it is the former who must channel these tools toward the socially acceptable end to which the organization is committed.

Three points need to be made here. First, one cannot effectively use a tool without understanding it and how it works. A scalpel is a useful tool in the hands of a skilled surgeon; otherwise, it is just a deadly weapon. A manager who does not understand financial information cannot make the best use of it and may well lead the organization to its demise by making bad decisions or none at all.

Second, one cannot effectively communicate with others without using a common language and knowing the syntax of that language. Therefore, a CEO cannot effectively communicate with an accountant or chief financial officer if he or she has no understanding of what they are talking about or the industry convention that governs how they operate. Communication goes both ways. Perhaps the less important direction is from the CEO or other managers to the CFO and the accountant, and the more important is often from the latter to the former.

Those who deal with financing and accounting have useful information about what expenditures can be charged to a contract, how projects must be designed so that costs can be shared in keeping with accounting principles, and all these can affect project design and organizational strategies.

A third point relates to an event that occurs much too often. When financing is seen as an end in itself, the nonprofit becomes not a for-profit firm, but one that is likely to deal in questionable transactions. Any number of cases studies of fund-raising abuses involving sophisticated fund-raising strategies—as recently alleged in the field of conservation—can be used to teach these lessons.

3. *The management must view the organization as a competitor in a world where potential donors have alternative nondonative uses for their dollars and where the number of organizations seeking these dollars is rapidly growing.* Moreover, prospective donors seek more and more information before making a decision and such information is increasingly available partly because of law and particularly because of the Internet access that organizations like Guidestar provide.

Here a principal teaching tool is the Form 990 that all organizations with revenues over $25,000 annually must file. A review of this form will make managers aware of the financial transparency required of nonprofit management and how readily available negative impressions are to the public that cares. But more than anything it will awaken senior managers to what, by virtue of law, they must report and how their organization is evaluated.

4. *Successful managers learn less about how to create the numbers in a budget and more about how those numbers are created, how they impact decisions on all levels, how they direct the future of the organization and the likelihood that a vision will be realized or magnified.* A skillful CEO learns how to use a budget to accomplish long- and short-

run objectives and appreciates that an approved budget communicates a diagram of the path the leadership intends. Good CEOs are not mesmerized by budget numbers or the process by which the numbers are created. A budget communicates an idea with numbers and dollar signs attached.

Even experienced senior managers who have done budgeting can learn a great deal through exploring the budgets of other organizations in a classroom setting where the executive is required to role-play. How did this budget come about? What is the thinking behind it? Does it help the organization to meet its goals? Which goals, long or short term? What is the nature of the revenues that are projected, are they reliable, are they transitory, or are they based on an expected permanent flow? What does this budget tell you about the organization when compared over the years with the same organization or with similar organizations?

5. *Successful financial management honors and respects the force of accountability.* Respect for accountability leads to the development of procedures over which the use of the smallest of resources is controlled and there is no ambiguity about by whom, when, and under what conditions. Good financial management is conducted under a hierarchy where the rules are clear, strict, and, yet, functional. Accountability occurs continuously and ultimately through audits—many of which may not be voluntary. Donors and contractors often retain the right to audit the use of their contributions. Failure to set up stringent rules of accountability will always be an open invitation to corruption—embezzlement being only the most glaring form of such corruption.

This concept of the vulnerability of an organization to corruption when the management is financially slack or ignorant can be taught using the examples of a number of embezzlement or misappropriation of funds cases that come up every year—even in closely watched organizations such as labor unions or religious organizations. Management must appreciate the extent to which its laxity contributes to the probability that such events will occur.

6. *Every successful manager needs to understand financial statements.* Basically, these fall into two types—those that are used only for internal purposes and those that are used for public and legal purposes such as the annual report to the public, Form 990, and other forms that must be filed with the government. The truth is that many CEOs dislike calculating ratios and many distrust them. Indeed, ratios often portray an incomplete or inaccurate picture of the organization. But they do provide an important indicator for understanding and discussing real resources in organizational planning sessions. In addition, there is no way to prevent the public from calculating these numbers in order to make judgments about the organization.

Teaching reluctant managers about financial statements is often a trying enterprise requiring pedagogical imagination. Elsewhere (Bryce 2000a), I have experimented with a conversational style of accomplishing this objective. It recognizes that most nonprofit managers dislike calculating ratios and are distant from accounting, but after a couple of bad experiences will acknowledge that these attitudes do them no good. Most become more disposed after having grasped the conversational simplicity and relevance of these concepts. The suggestion here is to begin with a comprehensive conversation about financial statements before delving into their meanings.

7. *Every top manager must appreciate that for a nonprofit, unlike a firm, the structure of finances—both expenditures and revenues—have very serious implications for the organization because they are used by the IRS to determine the tax-exempt status of organizations.* They are also used by states to determine not only tax-exempt status but eligibility for relief from various fees and for inclusion in certain preferred classes particularly for bidding and state aid. There is no denying that maintenance of the tax-exempt and privileged status of a nonprofit is the responsibility of top management. Federal and state laws allow personal penalties to be imposed on managers whose behavior (or lack of it—called "omissions") leads to these unintended consequences.

One way of teaching the principles of this point is for the instructor to itemize the sources of income of a major nonprofit (one that is likely to be exploiting many revenue sources) and asking what the implications are for each source. The implications involve not only putting the nonprofit at financial risk, but also putting donors and partners at risk of losses in their investments or confidence. It may also expose them to legal penalties.

8. *The fact is that sophistication and the need for resources mean that the successful nonprofit manager must go beyond traditional public appeals and the seeking of grants.* An endowment is a useful tool, and is revenue from charging fees—called "business revenues." But what should the manager learn? Concerning endowments, investment and withdrawal policies should be part of the board minutes. Methods for choosing investment advisers and for giving them broad directions should be agreed upon and in the record. Like business revenues, these types of earnings can have tax implications, and business revenues can affect the tax-exempt status of the organization in ways other than the complete loss of such exemptions. Business revenues require an entirely different form of accounting. Business revenues also invite public scrutiny and even claims of unfair competition (often unjustifiably in this author's view).

How can these concepts be taught? One way is to look at businesses run by nonprofits. But perhaps a more productive way is for student participants to look at endowments and how they are managed. The National Association of College and University Business Officers annually produces data on hundreds of college endowments. This is an excellent beginning point.

9. *Management must appreciate that in finance and accounting everything is not up to managerial discretion. There are rules for reporting that accountants must follow.* These rules constrain the discretion of the accountants. Their violation constrains the ability of the organization to work with outside agencies from banks to governments, from potential contractors to potential partners. Violations of accounting rules show up in audit statements and will seriously reduce the ability of the organization to raise funds from foundations and large donors. Some accounting and expenditure violations are outright unlawful. These include violation of donor restrictions and improper accounting for them.

This point is clearly related to point 2, but it is different in substance and teaching approach. What is involved here is not so much the development of an attitude as a familiarity with specific rules. It is one thing to know that the accountant may have something to contribute regarding how a fund-raising campaign should be designed so as to meet the joint cost allocation rules between fund-raising and education; it is another thing for the senior manager to take time to become familiar with the key rules so that questions may be properly framed to stimulate not just an appropriate response but one that invites a conversation about how to proceed in order to meet legitimate objectives of our imagination and yet remain rooted in the rules.

10. *Finally, the discussion can be capped with one statement*: Without money and its proper management, no mission, no matter how worthy and honorable, can be sustained and grow. This is the Achilles' heel of many who are drawn to nonprofit management. They hate fund-raising, but they want to do great things. The latter is unattainable without the former.

On a personal note, I have found that introducing fund-raising from the perspective of corporations and what they must consider and what the applicant should consider "piques the interest" of MBA students and senior managers. Here are some principles I try to develop and explore with respect to raising funds from corporations, and only afterward I delve into details. Why does this approach work? Probably because it places fund-raising on the level of an economic negotiation and transaction and elevates it above the level of pleading or begging.

Priorities. It is important to remember that corporations, no matter how benevolent, do not see any single nonprofit as a high priority. Each dollar that goes to a nonprofit is one less that goes to shareholders in the form of dividends, to executives and employees in the form of compensation, or to the corporations for reinvestment or to pay its debt. Giving—especially when deductible only if the corporation has a profit and only up to 10 percent of that profit per year—is not a priority for most corporations.

Competition. Nonprofit leaders must recognize that fund-raising is very competitive. The average corporation gives less than 2 percent of its net annual income to charities of all types. The presumption that the capacity to give is automatically increased by the profitability of a corporation is simply not valid. Each nonprofit is competing for a small share that increases slowly and has many claimants.

Specific Preferences. Corporations have strong preferences for specific charities. Each operates under sets of preferences of its directors, employees, executives, and shareholders. Corporations often give to enhance consumer loyalty, to enhance corporate image, and to participate in the welfare of the communities in which they are located or where they want to do business. It helps for a nonprofit to link its request for funds to a strong business interest. How does giving to nonprofit A relate to the corporate mission? A case must to be made that the existence of the college results in specific benefits to the corporation. The corporate mission, particularly as it relates to its charitable giving, is never a secret; asking outside of this purpose is usually futile.

Necessary Approvals. In the final analysis, corporate assets belong to shareholders. They are not any corporate officer's to give. It is helpful to appreciate that the person to whom a request is directed usually cannot make the decision alone. The case made to the corporate contact must be persuasive at every level to which the appeal is made, and nonprofit leaders must be prepared to help their corporate contacts to sell their case to internal decision makers.

Tax Benefits. For most corporations, the actual tax benefit from making the typical contribution may be small unless it involves a major type of research equipment given to a college for educational purposes. Furthermore, there are some types of gifts that cannot be deducted and some types of property that bring only a very low, if any, tax deduction. Some assets are better being disposed of in discount sales rather than given away. Therefore, any appeal should not rest solely on so-called tax write-offs. Tax benefits are important, but not as important as the clarity of a mission and its usefulness to the community. While it is useful to be well informed about tax law related to corporate giving, it is even more important to understand the limited appeal of arguments based upon this rationale.

Fiduciary Responsibility. Savvy corporate donors are more impressed by well-presented balance sheets and revenue and expense statements than they are by budgets. Budgets tell the corporate donor something about the ambition of the college and what it proposes to do with its gift. However, financial statements reveal much more about an organization's actual performance and track record. Corporate donors want to know whether an organization is capable and can be trusted to complete successfully any project for which it seeks funding.

Documentation. The corporation may ask the nonprofit not only for its financial statements but also for a copy of its charter, and, where property is involved, the corporation may also ask for a promise that the property will be used by the non-profit for nonprofit (as opposed to for-profit) purposes and will not be sold or used for lobbying purposes. Donations used for these purposes may reduce or cancel any tax deduction the corporation may take.

Patience. Corporate giving, except in extraordinary situations such as disasters, comes from years of patience and nurturing. Emotional appeals are usually unproductive and distracting to what is essentially a business decision. Patience and grace are more likely to be rewarded.

Appropriate Channels. Most corporations give through a corporate foundation. These foundations are normally required to make certain levels of contributions every year in order to maintain their status. They are also the primary source of information about the types of programs that interest the corporation. Development professionals should always obtain a copy of the annual report of the corporate foundation and read it thoroughly. Any appeal for corporate giving should be carefully tailored to the guidelines of the foundation and informed by its report of past activities and preferences.

Employee Influence. Corporations often make gifts in response to employee initiative and interest. Some are in the form of matching gifts. It is important not to underestimate the influence that employees can have. In fact, many successful appeals are not initiated with corporate officers but at other employee levels. A college can enhance its contacts with a corporation in a number of ways, including having a corporate employee serve as a college faculty member or administrator. Such a link can prove invaluable to a successful request for funds.

Stewardship. Once a gift is made, it is absolutely critical that the college exercise good stewardship in its use, especially if the college hopes to seek additional funds from the corporation or its corporate associates for other purposes. No corporation wants to be embarrassed or disappointed. The college must deliver on any promises associated with the gift, routinely report to the donor about how its gift is being used, and document the specific outcomes of the gift.

Teaching the above point about fund-raising can be both productive and fun. A good approach is for the executive to pick a cause (other than the one he or she is involved with), search out appropriate corporate prospects, and design a fund-raising strategy to convince that prospect. Obviously, it is easier if the choice involves a cause directly related to the executive; but a purpose of this task should be to expand the challenge and to learn from what others must do.

FROM PERSPECTIVE TO CONTENT

The above discussion focuses on perspective because a major source of the resistance of nonprofit managers to learning more about finance and economic decision making is attitudinal. In this section, we focus on some key concepts that need to be grasped by all senior managers. Note that the point is not to develop the concept but to argue why it is important.

1. *Time Value of Money.* This concept is important in answering questions such as how much management must put up today or over a given period in order to meet a financial target in some designated period. Time value of money is important in all financial target setting and in most financial decision making between alternative uses or investment of funds.

2. *Budgeting.* A clear distinction should be made between budgeting in the public sector and budgeting in a nonprofit. A budget in a public agency is law, but in a nonprofit it is a financial plan of action that makes it more fungible, susceptible to discretion, and affected by each contract or grant the organization receives. Understanding how each senior manager affects the overall organizational budget is important. The truth is that the budget of a nonprofit organization is far closer to the budget of a firm of similar size than it is to government. As in a firm, it can be an effective instrument of organizational control and direction. There is no substitute for understanding why actual performance varies from what is budgeted or planned. To the astute nonprofit manager, this is more than a budgetary exercise; it speaks to past, present, and future planning needs. A budget used as a planning device is a powerful managerial tool.

3. *Understanding Costs.* An organization must work hard to raise revenues—but it has no control over the revenues it raises. The revenues are determined by the responsiveness of donors, grantors, and clients. But an organization can control costs—even fixed costs can be controlled at some point before they are decided upon and fixed. A considerable amount of the budgeting exercise in nonprofits, as in firms, needs focus on understanding the cost implications of decisions and how they affect the financial health of the organization.

4. *Understanding Revenues.* Fund-raising is clearly important here. But we have to be careful. In many countries, fund-raising in the form of fund-raising from individuals makes little sense and offers little promise. In many such countries, fund-raising has more to do with convincing governments (principally foreign), foreign nonprofits, and foreign corporations than with convincing local governments or residents. Some of these constraints have led to imaginative forms of fund-raising, for example, in conservation, when foreign corporations use local profits that they cannot repatriate to obtain easement on land.

In a country such as the United States, understanding revenues means understanding a variety of revenue sources and not only how they impact available funds, but how they constrain the organization, how they must be accounted for, and what the tax implications (including implications on the tax-exempt status of the organization) are for various sources of funds.

5. *Financial Statements and Financial Ratios.* The financial statements of a nonprofit organization are different from those of a firm or a government agency. The issue is not so much the ratios as it is the understanding of the entries on the balance sheet, the revenue and expense statement, and the statement of changes in financial position, and how these changes impact the organization. The utility of ratios is a derivative of the understanding of the entries themselves.

In this author's view, cash availability and cash equivalents and their flows are often overlooked as a financial metric. Concentrating on liquidity ratios as if the organization were a business often misses the point. When an organization does not generate a steady flow of cash, knowing the amount and pattern of that cash flow is important. Organizations pay bills with cash—not with promises to send it.

DUE DILIGENCE AND THE ETHICS OF FINANCIAL TRANSACTIONS

The failure of managers to conform to financial decency and ethical codes can, in my view, be attributed to three sources: (1) the invitation that the laxity and ignorance of superiors extends to such managers, leading them to believe that they can get away with it, (2) the moral discrepancy of the manager, and (3) the failure of due diligence. Attention to the points of the earlier sections of this chapter may ameliorate the environment that invites malfeasance by managers; the second, only God can solve; and the third is within the power of management including the trustees, and that is the subject of this final section. As before, we not only state the problem and issues but suggest how they may be taught.

Due diligence has to do with the obligation of trustees and managers to be informed and to exercise prudent judgment over all assets of the organization. This means that each manager or trustee must exhaust every effort to express an honest and informed judgment on all transactions that may materially impact the organization's welfare.

Existing ethical codes are not substitutes for diligence. To date, no one has accused the directors of Enron of having acted unethically. There is general belief, however, that they have failed in their duty of diligence and that this failure continues to result in severe financial hardship and widespread damage to the company, its investors, its employees, and its sector.

In like fashion, the failure of due diligence shook the foundations of the United Way, and, recently, the American Red Cross. In the former, the lack of diligence of the board over transactions enabled extensive unethical acts of an expansive executive. In the latter, the sufficient exercise of due diligence might have prevented the elaboration of promises not fully met but that were not illegal and were fully consistent with increasing the capacity of the organization to carry out its charitable mission. Due diligence, therefore, is an engine that drives both ethics and efficiency.

The issue of due diligence arises whenever a financial transaction generates questions such as: How could this have happened? How could this have gone undetected for so long? Why didn't they catch it? How can directors deny not knowing? Shouldn't they have known? Were they not sufficiently curious to have asked questions? Were they sleeping at the wheel? Were they not paying attention? How could they sign a document and claim not to know that it is inaccurate or incomplete? How, given past history, could they not have been alert? Are they finding a scapegoat in the hailstorm? Are they really that stupid?

The need for due diligence over financial matters is increasing. Indeed, the more complex an organization and the more successful we are in insisting on ethical behavior, the more important is due diligence in monitoring and disciplining financial decisions. As nonprofit transactions become more complex, this tool must be sharper and more informed and it is more incumbent on trustees and managers to acquire the curiosity, information, and skill to evaluate strategic and financial decisions.

In many of these financial transactions, ethical codes alone may give incorrect guidance. Take the fund-raising ratio commonly used as an ethical standard. These ratios are computed as the dollars raised in a given year divided by the dollars expended in that year. A high ratio, sometimes called *yield*, is assumed to be good. High ratios are often obtained without any ethical or professional breach.

But high fund-raising yields are often explainable not by current expenditures but by past expenditures during years when managers are likely to have been criticized by donors, watchdog agencies, and unwitting trustees for having low ratios and failing ethical standards or best practices. This is because today's fund-raising yield is often the product of years of cultivating contacts, channels of communications, and the confidence of donors. As a result of accounting rules, there may be a delay between the promise of a donation and its recognition in the financial statement. Were these low-yield years so detrimental? Were they truly violations of ethics? Would the organization truly be better off by adherence to the standard? Here the issue is not ethics, but the exercise of due diligence—getting behind the ethical screen.

As ethical codes, acceptable professional practices are also no substitute for due diligence. For example, a manager (not just the accountant) may choose among several professionally acceptable ways to allocate shared or common costs between fund-raising and other activities. What percentage of the common costs goes to fund-raising and what percentage to the other activity will affect the fund-raising ratio. This is true even though the accounting profession has guidelines regarding how common costs between fund-raising and education are to be shared. As I have discussed elsewhere, these professional rules can be satisfied through managerial strategies that are totally ethical and acceptable, but each has a different impact on the resulting ratios.

Due diligence is a strategy to reduce the risk of failure as well as the embarrassment of discovering what underlies spectacular success. Due diligence is driven by a quest for information and a curiosity that questions. It is asking why, how, when, and with what consequence, even when choices are clearly ethical and results clearly satisfactory. Hence, it takes due diligence to determine if and when the choice that yields the best quantitative fund-raising yield ratio is preferable, given an organization's strategic station. Due diligence is required even when all choices are acceptable.

How does an organization develop a culture of financial diligence among managers and trustees? Cultivating a culture of financial diligence is more akin to teaching art and music appreciation than to training accountants or financial officers. It is less the teaching of how to do it than why it is done and what the ultimate aesthetic effects are. It begins by recognizing the content of financial information just as the critic understands the material with which the artist must work. But, as the successful artist must share his or her work and open it to viewing and criticism, so must financial information be shared and a tolerance for open and frank discussion be instilled; for unlike the audience, non-profit managers and trustees are held legally and personally responsible for what they should have seen or heard but failed to do so. Therefore, instilling a culture of diligence involves encouraging a dialogue about "what if" in the exploration of every financial or strategic decision. It must seek to understand both the operational and ethical implications of financial strategies.

Due diligence is a continuous process. In the budgeting process, for example, due diligence calls for explanations about why and how certain expenditures or revenue estimates are arrived at and how realistic they are. During the course of the year, variances from these estimates need to be assessed, but with an intelligence that demands explanations not only for things that seem bad but also for things that seem good. Due diligence goes beyond the numbers. It is not an exercise in arithmetic but in logic. It is not about numbers but about meaning and implications.

Finally, due diligence is not motivated by concepts such as competence, commitment, or confidence. The reason is simple. Due diligence requires the exercise of these. Thus, the appointment of a financial executive, or chief executive officer, or a member of the board should occur only after the exercise of due diligence to establish confidence in his or her competence and commitment. Once the person is appointed, then the exercise of due diligence should uncover whether such confidence continues to be warranted. These concepts are the result, not the source, of due diligence.

The legal source of due diligence is the duty of care. In virtually every state, officers and trustees are legally required to oversee the transactions of a nonprofit organization and to make informed judgments about the use of the organization's assets to raise, invest, and to expend funds. Due diligence, therefore, is a central concept in nonprofit financial strategies and decision making. The key is to develop and to share financial information, to be able to assess that information, to have the curiosity to ask for explanations and additional information on a timely basis, and to recognize that, in the end, the failure of due diligence is costly. Perhaps we can learn from Enron.

CONCLUSIONS

The truth is that while a growth in the demand for new nonprofit leaders is a very reasonable assumption, there is no reliable forecast as to how many to recruit and train to meet the expected rising demand for such leaders.

Therefore, this chapter recognizes that there will be a net increase in the demand for leaders of nonprofit organizations, although it has no forecast of the number of new persons that must be trained to fill these slots throughout the world. Thus, the issue for executive training of nonprofit leaders is not how to consolidate or retrench, it is how to expand, but with some core competence that will maximize the mobility of nonprofit leaders among various types of nonprofit organizations while assuring a foundation for the successful management of any one of these organizations.

It then proceeds to suggest what this author believes is the foundation knowledge—at least in finance and financial management—that must be imparted to these prospective leaders and why. The chapter emphasizes core concepts. It concludes with the acknowledgment and discussion of an overarching ethical imperative encapsulated in the concept of due diligence.

Obviously, the way that any training institution proceeds to train the leaders entrusted to it will depend upon the competence and interest of those it can recruit to teach such courses and also upon the nature of the demand within the market area of the training organization—the stakeholders. This notwithstanding, it is arguable that without certain core competencies (at least in finance) the leader may be ill prepared to lead, and that is what this chapter is all about.

In closing, we refer to a study by Herman and Renz (1998), who find that, in addition to good boards, the more effective nonprofit organizations also use more effective procedures and strategies. Therefore, the bottom line for educational programs is the dissemination of an attitude that constantly explores the most effective strategies and procedures, and this is the ultimate goal in educating the new nonprofit manager.

REFERENCES

Bryce, H. (2000a). "Financial Statements as Tools of Conversation and Control." In *Financial and Strategic Management for Nonprofit Organizations*, ed. H. Bryce, 493–534. San Diego, Jossey-Bass.
———. (2000b). "Teaching Nonprofit Management and Finance in an MBA Program." Paper presented the annual meeting of the Academy of Business Education, Bermuda, September 22–23.
———. (1993). "The Liberally Educated Manager." *Liberal Education* (Fall): 59–61.
Cook, J.B. (1988). "Managing Nonprofits of Different Sizes." In *Educating Managers of Nonprofit Organizations*, ed. M. O'Neill and D. Young, 101–116. New York: Praeger.

Cyert, R. (1988). "The Place of Nonprofit Management Programs in Higher Education." In *Educating Managers of Nonprofit Organizations*, ed. M. O'Neill and D. Young, 33–50. New York: Praeger.

DiMaggio, P. (1988). "Nonprofit Managers in Different Fields of Service: Managerial Tasks and Management Training." In *Educating Managers of Nonprofit Organizations*, ed. M. O'Neill and D. Young, 51–70. New York: Praeger.

Freeman, R.B., and J.A. Hansen (1983). "Forecasting the Changing Market for College-Trained Workers." In *Responsiveness of Training Institutions to Changing Labor Market Demands*, ed. R.E. Taylor, H. Rosen, and F.C. Pratzner, 79–100. Columbus, OH: National Center for Research in Vocational Education.

Goldstein, H. (1983). "The Accuracy and Utilization of Occupational Forecasts." In *Responsiveness of Training Institutions to Changing Labor Market Demands*, ed. R.E. Taylor, H. Rosen, and F.C. Pratzner, 39–70. Columbus, OH: National Center for Research in Vocational Education.

Guidestar. www.guidestar.org.

Herman, R.D., and D.O. Renz. (1998) "Nonprofit Organizational Effectiveness: Contrasts Between Especially Effective and Less Effective Organizations." *Nonprofit Management & Leadership* 9 (1): 23–39.

Leduc, R.F., and T.W. McAdam. (1988). "The Development of Useful Curricula for Nonprofit Management" In *Educating Managers of Nonprofit Organizations*, ed. M. O'Neill and D. Young, 95–100. New York: Praeger.

Mirabella, R.M., and N.B. Wish. (1999). "Perceived Educational Impact of Graduate Nonprofit Degree Programs: Perspectives of Multiple Stakeholders." Research Report, *Nonprofit Management & Leadership* 9 (3): 329–331.

———. (2000). "The 'Best Place' Debate: A Comparison of Graduate Education Programs for Nonprofit Managers." *Public Administration Review* 60 (3): 219–231.

Wish, N.B., and R.M. Mirabella. (1998a). "Curricular Variations in Nonprofit Management Graduate Programs." *Nonprofit Management & Leadership* 9 (1): 1–2.

———. (1998b). "Nonprofit Management Education: Current Offerings and Practices in University-Based Programs." In *Nonprofit Management Education: U.S. and World Perspectives*, ed. M. O'Neill and K. Fletcher, 13–22. Westport, CT: Praeger.

CHAPTER 8

TEAM-BASED LEADERSHIP AND CHANGE IN THE CHRISTIAN CHURCH

REV. MICHAEL W. HONEYCUTT AND REV. CLAY SMITH

Toward what end is the Christian church shepherded by its leaders? How is this end articulated? Church organizations, like business organizations, are often guided in this effort by their formal mission statements. For the Christian church in particular, we believe this mission was articulated by Jesus Christ in the "great commission" found in the biblical book of Matthew wherein Jesus comments that "the church is to make disciples of all nations." Thus, the mission of the Christian church as an international institution and organization is as simple as that: make disciples of all nations. Yet pursuit of that mission takes various forms. And because leadership functions to keep the church faithful to that mission, the question before the leader is "How?"

What you will find in the pages that follow are our thoughts as practicing church leaders. First, we describe a new, emerging leadership model that has the potential to enable church leaders to shepherd more effectively. Second, we offer a real-life story (warts and all) of shepherding significant change in a typical church congregation. Many principles delineated in the first section are fleshed out in the second. Through both sections, it will be apparent that we openly appropriate leadership principles from other kinds of organizations, including those that have significant credibility in for-profit arenas. Our willingness to do this is based on our belief that "all truth is God's truth." In other words, because God has made *all* people in his image, his "truth" may be found even in the words of those who do not profess faith in the *same God*. And, of course, we also believe our ideas and thoughts to be applicable to more than just Christian church organizations. It is in this spirit of mutual respect that we invite you to join us as we explore leadership in the church—leadership that we believe remains faithful to Christian principles, offers concrete benefits to local church organizations, and seeks to be relevant to the culture in which we live.

A NEW MODEL FOR CHURCH LEADERSHIP

Leadership models at times serve as the latest fad in ministry. Often, without reflection, we employ a particular model simply because a leader we respect uses it. Yet, effective leadership requires not only reflection on the Christian principles of serving and leading, but also a keen understanding of how cultures work. Karl Barth, noted scholar and com-

134

mentator, encourages preachers to prepare for ministry "with the Bible in one hand and the newspaper in the other" (Stott 1982, 149). The same could be said for leadership in the church. We must be students of the Bible and of the people we hope to lead.

Envisioning a leadership model that speaks to our culture, in our opinion, involves rethinking traditional hierarchical models. We propose a different paradigm focused on collaborative or team-based leadership. The collaborative leadership paradigm calls the church to discern its position in contemporary society, grasp the tools available to the leader, and intentionally apply the team-based model. From the outset, we recognize that collaborative leadership is not found frequently as an intentional model throughout the church. It is a new and emerging paradigm, yet one growing in influence, however, especially as postmoderns join the leadership ranks. We propose this model as a catalyst for significant change in the way we lead and for positive impact on the effectiveness of our congregations.

The Church in Contemporary Society

In a society driven by markets and opportunity, why do people plug into a church? Some choose a church based on the ministries or programs it provides. Larger churches have distinct advantages over smaller churches in this arena. Larger churches can offer more activities for the family, more varied ministry opportunities, better staffed programs, and so forth. For others, however, a smaller church may provide a level of comfort in its "smallness."

Small churches may more readily give an opportunity to become involved and to have significant impact on the future direction of the organization. One such church, Covenant Community Church (CCC) in Scottsdale, Arizona, elected its first class of officers just over a year ago and attracts approximately 200 weekly attendees. The CCC routinely asks people who have been regular attendees for a period of months why they have made CCC their church of choice. Although the church leaders would like to hear "the outstanding preaching," nine times out of ten, people list the overwhelming sense of community and network of relationships that defines this particular church. It is also true that small churches seem to attract a few people with darker motives. Some, for example, find the smaller church a place to move along a single-minded agenda that is of personal importance whether or not that value is shared by others.

Yet, in a culture that increasingly reflects movement toward postmodernity, the quest for community is a consistent factor in church choice. Desiring a place to belong where one is known and knows others is a basic need for humanity. George Barna, cultural statistician, reports that community is one of the chief "felt needs" of the generation born after the mid-1960s (2001, 67). While writing this chapter at a local Starbucks, on the store window, we noted a marketing poster announcing a search for employees. Dominant text in the ad read in large letters, "Create Community." The postmodern culture is well in tune with this basic need and searches for a solution wherever it may be found, even through employment at the local Starbucks. For many people, the church is perhaps one of the most critical places to look for this sense of community. Recognizing the predominance of this sense of need helps the leader discern the set of expectations and desires people bring to the church. Understanding and appreciating the longing for community helps provide leaders with keys for effective leadership. Effective leaders must create a sense of belonging, participation, ownership, and movement. Belonging, participation, and ownership are self-explanatory. By creating a sense of "movement," we mean awareness among individual members that involvement in this particular church unites them with a movement of people around the world committed to participating in the overarching plan of God and to the larger mission of the church universal.

These elements are crucial for leadership within any church. Yet they are particularly essential in a small church. As stated above, large churches have much to offer the church consumer: varied ministries specific to any family need, the resources to staff and implement excellent programs, visibility within the community, sheer numbers of people, all of which can easily create the sense of movement mentioned above. But for the small church, without as many services to offer the newcomer, a sense of belonging, participation, ownership, and movement may prove to be the most fulfilling "hooks" available.

Belonging, participation, ownership, and movement, however, are not simple emotions that a leader can *produce* in the heart of another person. Church leaders, for instance, cannot manufacture a sense of "belonging" in another human being. But they *can* fashion the way their church community works together to foster the opportunity for that sense of belonging to emerge. As leaders, they can provide an *environment* in which these senses are welcomed and encouraged. Embarking on this journey of producing such an environment determines how we use the tools at our disposal. These tools include the shape of the leadership model we use; the way leaders interact with other leaders in the group, as well as the followers; how vision is enumerated, and ultimately mission pursued; and involvement of other key persons within the organization. In short, effective leaders must "lower the hurdle" for a plurality of people to have ample opportunity to belong, opportunity to participate, to see areas in which to take ownership, and grasp a greater sense of movement within the group. Lowering the hurdle to belonging, participation, ownership, and movement, however, has not always been the means of leveraging the church's influence in the lives of its members.

At times in the past, the church's position as a central societal institution provided for strong "leverage" in the lives of its members. For instance, an individual's standing in the church often had significant impact on standing within the broader community. Participation in the church opened and closed doors to other opportunities in various sectors of society. Leadership expert John Maxwell (1998) applies the concept of leverage directly to a leader by suggesting that people follow others in a position of authority when their livelihood is at stake. Church leaders had leverage and "positional" influence in the lives of its members, and in a sense, in society as a whole. Jesus himself used the metaphors of "salt" and "light" to describe the church's positive and preserving leverage or influence in society.

Contemporary culture has become more pluralistic since those days when the church held such a central societal role. Neither the church nor its leaders continue to hold the same leverage in the lives of members. For better or worse, the church takes its place in the "marketplace of ideas" along with health clubs, discussion groups, neighborhood homeowners associations, child sports teams, and the like. Involvement in church is not the key to community opportunity that it once was. Leverage must come through different means.

Tools Available to the Leader

Some valid leadership models involve a hierarchy of strong directive leadership from the top of the organization (e.g., from a chief executive officer [CEO]). In these situations, the vertical chain of command provides for the development of vision and the accountability for implementation. This paradigm of leadership offers much strength and has worked very well in several sectors of society. Yet it must not be assumed that this directive model of leadership from the top necessarily translates into a church environment or is equally effective with all types of people.

We believe that a better model for influence in the church exists—namely, one that relies on the tool of *persuasion*. We use persuasion in this context to mean "the intentional influencing of others toward a particular goal." Positional leadership may empower others to accomplish a task, but persuasive leadership engages others such that they "give you their heart" (Stanley, 2003, 117). Sydney Pollack, famous actor, director, producer, identifies the problems inherent in the exclusively positional model: "You can make people follow you by scaring them, and you can make people follow by having them feel obligated. You can lead by creating a sense of guilt. . . . But the problem is that you're creating obedience with a residue of resentment" (Bennis 1989, 157). In a volunteer organization, such as the church, it is nearly impossible to create an environment necessary for survival and growth (belonging, participation, ownership, and movement) using methods that accomplish tasks with a residue of bitterness and resentment. Persuasion and influence through vision and integrity provide the necessary leverage. The leverage we refer to here pertains to carrying out a particular vision and mission in a local church body. We are not speaking to moral or ethical issues that find their bedrock articulation in the Christian scriptures; nor are we seeking to describe the authority that Christ has given to church leaders to lead a group toward those bedrock Christian scriptural commitments. Rather, the leverage of persuasion articulated in this chapter speaks to the "hows" of carrying out the mission of Christ in a local church.

In order for a leader to be effective, Maxwell asserts, followers must buy into the leader himself before they buy into the vision the leader casts (1998, 145). The process of buy-in involves an assessment of the leader's integrity. Warren Bennis, Distinguished Professor of Management at the University of Southern California, describes this integrity as "congruity," or when "leaders walk their talk" (1989, 160). It has also been delineated as "when belief, conviction, action, and behavior align" (Stanley 2003, 118). The perceived integrity of a leader crucially affects a program of transition proposed for any church. One organizational leader has described the change process as a poker game. Each player has a limited supply of chips to lay down on a bet, and you cannot bet more chips than you have. The same image works for church leaders. When implementing change or leading in a direction that may prove uncomfortable for the church members, the leader must count his chips to ensure he has enough to "cash in" on this initiative or direction. Perceived integrity more often than not determines how many chips a leader has. For the small church, building integrity in the eyes of followers is critical because there is no image, program, or status of the church already established in the community. In a very real way, the integrity of the leader is transferred to the church as a whole. Thus, observed integrity, or alignment between belief and behavior, ultimately persuades followers (Stanley 2003, 118).

Another key element of integrity is simply the integrity of the leader's personality. The leadership style of the leader, in other words, must be true to his or her personality. Often those who study leadership make the mistake of assuming the kind of personality necessary for leadership. They suppose only the dominant, forceful, independent thinkers, who by the sheer force of will whip a group into excitement over a particular vision, can effectively lead. Leaders, they argue, must fit this *particular* personality type. Evidence, however, suggests that this should be reconsidered. In his insightful book *Good to Great*, Jim Collins argues that "Level 5" leaders are the most effective change agents. This kind of leader "builds enduring greatness through a paradoxical blend of personal humility and professional will" (2001, 20). Co-workers of Level 5 leaders consistently describe them as "quiet, humble, modest, reserved, shy, gracious, mild-mannered, self-effacing," and the like (2001, 27). In contrast, "Level 4" leaders are leaders who use charisma, personality, and often ego to stimulate a tenacious implementation of a clear vision in the pursuit of a more successful company. Collins's research concluded, however, that Level 5 leaders are the ones who leave their companies with an enduring positive legacy. One need not be the dominant hard-charger in order to effectively lead.

Clearly, contemporary leadership theory makes room for leadership from varied personality types. Bryan Chapell, president of Covenant Theological Seminary, one of North America's largest graduate theological schools, has frequently noted the risk-aversion characteristic of those born since the mid-1960s. His observations are shared by other leaders of educational institutions. Over the past twenty-five years, Covenant Seminary has seen its percentage of graduates taking solo pastorates upon graduation drop from over 50 percent to less than 10 percent. Various factors contribute to this statistic, yet it remains true that solo-leadership aversion characterizes this group. The hierarchical, take-charge, singular-leader model is not widely in use throughout this generation, nor does this model particularly resonate with them.

Providing effective leadership within the church calls for leadership from personal strengths, rather than from fitting into a leadership mold. Leaders are then free to lead from their own strengths rather than trying to borrow someone else's, reinforcing the belief that any personality type can serve as a leader (Trent, Cox, and Tooker 2004). In the church, this becomes particularly important as it reflects appreciation of who a leader is *as designed* by God. Being comfortable with the unique person God has created them to be gives leaders great freedom and peace to pursue a role with passion, absent the angst of morphing into someone they are not. Grasping a unique personality given by the Creator allows a leader to embrace his or her own humanity, including its limitations and weaknesses. This is especially relevant given the propensity of the members of Generation X (Gen X) and the subsequent Generation Y, or the Mosaic Generation as others have called them (born 1965–), to embrace authenticity and to expose weakness. This level of comfort supplies the leader with confidence to lead from her or his own strengths. Integrity of personality endears a leader to the Gen X crowd, creating room for authentic community. Covering over weaknesses, or trying to "be it all," breeds an environment of suspicion that may result in the leader being tuned out as a fake. Personal integrity, however, that allows a leader to lead according to his or her own personality, acknowledging limitations along the way, is a far more persuasive, and therefore a far more effective, leadership style.

Implementing a Collaborative or Team-based Model

Noting some of the cultural changes outlined above, Frances Hesselbein, chair of the Peter F. Drucker Foundation for Nonprofit Management and former CEO of the Girl Scouts of America, proposes for the nonprofit and business worlds a new model of leadership: the collaborative model. Her book of lessons learned, *Hesselbein on Leadership*, speaks of this model as the leadership "wheel of fortune." Instead of a CEO at the top of the pyramid with multiple layers of employees beneath, in which each layer lessens in power and information, Hesselbein envisions a series of concentric circles. At the center of a flat structure sits a CEO encircled by concentric rings of leaders dispersed throughout an organization. There is a "center, but no top or bottom" (Hesselbein 2002, 54). Thus, Hesselbein posits that "the days of turf battles, the star system, and the Lone Ranger are over," and that "the day of partnership is upon us" (2002, 55).

Societal change forced Hesselbein to propose changes in the business world. We suggest that those same cultural issues affect the church and encourage us to consider alterations to our models as well. Our experience and thought suggests that collaborative or team-based leadership is the best way to harness the leverage of persuasion for achieving an environment of belonging, participation, and ownership. On one hand, the model we propose is nothing new. Shared leadership through the ordained offices is the clear Christian scriptural teaching about how the church is to function. Yet, on the other hand, the collaborative, team-based leadership model is completely new. Many churches function with a pastor or primary leader as the vision creator, articulator, and implementer. Other leaders within the church serve to implement the *pastor's* vision. This is not the model we propose. Genuine application of this model includes collaboration not only in the implementation of a vision, but also team-based vision crafting and articulation (see Figure 8.1).

This model significantly flattens out leadership structure and diffuses power. Envision the typical organizational chart with the CEO at the top supported by cascading layers of vice president, division managers, and functional department managers. Power, influence, and information are concentrated at the top in the hands of the CEO, and each layer underneath has decreasing power, influence, and information. The farther down the organizational chart you may be, the less power, influence, and information you have. Your role,

Figure 8.1   **A Model of Collaborative Leadership in the Church**

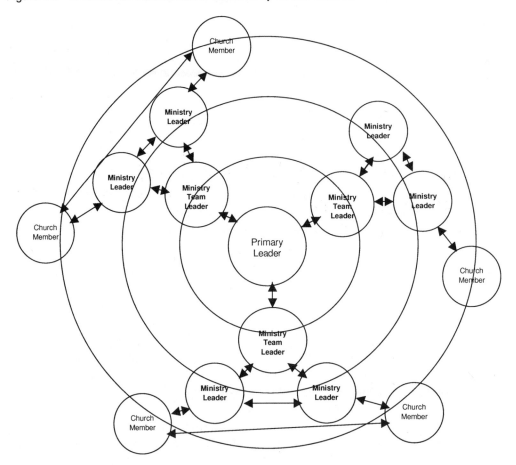

then, is to manage a particular area and pass up the chain of command information to be collected at the top where decisions are made. Although positional leaders must utilize inspiration, persuasion, and other tools in the hierarchical model, one significant currency available to a person to accomplish tasks and influence change in this model is *power*.

In the collaborative model adapted to the church, the structure is flat; there is minimal cascade of power and information. Dispersal and empowerment of *leaders* throughout the church is the distinguishing goal of this model. Delegated tasks and responsibilities function to help these leaders accomplish vision. The center or core of the model is usually the pastor. Concentric circles of *leaders* surround him or her, each with designated responsibilities. This primary leader need not be a single individual. Rather, even this core could function as a team in unique situations. For instance, Covenant Community Church has a clearly defined pastoral team, a senior pastor and associate pastor. These two leaders share this core function of leading the entire church. Practically, what this means is that preaching and vision articulation are shared, and the activities of the church are not arranged according to traditional hierarchy. Instead, the roles are defined according to passion and gifting. The senior pastor oversees worship and outreach, and the associate pastor is responsible for teaching and nurture. The teaching and nurture role at CCC includes functions traditionally reserved for the senior pastor, such as leadership development (including moderating the meetings of elders and deacons), pastoral care, administration of support committees (human resource management, finance, etc.), and even leading the due diligence process for the church's facilities planning and building initiative. This leadership team functions faithfully to the unique ways God has shaped each member of the team, not by fulfilling traditional hierarchical roles. Thus, collaboration even within the central core structure is possible, given the right leaders.

Achieving Belonging and Participation

Ministry team coordinators and team members make up concentric circles in the church. Indeed, the entire church body should find a place in the model. "Everybody needs a job," is a mantra of a pastor we immensely respect. The entire church serves in the leadership model; the only question should be "Where?" Coordinators involve ministry teams to generate *and* implement vision as shared values. Relationship and information supply the currency to run the model; relationship, not position, influences decisions. This model calls for thinking *across* the organization, not thinking *down* or *up* the organization. Leaders across the church serve to empower and support one another in a team structure that values the contribution and leadership each member brings. These teams embody a deep sense of participation and ownership as responsibility for mission and leadership within that team is delegated. "Disperse the tasks of leadership across the organization," Hesselbein recommends, "until there are leaders at every level and dispersed leadership is the reality" (2002, 89).

Achieving Shared Ownership

How then does a leader ensure that the dispersed leaders all lead in the same direction? Essentially, ownership of the vision supplies consistent direction. As primary leaders, not only must we collaborate on the leadership of the vision, but we must also collaborate on the vision itself. It need not be assumed that adopting this model means that all leaders are involved in all decisions. If, however, a leader can have his teammates shift personal pronouns, he has accomplished a monumental task. When the vision ceases to become "my" vision or "your" vision, and instead is embraced as "our" vision, ministries are strengthened and empowered for passionate implementation. Creating ownership in this collaborative vision does not call for the primary leader to give up the role of vision caster or innovator. But the leader does expend more energy to keep the vision in front of teammates to such an extent that accomplishment of the vision weaves itself into the sense of identity of the entire team. Mission becomes not simply a "team" goal but is owned as a *personal* goal for each and every member of the team. This may sound a bit frightening to many entrepreneurial leaders who grasp their vision as "my baby," fearful others may try to alter or manipulate it. This need not be so. Remember, persuasion is our tool. The task of the effective leader is to consistently speak the language of vision and mission such that all involved embrace the vision as a *personal* one. Leading from the position of persuasion is far healthier than from that of positional leverage. We do not want a team filled with players who participate with a "residue of resentment." We want players who own the vision.

It has been stated too many times to cite that leadership and management are not the same thing. In the church however, if for no other reason than having a small pool of hands to do the labor, leadership and management often converge. The collaborative mindset, therefore, must permeate the way we manage as well. Rather than the central figure always identifying problems and proposing solutions, this type of management sees solutions to problems bubbling up from the network of leaders actually doing the ministry (Gosling and Mintzberg 2003). Ideas about how to manage the work of the church and ideas about new ministries are proposed *and* implemented by the dispersed network of leaders. Ideas "get traction" through the passing of information across the organizational structure and by pulling together the network of relationships all committed to the same vision.

How does a church implement this shared ownership model and still retain a healthy respect for the ordained offices of the church? We believe that authority exercised in plurality helps promote the humility required to pursue collaborative leadership. Indeed, God does empower his ordained officers (elders and deacons) for spiritual authority and accountability for the welfare of the people under their care. Any leadership model implemented in the church must not compromise that central biblical commitment. However, spiritual authority can be exercised (and we would argue *should* be exercised) in a plurality of leadership so as to guard against the biases of any particular individual. Related to this, we believe that leadership requires substantial humility and a bedrock commitment to a common cause and vision. Specifically, it requires a bedrock commitment to the Christian belief that the ultimate authority over the church rests with Jesus Christ; and each leader and member of the church is accountable to his authority as head. Thus, shared leadership does not categorically undermine the authority of the officers of the church; it protects that authority from abuse.

Achieving Movement

Providing opportunities for belonging, participation, and ownership are critical to the church leader's task, especially in our current culture. Movement wraps these factors together. An individual's search for significance must find its answer here. She needs to become a part of a meaningful cause bigger and beyond herself. People search for this cause or movement in politics, social issues, music, art, and any number of other media. Movement creates awareness of opportunities to have significant impact in life (as a part of a greater cause than self) while it offers at the same time a pathway for individual involvement. A sense of movement within the church gives purpose to all the ministries we do and motivation to take part in those ministries.

Understanding how a sense of movement works has been perfected by activists with whom many in the "conservative" church will not agree. Gloria Steinem is one of those people. Although many in the "conservative" church (including ourselves) may be quite uncomfortable with the movement for which she has given her life, she certainly knows a great deal about leading a movement. Ms. Steinem, as quoted by Bennis, discusses the difference between leadership in a movement and corporate leadership by arguing that "movement leadership requires persuasion, not giving orders. There is no position to lead from. It doesn't exist. What makes you successful is that you can phrase things in a way that is inspirational, that makes coalitions possible. The movement has to be owned by a variety of people, not one group." (Bennis 1989, 159). Placing the church in the appropriate context of a *group* pursuing goals larger and more significant than any personal goal inspires and breathes life into any cause. The church is no exception. Becoming ingrown and stagnant poisons a church very quickly. Cause, or movement, mentality infuses the church with energy and vitality and feeds the desire for impact in the city and world.

Church Diversity and the Team-based Model

Gathering individuals into, and making progress as, a group pursuing a mission as encompassing as the Great Commission calls for courageous leadership. We believe that God has given church leaders the tool of persuasion as a means to foster belonging, participation, ownership, and movement among *diverse* individuals. Collectively, we bring to the church profound racial, ethnic heritage, gender, age, socioeconomic, and even personal lifestyle diversity. Yet our call is to work together to serve the single mission of the "great commission." Collaborative leadership embraces this singular mission by leveraging the diversity of the church. Team-based ministry leadership tethers God's people into a force of immeasurable influence. Implementing this new model in the church not only enhances each member's value to the ministry team, but also unleashes the gifts of the varied leaders God has placed within our congregations. We believe that implementing these principles can be rewarding for both leaders and church members. We also know that implementing an organizational change initiative to effect a transition to this model can be quite painful (at least in the short run), as the following case study attests.

SHEPHERDING CHANGE IN THE LOCAL CONGREGATION— A CASE STUDY OF EMPLOYING A TEAM-BASED MODEL

"It was the best of times; it was the worst of times." Charles Dickens's oft-quoted line from *A Tale of Two Cities* aptly describes my fourth year as senior pastor of Southwood Presbyterian Church (PCA) in Huntsville, Alabama.[1] After three quiet years of ministry leadership, my honeymoon came to an abrupt end as I sought to take this 1,400-member congregation through a number of significant changes. Initially, Rembrandt's painting, *The Storm on the Sea of Galilee*, was for me a visual depiction of what I sought for our congregation—"high adventure." A nice, romantic notion that a sea of criticism quickly disabused me of. I expected, of course, that my change initiatives would be challenged—and they were—but I did not expect the personal criticism that surfaced during that time. My preaching, my personality, and even my calling as a pastor and leader were called into question. And it was painful—to me and to my wife. David's prayer in Psalm 55:6, "Oh, that I had the wings of a dove! I would fly away and be at rest," was frequently in my heart if not on my lips. I have come to realize, however, that little of significance occurs without great difficulty. The positive transitions our congregation made during that year were little short of miraculous. Though still in the early stages of change, Southwood Presbyterian Church is even now a very different congregation, one, I believe, to be far more consistent with the biblical model of church and the team-based leadership model described above.

On the next pages, I will walk you through the transition process we have begun and are still engaged in. Along the way, the curtain will be pulled back to give you an insider's view of our successes and our failures. Stated simply, my thesis is this: Change is inevitable; the leadership of the church must learn to manage change to reduce the level of pain and increase the possibility of success. Do I believe that God was involved in this? Yes, as you will see. Humanly speaking, however, the "primary reason improvement issues fail or succeed is leadership" (Nelson and Appel 2000, 100). It is vitally important, then, that church leaders own their God-given responsibilities in this area, responsibilities that can be summarized as follows: assess the need for change; prepare for the change; implement and sustain the change. There is, of course, significant overlap among these tasks, but a linear relationship does still exist.

Assess the Need for Change

Key leadership must never accept the status quo—not because change in and of itself is good, but because the local congregation, left unchecked, tends to conform to its external culture. At the same time it remains unintelligible and ineffective in terms of reaching that rapidly-morphing culture. When that happens, the church not only loses the unique gift it has to offer but also loses the ability to give what it does have. And this can happen within congregations that wholeheartedly believe the Bible to be the standard for belief and practice. It happened at Southwood. Much like the culture in which we exist, we had become overly focused on meeting the needs of our members rather than helping our members reach out to meet the needs of the people in our community and beyond. Having relegated the great commission of Matthew 28:19 ("make disciples of all nations") to a minor role, we focused inward, speaking and ministering primarily to those who were familiar with biblical language and practices. The visitor, especially the uninitiated, felt out of place and out of our sphere of concern. The leadership of any church, then, must constantly study the word of God to more fully understand its standards for the church and compare those standards with the actual beliefs and practices of its congregation. Any gulf between the two indicates a need for change. At the same time, leaders must know the culture they hope to reach and fashion ministries in such a way that they are intelligible and appropriate not only to church members but also to the church's culture.

Once leadership embraces the need for change, the success or failure of assessing the actual change needed will depend to a great extent on the leaders' willingness to painstakingly take stock of the congregation's present situation. In *Good to Great*, Jim Collins identifies key concepts held by companies that have successfully navigated the murky waters of transitioning from good companies to great ones. One concept particularly applicable to the assessment stage of the change process is this: "You must maintain unwavering faith that you can and will prevail in the end, regardless of the difficulties, *AND at the same time* have the discipline to confront the most brutal facts of your current reality, whatever they might be" (Collins 2001, 13). In other words, do not gloss over, do not minimize, do not excuse the problems, but do not lose heart in the process. There is no guarantee, of course, that you or your church will survive a significant transition, but when God reveals shortcomings in our lives or in our congregations, he does so to bring about change. We can be confident then that the change is called for and that God will be with us in the journey, bringing about his desired result.

That kind of confidence helps us to be willing to take the much-needed hard look at ourselves and our congregation, but one thing more is necessary for a realistic assessment to take place: humility, extraordinary humility. No one likes to acknowledge shortcomings under his or her watch—especially when it becomes personal. But it must be done. Only then will leaders be willing to turn over rocks and look at the muck underneath; only then will leaders create a corporate environment that encourages honest, constructive criticism from others that will identify blind spots on the part of key leaders.

And that is where my own record becomes spotty. As we assessed the need for change at Southwood, there were times when I enjoyed a modicum of success in this area; there were also times I failed royally. At the outset of the assessment process, I invited members of our session (body of elders) to join me on what would become known as the vision committee. Four of twenty-six elders volunteered to serve with me, and together we began the roller coaster ride that has been exhilarating, exhausting, and exposing (how's that for alliteration?). There have been moments when we could hardly contain our excitement, there have been moments when we had difficulty finding the energy to press on, and there have been moments when we got a glimpse of each other's hearts—seeing both the beauty of humility and the ugliness of arrogance (mine especially).

The vision committee met almost weekly for about two months, then retreated overnight. The retreat resulted in conviction of personal and corporate shortcomings. Tears were shed as we confessed those shortcomings and sought God's wisdom for the future. It was a good start, but more soul-searching was needed. That happened for me while on a five-day personal retreat encouraged by the session. Staying in a guesthouse on the campus of Covenant Theological Seminary (my alma mater), I prayed, spent time reading the Bible, read a dozen books, and sought the counsel of former professors. Halfway through the week, I got to the bottom of the problem—we had little zeal for the "great commission." Seems simple doesn't it? But we had missed it, focusing the vast majority of our efforts on maturing the members of our congregation and meeting their needs, to the exclusion of reaching the lost. The assumption, of course, was that the members, as they matured, would reach out beyond our doors to the community, but it was not happening. Though we were growing, new members were almost solely transfers from other churches. Only a handful of people were joining as altogether new members of the Christian church. We were "sheep-stealers"—unintentionally of course, but "sheep-stealers" nonetheless. We had joined the ranks of 99 percent of all churches in this country, whose new members come primarily through "transfer growth" (Nelson and Appel 2000, 2). Our efforts to build the church, then, were far from successful. Focusing inward, we had effectively taken ourselves out of the game, and I was leading the way. That was a devastating realization, but it provided exactly the right motivation for desperately needed change, needed change that was, until that moment, unrecognized.

Returning home, I continued the assessment process by presenting my conclusions to the vision committee, session, diaconate, and other groups of key leaders, seeking their input. For the most part, that went very well. One major misstep I made, however, is worth mentioning, because it almost derailed the whole process. It also demonstrates the need for humility on the part of leadership. Early on, the vision committee decided that there were to be no sacred cows. Everything was up for grabs, everything was fair game for critique. It never occurred to me, however, that my preaching would be included in that list. For three years, I had never heard one criticism of my preaching style. No doubt it existed, but somehow it never reached my ears. Then, during one of the assessment meetings, someone outside the vision committee, representing several people, suggested I make some significant changes in the way I preached. I was completely caught off guard, but handled the comments reasonably well during the meeting. Later I sought the counsel of others, concluded that there was some truth in the critique, and made certain changes. When, however, that same critique surfaced again several months later by the same people, I became angry. When the critique was delivered to me by the vision committee, I shot the messengers. That just about ended the change process before it ever began. It took several months and numerous apologies on my part for those relationships to heal. The importance of humility in the face of criticism has been well stated in a letter from an experienced minister to a younger one: "It does not matter what happens to us, but our reaction to what happens to us is of vital importance" (Sanders 1994, 119).

Beneficial change begins with the ever-ready willingness on the part of leadership to confront the brute facts about a congregation. And that takes humility—humility to acknowledge that your church is not what it could be, that you are not the leader you could be, and that you need others in the congregation to reveal those shortcomings to you. Only then, when people know they can speak openly, constructively criticizing even your leadership, will you be able to adequately assess the need for change.

Prepare for the Change

Once the need for change has been thoroughly assessed (in truth, an ongoing process), leaders need to take great care to properly prepare for the change. Although many leaders hurry through this phase if they address it at all, significant change will not be sustained without significant effort at this point. Attempting to implement a new structure, a new direction, or a new ministry without taking time beforehand to prepare yourself, your key leaders, and your congregation—both intellectually and emotionally—will result in a failed change initiative.

It is paramount during the preparation stage that leaders take the raw, negative data from the assessment phase and convert it into a positive, compelling vision. Dissatisfied with where you are, it is time to show your members how far they can go, and to do so in a way that motivates them toward that destination. "Vision," writes Bill Hybels, "is a picture of the future that produces passion" (2002, 32). And that passion must begin first in the leader. For that to happen, the overarching vision must be large enough and important enough to elicit from that leader statements like, "I think I could give my life to this. I think maybe I was born for this" (2002, 33).

By the end of my five-day retreat, having already begun to move from assessment to vision, I was so convicted by our current state, and, at the same time, so passionate about our future direction that I included these words in a ten-page memo I gave to the vision committee: "I believe that we as leaders have two possible responses to the realization that we are failing to carry out the great commission: 1. we can repent and begin to live as true Christian disciples who risk boldly to reach the hurting world outside the church walls or 2. we can resign." Outside of the vision committee, I communicated that statement in the first person. Either way, it successfully conveyed the message that I was willing to stake my career on this budding vision—and, in the context of the fuller vision, it began to light fires in the hearts of our members.

As the vision matured, I began to describe it in terms of becoming a "missional church," one, in other words, that understands that God wants the church to be a missionary church in its own community—whether in Africa, Asia, or North America (Guder et al. 1998). We must, in other words, see our congregation, both corporately and individually, as placed in our particular community for the sake of that community. Rather than living primarily for ourselves, we must begin to identify ourselves, by word and deed, as servants of our community. Robert Lewis, in *The Church of Irresistible Influence*, states this vision in ways that stir our hearts as we see what can be: "*Can you imagine* the neighborhoods around your church talking behind your back about 'how good it is' to have your church in the area because of the tangible witness you've offered them of God's love? *Can you imagine* a large number of your church members actively engaged in, and passionate about community service, using their gifts and abilities in ways and at levels they never thought possible? *Can you imagine* the community actually changing . . . because of the impact of your church's involvement?" (Lewis and Wilkins 2001, 13–14)

Having a well-thought out, passion-igniting vision in place is a good first step in the preparation phase. More must occur, however, before that vision can be successfully communicated to the congregation. There are issues of timing, for instance. How long the senior pastor has been at the church has significant implications. Usually, during the first year, no major changes should be initiated. That time should be used to gain the trust of the congregation as you model for them a life of integrity, competency, and concern for their well-being, as discussed in the first section of this chapter. With one exception, I heeded that piece of advice given to me by a seasoned mentor. The one time I failed to do so, I was greeted by a torrent of passionate (and successful) arguments from members who saw themselves negatively affected by the proposed change. I quickly realized that until I had been a trusted part of the larger team for some time my vision would simply remain that—*my* change vision as opposed to a *shared* change vision.

On the other hand, if a senior pastor has been at a church three years or more without making a single major change, the difficulty of effecting change will be significantly increased. During the second and third years of a pastor's ministry at a given church, members expect change. When none comes, many assume that none will and may then leave because of disappointment or stay because they like the status quo. Those who stay begin to feel safe and may feel betrayed by change after that point. A pastor who initiates change after his third year should probably begin with one change and introduce it gradually. Unlike what I did. Waiting until my fourth year before encouraging major change, I introduced a "perfect storm" of significant initiatives—a second Sunday-morning worship service, a $2,000,000 youth facility (with a decidedly outward focus), and a fairly comprehensive urban renewal effort in one of the poorest areas of our city. Though the ship did not sink, it did take on water. And some of our members, rather than bailing water, bailed out. The positive results of that year far outweighed the negative ones (twice as many people joined the church as left that year, for example), but there were gut-wrenching moments, a few of which caused me to wonder if my more vocal critics were onto something.

A second timing-related issue is the length of time required for effecting the actual change. Churches, for various reasons, are typically slower to change than for-profit corporations. Alan Nelson and Gene Appel, in their book *How to Change Your Church Without Killing It* outline several reasons for this dynamic. First, "churches see themselves as tradition keepers, preservers of the past. A felt responsibility of the church is to perpetuate values of the historical church" (2000, 44). Second, the church is not as in touch with its "bottom line" as is the for-profit corporation. Because effectiveness in the church is more difficult to measure, the need for significant improvement is "rarely clearly perceived, unless there is a crisis" (2000, 44). Third, because "only 5 percent of pastors identify leadership in their gift mix, they are apt to either avoid change efforts, feel intimidated by lay leaders who promote change initiatives, or bungle improvement projects because they do not understand the leadership process" (2000, 45). Church leadership must, then, prepare more thoroughly and allow more time for implementation than for-profit corporations. Patience is indeed a virtue.

One more step is essential before communicating the vision—creating a sufficiently powerful guiding coalition. "In successful transformations," notes leading change expert John Kotter, "the president, division general manager, or department head plus another five, fifteen, or fifty people with a commitment to improved performance pull together as a team. . . . Individuals alone, no matter how competent or charismatic, never have all the assets to overcome tradition and inertia except in very small organizations" (1996, 6). A congregation, especially if it has seen initiatives come and go before, needs to see that the leadership as a whole has bought into the vision. That is where the coalition comes in. Ours initially consisted of the vision committee, the session, and the staff. A great deal of energy was expended to unite this coalition around the *missional* vision— one-on-one conversations, group meetings, a session retreat, and so forth. Additional leaders were later added as we sought to communicate and implement specific change initiatives. More meetings were held. And even then nothing came easily, but without that coalition fanning out through the congregation, carrying the same message, the hoped-for changes would have been stillborn. And it was only through such effort that the vision eventually became one that was collectively owned by the larger church as a whole.

Finally, we have reached the last stage of preparation—communicating the vision. And that begins with the primary leader. "How," asks Hybels, "does a leader best communicate a vision? By embodying it. By personifying it. By living it out" (2002, 38). The church leaders and the entire congregation had to see in me not only passion for the new direction but also a life that conformed to that passion. So as I began to describe the vision, I told stories, candidly confessing my previous lack of zeal for the "great commission" and demonstrating my reinvigorated concern for those who had not traditionally been served by our church. That began with the inner circle of the vision committee, moved outward to the entire session, then to the diaconate, then to other members who were influencers in the church, and finally to the congregation on Sunday mornings and in a variety of additional settings. Other members of the guiding coalition also began to chime in, communicating the same vision through their own stories. Within two months it was obvious to the congregation that the leadership had charted a new course for the future.

How did the congregation respond? Some immediately came on board, wanting to get started. Others assumed the worst—"leadership was abandoning the flock in favor of the community." Some left. Others, who had planned on leaving out of boredom before the new vision was cast, stayed. Many joined, telling us, "I want to be a part of a church like that." Shared ownership was growing. And the "movement" had begun.

We learned a number of lessons during that time. One was the necessity of repetition. Early on, the vision committee attended a conference on leading congregational change. There, Jeanie Duck, a leader in organizational practice, made a comment that stuck in our minds and proved true in our situation: "When the leader is getting sick of stating the vision, the congregation is just starting to get it." She went on to say that people need to hear the vision about eight times before they understand it. So we communicated the vision through many people in a variety of settings on a number of occasions. And because some members did assume the worst, we communicated very specifically what the vision is *and* what it is not, addressing head-on some of the voiced concerns. We also tried to state the vision in a way that is easily understood and difficult to forget. "Discipleship that faces outward" or "discipleship that faces the world" became a summary statement of our vision. That statement did two things: it addressed congregational concern that we were abandoning our calling to build up the current members of the church while it concurrently kept us moving in the right direction—outward toward members of the community who had not been traditionally served by our church. Finally, we were careful to help the congregation understand how we decided on the vision. "If leaders want to change the thinking and actions of others," writes Duck, "they must be transparent about their own. If people within the organization don't understand the new thinking or don't agree with it, they will not change their beliefs or make decisions that are aligned with what's desired" (2001, 27–28). So we worked hard to communicate the significance of the problem (a must if people are to desire change), and the way forward.

One caution is in order: Never demean the accomplishments of the congregation, past or present. Though the brute fact of your current situation must be pointed out and excitement about future direction must be inspired, leaders must not diminish the significance of congregational successes. That demoralizes the membership and denies the proud heritage of the particular church. When we introduced the vision to the congregation through "town hall" meetings, we celebrated the past with a video of member interviews, recalling the ministry of Southwood in their lives. It was a way of responding with gratitude to God for his many blessings in the past, and, thanks to many comments in those interviews, a way of looking forward to even better days.

The preparation phase requires extraordinary work. Leaders must convert the shortcomings discerned during the assessment phase to a compelling vision, consider when to implement that vision, form a guiding coalition strong enough to lead that vision, communicate that vision numerous times to many people in a variety of settings, and do all of this without demeaning the past. A tough task, but absolutely critical if change is to be implemented with the least amount of pain and the highest probability of success.

Implement and Sustain the Change

We are still very early in the process of implementation, but the perfect storm mentioned above (second worship service, construction of a youth facility, and urban renewal effort) did more than cause turmoil. Coming so quickly after introducing the vision, it also generated a great amount of excitement as the congregation realized the new direction was more than mere rhetoric. As Duck notes, "the time between the announcement of the plan and its implementation can and should be short" (2001, 22). Otherwise, many in the congregation will assume that the leaders are simply expressing a passing fancy and will pay little attention to exhortation for change.

Kotter (1996) also addresses this, positing that generating short-term victories and building off those gains is critical to the success of the larger change initiative. Thus, as we brought specific change initiatives to the congregation, we rooted them in the overarching vision of becoming a *missional* church—the second worship service gives more room for people we hope to reach; the youth facility, placed intentionally across the street from our sanctuary, appeals not only to our current young members but also to the nonmember youth in our community who might (at first) be intimidated by a more formal church sanctuary; and the urban renewal effort enables us to reach out in word and deed to people who have significant personal needs relative to daily survival and (traditionally) little to do with church. With those initiatives under way, we had short-term victories to celebrate, the importance of which can hardly be overstated. "Most people," writes Kotter, "won't go on the long march unless they see compelling evidence within six to eighteen months that the journey is producing expected results. Without short-term wins, too many employees give up or actively join the resistance" (1996, 11). We publicly highlighted those successes, especially on Sunday mornings. There were reports, testimonies, letters of thanks, and a groundbreaking for the "Lodge," our youth building. At the same time, we stayed away from any suggestion that the task was nearly complete. As Kotter has noted, "Until changes sink deeply into the culture, which for an entire company can take three to ten years, new approaches are fragile and subject to regression" (1996, 13).

What is next? A system of accountability. "Collins talks about the need to 'put thorns in our laurels.' That way, when we go to sit on our laurels, we'll feel pain" (Nelson and Appel 2000, 27). We must put in place a way to measure our success, a system that will let us know if we are becoming in practice what we are proclaiming in word. We need a system of accountability that will reward us with pain and discomfort when we fail to fulfill our vision of "discipleship that faces outward." Maybe thorns are not such a bad thing after all. For now, my vision committee—a pretty thorny lot—rightly reminds me on a regular basis that we have only begun to move in a more *missional* direction. It will take years of working together to make that vision a part of our corporate culture. But it will be worth it.

CHANGE AND TEAM-BASED LEADERSHIP—SOME CONCLUDING THOUGHTS

A leader must embrace change—whether large or small. It is a part of the job. And he or she must understand how to bring it about. When I (prior to entering the pastorate) owned a real estate development firm in Myrtle Beach, South Carolina, I started a 250-unit residential community by building two model homes. A local firm supplied the furniture for these models, at their expense, based on our commitment to refer home buyers to them when they sought to purchase furniture. My salespeople, however, thought the prices were too high for our home buyers and began referring people to another furniture store with lower-priced goods. As president of the company, I assumed that a simple directive to change that practice would suffice. I was wrong. The only thing that changed was the way in which they continued to direct home buyers to their choice of a furniture store—quietly, that is, so I would not find out about it.

Leaders utilizing a hierarchical leadership model know that power alone is rarely enough to influence any directive, much less one that involves significant change. That truth is more pronounced in the church, where most ministry must be accomplished by volunteers. A team-based leadership model, in which all members can have some sense of belonging, participation, ownership, and movement, is more likely to exert influence throughout the congregation than is a strictly hierarchical model. That understanding is crucial, because implementing important change in the church, whether a new ministry, a new building project, or a new vision, requires the involvement of a tremendous number of people. And the more significant the change, the more this model of leadership can help.

Once we identified the needed change at Southwood Presbyterian Church, we attempted to involve a number of people in the persuasion process, as we moved farther and farther outward from the center. After each member of the vision committee passionately and personally embraced the new vision, we met with the session, the diaconate, groups of members who were influential in their circles within the congregation, and finally the entire congregation. Our goal was not only to gain agreement with the vision, but also to gain involvement (in each circle, as depicted in Figure 8.1) in the persuasion process before the implementation phase began. By the time we began to implement the vision, many were on board and ready to go. And we were able to start with three very visible expressions of the new vision that generated enthusiasm for that vision—the second worship service, the youth facility, and the urban renewal effort.

This team-based leadership model is not only helpful within the congregation, however. It is also more appealing to those outside the church, people we long to see join the church. It fits the mindset of those in our postmodern culture who seek a deeper sense of community. The results of this kind of leadership model—a sense of belonging, participation, ownership, and movement—also describe very well the nature of a disciple. At the same time, it is an excellent expression of the Christian emphasis on servant leadership, a kind of leadership that requires a deep level of humility. With that said, is the team-based leadership model easy to institute, in a church organization or otherwise? Of course not. Nothing worthwhile ever is.

NOTE

1. This case study chronicles the experiences of Mike Honeycutt (co-author of this chapter) in leading a significant change initiative in a large church via a team-based leadership model. For purposes of clarity and effect we have chosen to convey the case in the personal voice of Rev. Honeycutt.

REFERENCES

Barna, G., and M. Hatch. (2001). *Boiling Point.* Ventura, CA: Regal.

Bennis, W. (1989). *On Becoming a Leader.* New York: Addison-Wesley.

Collins, J. (2001). *Good to Great: Why Some Companies Make the Leap . . . and Others Don't.* New York: Harper Business.

Duck, J.D. (2001). *The Change Monster.* New York: Three Rivers.

Gosling, J., and H. Mintzberg. (2003). "The Five Minds of a Manager." *Harvard Business Review* 11: 54–63.

Guder, D.L. ed. (1998). *Missional Church: A Vision for the Sending of the Church in North America.* Grand Rapids, MI: William B. Eerdmans.

Hesselbein, F. (2002). *Hesselbein on Leadership.* San Francisco: Jossey-Bass.

Hybels, B. (2002). *Courageous Leadership.* Grand Rapids, MI: Zondervan.

Kotter, John P. (1996). *Leading Change.* Boston: Harvard Business School Press.

Lewis, R., and R. Wilkins. (2001). *The Church of Irresistible Influence.* Grand Rapids, MI: Zondervan.

Maxwell, J.C. (1998). *The 21 Irrefutable Laws of Leadership: Follow Them and People Will Follow You.* Nashville, TN: Thomas Nelson.

Nelson, A., and G. Appel. (2000). *How to Change Your Church Without Killing It.* Nashville, TN: Word.

Sanders, J.O. (1994). *Spiritual Leadership.* Chicago: Moody Bible Institute.

Stanley, A. (2003). *The Next-Generation Leader.* Sisters, OR: Multnomah.

Stott, J. (1982). *Between Two Worlds.* Grand Rapids, MI: Eerdmans.

Trent, J., R. Cox, and E. Tooker. (2004). *Leading from Your Strengths: Building Closely Knit Ministry Teams.* Nashville, TN: Broadman & Holman.

PART III

LEADERSHIP IN GOVERNMENT ORGANIZATIONS

CHAPTER 9

NOTES FROM THE BELLY OF THE BEAST

Leadership Challenges in the Federal Government

RICHARD F. CULLINS

"We'll never be the same after 9/11" seemed to be the mantra after the excruciating events in 2001. True enough: 9/11 began a series of subsequent events that have changed the fundamental fabric of the federal government. Since 9/11, we have had wars in Afghanistan and Iraq, police action in Liberia, saber rattling from North Korea, discord in relations with our closest international partners, a tentative economy, and the largest restructuring of government since Franklin Roosevelt was in office. Add to this a rising call for accountability, the need for agencies of the federal government to operate more like private sector businesses, drives toward pay-for-performance, burgeoning unionization, galloping technological advancement, large numbers of baby boomer retirements, a relative disinterest in government jobs among young people, and the omnipresent blanket of Washington politics. A picture emerges of the types of challenges faced by current executives and managers. It is a playing field of ambiguities and managerial paradoxes that must be negotiated carefully and tactically if leaders are to be successful for the foreseeable future.

This chapter will consider the leadership challenges to agencies of the executive branch of government. "Agencies" are defined herein as cabinet-level departments and their subagencies. Many of the challenges discussed are tied, and not coincidently, to the *President's Management Agenda* (Executive Office of the President 2002). That agenda has broad implications for federal civil servants.

A new model of leadership may be required if tomorrow's federal leaders are to be successful. This chapter will explore current challenges facing those leaders. It will also review some thoughts in the literature on leadership over the past decade in contrast to the current operational environment to determine whether leadership strategies and precepts of the recent past still apply.

Leadership is an elusive concept. We know it when we see it. And we are keenly aware when it is absent. It is those not-so-rare occasions when we have the chance to observe leadership directly—when one is highly successful or fails in a big way—that we get the best perspective on when and how leadership works along with those anecdotal characteristics that contribute to one's success or failure. Nonetheless, many models of leadership have been put forward.

THE NATURE OF LEADERSHIP

Much has been written on the subject of leadership. Many authors present theorized "formulas" for developing leadership. Three representative examples are discussed below.

Kouzes and Posner (1995, 9–14) posited Five Fundamentals of Exemplary Leadership:

- Challenge the process
- Inspire a shared vision
- Enable others to act
- Model the way
- Encourage the heart

In sum, these attributes perhaps translate, simply, to: be creative in envisioning new ways of working; share that vision with your workforce in a committed and communicative fashion; empower your employees to help create your collective vision; model the behavior you envision; and support, encourage, and care about those who work for you. The authors' work provides a wide and smart array of strategies one might employ in the pursuit of superior leadership but offers little in the way of when and under what circumstances those strategies might be employed.

Zaccaro and Klimoski, in the introduction to their contribution to the literature, suggest the following:

> Leadership has been a major topic of research in psychology for almost a century and has spawned thousands of empirical and conceptual studies. Despite this level of effort, however, the various parts of this literature still appear disconnected and directionless. In our opinion, a major cause of this state of the field is that many studies of leadership are context free; that is, low consideration is given to organizational variables that influence the nature and impact of leadership. Such research, especially prominent in the social and organizational psychology literatures, tends to focus on interpersonal processes between individual, nominally leaders and followers. Studies that explicitly examine leadership within organizational contexts, particularly from the strategic management literature, seem incomplete for other reasons. They typically ignore the cognitive, interpersonal, and social richness of this phenomenon, in that they fail to come to grips with processes that would explain or account for outcomes. While model building in the strategic management literature is typically focused on the examination of leadership occurring at upper organizational levels, any insights offered regarding the selection, development, and training of potential leaders are not often grounded in strong conceptual frameworks having significant empirical support. (Zaccaro and Klimoski 2001, 3)

Zaccaro and Klimoski (2001) go on to put forth principles and models of leadership that are context based, that is, they ask the reader to consider the social, political, economic, technologic, personnel, and personal concerns in play in their operating environment when determining how to best lead the organization.

Palus and Horth take a competency-based approach to leadership. Their approach focuses on individual challenges and the competencies that can be brought to bear in order for leaders to fully explore the challenge before them and to collaboratively craft solutions. Their competencies are:

1. *Paying attention:* using multiple modes of perception to understand a complex situation;
2. *Personalizing:* tapping into your and others' unique life experiences and passions to gain insight and create energy to tackle group challenges;
3. *Imaging:* making sense of complex information, constructing ideas, and communicating effectively by using all kinds of images, such as pictures, stories, and metaphors;
4. *Serious play:* generating knowledge through free exploration, improvisation, experimentation, levity, and play;
5. *Co-inquiry* (or collaborative inquiry): dialoguing within and across community boundaries of language, culture, function, and professional discipline;
6. *Crafting:* synthesizing issues, objects, events, and actions into integrated, meaningful wholes. (Palus and Horth 2002, 3)

It might be said that these competencies, when put to use, build context around the challenges on which they have been brought to bear. From these few examples dating from 1995, 2001, and 2002, respectively, it appears that there is increased emphasis on the context of leadership and less on the attributes of leaders themselves.

LEADERSHIP ISSUES IN THE FEDERAL GOVERNMENT

The approaches to leadership outlined above can all be helpful guides to government leaders, although Zaccaro and Klimosky's (2001) work comes closest to the mark in the context of the public sector and particularly at the federal level. Government leaders operate in a highly political atmosphere. Policy is arrived at through the political process and depending on the party in power is often tinged with ideology. When policy is enacted at the agency level, it is sometimes at odds with personal and political views held by some employees at all levels within a given agency. Executives are expected to support the views of agencies' top executives, who are generally political appointees. Executives, for the most part, support the views of these leaders or they do not last long. But often their support is tentative and without unflinching support. One often hears in government, albeit covertly, words to the effect, "We can outlast this administrator," suggesting less than full support for the occasional mandated and/or partisan policies and programs that may be at odds with careerists' personal and professional perspectives.

Aberbach and Rockman refer to these situations as "responsiveness dilemmas" and suggest that: "In practice it is probably impossible for any set of bureaucratic agents in a truly democratic and constitutional system simply to follow the dictates of their political superiors" (2000, 89).

There is also the notion that the federal bureaucracy is not comparable to private indus-try on multiple levels. Donahue (1999) discusses four characteristics of the federal govern-ment that set it apart from the private sector: scale, complexity, monopoly, and indirect accountability. Scale is the sheer size of the federal government with over 4 million em-ployees and $1.7 trillion in spending in 1998. Complexity is the vast range of services provided and the infrastructure to support it. Donahue (1999) suggests that the stability in government structure and services expected by the public (e.g., that Social Security checks will be sent on time) inhibits the amount of innovation agencies might consider. Monopoly is the fact that the federal government has, for the most part, no rivals for the work that it does. Indirect accountability is the government's lack of direct accountability to an equiva-lent of stockholders, boards of directors, and direct customers. Donahue offers that:

> Creativity, boldness, intuition, and initiative tend to rank lower in the pantheon of virtues than do continuity, predictability, accountability, and impartiality. Com-pared with a solitary entrepreneur or a small private company—indeed, compared with a large private company—the federal government is not built for flexibility. (Donahue 1999, 2)

So, while the leadership models above do not take these matters directly into consid-eration, they are still useful models for leadership development. But there is more room in the literature for discussion of how leaders at the agency level might perform in politi-cal environments. Several key challenges to government leaders are discussed below. They are not the only challenges. Americans are concerned about terrorism, possible changes to Social Security, medical care, education, the environment, and many other issues. Those discussed below are, for the most part, key issues *within* federal service. They are issues critical to the fluid operation of the government itself.

FEDERAL CHALLENGES

People

Paul Light (2003) believes the state of health of public service is dire. He cites increasing layers of bureaucracy, decreased training and development, and recruitment difficulties due to disaffection with public service. From the inside of government these issues are obvious and trying. According to the U.S. Office of Personnel Management (2000), the average age of federal employees in 2000 was 45.05. Given the issues raised by Light (2003) and the likely retirements of vast numbers of baby boomers over the next seven to ten years, the federal government is facing a major crisis in employment. *The President's Management Agenda* (Executive Office of the President 2002) has set Strategic Manage-ment of Human Capital as its first priority. *The President's Management Agenda* states,

"Approximately 71 percent of the government's permanent employees will be eligible for either regular or early retirement by 2010 and then 40 percent of those employees are expected to retire (2002, 13)." Younger workers have seen what the private sector offers— better pay, flexible work schedules, flexible benefit plans, modern workplace environments, health clubs, child care, and casual work atmospheres. They have also been raised on the belief that government is bloated and wasteful. One of the themes of the 1994 "Republican Revolution" was reduction of the size and scope of federal government. The Clinton administration followed with "Reinventing Government" and the arbitrary reduction in the size of government by some 300,000 employees. As Stephan Barr of the *Washington Post* notes, "Stories of waste fraud and abuse attract far more attention than 'good' government" (2003, B2). Barr cites other alienating aspects of federal employment including the lack of meaningful recognition, turf battles, continuing assaults on job benefits by Congress, fluctuating program direction and underfunding, stifling of entrepreneurial sprit, and long commutes that are off-putting to would-be federal employees.

Leaders in the federal government will have to develop new strategies to attract new talent and will have to find ways to alter perceptions they have helped to create. This means changes in policy at all levels of government and new thinking about modernizing the federal workplace. One way this might occur could be through a national call to service akin to the Kennedy-era efforts chronicled in David Halberstam's 1972 book, *The Best and the Brightest.* However, the 1960s were a different time. There was a pervasive sense of idealism at the time. We live in a more cynical and skeptical era and both the message and the messenger for a contemporary call to public service will require thoughtfulness and leadership at its very best.

Human resources reform is badly needed in government on a number of levels. Over the past decade many agencies have established different pay plans and some agencies are now excepted service (have their own personnel and pay systems—excluded from the federal personnel system). Many unions have negotiated pay systems within pay systems. This has created huge disparities in pay within and among agencies for individuals who perform very similar duties. It has created morale problems, reduced confidence in leadership, and undermined recruitment for top talent.

Most of the current new pay systems have some variation of pay-for-performance. Pay-for-performance is premised on small annual pay increases supplemented by additional percentage increases for the highest performers. The Civil Service General Schedule pay system, still in use in some agencies, is based on a range of pay "steps" within fixed grade levels. Years of service, for the most part, determine at which step an individual is paid. The Civil Service pay system treated everybody the same way, even low performers. For many years high performers could receive "merit pay" (a one-time bonus) or step increases (a jump to the next incremental pay level, ahead of the normal schedule) for high performance. Bonus amounts varied from agency to agency based on available funding. Many federal employees feel that pay-for-performance is unfair because the optional percentage increases go into annual base pay and will be meted out on a basis other than high performance, say, to favored employees or to avoid grievances.

Other criticisms have to do with the mechanics of pay-for-performance. How do we measure performance, particularly when agency performance metrics are inadequate? How do we measure the performance of teams? Do we recognize team performance or individual performance? The formation of teams has been emphasized in government agencies for, roughly, the past twelve years. Clearly, on any team there are individuals who do more or less than others. How is a supervisor going to evaluate the performance of an employee who has been working on a team in another part of the organization? The form of pay involved is also a problem. Will it be a one-time payment? How much? Many federal workers oppose one-time payments, even sizable ones, as they do not represent a pay raise. How does an organization or an individual determine, objectively, who the top 20 percent of employees are? What if, in actuality, 50 percent of employees met and exceeded specific performance goals? Finally, and perhaps most important, will pay-for-performance change behavior? Will people be more productive? Leaders will need to find answers to these questions if pay-for-performance is to work. Otherwise it will end up on the scrap heap of experiments with federal employee remuneration and motivation.

Federal leaders will need to work together to build a new, people-friendly, national personnel system. Further balkanization of pay systems will only make federal service increasingly unattractive to potential employees. At the agency level, leaders are stuck with making questionable pay systems and union agreements work in the near term. They can aid themselves by employing some of the private sector human resource practices arrived at over the past twenty years such as nonmonetary recognition, making work less formal (but not less effective), and providing comfortable work environments that have a progressive, campus like feel instead of the stodgy, bureaucratic, institutional facilities they are, for the most part. Some new practices have already been widely employed, such as flexible schedules, time-off awards, and telecommuting. Most agencies now provide day care. But, still, the federal government is well behind the private sector in workplace modernization.

Herzberg (Herzberg, Mausner, and Snyderman 1959) developed a two-factor theory of motivation called dissatisfiers-satisfiers or extrinsic-intrinsic factors. Herzberg's theory holds that employee dissatisfaction can occur when there is a set of "extrinsic" conditions, or the job context, that are not present. If the conditions are present, they may not motivate employees, but if not present, will result in dissatisfaction. Such conditions are called dissatisfiers. These include such factors as salary, job security, working conditions, operating procedures, status, and quality of relations with supervisors, peers and subordinates. Each of these factors has been under attack in the federal sector. Job satisfaction in the federal government is on the decline. Tobias observed:

> Federal employee job satisfaction is declining, according to a survey released recently by the National Partnership for Reinventing Government and the Office of Personnel Management. In 1998, 62 percent of employees answered "favorable" to the question "Considering everything, how satisfied are you with your job?" but in 1999 the response was 60 percent. The 1999 federal employee rating was 2 percentage points below the 62 percent average private-sector favorable response rate.

> Federal managers are not competing against average companies for talent. They must create a significantly higher level of job satisfaction in order to offset the competitive pay disadvantage. (Tobias 2000)

Training and development are keys to success in any organization. It is also commonly held that training and development are the first to go in tight budget times. To attract and retain people, now and in the future, the federal government will at least have to keep pace with the private sector. College graduates today have grown up with technology. In the past twenty years, technology for training and development has changed radically. Distance learning, e-learning, and blended learning have all become ubiquitous in the private sector. While the federal government is making progress through its e-government initiative, individual agencies are woefully behind the power curve. In the past several years, budgets have been slashed and training dollars diverted to agencies' operational necessities. Many agencies continue to send employees to distant training facilities for classroom-based learning. Budgetary planning is too often based on immediate fiscal year priorities rather than long-term infrastructure investment. As a result, many agencies are in continual catch-up mode. In an era when technology is rapidly evolving, playing catch-up is no longer viable. If the federal sector wants to attract young people in the numbers that will be required, they will have to demonstrate a long-term commitment to human resource development as a function of the strategic management of human capital. In order to become fluid in their response to emerging new business requirements, federal agencies will have to constantly retrain employees on new systems and processes if they are to operate more like businesses.

Human resource development is expensive, but it is indispensable if we are to have tomorrow's leaders and doers. Today's leaders not only must make sure we have enough employees, but also must assure that they are equipped with the knowledge, skills, and abilities to build the responsive, flexible, modern government the American people expect.

While unions have seen a thirty-year decline in the private sector, they have expanded considerably in government. State, local, and federal government employees now account for almost half of all union members. The National Center for Policy Analysis (1998) reported that 37 percent of government workers belong to unions, compared to about 10 percent of private sector workers. While one may argue that unionization of the federal government is either positive or negative, it is clear that it makes things more complex. Unions are capable of exerting much pressure and have demonstrated an ability to stop work on projects, whatever their merit, until bargaining is complete, often a lengthy process depending on the issues under negotiation and the current political environment. Then, too, union members can halt activities through malicious compliance, slowdowns, and other strategies. While the unions argue that they are protecting the rights of their employees, it is also clear that such efforts often play havoc with schedules, can increase costs, and disrupt progress. Leaders are still learning how to work most productively with unions in the federal sector. It requires great skill, creativity, the ability to deal with ambiguity, and the ability to keep the organization's agenda moving forward.

People are the key element in government innovation, and leaders will have to navigate "people issues" wisely and fairly, now and in the future, if the nation's governance is to keep pace with, and more closely reflect, growth and change in the private sector.

Government Performance

The Government Performance and Results Act (GPRA) (1993) may be the progenitor of one of the biggest single changes in the way the federal government works even though it was premised on the belief that "waste and inefficiency in Federal programs undermine the confidence of the American people in the Government and reduces the Federal Government's ability to address adequately vital public needs." The GPRA requires agencies to submit five-year strategic plans for performance improvement to include measurable outcomes. It is still an evolving element within government. In the ten years since its enactment, progress has been slow but sure. There are problems. Kamarck (2003) remarks that agencies rather than individual managers have been held accountable for achieving program goals. Then, too, the identified measurements often quantify results that provide little information as to the real impact the improvement may have had. For example, the U.S. General Accounting Office reported that the U.S. Department of Agriculture (USDA), in attempting to meet the FY 2000 Planned Outcome of "Reducing Hunger and Ensuring Food for the Hungry" saw this result:

> USDA reported continued progress in FY 2000 toward achieving this outcome and that its performance exceeded that of FY 1999. For example, the department reported meeting its goal for distributing food nutrition education information to low-income Americans. USDA's FY 2002 departmental performance plan contains general strategies for achieving this outcome—such as the strategy to "effectively deliver assistance to eligible people" that provides little insight into how progress is to be achieved. (GAO 2001a)

From the data available, it appears USDA did provide food information to a certain number of people effectively, but what impact did that have on reducing hunger? In USDA's defense, such constructs (i.e., reducing hunger) are difficult to measure. This is true of many services provided by the government. Agencies are then reduced to indirect measures that suggest success rather than truly measure bottom-line results. One can review most GAO assessments of GPRA progress and find example after example of performance metrics that are flawed or fail to adequately measure progress toward agencies' goals.

The U.S. General Accounting Office looked at the use of performance-based incentive measures in DOE contracts designed to help improve contractor performance. They found that:

> Despite this progress in implementing contract reforms, it is unclear whether contractor performance has improved. Instead of measuring outcome-oriented per-

formance results, DOE has primarily gauged progress by measuring its implementation of the contract reform initiatives and by reviewing performance measures in individual contracts. Therefore, objective performance information on
overall results is scarce. (GAO 2003a)

As often observed in government performance metrics, they can be well intended yet
misapplied. One must believe that if performance measures are *not* employed it is difficult to demonstrate any actual quantitative progress. Qualitative narrative offers too many
opportunities for inflating actual progress. The real problem may be the confluence between politics and measurement. Agencies tend to pick highly visible goals, and they
may be opting for measures that best meet their political goals. It may be that such goals
do not often lend themselves to rigorous measurement. Then, too, when an agency is
aware they have a continuing problem, they may not choose to measure a goal in ways
that may reveal continuing lack of progress.

The General Accounting Office's assessment of the Department of Defense's (DOD)
Planned Outcome "U.S. Forces are adequate in number, well qualified, and highly motivated," is illustrative:

> DOD's performance measures do not adequately indicate its progress toward achiev-
> ing the outcome of ensuring that U.S. Forces are adequate in number, well quali-
> fied, and highly motivated. DOD's performance measures still do not fully measure
> how well DOD has progressed in developing military personnel or the extent to
> which U.S. military forces are highly motivated. With the exception of the enlisted
> recruiting area, DOD does not identify specific planned actions that it or the ser-
> vices will take to assist them in meeting unmet performance targets in the future.
> Also, DOD's performance report discusses generally the difficulties of the current
> retention environment but the report contains little clear articulation of specific
> actions or strategies being taken to improve future retention. (GAO 2001b)

The government has made some significant strides over the past several years in creating the infrastructure to manage much more effectively. In addition to GPRA, the Chief
Financial Officers Act and related legislation have promoted the use of more stable accounting practices. Agencies are adopting best practices such as cost accounting systems
and labor distribution reporting to better manage resources. Information technology reform has provided a much better environment for information technology acquisition choices
and management. Agencies will be working on evolving and integrating these tools so they
are able to ask and answer a far broader array of business questions than ever before.
Endless hours of staff work will be replaced with one or two brief database queries. Leaders will have enormous amounts of information at their immediate disposal.

However, several issues will have to be addressed before this will be possible. First,
these systems and tools are in the formative stages of development in many cases. They
require an enormous amount of time and resources to implement. Some private industries have taken decades to arrive at systems that finally meet their needs. These systems
and tools are new to government and will take more time to learn to use to best effect.

Then, from a knowledge management perspective, leaders will have to determine what business questions they want answers to in order to configure the systems and populate them with data appropriate to answer those questions. It sounds like a simple proposition but has proved difficult for many organizations, hence the evolution of "knowledge management" as an academic, as well as an applied, field of study. This entire infrastructure must then be integrated into a culture of continuous performance improvement and must be joined at the hip with performance metrics and agency strategic plans and goals. It will take some time for agencies to use these tools with some ease. While it is a high-risk transition, it also promises to transform government management and vastly improve the speed at which government operates.

Many external issues influence performance over the period of a five-year plan—economics, politics, and national and world events. The economy has been weak since March 2000, although, as of December 2003, has shown indications that it may be rebounding. The events of 9/11, the wars in Afghanistan and Iraq, and worldwide terrorism have certainly rearranged everyone's priorities. The national leadership can and does change, as do their priorities. If recruitment and retention were difficult for the Department of Defense in 2001, what effect do unplanned year-long tours of duty in Iraq and Afghanistan do to recruitment and retention in 2004 and beyond? Realities change, and, therefore, what is measured, how it is measured, and the desired results may need to be redefined to meet dynamic new realities over the period of a multiyear plan. Leaders are being, and will continue to be, challenged to define metrics carefully and in ways that attentively balance political goals with true progress on fundamentals of an agency's operation. Even then, last year's results must be examined more in the context of today and tomorrow rather than yesterday. Finally, all the systems, tools, and information infrastructure used to better manage the organization will require constant attention and adjustment to assure they keep pace with changes in the social, political, and economic environment.

Business Management

Beginning perhaps with the publication of John Naisbitt's (1982) *Megatrends* and Peters and Waterman's (1982) *In Search of Excellence* there has been an international trend toward business, government, and social reengineering based fundamentally on competition for economic dominance. In the early 1990s, "re-engineering" and "reinventing" became the themes for improving performance across the spectrum of organizational life. Vice President Gore's National Performance Review, which became the National Partnership for Reinventing Government, stimulated a lot of thinking and action toward streamlining government and creating a more businesslike environment in the federal government. Franchising, fee-for-service, and performance improvement became part of the public lexicon as well as innovative ways of redefining government services. Government began thinking of its stakeholders and customers rather than simply providing services and developing regulations. In many cases government partnered with the industries they regulated to fundamentally change the ways in which government and industry worked. For example, the

Occupational Safety and Health Administration (OSHA) was able to make a shift away from strict regulation and enforcement into, for the most part, a consulting organization (Cullins 1998). It worked with the industries it regulated to have them voluntarily, and with OSHA's assistance, improve health and safety in the workplace. From 1992 to 1996 injuries and illnesses declined steadily using this strategy.

Beyond this kind of progress are some sizable challenges to the vision of federal government operating like a business. One must first recognize that there is a fundamental difference between government and the private sector. Government agencies operate on annual appropriations from Congress that can fluctuate based on competing federal requirements. Thus, many new initiatives generally must come out of existing, redistributed funding. Supplemental appropriations are not uncommon when special needs emerge, but that is the exception, not the rule.

Another vexing problem is the federal budget and budgetary process. The General Accounting Office (2003b) reported that mandatory government programs, programs that are enacted by public law, for example, Medicare/Medicaid, and Social Security, have increased from roughly 26 percent of the federal budget in 1962 to 56 percent in 2002. Concurrently, discretionary budgets, the amount appropriated by Congress to operate government agencies, have dwindled from 68 percent of the federal budget in the same time period to 36 percent. This translates to less money available for new as well as existing programs. Individual agencies are even worse off. For example, in FY 2004, the Federal Aviation Administration's (FAA) fixed mandatory costs (payroll, utilities, rent, communications) are more than 82 percent of the operating budget. Much of the remainder goes to training, travel, contract support, and administrative reforms.

Agency budgets are typically planned two years out. So, if key budget drivers change within that two-year period, agencies may be stuck with planned funding levels, rather than need-based budgets. The timing of budget enactment is also a problem. Often Congress fails to agree on one or more departmental budgets before the beginning of a given fiscal year. When this occurs, Congress typically passes a continuing resolution that allows departments and agencies to operate at the previous year's funding levels until a budget is passed. With some frequency, departments and agencies may operate under a continuing resolution for months. Such delays create difficulties in program planning and execution. So, government agencies do not have the financial flexibility that many for-profit private organizations may have. As a result, performance measures must be adjusted accordingly to reflect new planning and funding realities.

Government agencies are looking at new ways of generating revenue. Franchising allows agencies to charge for certain services and to reinvest 4 percent of earned revenue, primarily from their own or other agencies, into capital improvements. Fee-for-service (Dizard 2002) is growing in the federal government. In some cases this takes the form of a working capital fund. Such funds are used within agencies to fund common needs. Generally, appropriated funds are tapped at the department or agency level before annual budget distributions are made to suborganizations. The Environmental Protection Agency uses a working capital fund for about $125 million in computing services. Suborganizations then have annual use of computer services at no additional expense.

The FAA has a different approach to fee-for-service. It has charged overflight fees for nations flying through U.S.-controlled airspace in the recent past. Currently these fees are not charged due to litigation. Congress has allowed overflight fees by law in FAA's recent Reauthorization Bill but the details of how the process will proceed in the future are still being resolved. Those fees have gone primarily to DOT's Essential Air Services initiative—subsidies that allow remote smaller airports and aircraft access to the larger hub airports. The FAA may expand the use of such user fees in the future, and this will be a model for all other agencies that provide marketable services. The potential for a consistent revenue stream through user fees rather than an annual appropriation is inviting. Getting there will be problematic. Unlike the private sector, agencies must seek approvals from Congress for such actions. Approvals take time and are fraught with legal and legislative entanglements that take years not days or months.

So far such programs have promise but are a source of some concern. Who should be charged and for what? Currently the American people pay for almost all air traffic services. When the FAA first broached the idea of user fees for a broad array of domestic air traffic control services, the agency met with mixed sentiments. The airlines appeared, at the time, indifferent. The impression was they would simply pass along costs to customers. General aviation, the community of private pilots, was much opposed to user fees. They believed that the cost of flying was already quite high, and many felt it would destroy private aviation. So, as leaders look for creative new solutions to funding and managing programs, they will have to partner with stakeholders to help co-create those solutions so that all diverse opinions can be heard and addressed. Then there is a question of partnering. While federal leaders can and should work with their "customers," they must be careful not to compromise safety and regulatory responsibilities in the resulting agreements, policies, and procedures.

The idea that government should operate more like a business is a popular concept and plays well at the highest levels of government and certainly with the American people. Leaders will have to determine the limits of this concept in the federal government. Public service is just that—service to the public. As Paul Light reported in a Brookings Institution survey of federal workers, 31 percent of federal workers indicated that they came to work exclusively for the money. In a subsequent 2002 survey, that number rose to 41 percent. Light reports that 50 percent of private-sector employees surveyed work exclusively for the money, and he notes that "this is one area where federal employees are becoming more businesslike and it's troublesome" (Light 2002). Public service is in danger of losing its gravitas. As leaders choose to move toward more businesslike practices, they should ensure that employees are fully aboard and fully invested as public servants in those endeavors.

Outsourcing

For decades there has been debate about the outsourcing, or contracting out, of much of the work that federal employees perform. It is largely a partisan issue. Pro-labor Democrats want to keep jobs in a government that now has many unions. Pro-business Republicans believe that as many jobs as possible should be contracted out. Outsourcing is a key tenet of the current administration's management agenda. *The President's Management Agenda* includes the following:

> Nearly half of all federal employees perform tasks that are readily available in the commercial marketplace—tasks like data collection, administration, support, and payroll services. Historically, the government has realized cost savings in a range of 30 to 50 percent when federal and private sector service providers compete to perform these functions. (Executive Office of the President 2002)

Needless to say that outsourcing has been, and will continue to be, controversial. It holds opportunity for the business community and is a source of concern for many federal employees. Historically, agencies have been required to use the Office of Management and Budget Circular No. A-76 (A-76) (Executive Office of the President 2003b) process to determine what part of the work that agencies do could be done better and more economically by a private-sector provider. A-76 is a rigorous cost comparison process. Agencies have used it sparingly until recently. It was thought by government employees and private sector interests alike to be a lengthy and cumbersome process until a May 2003 major revision. It is too soon to tell whether the streamlined process will prove a significant improvement. However, the streamlined A-76 process and pressure from the White House and Congress to outsource create a responsiveness dilemma for many agency leaders. They will be expected to support the process. Currently, activity on A-76 studies is elevated but not aggressive. The degree to which outsourcing is pursued will likely be determined by the outcome of the 2004 presidential election.

From their beginnings shortly after September 11, the Department of Homeland Security, and particularly its Transportation Security Administration (TSA), have contracted out their personnel and training services, as well as much of their frontline operational services. The list of contractors working on TSA contracts (USTSA 2003) is a veritable who's who of major technology and service firms. Lockheed Martin has a $350 million contract for airport security. Cooperative Personnel Services has a $554 million contract for recruitment and hiring. Accenture has a $215 million contract for personnel services. And Unisys has a contract with a potential ceiling of $1 billion for information technology development, support, and security. Many of the TSA contracts were let without significant competition. Given the environment of the time, one could argue that such practices were a temporary necessity. However, in the two years since, Congress has noted that there is too much latitude for waste and mismanagement and is reviewing TSA's procurement practices and history.

Many federal employees speculate that the TSA model is one that the executive branch would like to export to other agencies. When one considers the magnitude of the exodus from public service over the next decade, the absence of development programs, lack of any coherent recruitment plans, and lack of attention it appears to be getting from the Bush administration or Capitol Hill, it does appear to be a possible strategy. It is a plausible consideration given the dearth of attention paid to these issues except by academics and think-tank personnel. Fortunately, there is enough diversity of opinion on the subject on Capitol Hill that any attempt to pursue such a strategy would likely be met with considerable opposition.

The Bush administration believes the revised A-76 process will speed up outsourcing. Much of the dilemma centers on what kind of work the government should do and what might be contracted out—a determination of work that is "inherently governmental." The OMB defines this determination as follows:

> An inherently governmental function is a function which is so intimately related to the public interest as to mandate performance by Government employees. These activities require the exercise of substantial discretion in applying government authority in making decisions for the government. Inherently governmental activities normally fall into two categories: the exercise of sovereign government authority or the establishment of procedures and processes related to the oversight of monetary transactions or entitlements. (Executive Office of the President 2003b)

The debate continues over the precise meaning and interpretation of the criteria of the government's definition of "inherently governmental." The government criteria suggest that contractors can do much of the staff work done by federal employees. Often, simply conducting the kind of staff work required demands a broad historical understanding of many agency issues, political considerations, and subtleties a contractor may not possess without several years of exposure. Can they acquire the knowledge? Yes, with time, but how much and how long will a contractor stay? Job-hopping is far more prevalent than it was twenty years ago in the private sector. Most federal employees are careerists and after years of service can be relied on for their corporate memories. Stability is very important in government. Can government afford high annual turnover rates in jobs where a working knowledge of the core functions of an agency is essential to the conduct of it operations? Leaders are going to have to navigate this territory carefully. Clearly, exercising the requisite "discretion in applying government authority" in the A-76 process is an area rife with responsiveness dilemmas. Some managers will wish to protect employees and retain staff and control. It is, conversely, an opportunity to replace a rapidly aging workforce with a younger talent pool of hungry and motivated contractors. Leaders will have to be able to determine which direction is best for their organizations, their agencies, and their departments of the federal government.

Accountability

Accountability is not the federal government's strong suit. A leader is more likely to be moved or removed for a political gaffe than for failure to show results. Many issues that are not in a leader's direct control can have negative effects on schedule, cost, and performance. Often, program delays can be attributed to contractual limits, contractor protests and litigation, and unforeseen glitches in hardware or software, for example. Government executives understand these pitfalls and for the most part appear to allow for readjustments unless there is some direct and major causal error that can be associated with a key functionary.

Accountability is a lynchpin for performance improvement, but few talk about what accountability looks like for government employees. Traditionally, it has meant letters of reprimand, rotation to a different position, pressure to retire, or, in severe cases, removal. The government has not shown significant interest in organizational learning, which can work exceedingly well, particularly in an environment of continuous performance improvement. Agencies of the federal government operate in an essentially political environment—agencies are part of the executive branch and get their funding from the legislative branch. Both branches have high expectations, and, when problems arise in highly visible cases, they sometimes demand specific action, usually of a disciplinary nature against individuals. Agencies are obliged to show that problems have been corrected and parties dealt with in these cases and usually respond accordingly. It is the lesser failures that are often not dealt with.

Accountability has a downside. Leaders who do hold individuals responsible may find themselves as targets for grievances by those they hold accountable. Whether such grievances have merit or not, there is an unwritten rule in government that leaders at all levels must not accumulate grievances. An executive or senior manager with several grievances is often seen as ineffective and can be shuffled to a different or lesser position regardless of the merits of the grievances. Senior managers do not like controversy. As a result, many executives and senior managers avoid grievances carefully or settle them swiftly. Too often this translates into quiet financial settlements or promotions for individuals who mounted grievances based on spurious, retaliatory accusations because they know they can. This is a truth in the federal government that few will publicly acknowledge. It is also almost impossible to document and thus persists. It has a demoralizing effect on other employees and undermines confidence in leaders' abilities and credibility. And, it makes real accountability problematic at times. It is a sinister reality that leaders must face. Do I make frivolous grievances go away, or do I stand up to false or questionable claims when they arise and bear the consequences? In their defense, leaders can be distracted from doing much good by having to attend to multiple personnel issues. Certainly, many, if not most, grievances are legitimate. But some see the process as a way toward promotion or a quick and sizable financial "pay-day." It is an issue requiring conscious attention.

The notion of collectively looking at mistakes and learning from the experience, organizational learning, is not a new concept, but it has not been widely embraced by the bureaucracy. Senior program managers still miss deadlines and schedules go unmet, but generally no one is held accountable in ways the private sector uses as a matter of course. In the current pay-for-performance environment, pay increases are based on organizational and individual performance, but generally the amounts in question will not likely dramatically increase performance. Instead, it will likely cause widespread dissatisfaction.

A definition of organizational learning suggests that it can be useful in the emerging transformational, integrated data systems, performance-driven government of tomorrow. Dixon defined organizational learning as "the intentional use of learning processes at the individual, group and system level to continuously transform the organization in a direction that is increasingly satisfying to its stakeholders" (1994, 5). While malfeasance and other illegal activity must be punished, leaders should explore accountability strategies for lesser infractions that are more consistent with progressive management. Organizations would benefit by beginning with organizational learning. The practice of organizational learning goes well beyond accountability, however. When applied properly it can be a powerful tool for managing the organization.

Globalization

We live in a very dynamic world today. It is more one world than it was even ten years ago. People move about the planet at will. We are all connected via the Internet. Global markets are inextricably linked. Globalization is a reality. Those who fight it will be met with failure at every turn. It will do nothing but progress. Leaders will have to find ways of making it fair, equitable, and positive in our country and in the world. Leaders must be mindful of the implications of policy setting. For example, Chinese products have flooded our national marketplace. While less-expensive, quality merchandise is desirable, what problems might that create for us later? As China grows into a much stronger regional economic and political power, they will also grow technologically and militarily. While there have been major reforms in China over the past twenty years, it is still a totalitarian, communist state with pronounced human rights issues. China has made known its desire to formally reincorporate Taiwan into the People's Republic. Leaders should be asking what effects our economic policies, in fact all our national and international policies, will have on the United States, regions of the world, and the global community of nations. We tend to focus on one international problem at a time, for example, Afghanistan and Iraq. Leaders may need a more unified political and economic international policy on globalization. This is not simply an issue for Congress or the executive branch. Individual agencies, individual states, and business and industry need to deal with other countries on a myriad of issues such as economic development, business and industrial development, and many kinds of international assistance. Leaders will have to work cooperatively with their international counterparts to help assure that we are collectively working, to the greatest possible extent, to improve international conditions and make globalization positive, particularly for the poorer nations of the world.

Electronic Government

Electronic government or "e-government" is clearly the future for many of the services that the federal government provides. Much can and has been done to use Internet technology to provide such services. "The Official Web Site of the President's E-Government Initiatives" (USGSA 2003), or "e-gov," catalogs fifteen major initiatives across the government in nine agencies. Three will be discussed below to acquaint readers with the kind of information and services currently available. FirstGov.gov, is perhaps the best known of the sites and is managed by the General Services Administration. It is essentially a single portal to sites in state and federal government, the District of Columbia, and to U.S. territories. Six million people access the site each month. E-training, according to the e-gov Web site, says it is "considered the number one most visited on-line training site in the world" (USGSA 2003). And, IRS Free File provides access to on-line tax preparation and filing. Few could argue that such services save time and money and improve access to government for our citizens.

There is another side to electronic government. It results in job loss—a by-product likely to expand in the future. The Internal Revenue Service (Gruber 2004) announced it would involuntarily separate 2,400 employees because electronic filing had eliminated positions that, heretofore, were processing filings manually. Virtually all agencies now have Web sites that provide general information about the agencies' missions and services and often more specific information. As more and better integrated data becomes available and e-gov initiatives proliferate, there will likely be commensurate reductions in jobs. Whether this is a positive or negative eventuality probably hinges on one's source of employment. Most federal employees would likely prefer to keep their jobs. Contractors most likely find the proposition attractive.

It makes sense to decrease the cost of government through automation where possible. It will be left to government leaders to manage e-gov responsibly and to make good business decisions. It is also important to treat federal employees fairly. Retraining federal employees for other jobs should be the choice of first resort. If no positions are available, then they should be helped through comprehensive outplacement programs. E-government is a very positive development in the federal government. Leaders will have to examine their needs and make reductions in force decisions related to e-gov initiatives carefully so as not to tarnish e-government's image. There is also a potential danger in dehumanizing government services. Most of us bristle when we call organizations for information and get annoying and lengthy recorded messages and must navigate our way through multiple recorded options. Business and industry can perhaps afford to raise our ire. The federal government cannot.

IMPLICATIONS FOR PROGRESSIVE LEADERSHIP

Contemporary federal leadership must include even more attention to the political, economic, and social context in which we find ourselves in the new millennium. Leaders must be savvy about ideas and people, but also about relationships across organizational and agency boundaries and the politics of those relationships. Good judgment must be tempered with political realities at times. Many of the leadership challenges discussed in this chapter are recent concerns. Some have been around in one form or another for some time. These challenges are all complex, difficult problems that demand complete understanding of the problems themselves, a vision of how they should be dealt with at the agency level, astute political skills and understanding, and followership of a high order.

The National Commission on the Public Service (2003), commonly referred to as the Volker Commission, was formed to assess the state of public service. Their published findings and recommendations include structural changes to government organizations, realigning the Senior Executive Service, and improving the measurement of government performance. Many of their recommendations are bold and creative, such as reorganizing departments and agencies into a limited number of executive departments with very specific missions. The commission made the following recommendations on leadership in government:

- The President and Congress should develop a cooperative approach to speeding and streamlining the presidential appointments process.
- Congress and the President should work together to significantly reduce the number of executive branch political positions.
- The Senior Executive Service should be divided into an Executive Management Corps and a Professional and Technical Corps.
- Congress should undertake a critical examination of "ethics" regulations imposed on federal employees, modifying those with little demonstrated public benefit.
- Congress should grant an immediate and significant increase in judicial, executive, and legislative salaries to ensure a reasonable relationship to other professional opportunities.
- Congress should break the statutory link between the salaries of members of Congress and those of judges and senior political appointees.

These proposals are leadership challenges in their own right. While it is difficult to disagree with such an esteemed body, these challenges will be very difficult to accomplish concurrently with the leadership challenges discussed throughout this chapter. The commission proposes radical change in a period of economic instability, competition for fewer resources, and turbulent national and international times. Perhaps what is needed for now is a measured attack on the key challenges of which we are already aware. If solutions can be found for some of the critical challenges in the current system, government can be made to work better. If creative solutions cannot be found, the problems may be more political than administrative.

The above leadership challenges: people, government performance, business management, outsourcing, accountability, globalization, and e-government, will not be resolved or addressed by restructuring and reorganizing, although there is a lot of new and progressive thinking in the Volker Commission report. Aberbach and Rockman (2000) point to the "web of politics" that faces federal managers and leaders. The fabric of our government and the structure of governance have grown increasingly political in nature. Leaders are keenly aware of others' agendas and tend to business based on that influence. While this is not inherently a bad thing, it can be situationally bad for individual agencies. Many of the issues discussed in this chapter stand unresolved because they are across-the-board political agendas rather than reasoned and well-thought-out managerial agendas. Leaders can lose their professional compass and instead follow others' agendas in the name of politics and the furtherance of their own careers. It is a conundrum faced by every leader in government at one time or another.

Our form of government and its administration are among the best in the world. It was designed to be cumbersome so that decisions would be made with considered thought and attention at multiple levels. Debate and alternate perspectives have been hallmarks of the democratic process. We have perhaps swung too far into the realm of political leadership vs. managerial leadership. Perhaps the federal government's biggest challenge is leadership itself.

REFERENCES

Aberbach, J., and B. Rockman. (2000). "Responsiveness Dilemmas." In *In the Web of Politics: Three Decades of the U.S. Federal Executive*, 87–99. Washington, DC: Brookings Institution Press.
Barr, S. (2003). "Uncle Sam May Want You, but Do You Want Uncle Sam?" *Federal Diary, Washington Post*, April 21: B2.
Cullins, R.F. (1998). "The Promise and Practice of the National Performance Review." In *Accountability and Radical Change in Public Organizations*, ed. R.R. Sims, 145–165. Westport: Quorum Books.
Dixon, N. (1994). *The Organization Learning Cycle*. Berkshire, UK: McGraw-Hill.
Dizard, W.P. (2002). "EPA Gets Grip on Fee-For-Service Accounting." *Government Computer News*, July 15. www.gcn.com/21_19/manager/19272–1.html.
Donahue, J.D. (1999). *Making Washington Work*. Washington, DC: Brookings Institution Press.
Executive Office of the President. Office of Management and Budget. (2002). *The President's Management Agenda, FY 2002*. www.whitehouse.gov/omb/budget/fy2002/mgmt.pdf.
———. (2003a). "The Government Performance and Results Act of 1993, Sec.2, (a) (1)." www.whitehouse.gov/omb/mgmt-gpra/gplaw2m.html.
———. (2003b). Circular no. a-76. www.whitehouse.gov/omb/circulars.
Gruber, A. (2004). "IRS Announces Major Overhaul, Layoffs." *Government Executive* (January). www.govexec.com/dailyfed/0104/010704a2.htm.
Halberstam, D. (1972). *The Best and the Brightest*. New York: Random House.
Herzberg, F., B. Mausner, and B. Snyderman. (1959). *The Motivation to Work*. New York: Wiley.
Kamarck, E.C. (2003). "Public Servants for Twenty-first Century Government." In *For the People*, ed. J.D. Donahue and J.S. Nye, 134–151. Washington, DC: Brookings Institution Press.
Kouzes, J.M., and B.Z. Posner. (1995). *The Leadership Challenge*. San Francisco: Jossey-Bass.
Light, P.C. (2002). "A Workforce at Risk: The Troubled State of the Federal Public Service" (briefing, Brookings Institution, Washington, DC, June 2). www.brookings.edu/comm/transcripts/20020627.htm.
———. (2003). Measuring the Health of the Federal Public Service. In *Workways of Governance*, ed. R.H. Davidson, 90–120. Washington, DC: Brookings Institution Press.
Naisbitt, J. (1982). *Megatrends: Ten New Directions Transforming Our Lives*. New York: Warner Books.
National Center for Policy Analysis, Idea House. (1998). www.ncpa.org/pd/unions/aug98c.html.
National Commission on the Public Service. (2003). *Urgent Business for America: Revitalizing the Federal Government for the 21st Century* (January). www.brookings.edu/gs/cps/volcker/reportfinal.pdf.
Palus, C.J., and D.M. North. (2002). *The Leader's Edge*. San Francisco: Jossey-Bass.
Peters, T., and R. Waterman. (1982). *In Search of Excellence*. New York: Warner Books.
Tobias, R.M. (2000). "Job Satisfaction Has Market Value." *Government Executive*, May 27. www.govexec.com/features/0600/0600manage.htm.

United States Department of the Treasury, Internal Revenue Service, Newsroom. 2004. *IRS Plans New Steps to Improve Operations, Shift Jobs to Front-Line Positions* (January 7). www.irs.gov/newsroom/article/0,,id=119136,00.html.

United States Office of Personnel Management. (2000). *Demographic Profile of the Federal Workforce.* www.opm.gov/feddata/demograp/table10.pdf.

United States General Accounting Office. (2001a).*Report to the Ranking Minority Member, Committee on Governmental Affairs, U.S. Senate, Department of Agriculture, Status of Achieving Key Outcomes and Addressing Major Management Challenges* (GAO-01–823). (August), www.gao.gov/new.items/d01761.pdf.

———. (2001b). *Report to the Ranking Minority Member, Committee on Governmental Affairs, U.S. Senate, Department of Defense, Status of Achieving Key Outcomes and Addressing Major Management Challenges* (GAO-03-98). June. http:www.gao.gov.

———. (2003a). *Performance Accountability Series: Major Challenges and Program Risks* (GAO-03–100), Department of Energy (January). www.gao.gov.

———. (2003b). *Major Management Challenges and Program Risks: A Governmentwide Perspective* (GAO-03–95). http://www.gao.gov.

United States General Services Administration (USGSA). (2003). *E-Gov and IT Accomplishments.* (November) www.whitehouse.gov/omb/egov/about_glance.htm.

United States Transportation Security Administration (TSA). (2003). Business Opportunities, *Contractor Fact Sheet.* www.tsa.gov/public/display?theme=27.

Zaccaro, S.J., and R.J. Klimoski. (2001). *The Nature of Organizational Leadership.* San Francisco: Jossey-Bass.

CHAPTER 10

THE ACHIEVEMENTS AND CHALLENGES OF MILITARY LEADERSHIP

CHRISTOPHER TAYLOR

MILITARY LEADERSHIP

The historical achievements and ongoing challenges of military leadership are both glorious and sometimes tragic. Throughout the history of warfare, there are stories of triumph and defeat, of life and death, and of personal sacrifice, self-discipline, and selfless service. There is something different about the warrior profession, and, in a warrior community, it is the responsibility of everyone who has served, is serving, and will serve to protect those values that make the profession at arms separate from other professions. But *why* is this profession so different? What makes these achievements and challenges different from others? It is because the very nature of warfare demands that the individual marine, sailor, soldier, or airman subordinate his own personal welfare to that of the welfare of the many; the security of the nation, even at the risk of his own life, and the very specific trust given him by citizens. The achievements of the world's militaries have been realized through the hard work of ordinary men and women who have lived and died serving their nations. In many cases they carry the scars of war: lost limbs, nightmares, chemical illness, and post-traumatic stress disorders. In every case, the experience has changed them forever.

TOP-DOWN OR BOTTOM-UP VIEW?

Usually, a retired three- or four-star general or admiral, or a very "salty" colonel writes on military leadership. They have had successful careers and time to reflect on their own leadership experiences, and how those experiences shaped both their military and post-military lives. That will not be the case in this chapter. I spent thirteen years as a United States Marine and left with the rank of staff sergeant. A bottom-up view seems more appropriate considering the level at which I served. With that in mind, my view on the achievements and challenges of military leadership may lead you to the same place, just using a different path.

In order to celebrate the achievements of military leadership, one must first understand what it is.

WHAT IS MILITARY LEADERSHIP?

For centuries, historians, teachers, political figures, and others have used military leadership and leaders as examples of what a leader can accomplish (Taylor & Rosenbach 2000).

> The United States Army defines leadership as "influencing people by providing purpose direction, and motivation while operating to accomplish the mission and improving the organization." (FM 22–100 Army Leadership "Be, Know, Do")

Movies about World War II, Korea, Vietnam, and Somalia have added to the image of military leadership. We generally show great respect and deference toward successful military leaders because they have defended our country and our way of life. Generals and admirals conjure up visions of battlefield glory, of stoic decision making, and of loneliness. The roles of John Wayne in *In Harm's Way* or Gregory Peck in *12 O'Clock High* are classic examples, but more recently, movies such as *Saving Private Ryan*, *Band of Brothers*, and *Blackhawk Down* have detailed the leadership experience at the lowest levels. What is it that makes the military brand of leadership seemingly different from other forms? If you were to ask a general, you would receive one answer, and if you were to ask a sergeant, you might get another. In any case, several true differentiators put military leadership in a class by itself. Some of those differentiators are: (Malone 1983)

1. *The commander for whom a new soldier, sailor, airman, or marine will serve has no say in the interview or selection process.* Service members are assigned to units based on a military occupational specialty (MOS) and the needs of those units. Commanders do not get to run "want ads," and there are no draft days or trades to be made. You get what you get, and you have to develop those people to the best of your abilities (and theirs) in support of unit goals.

2. *Service members have signed a contract.* Not only have they signed a contract, but they have signed one for three, four, or six years. You cannot fire them (except through a court-martial), and you cannot lay them off. Conversely, they are not allowed to strike or quit. And it is an unlimited contract, with a requirement that you may have to risk or lose your life in the defense of your country.

3. *Military commanders have a much greater personnel turnover rate.* Because of the enormity of the services, the burden of personnel management can be nearly overwhelming. While there are reenlistment bonuses, they are not generally designed to keep a person in a particular unit, but rather to stay in a particular job or MOS. Just as it seems you have assembled a great team, it is time for one or more of your key players to rotate to another unit or end their service contract.

4. *Service members are a lot younger at all levels of responsibility than are their counterparts in business.* The average age of a service member is twenty-one. A young corporal or sergeant is responsible for, and to, between four and thirteen direct reports. A young staff sergeant can lead as many as forty. The very numbers of people require a true commitment to leadership.

5. *Military commanders have more power than any civilian boss does.* Commanders can fine, restrict, and put service members in jail depending upon the infraction. The Uniform Code of Military Justice (UCMJ) is far more restrictive than civilian law. A civilian worker who misses a week's work without authorization will likely be docked the pay or be fired, but not put in jail or restricted to his home for a month.

6. *Military commanders' responsibilities to their troops do not end at 5 o'clock each day.* A commander is accountable for and responsible to the people he leads twenty-four hours per day. Civilian bosses do not get calls at 2 A.M. about car accidents, an employee's family problems, or unit activations.

7. *Military commanders control the time of the people they lead twenty-four hours per day.* There is no overtime granted, there is no eight-hour workday, and there are no guaranteed weekends off in the military. You simply work until the mission is accomplished.

Perspective here does matter because it is important to detail the subtle and not-so-subtle differences between military and civilian leadership to establish a baseline for comparison.

To a young corporal who is a fire team or squad leader, the concept of leadership is quite black and white. It is about right and wrong, good and bad, and honor and dishonor. The simplicity of these choices guides the young military leader in his every action. The noncommissioned officer who takes his job as a junior leader seriously will vehemently defend a choice made based on these simple contrasts, and do so loudly (Taylor and Rosenbach 2000). In many cases, young military leaders serve as the example of the basic tenets of good leadership and remind us of our beginnings in the profession at arms. Dependability, decisiveness, integrity, justice, and knowledge are leadership traits learned in boot camp and applied every day by a leader at the "eyeball" leadership level, where the work takes place, and where the troops get dirty (Malone 1983). Granted, it is easier for the young military leader to live the core values because he does not yet have to deal with the organizational and strategic political pressures that enter into the decision-making equation for a general or admiral, but the example is what matters.

Some of the services have distilled what they inculcate into three words that express their core values. For the Marine Corps and Navy, these are "honor, courage, commitment" (U.S. Marine Corps 1995) and for the Army, they are "be, know, do" (U.S. Army 1999). Young military leaders particularly make use of these values in their decision-making processes, and openly refer to them when justifying various choices they have made. There is a great lesson in this: If you are a service chief, make sure you understand the values by which you are asking your warriors to live, because they will live those values, and they will live them with pride and audacity.

Three-word value statements are wonderful reminders of the actions all military leaders should strive to perform daily, but in order for these statements to mean anything, they must be supported by specific scholarship of the set of values that are the foundation of the military organization that they serve.

There are many traits that are developed continuously in young and old military leaders alike, and some would debate a list of basic traits, but following are those that should be included on any list.

> *"Success in battle is not a function of how many show up, but who they are."*
> General Robert H. Barrow

Character

Character is that nearly all-inclusive trait that defines the person. While there certainly exist those with bad character, here we are concerned with good character. The development of character begins in the home, and should be complemented in school and polished through life experience. The military leader with good character seeks and accepts responsibility, admits when he is wrong, and takes responsibility for his actions (Taylor and Rosenbach 2000). He gives credit to the people who have successfully executed the plan, he is loyal until honor is at stake, he is humble yet forceful, and fair in all his dealings, and he puts the mission and troops before himself. If his everyday actions are guided by these principles, then all those around him are drawn to him, respect him, admire him, and seek to emulate him because they know he is a true leader. If this is true, then he will naturally be referred to as a "person of character" and therefore will engender trust and commitment even on the toughest days, because at the eyeball level of leadership, character is that which is observed, not lectured. It is the prolonged observance of sound character that leads to successful early character development in young military leaders.

Discipline

For a young marine recruit, "discipline" is defined as "the instant and willing obedience to all orders." This concept can be realized only if the leader asking for the discipline is disciplined herself. If a commander expects instant and willing obedience but has yet to get her hands dirty, and is living in far better conditions than the troops, she may find that her demand for instant obedience meets with a lackluster response. Certainly, the majority of young leaders will rally the troops to carry out the orders given even by a poor leader, but it will not be because they respect the person giving the orders. Rather, it will be because they see themselves as "keepers of the gate" and they believe in the organization and will look beyond the current environment to support its goals and values (Taylor and Rosenbach 2000). In that case, who demonstrates the greater discipline, the leader or the led? However, the leader who through every action shows an unwavering commitment to mission accomplishment and troop welfare (concurrent with mission accomplishment) never suffers this problem. She further creates an environment whereby the time gap between order and action is reduced to instant obedience, which can mean lives saved on the battlefield.

In a letter to John Banister of the Continental Congress from Valley Forge, General George Washington wrote,

... without arrogance or the smallest deviation from truth, it may be said that no history now extant, can furnish an instance of an Army's suffering such uncommon hardships as ours have done, and bearing them with the same patience and fortitude. To see men without clothes to clothe their nakedness, without blankets to lie on, without shoes, by which their marches might be traced with the blood from their feet, and almost as often without provisions as with; marching through frost and snow, and at Christmas taking up their winter quarters within a day's march of the enemy, without a house or hut to cover them till they could be built, and submitting to it without a murmur, is a mark of patience and obedience which in my opinion can scarce be paralleled. (Library of Congress—April 21, 1778)

In that same spirit, the 1st Marine Division some 180 years later at the "Frozen Chosin" Reservoir, in subzero temperatures, fought eight Chinese divisions for seventy-eight miles through the mountains of Korea in a breakout to the sea and safety. Even with the 8 to 1 odds, the marines brought out every piece of equipment and all wounded, and nearly all of the dead.

The leader who demands discipline must first have self-discipline and understand the hardships he puts on his troops. He must seek to support them in their mission in every way possible. He understands that no plan is successful unless executed properly and that to be successful, the discipline of good men who first believe in their leader is necessary.

Courage

Both moral and physical courage are required for a military leader to be successful and provide the proper example to young leaders. There are countless examples of physical courage through the history of warfare. Read any Medal of Honor, Navy Cross, or Distinguished Service Cross citation and you will see someone who demonstrated tremendous physical courage. At the eyeball level of leadership, the standard for courage is the act that risks life or limb for the sake of others (McCain 2004). Courage, a subtrait of character, is a trait that develops over time (Taylor and Rosenbach 2000). Physical courage is supported by physical fitness and an awareness of one's physical capabilities, but there is no guarantee that a physically fit person will choose to engage in a courageous act. Confidence does grow out of physical fitness. Examples of moral courage may be no fewer, but far less documented. Moral courage takes the military leader to the crossroads of decision making. In many cases, it presents the dilemma of deciding among a range of bad options. Sometimes moral courage forces a leader to take a course of action that will cost lives no matter what. The right decision, such as to hold a position rather than fall back, may be the right moral decision, but may be very costly in lives. Alternatively, it may force a leader to decide between what is right and what reflects personal gain or loss. It is this split-second decision that will both send a message to those around him and set the tone for future decision making. In any event, a lack of moral courage in the military leader can needlessly cost lives. One life lost is too many, let alone thousands of lives.

For those who lead in the military, it is demanded that moral courage take center stage. A commander who fails the test of moral courage instantly mutes his personal and professional growth, and everyone in the troop will see it, because they see everything. Where does a morally courageous decision reside? First, it is in the planning, where decisions and actions can be debated to some degree and where it is the responsibility of all involved to ask questions and offer alternatives that accomplish the mission and reduce the risk of life. Moral courage also lives in those situations on the battlefield where planned action diverges from necessary action. Small-unit leaders invariably are placed in a position where they must near-instantly decide to pursue an alternate course of action to achieve a stated goal. If a commander issues orders that clearly put the mission and troops at unnecessary risk, should a subordinate leader alert the commander to such risk? The answer is a resounding yes. All leaders should be taught that speaking up in such a situation is not just encouraged, it is their obligation. To do less is a failure of moral courage on the part of a subordinate. Moreover, should a leader scold or ridicule the subordinate who brings up such matters in good faith, the leader must expect never to receive the potentially valuable counsel of his subordinates again. For any leader, honest feedback is invaluable and such open discourse between the leader and the led has saved countless lives. Only recently has the culture in the military really allowed for such an open exchange of this nature.

An example of moral courage can be found in Marine Corps history. Brigadier General "Red Mike" Edson, recipient of the Medal of Honor and two Navy Crosses, demonstrated that he was willing to forgo his own advancement for what he believed was right (U.S. Marine Corps 1995). He had spent more time overseas in World War II than any other marine officer and was thought to be a strong candidate for commandant. However, after World War II, there were "Armed Forces Unification" hearings, which debated whether to combine each of the services into one. Edson felt strongly against the unification and wanted to speak out about it because it would affect the way wars were fought forever. To avoid bringing criticism upon the Marine Corps, he *retired*. He was about to be recommended as the next commandant, but he retired because he felt it his obligation to pursue what he thought was right rather than what was best for his career. It is said that this act was the greatest contribution to the unification deliberations. We should all be so strong in moral courage (U.S. Marine Corps 1995).

Commitment

It is the spirit of determination and dedication that leads to professionalism and the mastery of the art of war (U.S. Marine Corps 1995). It is the willingness to endure sacrifice to achieve a standard of excellence in all endeavors—both in life and the profession at arms. It is the trait that drives the warrior to learn and embody all the other leadership traits, no matter the cost. That commitment begins with the oath taken by all service members; another difference between military and civilian leadership. Read the oaths below, and ask yourself whether something similar would be well received or enforceable in the business world.

OATH OF OFFICE

I, _____, do solemnly swear (or affirm) that I will support and defend the Constitution of the United States against all enemies, foreign and domestic; that I will bear true faith and allegiance to the same; that I take this oath freely, without any mental reservation or purpose of evasion; and that I will well and faithfully discharge the duties of the office on which I am about to enter. So help me God.

OATH OF ENLISTMENT

I, _____, do solemnly swear (or affirm) that I will support and defend the Constitution of the United States against all enemies, foreign and domestic; that I will bear true faith and allegiance to the same; and that I will obey the orders of the President of the United States and the orders of the officers appointed over me, according to the regulations and the Uniform Code of Military Justice. So help me God.

Taking the oath is but the beginning of commitment. Captain Sam Gibbons demonstrated his commitment on D-Day in Normandy, 1944 (U.S. Army 1999).

Prior to the amphibious landings at Normandy in June 1944, the 82nd and 101st Airborne divisions parachuted in and were horribly blown off course. Paratroopers found themselves lost in unfamiliar countryside and spent the night searching for their comrades and their units so they could push to their respective targets. These soldiers had been trained well, and through discipline and initiative and a clear understanding of the mission, were able to recover. How could this happen under such trying circumstances? Because every soldier had been trained to act instead of waiting to be told what to do. This is the essence of military leadership: decentralizing command to the lowest levels to enable that direct level to operate regardless of the circumstances.

A young officer, Captain Sam Gibbons of the 505th Parachute Infantry Regiment massed together twelve soldiers from different units and proceeded to liberate a tiny village which turned out to be outside the divisions' area of operations. He then headed south to his original objective to destroy a bridge nearly fifteen kilometers away with the same group of soldiers and no demolitions equipment. He later remarked, "This certainly wasn't the way I had thought the invasion would go, nor had we ever rehearsed it in this manner." Nonetheless, he gathered soldiers and moved to his objective. Why go if you do not have the tools to do the job? Because in combat, you find a way to accomplish the mission, and there is no hope of that if you are not on the objective. Stories like this were reported throughout the countryside. Soldiers were doing what soldiers do—move to the target and accomplish the mission.

Honor

This is the quality that embodies the soul (U.S. Marine Corps 1995). It is the moral compass by which we live. It is the ultimate in ethical and moral behavior: to never lie, cheat, or steal, and to hold oneself to the highest standard of integrity. Honor is living up to the oath taken upon entry into the military, and it is actionable; doing what is right. It belies a compassion for human life and dignity and demands the warrior be accountable for all actions, whether someone is watching or not. It is the beacon by which others will guide their actions, and it should be perpetually defended. They do not call it the Medal of *Honor* for nothing. Just ask Jimmy Howard (Malone 1983).

Staff Sergeant Jimmy Howard was a platoon sergeant with C Company, 1st Reconnaissance Battalion. This was the early days of the United States' involvement in Vietnam, and Howard's team was sent to Hill 488 west of Chu Lai to stem the advance of the North Vietnamese. Howard landed with fifteen Marines and two Navy corpsmen. For two days, the platoon called in artillery and air strikes on the enemy positions and was doing a good deal of damage. The North Vietnamese felt the pain and moved a *battalion* of 250 men to Hill 488. This was reported by an Army Special Forces unit. Headquarters radioed to Howard and suggested he exfiltrate, but Howard believed he had one more day before he would need to do that. He was wrong.

Knowing he was to be attacked, Howard briefed his men, reinforced his position, and waited. At about 2200 (10:00 P.M.), one of the Recon Marines slowly lifted his weapon, pointed it toward a bush, and fired. The bush reeled back and thrashed not twelve feet away. Other Marines joined in, threw grenades, then scrambled back up the hill to the main perimeter. As they ran, grenades detonated all around them and small arms fire followed. The other listening and observation posts also made their way back to the perimeter. In that initial barrage from the enemy, every Marine and Corpsman was wounded. The North Vietnamese followed this with a well-coordinated attack. In some cases, they were but twenty feet from the Marines. Realizing his situation, Howard called headquarters for an immediate extraction. He was told he would have to wait until morning. He again briefed his men, but was unsure as to how they would react. They reacted with the resilience and courage that Recon Marines have been demonstrating for decades; they fought harder. When both sides took the time to regroup, it was under a moonless sky. As the night went on, North Vietnamese soldiers began to yell at the Marines, "You die in one hour Marine!" The Marines asked Howard if they could yell back. He told them to yell whatever they wanted, and they cut loose with phrases not fit to print here. In another instance, when the North Vietnamese would yell, the Marines simply laughed at them aloud, and the Viet Cong went silent. Here were fifteen Marines and two Navy Corpsman, outnumbered 20 to 1, and they were laughing at the enemy.

At about 0100 (1:00 A.M.), an Air Force flare ship radioed to Howard. Howard talked them in, and when they dropped the first flares to illuminate the area, the Marines were awe-struck. There were hundreds of North Vietnamese all around them. One Marine recalled that it looked as if an anthill has blown apart.

With the light, American gunships and jets swooped down on the North Vietnamese and engaged. Unfortunately for Howard, he and his men were desperately low on ammunition. To make each round count, the Marines would throw *rocks* into the bushes. The enemy would think it was a grenade, run into the open, and be shot with one round by a Marine, a great tactic that worked repeatedly.

The Marines fought through the night. At about 0300 (3:00 A.M.), headquarters heard Howard's radio go dead, and feared the worst. The radio went dead because Howard had been shot in the back and was unable to move his legs. Even in this condition, Howard directed his Marines. He encouraged them, telling them they need only make it to daylight and their fellow Marines would arrive. Indeed, that was true. As daylight broke, an infantry company landed in helicopters. One of the helicopters was shot down. It wasn't until noon that the reinforcements reached Jimmy Howard's position, and when they did, Howard and his men had only eight rounds of ammunition between them. EIGHT!

Resilience, confidence in one's training and leadership, and courage, when set as the daily example lead to accomplishment of the mission even in the face of overwhelming odds. Jimmy Howard's story proves it.

This is but a basic list of essential traits (and examples of those traits in action) the military leader must possess to be effective in both peacetime and war. The absence of any one of these leaves a gap in the defense of a unit. Poor leadership is a cancer that spreads through an organization, and it can potentially cost lives. The leader who practices each of these traits may never be written about in the annals of military leadership but will always be respected in the hearts of the men and women he or she leads and serves.

In all of this, military leadership resides at different levels (U.S. Army 1999). First, it exists at the "direct" level, that is, the level where soldiers, sailors, airmen, and marines fight. In the enlisted ranks, this is typically from private to staff sergeant (pay grades E-1 to E-6) and in the officer ranks, from lieutenant to captain (pay grades O-1 to O-3). Past the direct level is the "organizational" level, where leaders influence hundreds or thousands of service members. These leaders have staffs that support the warriors at the direct level. Finally, there is the "strategic" level, where the military service chiefs and their civilian leaders cooperate to create sound policy, allocate appropriate resources, and provide a vision for the future. We will explore these in more detail.

Direct leadership is the leadership that occurs at the eyeball level. Where a fire team leader trains his team, a squad leader trains his squad, a platoon commander leads his platoon, and a company commander employs all of them in support of a battalion operation. Of course, there could be any combination of the above, but from the battalion level (roughly 600–800 warriors) down, operations are conducted in direct contact with the enemy, where the rubber meets the road, so to speak. In direct leadership, men and women quickly see what works and what does not, and learn how to maneuver and attack "on the fly" because of their relative proximity to the enemy. In peacetime operations, direct level operations provide a think tank, a training center, a crucible where young leaders study, make mistakes, and learn. It is at this level where the warrior is trained for war, and where personal growth and confidence flourish. As a young marine corporal, I was first privileged to lead a fire team (four marines), then a squad (thirteen marines), a rifle platoon (forty marines), and then a security platoon (ninety-six marines). In those first five years, I learned more about leading people than at any other time. Why? Because I had leaders who allowed me to actively find myself, make mistakes, and learn from them.

Therein is the challenge to the young military leader. It is not merely having the experience, but what you do with it as you grow. I was twenty-five years old and had up to ninety-six young marines for whom I was responsible. Where else does one get that kind of responsibility but in the military?

Organizational leadership (U.S. Army 1999) generally begins at the regimental level and continues to the highest operational level, although there is some overlap between the higher echelons of the organizational level and the strategic level. The leadership skill set is the same at the organizational level as at the direct level, but it differs in degree. Organizational leaders deal with greater complexity, more uncertainty, more people, and a greater number of unintended consequences. While there is more direct leadership at the lower level, organizational leaders more often influence their people through policy making and systems integration than through face-to-face contact. It is imperative that organizational leaders leave the office to see what effect their policies have on the people who implement them. It is also imperative to do a gap analysis between the information the staff provides and what is actually happening, better known as "ground truth," because, ultimately, it is the person whose name has "commanding officer" or "commanding general" after it who is both accountable for and responsible to the men and women being led.

Strategic leadership (U.S. Army 1999) occurs at the highest levels of the government and the military. The level of uncertainty and responsibility is greatest at this level, and the policy making here affects global politics. Strategic leaders may not see the fruits of their labor on their own watch in the organization. Because the decisions of strategic leaders may reach hundreds of thousands to millions of people, the demands of the job require them to develop fully the subordinate leaders around them. "Sanity checks" are required daily, and skilled subordinate leaders are necessary to give strategic leaders the feedback they need to make good policy decisions. Leadership at these levels demands men and women of exceptional decision-making ability and forward thinkers who deal well with uncertainty at any level.

The very nature of military service affords both junior and senior leaders the chance to develop and hone leadership skills. The integration of these three levels of leadership must be seamless to achieve the goal: fighting and winning wars.

ARE MILITARY LEADERS BORN OR MADE?

> *"The essence of loyalty is the courage to propose the unpopular, coupled with determination to obey, no matter how distasteful the ultimate decision. And the essence of leadership is to inspire such behavior."*
> Lieutenant General Victor A. Krulak

Ah, yes, the age-old question: Are great leaders born or made? This one question and the exploration of its answer have been sources of income for many an author, a remarkable number of whom have never served (or led), but rather are academics who observe, but have never felt the heat of battle or the challenge of life and leadership in the hard school of the warrior. There seems to be a desperate quest to show clearly that leaders are either born or made, but that is a fool's journey. The answer to the question is "both."

Much of what makes a leader good is the same as what makes a person good. Those skills are first built in the home, starting at a very young age. However, beyond that, recruit training and officer candidate school (OCS) seek to inculcate into future leaders the traits discussed earlier in the chapter and have achieved amazing success in doing so. Many are the mothers and fathers who have seen their troubled or unfocused children leave home for boot camp or OCS and return as truly changed people. The U.S. Marine Corps touts the transformation with audacity and pride, and its battle history cements the claim. While each armed service has different criteria for its recruits, the basic premise is the same: to strip away the pseudo-individualism that seems so safe for young people and to replace it slowly with an ethos of honor, courage, and commitment to one's country, to selfless service, to fellow service members, and finally to ones self—one's *new* self.

Millions of people happily tell the story of who they were before the military and who they have since become. There will always be people who are not suited for the profession at arms, but in general, it can be said that the reinforcement of "right and wrong" in the various recruit training commands serves to enhance positive personality traits and diminish those that are negative. In this format, leaders can be "made" or the "natural leader" can be improved. From examples of courage, honor, and commitment, junior leaders learn what is expected of a good leader (U.S. Marine Corps 1995). What they choose to do with those examples when given the opportunity to lead is the measure of the esteem they accord the leaders who taught them and who have been their examples. This is where an individual's character development over the course of his life and his willingness to accept a higher calling can help ensure that he will carry out this commitment.

Military indoctrination offers another valuable experience: followership. No leader can reach his full potential unless he has the opportunity to follow another's direction. The experience of followership inevitably allows the future leader to see the result of both great and poor leadership and the effects of both on an organization. It is simply indispensable. Once someone has followed, he will better understand how to plan, motivate, guide, and mentor—and how to lead with passion. Again, this can all be "made."

Beyond the art of leadership, there is the related art of battle command (U.S. Marine Corps 1995). A born leader, or perhaps better said, one who receives her early leader training at home at a very young age, is one whose abilities allow her to see the battle more clearly and faster than another. She quickly ingests and processes information, and makes decisions with little time and incomplete information. She is the one who surpasses the baseline of leadership. She is the one who leads from the heart rather than mechanically following a philosophy. This is where character and commitment to service collide and catapult a good leader to the ranks of a great leader. A "born" leader more readily identifies opportunities to destroy the enemy before he destroys you, she understands the battlefield three and four moves ahead, but can maneuver in any direction when the flow of the battle changes. Does this make her a better leader? Yes, but it does not make the "made" leader a bad leader. This is why the answer to the question,

"Are military leaders born or made?" is that they are both born and made. Continually raising the baseline of leadership for everyone and achieving goals makes leadership better as a whole, but there will always be those who have some advantage physically, mentally, or spiritually, and this will spring them to the top by consensus. That should be embraced so long as opportunity is available to all, because you never know at what stage a "made" leader realizes she is a "born" leader.

Born or made is not the point. Nearly all aspiring leaders arrive at their initial formal leadership training with some inherent leadership traits, based on their home life, school, sports, boy scouts, and so forth. It is the goal of military leadership training to hone these fledgling traits into the traits of a capable military leader. Among those, some will have the ability and may be afforded the opportunity to become capable and respected combat leaders—Chesty Puller, Red Mike Edson of the Raiders, Manila John Basilone, and Bill Hawkins all come quickly to mind. And among those, a very few might have the ability to become higher level combat commanders, the Grants, Lees, Eisenhowers, Pattons, Bradleys, and Vandegrifts of history.

Leadership traits have been identified as the key elements to success on the battlefield. The military leader *should* be defined precisely by these traits (and others). If a leader lives these traits, then he by definition is a good leader. However, opportunity plays a significant role in the development of leaders. Those who are in the right place at the right time, and who are successful (but perhaps no better in leadership skills than those who have yet to realize an opportunity) are almost always rated higher and promoted to further command or to a staff position. Those promotions provide the opportunity to develop more skills that prepare them for even higher-level command in the future. Luck—defined by some as "when opportunity meets preparation"—seems to be involved. If this definition is true, then luck can be controlled to some extent. Accepting challenging assignments, committing to a lifelong professional education program, and living the core values of the military continue the development of the military leader and will provide greater opportunity.

Military leaders *must* be both born and made. There is the subtle inference of a baseline of leadership when someone is called a leader, and perhaps even more so, when someone is called a "born leader." The military model offers the opportunity for growth so that all may explore which category they fall into, but in the end, the question is pointless. If continually practiced, the leadership traits and principles listed in this chapter can establish anyone as a leader with whom anyone else would be proud to serve. It is not the quest to define military leadership that should consume our time, but how to develop and sustain it.

As a testament to the success of military leadership, consider the following two incidents, which occurred just after the bombing of the Marine barracks in Beirut in October 1983. As the media swarmed upon the bombed barracks, a young lance corporal was sifting through the carnage desperately searching for his friends, his fellow marines and sailors. He was approached by reporters and barraged with questions. "Should the United States be here? Are you scared? Should the Marine Corps be here?" This young lance corporal's response was, "I am a United States Marine, where else should I be? If anyone should be here, it should be marines" (U.S. Marine Corps 1995). In another instance, a young marine named Jeffrey Nashton was in the hospital after the bombing, and he was unable to hear much and had been temporarily blinded. Then Commandant General P.X. Kelley leaned over his hospital bed and said something to the marine. With reporters looking on, and unable to speak, the young marine reached up, felt the four stars on his commandant's collar, and motioned for something with which to write. He wrote, "Semper fi," Latin for the Marine Corps motto, "Always faithful."

These two stories demonstrate the effect good leadership can have from top to bottom in an organization. The young marines mentioned above had no other concern but their brother marines, their corps, and to be true to their oaths and the nation.

Historical examples are not the only examples to which we can turn. The following is a very recent heroic example of honor, courage, and commitment in action.

Operation Iraqi Freedom, 2003

On May 13, 2004, Lance Corporal Joseph Perez was awarded the Navy Cross, the nation's second highest award for valor, for his actions on April 4, 2003.

While operating as the "point man" as a member of Company I, 3d battalion, 5th Marines, 1st Marine Division, I Marine Expeditionary Force, Lance Corporal Perez's platoon came under heavy enemy fire. As the point man of the lead squad, he was the most exposed member of the platoon. Taking the majority of the fire, he responded without hesitation and immediately engaged the enemy with his rifle and concurrently directed the fire of his squad. He led a charge down a trench from which the enemy was firing, threw a grenade that neutralized the trench, and then fired an AT-4 (84mm man-portable anti-tank weapon) into a machine gun bunker, destroying the enemy. These actions allowed his squad to close with the enemy and secure their position. As he continued to lead his squad, he engaged the enemy with precision rifle fire, but was wounded in the shoulder and torso. Despite his serious injuries, Lance Corporal Perez directed the squad to take cover, and further directed their fire onto the enemy, allowing the squad to reorganize and destroy the remaining enemy.

The importance of this story and the thousands like it is that it illustrates that military leadership's culmination and ultimate measure of success are revealed in what junior leaders do while under fire. In this case, Lance Corporal Perez continued to lead even though he was wounded. He directed his squad efficiently, and, when it came down to it, he was willing to sacrifice selflessly for them. Even though he was injured, his team had been trained and led so well that in the heat of battle, they understood the intent of the mission and were able to carry on and accomplish it. Therein lies the true testament to military leadership.

The Challenges of the Twenty-first Century Military Leadership

> *"If we wish to think clearly, we must cease imitating; if we wish to cease imitating, we must make use of our imaginations. We must train ourselves for the unexpected in place of training others for the cut and dried. Audacity, and not caution must be our watchword."*
> J.F.C. Fuller

In the past ten years, the operations tempo of the military has increased dramatically. More and more, service members are called away for duty as the mission set for the military grows. Whereas decades ago the call was made in time of war, today's military is called on to perform peacekeeping missions, humanitarian actions, drug interdiction, and to provide protection at the Olympics (Taylor and Rosenbach 2000). During this incredible expansion of missions, the military was reduced by a substantial amount and new technology was introduced, which required extra training time before deployment, further reducing the time service members could spend with their families. This stepped-up pace puts a strain on military families and creates retention problems.

These changes have also affected recruiting efforts. As technology improves in the military, the services must attract recruits who can master that technology and contribute to its ultimate evaluation. Further, recruiters today are faced with greater challenges because they are now competing with a society that has distanced itself from selfless service and moved toward more profit, more self-wealth, and less personal interaction. Each service must deal with officer retention issues. In this technological age, there is a greater demand from the private sector for intelligent, disciplined, well-trained young men and women who have had great leadership experience. The private sector pays well, and even though there has been great volatility in the job market over the past five years, and job security is not guaranteed, young officers have families and they realize the value they add to private-sector companies, especially defense contractors, so the lure of more money and less hours away from home is tempting.

All of these things demand a supplemental set of leadership skills and behavior for those who would command in today's military. While honor, courage, commitment, integrity, selfless service, and character will always remain at the forefront of required traits, a subset may include strong cognitive skills, the ability to deal with ambiguity, intellectual flexibility, self-awareness, and a better understanding of organizational behavior and climate. This subset can greatly enhance the ability of a leader to influence people and to gain collective commitment to the unit goals, and to operate under the most trying of circumstances, all the while making the unit stronger.

Why is this subset so important? The intellectual demands that technology places on warriors in both training and war will compound the stress on battlefield decision makers, and thus leadership will even more determine who wins and who loses (Taylor and Rosenbach 2000).

In order to prepare tomorrow's commanders to efficiently and effectively lead, the services must continue to provide career-long educational opportunities that support the needs of service members, but also close the gap between new technology and current skill sets. Along with continuous educational opportunities, there must be more opportunities for younger leaders to take on responsibility at varied levels, and efforts to identify the "stars." As we have said before, this may not be altogether fair to late bloomers, but by providing more opportunities, more leaders get the chance to prove themselves and compete fairly for the finite promotions and advanced schooling billets that will take them to the next level of leadership.

A further challenge to each of the services is to ensure that techniques for evaluating and assessing individuals and groups and units are innovative. An example might be 360-degree feedback (Taylor and Rosenbach 2000). While at first glance this may seem too cumbersome for an organization like the military, the corporate world has proved its effectiveness when implemented properly, and thus far, no company has gone out of business from using this technique. Through better assessment techniques, the needs of individuals and units can be met, resulting in a stronger and more focused unit.

Perhaps the greatest challenge to the military is dealing with the inherent perception of tension between troop welfare and mission accomplishment, and maintaining a warrior mentality while paying attention to cognitive and organizational needs in developing leaders. In peacetime, the superficial contrast between troop welfare and mission accomplishment is often seen as making the troops feel better (i.e., sleeping in a warm barracks or some extra time off) versus staying in the field one more night in the freezing rain and training to standard. This is not, nor should it ever be, the stated choice. Troop welfare and mission accomplishment can be seen as the same in this case. In the preparation for war, there can be only one criterion for troop welfare and that is to train every soldier, sailor, airman, and marine to his or her fullest potential so that they succeed as warriors on the battlefield. Curiously, this is sometimes seen by junior service members as a lack of caring for their well-being. This could not be further from the truth. As a leader of warriors, the primary metric for determining troop welfare is survival on the battlefield and all the preparation that comes with that.

Continually instilling the warrior spirit—the "can do" at all costs spirit that has served our great forces for over two hundred years—must now be enhanced with those supplemental skills of creativity, embracing change, agility, and self-awareness because the battlefield, the people who fight on it, and the weapons used have changed, and these skills are paramount for any leader to successfully win battles.

Finally, military leaders will have to better understand the role of the media in future operations. During Operation Iraqi Freedom, the world was given unheard-of access to the front lines through embedded reporters. For the most part, this was good for the military, because it clearly portrayed the conditions under which our service members fought and it gave Americans an opportunity to better appreciate the men and women who serve in uniform. However, embedded media, near-unlimited access and technology can also swiftly depict a breakdown in leadership as seen by the Abu Ghraib prison scandal. Thousands of pictures, video, and hundreds of reports gave the American people and the world a view of poor leadership that affected policy, may have contributed to kidnappings and beheadings, and allowed us to catch a glimpse into the unprecedented abdication of responsibility throughout the chain of command, and the subsequent lack of accountability, except at the lowest levels. While Abu Ghraib continues to be investigated, the media's ability to disseminate the incident to the world so quickly clearly poses a challenge to all levels of military leadership as to how to effectively respond to immediate and powerful scrutiny from the government and citizens.

EPILOGUE

"The time always comes in battle when the decisions of statesmen and of generals can no longer effect the issue and when it is not within the power of our national wealth to change the balance decisively. Victory is never achieved prior to that point; it can be won only after the battle has been delivered into the hands of men who move in imminent danger of death."

S.L.A. Marshall

Military leadership has been and most likely will be the most intensive leadership training anyone can receive. In the military, leadership training is ingrained at all levels through education, example, and opportunity. The achievements of military leadership can be debated, but what is true is that it has given us a free and democratic society, it has given back to that society people of moral and physical courage, audacious decision makers, precise planners, and selfless public servants. It has created a subset of society that has been prepared to "fight fires" (Weick 1996), that is, to react aggressively to unforeseen circumstances with wisdom, innovation, effective communication, and an intellectual flexibility that allows a free-flow of simultaneous approaches and adjustments, to solve the problem quickly, minimizing the attack, and confounding the enemy (U.S. Marine Corps 1995). It is these men and women who have held steadfast to a set of core values even when society's moral barometer has slipped, and temptation to follow is great. It is in these young and not-so-young leaders that we have helped sustain our way of life and provided a shining beacon from which the world can fashion their own freedom and democracy. It is in these exceptional men and women that we will continue to grow and evolve as a society. Finally, it has given the opportunity to lead where other sectors cannot. Military leadership decentralizes the decision-making process to the lowest levels (U.S. Marine Corps 1995), making direct-level leadership stronger, therefore making organizational and strategic leadership stronger.

Four simple rules have helped bring about stellar military achievements (Katzenbach and Santamaria 1999):

1. Overinvest at the outset in inculcating core values.
2. Prepare every person to lead, including frontline troops.
3. Attend to troop welfare, first as it applies to winning battles, then as it pertains to social needs.
4. Use discipline in a positive manner to instill pride.

Military leaders should strive to create leadership "muscle memory." That is, they should daily practice the fundamental tenets of leadership, live the core values, and continually educate themselves until leadership is so ingrained it may be considered natural behavior. Only then will the leader be able to improvise freely and successfully exploit both his full potential and that of the men and women he leads (Pagonis 1992).

Figure 10.1 **The Army Leadership Framework**

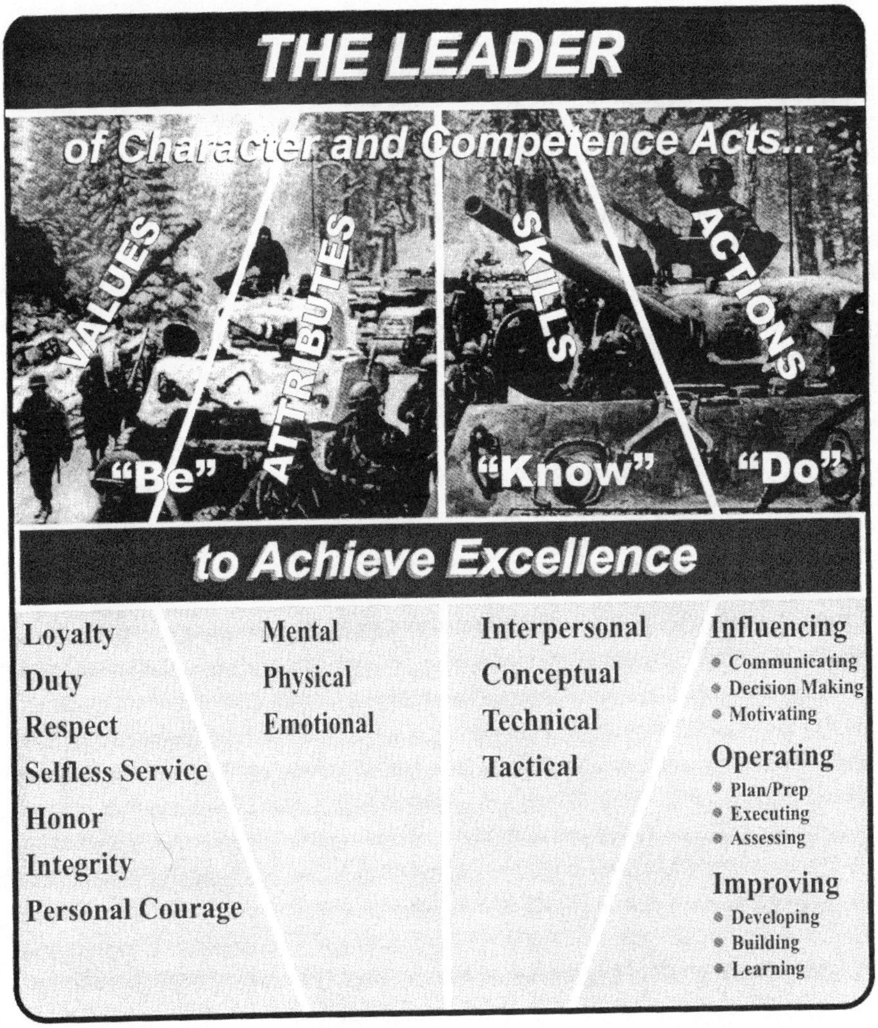

My thirteen years as a marine changed my life. In that time, I was allowed to take chances and make mistakes, then given the opportunity to learn from them. I was held accountable for my actions and for those of the men I led. As I approached the top of one leadership level, I was shown the open door to the next. At every step, I had leaders who led with pride, courage, unselfishness, compassion, and a firm hand when necessary. The benefit to me was personal growth, the patience to consider all perspectives, a honed set of leadership and decision-making skills, and a newfound passion to live by a set of values that can help change any organization, and the world. One person can make a difference, but a whole lot of people can make a whole lot of difference, and no greater leadership training ground can be found than in the military. (See Figure 10.1 for an example of one military branch's leadership training framework.)

REFERENCES

Barrow, R.H. (General) (1981). Remarks Given to the Pennsylvania House of Representatives on June 2, 1981.

Fuller, J.F.C. (1936). "Generalship: Its Diseases and Their Cure." Harrisburg, PA: Military Service Publishing.

Katzenbach, J., and Santamaria, J. (1999). "Firing Up the Front Line." Cambridge, MA: *Harvard Business Review.*

Krulak, V.A. (Lieutenant General) (1986). "A Soldier's Dilemma." Quantico, VA: Marine Corps Gazette.

Malone, Dandridge M. (1983). "Small Unit Leadership—A Commonsense Approach." Toronto, Canada: Presidio.

Marine Corps Warfighting Publication 6–11. (1995). "Leading Marines." Washington, DC: U.S. Marine Corps.

Marshall, S.L.A. (1978). "Men Against Fire." Gloucester, MA: Peter Smith.

Pagonis, W.G. (1992). "Leadership in a Combat Zone." Cambridge, MA: *Harvard Business Review.*

Taylor, R.L., and R.E. Rosenbach. (2000). "Military Leadership—In Pursuit of Excellence." 4th ed. Boulder, CO: Westview.

U.S. Army Field Manual 22–100 (1999). "Army Leadership—Be, Know, Do."

Weik, K. (1996). "Prepare Your Organizations to Fight Fires." Cambridge, MA: *Harvard Business Review.*

Washington, G. (1778). "A Letter to John Banister of the Continental Congress: April 21, 1778." Valley Forge: Library of Congress.

CHAPTER 11

LEADERSHIP CHALLENGES IN EDUCATION

Improving Administrative Decision Making

SERBRENIA J. SIMS AND RONALD R. SIMS

Education will continue to be a major priority for enhancing political, social, and economic objectives for most people in the United States and around the world. With this in mind, the challenges for today's educators and educational leaders are vast and therefore require a systematic approach to achieving a satisfactory solution. Educational leaders must become adept at monitoring local, state, federal, and global environments in order to accurately forecast political and social problems that will impact their school or school system. This chapter discusses a systematic approach in the form of the balanced scorecard, which the authors believe will allow educators and educational leaders to best respond to ever-changing and demanding challenges. Before discussing the balanced-scorecard approach and its application to educational systems, the chapter will first take a brief look at seven trends that will have an impact on schools and educational leaders in the coming years.

TRENDS IMPACTING SCHOOLS AND EDUCATIONAL LEADERSHIP

The educational environment has experienced rapid change over the past few years, and there are increasing signals of more change on the horizon. Educational leaders have offered numerous perceptions of problems expected to plague the educational system in future years. Seven of the many trends that will have an enormous impact on schools and educational leadership are discussed below. These trends are: student achievement, funding, teacher quality, accountability and standards, student body composition, technology, and educational choice.

Student Achievement

There is an increased mandate for educational leaders to enhance student achievement in schools. David Perkins and colleagues at Harvard Project Zero introduced the concept of Smart Schools to guide student achievement. The Smart Schools concept is based on two guiding beliefs. The first belief is that learning is a consequence of thinking, and all students can learn good thinking. The second belief is that learning should include deep understanding, which involves the flexible, active use of knowledge. These two principles provide a structure for schools with a vision of a learning community that produces students who are critical thinkers. This vision serves as a starting point for strategically managing obstacles that could impede educational achievement. There are seven key principles in a Smart School:

- *Generative Knowledge.* Educational leaders must carefully scrutinize disciplinary and interdisciplinary content to determine what is most beneficial to students.
- *Learnable Intelligence.* It is expected that students will learn ways of thinking that can boost their performance. Therefore, the integration of higher order thinking skills into all subject matter is critical.
- *Focus on Understanding.* Emphasis is placed on student work that requires the student to demonstrate deep understanding in contrast to rote memorization and narrowly defined objectives.
- *Teaching for Mastery and Transfer.* Teachers must use techniques such as modeling, scaffolding, and concept mapping to help students bridge what they already know to new concepts. This will increase the likelihood that students will learn new concepts and use them in their day-to-day lives.
- *Learning-Centered Assessments.* Assessments should function as a reflective and evaluative tool for learning that creates an environment in which students take on the responsibility for their own learning.
- *Embracing Complexity.* Learning situations must be created that will enable students to build skills and tolerance for complex situations and problems.
- *The School as a Learning Organization.* Schools should be places of growth for students as well as for faculty and administrators. All members of a school's community should be involved in the process of goal setting and monitoring; thereby creating a dynamic educational system that responds to change in a positive, proactive manner (Presidents and Fellows of Harvard College 2003).

Funding

The projected deficit in the U.S. federal budget could range from $2 trillion to $4 trillion. The result will be the absorption of the education budget by local taxpayers as contributions from the state and federal government dwindle. This will make it difficult for state and local educational budgets to fund needed construction of new schools, increase staffing, and meet the short- and long-term objectives of the No Child Left Behind Act (Cetron and Cetron 2004) signed by President Bush in January 2002. Educational leaders must fund more and more initiatives with less and less money.

Teacher Quality

Educational leaders must continue to focus their attention on teacher quality and the shortage of qualified teachers available for employment. In today's society, teachers are expected to know more and be able to do more than their predecessors, oftentimes with less pay. Therefore, many college-age students are electing not to enter the field of teacher education, which has resulted in an aging teacher workforce. Educational leaders must manage ways to attract and retain qualified candidates to the teaching profession. Why is this important? Darling-Hammond (2000) discusses the correlation between teacher qualification and student achievement. She explains that in states such as North Carolina and Connecticut, where efforts to upgrade the quality of teacher preparation, teacher quality, and test-based accountability were implemented, scores on the National Assessment of Educational Progress had increased significantly.

Accountability and Standards

The No Child Left Behind Act significantly strengthened the federal government's role in K-12 education. Prominent components of this act include:

- Raising student achievement for all students.
- Closing the achievement gap.
- Revising standards that require that states hire only "highly qualified" teachers.
- Raising reading proficiency of young children in K–3.
- Utilizing research to support new programs and practices.
- Raising the amount of federal funding to support high quality professional development and teachers in the classroom.

In order to execute these reforms, states will be required to implement reading and math assessments in grades 3–8 and at least once during grades 10–12 beginning in the 2005–6 school year. In addition, by school year 2007–8, all students must be tested in science at least once. These tests must be aligned with state academic standards, must produce results that are comparable from year to year, and must show whether students are meeting state standards, and the results must be reported widely. If these requirements are not met, penalties will be imposed (ETS 2004).

Student Body Composition

More school divisions can expect a dramatic increase in the number of school-age children over the next two decades, resulting in the need to hire more teachers. At the same time, the demographic makeup of the population of school-age children will change. Over the next twenty years, it is expected that a decline in white students will occur, African-American and Native American student populations will remain steady, Asian Americans will increase from 4 percent to 6.6 percent, and the Hispanic population will increase by 60 percent. In addition, many students will be returning to school to pursue new interests. It is predicted that today's students will pursue an average of five occupations during their lifetimes, resulting in a continuous need for advanced training after normal school hours. In addition, more adults are electing to participate in lifelong learning to remain healthy and energetic during retirement.

Technology

Advances in technology (primarily computers and the Internet) are driving change in the workplace. For a good career in almost any field, computer competence is becoming mandatory. Ongoing training for teachers and education administrators will be mandatory in order for them to keep pace with rapid advances in technology fields. Additionally, educational leaders must find ways to make sure schools are state-of-the-art technologically (e.g., wired and staffed appropriately).

Educational Choice

Although a controversial issue, educational choice will continue to be a driving force for educational change. Educational choice or vouchers are financial incentives that parents can use to pay for their child's education at a school of their choice either private or public. Supporters of vouchers see them as a way of restoring choice to parents to give their children a better education than they might receive in their neighborhood public school. On the other hand, opponents see vouchers as a way to undermine public education by competing for needed resources (ETS 2004). In either case, it appears that more or less educational choice is a trend that will test schools and educational leaders for years to come.

In addition to the seven challenges identified above, school leaders must continue to balance, forecast, and respond to the continuous demand of creating students who are critical thinkers and creative individuals. The complex environment in which educational leaders must work necessitates a fundamental shift toward a logical, systematic approach to managing problems. In this context, the concept of strategic management and its underlying principles has come to be seen as the launching pad for excellence, and the balanced scorecard as the solution.

THE BALANCED SCORECARD: WHAT IS IT? AND CAN IT HELP EDUCATIONAL LEADERS?

The balanced scorecard is a customer- and performance-based, results-oriented strategic management system first introduced by Robert S. Kaplan and David P. Norton in 1992 in an effort to assist companies in tracking financial progress while monitoring other areas identified as necessary for growth. A balanced scorecard enables employees, managers, stakeholders, and the public to focus on an organization's performance outcomes and the relationship between the underlying strategies that are deployed to achieve those outcomes. In addition, the balanced scorecard is a planning and process improvement system aimed at focusing and driving the change process. The basic idea behind the balanced scorecard, as developed in the private sector, is that indicators of financial performance, by themselves, are not enough to analyze and determine an organization's ability to achieve its goals. In the public sector, this translates into the idea that a narrow focus on program outcomes does not tell the full story on the agency's ability to achieve its stated objectives or policy (Texas Education Agency 2004).

The balanced scorecard is a set of measures designed to examine an organization's performance from four perspectives:

1. Measuring organizational business unit or departmental success.
2. Balancing long-term and short-term actions.
3. Balancing different measures of success:
   a. Financial.
   b. Customer.
   c. Internal operations.
   d. Learning and growth.
4. Tying strategies to measures and actions.

Simply put, the balanced scorecard is a customer-based planning and process improvement system aimed at focusing and driving change processes. It does this by translating strategy into an integrated set of financial and nonfinancial measures that both communicates the organizational strategy to the members and provides them with actionable feedback on attainment of objectives.

The balanced scorecard satisfies the individuals who are comfortable with financial or quantitative measures and serves the needs of those responsible for change that are concerned with the drivers that affect future performance. The balanced scorecard measures focus on key aspects of operations, for an organization, a subunit, or even an individual. For each organizational unit or level, the approach involves identifying several key components of operations establishing SMART (Specificity, Measurability, Attainability, Relevancy, and Time-sensitivity) goals for these, and then selecting measures to track progress toward the goals. In doing so, the measures as a whole provide a holistic view of what is happening inside and outside the unit or level so that each participant can see how his or her individual activities contribute to the overall mission. In addition, tying rewards to these measures motivates greater efforts toward their attainment.

At the organizational level, the balanced scorecard typically would include at least the following four components, though the exact number and nature would depend on the organization's specific goals and circumstances (Kaplan and Norton 1996a):

1. Customer perspective: How do our customers see us?
2. Internal business perspective: What must we excel at?
3. Innovation and learning perspective: Can we continue to improve and create value for our customers?
4. Financial perspective: Do we get the best deal for our school system?

Each of the four perspectives is linked to the others and is the vehicle to aligning change strategy and realizing the vision. Figure 11.1 shows how these components, or

Figure 11.1 **Balanced Scorecard: Strategic Perspectives**

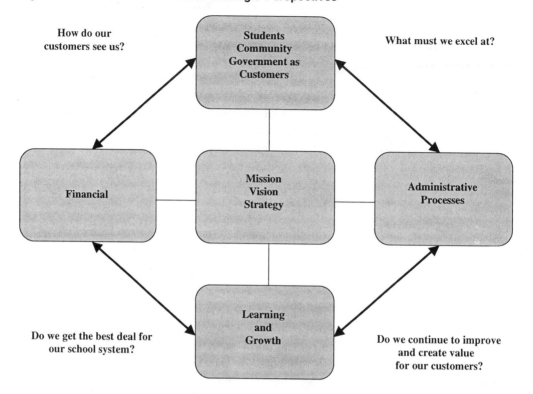

perspectives, interrelate to provide an integrated picture of the organization. The customer perspective tracks how well the organization is meeting the expectations of its customers, because they are the ones who pay for its costs and provide its profit. This perspective does not end with identifying current needs, but demands anticipating what customers may require in the future. The internal business perspective focuses on the internal processes that will deliver the objectives related to satisfying current and future customer demands. This perspective expands the focus beyond just improving existing processes to defining a complete internal process value chain. The emphasis of the innovation and learning perspective is the organization's ability to sustain and increase its ability to satisfy customer demands. Finally, the financial perspective tracks how well the organization is translating its operational results into financial well-being. More will be said about these in the next section.

Over the past decade, a considerable number of articles and books have discussed the balanced-scorecard approach in the for-profit sector (see, for example, Kaplan and Norton 2000; Berkman 2002). More generally, writers on the subject have reported that the balanced scorecard has been found to provide the following major benefits across the range of users:

1. Promoting the active formulation and implementation of organizational strategies;
2. Making organizational strategies updated and highly visible;

3. Improving communication within the organization;
4. Improving alignment among divisional and individual goals and the organization's goals and strategies;
5. Aligning annual or short-term operating plans with long-term strategies;
6. Aligning performance evaluation measurement and long-term strategies.

Though a wide variety of for-profit organizations have benefited from using the balanced scorecard, only a few applications by educational institutions have been reported to date. The balanced scorecard increases the likely success of a school or school system change effort as it assists educational leaders and others in communicating a change strategy or plan to key stakeholders. School or school system change strategies or plans may look nice in the end, but they simply are worthless and will increase the likelihood of failure of a change effort unless they impact the stakeholders who must execute the plan. A balanced scorecard provides educational leaders with a vehicle to counter four barriers to school or school system change execution:

1. *Change vision barrier.* No one in the school or school system understands the change strategies or plans.
2. *Stakeholder barrier.* Most stakeholders have objectives or interests that are not linked to the change strategy or plan of the school or school system.
3. *Resource barrier.* Time, energy, and money are not allocated to those things that are critical to the school or school system change effort. For example, budgets are not linked to school improvement or change, resulting in wasted resources.
4. *Administration barrier.* Administration spends too little time on change strategy or plan and too much time on short-term tactical decision making.

Using the four perspectives in the balanced scorecard allows the administrator to take a systems view of a school or school system and avoid taking a myopic view of a planned change initiative.

DESIGNING A BALANCED SCORECARD FOR A SCHOOL: AN IMPLEMENTATION MODEL

Assuming that one is convinced that the balanced scorecard can be useful to educational leaders as they face multiple challenges and school or school system change initiatives over the next few years, how does one go about implementing it? Answering this question requires attending to two subordinate issues: what specific items to include in the scorecard, and what development and implementation process to use. As these issues are discussed in the next two sections, attention should be given to establishing goals and strategies for achieving the goals. The goals of an organization are its self-determined purposes or tasks. They generally address what is being satisfied, who is being satisfied, and how they are being satisfied. On the other hand, strategy is a plan or method of achieving stated goals. It is a plan to strengthen the organization's position, satisfy customers, and improve performance. Strategy is the method of achieving the organization's goals in a competitive, accountable focused environment.

Assuming that of all the stakeholders with an interest in K–12 education, principals (of course, other school stakeholders such as teachers could also be queried) should have thought as much as anybody about the change and other challenges to schools and strategies for meeting them. Thus, an appropriate first step would be to undertake a survey of these school leaders on the subject. One suggestion would be to develop a two-part questionnaire or survey to be completed by the principal. The first part should provide an explanation of the balanced scorecard and its four typical perspectives, or components. The second part should contain five blank tables, each with one column for goals, and another for measures. The first four tables should be named after the four typical perspectives. The fifth should be unlabeled, so respondents can introduce perspectives that they believe to be important. The respondents should also be invited to change the first four tables' labels to ones that they consider more appropriate. For each perspective, the respondent should be asked to identify up to five goals that he or she believes a school should have, and for each goal, one or more relevant performance measures. There also should be several demographic questions.

To reduce clutter once data are gathered from respondents, common terms should be used to capture responses of similar content. These terms should be developed through a process of discussion and consensus between those individuals responsible for analyzing the survey data. Tables 11.1 through 11.4 provide samples of some suggested goals and related measures for the four typical perspectives.

An important consideration in the grouping process should be preserving the richness of the responses. Items (especially goals) that seem to contain subtle differences should be kept separate (e.g., "maintain high quality programs" versus "academic excellence"). A brief overview of each of the components is offered below.

Customer Service

The customer perspective tracks how well the organization is meeting customers' expectations. In Table 11.1, sample suggestions are grouped in four subsections. The first subsection focuses on the stakeholders and reveals a broad view of who the schools' "customers" are. They include students, the public (government, taxpayers, etc.), the teachers, and parents. A wide range of goals is suggested for each of these stakeholders. Relating to students, for example, suggested goals range from developing high quality students to improving student admissions to college and employment.

The remaining three subsections summarize goals and measures that apply across multiple stakeholders. For example, "academic excellence" (from the second subsection) and "reputation of school programs" from the third subsection) are potentially relevant to students and their families as well as to teachers and the community.

Table 11.1

Sample School Principals' Suggested Goals and Measures for the Customer Perspective

Goals	Measures
The stakeholders: Students, public/community, teachers, and parents	

1. Students

Goals	Measures
Student quality	• Quality of teaching and advising • Pre-post tests • GPA over time • Curriculum quality
Graduate high-quality students	• Quality and appropriateness of each student's knowledge upon graduation • Quality of teaching and advising • Quality and timeliness of placements/admissions (both employment and college) • Outcomes assessment (1, 3, 5 years after graduation) • Quality and no. of colleges recruiting students • No. of students employed upon graduation
Admission of students in colleges/universities	• Admission rate • Survey of colleges/universities • Standardized test scores (SAT, ACT) • Quality of colleges/universities where admitted • Scholarships
Student satisfaction	• Dropout rate as % of students • Student retention (nonfailing) rates • School academic climate • No. of complaints or positive sentiments reported • Direct current student survey of satisfaction • High graduate exit surveys • Alumni retroactive ratings of their experience

2. Teachers

Goals	Measures
Teacher satisfaction	• Teacher ability to participate in those decisions affecting them • Encouragement given teachers to engage in developmental activities (e.g., relevant professional development—support to take additional courses, attendance at professional conferences) • Effectiveness of orientation and inculcation process, for new teachers • Availability of well-defined personnel policies and procedures available to teachers • Comfortable classroom, teachers' lounge, and technology support • Administrative support of teachers

3. Parents

Goals	Measures
Parental satisfaction	• Satisfaction with student's education/learning experience • Response to surveys

(continued)

Table 11.1 *(continued)*

Goals	Measures
	• Focus groups
	• Participation in school-sponsored activities
Quality programs: Quality of students and teachers, quality of teaching	
Academic excellence	• Quality of students—standardized testing, PSATs, etc.
	• Quality of teachers—% with masters/certifications
	• Community surveys
	• Retention rates of students
	• College admission rate of students
	• Number of graduates
	• Accreditation status
	• Self-evaluation reports
	• Awards for academic excellence
Teaching quality	• How teaching skills are perceived by students and parents
	• Qualifications of faculty
	• % of certified teachers
	• Student evaluation of teachers
	• Parent evaluation of teachers
	• Focus on up-to-date teaching practices
	• Innovative teaching strategies
Curriculum	• Students' understanding of course/program objectives
	• Variety of teaching and learning methods
	• Use of technology in the classroom/learning
	• Curriculum integration across disciplines
	• Alignment of curriculum with assessments
	• Character/citizen development component within curriculum
A teaching focus	• Student-teacher ratios
	• Rewards for good teaching
	• Percentage of budget devoted to teacher development
Program and teaching innovations	• Quality of instruction
	• Quality of advising/counseling
	• Extracurricular activities
Public image: Value added of programs, reputation of school	
Seen as providing "value" for the funds allocated/per student costs	• Student and parent perceptions
	• Cost per student compared to other schools
Reputation of school	• Employment rates of high school graduates
	• State and national rankings
	• Internal survey of students
	• Accreditation
	• Reputation among peers and stakeholders
	• Acceptance of former students in colleges/universities
	• Number of students receiving scholarships
	• Discipline reports

Outstanding customer/ school image	• Graduation rates • College/university admission rates • Quality of colleges/universities accepting students • Recognition of teachers • Reports from key public groups
Quality service and continuous improvement	
Service to the school/ system	• Adequacy of participation in schoolwide activities • Quality of relationships between administrators, teachers, parents, support staff, and others
Quality of support services	• Ease of communication • Extent that student advising/counseling and administrative processes are student-centered, effective, and efficient • Adequacy of library for students • Responsiveness of support personnel to assisting in meeting student's needs

Internal Business Perspective

The internal business perspective focuses on how well operations are satisfying customer demands (see Table 11.2). The suggested goals and measures focus on different aspects of operations and are presented under five subheadings: teaching/learning experience; curriculum/program excellence and innovation; quality and currency of teachers; efficiency and effectiveness of service; and strategic issues. Again, the wide variety of suggested sample goals and measures indicates the scope of issues that might arise from a survey and could be considered along with the potential responses to them as part of a school improvement or change effort.

Innovation and Learning Perspective

This perspective emphasizes the organization's capacity to sustain and increase its ability to both satisfy customer demands and improve process efficiency and effectiveness. In Table 11.3, sample principals' suggestions are grouped into two subsections: teaching/learning excellence and innovation and quality service and continuous improvement. In the first subsection, the suggested goals are related to the teachers, technology, programs, and curricula as well as teaching and pedagogical improvements.

Financial Perspective

The financial perspective tracks how well the organization is translating its operational achievements into financial results. As the sample data in Table 11.4 show, sample principals viewed this component as investing in human capital and a school's financial viability. An examination of the suggested goals and measures reveals a wealth of ideas for schools

Table 11.2

Sample School Principals' Suggested Goals and Measures for Internal Business Perspective

Goals	Measures
Teaching/learning experience	
Teaching excellence	• Student satisfaction • Teacher acquisition of competencies, skills, knowledge over time • Use of latest technology • Teaching awards • No. of students graduating • College/university admission of graduates • Student evaluations • Peer review • Outside reviews
Excellence in developing learning and learning skills (classroom experience that prepares students for success)	• National scores on exit exams • Evaluations by external reviewers and employers • Grade point standards • Opportunities for writing and oral presentations • Improved math skills • Number of students going to college/universities
Develop state-of the-art teaching facilities/ classrooms	• Inventory of teaching/learning facilities/ classrooms • Computer labs • Presentation capabilities
Information technology currency, usage, and applications	• Students' degree of access to technology • Degree of deployment of technology in learning experience • Currency and appropriateness of hardware/software • Internet access/use
Curriculum/program excellence and innovation	
Curriculum excellence and innovation	• Degree to which curriculum is up-to-date with educational, employer, and broader community trends • Regular feedback from employers and colleges/universities • Accreditation • Periodic review of each course/program
Introduction of new courses/innovations	• Actual versus planned • Number within past 3–5 years • Concept to implementation time
Quality and currency of teachers	
Quality teachers	• Teacher credentials • Teacher development plans • Teacher appraisals
Currency of teachers and classroom materials/ experiences	• Faculty development outcomes • Utilization rate of multimedia in classroom

Efficiency and effectiveness
of service

Production efficiency	• Failure/dropout rates of students • Teaching load management • Percentage of students graduating • Teaching costs/student • Administrative costs/student • Percentage of budget dedicated directly to learning • Allocation and use of equipment and supplies • Analysis of use space
Student services effective- ness, including advising/ counseling	• Type and number of services provided • College and employment placement services and opportunities • Quality of instruction and advising/counseling • Effective use of Internet
Positive climate	• Degree to which staff is professional, friendly, and helpful • Quality of library • Degree of access to technology
Increased diversity	• Minority recruiting (teachers, support staff, and administrators) and mentoring • Number of male and minority teachers

Strategic issues

Ability to change	• Curriculum and pedagogy currency • Success of accepted reforms/changes • Number of new/revised courses/programs to meet needs and demands of various stakeholders
Shared expectations and collaborative relations	• Buy into goals and harmony in internal operations • Constituency/stakeholder feedback
Mission updates	• Situation analysis • Modification methods
Positioning of school	• Match with mission • Establishment of image with stakeholders • Measures of students' knowledge

Table 11.3

Sample School Principals' Suggested Goals and Measures for Innovation and Learning Perspective

Goals	Measures
Teaching/learning excellence and innovation	
Teacher development	• Self-reports • Degree to which continuous teacher development is expected, encouraged, suggested, and evaluated

(continued)

Table 11.3 *(continued)*

Goals	Measures
	• Expenditures for teaching enhancement • Teacher evaluations by students/administrators • Teaching assessment
Technology leadership (use, development, application)	• Number and types of activities • Student and teacher satisfaction • Degree to which technology is used in specific courses • Speed of introducing technology and technology adaptation • Expenditures for hardware, software, and maintenance
Technology/learning	• Number of innovations incorporated into classroom • Methods update • Level of equipment • Degree of multimedia presentations • Teaching assessments • Implementation of alternatives to traditional lecture/discussion classes • Quality of instruction • Quality of advising/counseling • Number of ongoing instructional development initiatives
Program and curricular innovations/improvements	• Extent of curriculum revision • Number of new initiatives • Rate of change in curriculum • Reports of continuous improvement committees • Formally approved curriculum changes • Innovation versus competitors (e.g., other schools)
Pedagogy enhancement	• Course revision/development • Field trips • Attendance at pedagogy workshops • Interaction with community/business/employers • Development of assessment technique/device for innovation
Value-added learning	• Pre- and post-learning measures • Learning portfolio
Increased teacher reputation	• Rankings of teachers with peers in other schools • Ability to recruit top candidates
Quality service and continuous improvement	
Service to the school/system	• Adequacy of participation in schoolwide activities • Quality of relationships between administrators, teachers, parents, support staff, and others
Quality of support services	• Ease of communication • Extent that student advising/counseling and administrative processes are student-centered, effective, and efficient • Adequacy of library for students • Responsiveness of support personnel to assisting in meeting student's needs

Table 11.4

Sample School Principals' Suggested Goals and Measures for the Financial Perspective

Human capital investments

Maintain/enhance salaries to retain and attract quality teachers	• Salaries relative to peer groups • Schools attended by job applicants • Teacher satisfaction • Teacher turnover rate
Provide adequate resources for teacher development	• Dollars for travel, technology support, etc. • Dollars/teachers • Program for release time and sabbaticals

Financial management

To be financially sound	• Balanced budgets • Extent budget submissions cover all essential requirements • Efficiency and effectiveness of budget allocations spending
Be perceived as responsible stewards of the resources under our control (resource accountability)	• Effective stewards of school resources entrusted to us • Effectiveness of methods of monitoring our supplies and equipment • Degree to which expenditures are essential • Ability to direct resources to programmatic needs • Efficiency and effectiveness of use of resources given school mission • Graduates' track record
Succeed	• Rate of increase in number of employees to students • Teacher-student ratio • Rate of change of survival measures
Prosper	• Growth in quantity and quality of students • State and national ranking • Percentage of surplus fund balance of operating budget • Increased budget • Increased teacher lines
Survive	• Budget maintenance • Enrollment trend • Relevance preference by parents of students • Spending relative to budget
Stable	• Ups and downs in enrollment

to increase their financial viability. It also suggests areas deserving of increased effort. For example, there could be considerable emphasis on perceived and actual budget and financial accountability.

DEVELOPING AND IMPLEMENTING A BALANCED SCORECARD IN A SCHOOL

Consistent with the observation that few schools have applied the balanced scorecard to date, a search of the literature reveals no real systematic study of such experiences. In the absence of such an analysis, the experiences from the for-profit sector can provide a useful point of departure. These experiences suggest that the entire design and implementation process can easily take up to two years or more, with the component steps illustrated in Table 11.5.

Prior to considering the details of the schedule, it is instructive to take a holistic view of the entire process. Kaplan and Norton (1996b) suggest that designing and implementing a balanced scorecard comprises four related stages: (1) translating the vision and gaining consensus; (2) communicating the objectives, setting goals, and linking strategies; (3) setting targets, allocating resources, and establishing milestones; and (4) feedback and learning. An important component of the feedback/learning stage is post auditing the performance measures' continued applicability. Both the audit process and results can provide an opportunity for double-loop learning by collecting data about the strategy, reflecting on whether the strategy is working and appropriate in light of new developments, and soliciting ideas broadly about new strategic opportunities and directions in the school or school system.

Beyond attending to each stage, it is important to avoid two common mistakes (Kaplan and Norton 1996a, 284–285). First, some people regard the balanced scorecard as merely a performance measurement system. In actuality, the design of performance measures is an integral part of the strategic planning process. These measures help to communicate the organization's strategies and goals, motivate actions to these, and provide guidance and feedback to their attainment. Thus, to reap the full benefits of the balanced scorecard, a school or school system needs to first define its mission, determine major program or curriculum objectives, and select strategies. And because effective implementation of strategies requires coordinated actions by all members of the school, widespread participation or involvement by stakeholders in the process of identifying missions, objectives, and strategies is crucial to ensure full and open communication of needs, concerns, and ideas, and to nurture feelings of "ownership" in the change outcomes.

The second common pitfall to be avoided is simply adopting the balanced scorecard from, say, a peer school from another school district. The problem with that approach is that each school has its unique set of characteristics (e.g., number and backgrounds of students, number and mix of teachers, level of resource availability), and, accordingly, its mission and associated objectives and strategies reflect these circumstances. A school that simply transplants another school's balance scorecard not only runs the risk of trying to put a square peg in a round hole; more important, by omitting the scorecard's developmental process, it is sure to limit the understanding and acceptance, and thus effectiveness, of the scorecard.

Shifting attention back to the schedule (Table 11.5), a retreat is a useful way to shelter the stakeholders from day-to-day concerns so they can focus on the long-run issues of school vision, mission, objectives, and strategies. Having developed a generally accepted mission statement and set of objectives and strategies, a task force can be formed, consisting of well-regarded representatives from all major stakeholder groups (e.g., administration, teachers, staff, students, and the outside community such as parents). This task force

Table 11.5

A Sample Schedule for the Development and Implementation of a Balanced Scorecard for a School

Months 1–2	A strategic planning retreat involving everyone in the school is held to identify strategic issues and to discuss possible solutions. The purpose of this meeting is to form consensus regarding the vision and strategic goals and objectives. A second retreat meeting is held if necessary.
Months 3–4	A strategic planning committee (preferably including the principal) is formed with the charge to formulate objectives for each perspective in the school's balanced scorecard.
Months 5–6	Using the balanced scorecard as a communication tool, the strategic planning committee seeks comments on and acceptance of the school's balanced scorecard from school members.
Month 7	The strategic planning committee revises the balanced scorecard in response to comments from school members.
Months 8–9	The revised balanced scorecard is communicated to the school members (departments and individuals). Each member is required to develop an individual balanced scorecard that supports the schoolwide goals and objectives.
Months 10–11	The strategic planning committee reviews individual and departmental balanced scorecards, suggesting possible revisions of the individuals, as well as the school's balanced scorecards.
Month 12	The school formulates a five-year strategic plan based on finalized balanced scorecards. The first-year plan is expanded into the annual operating plan for the coming year.
Months 13–24	Individual departmental and school progress is reviewed quarterly to identify areas that require attention and additional effort.
Months 25–26	The school evaluation committee evaluates each member's performance, based on the individual balanced scorecards, for the past year and makes recommendations relating to retention, tenure, promotion, salary increases, or other rewards. The strategic planning committee revises the school's balanced scorecard and the five-year strategic plan according to internal and external scanning of the school's conditions and changes in the environment. In helping to revise the strategic objectives of the balanced scorecard, the strategic planning committee identifies as many strategic issues as possible, and, for each of these issues, considers possible solutions that can be employed by the school.

can be charged with identifying more specific goals under each of the major components, or perspectives, agreed to by the school constituents as being appropriate (these can be the four components in the illustrative scorecard, a subset of those, all of them plus others, etc.). Frequent two-way communication between this task force and the various stakeholder groups is needed to ensure agreement with, and acceptance of, the final product.

Next would be selection of the performance measure(s) for each specific goal. Because these measures have more immediacy to certain school members or stakeholders than to others, it is desirable to seek even more widespread participation in this step. One possibility is to form a task force for each component and to instruct these groups to work under three guidelines (Kaplan and Norton 1996a, 148–151, 305):

1. The performance measure(s) selected should be positively related to degree of attainment of the related goal; as the latter increase, the former also should increase.
2. The performance measures should be focused on outcomes. Outcome measures tend to be prepared only periodically and often are not sufficiently timed to alert remedial action. Performance drivers also need to be included to serve as leading indicators of outcomes. To illustrate, the ability to balance the budget can be an outcome measure for a school. But the number of teachers (or students) can be a performance driver, as it will affect both the school's budget allocation and expenditures.
3. The number of performance measures should be kept low so as not to diffuse attention and create confusion. Many instances of performance measure proliferation result from people confusing the diagnostic and strategic purposes of such measures. For example, a school's budget surplus can be a diagnostic measure, as it can indicate potential cash-flow difficulties. But having an adequate budget surplus provides no indication whether the school is attaining its more fundamental or strategic goals (e.g., increased quality of instruction).

KEYS TO MANAGING CHANGE PROJECTS AND IMPLEMENTING THE BALANCED SCORECARD

The balanced-scorecard approach to strategic management of problems or issues is grounded on two premises. First, SMART goals must be established with the aid of multiple stakeholder groups, employees, and educational leaders. Second, there is a cause-and-effect relationship between the achievement of stated goals and the quality of employees hired, administrative processes put in place, support for educators and students, and accountability for performance (TEA 2004). As educational leaders identify key administrative initiatives, more quantitative measures such as the balanced-scorecard equation should be used.

The Equation

Educational leaders and others involved in school system change should look at the successful implementation of the balanced scorecard as an equation:

Success = Measurement × Technique × Control × Focused persistence × Consensus

Measurement

First of all, success is a function of what *Measurement* you use. If you do not measure the right things and the measures do not reflect what is really going on, much will be done in a school or system, but little will be accomplished.

Technique

Second, what *Technique* or methods also have a significant bearing on success? Techniques fall into two categories:

- *Large-scale, or major techniques.* Examples include restructuring, tying teachers pay to measurements (e.g., student performance on government-mandated standardized tests), adding resources (dollars and people), adding or changing customers or products, reengineering processes such as curriculums, change of strategy, addition or change of teachers' or administrators' core competencies, and so on.
- *Small-scale, or minor techniques result in small changes in drivers.* Examples include motivational speeches, problem-solving teams focused on how best to integrate technology into classrooms, graphs displayed to teachers on student performance on standardized tests on bulletin boards, and so on.

The key to educational leaders' use of these techniques is for them to realize that if major improvements in balanced scorecard measures are needed, then large-scale change techniques must be used. This fact usually causes great distress in a school or school system because many stakeholders think major improvements can be made only by tinkering with the school or school system, instead of making fundamental changes. If educational leadership is willing only to use small-scale techniques, then they must expect only modest improvements in balanced-scorecard measures.

Control

Another part of the equation is *Control.* Once educational leaders have brainstormed to create a list of possible actions that might accomplish their goals, these actions need to be categorized into four levels of action:

- Level 1 action: in control of action, and effects are inside the school;
- Level 2 action: in control of action, but effects are outside the school;
- Level 3 action: not in control of action, but it affects the school driver(s);
- Level 4 action: not in control of action, but does not affect your driver.

For educational leaders to be successful:

- They have to concentrate on level 1 and 2 actions;
- They have to gain control of, or compensate for, level 3 actions;
- And if they do not have sufficient control over the actions necessary to achieve their goals, then they must lower their expectations of what they can accomplish and either set a lower target or abandon the target altogether.

Focused Persistence

Focused persistence, otherwise known as project management, is another key in the equation. Project management includes having a timetable (beginning and end) for each task, periodic reviews of accomplishments, resources and people who are assigned to each task, and, most important, who have a sincere drive to accomplish the tasks. The use of such tools as Gantt charts, PERT charts, and so forth, is essential in this process. (A Gantt chart is a graphical representation of the duration of tasks against the progression of time. A Program Evaluation and Review Technique [PERT] is a method to visually represent a project.)

Consensus

The last, but equally critical, factor is *Consensus*. The best-laid plans, along with a thorough knowledge of measures, drivers, and with sufficient resources will fail if there is not enough agreement among those with sufficient power to block balanced-scorecard implementation. Key power brokers need to be involved in decision making, and as many others as possible in the various stages and steps outlined here. Among some opportunities for involvement are:

- Communication on the importance and status of the project;
- Participation in planning and decision making;
- Implementation of action;
- Suggestions for improvement.

Keeping in mind these factors when implementing the balanced scorecard will substantially increase the chances of successful change in school systems. Though every factor in the equation above need not be perfect, and each can compensate for another, all must be present to some extent for the balanced scorecard to be successfully implemented.

Based on the preceding discussion and the illustrative sample design/implementation schedule, it is obvious that the time span between the start of the process and the harvesting of initial results can be considerable. Given the mounting challenges to schools and education, there is little time to lose in implementing the balanced scorecard or similar approaches to promote and support change.

CONCLUSION

As highlighted throughout this chapter, the balanced-scorecard approach offers educational leaders a better vehicle for addressing the unprecedented levels and calls for school change as well as escalating expectations. Meeting the seven trends or new challenges in an era of shrinking resources will require educational leaders to undergo fundamental changes and to continuously seek ways to create future value. This chapter has provided a workable explanation of the balanced-scorecard approach and suggests how educational leaders can use it to manage change.

Increasing educational leaders' skills in using tools such as the balanced scorecard can do nothing but increase the likelihood of successful administrative decision making and change in schools and school systems. The balanced scorecard reflects the values of a school or school system, and therefore requires the support of all school representatives and key stakeholders. One of the benefits of the balanced-scorecard process is that it forces interested individuals and stakeholders to sit down and articulate the vision of the school or school system before moving to an action plan. By doing this, decisions on change goals that are imperative to realizing the vision can be more easily made. From these goals, measurements can be chosen. These measurements are the critical part of the balanced scorecard because "what gets measured gets managed" and what gets effectively managed enables educational leaders to make better administrative decisions.

REFERENCES

Berkman, E. (2002). "How to Use the Balanced Scorecard." *CIO Magazine*, May 15: 7–9.

Cetron, M., and K. Cetron. (2003/2004). "A Forecast for Schools." *Educational Leadership* 61: 22–29.

Darling-Hammond, L. (2000). "Teacher Quality and Student Achievement." *Education Policy Analysis Achieves*, January 1. www.cpaa.asu.edu/epaa/v8n1.

Educational Testing Service (ETS). (2004). "About ETS State and Federal Relations." www.ets.org. September 4.

Kaplan, R., and D. Norton. (1996a). "Using the Balanced Scorecard in a Strategic Management System." *Harvard Business Review* 74: 75–85.

———. (1996b). "Strategic Learning and the Balanced Scorecard." *Strategy and Leadership* 24: 19–24.

———. (2000). *The Strategy-focused Organization: How the Balanced Scorecard Companies Thrive in the New Environment.* Boston: Harvard Business School Press.

Presidents and Fellows of Harvard College. (2003). Smart Schools. www.pz.harvard.edu/research/smartsch.htm.

Texas Education Agency (TEA). (2004). "TEA Balanced Scorecard." www.tea.state.tx.us/stplan/bsc.html. September 6.

CHAPTER 12

LEADERSHIP CHALLENGES IN LOCAL GOVERNMENT

Economic Development, Financial Management, and Ethical Leadership

WILLIAM I. SAUSER, JR., LANE D. SAUSER, AND JOE A. SUMNERS

In an effort to help prepare local government leaders for the challenges they will face in the twenty-first century, in 1998, William Sauser prepared a short list of examples of the kinds of issues being dealt with by public officials.[1] That list included (a) public demands for accountability; (b) organizations under siege; (c) unfunded mandates and regulations; (d) the "New Federalism"; (e) a technology explosion; (f) changing standards, laws, and procedures; (g) time compression; (h) election cycles; (i) litigiousness; and (j) a lack of resources. Most of these issues continue to plague local government leaders, of course! But to this list we must now add three more key issues: economic development, financial management, and ethical leadership. In this chapter, we address each of these three issues in turn, and provide practical advice for leaders in the public sector who find themselves face-to-face with these challenges. Our suggestions are particularly pertinent to smaller local jurisdictions that often lack the resources available to large metropolitan governments.

LEADERSHIP FOR COMMUNITY AND ECONOMIC DEVELOPMENT

Citizen Leaders

Alexis de Tocqueville, the French count who visited the United States in 1831, found that European settlers were creating a society different from the one they knew in Europe. He found communities formed around an uncommon social invention—small groups of common citizens coming together to form organizations that solve problems. Tocqueville observed three features of how these groups operated. First, they were groups of citizens who determined they had the power to decide what a problem was. Second, they determined they had the power to decide how to solve the problem. Third, they often decided that they would themselves become the key actors in implementing the solution. From Tocqueville's perspective, "these citizen associations were a uniquely powerful instrument being created in America, the foundation stones of

American communities."[2] These same features characterize many of today's high-achieving communities.

All over the United States, citizen leaders are finding new ways to address community challenges. A new leadership model is emerging that is more inclusive, more connected, and more collaborative than ever before.[3] This emerging leadership model recognizes that the quality and quantity of a community's citizen engagement and "social capital"[4] directly impact both quality of life and economic opportunity—which are inseparably linked. It recognizes that leadership is not confined to elected officials, business leaders, and those with specific titles. The new leadership model recognizes that a community cannot do its work with just a few people. Rather, citizens from all walks of life have an important role in making difficult choices for their community and everyone has something to offer—individual knowledge, perspectives, and talent—to the leadership of the community. In other words, today's successful communities tend to be full of leaders.

David Mathews, president of the Kettering Foundation, in summarizing the findings of the foundation's research on community politics, says:

> What stands out in the high-achieving community is not so much the characteristics of the leaders as their number, their location and, most of all, the way they interact with other citizens. The high-achieving community had ten times more people providing leadership than communities of comparable size. This [high-achieving] community is "leaderful"; that is, nearly everyone provides some measure of initiative. And its leaders function not as gatekeepers but as door openers, bent on widening participation.[5]

Social Capital and Economic Development

In 1958, Edward Banfield published *The Moral Basis of a Backward Society*, a study of underdevelopment in a village at the southern tip of Italy. "The extreme poverty and backwardness," he wrote, "is to be explained largely (but not entirely) by the inability of the villagers to act together for their common good."[6]

In 1970, Italy established local governments in its twenty regions and turned over to them many of the functions of the central government. Robert Putnam studied the performance of these new governments and found that governments in the prosperous north of Italy outperformed the ones in the more impoverished south. He found the north's secret to be "civic virtue"—an ingrained tendency to form small-scale associations that create a fertile ground for political and economic development. According to Putnam, civic virtue both reveals and engenders trust and cooperation in the citizenry, and it is these qualities—which he called "social capital"—that make everything else go so well.[7] A wealth of more recent international research shows social capital to be an important factor in economic development.[8] A World Bank study concludes that "social capital is the glue that holds societies together and without which there can be no economic growth or human well-being."[9]

The rationale for these findings is clear. Economic development requires a foundation upon which to build. It is well understood that a physical infrastructure—roads, water, gas, electricity, and sewers—is necessary for economic growth. At least as important is a community's civic infrastructure of strong and diverse local leadership, vital community institutions, public involvement, and a community mindset of pride and optimism. A strong community supports and sustains a strong economy.

Citizen Leadership in Rural Southern Communities

The following examples illustrate how community leaders in several economically challenged rural communities in the southern United States have addressed their problems. These stories illustrate the strong connection between a community's civic life and its economic development. They show how the traditional notion of the community leader—often a mayor—as chief community problem solver is giving way to the model of the community leader as catalyst, connector, and consensus builder. The successful community leader recognizes that one person, or only a few persons, cannot adequately deal with today's community and economic development challenges. Successful leadership requires mobilizing the talents of every segment of the community.

Tupelo, Mississippi

Vaughn Grisham, in a study of Tupelo, Mississippi, demonstrates how that community's vigorous civic life provided the foundation for an economic revival during the past half century.[10] During that period, Tupelo and Lee County, Mississippi, rose from the depths of poverty to become a model for community development. In 1940, Lee County was one of the poorest counties in the nation. The county's largest employer, a garment factory, had closed in 1937 after a bitter labor strike. That event deeply divided Tupelo and left a residue of anger and mistrust between the town's workers and its leaders.

One person, George McLean, the editor of the *Tupelo Daily Journal*, provided the leadership that sparked the evolutionary transformation of Tupelo. He wrote editorials, cajoled, and eventually convinced local businessmen and farmers that, if they worked together, Tupelo could become much more than it was. This is typical of successful community development efforts. In the early stages of community development, there is often a champion, or catalyst, who is completely dedicated and who pushes the effort forward. In Tupelo, McLean was that person. But McLean knew that even the best ideas will fail if they are not connected to, informed by, and "owned" by a larger body of participants.

First, McLean convinced local businessmen that it was in their interests to help the region's farmers. He reasoned that the more prosperous the area's farmers, the more money they could spend in Tupelo stores. Thus, Tupelo's businessmen determined to find a way to help to relieve the economic hardships that were making lives of the county's farmers so difficult. Their solution was to form a cooperative, with local citizens investing financial capital in the creation of a regional dairy industry. The dramatic success of this dairy program reinvigorated Tupelo. It erased any doubts that a grassroots economic development project could work.

In 1946, Tupelo created a series of "rural community development councils" (RCDCs) to provide a structure for involving farmers in the development of their own communities. The RCDCs worked much like New England town meetings—they provided a forum where members of the communities in northeastern Mississippi could come together and decide upon their priorities.

Tupelo leaders next decided the city needed a new organization to be the community's vehicle for investing in itself on a continuing basis. In 1948, eighty-eight of Tupelo's leaders formed the Community Development Foundation (CDF). Anyone willing to pay the dues—which varied according to one's income—could join. The CDF was built on the philosophy that the citizens of Tupelo were responsible for creating their own future; however, the CDF also recognized from the beginning that neither it nor the community as a whole held all the answers. They consistently sought outside advice and assistance when needed.

The network of organizations cultivated by the CDF has shaped community life in Lee County—especially the RCDCs. They provide ordinary citizens with instruments for influencing community decisions. With each new success, the community has looked to take on the next challenge. This model of citizen leadership continues today—with astounding results. Today, Lee County is the second-wealthiest county in Mississippi and is home to more than 200 highly diversified manufacturers. The county's poverty rate is approximately one-half the national average. The school system has received numerous awards, and Tupelo has twice been named one of ten all-America cities by the National Civic League.

It is noteworthy that while most of the state was torn apart by racial division during the struggle for civil rights, the Tupelo community held together. As early as 1961, Tupelo's recreation department began refusing to allow any of the sports teams it sponsored to compete against communities that maintained segregationist policies. In 1965, Tupelo became the second community in the state to sign a school antidiscrimination agreement and to desegregate its schools that autumn without incident.

The Tupelo experience shows that as the attitudes of people within the community change, the attitudes of people outside the community also change. Tupelo, for example, has been able to attract new business and industry because people see it as a place worthy of investment. Economic development came about because community development— the ability of citizens to identify and work together on issues of common concern— made it possible.

Uniontown, Alabama

Uniontown, a community of about 3,500, is located in the heart of Alabama's Black Belt, named for a deposit of dark, fertile soil extending from Mississippi's border through the heart of Alabama. This region, once the backbone of the state's agricultural economy, is now plagued by pervasive poverty and economic stagnation—the worst in the nation by most standards and considered by some to be at or below the level of many Third World nations. An area of urgent need, the region faces declining population, inadequate health care, substandard schools, and weak business development. Uniontown is one of the poorest of the many poor communities in the Alabama Black Belt.

Auburn University initiated an outreach project to assist the community beginning in 1999.[11] Auburn University's Economic Development Institute first provided assistance by helping create a strategic plan for the community. Auburn next recommended the creation of a Community Development Corporation (CDC) as a way to obtain broader public involvement and to provide a structured organization capable of implementing some of the strategic plan's recommendations. The CDC was created, but with the mayor serving as president and appointing all CDC members. The mayor also tended to dominate meetings. Citizens who attended strategic planning or CDC meetings often took a passive role and appeared reluctant to express their viewpoints in front of others. They tended to look to a leader—the mayor or the outside experts from Auburn—for answers to community problems. Although the CDC met regularly, it was mostly unsuccessful in its efforts to broaden public engagement, develop leadership capacity, or improve the community's quality of life.

In the fall of 2000, the incumbent mayor was defeated in his bid for reelection and his successor was not enthusiastic about the city's strategic plan. The new mayor rightly felt that the group that created it was not representative of the whole community. He also was skeptical about using the CDC (comprised of the former mayor and his supporters) as the vehicle for promoting community and economic development. Any momentum that Auburn University had gained in its community-building efforts was stalled.

With the mayor's defeat, Auburn decided to try a different approach. The new focus was less explicitly on problem solving and much more on facilitating dialogue, listening, and responding to the needs of Uniontown citizens as they defined them. Instead of working through the city's mayor, the Auburn team decided to more actively engage ordinary citizens. To do this, Auburn identified and recruited about twenty-five individuals representing all segments of the community to participate in a focus group. This biracial group of citizens representing a wide range of age groups, income levels, and occupations continues to meet on a biweekly basis. In order to create a sense of shared identity, the citizens gave their group the name "Uniontown Cares."

Since the creation of Uniontown Cares, citizens have taken advantage of new public space to talk about community issues in a deliberative way, identify and take ownership of community problems, and connect with one another and with their community. As members of the Uniontown community discussed local problems, they began to realize their capacity for doing something about them. Talk was turned into action. And these actions led to results—cleanups of parks and cemeteries, creation of an Alcoholics Anonymous chapter, and creation of an adopt-a-park program, among many other successes. Those residents who were engaged through Uniontown Cares began to feel good about themselves and their sense of efficacy increased. They came to see themselves as citizens who could do something to improve the quality of life in their community.

The new mayor is participating as a member of the group, and the dynamics of local politics have changed for the better. Uniontown Cares is making a difference, and others in the community are beginning to notice. More and more members of the community have joined the group. In fact, the group has outgrown its original city hall meeting room and has moved to a new public library—which Uniontown Cares members helped renovate and stock with new books and computers.

The horrendous problems of the Alabama Black Belt remain. But for the people participating in Uniontown Cares, things are looking better. They see themselves as citizens instead of victims, as public actors instead of clients of services. They see that they can control many things about their lives and community. They are creating small ripples of hope in a community where hope has been in short supply.

An important lesson from the Uniontown experience is that government alone cannot solve the types of problems facing many of our nation's economically challenged communities. Dealing with such problems clearly requires a collaborative approach by government, citizens, multiple community institutions, and external resources. Relying solely on government—or outside experts—can relegate people to the sidelines and stifle the community-building process.

Demopolis, Alabama

Demopolis, Alabama, is a community that has seemed to avoid many of the problems of its Black Belt neighbors. In the late 1960s, when Alabama schools finally desegregated, Demopolis leaders—white and black—made the decision to work together to support an integrated city school system. In most other Black Belt communities, whites almost completely abandoned public schools, choosing instead to create a dual school system through the creation of all-white private academies. Today, almost every Black Belt community in Alabama maintains a segregated school system, with blacks attending public schools and whites attending private academies. But not in Demopolis! Demopolis citizens are very proud of their excellent schools and remain committed to supporting a racially diverse public school system. Not coincidentally, Demopolis is a socially and economically vibrant community and one of eight Alabama communities selected to participate in the Alabama Communities of Excellence program. While other Black Belt communities were coming apart, the Demopolis community chose to come together—and that made all the difference.

Morrilton, Arkansas

In 1999, executives of the two largest employers in Morrilton, Arkansas—Levi Strauss and Arrow Automotive—announced the closing of their plants.[12] These announcements, which occurred within seven days of one another, represented a loss of over 1,000 jobs, or about half the manufacturing jobs in the community. The plant closings sent shock waves throughout the small Arkansas community. However, a small group of citizens had been aware of the possibility of plant closings and had been meeting with the Conway

County Industrial Development Corporation (CCIDC) to develop a plan of action. With the plant closing announcements, the effort took on new urgency and attracted broad community involvement. The CCIDC also invited state economic development agencies to contribute to the planning process. Thus, a coordinated effort of local and state entities pitched in to decide how the community would respond to the plant closures. Local leaders brainstormed about a variety of possibilities and decided that attracting a "call center" might be the best economic opportunity for the community in the short run. Within one year, the CCIDC had attracted a new call center facility that employed 350 people. The community, with the assistance of state agencies, continued to work hard to follow up on strategies to create more jobs for the region. They were able to recruit a telecommunications company that bought the former Arrow Automotive facility and a local packaging plant purchased the Levi Strauss plant—replacing many of the community's lost jobs.

The catalyst for this economic resurgence was engaged community leadership that responded to the economic challenge, not with resignation, but with action. Local leaders pulled together, sought outside assistance, made decisions, and doggedly pursued their plan to achieve success.

Concluding Thoughts on Economic Development

The experiences of these economically challenged southern communities suggest that a critical component of a community's economic strategy must be to take steps to strengthen civic life. This means building the "connections" among citizens, groups, and institutions within the community. Successful communities recognize that their destiny is largely in their own hands. Although outside help is sought when appropriate, they do not wait for outsiders to save them, nor do they just sit around and wait for things to get better. Successful communities take the attitude that "nobody knows or cares about our community like we do" and "if we don't do it, it won't get done." High-achieving communities are full of leaders who work with others to identify all local assets and attempt to connect them in ways that multiply their power and effectiveness.

LEADERSHIP IN FINANCIAL MANAGEMENT

There are some 83,000 governments nationwide in the United States. This number includes one federal government, fifty state governments, and thousands of cities, counties, and single-purpose local governments, such as school, water, and transportation districts.[13] Most of these local governments serve relatively small communities. Consequently, elected officials and administrators serve in a part-time capacity. Many lack professional training in the area for which they are responsible, and many do not have the experience of having served in governments with greater resources and capacities. Financial management is typically the one government function that causes the most problems for them and where mistakes are most costly.[14] Governments across the country have taken a number of different approaches to improve their financial management processes. Here we offer ten ways that local government leaders, particularly in smaller jurisdictions, can better manage the finances of their community.

1. Hire and Retain Competent Staff

Mayors, city council members, and county commissioners frequently fail to realize how important it is to employ competent individuals. This is true in any city or county department or function, but it is especially true for the city or county clerk/administrator's and finance director's office. The operation of even the smallest government typically involves millions of dollars. The accounting for these resources and the administrative requirements of running a local government are complicated. Employing and retaining competent, well-trained, well-compensated administrative employees is an important component of sound financial management.

Just what do these financial administrators do? They (a) determine the costs of people, goods, and services; (b) determine how much revenue is expected from each revenue source; (c) establish and maintain the information processing systems; (d) accumulate, report, analyze, and interpret the information through these systems; and (e) process financial resources—meet the payroll, pay the bills, and collect the revenues. These are functions critical to the overall management of the jurisdiction. Sound financial management makes possible the provision of all other services. Poor financial administration puts every government service or program at risk.

2. Plan Ahead

Local government officials do not like financial surprises. The less the jurisdiction gets involved in planning—whether it is capital budgeting, land use planning, or strategic planning—the more likely it is that there will be surprises. It has been said that the lack of planning is tantamount to planning to fail.

Our political system tends to force us to manage government affairs along a timetable that matches the election cycle, therefore planning and decision making tend to have a four-year or shorter focus. However, governments have a longer life expectancy than any business and can really benefit from planning. Proper planning is essential if city councils, mayors, and county commissioners want to avoid the kind of surprises that can have a negative financial impact. Proper planning should be applied in at least two areas: budgeting and operations.

The budget is a plan that should allow for both anticipated and contingent expenses. Councils and commissions often get trapped into looking only at anticipated revenues and funding requests from the various departments. They forget to anticipate funding needs that come up sporadically and unannounced. These may be different items each year, but seem always to appear in one form or another annually. Some common examples of these unexpected spending needs are: (a) damage to public buildings and property caused by severe weather, (b) insurance premium increases, (c) unanticipated legal expenses, (d) reduced revenues, and (e) unbudgeted personnel overtime. Annual budgets should include some amount to cover these expected "unexpected" items.

A second form of planning should take place in the review of operations. Changes should be implemented where needed. From time to time government leaders must take a step back and look at how the entire local government organization goes about its operations. It is too easy to continue to carry on because "we have always done it this way." By nature, managers and employees do not like change. However, it may be necessary to embrace technology and consider some different ways of doing business. It is a worthwhile effort to review staffing patterns and needs and to evaluate the condition of and need for equipment in various departments. As part of the planning process, the condition of the jurisdiction's buildings, jail, water, sewer, and other infrastructure should be reviewed. A plan should be developed to address needs and set priorities.

3. Budget Wisely

An essential component of government finance is the preparation of an annual budget. The budget should be adopted by the commission or council prior to the beginning of each fiscal year. The adopted budget serves as a control over spending and as the policy guideline for all funds and departments. A budget is based on anticipated revenues and expenditure projections. Too often, budget preparers in small jurisdictions focus mostly on the spending side and devote less attention to the revenue side of the budget. The budget is a plan for operations in which the level of expenditures is dependent on revenues available. It is critical that revenue sources and patterns be analyzed to determine trends so that the government is not in the position of relying on revenues that will not be realized.

It is a common practice in government to use what is known as the incremental approach to budgeting. Basically this means that last year's budget is the starting point, and small modifications are made to prepare the new budget. This is not necessarily a bad practice; however, it assumes little change and creates a situation where the future tends to be a perpetuation of the past. Some activities may be receiving a larger proportion of the budget than is warranted. This problem is tied to earlier lack of planning. Funding allocations should be examined to ensure that spending patterns accurately represent the jurisdiction's priorities.

4. Carefully Attend to Budget Implementation

The budget should be viewed as *the* plan of operations for the year. Some jurisdictions adopt a budget in October and do not really look at it again until the end of the fiscal year approaches and the clerk/administrator reports that "we are about out of money." In these cases, the budget is not being used as a guide, and it may be too late to bring finances back in line. Fiscal managers should have access to financial information on a periodic basis—monthly or at least quarterly. Departments must be held accountable. If there is overspending, corrections can be made early enough to discontinue spending over budget, or funds can be reallocated to prevent a shortfall.

Even the best intentions of following the budget may break down when it comes to saying no. As the fiscal year marches on, requests for funding not anticipated in the budget often arise from citizens and department heads. For fear of the political conse-quences, local elected officials find it difficult to say no. However, the public expects and appreciates fair and reasonable budgetary restraints. Allowing the local government to get into fiscal disarray is probably a greater cause of defeat at election time than holding the line on expenditures.

Another threat to budget maintenance is the assumption on the part of members of the council or commission that fiscal management is completely in the hands of the clerk/administrator and chief elected leader. Even where these individuals are capable and are doing a good job, they must have the support and input of the commission or council as a whole in order to maintain the integrity of the jurisdiction's financial position.

5. Create a Rainy Day Fund

Nationally, local governments have typically been able to benefit from some revenue increases from year to year. At budget time, the council or commission simply antici-pates revenues and budgets the last anticipated penny, and then prays that nothing out of the ordinary comes along. The practice of budgeting and expending all anticipated rev-enues is very risky. Governments have been able to avoid financial crises brought on by unanticipated expenditures and serious cash-flow problems by building and maintaining an unreserved fund balance or rainy day fund. Balancing current needs and setting aside a reserve is difficult, but not impossible.

How is a reserve or rainy day fund established, and how much is enough? The first step in establishing a reserve is for the governing body to agree that this is a priority. Council/commission members must agree that they will work together and resist using the reserve except for an extreme need. It is very difficult to establish a significant re-serve immediately, so setting a goal such as half a percentage point or one percent per year is one way to get started. Another method is to dedicate the increase in one or more current revenue sources to establish and build the reserve. Place any windfall or unex-pected additional revenues into a reserve. Traditionally, two methods have been used by finance officers in determining the appropriate size of the reserve: (1) allocating finan-cial resources equal to a percentage of annual operating expenditures, or (2) allocating financial resources equal to a certain number of months' operating expenditures.

A common question is: Just how much should be placed in reserve? The "right amount" of reserve is a question open to some debate, particularly in the general fund. Bond raters and others often use "rules of thumb" to measure the adequacy of reserves in the general fund. For example, 5 percent of annual operating expenditures is a commonly cited minimum amount. Others argue that reserves should equal no less than one month's operating expenditures. This works out to 8.3 percent. Others seem to think that three months' expenditures is an adequate reserve. Care must be taken to avoid applying these rules of thumb without taking actual operating conditions into account.

One important consideration is the reliability of a government's revenue sources. Some revenue sources are traditionally quite stable (property taxes) while other revenues can vary widely depending on economic conditions (sales taxes). If the government depends on less-reliable revenue sources, then a significantly higher reserve should be maintained to stabilize funding. Another important factor is the timing of cash inflows and outflows. Governments whose cash flows are less predictable may need relatively higher levels of reserves to maintain liquidity than those with highly predictable cash inflows and outflows. A third consideration is the amount of resources available in other funds. When additional resources are available in funds other than the general fund, then a lesser amount of unreserved fund balance may be needed in the general fund. It is less likely that operating transfers from the general fund will be needed to supplement inadequate funds elsewhere.

Thus, how much reserve to maintain depends on several factors. These include the reliability of revenues, the timing of cash flows, and the soundness of other funds. The level established should be directly linked to the degree of uncertainty the jurisdiction faces; the greater the uncertainty, the greater the reserve needed. Can a government have too high a reserve? Some citizens and taxpayer watchdog groups believe that a government should not raise money until it is needed. Therefore, some users of government financial statements object to what they perceive as an excessive amount of reserves, arguing that high levels of reserves indicate overtaxation. Nevertheless, we believe local governments should find a way to start establishing that reserve or rainy day fund, particularly in cases where the jurisdiction relies on highly variable revenue sources.

6. Manage Risks

One way to avoid financial surprises is to develop a risk management program. Failure to be concerned about various risks can have a significant impact on the financial health of the local government. Risk management includes following best safety practices and perhaps a targeted program designed to limit accidents or events that may give rise to a workers' compensation claim or a lawsuit. By managing risk, the jurisdiction's exposure to financial loss can be reduced.

A significant expense for local governments is the cost of workers' compensation benefits for employees. Most jurisdictions continue to see significant increases in the cost of workers' compensation and liability insurance. Some of the increases are due to factors beyond their control, but some can be avoided, primarily through programs designed to prevent events that give rise to workers' compensation or liability claims. Insurance companies base premiums for insurance on a number of factors, and one of the most prevalent and costly is loss history. Most insurers charge higher premiums to businesses and governments with a history of excessive claims or losses. A commitment by the city or county to try to reduce claims and promote safety among all employees can pay dividends in terms of insurance savings.

7. Avoid Political Conflicts

An argument can be made that of all the reasons that local governments get into financial difficulties, political differences among council or commission members may be the most prevalent. Some councils/commissions cannot achieve a reasonable level of political unity. There is constant bickering and backstabbing, and a lot of wasted energy goes into finding ways to discredit one another. In such cases, individual members insist on promoting their individual political agendas rather than pursuing common goals for the jurisdiction. It is very difficult to accomplish anything—and that includes financial stability and soundness—under these conditions.

A certain amount of political disagreement is healthy and appropriate; our political system in the United States is built on it. When these differences are carried to the extreme, however, serious problems become evident. If the governing body presents a highly divided front, it is next to impossible to convince the taxpayer that the government is doing what is best for the jurisdiction. The media and the public like nothing better than to witness and read about strife among local governing body members, which seems to prove that sound fiscal management cannot possibly be achieved.

8. Diversify Revenue Sources

Heavy dependence on a single revenue source increases the risk of financial problems for the jurisdiction. For example, credit analysts do not look upon overreliance on a local sales tax favorably because these revenues are susceptible to swings in the business cycle. Up to a point, credit analysts generally consider revenue diversification a sound approach. Having in place an income or sales tax, which can reduce a government's dependence on a single revenue source, such as the property tax, adds elasticity to the revenue structure and is generally regarded as a positive step. Ideally, a balance between these major revenue sources should be established. The property tax is considered to be the foundation of the local government revenue structure due to its reliability and predictability. Credit analysts view this favorably because it indicates that the government has a steady source of revenue to meet its debt service obligations and to fund government operations. Reliance on other revenue sources may not provide the same level of stability.

Current trends in revenue collection require governments to shift to a greater reliance on user fees. User fees enable the local government to better align the benefits received with those who pay for the service. User fees should be set at levels that will allow a local government to recover the costs of providing a service—including direct labor costs, administrative costs, supplies and materials costs, and appropriate indirect costs. An optimal revenue structure should include a balance among the major taxes. Taxes should be as broadly based as possible to allow for lower tax rates. Diversity in the revenue structure is desirable for political and social reasons.

9. Promote Economic Development

Another problem that relates to the revenue structure of the local government is an inadequate tax base. Even if sound financial management practices are in place, good management will not by itself generate additional taxes. The tax base may be diminishing because there is just not enough economic activity in the jurisdiction to generate sufficient tax revenues. County commissions and city councils can get actively involved in efforts to expand local economic activities, as we have noted above. Local government leaders should form a strong working relationship with the local chambers of commerce and support and promote their activities. The business community and civic leaders should be tapped to promote the jurisdiction's resources and attract industrial and commercial development. Joining forces across county and city lines may be more beneficial than a more competitive strategy. Increased regional activity and development can produce benefits for more than one jurisdiction.

As policy makers, local officials need to be aware when they are in competition with nearby jurisdictions for economic development projects. Fear of developing a less competitive tax climate than neighboring jurisdictions has caused many local governments to raise revenues by imposing additional user charges and fees rather than by raising major tax rates. This can result in a more balanced tax and revenue system and may ultimately benefit a local government's residents as well as enhance economic development efforts. Important questions to ask are: Would a tax or other revenue change force a business to leave? Have any businesses complained of heavy tax burdens and financial difficulties? Would tax incentives offered to business undermine revenue stability? Would a tax or other revenue change contradict past policies including the granting of tax abatements to businesses? It is critical that local government officials understand the business climate and the linkages between revenues and economic development.

10. Seek Expert Advice

A final recommendation for sound financial management is to seek advice and counsel from a number of sources that are readily available. It is not unusual for newly elected officials to exclaim after several months in office, "There is a lot more to this job than I thought when I was running for office!" The functions and responsibilities are many and varied. Additionally, council and commission members and other elected officials must face the political and legal consequences of their individual and collective decisions. Sometimes not knowing where to get the answers and not taking the time to do so can create major problems. The political, legal, and financial implications can be significant. What are the resources at hand? Obviously, a league of municipalities, association of county commissions, or similar professional organization is a tremendous resource. Such organizations typically feature an exceptional staff that is available to assist local governments and possesses the knowledge that comes from working with and for local governments every day. The very problem your jurisdiction is wrestling with may not be as unusual as you think.

The city or county attorney is also a key resource. Even for small jurisdictions, an attorney should be retained to serve this function. This individual should be required to attend every meeting of the local governing body. If there is a question about the legality or legal implications of a decision, the attorney should be consulted. Before entering into a contract, the governing body should have it reviewed by its attorney. The jurisdiction's personnel policies and procedures should be reviewed to ensure that the local government is in compliance with state and federal laws. The cost of legal action, whether you are in the right or wrong, can be significant.

Another important resource is the city's or county's CPA or independent accounting firm that is responsible for the annual audit. This can be a resource in guiding financial decisions. If the local government is the recipient of grant monies, the granting agency is another important resource. Consult the agency if there are questions about allowable costs. Audit findings of disallowable costs and having to pay monies back can be costly mistakes.

Yet another valuable resource for local officials is the state ethics commission. The three most common ways that officials violate the ethics law are using the position to obtain personal gain for the official or for a family member; using public equipment, facilities, or employees to benefit the official; and voting on matters in which the official or a family member can gain financially. If the official is unsure about a specific action, it is better to contact the ethics commission for a ruling before taking such an action. There is nothing worse than reading about an ethics violation when the violator is you!

Concluding Thoughts on Financial Management

Managing the fiscal resources of local governments, especially small jurisdictions, can be extremely challenging. Often, elected officials are not trained in this area and must turn to other sources for expertise and workable solutions. The ten recommendations cited here provide a good map for municipalities and counties to avoid financial troubles.

ETHICAL LEADERSHIP

Ethics has to do with behavior—specifically, one's moral behavior with respect to society. The extent to which one's behavior "measures up" to societal standards is typically used as a gauge of one's ethicality. There are a variety of standards for societal behavior, of course, so ethical behavior is often characterized with respect to certain contexts. In the context of "doing the local government's business," ethics has to do with the extent to which a person's behavior "measures up" to such standards as the law, local government policies, professional association codes, popular expectations regarding "fairness" and "rightness," plus one's own internalized moral standards.

Standards of Behavior

"The law" (including statutory, administrative, and case law) is one important and legitimate source of ethical guidance, of course. Federal, state, and local laws establish the parameters within which the local government's business is done. Violation of the law is almost always considered unethical behavior (with the possible exception of "civil disobedience" as a mechanism for putting the law itself on trial). One who pursues the local jurisdiction's business outside the law is considered to be following an "obstructionist" approach to ethics. Such an individual would almost certainly be labeled an "unethical local government leader."

A second important source of authority consists of the formal policies of the local government. These are standards for behavior established by the organization, and all elected and appointed officials, as well as all public employees within the jurisdiction, are expected to follow them. Typically they are in alignment with the law (which takes precedence over them) and spell out in detail "how things are to be done around here." *All* employees are expected to adhere to these organizational policies! It is very important that leaders at the highest level of the local government set the example for others by working always within the law and the policies of the jurisdiction.

Likewise, another important source of ethical guidance consists of the codes of behavior adopted by professional associations, such as the league of municipalities, the association of county commissions, and the state and national associations of city managers. These are often "aspirational" in nature, and frequently establish higher standards for behavior than the law requires. Members of a professional association typically aspire to meet these higher standards in order to establish and uphold the reputation of the local government as professionally managed.

A fourth type of standard—often unwritten and "commonly understood"—is the community's conceptualization of morality. These social mores, based on commonly held beliefs about "what is right and what is wrong" and "what is fair and what is unfair" can be powerful determinants of one's reputation in society. Behavior that—in the strictest sense—meets legal requirements, jurisdictional policies, and even professional standards may *still* be viewed by the general public as unfair and wrong.

Yet a fifth set of standards are those of the individual conscience. "Highly ethical" local government leaders typically have moral standards that exceed all four of the lesser standards listed above. These values, learned early in life and reinforced by life's experiences, are internalized standards that are often based on individual religious and/or philosophical understandings of morality.

Ethical Dilemmas

An ethical dilemma is a situation with a potential course of action that, although offering potential benefit or gain, is also unethical, in that it would violate one or more of the standards described above. The key question for the local government official, of course, when presented with an ethical dilemma is: "What do you do?" It is one's behavior that determines one's reputation for ethicality, after all. Ethical leadership is exhibited when ethical dilemmas are resolved in an appropriate manner.

Here is a sampling of some of the ethical dilemmas that frequently arise in the context of doing the local government's business:

- Providing a service you know is harmful or unsafe
- Misleading someone through false statements or omissions
- Using "insider information" for personal gain
- Playing favorites
- Manipulating and using people

- Benefiting personally from a position of trust
- Violating confidentiality
- Misusing public property or equipment
- Falsifying documents
- Padding expenses
- Taking bribes or kickbacks
- Participating in a cover-up
- Committing theft or sabotage
- Committing an act of violence
- Committing substance abuse
- Committing acts of negligence or inappropriate behavior in the workplace

Poor Ethical Choices

Why do people sometimes make poor choices when faced with ethical dilemmas? One set of reasons has to do with flaws of *character*. Such character defects include malice (intentional evil), sociopathy (lack of conscience), personal greed, envy, jealousy, resentment, the will to win or achieve at any cost, and fear of failure. There also may be flaws in an *organizational culture* that lead even "good" people to make poor ethical judgments.

Weaknesses in organizational culture include indifference, a lack of knowledge or understanding of standards on the part of officials or employees, poor or inappropriate incentive systems, and poor leadership, including the use of "mixed signals" such as:

- "I don't care how you do it, just get it done!"
- "Don't you ever bring me bad news!"
- "Don't bother me with the details; you know what to do."
- "Remember, we always meet our budget somehow."
- "Can't you find some way to get this accomplished?"
- "No one gets injured on this worksite . . . period. Understand?"
- "Ask me no questions, I'll tell you no lies."

Statements such as these, given by public managers to their subordinates, too often imply that unethical behaviors that obtain the intended results are acceptable to the local government. While it may be difficult—other than through means of termination or other sanctions—to rid the organization of employees with character flaws, improving a poor organizational culture is *clearly* a matter of leadership.

Establishing a Strong Ethical Culture

Local government leaders who wish to take proactive measures to establish and maintain an organizational culture that emphasizes strong moral leadership are advised to take the following steps:

1. *Adopt a code of ethics.* The code need not be long and elaborate with flowery words and phrases. In fact, the best ethical codes are stated simply in language anyone can understand. A good way to produce such a code is to ask all employees of the jurisdiction to participate in its creation. Identify the moral beliefs and values of the officials and employees of the local government and codify them into a written document that all can understand and support. Post the ethics code in prominent places around the worksite. Make certain that all officials and employees subscribe to it.

2. *Provide ethics training.* From time to time the local government leadership should conduct ethics training sessions. These may be led by experts in ethics, or they may be informal in nature and led by the leaders and/or employees themselves. A highly effective way to conduct an ethics training session is to provide "what if . . ." cases for discussion and resolution. The leader presents a "real world" scenario in which an ethical dilemma is encountered. Using the jurisdiction's code of ethics as a guide, participants then explore options and seek a consensus ethical solution. This kind of training "sharpens" the written ethical code and brings it to life.

3. *Hire and promote ethical people.* This, in concert with step four below, is probably the best defense against putting the local government at risk through ethical lapses made by employees with character flaws. When making human resources decisions, it is critical to reward ethical behavior and punish unethical behavior. Investigate the character of the people you hire, and do your best to hire people who have exhibited high moral standards in the past. Base promotional decisions on matters of character in addition to matters of technical competence. Demonstrate to your public employees that high ethical standards are a requirement for advancement in the jurisdiction.

4. *Correct unethical behavior.* This is the complement of step three. When the organization's ethical code is breached, the employee(s) responsible must be punished. Many local governments use "progressive discipline," with an oral warning (intended to advise the employee of what is and is not acceptable behavior) as the first step, followed by a written reprimand, suspension without pay, and termination as further disciplinary action if unethical behavior persists. Of course, some ethical lapses are so egregious that they require suspension—or even termination—following the first offense. Through consistent and firm application of sanctions to correct unethical behavior, the local government leaders will signal to all employees that substandard moral behavior will not be tolerated.

5. *Take a proactive strategy.* Community leaders who wish to establish a reputation for ethicality and good relations with the citizenry will often organize and support programs intended to "give something back" to the community. Programs that promote continuing education, wholesome recreation, good health

and hygiene, nutritious diet, environmental quality, adequate housing, and other community benefits may be undertaken in an effort to demonstrate the extent to which the local government promotes care and concern for human welfare. Seeking out and adopting "best practices" from other jurisdictions is also a proactive strategy.

6. *Conduct a social audit.* Most local governments are familiar with the process of financial audits. This concept can also be employed in the context of ethics and government responsibility. From time to time local government leaders might invite responsible parties to examine the jurisdiction's purchasing, service provision, citizen relations, and human resources functions as well, with an eye toward identifying and correcting any areas of policy or practice that might raise ethical concerns.

7. *Protect whistle blowers.* A "whistle blower" is a person within the organization who points out ethically questionable actions taken by other employees—or even by managers and local officials—within the jurisdiction. (The term is borrowed from the athletic arena, where referees "blow the whistle" when a foul is committed.) Too often whistle blowers are ignored—or even punished—by those who receive the unpleasant news of wrongdoing within the local government. All this does is discourage revelation of ethical problems. Instead the whistle blower should be protected, and even honored. When unethical actions are uncovered within a jurisdiction by one of its own employees, that is the time for local government leaders to step forward and take corrective action (as described in step four above). Employees observe and learn from one another. If the elected and appointed officials of a local government "turn a blind eye" toward wrongdoing, a signal is sent to everyone within the jurisdiction that ethicality is not a characteristic of their government's organizational culture.

8. *Empower the guardians of integrity.* The local government leader's chief task with respect to establishing a culture of ethicality is to lead by example and to empower every member of the organization to take personal action that demonstrates the governing body's commitment to ethics in its relationships with citizens, suppliers, employees, and other government entities. Turn each employee of the jurisdiction, no matter what that individual's position in the organizational hierarchy, into a guardian of the government's integrity. When maliciousness and indifference are replaced with a culture of integrity, honesty, and ethicality, the local government will reap long-term benefits from all quarters.

A Checklist for Making Good Ethical Decisions

A local government leader who takes seriously the challenge of creating a strong ethical culture for the jurisdiction must, of course, make good decisions when faced personally with ethical dilemmas. Here is a "checklist" a public leader might wish to follow in deciding what to do when presented with an ethical dilemma:

1. Recognize the ethical dilemma;
2. Get the facts;
3. Identify your options;
4. Test each option: Is it legal, right, beneficial? Note: Get some counsel!;
5. Decide which option to follow;
6. Double-check your decision;
7. Take action.

A key step in this checklist is number six: Double-check your decision! When in doubt consider how each of the following advisers might guide you. (Or, better yet, *ask* your most trusted advisers!) Then take the action that would allow you to maintain your reputation as a public servant who adheres to the highest ethical standards:

- Your attorney
- Your accountant
- Your electorate
- Your colleagues in government
- Your political supporters
- Your family
- The newspaper
- The television news
- Your religious leader
- Your Deity

How would you feel if you had to explain your decision—and your actions—to each of these parties? If you would not feel good about making a detailed explanation to each of them, then it is quite likely that you are about to make a poor decision. Double-check your decision in this manner before you take any action you may later regret.

Concluding Thoughts About Ethical Leadership

A local governing body's reputation for leadership may take years—even decades—to establish, but it can be destroyed in an instant through unethical behavior. That is why it is so important for local government leaders to be very careful about the things they say and do. Remember: The public is always listening and watching! Taking the time and effort to establish and maintain an organizational culture of morality, integrity, honesty, and ethicality will pay important dividends throughout the history of the jurisdiction. While "taking ethical shortcuts" may appear to lead to gains in the short term, this type of leadership strategy almost always proves tragic in the longer term.

Every local government leader will be faced at one time or another with an ethical dilemma. Many face even daily temptations. How the leader manifests moral integrity when faced with ethical dilemmas sets the tone for everyone else in the organization. This is why it is so important to "walk the talk" by making good ethical decisions every day. Understanding and applying the concepts presented in this chapter will enable you, as a local government leader, to create and maintain an ethical culture in your jurisdiction. As Carl Skoogland, the former vice president and ethics director for Texas Instruments, recently advised, if you want to create an ethical organization, you must *"know what's right . . . value what's right . . . and do what's right."*[15]

SUMMARY

We have sought in this chapter to provide pragmatic advice to local government leaders as they wrestle with three key issues: economic development, financial management, and ethical leadership. We recognize that these are but a few of the many challenges facing local government officials, but we also believe that they are three of the most critical. Local government is the closest to the people, and in many ways the most critical to their well-being. By working in tandem with the citizenry and business community in economic development, by following the ten steps we recommend to assure good financial management, and by taking the suggestions we offer to create an ethical climate within which the local government's business is done, our readers can do much to improve the lives and circumstances of their local citizenry. We encourage local elected and appointed public officials to take their leadership responsibilities seriously and work toward the betterment of all citizens in the jurisdiction.

NOTES

1. William I. Sauser, Jr., "Staying Sane in an Ever Changing World," in *Accountability and Radical Change in Public Organizations*, ed. Ronald R. Sims, 243–269 (Westport, CT: Quorum, 1998).

2. John McKnight, *The Careless Society, Community and Its Counterfeits* (New York: Basic Books, 1995), 117.

3. Southern Growth Policies Board, "Reinventing the Wheel: Report on the Future of the South 2003." The SGPB adopted the following regional objective in 2003: "Build the civic capacity of Southern communities to respond to emerging opportunities and challenges with new models of leadership, engagement and social capital."

4. According to Robert Putnam, "'social capital' refers to features of social organization, such as networks, norms, and trust that facilitate coordination and cooperation for mutual benefit." (Robert D. Putnam, "The Prosperous Community, Social Capital and Public Life," *American Prospect* 4 (13): March 21, 1993.) Putnam regards social capital as the foundation for successful community building. In contrast to all other concepts related to development, social capital is unique in that it is *relational.* "Whereas economic capital is in people's bank accounts and human capital is inside their heads, social capital inheres in the structure of their relationships. To possess social capital, a person must be related to others, and it is these others, not himself, who are the actual source of his or her advantage. As an attribute of the social structure in which a person is embedded, social capital is not the private property of any of the persons who benefit from it. It exists only when it is shared" (Deepa Naraya, *Bonds and Bridges, Social Capital and Poverty* [World Bank, Poverty Reduction and Economic Management Network, Poverty Division, 1999], 6).

5. David Mathews, "The Little Republics of American Democracy," *Connections* 13 (2) (March 2003): 2–6. The quotation is from page 6.

6. Edward Banfield, *The Moral Basis of a Backward Society* (New York: Simon and Schuster, 1958).

7. Robert Putnam, Robert Leonardi, and Raffaella Y. Nanetti, *Making Democracy Work: Civic Traditions in Modern Italy* (Princeton, NJ: Princeton University Press, 1992).

8. See Bryan J. Kurey, "It Takes a Village: Social Capital and Development in Rural China," MA thesis, George Washington University, May 2000, and Stephen Knack, "Social Capital, Growth, and Poverty: A Survey of Cross-Country Evidence," Social Capital Initiative Working Paper No. 7, World Bank, Social Development Department, Washington, DC, 1999.

9. Christian Grootaert and Thierry Van Bastelaer, *Understanding and Measuring Social Capital: A Synthesis of Findings and Recommendations from the Social Capital Initiative.* Social Capital Initiative Working Paper No. 24, World Bank, Washington, DC, 2001.

10. See Vaughn Grisham, Jr., *Tupelo: Evolution of a Community* (Dayton, OH: Kettering Foundation Press, 1999) and Vaughn Grisham and Bob Gurwitt, *Hand in Hand: Community and Economic Development in Tupelo* (Washington, DC: Aspen Institute, 1999).

11. For an expanded version of this section see Joe A. Sumners, "Shared Learning with Uniontown: Lessons in Community Development," *Connections* 13 (2) (March 2003): 16–18.

12. See R. Lawson Veasey and Kelly Hawkins, "The Ebb and Flow of Global Competition: Morrilton, Arkansas, the 'Phoenix of Small Town America,'" *Arkansas Business and Economic Review* 32 (4) (Winter 2000): 9–12.

13. David Osborne and Ted Gaebler, *Reinventing Government: How the Entrepreneurial Spirit Is Transforming the Public Sector* (Reading, MA: Addison-Wesley, 1992): xxi.

14. Harry P. Hatry, "Would We Know a Well-governed City If We Saw It?" *National Civic Review* 75 (1) (May–June, 1986): 142–146.

15. Carl Skoogland, "Establishing an Ethical Organization." Plenary address at the Conference on Ethics and Social Responsibility in Engineering and Technology, New Orleans, LA, October 16, 2003.

PART IV

Leadership Across Multiple Organizational Contexts

CHAPTER 13

DEVELOPMENTAL-SERVANT LEADERSHIP FOR HUMAN RESOURCE PROFESSIONALS

JERRY W. GILLEY AND ANN GILLEY

Contemporary organizations are strongly in need of leadership that is broad and deep in terms of both philosophical underpinnings and required business-related skills. This is particularly true of the human resource (HR) leaders within contemporary organizations, as focus has shifted to emphasize the critical role that human resources play in long-term organizational success. Traditionally, human resource professionals are responsible for providing services such as administration of personnel records and activities, payroll management, compensation and benefits management, employer relations, training and development, employee compliance and outplacement services, recruiting and staffing. Human resource professionals need to provide expanded services to meet the constantly growing needs of their organization (Fiorelli, Longpre, and Zimmer 1996), including business consulting, employee communications, feedback, change management, and organizational redesign to serve the needs of tomorrow's businesses. These expanded services satisfy the needs and wants of both internal and external stakeholders by providing them value-added results.

According to Hesselbein, Goldsmith, and Beckhard (1995), today's HR leader is not the leader of the future. They suggest that a number of changes will take place requiring HR leaders to adjust their behavior and efforts. First, HR leadership will be shared throughout an organization rather than residing at the top of organizations. Second, individual leadership will be replaced by team leadership. Third, tomorrow's HR leaders will be more likely to ask questions than to give directives. Fourth, HR leaders will be more likely to identify and live with paradoxes than to look for and accept simple solutions. Fifth, charismatic leaders will be less important than those who have the ability to achieve results. Sixth, global thinking will replace an exclusively domestic focus. Seventh, interest in questions and learning will replace focus on solutions and answers. Consequently, tomorrow's HR leaders must discover ways of incorporating these changes into their respective practices.

Transforming the traditional HR function into a cutting edge, responsive, results-based entity requires HR professionals to adopt a new set of guiding principles (Fiorelli, Longpre, and Zimmer 1996, 49), including:

- focusing on business processes such as marketing, manufacturing, accounting, and so forth

239

- learning through collaboration and teamwork
- global orientation with local implementation
- enhanced commitment to people while meeting business needs, and
- measuring the value of every HR activity

Guiding principles provide direction and focus for HR professionals. They also establish a value-based approach critical to creating an organizational culture supportive of employee growth and development and organizational results.

Although HR professionals may be experts in HR practices, they will be of little value to the organization unless they are able to adapt their practices and business conditions. Ulrich (1997) suggests, therefore, that HR professionals add value to the organization by providing leadership that demonstrates their understanding of business operations. As a result, HR professionals need to gain operational experience in functional areas such as marketing, finance, operations, or sales. Operational understanding allows HR professionals to generate pertinent, practical solutions for their clients.

Nadler and Wiggs (1986) identified several characteristics of effective HR leaders. They contend each is essential to the development of a comprehensive and competent HR program. First, HR leaders plan HR activities that enhance learning, performance improvement, and organizational development. Such activities are targeted at employees, managers, and organizational leaders to improve organizational performance and effectiveness. Second, HR leaders establish goal priorities for the HR activities over a one- to five-year time span and should be linked with the organization's overall strategic plan and initiatives. Third, they identify the most appropriate organizational structure. They further decentralize the HR function within other operating units and divisions as needed. Fourth, HR leaders effectively communicate their ideas and vision of the organization. Fifth, they identify and develop effective information systems as a means of establishing good internal and external data sources. Sixth, HR leaders develop a mission-oriented position description for their professional staff, which includes specific performance outputs, activities, and standards. Seventh, they develop technical competence and practical expertise. Eighth, HR leaders allow others (organizational leaders, managers, and employees) to become a part of the HR decision-making process by providing opportunities for greater involvement and responsibility. Ninth, HR leaders must be role models of developmental-servant leadership.

The collective thinking of these theorists and practitioners clearly indicates the need for a new model of leadership to be embraced by the professional HR community. Only in this way will the HR leaders of tomorrow be able to meet the increasing demands outlined above. Developmental-servant leadership provides just such a leadership approach.

WHAT IS HR DEVELOPMENTAL-SERVANT LEADERSHIP?

Today's human resource functions require a new type of leader—one who realizes that organizational renewal and competitive readiness are totally dependent on employees prepared for future challenges, new work assignments, ever-increasing competition, life-long learning and change, and continuous growth and development. Therefore, we must differentiate leadership's myths and misconceptions. First, management and leadership are not the same thing. Management focuses on maintaining systems and processes, while leadership involves vision and influencing people to follow (Maxwell 1998). Second, leadership is not about the position one holds but about influencing others to contribute their expertise, perform beyond their abilities, and continually grow and develop. Third, many leaders are entrepreneurs who possess persuasive abilities. However, not all entrepreneurs are leaders. Entrepreneurs are often independent, self-centered, anarchistic, and lacking the long-term influence over others that leaders enjoy. Fourth, effective leaders are not compelled to constantly demonstrate their superiority or knowledge, realizing instead that their employees are more knowledgeable and experienced than they are regarding certain organizational issues and processes. Accordingly, they are subordinate to their employees, reinforcing the servantship philosophy so critical to HR professionals. Finally, true leadership occurs when one is able to articulate and inspire passion around a vision, broaden and elevate the interests of employees, generate awareness and acceptance of the purposes and mission of the group, and motivate people to look beyond their own self-interests for the good of the whole group.

To meet these challenges, HR professionals establish conditions under which employees can develop, transform, grow, and flourish. Accordingly, we refer to such HR professionals as *developmental-servant leaders*. Boyett and Boyett (1995, 186) discuss several characteristics of developmental-servant leaders, who:

- are servants first—driven by the need to learn and serve,
- lead by listening—to their followers,
- help people articulate their own goals—and that of the group by reaching consensus on a common will,
- inspire trust—via their actions, beliefs, and value placed on followers,
- take people and their work seriously—exhibiting commitment to employee growth, development, and ability to be self-led.

Collins (2001, 20) refers to this leadership style as *Level 5 Executive Leadership*, which "builds enduring greatness through [a] paradoxical blend of personal humility and professional will."

As developmental-servant leaders, HR professionals make several assumptions that guide their actions and behaviors. Human resource professionals assume that every employee can be trusted to perform to the best of his/her skills and abilities, has the right to be informed about the decisions of the organization, its mission and strategy, and prefers to be an involved contributor rather than a passive observer. They also believe that employees are willing to take risks if the organization establishes a safety net, enjoy teamwork and group harmony, are improvable, and want to grow and develop. Further, they believe that employees prefer to feel important, needed, useful, successful, proud, and respected, that they desire to develop a positive relationship with leaders, managers, and co-workers, prefer meaningful, challenging work, desire to be appreciated and recognized for their accomplishments, and prefer responsibility to dependency and passivity. Finally, employees prefer a self-directed leadership approach to an authoritarian approach and want the organization to become successful and to meet its strategic business goals and objectives (Maslow 1998).

When HR professionals adopt a developmental-servant leadership approach, they advocate, encourage, and support employees and accept their overall and career development responsibilities by working tirelessly to help others grow and develop. Moreover, they adopt a personal philosophy of humility and a willingness to work for the betterment of others. They assist employees as they struggle to become the best they can be and share organizational success with them. They make certain that other decision makers in the organization are aware of their employees' contributions to achieving desired organizational results, accept responsibility for their failures, celebrate their successes, and engage employees by expressing interest in their careers and professional contributions. Above all, developmental-servant leaders operate without regard for their own well-being or career advancement because they believe that their employees are the organization's most important asset.

In the final analysis, a developmental-servant approach requires leaders to encourage employee growth and development above and beyond oneself, which is perhaps the most difficult aspect of leadership. Quite simply, the lasting value of a developmental-servant leadership is measured by a person's ability to help others succeed without regard for creating a personal legacy. Maxwell (1998, 215) calls this the *law of legacy*, whereby an HR professional's lasting value is measured by succession. He further contends that "a legacy is created only when a leader puts his/her organization into position to do great things without him/her" (1998, 221). Most important, developmental-servant leaders are servants because it is the right thing to do.

Developmental-servant leaders involve and engage employees at all levels, building collaborative, trusting partnerships to craft and implement a challenging vision. Developmental-servant leaders advocate for, encourage, and support employees. A developmental-servantship approach exudes a personal philosophy of humility compounded with a tenacious willingness to work for the betterment of others despite the necessity to make difficult decisions.

As developmental-servant leaders, HR professionals are dedicated to creating a culture that supports, encourages, guides, and directs the organization as it addresses ever-changing market conditions. In short, HR professionals must exhibit several key characteristics. They are servants first—driven by the need to learn and serve. They lead by listening to employees and helping them articulate their own goals—and those of the group—by reaching consensus on a common will. As such they inspire trust—via actions, beliefs, and value placed on employees.

Developmental-servant leadership does not mean that HR professionals are weak or unable to make difficult decisions. It simply infers a personal philosophy of humility and a willingness to work for the betterment of others. As developmental-servant leaders, HR professionals help their organization by assisting, growing, and developing its most important asset: its people. Quite simply, servantship means being a caretaker without regard for one's own personal needs or the rewards that are typically afforded leaders responsible for the professional lives of others—a tremendous responsibility, and one that should not be taken lightly.

Human resource professionals delegate tasks and responsibilities to others because they are secure with themselves and realize that opportunities for growth and development stimulate employees. Leaders also understand that they will receive credit for a job well done because part of their job is being delegated. Furthermore, they are supportive of their employees' careers and professional lives. As such, employees are willing to discuss important issues openly and honestly, without fear of negative repercussions or reprisals, and are willing to become vulnerable and exposed rather than guarded and controlled. When this type of behavior is evident, *honesty and openness* will be mutual on the part of leaders and employees.

TEN PRINCIPLES OF DEVELOPMENTAL-SERVANT LEADERSHIP

Ten principles of developmental-servant leadership guide HR professionals (Gilley and Maycunich 2000a). The ten principles are clustered into four categories:

1. relationship-oriented principles,
2. employee-oriented principles,
3. performance-oriented principles, and
4. organizationally oriented principles.

Each of these categories and the related principles are discussed at length below.

Relationship-oriented Principles

Relationship-oriented principles emerge when developmental-servant leaders work closely and amicably with managers and employees. The application of these principles enables HR professionals to demonstrate trustworthiness and respect, encourage collaboration, improve interpersonal relationships, and build teamwork. Relationship-oriented principles are personal accountability and trustworthiness:

- *Personal accountability* occurs when HR professionals understand they are responsible for their own behavior, actions, and organizational results, including the policies, procedures, incentives, interventions, and plans they advocate and implement.
- *Trustworthiness* is based on truth, integrity, respect, and character. Integrity implies open, honest, and direct communication, and avoidance of hidden agendas that discourage positive working relationships, while respect involves believing in others and holding them in high regard.

Employee-oriented Principles

Employee-oriented principles reaffirm that without employees and their contributions, organizations would not be able to achieve their strategic business goals and objectives. Again, this demonstrates that employees are the organization's most important assets. Logically, HR professionals serve as employee advocates and conduits of their self-esteem. Employee-oriented principles are employee advocacy and employee self-esteeming:

- *Employee advocacy* is based on an HR professional's willingness to develop others' abilities to assume new roles and responsibilities, which is quintessentially a growth and development strategy.
- *Employee self-esteeming* is based on the tremendous need of organizational leaders (including HR professionals) and employees to feel confident about themselves and their experiences, skills, and abilities.

Performance-oriented Principles

As developmental-servant leaders, HR professionals rely on performance-oriented principles to improve employee performance and productivity and help their organizations achieve the business results needed. These principles provide a basis for excellence by allowing HR professionals to communicate their expectations in a clear, motivational, and inspirational manner. Performance-oriented principles are performance partnership, organizational performance improvement, and effective communications:

- *Performance partnership* is based on the belief that employees are more willing to be supportive of growth and development activities when they are actively involved in their establishment.
- *Organizational performance improvement* is based on the practice of achieving organizational results through people. Accordingly, HR professionals create work climates and environments in which employees are encouraged to demonstrate creative solutions to complex problems, challenged to perform at maximum levels, required to participate in growth and development interventions, engaged in quality initiatives, and asked to participate in continuous organizational improvement activities.
- *Effective communications* require HR professionals to use all means of interpersonal communications available to stimulate and challenge employees at all levels to perform to the best of their abilities and to grow and develop.

Organizationally Oriented Principles

Organizationally oriented principles are those that developmental-servant leaders use to help other organizational leaders create work climates, environments, and organizational cultures that foster employee growth and development. These principles involve organizational consistency, holistic thinking, and organizational subordination.

- *Organizational consistency* requires HR professionals to filter decisions through a set of guiding principles that control and influence their actions. In this way, they demonstrate consistent behavior and decision making—avoiding the latest fads and trends typical of so many organizations.

- *Holistic thinking* requires HR professionals to collaboratively create and articulate a vision for their organization and identify an actionable game plan to achieve this vision. Holistic thinking consists of three elements:

  1. *Visionary thinking* allows employees to focus on a common set of goals and outcomes that gives their daily activities serious meaning and determines an organization's success.
  2. *Strategic thinking* is the ability to direct one's attention to an organization's future. It includes the ability to anticipate business trends and processes, and break them down into manageable units for others to understand and implement.
  3. *Critical reflective thinking* is the ability to understand one's values and beliefs, and to know why one behaves in a particular manner.

- *Organizational subordination* is simply a process by which HR professionals place the contributions, involvement, and loyalty of employees above those of the organization. By doing so, they attempt to guarantee organizational subservience to employees' efforts to improve efficiencies, productivity, and approaches essential to competitive readiness and organizational renewal. Quite simply, developmental-servant leaders *get out of the way*, allowing employees to work effectively and efficiently, enabling them to demonstrate insightful, creative, and innovative approaches to organizational problems and performance difficulties.

Gilley, Boughton, and Maycunich (1999) believe that developmental-servant leaders demonstrate organizational subordination by eliminating policies, procedures, and structures that interfere with, prevent, or discourage employee growth and development, and by eliminating organizational structures that inhibit two-way communication. Additionally, they display organizational subordination by eliminating negative and personally demanding work climates, creating organizational cultures in which employee growth and development are encouraged and sponsored, creating performance management systems that foster employee growth and development, and creating work environments in which continuous learning and change are the norm. As developmental-servant leaders, HR professionals demonstrate organizational subordination by transforming performance appraisals into developmental evaluations that support employee growth and development, creating compensation and reward systems that recognize and reward employee growth and development, selecting managers and supervisors for their employee development and interpersonal skills, rather than their personal performance records, and eliminating political favoritism and replacing it with a performance-oriented promotion system based on continuous employee growth and development. Finally, they display this principle by encouraging employee career development and linking it with long-term human resource planning initiatives, selecting employees based on their readiness to learn, change, grow, and develop, and linking employee growth and development to the organization's mission and strategy.

DEVELOPMENTAL-SERVANT LEADER AS STRATEGIC BUSINESS PARTNER

When HR professionals internalize the ten principles of developmental-servant leadership, they are capable of becoming strategic business partners responsible for building relationships, championing employee growth and development, and improving organizational performance capacity.

As *strategic partners*, HR professionals have the ability to communicate the benefits that change strategies and innovations provide for the organization, while concurrently ensuring a shared understanding of the critical factors that affect organizational competitiveness. Strategic partners possess a thorough understanding of business fundamentals, core processes, operations, and procedures. As a result, HR professionals are able to establish connections between departments within an organization by communicating the value and importance of teamwork. When cooperation such as this is present, the affected parts of the organization work together in harmony.

Some HR professionals fail to be perceived as valuable because their programs and services are not linked to the organization's strategic business goals, while others falter because HR professionals do not properly communicate the value and benefits of their interventions and initiatives to decision makers within the firm. Although these are contributing factors, most HR programs suffer from a poor image because organizational leaders, managers, and employees do not view HR departments and their professionals as vital, contributing members of the firm. At this point, HR is unable to improve the organization's performance, quality, efficiency, or productivity, or help it accomplish its strategic goals and objectives.

To be effective, HR professionals need to become proactive in their efforts to change the negative perceptions of themselves and their programs. They need to discover ways of enhancing their credibility, and, thus, their effectiveness. One approach is for HR professionals to become strategic business partners. A strategic business partner is a person who "takes part" with others, and partnerships involve the "parts" we each play in our work. Partnerships are essential to the success of any organization.

There are two primary elements of partnership: *purpose* and *partnering* (Bellman 1998). Purpose defines "why" a partnership is needed, and provides a focus and direction for the partnership. Without a purpose, no partnership exists. Purpose may be quite clear and explicit, such as that imposed by an organizational leader or manager (client), or implicit, such as a mutual exploration of a purpose about to be defined. Purpose, in essence, brings us together. Partnering occurs when HR professionals and clients pursue a common purpose together. Partnering exemplifies the visible and invisible dynamics between HR professional, client, and purpose, the result of clarifying roles and focus. It also embraces underlying assumptions, trust and risk, shared values, and expectations. Much that is key to partnering often goes unexpressed. Bellman (1998) suggests that HR professionals and clients who attend to purposes but neglect partnering often fail in their work altogether.

Strategic business partnerships are intra-organizational alliances formed in which HR professionals align themselves with organizational leaders, managers, supervisors, and employees to help the organization achieve its strategic business goals and objectives as well as to ensure successful completion of the firm's overall strategic plan. Strategic business partnerships are long-term-oriented and interdependent, allowing HR professionals to better understand and anticipate their clients' needs. These partnerships help HR professionals develop a responsive attitude, which is necessary for them to become customer service-oriented. HR professionals as strategic business partners break down the walls between themselves and their clients. As a result, lasting commitments are forged and investments are made in learning, performance, and change efforts. Partnerships encourage HR professionals to fully understand their clients and the value they bring to an interaction. Consequently, HR professionals become immersed in their clients' performance problems, needs, concerns, and expectations.

Strategic business partnerships give HR professionals the opportunity to develop personal relationships with clients. Alliances allow HR professionals and clients to build trust and develop a shared vision of the future through a free exchange of ideas, information, and perceptions. Larry Wilson, founder of the Wilson Learning Corporation and Pecos River Learning Center, believes that strategic business partnerships also promote establishment of working relationships based on shared values, aligned purpose and vision, and mutual support.

In creating strategic business partnerships HR professionals demonstrate both a willingness to intimately know those they serve and their ability to learn from clients. Furthermore, partnerships are based upon the business and performance needs of clients, not of the HR program. Becoming a strategic business partner allows HR professionals to direct all efforts at satisfying their clients, including designing and developing services in accordance with their clients' expressed interests, as well as to provide consulting activities that improve the organization and its competitive readiness.

Creating strategic business partnerships enables HR professionals to address various demand states facing their programs. Demand describes the number of clients who have the capacity and willingness to exchange their time, effort, and commitment for a program or service offered by the HR department. Over time, demand will change for every program or service offered by HR. To be effective, HR professionals must know how to identify ever-changing conditions and how to react. Creating strategic business partnerships promotes HR professionals' response to client demands by altering, changing, or improving their interventions and services.

Better management of limited financial and human resources is another reason for creating strategic alliances. Partnerships help HR professionals decide which programs or services provide the highest value and have the greatest impact on the organization. Armed with this information, HR professionals are in a better position to appropriate resources that maximize organizational performance and results.

Finally, creating strategic business partnerships produces economic utility, which is measured in terms of increased organizational performance, revenue, profitability, quality, or efficiency. Overall, strategic alliances afford HR professionals and their clients opportunities to work in harmony for the purpose of improving the economic viability of the organization. A healthy organization benefits all.

Steps in Becoming a Strategic Business Partner

The four strategies critical for becoming a strategic business partner are to establish credibility, develop a customer service strategy, exhibit business acumen, and demonstrate organizational knowledge.

Establish Credibility

The first and most important step in becoming a strategic business partner is to establish credibility within the organization. Improved credibility results from HR professionals' ability to demonstrate professional expertise as well as their understanding of organizational operations and culture. In this way, HR professionals are able to provide real value to the firm.

Additionally, HR professionals establish credibility within organizations in numerous ways. First, they demonstrate the ability to solve complex problems, which results in improving one's ability to satisfy client needs and expectations. Second, they exhibit professional expertise along with understanding of organizational operations and culture. Doing so enables HR professionals to establish respect for their insight and particular area of expertise. Third, credibility can be transferred, most commonly by third-party referrals. This is often referred to as a network, which is a collection of individuals who can introduce HR professionals to key organizational decision makers while keeping them informed. Fourth, credibility can be developed via reputation, commonly by delivering results. In essence, credibility must be earned.

Credibility can also be established through an appropriate understanding of differing roles. Within a partnership, clients are accountable for results, clarity of vision and values, managing resources (time, energy, money, human talent, materials, equipment, environment), creating structures and systems, and strategic decision making. Ulrich (1997, 253–254) points out that HR professionals need to demonstrate several behaviors in order to enhance credibility. First, they need to be accurate in all HR practices. This includes analysis activities (performance, needs, causal, organizational), design of HR programs and services, recruiting and selection, job design, performance appraisals and management activities, compensation and benefits, and performance and organizational development consulting. Second, HR professionals need to be predictable and consistent, that is, dependable and reliable so that decision makers have confidence in their actions and recommendations. Third, they must meet their commitments in a timely and efficient manner. Fourth, HR professionals need to establish collaborative client relationships built on trust and honesty. Fifth, they must express their opinions, ideas, strategies, and activities in an understandable and clear manner, and at the most appropriate times. Sixth, they need to behave in an ethical manner that demonstrates integrity. Seventh, HR professionals must demonstrate creativity and innovation. Eighth, they need to maintain confidentiality. Ninth, they need to listen to and focus on client problems in a manner that brings about mutual respect.

The HR professional's role exudes competence combined with adaptability in its focus on client needs. This role encompasses clarity regarding one's contributions, awareness of the organization's needs, developing alternatives, revealing new perspectives, modeling risk taking, and knowledge of the consulting process—all while honoring one's personal purpose, vision, values, and core beliefs. When appropriate roles are executed, trust and confidence emerge, which deepens relationships and bridges performance uncertainty. Over time, improved efficiency results, as collaboration and cooperation replace competition and conflict.

Develop a Customer Service Strategy

The second step in becoming a strategic business partner is for HR professionals to develop a customer service strategy that satisfies their stakeholders' needs and expectations. Such a strategy ensures that HR programs and services are designed in accordance with the stakeholders' expressed interests, which assures that the HR department focuses on maximizing organizational performance. As a result, HR departments will be supported as well as defended by stakeholders during difficult economic periods, and HR is viewed as essential to the firm's long-term success.

A stakeholder can be defined as anyone who has something to gain or lose as a result of an interaction with human resources. These gains and losses collectively frame needs and become the target for performance improvement interventions and change initiatives. The typical stakeholders of HR include:

- *Managers* are primary customers because they endure the cost of programs and services and reap the benefits.
- *Employees* are those who participate in programs and services.
- *Senior managers* expect programs and services to return value and help the organization achieve its goals.
- *Organizations* need the skills, abilities, and capabilities of employees to produce and deliver high quality products and services at a profit, and rely on employees' capabilities to remain competitive.

As such, each of these constituencies has a critical stake in the services provided by HR professionals.

A customer service strategy that satisfies stakeholders' needs and expectations consists of six steps (Gilley and Maycunich 1998):

1. *Establishing a customer service philosophy* requires HR professionals to be true developmental-servant leaders, willing to place the business and professional needs of their clients above their own.

2. *Creating a customer service environment* demonstrates willingness to listen to clients, respond to their demands, and work with them in a collaborative manner.

3. *Creating customer service opportunities* requires face-to-face interaction, the result of unwavering dedication to client satisfaction.

4. *Implementing customer service* requires HR professionals to become active participants with clients rather than passive observers, and embodies ample questioning, listening, and facilitating skills that lead to viable recommendations and solutions.

5. *Evaluating the utility and shortcomings of customer service* involves feedback from clients regarding their satisfaction with HR interventions and initiatives.

6. *Implementing areas for improvement in customer service* is always based upon the feedback received from clients.

Ultimately, an effective customer service strategy becomes a guiding principle for HR professionals, which directs their decisions and actions.

Exhibit Business Acumen

The third step in becoming a strategic partner requires HR professionals to demonstrate an understanding of business strategies, goals, tactics, and financial performance. Consequently, HR professionals need to acquire a knowledge of business fundamentals, systems theory, firm culture, and politics. An awareness of how organizations work is essential for HR professionals and enables them to think the way their clients do. This understanding requires knowledge of how things get done and how decisions are made inside a firm. Human resource professionals possessing business understanding are better able to facilitate change without disrupting the firm's operations.

Human resource professionals add value by understanding business operations, thus allowing HR personnel to adapt their practices and activities to changing business conditions. Although HR professionals may be experts in learning, performance, and change initiatives, these skills will be of little value to the organization unless the HR professionals are able to adapt their practices to fluctuating business conditions and circumstances. Consequently, HR professionals need to gain experience in functional areas such as marketing, finance, operations, or sales to generate pertinent, practical solutions for their clients.

As a member of the organizational family responsible for its improvement, HR professionals promote business initiatives that help the firm improve its competitive readiness, performance capacity, and renewal capabilities. They design and implement programs and services that enhance employee productivity and performance, which leads to overall organizational improvement.

Demonstrate Organizational Knowledge

Although most traditional HR professionals are experts in their respective disciplines (such as compensation, recruiting and selection, payroll administration, training and development), they add little value to the organization unless they are able to adapt their practices to economic conditions or link learning to the organization's business strategy (Brinkerhoff and Apking 2001). Consequently, it is essential that HR professionals demonstrate their operational experience in functional areas such as operations, finance, marketing, manufacturing, quality control, and strategy. Demonstrating ones organizational knowledge further improves a transformational professional's impact and influence (Fuller and Farrington 1999). Human resource professionals who develop a knowledge of organizational fundamentals, systems theory, organizational culture, and politics reveal an understanding of organizational philosophy that guides action. Furthermore, it is critical for HR professionals to think the way their clients do, understand how things get done inside the firm, and how and why decisions are made.

Ulrich (1997) suggests that HR professionals add value to the organization by understanding the organization's operations, which allows them to adapt their practices and activities to changing environmental conditions. He states that HR professionals must possess financial and organizational understanding in order to generate pertinent, practical solutions for their employees.

Organizational knowledge permits HR professionals to be credible members of the firm who are responsible for its improvement. By understanding organizational operations, HR professionals can recommend initiatives that help the organization improve its competitive readiness, performance capacity, and renewal capabilities. They can encourage developmental programs that motivate employees to increase their personal productivity and performance, which leads to overall organizational improvement. As a result, effective HR professionals adapt their practices, procedures, products, innovations, and services based upon this knowledge, which allows them to better serve their clients.

Strategic Partner Subroles

The final step in becoming a strategic business partner occurs when HR professionals engage in several subroles that enable them to respond to unforeseen contingencies and sensitive issues, to provide appropriate solutions to complex problems, and to conduct a wide range of activities designed to modify or enhance results. These subroles include: *relationship builder, influencer, consensus and commitment builder, employee champion, performance engineer, change agent, problem solver*, and *analyst*.

Relationship Builder

Few HR professionals develop successful alliances with organizational leaders, managers, or employees. As a result, they often lack credibility with critical groups, which creates an environment of mistrust and cynicism. Human resource professionals who act as developmental-servant leaders develop relationships that enhance their credibility and influence within the firm.

Building collaborative relationships allows HR professionals to develop trust and honesty, which breaks down barriers to communication, reinforces the investments made in learning, and forges lasting commitments to change. Collaborative relationships enable HR professionals to develop the responsive attitude necessary for them to become customer service-oriented.

Collaborative relationships are synergistic by design, long-term-oriented, and mutually beneficial alliances to help the organization successfully achieve its goals and objectives. Such relationships enable HR professionals to acquire the responsive attitude necessary for them to better understand and anticipate employee and organizational needs.

Human resource professionals become competent *relationship builders* by turning assertions into questions, giving clients options, making meetings and reports meaningful, helping clients implement solutions and interventions, being accessible, and always, always adding value (Gilley and Coffern 1994). Human resource professionals enhance relationships by encouraging the development of critical thinking skills that improve clients' professional practices and result in better approaches to accomplishing work.

Influencer

As *influencers*, HR professionals are directive in their efforts to influence client thinking, initiate change, or provide specific recommendations that address difficult performance problems. Human resource professionals need to guard against their own personal biases and overpowering opinions, remaining receptive to others' views, ideas, and recommendations in order to be successful in the influencer subrole. Simultaneously, they encourage organizational members to take risks in order to achieve their goals and objectives.

Consensus and Commitment Builder

Burke (1992) suggests that HR professionals serve as *consensus and commitment builders* among organizational leaders and decision makers to facilitate lasting and needed change. In this role, HR professionals use a participatory, synergistic approach and collaborate with employees in a cognitive, perceptual, and action-taking process to solve problems (Lippitt and Lippitt 1986). This requires them to become active participants in the problem-solving process. Consensus and commitment builders use a partnership approach to focus their attention on identifying problems, evaluating, selecting, and carrying out alternatives, providing sound and convincing recommendations, and presenting them persuasively.

Serving as consensus and commitment builders requires HR professionals to establish a collaborative working relationship with employees (Gilley and Boughton 1996). Turner (1983) contends that an effective relationship becomes a collaborative search for acceptable answers to employees' real needs and concerns. This mutually beneficial relationship embodies trust and a readiness for change.

Employee Champion

Human resource professionals are in a unique position to serve as *employee champions* (Ulrich 1997). In this role, HR professionals explore the correct balance between work expectations and resources, identify legitimate demands on employees, and help workers to focus by setting priorities. Employee champions also develop creative ways of leveraging resources so that employees do not feel overwhelmed by the demands of the job.

Challenging work demands force employees to respond appropriately by allocating resources in an efficient, effective manner. Ulrich (1997, 135) identified ten questions to determine whether employees and firms are responding appropriately to demand situations:

1. Do employees control key decision-making processes that determine how work is done? (*control*)
2. Do employees have a vision and direction that commits them to working hard? (*commitment*)
3. Are employees given challenging work assignments that provide opportunities to learn new skills? (*challenging work*)
4. Do employees work in teams to accomplish goals? (*collaboration, teamwork*)
5. Does the work environment provide opportunities for celebration, fun, excitement, and openness? (*culture*)
6. Are employees compensated and rewarded for work accomplishments? (*compensation*)
7. Do employees enjoy open, candid, and frequent information sharing with management? (*communication*)
8. Are employees treated with dignity while differences are openly shared and respected? (*concern for due process*)
9. Do employees have access to and use of technology that makes their work easier? (*computers and technology*)
10. Do employees have the skills necessary to do their work well? (*competence*)

Answers to these questions (1) determine the adequacy of employee *control*, (2) identify employee *commitment* to the organization, (3) indicate whether the firm provides *challenging work* for employees, (4) reveal the degree of employee *collaboration and teamwork*, (5) illustrate the adequacy of organizational *culture*, (6) determine the quality of the *compensation* and reward system, (7) identify the quality and quantity of organizational *communications*, (8) indicate the *concern for due process*, (9) determine the adequacy of *technology*, and (10) reveal overall employee *competence* (Ulrich 1997).

Performance Engineer

Performance improvement is the ultimate goal of and therefore a critical responsibility of HR professionals (Gilley and Maycunich 2003). As *performance engineers*, HR professionals participate in performance improvement initiatives for the purpose of helping employees develop diagnostic skills to address specific performance problems, and focus on *how* things are done rather than on *what tasks* are performed. This requires HR professionals to examine organizational structure, job design, work flow, performance appraisal and review, employee attitudes, performance management procedures, performance standards, and quality improvement processes (Ulrich, Zenger, and Smallwood 1999; Rummler and Brache 1995). Such analysis enables HR professionals to develop a greater understanding of the necessary actions required to improve individual and organizational performance.

Performance engineers improve performance best by implementing an organization-wide performance management system (Fuller and Farrington 1999). The goal of such a system is to guarantee that the right individuals have the knowledge, skills, motivation, and environmental support to do their jobs successfully. Dean (1999) suggests that performance management relies on performance, causal, and root-cause analysis to identify current and desired performance, while taking into account the impact of the organization and work environment, motivation system, employees' competencies, material resources, and appraisal systems. Quite simply, Gilley and Maycunich (2000b) suggest that performance management identifies breakdowns within an organizational system and appropriate interventions useful in achieving desired performance results.

Change Agent

As *change agents*, HR professionals improve effectiveness and responsiveness via organizational transformation. In short, change agents facilitate and manage change, which is sometimes referred to as change management. According to French, Bell, and Zawacki (1999), change management is not a "fix-it" strategy but rather a continual way of managing organizational change that, over time, becomes a way of organizational life. Change management involves goal setting, action planning, monitoring, feedback, and evaluating results (Beer 1997).

Change management is also a systems approach that closely links employees to technology, organizational processes, and change. Employee demands for better work environments and participation in decision making, ever-changing economic conditions, and market competitiveness force organizations to adjust to constantly mobile marketplaces.

Change agents initiate collaborative forums allowing employees to function as vital contributing human beings instead of resources in the productivity process (Burke 1992). They provide opportunities for all employees, and the organization itself, to develop their full potential. Change management increases organizational effectiveness by helping organizations achieve their strategic organizational goals and objectives. Employees find the environment exciting, the work challenging, and they have multiple opportunities to influence the way in which they relate to work, the environment, and the firm.

As change agents, HR professionals are the captains of the change process, which includes (1) developing and communicating a change vision, (2) creating a sense of urgency for change, (3) facilitating organizational change, (4) solving problems, and (5) performing analysis.

Developing and Communicating a Change Vision. Without a shared sense of direction, interdependent employees may constantly conflict, whereas a shared change vision clarifies the direction of change and helps them agree on its importance and value (Quatro, Hoekstra, and Gilley 2002). Kotter (1996, 70) suggests that HR professionals create a change vision in order to direct their efforts and develop strategies for achieving that vision. *Vision* is a picture of the future with some implicit or explicit commentary on why people need to strive to create that future. He believes that an effective change vision serves three important purposes, it:

1. clarifies the general direction for an organization,
2. acknowledges that sacrifices will be necessary to achieve desired particular benefits, and
3. coordinates the actions of different employees by aligning them in a remarkably efficient way.

Creating a Sense of Urgency for Change. Many organizations fail to adapt quickly to external conditions because they do not recognize the signs of intimate danger. Gilley and Boughton (1996) refer to this period as organizational equilibrium, because the stress levels are low and productivity is adequate. However, they warn that this period occurs when the organization becomes too comfortable and fails to maintain its competitive spirit. If allowed to last too long, results may be disastrous. Kotter (1996) adds that change usually goes nowhere when organizational leaders are comfortable with the status quo and lack the power, enthusiasm, credibility, and influence to communicate a need for change. It is equally difficult to energize employees when complacency is high.

Kotter (1996, 44) identified nine ways that HR professionals may raise the level of urgency:

1. Create a crisis by allowing a financial loss, expose HR professionals to major weaknesses, or allow errors to blow up instead of being corrected at the last minute.
2. Eliminate obvious examples of excess (e.g., company-owned condos or airplanes, executive dining rooms).
3. Establish revenue, productivity, customer satisfaction, and cycle-time targets so high that they can't be reached via operations as usual.
4. Stop measuring sub-organization performance based solely on narrow functional goals and insist that more people be held accountable for broader measures of financial performance.
5. Make available more data about customer satisfaction and financial performance.
6. Insist that people interact regularly with unsatisfied customers and disgruntled stakeholders.
7. Use consultants and other means to provide more relevant data and honest discussion at meetings.

8. Promote honest discussions of problems in company newsletters and senior administrators' speeches, and stop senior administrators' "happy talk" about real, serious problems.
9. Provide employees with information on future opportunities, on the rewards for capitalizing on those opportunities, and on the organization's current inability to pursue those opportunities.

Although each may generate results, the first four are perceived primarily as negative attempts to raise the urgency level and the last five are perceived as positive means for raising the urgency level.

Facilitating Organizational Change. HR professionals are responsible for implementing change and guaranteeing that change is supported at the operational level of the organization (Ulrich 1997; Burke 1992). Rothwell (1996, 217–221) maintains that HR professionals have the ability to implement or coordinate implementation of organizational development strategies, integrating them with strategic plans, politics, work processes, culture, structure, and employee input into decisions.

Human resource professionals also participate in implementing solutions while serving as linkages between important employee groups (Ulrich, Zenger, and Smallwood 1999). Without these key connections, implementing change will not occur, regardless of the developmental-servant leader's efforts. Another way of implementing change is to assemble a guiding coalition (Kotter 1996) of leaders, managers, and employees who are supportive of the change.

Problem Solver

Many organizations rely on internal problem solvers, which should include HR professionals, to identify and solve their problems. As *problem solvers*, HR professionals make certain that the perceived problem is indeed the one that needs solving. Ineffective HR professionals spend the majority of their time providing solutions to problems that do not exist rather than determining the accuracy of the problem. Problem solvers take an active role in the change process and rely on their objectivity to help them evaluate existing problems and explain possible solutions.

Analysts

Nilson (1999) and Rossett (1999) contend that as developmental-servant leaders, HR professionals serve as analysts responsible for determining the need for performance improvement interventions and change initiatives. As *analysts*, HR professionals define the current and desired states as a way of identifying the need for change (Fuller and Farrington 1999). Effective HR professionals analyze the business issues facing an organization to identify the root causes for change. These approaches determine whether the root cause is a gap caused by the firm, its people, their behavior, consequences of performance, feedback, or other environmental factors. After the root causes have been identified, HR professionals validate them in a reliable manner, such as through observations, interviews, and the like (Rossett 1999). Further, HR professionals communicate with clients about the need for change in a straightforward and understandable way. They examine the organizational system, obtain permission to proceed with a change analysis, define business issues with their clients, and decide what measures will be used to gauge the change initiative's rate of success (Gilley and Maycunich 2000a). Finally, Clark and Estes (1996) suggest that HR professionals can avoid being distracted by irrelevant behaviors that will negatively affect implementing change by focusing on the results that need to be achieved to meet business goals.

KEY BENEFITS FOR BOTH HR PROFESSIONALS AND THEIR ORGANIZATIONS—SOME CONCLUDING REMARKS

One of the primary benefits of a developmental-servant leadership approach is having the right people, with the right competencies, in the right place, at the right time. Consequently, it is important to select and develop human resources necessary to meet the business goals and objectives facing an organization now and in the future. Specific strategies that bring about desired results include (Fiorelli, Longpre, and Zimmer 1996, 48):

1. creating competitive advantage through people and processes, and
2. building competencies in people and the organization.

To create competitive advantage through people and processes, growth-oriented organizations employ and support developmental-servant leadership. In this way, organizations treat their employees as their most valuable component in achieving organizational renewal and competitiveness.

As developmental-servant leaders adept at developing strategic business partnerships, HR professionals are in a position to influence the direction of the organization as well as to enhance the value of HR programs and services. Strategic business partnerships are synergistic, mutually beneficial, and long-term-oriented. These relationships require HR professionals to develop a responsive, customer service orientation that better understands and anticipates client needs. The principal benefits to organizations are improved performance and efficiency, while HR professionals enjoy increased credibility and influence within the firm. Strategic business partnerships satisfy the needs of internal and external clients alike, while positioning HR professionals in a more positive light within the organization as "selfless" professionals intent on developing the capabilities of the organization and its employees.

REFERENCES

Beer, M. (1997). "The Transformation of the Human Resource Function: Resolving the Tension between a Traditional Administrative and a New Strategic Role." In *Tomorrow's HR Management: 48 Thought Leaders Call for Change*, ed. D. Ulrich, M.R. Losey, and G. Lake, 84–95. New York: Wiley.

Bellman, G. (1998). "Partnership Phase: Forming Partnerships." In *Moving From Training to Performance: A Practical Guide*, ed. D.G. Robinson and J.C. Robinson, 39–53. San Francisco: Berrett-Koehler.

Boyett, J.H., and J.T. Boyett. (1995). *Beyond Workplace 2000: Essential Strategies for the New American Corporation*. New York: Dutton.

Brinkerhoff, R.O., and A.M. Apking. (2001). *High Impact Learning: Strategies for Leveraging Business Results Through Training.* Cambridge, MA: Perseus.

Burke, W.W. (1992). *Organizational Development: A Process of Learning and Changing.* Reading, MA: Addison-Wesley.

Clark, R.E., and E. Estes. (1996). "Cognitive Task Analysis." *International Journal of Educational Research,* 25 (3): 403–417.

Collins, J. (2001). *Good to Great: Why Some Companies Make the Leap . . . and Others Don't.* New York: Harper Business.

Dean, P. (1999). "Designing Better Organizations with Human Performance Technology and Organization Development." In *Handbook of Human Performance Technology: Improving Individual and Organizational Performance Worldwide,* ed. H.D. Stolovitch and E.J. Keeps, 321–334. San Francisco: Jossey-Bass.

Fiorelli, J., E. Longpre, and D. Zimmer. (1996). "Radically Reengineering the Human Resource Function: The National Semiconductor Model." *Organizational Development Journal* 14 (1): 48–49.

French, W.L., C.H. Bell, Jr., and L. Zawacki. (1999). *Organizational Development: Behavioral Science Interventions for Organizational Improvement.* Englewood Cliffs, NJ: Prentice Hall.

Fuller, J., and J. Farrington. (1999). *From Training to Performance Improvement: Navigating the Transition.* San Francisco: Jossey-Bass.

Gilley, J.W., and N.W. Boughton. (1996). *Stop Managing, Start Coaching: How Performance Coaching Can Enhance Commitment and Improve Productivity.* New York: McGraw-Hill.

Gilley, J.W., N.W. Boughton, and A. Maycunich. (1999). *The Performance Challenge: Developing Management Systems to Make Employees Your Greatest Asset.* Cambridge, MA: Perseus.

Gilley, J.W., and A.J. Coffern. (1994). *Internal Consulting for HRD Professional: Tools, Techniques, and Strategies for Improving Organizational Performance.* New York: McGraw-Hill.

Gilley, J.W., and A. Maycunich. (1998). *Strategically Integrated HRD: Partnering to Maximize Organizational Performance.* Cambridge, MA: Perseus.

———. (2000a). *Beyond the Learning Organization: Creating a Culture of Continuous Growth and Development through State-of-the-Art Human Resource Practices.* Cambridge, MA: Perseus.

———. (2000b). *Organizational Learning Performance, and Change. An Introduction to Strategic HRD.* Cambridge, MA: Perseus.

———. (2003). *Strategically Integrated HRD: Six Transformational Roles in Creating Results Driven Programs.* Cambridge, MA: Perseus.

Hesselbein, F., M. Goldsmith, and R. Beckhard, eds., (1995). *The Leaders of the Future.* San Francisco: Jossey-Bass.

Kotter, J.R. (1996). *Leading Change.* Boston: Harvard Business School Press.

Lippitt, G., and R. Lippitt. (1986). *The Consulting Process in Action,* 2d ed. San Diego: University Associates.

Maslow, A. (1998). *Maslow on Management.* New York: Wiley.

Maxwell, J.C. (1998). *The 21 Irrefutable Laws of Leadership: Follow Them and People Will Follow You.* Nashville, TN: Thomas Nelson.

Nadler, L., and G. Wiggs. (1986). *Managing Human Resource Development: A Practical Guide.* San Francisco: Jossey-Bass.

Nilson, C. (1999). *The Performance Consulting Toolbook: Tools for Trainers in a Performance Consulting Role.* New York: McGraw-Hill.

Quatro, S.A., E. Hoekstra, and J.W. Gilley. (2002). "Holistic Model for Change Agent Excellence: Core Roles and Competencies for Successful Change Agency." In *Changing the Way We Manage Change,* ed. R. Sims, 55–84. Westport, CT: Quorum Books.

Rossett, A. (1999). "Analysis for Human Performance Technology." In *Handbook of Human Performance Technology: Improving Individual and Organizational Performance Worldwide*, ed. H.D. Stolovitch and E.J. Keeps, 139–162. San Francisco: Jossey-Bass.

Rothwell, W. (1996). *Beyond Training and Development: State-of-the-Art Strategies for Enhancing Human Performance*. New York: AMACOM.

Rummler, G.A., and A.P. Brache. (1995). *Improving Performance: How to Manage the White Space on the Organizational Chart*. San Francisco: Jossey-Bass.

Turner, A.N. (1983). "Consulting Is More Than Giving Advice." *Harvard Business Review* 61 (5): 120–129.

Ulrich, D. (1997). *Human Resource Champions*. Boston: Harvard Business School Press.

Ulrich, D., J. Zenger, and N. Smallwood. (1999). *Results-Based Leadership: How Leaders Build the Business and Improve the Bottom Line*. Boston, MA: Harvard Business School Press.

CHAPTER 14

ENGAGING PEOPLE'S PASSION

Leadership for the New Century

DIANA BILIMORIA AND LINDSEY GODWIN

> *The final test of leaders is that they leave behind in*
> *others the conviction and the will to carry on.*
> Walter Lippmann

As the curtain of each new era lifts, the world stage shifts and changes to create its new set against which the drama of business must be played. The global and diversified stage that is being unveiled today presents business leaders with very different circumstances than those that leaders faced even a decade ago. The old rules of business are quickly slipping into obsolescence. The old model of organization, complete with its specialized job positions, formal hierarchy, standardized rules and operating procedures, and set boundaries served as a static blueprint from which leaders could plan out courses of action. In that model, leadership and management were synonymous. In the emerging century's new organizational model, however, the same clear-cut directions are not provided for leaders. Capturing this evolution of management and leadership, Bennis notes that:

> There is a profound difference between management and leadership, and both are important. To manage means to bring about, to accomplish, to have charge of or responsibility for, to conduct. Leading is influencing, guiding in a direction, course, action, opinion. The distinction is crucial. . . . Leaders are people who do the right things and managers are people who do things right. Leaders are interested in direction, vision, goals, objectives, intention, purpose, and effectiveness—the right things. Managers are interested in efficiency, the how-to, the day-to-day, the short run of doing things right. (Bennis 1997, 6)

Leaders today face organizations that are flatter, more networked, flexible, diverse, and continually influenced by the globalization forces at play in the world. With this new model come new challenges and organizational priorities that extend beyond profit management and include a broader definition of what a successful workplace means. Organizations today also face increased emphasis on employee well-being, environmental protection, equitable treatment for all workers, and concerns for socially responsible business practices (Lipman-Blumen 1996). In such a fluid and diverse environment, effective leadership is more vital than ever if organizations are not only going to survive, but thrive. Leaders no longer have an effective blueprint for what their organization should look like nor does the new organizational model automatically equate management with leadership. Instead, today's organizations realize that effective leadership not only exists, but is needed at every level of the organization.

Developing more effective leaders is not just good advice for creating a successful organization, it is a vital prerequisite. In the tumultuous, globalizing environment that organizations face today, effective leaders must move their organizations forward, unleashing the best within others even during difficult times. And many would argue that today's world is increasingly difficult, as it is a "time marked by two contradictory forces, interdependence and diversity, pulling in opposite directions" (Lipman-Blumen 1996, 3). While the globalization of markets has led to increased reliance on networks and relationships around the globe, it has also amplified the variety that exists within these networks. "The leadership challenge at the very top of complex organizations appears sometimes to be almost overwhelming. Establishing and implementing sensible strategies for business is rarely easy. In many situations today the technological, competitive markets, and economic and political uncertainties make strategic decision making horrendously complicated . . . thousands of executives around the world are facing just these kinds of challenges today" (Kotter, 1998, 13).

The new paradigm of organizing, characterized by increased global connectivity, diversity, lean operations, and speed of responsiveness, has slowly been emerging over the past several decades, but it now provides the backdrop against which leaders must act everyday. As illustrated in Table 14.1, Caproni captures the new dynamics that leaders face today when they must create stability in the midst of an ever-changing world. Primarily, these dynamics indicate the need for leaders to act with enhanced inclusion and engagement of others, flexibility, responsiveness, openness, ethicality, and proactivity. Furthermore, even in the face of the new tensions and challenges, leaders are held to a high standard of behavior; they are regarded as role models for, and living images of, the values to which society and organizations proscribe.

To effectively address the various pressures that can so easily emerge and overtake organizations in today's seemingly chaotic postindustrial world, leaders must create a compelling contagion of positive emotion in organizations, offering inspiration, hope, stimulation, and productive challenge to organizational members, and countering unproductive spirals of anxiety, doubt, anger, fear, despair, and cynicism (Boyatzis et al. in press). The ripples of effective leadership are felt not only throughout an organization, but also beyond. Yet, those positive waves must begin somewhere, and in this chapter, we suggest that they begin with the leadership act of igniting the passion within others. As the poet and philosopher Henri-Frédéric Amiel wrote, "Without passion man is a

Table 14.1

The Changing Face of Leadership

Old organization	New organization	Consequences for leaders
Stable, predictable environment	Changing, unpredictable environment	From routinization to improvisation, adaptability, and flexibility
Stable and homogenous workforce	Mobile and diverse workforce	From one-size-fits-all styles to multiple styles
Capital and labor-intensive firms	Knowledge-intensive firms	From machine and industrial relations models to learning models of organizations
Brick-and-mortar organizations	Brick-and-click organizations and e-commerce	From managing relationships face-to-face to managing with technology
Knowledge and product stability	Knowledge and product obsolescence; mass customization	From routinization to improvisation, adaptability, and flexibility
Knowledge in the hands of a few	Knowledge in the hands of many	From manager as expert to manager as a creator of context that enhances learning
Stability of managerial knowledge and practices	Escalation of new managerial knowledge and practices	From a focus on learning to a focus on learning and unlearning
Technology as a tool for routine tasks	Escalating information and communication technologies	From using technology for tasks to using it as a key leadership resource for wide-scale changes
Local focus	Local and global focus	From one-size-fits-all styles and standards to multiple
Bureaucracy	Networks	From command and control to relationship building and fluid organizational boundaries
Managers as fixed cost	Managers as variable cost	From security to pay for performance
Predictable, trajectory careers	Multiple careers	From employment to employability
One-breadwinner families	Dual and triple career families	From emphasis on traditional family roles to an emphasis on fluid family roles, flexible work schedules, and work/life balance

Source: Caproni 2001.

mere latent force and possibility, like the flint which awaits the shock of the iron before it can give forth its spark" (*Columbia World of Quotations* 1996). Similarly, unless leaders can tap into their followers' passion, they have not truly begun to lead their organization toward what is possible.

Indeed, the job description of today's leaders has changed in comparison with the past, with organizations and society alike raising the bar regarding their expectations of leaders. Therefore, given the increasing importance of leadership in today's organizational context, it is necessary that new frameworks be developed to help clarify and prepare individuals for effective leadership. The purpose of this chapter is to give an overview of the five elements comprising effective leadership in the emerging century's new business paradigm. By engaging people's passion in positive and constructive change, leadership enables people, organizations, and society to address and transcend the tensions, challenges, constraints, and pressures posed by a rapidly shifting, constantly changing, and information-sensitive world. The model of "Engaging People's Passion" provides a coherent lens through which we can look at the factors necessary for effective leadership in the postindustrial age, by showing how leadership must encompass a balance between vision and the fundamental truth, inspiring core values, an engaging and inclusive style, emotional intelligence competencies, and courage.

ENGAGING PEOPLE'S PASSION

> *A vivid imagination compels the whole body to obey it.*
> Aristotle

Like a turbine, change often churns up a myriad of emotional reactions. Therefore, as change continues to be an ever-present reality within the new organizations of today, leaders must expect that feelings of excitement and hope for the future will naturally be coupled with feelings of frustration and confusion for the ambiguity that accompanies any change. While negative reactions from some may be normal, it is the true leader who realizes that nurturing the positive emotions and tapping into people's passions for a better tomorrow are what will result in a successful and sustainable change. Indeed, as research shows, "building and sustaining momentum for change requires large amounts of positive affect and social bonding—things like hope, excitement, inspiration, caring, camaraderie, sense of urgent purpose, and sheer joy in creating something meaningful" (Cooperider and Whitney 2001, 22)

To ignite others' passion, leaders must present a core leadership message that others find compelling and consistent. Jack Welch, former chief executive officer (CEO) of General Electric, refers to this core message as the leader's teachable point of view (Slater 1998). The core leadership message is the overarching story and meaning that the leader conveys, in every interaction, whether with one person or with many. It reveals not only what the leader wants to accomplish and how, but also who the leader is. In this sense, the core leadership message comprises the essence of the leader's story that brings others on board with them. As Carly Fiorina, CEO of Hewlett-Packard, who was

Figure 14.1   **Engaging People's Passion: Effective Leadership for the New Century**

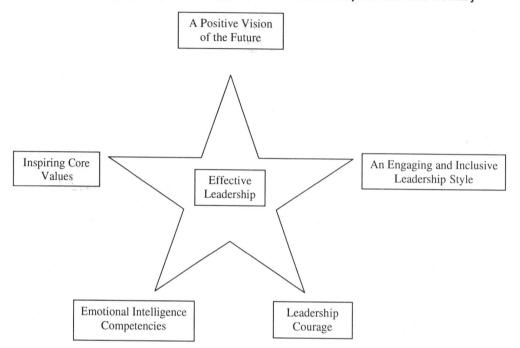

named five years in a row by *Fortune* magazine as "the most powerful woman in American business," reflected upon her success in a 2003 interview, she stated:

> I would say three things [make a difference]. One is that it doesn't matter whether I'm talking to two people, 10 people, or thousands of people. I think about it as if I were speaking to just one person. Every communication is a conversation that has to be real, in which something real is conveyed. The second thing is I try to speak to the essence of things . . . of what matters. And the third thing is I try to communicate from my heart, as well as my head. You can't be persuasive if you don't believe what you're saying. You can't persuade unless you are, yourself, convinced. And conviction is not only about understanding the facts, the figures and the intellectual aspects of it, but it also comes from the heart and the gut. All my experience says that people are their most effective when they are saying what they believe and being who they really are, not when they're saying something they don't believe or trying to be something they're not. (Fiorina 2003, 32–33)

Five elements comprise the core leadership message to make it compelling in engaging people's passion (see Figure 14.1 above). They are (1) a positive vision of the future, (2) inspiring core values, (3) an engaging and inclusive leadership style, (4) emotional intelligence competencies, and (5) leadership courage. In the following sections, we describe each of these elements in detail, providing examples of how each enables effective leaders to engage others' passion to bring out positive and sustainable change in a tumultuous world.

A Positive Vision of the Future

"Where there is no vision, the people perish."
Proverbs 29:18 as quoted by John F. Kennedy, November 21, 1963.

"I skate where the puck is going to be, not where it is or has been."
Wayne Gretzky, hockey champion

Just as travelers on a voyage must know where they are going if they are to successfully reach their destination, organizations need a vision for their journey into the future. Leadership has been defined by some as the ability to create a compelling vision, to translate it into action, and to sustain it (Bennis and Nanus 1985). Indeed, the nature of leadership vision has been the fodder for many authors. While various definitions for "vision" exist, a vision is typically described as being an ideal future image of the organization that represents or reflects the shared values to which the organization should aspire (House and Shamir 1993; Bennis and Nanus 1985; Kouzes and Posner 1987).

A vision can serve many purposes within the organization: it compels, clarifies, uplifts, and directs. A vision not only captivates people's attention, it inspires them to want to help move the organization toward its desired goal. It transforms organizational purpose into individual and collective action. Most important, a vision catapults an organization from its current reality into a desired future.

The importance of having a leadership vision has been supported empirically. For example, a study that explored the impact of vision on organizational growth found that vision significantly affects organizational-level performance (Baum, Locke, and Kirkpatrick 1998). As prior leadership authors have suggested, visions can distinguish the new directions to be pursued from the old while moving people to action (Galbraith and Lawler, 1993).

A key component of an effective leadership vision is a *positive view of the future* of the organization. The envisioned future presents a clear and compelling ideal state to which the organization can aspire. Of course, while future oriented, a vision is not entirely divorced from an organization's current reality. Powerful leadership visions are actually rooted in the organization's core purpose, which is the fundamental reason for the organization's existence, the organization's reason for being (Collins and Porras 1996).

An examination of the content of vision statements of exemplary leaders found that they are often inspirational, optimistic, and future oriented (Bennis and Nanus 1985). Because it allows people to pursue dreams and new possibilities, being future focused has been a characteristic attributed to effective leaders (Hickman 1992; Morden 1997). Mary Parker Follett, a forward thinker on leadership in her own day, states that it is the leader who "can organize the experience of the group . . . it is by organizing experience that we transform experience into power. The task of the chief executive is to articulate the integrated unity which his business aims to be . . . the ablest administrators do not merely draw logical conclusions from the array of facts . . . they have a vision of the future" (1987, 169). Part of having an envisioned future for the organization reflects the fact that effective leaders not only have their finger on the pulse of the organization today, but also have an eye toward the long-run possibilities for the organization. Contrasting the roles of manager and leader, Jack Welch has suggested that organizations need leaders rather than managers, since leaders, "inspire with a clear vision of how to get things done. . . . Managers slow things down, leaders spark the business to run smoothly, quickly. Managers talk to one another, write memos to one another. Leaders talk to their employees, *with* their employees, filling them with vision, getting them to perform at levels the employees themselves did not think was possible. Then they get out of the way" (Slater 1998, 29).

Beyond anecdotal stories, scientific evidence supports the assertion that creating an affirmative vision of the future results in positive outcomes. In medicine, the placebo phenomenon has been cited as an example of how the belief that a treatment will have positive impacts actually leads a person to experience positive impacts regardless of the substance of the treatment (White, Tursky, and Schwartz 1985). Similarly, in the social sciences, the classic, empirically tested Pygmalion study illustrates the fact that having a positive expectancy of an individual can significantly affect how that person is perceived (Rosenthal and Jacobson 1968). In this study, teachers were randomly given either a positive image of a new student or a negative one, with results showing that differences in the student's performance emerged not on the basis of his or her objective intelligence, but rather on the basis of the teachers' subjective image of the student (for a review of other studies verifying affirmative expectancy outcomes, see Rosenthal and Rubin 1978).

Of course, sometimes the anecdotal stories are more compelling than science. Indeed, the effect of having a compelling vision for the future has been the material for the fairy tales of enterprise. There are many examples of powerful dreams leading to unimagined outcomes, such as Ford's future vision in 1907 to democratize the automobile industry, with his bold, fortuitous statement, "When I'm through . . . everyone will have one"; or Sony's vision in the 1950s to change the worldwide image of Japanese products as being of poor quality (Collins and Porras, 1996). Today, visions for a better future, combined with a business's core purpose, continue to propel organizations toward betterment. Take the story of chairman and CEO of Interface, Inc., Ray Anderson, as one example. Interface, Inc. is a Fortune 1,000 company with 24 factories, sales offices in 110 countries, 6,750 employees, a supply chain heavily dependent on petrochemicals, and annual sales of US$1.1 billion (Wong 1999). From its beginnings in 1973, the company has grown to become the world's largest manufacturer of carpet tiles and upholstery for commercial interiors. Recently, Ray Anderson presented a new vision to carry the company into the new millennium. Today, Interface's core vision is not only about making carpets—"it's about becoming a leading example of sustainable and restorative enterprise by 2020 across 5 dimensions: people, planet, product, process and profits" (Wong 1999). Anderson (1992) is working to articulate his vision of making Interface a truly sustainable and restorative company, with statements like:

> I have challenged the people of Interface to make our company the first industrial company in the whole world to attain environmental sustainability, and then to become restorative. To me, being restorative means to put back more than we take, and to do good to the Earth, not just no harm. (Anderson 1992)

By articulating a vision for the company that incorporates, yet extends the organization's core purpose, Anderson has been a catalyst for a new business model not just for Interface, but for other organizations that want to push their industry toward sustainability. The company developed the "Evergreen Lease" through which it aims never to lease rather than sell carpet, which will allow Interface to be able to collect its old carpet tiles and recycle them into new ones, building customer loyalty while driving down material costs (Fishman 1998). Trying to lead by example, Interface currently practices in-house recycling, makes carpet from recycled soda bottles, and even recycles discarded carpet from other manufacturers (Online Ethics Center for Engineering 2003). Anderson continues to push forward his vision for the company, admitting that there is still more work to be done in order to create a truly green company, and proposing that the organization eventually attain "closed-loop recycling," in which there will be no waste products or pollution produced (Online Ethics Center for Engineering 2003). Illustrating the truly optimistic, future-oriented nature of visions, Anderson says, "I want to pioneer the company of the next industrial revolution," pushing all industries to move from the current linear process of raw materials, energy, product, packaging, marketing, waste to cyclic capitalism where companies actually consume their own waste (Fishman 1998).

Merely having a vision that includes a positive state of the envisioned future is not enough unless the leader articulates the vision compellingly (House 1977; Kouzes and Posner 1987). Researchers have explored the various mechanisms though which leaders can communicate their vision throughout the organization—from written memos to speeches and pep talks—however, most research agrees that an effective leader uses a variety of forms of interpersonal communication to express vision (Bass 1985; Kouzes and Posner 1987; Conger and Kanungo 1987). Even on clean, crisp stationery, one can imagine how different an impression Martin Luther King's famous vision statement, "I Have a Dream," would have made on followers if it had been communicated via a memo or sent electronically via e-mail; the message might not have held the same power as it did coming from the impassioned leader himself. Regardless of what method leaders use to convey their vision, they have to make sure that their followers not only understand it, but also support it. As Kouzes and Posner write, "The image that the followers develop in their minds is highly dependent upon the leader's ability to describe an apple so that it appears as an apple in the minds of others" (1987, 100).

Additionally, the leader must make sure that the followers indeed want apples and not oranges. A leader's vision is not just a static statement, but rather a relationship with his or her followers—it is a co-created image for the future of the organization. In a study exploring successful public figures in the United States, Bennis and Nanus (1985) found that these leaders created a vision that others could believe in and adopt as their own. As reflected in the words of Jack Welch, "Somehow, the leader and the led have to define a vision that everyone can share" (as cited in Tichy and Sherman 1994, 181). Just as one cannot force a river to flow backward, effective leaders do not try to force their followers to go where they do not want to go, but rather they influence and direct the course that already exists.

Behind every great vision is great passion. Hegel once said, "Nothing great has been and nothing great can be accomplished without passion" (1971, 235). Emerson said that "Nothing great can ever be achieved without enthusiasm" (1981, 240). Thus, to help create the strongest current moving toward a positive future, leaders must tap into the passions of their followers, not just their intellect and reasoning. By doing so, they ensure that people are not only on board with the vision, but they will have the energy and excitement to travel a sometimes difficult course, to ensure that the vision comes to fruition.

Creating a shared vision does not mean that there will be no challenges to that vision. At times, an effective leader must be able to articulate the vision of the future even in the face of opposition. What if Henry Ford had been deterred by the bank president who thought that, "The horse is here to stay, the automobile is a novelty"? What kind of world would we live in today if aerospace leaders did not hold fast to their future-oriented visions when the *New York Times* wrote in 1936, "A rocket will never be able to leave the earth's atmosphere." Or, how different would our lives be if leaders in the computer business did not continue to present their future visions when other technology leaders at the time were saying, "There is no reason for any individual to have a computer in his home" (Winter 2000)?

Just as these visionary leaders of the past used passionate visions of a positive future state to propel their companies and industries in uncertain times, a passionate vision is a necessary bulwark against the challenges inherent in the new organizational paradigm. Sustainable success within the new, tumultuous, global stage similarly requires a compelling, positive vision to engage and unify people across boundaries and differences.

Inspiring Core Values

> *What we must decide is perhaps how we are valuable rather*
> *than how valuable we are.*
> –Edgar Friedenberg

Just as a vision guides an organization, something must help guide the vision. A leader's vision is not born in a vacuum, rather it needs to be rooted in the values of the organization. Values are an organization's essential and enduring tenets that act as the general guiding principles for all organizational decisions, and that cannot be compromised for financial gain or short-term expediency. Values indicate what the organization stands for, on what it will never compromise, what the expectations are for everyone in the organization, and what the organization wants to be remembered for. While values may seem intangible, they are a necessary component of any effective leadership. Jack Welch articulated this by commenting:

> The most effective competitors in the twenty-first century will be the organizations that learn how to use shared values to harness the emotional energy of employees. As speed, quality, and productivity become more important, corporations need people who can instinctively act the right way, without instructions, and who feel inspired to share their best ideas with their employers. That calls for emotional commitment. You can't get it by pointing a gun. You can't buy it, no matter how much you pay. You've got to earn it, by standing for values that other people want to believe . . . and by consistently acting on those values." (as cited in Tichy and Sherman 1994, 195)

Effective leaders become the living models of the values they espouse; in other words, they must "walk the talk." Echoing this sentiment, former cabinet secretary John Gardner attested, "It is not to find better values, but to be faithful to the values we profess" (1963, 53). Balancing the tension between espoused values, or what we say we believe, and values in use, what we actually do, is an ongoing challenge for any leader (Argyris 1977). Leaders who are effective, however, lead by example, paying attention to their values in use as much as they do to espoused values (Kouzes and Posner 1987). To be role models, leaders not only must manifest a set of values that support the organizational vision, but also must make their rationale and position on these values clear to all. Effective leaders personally embody the values, pushing visibly for the kind of engagement, personal involvement, and policy actions that support the values.

Consider the actions of Maulden Mills CEO Aaron Feuerstein in the face of a devastating fire in 1995 that left his organization, and indeed an entire community that depended on the mill for work, in shambles. Reflecting his deeply held value that the company was more than a business, it was also a home and livelihood to its workers, Feuerstein, a leader who valued his workers as family, translated his value into action when he made a decision that shocked and inspired others around the country. He announced that Maulden Mills would rebuild in the same place, so as not to export the business out of the country in search of cheap labor, and vowed that all employees would be paid their full salaries during the two months it took to rebuild, stating, "I think it was a wise business decision, but that isn't why I did it. I did it because it was the right thing to do" (CBSNews.com, July 2003). Leading with his values, Feuerstein continued making decisions that were in his workers' best interest even as the company faced bankruptcy. By enacting his values through the actions he took, he inspired a passion within his workers, his consumers, and the wider business community. At a time when it seems that stockholders are viewed as the only stakeholders, suddenly here is an example of a business leader acting upon his values and choosing to define his stakeholders more broadly, to include his workers and the community his company was embedded in. Although Feuerstein recently stepped down as CEO, Maulden Mills has been a literal phoenix, rising from the ashes, having since reduced its debt by over half and emerging from Chapter 11 (Pope 2004).

A company does not have to face a crisis to act upon its values, but rather can live every day as a fulfillment of them. Take the Body Shop, a retailer of naturally based skin, hair, and makeup products, as an example. This company not only knows its values and acts upon them, it also proudly articulates them to its customers, allowing them to make informed decisions about purchases from the company as well. The company engages in an interesting process called "social auditing," producing annual documents that reflect the company's performance on environmental, animal protection, and social issues (Sillanpaa 1998). The company's home page has a banner called "Our Values" that proudly displays the words of Margaret Mead: "Never doubt that a small group of thoughtful, committed citizens can change the world. Indeed, it is the only thing that ever has." With a quick mouse click, a new page appears that outlines the organization's entire value code:

- We consider testing products or ingredients on animals to be morally and scientifically indefensible.
- We support small producer communities around the world who supply us with accessories and natural ingredients.
- We know that you're unique, and we'll always treat you like an individual. We like you just the way you are.
- We believe that it is the responsibility of every individual to actively support those who have human rights denied to them.
- We believe that a business has the responsibility to protect the environment in which it operates, locally and globally.

The Body Shop not only states its values on its Web site, it also displays them proudly as logos, or badges of honor, in its stores and on its products so that customers have no question that the company is against animal testing, supports fair trade, wants to activate self-esteem, defend human rights, and protect our planet. Every decision in the company, from marketing to manufacturing, is held up to these standards the organization has defined as its values (The Body Shop). As Anita Roddick, the founder of the Body Shop states, "On the whole businesses do not listen to the consumer. Consumers have not been told effectively enough that they have huge power and that purchasing and shopping involve a moral choice" (Jones 2004).

"Valuing values," as the Body Shop does, may result in more than just making it a friendly company. Current trends suggest that companies that are run with the long-term view of their stakeholders in mind, and that actually incorporate their stakeholders' (including shareholders, customers, and employees) values into the organization actually will increase their competitiveness (Sillanpaa 1998). We suggest that values are an avenue for tapping into the passions of the various stakeholders, and by embracing those values, the organization generates energy for movement into the future from all constituencies: workers want to work there, customers want to shop there, and investors want to invest there.

Effective leaders also realize that values are not static anchors that never change, rather they review and renew values as necessary for the organization to remain vibrant and to remain aligned with new visions as they evolve. While this act is just as important as articulating the values, it is often overlooked. To ensure that the currently espoused values are still a good rudder for the organization, they need to be examined and reaffirmed. As Ruth Davidson Bell claimed, "Each time we rethink our values we reaffirm them or begin to change them" (*Columbia World of Quotations* 1966). Even as an organization's values may change, maintaining a sense of strong values helps unite the diverse and disparate workforce and stakeholders that leaders face today. Building support around a common set of values serves the leader in many ways, in that strong values lead to congruence with actions, as well as provide an impetus toward behaviors that will move the organization toward its desired vision (Kouzes and Posner 1987).

An Engaging and Inclusive Leadership Style

> *The wicked leader is he who the people despise. The good leader is he who the people revere. The great leader is he who the people say, "We did it ourselves."*
> Lao Tsu

While the message leaders communicate matters, the way they go about communicating it matters as well. The organizational culture that a leader creates and sustains can mean the difference between an organization's getting by and its truly excelling. Having an engaging and inclusive style of leadership is key when trying to translate an organization's vision and values into sustainable work practices.

Style is thus yet another feature that distinguishes effective leaders from effective managers. Goleman outlines six leadership styles that seem to emerge within organizations: Coercive leaders demand immediate compliance. Authoritative leaders mobilize people toward a vision. Affiliative leaders create emotional bonds and harmony. Democratic leaders build consensus through participation. Pace-setting leaders expect excellence and self-direction. Coaching leaders develop leaders for the future (Goleman 2000, 79). While each style has its particular strengths, research has shown that leaders who "have mastered four or more styles—especially authoritative, democratic, affiliative, and coaching—have the very best climate for business performance. And the most effective leaders switch, flexibly among the styles as needed." (Goleman 2000, 87). Like barometers, it is important that leaders become sensitive to how their style is impacting the organization. This sensitivity will allow them to calibrate and adjust their style in a way that connects with others.

Whatever style preference leaders have, it is through a style that manifests engagement and inclusion that energy, enthusiasm, high investment, and the desire to excel are created. Effective leaders encourage and empower others to achieve and stretch. They establish challenging performance standards and provide opportunities for growth, encouraging the development of passion in others. Perhaps just as important, they make work meaningful and fun—inspiring people to be present, to contribute, and to serve.

Take Southwest Airlines as an example. This is a company that values fun, service, passion, family, hard work, and engagement. Herb Kelleher, chairman of Southwest, has leveraged his personal leadership style of engagement and inclusion to institutionalize it as an organizational principle. This is illustrated in Kelleher's statement:

> You can't just lead by the numbers. We've always believed that business can and should be fun. At far too many companies, when you come into the office you put on a mask. You look different, talk different, act different—which is why most business encounters are, at best, bland and impersonal. But we try not to hire people who are humorless, self-centered, or complacent, so when they come to work, we want them, not their corporate clones. They are what makes us different, and in most enterprises, different is better." (1974, 20)

The inspirational style that Kelleher embodies is perhaps best reflected in the words of his own employees who celebrated him on Boss's Day in 1994 in a full-page ad in *USA Today* by saying:

> Thanks, Herb
> For remembering every one of our names.
> For supporting the Ronald McDonald House.
> For helping load baggage on Thanksgiving and for giving everyone a kiss (and we mean everyone).
> For listening.
> For running the only profitable major airline.
> For singing at our holiday party and for singing only once a year.
> For letting us wear shorts and sneakers to work.
> For golfing at the LUV Classic with only one club.
> For outtalking Sam Donaldson.
> For riding your Harley Davidson into Southwest headquarters.
> For being a friend, not just a boss.
> Happy Boss's Day from Each One of Your 16,000 Employees! (Schwartz 1996)

Kelleher's unique style has resulted in numerous awards and recognitions, including being named the 1999 CEO of the Year by *Chief Executive Magazine*. The engaging and caring style that Kelleher fostered at Southwest is echoed in the words of one pilot, "Herb is one of the inspirations of this company. He is the guiding light. He listens to everyone. . . . If you've got a problem, he cares" (Gittell 2002, 56). However, he and his fellow leaders have been able to balance the caring style with sincerity and honesty, which also adds to a culture of inclusion, as reflected by another employee:

"Herb Kelleher and Colleen Barrett have both got credibility. It has taken them a while to get to that point. They've created that level of honesty with us. If it's bad, they will tell you it's bad" (Gittell 2002, 56). Indeed by having an inclusive and engaging personal style, Kelleher laid the foundation for the entire company to develop a culture in which individuality, creativity, and fun were not just accepted, but celebrated (Freiberg and Freiberg, 1998).

The importance of having an engaging and inclusive vision is heightened by the new organizational challenges that leaders face. As the workforce continues to diversify and become co-located across the globe, the establishment of a sense of unified purpose and excitement for a common vision is what will keep companies moving forward. Additionally, with the increasing mobility of the workforce, talented individuals are no longer tied to an organization that they do not enjoy, and thus an effective leadership style can help cultivate an environment that attracts, retains, and benefits from inspired, motivated employees.

Emotional Intelligence Competencies

The crisis is in our consciousness, not in the world.
J.K. Krishnamurti

As mentioned earlier, emotions are a human reality. In the old organizational context, however, our models of management painted a sterile picture of organizational life. The interactions between leaders and followers were reduced to prescriptions of command and control. As the dynamic nature of organizational life becomes integrated, and even celebrated in the new organizational model of today, we realize that leadership is embedded within relationships. And, effective leaders are those who can establish resonant relationships (Goleman, Boyatzis, and McKee 2002). A resonant relationship is one in which the leader is emotionally intelligent, meaning he or she is in tune with others, and creates a positive emotional connection with them.

Emotional intelligence is the capacity for recognizing one's own emotions and those of others, for motivating oneself and others, and for managing emotions well in oneself and in relationships with others, to result in improved work performance and enhanced collective effectiveness (Goleman 1998). The essence of emotional intelligence is effectively understanding and managing one's own and others' emotions. Research on emotional intelligence has shown that it is comprised of specific clusters of competencies which, if demonstrated, predict outstanding performance of leaders, managers, and executives (Boyatzis 1982; Spencer and Spencer 1993). These competency clusters include: self-awareness skills (e.g., emotional self-awareness, self-confidence); self-management skills (e.g., emotional self-control, transparency, optimism, adaptability); social awareness skills (e.g., empathy, listening, perspective taking); and relationship management skills (e.g., persuasion, conflict management, collaboration) (Goleman, Boyatzis, and McKee 2002).

As the global circumstances continue to give birth to emotional events such as September 11, 2001, today's leaders are increasingly being looked to in times of crisis and distress. At such times—when organizations are most vulnerable—effective, emotionally intelligent leaders have the opportunity not only to comfort their followers, but also to help them reemerge from the situation fortified and perhaps even stronger than before. Such a case was seen in the wake of the Twin Towers' collapse, when Kenneth Chenault, the CEO of American Express, demonstrated his effective leadership skills by acting emotionally intelligent in the midst of his company's emotional turmoil. Having assumed leadership of the company only months before September 11, Chenault found himself leading a company that had just experienced unfathomable loss. In a matter of hours after the terror attacks, Chenault said that he knew he needed to address, "the immediate needs of the employees and customers and then give the people a sense and some clear direction about how we were going to operate our business and the company, not just in the short term, but the moderate and long term" (Ingram 2002). His composure, coupled with sincere concern, illustrated an important resonant quality in crisis situations, which is to be able to put one's own fears and anxieties aside in order to serve and lead others.

Realizing that effective leadership does not happen at arm's length, Chenault spent countless hours with his employees. As one employee stated, "He was there, and he was in the middle of it" (Byrne and Timmons 2001). Additionally, Chenault did not try to be a man hiding behind a stoic mask, rather he paid heed to his own emotions as well as to those of his grief-stricken employees in person (Bloom 2001) during a meeting of 5,000 employees who gathered in downtown New York City to begin their healing process. He would embrace upset employees, saying, "I represent the best company and best people in the world. You are my strength and I love you" (Bloom 2001, 20). One American Express board member commented after this meeting, "The manner in which he took command, the comfort and the direction he gave to what was obviously an audience in shock was of a caliber one rarely sees" (Byrne and Timmons 2001). Additionally, at this meeting, Chenault also promised to donate $1 million of the company's profits (despite the fact that profits would decrease after the crisis) to the families of the American Express victims, showing his faith in the company financially, as well as his desire to support the company emotionally. Thus, both his actions—convening a meeting in downtown New York when others would not—and his words—honest and heartfelt—evoked a sense of hope in a time of uncertainty.

As Chenault exemplified, being emotionally intelligent can be a source of inspiration to an organization when it needs to be uplifted the most. Emotional intelligence not only moves people during crisis, but also can be a tool to help tap into the passion of others. When leaders are in touch with their own feelings and those of the people around them, they nurture the resonance between them. This resonance, or positive emotional state, in turn becomes a contagion of positive emotion that spreads to others within the organization. A positive emotional state is the buttress that supports a diverse workforce.

Leadership Courage

> *When you see what is right, have the courage to do it.*
> Chinese proverb

> *Courage is not simply one of the virtues but the form of every virtue at
> the testing point, which means at the point of highest reality.*
> C.S. Lewis

In a world where the news headlines are speckled with adrenaline-inducing topics that range from health crises, to corporate corruption, to terrorist alerts, the stakes for leaders seem higher than ever. Leadership has always been about making choices, but the decisions that leaders must make today are increasingly challenging as the world becomes not only more interconnected but also more prone to publicizing every misstep organizations make. Terry Anderson, formerly a U.S. hostage in Iran stated, "People are capable of doing an awful lot when they have no choice. . . . Courage is when you have choices" (*Columbia World of Quotations* 1992). Therefore, in recognition that making the right decision when the world is watching, the final point on the five-star model of leadership is courage.

Increasingly, courage has emerged as a new topic in the area of leadership and as a necessary characteristic of effective leaders. As Robert Staub writes in his article appropriately titled "Courage and Leadership Go Hand in Hand":

> Courage is the key to accessing, developing and engaging three of the great drivers of leadership effectiveness: integrity, passion and intimacy . . . [because] all of them require stepping beyond our personality, ego structure and habitual patterns. . . . It takes courage to face our fears, doubts and to then act. . . . Yet, to lead with integrity, to learn quickly, to generate and transmit learning, and to implement effectively requires moving through the pain, uncertainty and discomfort of changing our thinking and behavior. (Staub 2003)

Other scholars have also begun pointing to courage as a defining trait for effective leaders today. For example, in discussing the important leadership attributes that extend beyond technical competence, Scarnati (1999, 327) highlights courage as, "having the conviction and fortitude to stand up for what you believe." Kanter (1999) proposes that qualities such as courage, traditionally seen as soft qualities, will become increasingly valued within companies in the emerging century. Through the articulation of new visions and values, leaders are effectively asking organizations and the people around them to change, which can seem like a daunting, if not scary proposition in today's marketplace. Additionally, sometimes visions for positive, long-term change may have to be translated through organizational revisions such as downsizing, job reallocations, or loss of short-term profit margins. Courage, therefore, is another necessary behavior for effective leaders to employ as they wade through the ever-shifting, and, at times, ethically cloudy, waters of business. The old grad-school adage still holds true for top executives: What is right is not always going to be popular and what is popular is not always going to be right. Courage to do the right thing, even in the face of resistance or uncertainty, will definitely distinguish exemplary leaders.

Effective leaders demonstrate courage in a variety of ways. They make tough decisions about the business portfolio and resource allocation. When called upon to do so, they make hard choices involving people (e.g., retention, compensation, and advancement). Rather than ignoring problems, they confront them promptly, which sometimes means they have to put themselves on the line. They also stand firm when necessary. Many leaders know what the right thing to do is, but the difference between the average leader and the exceptional one is the courage to act on what they know is right, even when the decision is difficult. Jeffrey Pfeffer writes on why sustainable competitive advantage is so elusive to organizations:

> Everyone wants to earn exceptional returns, but to do it by doing what everyone else does and in the same way too. What our investigation of truly, innovative, entrepreneurial, and high-performing companies reveals is that they don't do what everyone else does. They have leaders at all levels of the organization, with the wisdom and courage to know what to do and how to do it. (Pfeffer 2002, 104)

While courage often comes at a price, it is not without its rewards. In 2002, *Time Magazine* named three women, Coleen Rowley of the FBI, Sherron Watkins of Enron, and Cynthia Cooper of WorldCom as its persons of the year thanks to their courage to speak out against the misconduct and unscrupulous actions of their respective organizations. "They took huge professional and personal risks to blow the whistle on what went wrong at WorldCom, Enron and the FBI—and in so doing helped remind us what American courage and American values are all about" (Lacayo and Ripley 2002). While these examples of courage resulted in the unraveling of organizational transgressions and the dissolution of confidence in these entities, other acts of courage have resulted in bolstered trust in corporations.

Take the story of the 1982 Johnson & Johnson Tylenol recall crisis as an example. After several deaths were linked to the victims taking Tylenol laced with cyanide, the leaders at Johnson & Johnson faced a major ethical and business decision regarding whether or not they would launch a massive national recall of the potentially tainted product. While the Food and Drug Administration argued against a total recall for fear that it would send an invitation to other criminals who wanted to send shock waves throughout the nation, Johnson & Johnson courageously decided to put profits, and perhaps their public image, aside in order to make the right decision. They began a massive recall of 31 million bottles of Tylenol, which cost the company over $125 million. Larry Foster, the vice president of public relations at the company during the crisis, said that he looked to the company's mission statement—which was the "Credo" of Robert Wood Johnson—for guidance during this difficult time. This statement reminded him that Johnson & Johnson aims to serve its customers, then its employees; next its responsibility was to the communities where its employees live and work; and finally to its shareholders, in that order (Cooke 2002). Thus, while they knew that they were not responsible for tampering with their product, they also knew that they were responsible for their customers' safety more so than they were responsible for the shareholders' wallets. However, by showing courage in the face of an unprecedented organizational and public health crisis, Johnson & Johnson was rewarded with continued public support and trust.

While not every decision leaders face is of a life-altering magnitude, the decisions they make do affect the lives of people within as well as beyond their organization's walls. Courage to stand one's ground on difficult issues can instill a sense of pride and loyalty with coworkers. When even one person shows courage during a challenging time, faith can be reinfused into the system and passion reawakened to make tomorrow better than today.

CONCLUDING THOUGHTS

Passion rebuilds the world for the youth. It makes all things alive and significant.

Ralph Waldo Emerson

The Engaging People's Passion Model of Leadership is designed to serve as a dynamic framework for today's leaders to reflect on what constitutes effective leadership in the world today. It is a guide for leaders' repertoire development, rather than being a static prescription for each leader in every situation. Because the global context that colors organizations today is so variable, each of the five elements is actually variable as well. Courage is enacted differently in each leader; the visions that are generated will be unique to each organizational context; what it takes to create an engaging and inclusive style will differ across settings. Each leader's path is going to look different as he or she strives for effectiveness. We suggest, however, that whatever the path may look like, leaders need to orient themselves toward sparking passion in others. The world is not going to decrease in complexity, and organizational life is going to continue to evolve as we increase our informational and relational networks. Change is the constant. The fuel that is going to catapult today's realities into tomorrow's successes is the passion that lies within each one of us. This passion is what can unite us in a seemingly chaotic world. Through a positive vision for the future, inspiring core values, using an engaging and inclusive style, employing emotional intelligence, and showing courage, effective leaders can tap into that passion and inspire us to create a better tomorrow together.

REFERENCES

Amiel, Henri-Frédéric. (1856). *Swiss Journal Intime*, entry for December 17, trans. Mrs. Humphrey Ward (1892).

Anderson, Terry. (1992). *International Herald Tribune*. Paris, May 6.

Argyris, Chris. (1977). "Double Loop Learning in Organizations," *Harvard Business Review*, 55: 115–25.

Bass, B.M. (1985). *Leadership and Performance Beyond Expectations*. New York: Free Press.

Baum, J.; E. Locke; and S. Kirkpatrick. (1998). "A Longitudinal Study of the Relation of Vision and Vision Communication to Venture Growth in Entrepreneurial Firms." *Journal of Applied Psychology* 83:1, 43–54.

Bennis, W. (1997). *Learning to Lead: A Workbook on Becoming a Leader.* New York: Perseus.

Bennis, W., and B. Nanus. (1985). *Leaders: The Strategies for Taking Charge.* New York: Harper and Row.

Bloom, J. "CEOs: Leadership through Communication." (November 26, 2001). *PR Week.* Section: CEO Survey 2001, p. 20.

Body Shop. www.bodyshop.com.

Boyatzis, R.E. (1982). *The Competent Manager: A Model for Effective Performance.* New York: Wiley.

Boyatzis, R.; D. Bilimoria; L. Godwin, M. Hopkins, and T. Lingham. (In press). "Effective Leadership in a Crisis: Using Emotional Intelligence to Inspire Resilience." In *9/11: Public Health in the Wake of Terrorist Attacks*, ed. R. Gross, Y. Neria, R. Marshall, and E. Susse. New York: Cambridge University Press.

Byrne, J., and H. Timmons. (2001). "Tough Times for a New CEO." *Business Week*, October 29: 64. www.businessweek.com/magazine/content/01_44/63755001.htm.

Caproni, P. (2001). *The Practical Coach: Management Skills for Everyday Life.* Upper Saddle River, NJ: Prentice Hall.

CBS News.com. (2003). "The Mensch of Malden Mills." *60 Minutes.* July 3. www.cbsnews.com/stories/2003/07/03/60minutes/main561656.shtml.

Columbia World of Quotations. (1996). New York: Columbia University Press. www.bartleby.com/66.

Collins, J.C., and J. Porras. (1996). "Building Your Company's Vision." *Harvard Business Review* (September/October): 65–77.

Conger, J., and R. Kanungo. (1987). *Charismatic Leadership: The Elusive Factor in Organizational Effectiveness.* San Francisco: Jossey-Bass.

Cooke, J. (2002). "PSU Alumnus Recalls 1982 Tylenol Murders." *Digital Collegian.* October. www.collegian.psu.edu/archive/2002/10/10–18–02tdc/10–18–02dnews-06.asp.

Cooperider, D., and W. Whitney. (2001). "A Positive Revolution in Change: Appreciative Inquiry." In *Appreciative Inquiry: An Emerging Direction for Organizational Development*, ed. D. Cooperider, P. Sorensen, T. Yaeger, and D. Whitney, 5–30. Champaign, IL: Stipes.

Emerson, R.W. (1981). *The Portable Emerson.* New York: Penguin Books.

Fiorina, C. (2003). Interview *Continental Magazine.*

Fishman, C. (1998). "Sustainable Growth-Interface, Inc." *Fast Company.* April. www.fastcompany.com/online/14/sustain.html.

Follett, M.P. (1987). *Freedom and Co-ordination: Lectures in Business Organization*, ed. L. Urwick. London: Management Publications Trust, Ltd.

Freiberg, K., and J. Freiberg. (1998). *Nuts! Southwest Airlines' Crazy Recipe for Business and Personal Success.* New York: Bard.

Galbraith, J., and E. Lawler. (1993). *Organizing for the Future. New Logic for Managing Complex Organizations.* San Francisco: Jossey-Bass.

Gardner, J.W. (1963). *Self-renewal: The Individual and the Innovative Society.* New York: Harper and Row.

Gittell, J.H. (2002). *The Southwest Airlines Way: Using the Power of Relationships to Achieve High Performance.* New York: McGraw-Hill.

Goleman, D. (1998). *Working with Emotional Intelligence.* New York: Bantam Books.

———. (2000). "Leadership That Gets Results," *Harvard Business Review* (March/April): 78–90.

Goleman, D., R.E. Boyatzis, and A. McKee. (2002). *Primal Leadership: Realizing the Power of Emotional Intelligence.* Boston: Harvard Business School Press.

Hegel, G.W.F. (1971). *Philosophy of Mind, Part 3: The Encyclopedia, Section 1*, "Mind Subjective," par. 474, 235. Oxford: Oxford University Press.

Hickman, C.R. (1992). *Mind of a Manager, Soul of a Leader.* New York: Wiley.

House, R.J. (1977). "A 1976 Theory of Charismatic Leadership." In *Leadership: The Cutting Edge*, ed. J.G. Hunt and L.L. Larson, 189–207. Carbondale: Southern Illinois University Press.

House, R. J., and B. Shamir. (1993). "Toward the Integration of Transformational, Charismatic and Visionary Theories of Leadership." In *Leadership Theory and Research: Perspectives and Directions*, eds. M. Chemers and R. Ayman, 81–107. San Diego, CA: Academic Press.

Ingram, L. (2002). "Thinking Outside the Blue Box." *Continental* (June): 31–33.

Jones, M. (2004). "A New Way of Doing Business: Interview with Anita Roddick." *Share International*. www.shareintl.org/archives/social-justice/sj_mjnew.htm.

Kanter, R.M. (1999). "Change Is Everyone's Job: Managing the Extended Enterprise in a Globally Connected World." *Organizational Dynamics* 28(1): 7–23.

Kelleher, H. (1997). "A Culture of Commitment." *Leader to Leader* 4: 20–24.

Kotter, J.P. (1988). *The Leadership Factor.* New York: Free Press.

Kouzes, J., and B. Posner. (1987). *The Leadership Challenge.* San Francisco: Jossey-Bass.

Lacayo, R., and A. Ripley (2002). "Persons of the Year 2002." *Time* (December). www.time.com/time/personoftheyear/2002/polyintro.html.

Lipman-Blumen, Jean. (1996). *Connective Leadership: Managing in a Changing World.* Oxford: Oxford University Press.

Morden, Tony. (1997). "Leadership as Vision." *Management Decision* 35 (19): 668–676.

Online Ethics Center for Engineering, Case Western Reserve University. (2003). "Ray C. Anderson: From Captain of Industry to Champion of Sustainable Development." http://onlineethics.org/environment/rcanderson.html#notable.

Pope, J. (2004). "Ex-Im Bank Backs Former Malden Mills CEO's Request." Associated Press Release. January 8. www.boston.com/business/articles/2004/01/08ex_im_bank_backs_former _malden_mills_ceos_request/.

Pfeffer, J. (2002). "To Build a Culture of Innovation, Avoid Conventional Management Wisdom." In *Leading for Innovation*, ed. F. Hesselbein, M. Goldsmith, and I. Somerville, 95–104. San Francisco: Jossey-Bass.

Rosenthal, R., and L. Jacobson. (1968). *Pygmalion in the Classroom.* New York: Rinehart and Winston.

Rosenthal, R., and D.B. Rubin. (1978). "Interpersonal Expectancy Effects: The First 345 Studies." *Behavioral and Brain Sciences* 3: 377–386.

Scarnati, J.T. (1999). "Beyond Technical Competence: The Art of Leadership." *Career Development International* 4 (6): 325–336.

Schwartz, K. (1996). "Tangy Touch in Sky." *South Coast Today.* www.s-t.com/daily/11–96/11–17–96/m10bu066.htm.

Sillanpaa, M. (1998). "The Body Shop Values Report. Towards Integrated Stakeholder Auditing." *Journal of Business Ethics* 17 (13): 1443–1457.

Staub, R. (2003). "Courage and Leadership Go Hand in Hand." *Business Journal* (June 6). www.bizjournals.com/triad/stories/2003/06/09/smallb3.html?jst=s_rs_hl.

Slater, R. (1998). *Jack Welch and the G.E. Way: Management Insights and Leadership Secrets of the Legendary CEO.* New York: McGraw-Hill Trade.

Spencer, L.M., Jr., and S.M. Spencer. (1993). *Competence at Work: Models for Superior Performance.* New York: Wiley.

Tichy, N.M., and S. Sherman. (1994). *Control Your Own Destiny or Someone Else Will.* New York: Harper Business.

University of Cambridge, Institute for Manufacturing. www.sustainablepss.org/casestudies/interface/interface.php.

White, L., B. Tursky, and G. Schwartz, eds. (1985). *Placebo: Theory, Research and Mechanisms.* New York: Guilford Press.

Winter, B. (2000). "Good News: 'Expert' Predicts We Can't Win!" *Editor.* January. www.lp.org/lpnews/0001/fromtheeditor.html.

Wong, M. (1999). "Case Study No. 8–Interface–Evergreen Carpet Leasing System."

CHAPTER 15

"HR-MINDED" LEADERSHIP

Five Critical Areas of Focus for Contemporary Organizational Leaders

SCOTT A. QUATRO

BUILDING THE CASE FOR "HR-MINDEDNESS"

The past two decades have witnessed a tremendous advancement in the fundamental nature of the world economy. In short, globalization is increasingly driven by services-based and technology-based industries and firms (Downes and Heap 2002; Farrell 2003) that require a more highly educated and motivated workforce than at any other point in history. Concurrent with this has been a significant increase in the relative affluence of the citizens and employees in the world's most developed nations. As a result, these employees are no longer motivated by lower-order needs, but rather operate as a workforce in search of aggregate self-actualization (Abramson and Inglehart 1995). As such, these employees are increasingly desirous of reconciling their daily work lives to their higher-order beliefs (Herman and Schaefer 2001; Neal 2000) and related instrumental and terminal values (Rokeach 1973). Combined, these two realities pose a tremendous challenge for leaders in contemporary organizations: attracting, developing, and retaining an increasingly sophisticated, principled, and highly skilled employee base.

This chapter posits that contemporary organizational leaders, regardless of their functional or line responsibilities, must become "HR-Minded" leaders who are unswervingly focused on the strategic importance of holistically engaging and leveraging their human resources. Doing so requires that leaders focus on the following five critical leadership practices:

1. *Developing a Compelling Strategic Vision.* Leaders must facilitate the process of vision dialogue and articulation, and this vision must be both strategically sound from a competitive advantage standpoint and compelling from a human motivation standpoint.
2. *Designing Engaging Jobs.* Leaders must recognize that their organizations are only as engaging as the jobs in which their employees live and breathe everyday, and design jobs that holistically engage these increasingly sophisticated employees.

3. *Instilling a Sound Organizational Conscience.* Leaders must recognize the moral and spiritual normativity that guides the beliefs and behaviors of their employees, and ensure that their organization conducts its primary business activities such that they are seen as morally and spiritually sound by their increasingly principled employees.

4. *Leveraging Organizational Knowledge.* Leaders must understand the truth that organizational knowledge is a critical asset in today's evolved economy, and build an organizational infrastructure to harness and grow that asset.

5. *Building Change Capacity.* Leaders must recognize that the ability to proactively change as an organization is a legitimate source of competitive advantage, and spread the message that change capacity is not about "what" to change, but rather is all about "how" to change.

Those leaders who embrace these five areas of leadership practice and responsibility will lead their organizations into an increasingly successful future.

Each of these areas of leadership practice has been addressed quite thoroughly in the contemporary literature, and increasingly so as management and organizational theory as a whole has shifted to reflect a sharper focus on the critical role of human resources in driving organizational success. Many theorists have argued quite persuasively for leaders to focus more intently on the human resources component of their responsibilities, from both an operational (Bartel 2004; Becker et al. 1997; Greer, Youngblood, and Gray 1999; Ulrich 1997) and a strategic (Brockbank 1999; Collins 2001; Gilley and Maycunich 2000; Ulrich 1998) perspective. However, the literature to date has failed to explicitly treat each leadership practice discussed herein as uniquely critical *HR-related* practices and to integrate them into a unified model for *leadership* effectiveness (see Figure 15.1). Doing so specifically identifies these five areas as HR-related mandates that must be owned and driven by *all* organizational leaders, especially *non-HR* leaders. Put another way, the chief executive officer (CEO), chief financial officer (CFO), chief operating officer (COO), and even the chief information officer (CIO) of an organization must be as "HR-minded" as the chief human resources officer (CHRO), and perhaps even more so. And this is true at all leadership levels within an organization. All leaders, from front-line supervisors to middle managers to senior management, must become increasingly HR-minded in terms of their beliefs, behaviors, and priorities.

Individually, these five leadership practices each squarely focuses on the human element of organizations, and thus each has individual value as a driver of organizational success. As such, practicing any one of them as a leader will result in incremental gains in leadership effectiveness and organizational performance. But employed collectively these five leadership practices enable leaders, regardless of their organizational or industry context, to holistically engage and leverage their employees, and concurrently to effect sustained high performance. Thus, each of the five elements of HR-minded leadership serves as a *pillar* upon which overall leadership effectiveness and sustained organizational high performance is built. Each then is a *sine qua non* for HR-minded leadership—that is, without any *one* of the HR-

Figure 15.1 **The Five Critical Practice Areas of HR-Minded Leadership as Pillars of Leadership Effectiveness and Sustained Organizational High Performance.**

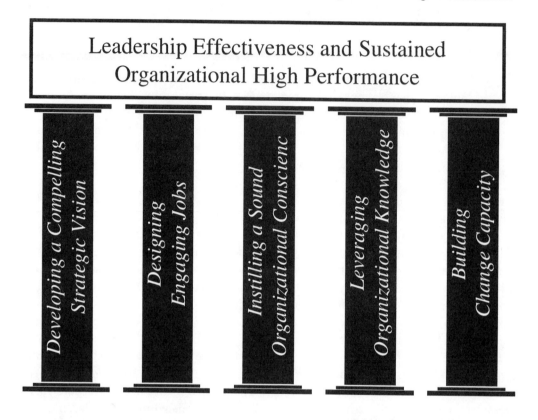

minded practices, leadership effectiveness is diminished and the sustainability of high performance is lessened. To this end, each of these five leadership practice areas is discussed in greater detail.

DEVELOPING A COMPELLING STRATEGIC VISION

Leaders must facilitate the process of vision dialogue and articulation, and this vision must be both strategically sound from a competitive advantage standpoint and compelling from a human motivation standpoint.

All organizational leaders have accountability for the development and stewardship of strategic vision. In terms of development, leaders simply must ensure that the organization has a well-developed strategic vision in place at all times. This is usually not a difficult component of the strategic vision mandate for leaders to embrace. Acting as steward of the vision is another matter altogether. The literal meaning of the word steward is "to manage another's property, finances, or other affairs." Thus, the act of stewardship involves accepting responsibility for something that belongs to someone else. When this component of the strategic vision mandate is elucidated, most leaders suddenly become less willing to embrace this particular HR-related leadership practice.

To be sure, this makes sense. It is inherently risky for leaders to accept accountability for the successful realization of a strategic vision that really does not belong to them (and thus is not entirely controlled by them) in the first place. But this is exactly the mandate that HR-minded leaders accept when they employ the leadership practice of strategic visioning. And the very fact that the leaders are utterly dependent on their employees for the successful realization of the strategic vision is evidence of the true HR-related nature of this area of leadership practice. Put simply, if the human resources of the organization do not own and enthusiastically pursue the vision, it is doomed to failure.

Visioning for Competitive Advantage and Maximum Employee Motivation

Leaders must ensure the strategic soundness and related motivational pull of any vision that they develop and steward. That is, the vision must be oriented toward the achievement of an enterprise-wide (or business unit, function, or even work-team level, depending on the role within which the leader is operating) objective that will enable the organization to achieve sustainable competitive advantage in the marketplace and compel the employees of the organization to accept ownership for realizing that objective.

Payless ShoeSource has long held a strong competitive position in the footwear retailing industry. By most accounts, Payless remains the largest shareholder (approximately 20 percent) of a fairly fragmented market. The firm has traditionally leveraged its core competencies in merchandise distribution and store operations to protect its strong position in the industry. However, opportunities for Payless to continue to grow the firm through expansion of its store base (either through acquisition or new store openings) have become very limited (at least domestically). The U.S. market can only support so many Payless stores, and it appears that the saturation point has been reached. At least, this was the conclusion reached recently by the senior leadership of the firm while facilitating the strategic visioning process for the organization.

The final product of this process was the articulation of a bold new vision statement for Payless—"To be one of the top ten admired retail brands in North America." In many ways this vision statement represents a significant departure form Payless's traditional strategy, but a departure that the senior leadership of the firm believed to be necessary in order to catalyze sustained high performance for the organization. As a deceptively simple yet insightful tool, the SMART acronym can be applied to test the strategic soundness of any vision (see Table 15.1).

Given a correct understanding of the five criteria upon which the "SMARTness" of a vision is evaluated, we can conduct such an analysis of the new Payless vision.

Table 15.1

Employing the SMART Acronym to Evaluate the Soundness and Motivational Pull of a Strategic Vision

Evaluation criterion	Key evaluative questions
Specificity	• Are the business-related challenges clearly delineated? • Are the industry and market scope clearly indicated? • Are the key value-chain activities clearly illuminated?
Measurability	• Are key performance metrics unambiguously stated? • Are various related metrics strongly inferred?
Attainability	• Is the overarching objective too easy to achieve? • Is the overarching objective too difficult to achieve? • Can current core competencies be leveraged?
Relevancy	• Is the overarching objective critical to sustained high performance? • Are hyperbole (hype) or banality (triviality) evident?
Time sensitivity	• Is a time frame unambiguously stated?

Specificity

Payless's new vision is quite specific. It clearly indicates the business-related challenge facing Payless; that is, traditionally Payless has been a very *recognized* retail brand but not an *admired* retail brand. These are very different things (although brand admiration does entail, at least in part, brand recognition), and specifically achieving strong brand *admiration* is clearly a critical means by which Payless can continue to grow sales in their established North American store base. Related to this, both the industry scope (retail brands) and market scope (North America) are clearly identified. Last, the key value-chain activities of brand management and customer service are strongly inferred, as these two value-chain activities are most strongly connected to public perception of retail brand admiration.

Measurability

Progress toward the realization of the new Payless vision can be easily measured. The firm has quite boldly and unambiguously stated that theirs will be a "top ten" most admired retail brand. The senior leadership has established a clear benchmark against which the performance of the entire firm will be evaluated. The fact that Payless has denoted specifically "retail brands" as their industry scope (as opposed to, for instance, all consumer brands) only further enhances the measurability of the vision. And key related metrics—such as customer satisfaction, price-quality perception, and same-store sales increases—are strongly inferred.

Attainability

This is arguably an area of significant weakness in terms of the new Payless vision. "Brand Payless" has traditionally been saddled with the baggage that goes along with being a discount retailer, primary among these being the Payless reputation as a great store for "cheap shoes," especially for "kids and middle-aged moms." While this reputation has served the firm well in growing its core North American business and has been intentionally leveraged by Payless for much of its history—as evidenced by the well-known, long-running Payless advertising campaign slogan "Doesn't it feel good to Payless"—the realization of the new Payless vision will require a fundamental shift in the minds of consumers. This will no doubt be a stretch for the firm on two major fronts. First, "Brand Payless" connotes exactly the reputation that the firm, at least in part, will need to shift away from. Thus, apart from changing the firm's primary brand name altogether (which would be ill-advised given the widespread recognition that the brand enjoys), the means by which this shift in consumer perception can be affected are complex indeed. Payless has (so far) chosen to reposition "brand Payless" by deemphasizing cost and highlighting the "fashionableness" of the brand—thus, the new advertising campaign slogan "Look smart. Payless." Second, the traditional core competencies of the firm—namely, merchandise distribution and store operations—are arguably tangential to the successful achievement of the new vision. Put simply, these existing core competencies are not as central, from a value-chain activity perspective, to achieving brand admiration as are brand management and customer service, and, clearly, neither of these latter two activities is a current internal strength for the firm. Therein lies the dilemma. Whether Payless can develop new core competencies in brand management and customer service, while continuing to maintain their strengths in "getting the right shoes, to the right stores, at the right time" and running a "tight ship" as far as store operations goes, is yet to be determined.

Relevancy

The new Payless vision has clear business relevance, and was quickly accepted by Payless associates throughout the firm as a highly credible and relevant statement of strategic direction for the organization as a whole. Domestic growth for Payless has come to a standstill, and aside from continued international growth opportunities beyond Canada, the principal way for Payless to grow corporate revenues is by selling more shoes through existing North American stores. Thus, the strong relevance of becoming a more admired North American retail brand becomes plain given an understanding of the firm's current competitive position. Simply put, realizing the new vision is perhaps the firm's best bet, and maybe even their only bet, for generating growth in their core North American business. Clearly, this is not a trivial vision, and also not one burdened by unnecessary hype or pie-in-the-sky "fluff." This vision is about ensuring the ongoing success of the largest family footwear retailer in the world.

Time Sensitivity

This is the most significant area of weakness relative to Payless's new strategic vision. The senior leadership failed to establish a specific time frame within which the new vision would be realized, or at least significantly readdressed. While some may argue that such time specificity is better established at the business-unit or functional levels of the organization, these more "operational" time frames are set in a more aggressive and concomitant manner when the overarching time frame for the vision has been clearly established as part of the vision statement itself. We all work better under pressure—it is simply the nature of human beings *and* organizations.

Employees Know How SMART the Vision Is

HR-minded leaders recognize that their employees are capable of performing an analysis such as the one just described. The fact is, most employees *immediately* gauge the SMARTness of a strategic vision upon first hearing it, whether this is explicit and fairly exhaustive as demonstrated above, or informal and cursory via a "hallway" conversation with colleagues. Either way, employees know whether a strategic vision is SMART, and they are much more willing to take ownership of that vision if this is the case. HR-minded leaders facilitate the visioning process with this truth in mind, ideally involving employees throughout the organization in dialogue as part of the visioning process, thereby better ensuring both SMARTness *and* buy-in.

DESIGNING ENGAGING JOBS

> Leaders must recognize that their organizations are only as engaging as the jobs in which their employees live and breathe everyday, and design jobs that holistically engage these increasingly sophisticated employees.

It is an unfortunate truth that few organizational leaders understand the critical role that effective job design can play in their overall leadership effectiveness. Too often leaders view job design as something outside their control, something that HR does and simply communicates to staff and line managers via formal job descriptions. The leader's only mandate then is to staff the jobs *as designed and inherited* from the organization's HR function. HR-minded leaders recognize the danger of such thinking, and rightly accept responsibility for ensuring that the jobs throughout their organization are as holistically engaging as possible.

Assessing the Motivating Potential of Jobs

Any job can be designed, or assessed and redesigned, to be more compelling. That is, any job can be inherently motivating for an employee to perform. It is all a matter of holistic engagement (see Figure 15.2).

Only jobs that engage the hands, mind, heart, and spirit of an employee are truly holistically engaging, and thus inherently motivating for employees. And each of these levels of employee engagement does not afford equal motivational impact, as conveyed in Figure 15.2. Arguably, only by engaging the heart and the spirit of an employee does an organization ever access half of that employee's motivation. This paints a sobering

Figure 15.2   **A Model for Assessing and Designing Jobs**

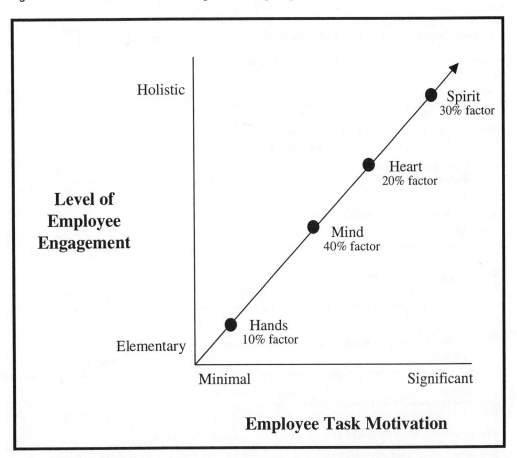

picture for most leaders, especially when they accurately recognize that most jobs continue to be designed and staffed with *only* hands and mind engagement, and too often only hands engagement, as design factors that are intentionally considered.

By assigning subscores of one to ten to each of the four design components (hands, mind, heart, spirit), and then multiplying these subscores by the factors assigned to each design component (hands = 10 percent, mind = 40 percent, heart = 20 percent, and spirit = 30 percent), an overall assessment of the level of holistic engagement and related employee motivation afforded by a particular job can be determined. Thus, the formula for determining the Holistic Engagement Score (HES) associated with a job is as follows:

HES = (*HandsScore* × .1) + (*MindScore* × .4) + (*HeartScore* × .2) + (*SpiritScore* × .3), with the highest possible HES being 10 and the lowest possible HES being 1.

Table 15.2 provides a more detailed overview of the HES methodology and a concrete example of employing it to assess the motivational pull of a job.

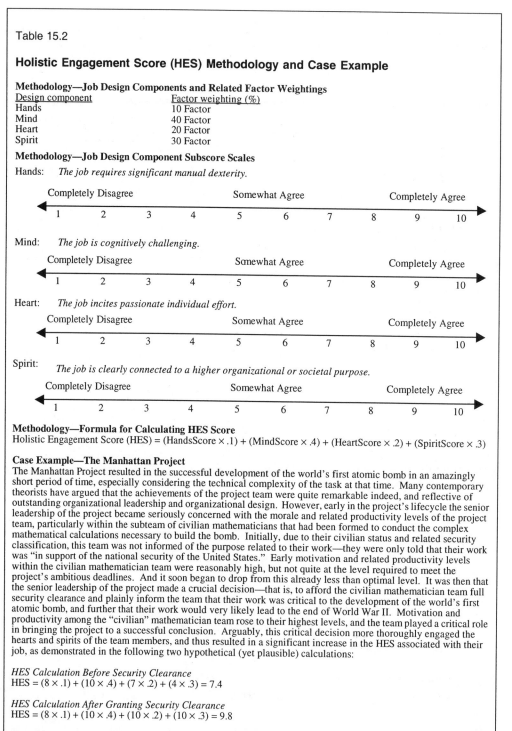

Table 15.2

Holistic Engagement Score (HES) Methodology and Case Example

Methodology—Job Design Components and Related Factor Weightings

Design component	Factor weighting (%)
Hands	10 Factor
Mind	40 Factor
Heart	20 Factor
Spirit	30 Factor

Methodology—Job Design Component Subscore Scales

Hands: *The job requires significant manual dexterity.*

Completely Disagree   Somewhat Agree   Completely Agree

1   2   3   4   5   6   7   8   9   10

Mind: *The job is cognitively challenging.*

Completely Disagree   Somewhat Agree   Completely Agree

1   2   3   4   5   6   7   8   9   10

Heart: *The job incites passionate individual effort.*

Completely Disagree   Somewhat Agree   Completely Agree

1   2   3   4   5   6   7   8   9   10

Spirit: *The job is clearly connected to a higher organizational or societal purpose.*

Completely Disagree   Somewhat Agree   Completely Agree

1   2   3   4   5   6   7   8   9   10

Methodology—Formula for Calculating HES Score

Holistic Engagement Score (HES) = (HandsScore × .1) + (MindScore × .4) + (HeartScore × .2) + (SpiritScore × .3)

Case Example—The Manhattan Project

The Manhattan Project resulted in the successful development of the world's first atomic bomb in an amazingly short period of time, especially considering the technical complexity of the task at that time. Many contemporary theorists have argued that the achievements of the project team were quite remarkable indeed, and reflective of outstanding organizational leadership and organizational design. However, early in the project's lifecycle the senior leadership of the project became seriously concerned with the morale and related productivity levels of the project team, particularly within the subteam of civilian mathematicians that had been formed to conduct the complex mathematical calculations necessary to build the bomb. Initially, due to their civilian status and related security classification, this team was not informed of the purpose related to their work—they were only told that their work was "in support of the national security of the United States." Early motivation and related productivity levels within the civilian mathematician team were reasonably high, but not quite at the level required to meet the project's ambitious deadlines. And it soon began to drop from this already less than optimal level. It was then that the senior leadership of the project made a crucial decision—that is, to afford the civilian mathematician team full security clearance and plainly inform the team that their work was critical to the development of the world's first atomic bomb, and further that their work would very likely lead to the end of World War II. Motivation and productivity among the "civilian" mathematician team rose to their highest levels, and the team played a critical role in bringing the project to a successful conclusion. Arguably, this critical decision more thoroughly engaged the hearts and spirits of the team members, and thus resulted in a significant increase in the HES associated with their job, as demonstrated in the following two hypothetical (yet plausible) calculations:

HES Calculation Before Security Clearance
HES = (8 × .1) + (10 × .4) + (7 × .2) + (4 × .3) = 7.4

HES Calculation After Granting Security Clearance
HES = (8 × .1) + (10 × .4) + (10 × .2) + (10 × .3) = 9.8

According to these calculations, the motivational pull of the jobs increased by 32 percent. The rest, as they say, is history.

The Employee is the "Product"

HR-minded leaders recognize that employee engagement is particularly important in contemporary organizations given the fundamental shift to a services-based economy, especially in the West. In a services-based firm, the employee is essentially the "product." Thus, the more engaged and motivated the employee, the higher the service quality they provide to consumers and customers.

The Employee Is Highly "Evolved"

HR-minded leaders also recognize that, regardless of organizational or industry context, their employees are increasingly motivated by the higher-order needs of esteem and self-actualization, given the relative level of widespread affluence afforded by contemporary Western society. And they further recognize that it is only through the heart and spirit that esteem and self-actualization needs are fully met. It is important to note that Abraham Maslow's thinking surrounding these universal human needs is largely misunderstood and misrepresented in contemporary organizations. The widely held belief that the way to afford employees esteem and self-actualization is to appeal only to their minds and self-serving desires (via intellectually challenging personal assignments, lucrative incentive-based compensation structures, and a "free-agency" approach to employment) is entirely off base in terms of Maslow's theory and related research findings. Maslow (1998, 8) himself actually referred to such thinking as "psychologically stupid" and "selfish." Rather, Maslow argued that it is only when employees are esteemed by others for passionately employing their giftedness (thus demonstrating heart engagement) in serving the greater organizational good that they approach self-actualization (thereby demonstrating spirit-level engagement). Put simply, the path to employee self-actualization is *selfless* exercise of heartfelt, passionate giftedness in the service of a cause that is much bigger than any single individual employee. According to Maslow (1998, 9), this was the case for every self-actualizing subject that he had studied; they were all "meta-motivated" by a cause or organizational purpose in which they literally lost themselves. Contemporary HR-minded organizational leaders must strive for this level of job engagement among their employees.

INSTILLING A SOUND ORGANIZATIONAL CONSCIENCE

> Leaders must recognize the moral and spiritual normativity that guides the beliefs and behaviors of their employees, and ensure that their organization conducts its primary business activities such that they are seen as morally and spiritually sound by their increasingly principled employees.

Contemporary employees are increasingly sensitive to the moral and spiritual soundness of their organizations. To employees operating in a highly prosperous and evolved economic system, this makes a great deal of sense and is consistent with the need for jobs to be more holistically engaging, as discussed above. HR-minded leaders recognize this phenomenon, and craft an organizational culture and surrounding infrastructure that reinforces morally and spiritually sound business activities.

The Contemporary Organizational Spirituality Movement as Catalyst

At its core, developing a sound organizational conscience involves leaders' enthusiastically embracing the contemporary spirituality in the workplace movement. Sidestepping this movement is no longer possible given the momentum it has gained over the past ten years. HR-minded leaders are cognizant of the fact that popular opinion supports the striking statistic that roughly four out of every five of their employees are fundamentally driven by their core spiritual beliefs on a daily basis, up from approximately one out of five just ten years ago. And these same employees are literally "praying" for their organizations to be likewise driven. Thus, for HR-minded leaders, the mandate to ensure the soundness of their organization's conscience is increasing.

The Legitimate Role of Traditional Organized Religion

An interesting dilemma faces HR-minded leaders who are willing to foster a spiritually influenced organizational conscience. That is, to do so under the auspices of "new age" spirituality alone, or to welcome the "age old" voice of traditional organized religion to the dialogue as well. In one of the more prominent and empirical works to date focused on contemporary organizational spirituality, the authors propose that the large majority of their study respondents viewed traditional religion as being inherently negative, commenting that "the descriptors used most often were *narrow, prescriptive, dogmatic, restrictive, closed, exclusive,* and so on" (Mitroff and Denton 1999, 40). In contrast, the authors claim, their study respondents "had a much more positive view of spirituality . . . to describe it they used such terms as *essence of life, spirit, soul expression, meaning, connection, interconnectedness, creative, creation, universality, cosmic oneness,* and so on" (1999, 40–41). The authors then go on to strongly infer that organizations and individuals that embrace the contemporary organizational spirituality movement in conjunction with traditional organized religion represent the "extreme" and even "dark" (1999, 58) aspects of the phenomenon.

To their credit, these same authors do present a religion-based model as a potentially viable means by which organizations can embrace spirituality, but by this point the divide between the "ideal" of new age spirituality and the "evil"[1] of traditional organized religion has already been clearly articulated. Unfortunately, this mindset concerning organized religion juxtaposed against spirituality is widespread in the literature, and arguably has been perpetuated by both the research methods employed to reach such conclusions and the largely secular-humanistic worldview of the researchers and study participants involved in investigating the phenomenon. Indeed, in an-

Table 15.3

The Normativity of the "Golden Rule" Across the Four Largest World Religions

"So in everything, do to others what you would have them do to you, for this sums up the law and the prophets."

Jesus

"Whoever believes in Allah and the life hereafter, let him be hospitable to his guest, and whoever believes in Allah and the life hereafter, let him not hurt his neighbor, and whoever believes in Allah and the life hereafter, let him say something beneficial or remain quiet."

Muhammad

"Man becomes great exactly in the degree in which he works for the welfare of his fellow-men."

Mahatma Gandhi

"All beings long for happiness. Therefore extend thy compassion to all. . . . He who wishes his own happiness . . . let him cultivate goodwill towards all the world."

Buddha

other recent and prominent study of contemporary organizational spirituality, the researchers admitted that their study sample (and hence, their study conclusion) was heavily skewed toward just such a population (Nash and McLennan 2001). Such bias has largely shut traditional organized religion out of the dialogue surrounding contemporary organizational spirituality, and the related leadership practice area of developing a sound organizational conscience.

Ironically, it is precisely the major organized religions that systematically teach and celebrate the very things (such as soul expression, meaning, interconnectedness, selflessness, and even cosmic oneness) that reinforce a sound organizational conscience, and that supposedly only new age spirituality embraces. And they do so with amazing "doctrinal" harmony, as demonstrated in Table 15.3 above.

The normativity of thought (both in comparison to one another and to "new age" spirituality) expressed by these words, each attributed to either foundational leaders or influential adherents of the four largest organized religions (namely Christianity, Islam, Hinduism, and Buddhism), is striking. And of course the potential value added of embracing these traditional religious "voices" in conjunction with the development of a sound organizational conscience is quite clear.

From a pragmatic standpoint, it may be sobering to reflect on the fact that fully 70 percent of the world's population claim to be adherents of these four religions (that is, Christianity, Islam, Hinduism, and Buddhism).[2] Put simply, leaders who embrace the contemporary organizational spirituality movement in conjunction with the development of organizational conscience *apart* from these traditional religions run the risk of marginalizing the spiritual experiences and heritage of almost three-quarters of their employees. Ironically, such exclusion of traditionally religious employees from the organizational conscience dialogue is in direct conflict with a cornerstone doctrine of the contemporary organizational spirituality movement itself—that is, inclusiveness. Most important, HR-minded leaders recognize that embracing traditionally religious employees as part of this dialogue will only result in a more sound organizational conscience, enhanced employee motivation, and sustained organizational high performance.

LEVERAGING ORGANIZATIONAL KNOWLEDGE

> Leaders must understand the truth that organizational knowledge is a critical asset in today's evolved economy, and build an organizational infrastructure to harness and grow that asset.

Countless theorists have vigorously proposed the merits of building learning organizations. They have done so on the grounds that organizations that learn better and faster than their competitors achieve stronger long-term performance. Such an argument is compelling indeed, especially given the pace of change in today's marketplace.

Consider, for example, the case of IBM. In the mid-1990s "Big Blue" was faced with the very real possibility of permanently losing its "blue-chip" status as one of the benchmark firms in American industry. The firm had relied too heavily and too narrowly on its core competencies in hardware manufacturing, research and development, and administrative discipline, and as a result had literally missed the shift from "big machines" (mainframes) to "smaller machines" (servers and personal computers) and bundled information technology (IT) services. Fortunately the board of IBM saw the writing on the wall before it was too late, and brought in Lou Gerstner, a marketer from Nabisco, as CEO. Gerstner's challenge was less associated with embracing the need for IBM to learn (and learn fast) as an organization, but more with leveraging the newfound knowledge that was generated via the learning that he catalyzed as the new leader intent on taking the firm in a critical new direction.

Therein lies the key, from an HR-minded leadership practice standpoint—that is, the primary challenge is not simply to foster ongoing organizational learning, but rather to understand how to leverage the increasing knowledge base of the organization. Doing so requires three distinct infrastructure components.

1. *Learning-Centric Performance Management.* Organizations intent on leveraging increasing organizational knowledge must first catalyze and reinforce learning at the individual employee level. They do so by building specific and measurable learning objectives into their performance appraisal tools and process, and orienting these learning objectives toward critical business needs. IBM's Gerstner started here by ensuring that the performance management process for the firm shifted toward the measurement of employee learning as a key assessment com-

ponent, especially for those employees in leadership roles. And these learning objectives were articulated to specifically reinforce the marketing and systems thinking knowledge and skills necessary to compete in the new IT market.

2. *Cross-Functional and Cross-Divisional Team Structures.* In addition to fostering increased learning at the individual employee level, organizations must employ cross-functional and cross-divisional team structures as much as possible, for both temporary project and permanent operational purposes. Doing so ensures that individual employee learning is not only enhanced, but shared with others on a regular basis. Gerstner ensured that these types of team structures, essentially unheard of in the traditionally compartmentalized IBM of old, were immediately put in place. Such teams eventually became the means through which IBM offered bundled IT services alongside hardware components, and led the drive toward increased services revenue for the firm as a whole. Today, an increasingly significant portion of IBM's revenues are generated by intangible IT services (bolstered by the mid-2002 acquisition of PricewaterhouseCoopers's consulting business) offered to clients via cross-functional and cross-divisional teams. It is somewhat ironic and perhaps even nostalgic to remember that IBM stands for "International Business Machines," given this fundamental shift in its business model.

3. *A Shared Corporate Knowledge Bank.* Despite the shift to an increasingly services-based business model, IBM still produces machines—and they use them to house their shared corporate knowledge bank. This database allows IBM associates anywhere in the world to share and access the best practices of the firm. And the expectation within the firm is that they will do so on a regular basis.

Combined, these three infrastructure components enable HR-minded leaders to measure and reward individual employee learning, foster team learning, and codify the increased knowledge associated with that learning. The end result of embracing this key area of leadership practice at IBM speaks for itself—the firm is once again considered to be at the leading edge not only of the IT industry but of American industry as a whole.

BUILDING CHANGE CAPACITY

Leaders must recognize that the ability to proactively change as an organization is a legitimate source of competitive advantage, and spread the message that change capacity is not about "what" to change, but rather is all about "how" to change.

For all the talk in the contemporary business world surrounding organizational change one would hope that leaders would finally be getting it. Unfortunately, many of them still do not. Far too many contemporary leaders willingly and admirably accept the mandate for building change capacity throughout their organizations but then proceed to focus on all the wrong things relative to this key area of leadership practice. This was certainly true of the leaders at an organization with which I worked briefly several years ago on a consulting basis.

"What" Versus "How"—The First Fundamental Misunderstanding

The disconnect was immediately clear to me when the CIO of the client organization (a Fortune 500 firm) leaned across the conference table during the initial meeting surrounding my proposed engagement with the firm and announced that he was "anxious to develop change capacity throughout the information system (IS) organization" and that doing so would "clarify our strategic direction in terms of IS service offerings." And further, that he was looking to me, as the external "change management expert," to develop the change capacity of the IS organization with this goal in mind. It was a classic case of the "what" versus "how" misunderstanding in the context of building organizational change capacity.

Like most leaders, the client CIO (an outstanding leader and executive in many respects) expected the wrong thing from building change capacity and was concurrently motivated to engage my expertise for the wrong reasons. As a change management consultant intent on assisting the client firm with building change capacity, I would not focus at all on "what" to change, but rather on "how" to change.[3] Building change capacity is in no way about determining a specific change in organizational strategic direction (a critical area of leadership practice unto itself, and a separate and distinct pillar of HR-minded leadership, as previously discussed in the section surrounding strategic visioning) but entirely about enabling an organization to effectively implement such a change. In short, it is all about enabling the organization to embrace and institutionalize change. I attempted to clarify this misunderstanding to the client leadership team, and even naively believed myself to have been successful when they all (including the CIO) shook my hand and enthusiastically agreed (or so I thought) to my making a formal proposal for an extended engagement on *my* terms—that is, that I would focus on the "how" and not on the "what." It was not until a post-proposal debrief meeting with the CIO two weeks later that I learned just how big, and strong, the "what" versus "how" misconception was, at least in this particular organization. It was during this meeting that the CIO communicated his profound disappointment that the "Embracing Change" training program that I had proposed as the core of the extended engagement would in no way produce tactical plans for changing the strategic direction of the firm's IS organization. He still did not "get it." And I did not get invited back for the extended engagement!

Change for Change's Sake—The Second Fundamental Misunderstanding

In addition to the "what" versus "how" blind spot, many contemporary leaders continue to believe that the way to build organizational change capacity is simply to drive as much change as possible, as quickly as possible, throughout their organizations. Rather than build change capacity, this results in increased change resistance. Leaders must take the time to demonstrate the legitimate business-related need for change, and focus on the "how" in terms of building organizational capacity to embrace and institutionalize change. Without such an approach, the leader's change initiatives are destined to fail.

One need only to look at the unprecedented "change wake" left behind by Durk Jager of Proctor and Gamble and Lloyd Ward of Maytag. Both of these leaders have been soundly critiqued in the popular business press, and in the leadership community at large, for their ill-advised change platforms. They each had remarkably short tenures as CEOs of their respective organizations (from two to five years), given the deep heritage of these companies (both firms have been in existence for at least seventy-five years, and leadership stability is a hallmark of each). Both of these leaders believed that the path to increased organizational change capacity was aggressive, and even unbridled, change. Granted, these mature organizations needed some fresh thinking and related initiatives to infuse them with new energy and vision. But not change for change's sake. Unfortunately, the tainted leadership legacies each left behind in their respective firms speak to the faulty nature of their thinking and their related lack of HR-mindedness relative to building change capacity.

THE "UGLY" TRUTH ABOUT THE NATURE OF EMPLOYEES—SOME SOBERING THOUGHTS FOR HR-MINDED LEADERS

The need for leaders to become increasingly HR-minded in terms of their leadership beliefs, behaviors, and priorities is clear. Only by focusing on the development of a compelling strategic vision, holistically engaging jobs, a sound organizational conscience, improved organizational knowledge management, and enhanced organizational change capacity are leaders able to effectively motivate an increasingly sophisticated and talented employee base. Thus, all leaders must see themselves as HR-minded leaders, regardless of their functional or line responsibilities.

An epiphenomenon, or by-product, of embracing HR-mindedness as a leader is the ability to better anticipate and effectively handle those inevitable situations when employees fail to perform up to expectations. Despite embracing and enthusiastically employing HR-minded leadership, not *all* of your employees will respond in kind, and even those who do will not *always* behave as the highly evolved, principled, sophisticated, and talented human resources profiled throughout this chapter. This is the "ugly" truth. Human resources are at once the most incredibly valuable yet fallible and unpredictable resource that leaders must effectively steward. As the old saying goes, humans are truly "fearfully and wonderfully made." And embracing the leadership practice areas outlined herein will better equip leaders not only to motivate and equitably assess their human resources, but also to deal more forthrightly and decisively with substandard employee performance and unacceptable employee behavior.

NOTES

1. The terms "ideal" and "evil," referring to spirituality and religion, respectively, are not quoted directly from another work. They are employed here to emphasize the polarity with which the two phenomena are generally treated in the organizational spirituality literature at large.

2. Several reliable sources can be cited for this demographic, including the International Database (IDB) developed in conjunction with the U.S. Census, and the Universal Almanac.

3. For a full discussion of the "how" of building change capacity see Quatro, Hoekstra, and Gilley (2002).

REFERENCES

Abramson, P.R., and R. Inglehart. (1995). *Value Change in Global Perspective.* Ann Arbor: University of Michigan Press.

Bartel, A. (2004). "Human Resource Management and Organizational Performance: Evidence from Retail Banking." *Industrial and Labor Relations Review* 57 (2): 181–194.

Becker, B.E., M.A. Huselid, P.S. Pickus, and M.F. Spratt. (1997). "HR as a Source of Shareholder Value: Research and Recommendations." *Human Resource Management* 36 (1): 39–47.

Brockbank, W. (1999). "If HR Were Strategically Proactive: Present and Future Directions in HR's Contribution to Competitive Advantage." *Human Resource Management* 38 (4): 337–352.

Collins, J. (2001). *Good to Great: Why Some Companies Make the Leap . . . and Others Don't.* New York: Harper Business.

Downes, H., and J. Heap. (2002). "World Productivity Congress." *Management Services* 46 (1): 8–11.

Farrell, D. (2003). "The Real New Economy." *Harvard Business Review* 81 (10): 104–112.

Gilley, J.W., and A. Maycunich. (2000). *Organizational Learning Performance, and Change: An Introduction to Strategic HRD.* Cambridge, MA: Perseus.

Greer, C.R., S.A. Youngblood, and D.A. Gray. (1999). "Human Resource Management: The Make or Buy Decision." *Academy of Management Executive* 13 (3): 85–96.

Herman, S.W., and A.G. Schaefer. (2001). *Spiritual Goods: Faith Traditions and the Practice of Business.* Charlottesville, VA: Philosophy Documentation Center.

Maslow, A. (1998). *Maslow on Management.* New York: Wiley.

Mitroff, I.I., and E.A. Denton. (1999). *A Spiritual Audit of Corporate America: A Hard Look at Spirituality, Religion, and Values in the Workplace.* San Francisco: Jossey-Bass.

Nash, L.L., and S. McLennan. (2001). *Church on Sunday, Work on Monday: The Challenge of Fusing Christian Values with Business Life.* San Francisco: Jossey-Bass.

Neal, J.A. (2000). "Work as a Service to the Divine: Giving Our Gifts Selflessly and with Joy." *Applied Behavioral Scientist* 43 (8): 116–133.

Quatro, S.A., E. Hoekstra, and J.W. Gilley. (2002). "Holistic Model for Change Agent Excellence: Core Roles and Competencies for Successful Change Agency." In *Changing the Way We Manage Change*, ed. R. Sims, 55–84. Westport, CT: Quorum Books.

Rokeach, M. (1973). *The Nature of Human Values.* New York: Free Press.

Ulrich, D. (1997). "Measuring Human Resources: An Overview of Practice and a Prescription for Results." *Human Resource Management* 36 (3): 303–320.

———. (1998). "A New Mandate for Human Resources." *Harvard Business Review* 76 (1): 124–134.

CHAPTER 16

LEADERS SPEAK

Success and Failure in Their Own Words

WILLIAM J. MEA AND SHAWN M. CARRAHER

What makes a leader? What elements of character make others want to follow them? In the end, what makes some leaders true successes and others failures? In this chapter we will look into what makes good and bad leaders. Rather than focus on theory, we have opted to hear from accomplished leaders themselves on leaders they had—good and bad—and the mark it left on them. Lively stories of personal experience with leaders will provide insight into some dynamic personalities who have made a difference in their respective fields. The stories of these competent leaders will be contrasted with the stories of those who aspired to leadership, but failed in some profound ways.

The chapter begins with observations on leadership that will frame our outlook. Afterward, we review a limited sample of theories that we use to shape the lens through which readers can view leaders' personal accounts. The next two sections contain the accounts of leaders—one on leaders who lead, and the other on leaders who ultimately fail. In the final section we draw conclusions about leadership as it is actually lived. We conclude that while many people are able to succeed, few are truly leaders in the sense that they make a positive and lasting difference.

BACKGROUND

Leadership is a providential combination of factors in which character, talent, and timing matter. Raw talent and the will to succeed are not enough. Many people have technical skills or interpersonal savvy, but the right blend of characteristics for leadership is rare. It is an extraordinary person in whom strength of purpose, technical competence, and solid character combine to face challenging events that give them the opportunity to serve as models for others.

Apart from our belief that character and timing set the stage for leaders, the authors of this chapter make no central theoretical statement on how people become leaders. In fact, leadership is thrust on some unlikely individuals. A good number of people with extraordinary gifts arrive at leadership. Other leaders are simply people with the right core characteristics, the right intent, the right situation, and the right timing. Some succeed in ways that are often surprising.

On the other hand, many people who aspire to leadership fail miserably. They show promise in one or more areas and may have technical virtuosity in many arenas. However, many who are given the opportunity for potential greatness squander it because a fatal flaw undermines and overrides their strengths.

Definitions of leadership are numerous and almost as varied and personal as the perspectives of the persons defining it. According to Stogdil (1974), differentiation of leaders from others in a society does not occupy the interest of all cultures. In our American results-focused culture it receives intense interest as individuals and organizations strive to achieve more than others. Leadership definitions can serve many purposes. For some it serves to provide theory development and for others, an attempt, perhaps unrealistic, to avoid the appearance of a particular value orientation. The authors of this chapter have a value orientation.

In this chapter we adopt Tead's (1935, 20) view, that leadership can be defined as "the activity of influencing people to cooperate toward some goal," along with Bass's (1961) view that successful leadership results in the creation of transformation in others. Leaders emerge because they can solve problems in times of stress (Mumford 1909) and great leaders emerge because their abilities are needed in conditions suitable for the particular ability they have (Stodgil 1974). Conflict, particularly warfare, economic competition among business concerns, and political ideologies, provides the situation in which leaders emerge and great leadership can be observed. Leaders orient others in their influence and motivate others to act with the expectation that their efforts will lead to worthy results.

APPROACH

Rather than confine our review to a particular industry sector or group of leaders, we took the broad approach and interviewed leaders in four arenas in which the authors have practical experience and access to experienced leaders. We conducted forty interviews with leaders who are recognized themselves as worthy representatives in their professions—the military, business, government, and politics. A number of them, named as contributors in a note at the end of the chapter, will be widely recognized, others not. Interviews generally lasted about one hour. Where it was not possible to conduct direct interviews or time constrained follow-up, we conducted telephone interviews and followed up with e-mail clarifications. In some cases, for political or personal reasons, an interviewee requested anonymity. Interviewees with past political involvement were particularly concerned that their statements might be misunderstood, taken out of context, or misapplied by a reader.

In brief, we asked two broad questions about leadership, covering successful leaders they admired and leaders who failed in some major aspect. The first question asked the respondent to describe the most-admired leader with whom they had worked and their leadership style. We asked further about what that leader did to inspire others, how they earned respect, and what in their personal background led them to be a leader. We asked them to illustrate with an example of a particular circumstance in which their actions reflected the nature of their inner qualities. In addition, we also asked each leader to identify a person in a recognized leadership position, who when given the opportunity to lead, failed in some significant way or had a flaw that made their leadership fail. A portion of information from the interviews is included in the next two sections.

LEADERS WHO LEAD, AND SUCCEED

This section contains the stories of leaders who succeeded, with accompanying interpretations. Not all of the interviews we conducted could be included in this chapter, but the key points are represented.

Military

There is no greater focus on leadership than in the military. Modern students of armed conflict study great historic battles such as Gaugamela, Lepanto, Austerlitz, the Wilderness, the Battle of the Bulge, and the Persian Gulf War. While they take an interest in the weaponry and tactics, the key focus is on the leaders themselves. Men like Alexander the Great, Don John of Austria, Napoleon Bonaparte, Robert E. Lee, George Patton, and Norman Schwarzkopf provide inspiration and models for others to guide their strategy and actions. The traits honed in battle become lessons to young people, captains of industry, and politicians. As you will hear from the following military professionals, what lies just underneath the surface in great leaders is an ability to focus on the mission and the people.

In his early career, General Terry Murray was executive officer to Colonel, later Brigadier General, Gary Brown who commanded the first regiment in the first division in Vietnam from 1987 to 1989. With this two-tour commander there was never a question among his subordinates of whether he shared the burdens or risks of life in the field. A master of tactics and people, he was bright, confident, and convincing both in and out of the field. Character core values of honor, commitment, and courage are what define the navy and the marines. Professional competence in technical methods, tactics, and leadership of warriors is absolutely essential to credibility and the welfare of one's unit. In preparation for, and during, a combat mission, Brown never lost his composure. Not a demonstrative man, he was honest with others in a way that inspired them to do their best. Brown was mission driven. Because his uppermost concern was his marines, with self-interest following well behind, the men in his command both loved and respected him. He exemplified the two essential qualities leaders must possess—character and competence.

General Murray noted that inspiring warriors come in all ranks. Master Gunnery Sergeant David Ankrom is one such leader who inspired Murray. In the early 1980s, Sergeant Ankrom, a decorated combat veteran of Vietnam, was operations chief at the

Washington Marine Barracks at 8th and I streets. He had an extraordinary ability to focus on "the mission." General Murray states that Sergeant Ankrom recognized that each man had a critical role to play in the mission—in this case, flawless military parades, especially the inspiring summer marine sunset parade. The ultimate point of emphasis for a marine is the ability to concentrate on the "moment at hand." Marine leaders learn to prepare well and recognize that once a tactical mission is engaged, poor execution of any key element can compromise the entire unit effort. In combat this means unnecessary death. Sergeant Ankrom always communicated in a manner that let people know where they stood in relation to him and to the mission. As a result of his ability to focus all the energies of the people surrounding him, once "the machine was in movement," it was clear that the unit and command would execute the mission flawlessly.

Air Force General Lee Wilson, while a young officer, served under former Air Force Chief of Staff General Ron Fogelman while Fogelman was still a colonel. Wilson's judgment is that leadership is an art form of adhering to one's beliefs and is also a condition of the heart. Convinced that leaders are born and not taught, General Wilson believes that leadership is defined by results and not how well liked by one's superiors one becomes.

Talleyrand is credited with saying that "I am more afraid of one hundred sheep led by a lion than one hundred lions led by a sheep" (personal interview with General Wilson). For Fogelman, leadership meant not just doing things right, but doing the right things with force. A formidable character who demanded much and spoke directly, he did not talk down to people. Even in heated situations where he thought someone had failed to execute properly, he never held on to the thought that someone was himself or herself a failure. Fogelman demanded no more of others than he would of himself. He demonstrated that fearless integrity is an indomitable force. In any setting, his superiors, peers, and subordinates turned to him for guidance. To those who reported to him, the worst punishment was feeling they had let Fogelman down. Following the 1996 bombing of Kobar Towers in Saudi Arabia, the secretary of defense is alleged to have demanded that military "heads should fall" for what ultimately was a civilian-directed policy. Federal executive leadership at the time, as with the bombings of the World Trade Towers (1993) and the USS Cole (2000) promised that those responsible would pay the price. Rather than serve as a conduit for misplaced blame, General Fogelman resigned when he could easily have moved ahead. If that administration's promise had been kept, perhaps almost 3,000 more in America would have lived past September 11, 2001.

Navy Captain Bill Hines served at the U.S. Naval Academy with Commander, later Admiral, Anne Rondeau. Hines described Rondeau as "the smartest Naval Officer I have ever known." She had the capacity and interest to engage in lively debate on any subject—history, naval matters, religion, sociology—and she knew what motivated people. Those over her did not intimidate her, and she was loyal and respectful. In an atmosphere that could appear mechanistic on the surface, she understood the dynamics of individuals and the pulse of units because people came first. While not unaware of human failings and hardened character flaws, she saw possibilities in young midshipmen in training where others did not see them. Rather than make excuses for those flaws, however, she demanded that young people come up to standard. Whether debating a technical matter or crafting young people's lives, she would challenge others to look deeper into the facts and examine their premises before drawing final conclusions—especially those that affected people's lives.

During Navy Commander Erik Anderson's first flight tour, he was led by a demanding, tough, and competitive commanding officer (CO). Known for "training as you fight," the CO instituted standard midnight briefs and flights. It earned him the nickname "Prince of Darkness" because of his eagerness to train in conditions that were as realistic as possible. Honor was a key component of his style—"You did what was right, despite the consequences." He took every opportunity to publicly acknowledge a job well done, but applied a compassionate discipline when necessary. Most squadrons have spirited young squadron officers with a penchant for getting into trouble. One case illustrates the prudent application of caring discipline to a junior office (JO) arrested by police for on-base intoxication. A number of junior officers grumbled openly when the JO was sent immediately to an alcohol rehabilitation program. Dissent in the ranks was short-lived, when after six weeks the JO returned to ranks, became the CO's greatest advocate, and claimed the hard decision saved him from alcoholism. As an effective parent's, the CO's hard but compassionate decision reformed the flight officer and demonstrated that character in a unit's leadership makes it stronger. The unnamed CO later was promoted to vice admiral.

This brief summary of interviewees' observations reveals that among outstanding military leaders professionalism is the ability to focus with intensity on the mission and the people. As General Krulak, former commandant of the Marine Corps stated, the job of a military leader is not the stewardship of things, but the leading of people. Integrity is what *prevents* one from doing wrong. Each of the military leaders described by our interviewees had straightforward moral courage, and their decisions were focused on "doing the right thing" versus creating the appearance of doing things right. The military leaders described above were men and women of conviction, who, even in trying circumstances, communicated in their actions a dedication to principles higher than themselves.

Business

The advances of Western institutions—democracy, capitalism, and science—provide the modern world's great capacity for harnessing human creativity for individual and collective advancement (D'Souza 2002). The chief cause of modern prosperity is human intellect—"discovery, invention, habit of enterprise, [and] foresight" (Bandow and Schindler 2003, 66), which are concentrated in free markets as a complex series of voluntary cooperative actions of buyers and sellers (Rosenberg and Birdzell 1986). Corporations are the institutions that make this possible, and their executives and management teams transform leadership into prosperity for employees and communities. Corporate leaders make economic success possible through the people they lead—through strategic focus, definition of priorities, and development of performance expectations—but they also lead by the values they communicate. While it may not lead to immediate short-term cents-per-dollar share results, long-term performance success accrues to leaders who focus on customer value, harness the capacity of a workforce they respect, and hold themselves responsible for corporate and public accountability. This section relates insights about effective business stewardship from experienced corporate leaders whose principle-driven success was formed by mentors who demonstrated the capacity to manage things as well as people.

Vice president of human resources at MASCO Corporation Dan Foley believes he has worked for some of the best industry leaders over the past thirty-five years. One individual, MASCO's late president, Raymond F. Kennedy, stands out as the best. Foley states that Kennedy walked through life with a combination of Irish humor, business insight, integrity, love of family, and a common touch. According to Foley, many executives known for being "fun" to work with fail as capable decision makers. Others are so focused on business as an end in itself that their people legacy is minimal.

Kennedy could cut through business nonsense more quickly than other senior executives—and did so with a smile and manner that left the person whose *ideas* were being brutalized feeling *respected*. Unimpressed with "the business elite," he had time for everyone who wanted a moment with him and genuinely cared about employees and customers as real people with real lives. His word was his bond, he could reduce data to its core points, and he forced other senior executives to focus on essentials. Even when he pushed subordinates, people loved him for his ability to do it with confidence. An example of Kennedy's capacity to lead is illustrated by a misunderstanding. He incorrectly blamed Foley, a seasoned labor negotiator and normally unflappable senior executive, for missing a conference speech. Devastated by the criticism, Foley contemplated resignation, but within minutes Kennedy appeared with a tear in his eye to apologize profusely, and, to Foley's growing embarrassment, to tell him all the things he admired about Foley as an executive. Kennedy showed a combined capacity to focus on business essentials and connect with people.

For former vice president and general council Richard Wall of Cerner Corporation, its former president Cliff Illig served as the most inspiring leader he ever encountered during his twenty-five years in the computer and software industry. Illig understood the potential of enterprise-wide software to revolutionize health care and promote health for this Kansas City–based $700 million firm. He took a long-term, enterprise view of the business and strove in every situation to do the right thing, even if it went beyond contract requirements with clients and commitment to people. No one situation provides an example of Illig's leadership capacity—but his steady ability to focus while listening and his unflappable talent for maintaining composure when others lost their tempers illustrate core characteristics. Wall feels that Illig's family training and religious values made him a man of integrity who could put employees and clients at the center of his business universe.

According to Arthur Amdurer, a former human resources information technology vice president, an unnamed mid-1990s president at the largest business unit of Simon and Schuster impressed him as the greatest business leader he had ever encountered.

Leading seven business units and 2,000 people, the executive focused first on ethics. His frequent feedback was positive and constructive, and it gained him the appreciation of his senior staff. His self-deprecating humor put others at ease. While he insisted on achieving numbers, he would not compromise his ethics. For example, on one occasion when his metrics shined, he learned of fraud in one unit. Rather than be unethical—he could easily have buried the failure in higher-level numbers—he chose to expose the fraud and thus himself to the appearance of failure. On another occasion, when Amdurer posed alternative options on a politically sensitive issue, the executive's response was an uncomplicated and principled—"What is the right thing to do?" Amdurer had never previously heard an executive ask this question in his twenty-five years' experience in industry. Amdurer believes that the president's principles were the result of his religious upbringing, as further evidenced in the executive's refusal to take advantage of opportunities that opposed his religious principles. He was asked to take on the additional responsibility of managing a magazine supportive of warfare, a position opposed to his convictions. In declining the responsibility, he risked ending his career, yet he maintained his honor.

David Smith, now a senior program manager at Lockheed Martin Information Technology, trained and developed a young and talented Tim Hohmann at Texas Instruments (TI) in the 1980s. Product marketing engineers at TI had to be capable of simultaneously developing strategy and marketing, working under tight budgets, designing new products, understanding technical customer applications, and managing product sales and profitability. Hohmann was a quick study whose contributions increased, yet without threatening his peers in the process. Ultimately, Hohmann moved up to the top position, swapping roles with Smith. Hohmann inspired the team to work together with energy while he conveyed respect for each team member and praised individuals for their unique contributions. In 1994, Hohmann went on to establish PLC Direct, now known as AutomationDirect, a company that sells high-technology automation products using a direct marketing model. Teams are given the authority to carry out needed actions and to discover methods to improve products, service, and prices. According to Smith, Hohmann made his company prosper by taking care of his people and making work both productive and enjoyable.

Jim Handlon, a former technology company executive and now president of Bottomline Partners, worked with MCI's late founder and CEO William (Bill) G. McGowan. McGowan combined technical know-how and interpersonal savvy in a manner that helped transform the telecommunications industry from what had been a monopoly industry. Handlon described McGowan as someone who focused people on using process improvement to create new technologies and services. The son of a second-generation Irish railroad engineer in the Pennsylvania coal region, Bill worked the railroads during his school days before attending graduate school at Harvard University. Warm, open, and approachable, Bill McGowan had the ability to connect with people from the top to the bottom of his organization. He would ask people at all levels to get involved in coming up with better methods by saying, "I need you to think about this and give it your best shot." Appreciating that not all initiatives have top authority, he understood how to "pull back the throttle," and was a master of thanking people in a genuine manner. His people knew where they stood, that they were genuinely respected, and that their contribution mattered.

Marty Goldberg, managing director of Change and Strategy Solutions at BearingPoint, worked for the late cofounder and chairman of Imperial Bancorp in Los Angeles, George Graziadio. Pepperdine University's Graduate School of Business now bears his name. He combined a striking blend of entrepreneurial capability and corporate know-how. Together with his long-term business partner, George Etlinge, Graziadio was a "builder" of businesses, organizations, and people. Motivated by a bright, optimistic vision that burned even brighter in hard times, he communicated to those around him how challenges were opportunities to become even stronger. During his prosperous career he went out of his way to surround himself with and support people "who made things happen." Development, forward thinking, and optimism were at his core. Fond of quoting Leonardo da Vinci, "He turns not back who is bound to a star," his actions gave vivid witness to the truth of that principle.

Walter Sechriest, marketing director at Deloitte, who managed supply chain management initiatives for the $2 billion agribusiness Delta and Pine Land Company, worked closely with its late CEO Roger Malkin. According to Sechriest, Roger had an extraordinary vision of the possibilities of genetic technologies in the global seed business as a means to increase plant yields. Having come from Wall Street, Roger moved to the Mississippi Delta and made it his community. He transformed the company from a small seed producer to the largest cottonseed enterprise in the world. While maintaining homegrown talent, he also recruited outsiders with business sense and the capacity to bring a third-party view to the company. Sechriest noted that even though he had no agribusiness experience, Malkin made a leap of faith in placing Sechriest in charge of major operations projects. Malkin provided hands-on coaching when requested, was a great listener, and stepped back tactfully to be a cheerleader. Malkin himself had been involved in prior ventures that failed and understood how to make the most of that learning. When Sechriest had to bring "bad news" to Malkin, there was no blame, but he always asked, "What is our work-around plan?" In essence, like other successful business executives, Malkin had the ability to take risks and to benefit from them, connect with others and build their confidence, and commit to business as a means to benefit those in his immediate environment as well as the larger community.

Similar to the experiences of our military interviewees, successful corporate leaders have an ability to focus on a mission and harness the energy of their colleagues and subordinates. Early character development and optimism makes a strong fundamental contribution to the success of business leaders. While the potential results of failure are not as severe as in a military context, similar interest in the success of people as a group is a driving factor. Successful business leaders communicate a clear vision for the future, have an understanding about how to get there, and get their people involved in reaching success. Our interviewees also felt that rather than drive people, successful business leaders believe in the genuine dignity and worth of their employees and demonstrate it through their actions.

Politics and Government

In this section we will review and consider observations on leadership in politics and government. This realm remains mysterious to military and corporate leaders. A former White House official in several administrations and frequent guest lecturer at the Washington Campus (a nonpartisan, nonprofit organization training Fortune 500 executives in the public policy process) would frequently say, "There is no bottom line in government." At the same time, successful government must achieve outcomes, but not outcomes that would translate in terms easily understood in business. In this section we will hear from leaders in politics and government about leaders who were truly successful.

We believe that skilled leaders in politics and government are keenly in tune with the emotions of others, and, like passionate poker players, they monitor how their own reactions play into winning. The skills that help make successful politicians predispose them to success in government. Unlike in business, where rational analysis is fundamental, emotional radar is critical for navigation in the arenas of politics and government. According to Nicholson (1998, 138), "human beings are hardwired to avoid loss when comfortable and scramble madly when threatened." Principles from evolutionary psychology hold especially true and provide a convincing model to frame interpretations in politics and government. Similar to entrepreneurs as well as to hunters of millennia ago, those who make a living in politics are keenly aware of threats. As leaders they channel their communications to energize others with their own willingness to take personal risk. People within bureaucracies, on the other hand, whether inside government or large corporations, are inclined to focus on protecting the interests of the structure itself. We have observed that professional civil servants want to contribute to making a difference. On the other hand, they sense change as a threat to stability and want to create emotional predictability within their institutions. Rosenberg and Birdzell, in an economic metaphor for this observation, note that, "In all well-ordered societies, political authority is dedicated to stability, security, and the status quo. It [government] is thus, singularly ill qualified to direct or channel activity intended to produce instability, insecurity, and change" (1986, 265). It takes extraordinary skill to bring together people to act with conviction, especially in politics, and, in some sense, in bureaucracies, where action is in many ways voluntary. We will examine some of the qualities described by current leaders in depicting great leaders they have known in politics and government.

Margaret Heckler, former congresswoman for sixteen years from Massachusetts, and during the second Reagan administration, secretary of the U.S. Department of Health and Human Services (HHS), later ambassador to Ireland, worked closely with President Ronald Reagan. She feels he was one of the few presidents ever driven by a philosophy. His experiences—living through World War II, the threat of obliteration by the Soviet Union, and labor union challenges—and also his reading gave him a clear vision for the world, which he was able to communicate as few others could. What appeared to be a natural ability to communicate complex ideas in simple terms were actually skills honed when he was the host of General Electric Theater. According to Ambassador Heckler, he toured plants throughout the United States and wrote his own statements to explain concepts in clear-cut terms that average people could understand and appreciate. He learned from his father about the misuse of welfare and from his mother the moral standards he lived by throughout his active political career. It is not well known that small interpersonal interactions could affect him profoundly. For instance, when he learned from a mother that her child needed a kidney to live, he assigned Heckler the task of using her HHS organization to locate the needed organ. As a result, the organization itself learned what could be accomplished during a human-focused dilemma. While he was caricatured as nothing more than an ideological free marketer, Reagan's belief that government should assist the truly vulnerable is little known.

Retired navy commander Chip Beck, also a retired clandestine services officer, worked internationally with numerous political and government figures. The three men he admired most met their untimely deaths because their leadership convictions would not allow them to give way to personal expedient options. William F. (Bill) Buckley, Beirut CIA station chief, was kidnapped and eventually tortured to death by Hezbollah terrorists in Lebanon. Cambodian General Khy Hak died with his family in the final day of combat at Phnom Penh at the hands of the Khmer Rouge. In Angola, Jonas Savimbi was assassinated by oppressors in the Popular Movement for the Liberation of Angola, following decades of guerilla war against Portuguese colonialism, Soviet control assisted by brutal Cuban invaders, and homegrown Marxist deceit. As stated by Beck, they all possessed keen intelligence, great capacity to organize, and a talent for translating theory into action and strategy into tactical warfare and political programs. In addition to tremendous physical courage and compassion for their troops, they led by example, exposing themselves to danger and privation. Their convictions, in the case of Savimbi disparaged in the press, were borne of compassion for subjugated peoples. As leaders, they guided the development of others and left legacies simply by doing what they believed was right rather than what was expedient. In each case these leaders sought to accomplish broader democratic justice for which they sacrificed their own lives.

Nancy Mohr Kennedy, who served President Reagan as assistant to the president for Legal Affairs and President George H.W. Bush as assistant secretary for Congressional Affairs at the U.S. Department of Education, was inspired while serving in the White House by her mentor, Max Friedersdorf. Friedersdorf taught his team members always to keep their word. For him, one's word is not only one's bond, but proximity to the president leads people to think that the words and actions of the president's staff are extensions of the president's intent. At times, misinterpretations of a president's or his staffs' reactions can lead to embarrassing results. Friedersdorf served his staff as a steady fatherly figure would. When the staff learned of President Nixon's cover-up, Friedersdorf helped the members of the staff to maintain their dignity; when President Reagan was shot, he consoled them. Kennedy was most impressed by the way Friedersdorf sought to keep a low-profile in a town where self-promotion goes unquestioned and to mentor his young staff—many of whom have now become senior veterans in congressional relations.

Sally Atwater, executive director of the President's Committee for People with Intellectual Disabilities, shared with us a personal view of the leadership of her husband, Lee

Atwater. Lee served as campaign manager for President George H.W. Bush and as chairman of the Republican National Committee until his death at age forty. He loved both the political arena and people, and was a born salesman with a desire to ensure that democracy serves the American people. Interning for a senator and studying history during college opened the door to a future political career to which Lee Atwater devoted the rest of his life. At age twenty-one he managed his first national campaign on college campuses. Lee believed in the need for a robust two-party system, which had been missing in his home state of South Carolina. On the occasions he lost a political contest, he studied his failures and persisted. His belief in democracy, his knowledge of people, focused energy and sense of drive, and loyalty to candidates and workers ranked him among the most notable leaders in American politics.

The skills that make a great leader in politics, according to Sally Atwater, are akin to but not necessarily the same as those that make a great leader in government. Madeleine C. Will, with whom Sally has worked, served as assistant secretary of Special Education and Rehabilitative Services at the Department of Education during the Reagan administration and is currently chairperson of the President's Committee for People with Intellectual Disabilities. Madeleine brings the compassion of a mother of a child with a disability and the patience of a mother of three. A strategic thinker with gracious people skills, she treats all people with dignity and self-worth. The programs that she initiated twenty years ago for people with intellectual disabilities (mental retardation)—early intervention, employment, transition from school to work for students with disabilities—still survive and serve as a basis for assisting American children with disabilities as well as a model for international programs. These qualities—patience, compassion, vision, and the practical ability to lead others in establishing federal programs—make her a commendable leader for others to follow.

Sam Diehl, staff director for the House Agriculture Subcommittee, worked in the past for Senator Rick Santorum of Pennsylvania. He believes the senator serves as a model leader in politics because he has the unusual capacity to keep his public persona and actions consistent with his personal beliefs. Politicians with personal outlooks similar to his often lend themselves to fractious debate, thus frequently undermining their cause. In contrast, Senator Santorum undertakes a thoughtful analysis of his own stands and the opposing views, and arrives at a principled position. Respectful of his colleagues, he earns the admiration of those with whom he disagrees—even as he engages them on issues that divide. Rather than surrounding himself with calculating staff seeking to move ahead quickly, he has a reputation for a dedicated staff that espouses his traditional beliefs. Evidence of his attention to their growth and mentoring are seen in a staff turnover that is extremely low. Senator Santorum's authenticity is evident in a response he gave about family-work balance. When questioned by one of the authors of this chapter about how he maintains a balance between work and family life, he responded, "I can only do perhaps eight percent of what my staff asks me to do . . . if I were to ignore my family, I could do two percent more . . . in twenty years when my name is forgotten, I want my children to remember I was with them."

Charlie Grizzle, assistant administrator for Administration and Resources Management of the U.S. Environmental Protection Agency in the second Reagan administration and in the George H.W. Bush administration, served with a superior career federal manager who was promoted to a senior political leadership position. Although a president needs to employ outsiders to bring in fresh ideas to government, they occasionally recruit from inside government. In this case, the president made the unusual yet prudent decision to elevate a career civil service employee to a political position. The individual exhibited keen interest in every agency program and worked diligently to master management and organizational issues. His inclusive management style ensured that even the most junior employees felt respected and a part of the organization's success. While willing to delegate responsibility to subordinate managers, his mastery made certain that subsidiary managers provided accurate information and acted with accountability. The unnamed executive moved on to an exceptional corporate career, demonstrating that sound leadership and management skills are broadly applicable across career settings.

Navy Captain Jim Dulin, a former navy pilot now in the corporate world, worked closely with Senator John Warner when the latter was secretary of the navy in 1975—principally while Secretary Warner was on tour in Antarctica. Secretary Warner was asked about how one leads a huge organization in which it was virtually impossible to be informed on all aspects of accountability. His reply taught Dulin a lesson that applied in his own later career as the commanding officer in Adak, Alaska, the largest military outpost between the Alaskan mainland and the Soviet Union. Specifically, one cannot do all things. In order to accomplish anything in large command circumstances, it is critical to select five major programs that can drive the success of others, and then to assign one's best people to carry out those programs with passion, drive, and a sense of positive expectations.

We have heard from a diverse group of leaders on great leaders in government and politics. On a national and international stage, political leaders who are successful believe in the capacity of democracy to bring about effective rule of law and the best chance of prosperity to their countrymen. Great leaders on the world stage see large opportunities and translate them into communications that build positive expectations and a belief that concerted common action will yield the promise of a better future. Within government bureaucracies, effective leaders "make peace with process" and by astute coalition building, they build success through informal channels. Instinct, mentoring, and painful failure build an individual's capacity to achieve authentic success by building parallel informal organizations. Perhaps the best training ground for learning these tactics is Capitol Hill. Under the tutelage of seasoned elders who survive repeated elections, political officials hone their capacity to build shifting alliances, weave elements of success through complex parliamentary processes, and build emotional antennae that sense the capacity to build coalitions. Translated into the workings of government bureaucracies, this means giving surface respect to rigid structures, while at the same time building an analogous system of personal influence. Give-and-take exchanges are employed behind the scenes to make progress on a few worthy initiatives. Unlike business, which is designed to be both rational and efficient, the founding fathers established political systems to live in a perpetual state of conflict that cancels out the potential abuse of power or the risk of acting too quickly. Much as in military and business, principled beliefs and focus on people help to achieve success. However, in politics and government, communicating the message clearly and building voluntary coalitions yield success.

Now that we have presented vignettes from the lives of distinguished military, business, and political and government leaders, we turn our attention to the contrasting side. True leaders inspire admiration and a desire to follow in humble imitation. Failed leaders also provide lessons, often ones that our interviewees preferred to forget.

LEADERS WHO FAIL

Failure as a leader makes for short bursts of exciting news, but does not often occupy the attention of people who study leadership. We found that our interviewees were surprised when we asked about noteworthy failures and their underlying causes. Although they wanted to forget them, they had numerous examples. Bad leaders are as influential as good ones. In this section we will offer some general reasons why people fail as leaders and then review experiences of failure in military, business, and political and government situations. We will offer fewer observations from leaders in this section because the themes of failure and its causes are more easily grasped than is the "formula" of leadership success.

The causes of failure in leadership, as in life, are many. As you will see in the experiences of the leaders described below, character is the chief cause of leadership failure. All human beings are flawed, and some flaws create greater vulnerabilities for failure in leadership positions. The human psyche has a way of insulating people from the ability to recognize their own flaws. There is a body of research proposing that when people are accurate in their self-assessment, they become depressed. The overuse of a particular leadership skill can also result in failure (Lombardo and Eichenger 2002). For instance, good leaders make every effort to take on challenging tasks, but if they lose sight of the capacity of their people to endure ongoing and unremitting stress, they fail the mission and their people. In addition, leaders can also attract and surround themselves with the wrong people as assistants (Sulowitz 2004), and thus prevent effective communications.

Military

According to recent polling data, military leaders are more trusted by the public at large than are political, business, or even church leaders. Samuel Johnson is attributed with saying, "An officer is much more respected than any other man with as little money" (U.S. Naval Academy 1992, 229). A mark of the esteem in which the military is held is the horror with which society acts when scandals erupt in their ranks. Being human beings, military leaders are just as subject as other members of society to failure through personal flaws, poor judgment, or poor training. The difference, of course, is that the military holds itself to a higher standard than society in general. Failure can come from human flaws, bad training, or adopting the wrong model for success. While military leaders can improve results by adopting elements of solid business best practices and techniques, the military is not a business. And although leaders can benefit from formulating their message based on keen instinctive insight into the needs of stakeholders, leaders will not be effective when adopting wholesale the principles of politics and government. The military has an entirely different value system, and the bottom line is principled victory in combat. There seems to be particular susceptibility to failure among leaders not directly focused on the military's core business, which is winning wars. There are numerous cases of egregious failure because the responsibility for leading men in combat is so profound. The most extreme cases involve moral failure.

According to U.S. Navy Commander Bryce Lefever, former psychologist with the Naval Special Warfare Development Group, failed leadership is instructive for future leaders. Institutional neurosis can emerge when leaders are committed more to personal advancement than to institutional core principles. Neurosis is a problem that arises when one avoids what one fears—neurosis causes a person to become precisely what they fear in the attempt to avoid it. In military institutions under flawed leadership, a neurotic shadow spreads quickly across the milieu of the leader who sets the wrong tone. For instance, when the wrong military leaders try to "operate like a business," it can lead to serious problems. In some cases the leaders have neither the technical training nor the people skills. In the absence of principled leadership that has an appropriate understanding of mission, trust deteriorates quickly and cannot be recovered. When "looking good rather than being good" becomes the focus—a situation more likely to be found in non-combat units—an unhealthy paranoia can develop in which troops work harder at working more and faster without getting any better results.

Command at sea is the most coveted role in the U.S. Navy. It carries profound leadership authority and responsibility, and, while technical failures can occur, it is quire rare to hear of failure in moral character. One naval officer we interviewed described a situation in which he observed both technical and moral failure. When a new executive officer (XO) reported aboard a large ship, calls from a business owner at the place of the officer's last foreign assignment claimed bill delinquencies. Because the XO had a senior rank and the confidence bestowed by it, he was able to deny financial problems. Other signs began to appear: The XO was quick to take credit for others' accomplishments and just as quick to eschew culpability when anything went wrong, promptly blaming his men. He enforced rules strictly with subordinates yet broke the rules himself. His dominating self-interest affected relationships with others, and their sense of loyalty eroded rapidly. Through sheer self-promotion with his CO, he obtained an excellent performance review and was promoted to a role of greater responsibility in a new shipboard command. Character flaws caught up with him years later, however. In a rare circumstance, he was court-martialed for malfeasance, found guilty, and separated from the naval service.

Military services expect more principled behavior than is the case for society at large. The oath of office that uniformed officers take upon promotion reminds them of the "special trust and authority" vested in them by the president and their duty to carry out faithfully the mission. As leaders they have both the power to direct and the duty to follow lawful orders. Placing one's self-interests above one's duty or the people in one's command results in failure. Confidence is an asset when directing others in a serious and perhaps dangerous mission. But the kind of boastful pride or sense of entitlement that would be acceptable in some business or political circumstances is an avenue to failure in military leadership. Only the correct order of obligations—to one's country, to one's unit, to one's team, and last, to one's self—leads to successful military leadership.

Business

Failures in business, both in economic terms and in terms of achieving genuine benefits for market stakeholders—the shareholders, communities, and employees—are legion. Success in business, on the other hand, is not just a matter of enhancing profit and loss statements or making returns to the shareholder. Business leaders are positioned in the economic center that drives the markets by which society must benefit. A business leader, according to one of our interviewees from a multinational corporation, must generate value to build a successful enterprise. Otherwise, shareholders, customers, employees, creditors, and the community are adversely affected. Producing quarterly financial returns must balance with the cost to the social fabric. If maximizing capital returns means unnecessarily stripping away long-term opportunities for families and communities, that success is questionable. The culture in which we live has become so comfortable with results at any cost that leaders like Attila the Hun (Roberts 1989) and the fictitious Tony Soprano (Himsel 2003) serve as an entertaining vehicle for discussing leadership. Executives who bring long-lasting *value to the company and industry they serve* are quickly forgotten in favor of those who raise quick profits and seek attention. Our interviewees cited numerous cases of failure. We will cover only a few, but the majority illustrated a focus on the self and quick profits regardless of the needs of employee, community, or customer.

In a large corporation with years of success in a broad spectrum of industries, one of our interviewees described a situation in which new leadership decided to partition and sell business components. The leader determined that it would maximize share value; regard for the impact on the communities and people who historically supported the business units was not considered. While it was true that change was needed and the stock soared, the new leader failed because he forgot that a true leader balances legitimate needs of all stakeholders to achieve the maximum good for everyone—shareholders, customers, or employees.

A former bank executive we interviewed worked with a senior executive at an insurance company division producing add-on services in support of the core line of business. While successful at growing his unit's revenue, he faltered when his lack of ability to work in concert with the line surfaced. Not only did he put the needs of his own division ahead of the rest of the business, he put his own personal needs for power, control, and visibility ahead of his division. If alert, he would have recognized that the very health of his division depended on its ability to work in tandem to support the entire mission. A classic case of hubris, this demonstrates that for some business executives, the drive to fulfill prideful ego needs sometimes trumps actual accomplishment of work—something rarely recognized until it is too late and harm has been done to the business.

According to one of our interviewees at a major publishing concern, a senior vice president who recruited him was utterly deficient in ethics. He focused only on what made him look good and would sacrifice anyone to save face. Insecure, he could not tolerate it when he appeared as if he did not know information or when he was not told something. Weaving webs of intrigue and sowing seeds of discontent, he would create conflict to make it look as if he were rescuing a situation. Lacking the personal discipline to inform himself and to keep up to date with any depth on business or human resource issues facing the company, he would just bluster his way through challenges to his credibility. With little focus on the core business, he would disparage other executives not under his influence rather than help them achieve the company's bottom-line numbers. Surprisingly, he still consults on human resource issues with executives in the publishing industry.

A junior expatriate executive with a now-defunct oil and gas company was charged to develop an on-line marketplace. Intelligent and gifted, he was considered a rising star. On one occasion, while leading a meeting of his team and customer invitees to discuss new products and services, he began to rant about how the team product that everyone had worked on intently for months was "just useless." His unsubstantiated opinion showed little regard for the harmful impact it would have on his team. His credibility was never regained as he continued to blame his team for communication problems. He duped the client into believing he was client-focused, he eventually went on to work for the customer company. He was fired in less than a year, however, as the customer learned to know him better. He failed to understand a fundamental principle in business, namely, that even the most gifted person in the company needs common sense, tactfulness, and respect for his team.

Financial markets do not distinguish between solid business leaders and ruthless knaves who happen to push the right product at the right time. While markets quickly winnow out poor products or deficient business models, ethically faulty business leaders can be successful in terms of short-term financial returns. The drive to deliver financial results on a quarterly basis, technical brilliance, and unscrupulous capacity to manipulate others for their own purposes can deliver the kind of outcomes that attract the press and new investors. This does not, however, deliver lasting results that change industries for the better or create opportunity for people and markets.

Politics and Government

Politics and government present a unique set of challenges for leadership. Where victory is the goal and the mission is clear in military situations, and where profit provides a benchmark for successful corporations, there is no bottom line in government and the sands are always shifting in politics. It offers no lavish rewards in terms of financial returns on effort, only power and position. Unlike wealth, which is limitless, there are limits to political power. In a zero-sum game for "political capital," vicious intramural fights occur regularly and only the most noteworthy extramural brawls attract headlines. Opportunities for building the politician's narcissism are astonishing, and challenges to meritorious service are abundant. W.F. Buckley noted, "The awful smell in the room is human vanity [which] is always a factor. . . . The candidates' problem is the absence of a true cause. . . . The benumbing challenge is to contrive a spiel in which the satisfaction of your own vanity plays a subordinate role" (2004, A-11).

One colleague of the authors, who served as a director of third world health care organizations in several previous administrations and in private industry, noted that Washington serves as a stage for officials' vanity. For some, character flaws such as conceit and the drive for power provide a prop that fuels their desire for more power as they rise in authority. At the same time, it wears away the fragile foundation on which they build influence. For some political and government officials, constructing an attractive vita takes precedence over the principles they espouse on the surface. In others, the raw jealousy leads them to engage in fratricidal vengeance within their own party against people they fear will get more praise. In others, obsequiousness toward one's superiors developed to a high art form serves only as a contrivance to achieve one's personal desires ahead of others.

One interviewee, with whom we discussed government officials' failures, described a dramatic example of what can occur. In this case, a clandestine services senior officer, simply by occupying the position he did, had great potential to benefit his country and allied nations. His climb to prominence was, as is often the case in Washington, accomplished by sheer devotion to his personal career advancement. Although people under his command were frequently in danger, he was driven by vanity and deception that focused on increasing his own professional advancement. Not above lying to colleagues, Congress, and investigators, he disgraced his nation by his actions while feigning patriotism that in truth did not exist. A key American ally of liberty died as a result of his inaction. It served no lofty intention other than the narrow self-interests he had set out to achieve from the beginning of his career.

According to one former senior political appointee from the Reagan and first Bush administrations, a serious shortcoming of many political appointees is that they become enamored with the trappings of their office. Over time, this leaves them less engaged in actively trying to lead their organizations in accomplishing a mission than in buoying their own empty sense of self-importance. Rank-and-file employees detect inflated egotism, and it results in a loss of respect for "leadership." In the worst situations, under the influence of scheming colleagues or rank and file, it can result in the undermining of an administration's agenda. Under these conditions, such "leaders" chase after "issues" they believe will give them public recognition rather than apply a disciplined approach to an unwavering mission.

According to one of our interviewees who came to politics three decades ago, while many who are driven by personal ambition reach the "top," they cannot sustain their leadership because their commitment is not genuine. They give up or find a job that pays better. It is because their commitment is based on ambition rather than on true principle. Ernest Lefever, founder of the Ethics and Public Policy Center, who has a half-century of think-tank and administration experience, observed that the main flaws of failed po-litical or government officials were arrogance, selfishness, and failure to keep promises. For him, they fundamentally lacked *courage*, the single virtue that makes all others virtues possible.

The juvenile vandalism involved in breaking the "W" keys off computer keyboards in the last change of administrations is only a minor act of outward aggression. It pales by comparison to the highly refined subterfuge employed to damage others. There are myriad ways to undermine one's opposing party or one's associate within the same party. A president can sign unpopular executive orders at the last minute that will bog down the following administration. An agency leader, rather than make a difficult decision, can commission a study that undoes an initiative with which he or she disagrees. Another crafty bureaucrat finds an element of a regulation that could create resource challenges or unpopularity. Rather than commit to action, the malefactor shifts accountability to another agency by drawing the colleague into the "opportunity." Laying landmines in the paths of others or planting viruses that proliferate at a later date are considered clever sport rather than scheming misdeeds among some. Some confidants lay in wait to under-mine the very political leaders they serve. One such type, labeled "usurpers" by Sulkowitz (2004), latches onto leaders only long enough to get their own needs met. Government officials are easy prey to charismatic yet calculating confidants who thrive under the protection of their power. When leaders open themselves to the influence of an adviser with a spotty sense of right and wrong, they can find themselves replaced by that indi-vidual. The reader may not be surprised to learn how frequently some covetous officials manufacture boldfaced lies when it suits their purpose. Given the natural widespread suspiciousness that comes with living in the nation's capital, spreading plausible lies while pretending to virtuously serve the group interest sows distrust among an official's colleagues, helping the borderline sociopath maneuver into situations where he may be considered the next choice for the position.

Moral equivalency, political expedience, and sham comradeship are highly crafted competencies among some political government officials—they accept them as being no more than tools of the trade. Vulgar self-service among the unscrupulous, in some cases, reaches its pinnacle in "public service." Recognizing the tendency of humans to be flawed, and wanting to prevent abuse of power, the founders wisely built in checks against abuse being concentrated in one branch of government. Despite the challenges noted, it appears that more young people with a well-formed sense of right are becoming attracted to service of their country.

DISCUSSION AND CONCLUSIONS

Now that we have heard from leaders about what makes someone a true leader, and why others fail, we believe it is useful to look below the surface to ask more deeply "*why* leaders fail" and not just how. Perhaps a larger question is better: "Why do people fail?" Both the question and the answer are psychological. An "achieve at any cost mentality," regardless of its effect on society or one's character, is bound to occur in a society that values short-term material goals over substance. Humans' capacity for self-deception is remarkable, and modern culture seduces many into an unhealthy drive to achieve surface recognition.

The cognitive map that serves as a guide for living is built upon assumptions formed early in life. It is a source of what we hold to be important and a source of vulnerability; it can be accurate or flawed, and the rules by which it operates are invisible (Rathus 1990). If one looks deeply into the formative past of people who "achieve at any cost," one is likely to find a fragile family system where profound distress and intense personal fears led to a tenuous self-concept. That self-concept, as in the case of a person who habitually cheats on a test or in business, is never built on a firm foundation and each ensuing act is one element in a lifelong struggle to seek self-affirmation. At the same time, real self-confidence evades individuals because their behavior is self-defeating. In the case of leaders who steer off course, power for power's sake alone and that is not subordinated beyond a higher goal than oneself becomes their undoing. Where accurate self-perception and well-formed conscience are missing, maladaptive drives and needs result in ruin for both leaders and those who are led.

Many people without solid family foundations also achieve worthy outcomes in subordination to the good of society. Unlike the conscience of failed leaders, however, they make a purposeful assessment of their vulnerabilities and a decision to serve others. What is it that successful leaders tap into as they lead others? All human beings have psychological needs and strivings for life that go beyond mere survival (Carson, Butcher, and Coleman 1988). Leaders tap into human needs for order, security, worth, hope, belonging, and approval. People need to feel that they contribute to worthy and attainable outcomes, that their best effort matters, and that they are valued more than the product they contribute. Effective leaders not only understand challenges but also see the possibilities that can be accomplished by united action, and in turn, they bind people together to achieve them.

Military service, and particularly armed conflict or training for it, provides a context in which great leaders emerge. Military life is not simply a profession of warfare, but a call to service for others—to one's country and fellow warriors. When it comes to leadership, morale is the key to victory. One cannot, as Commander Lefever says, make a unit succeed by improving efficiency by 1 percent while destroying morale by 100 percent. While both competence and character count, character is even more critical, according to General Murray. One can be slightly deficient in an area of professional competence and still get the job done and maintain the confidence of one's troops. One cannot be deficient at all in character and still maintain the confidence of the unit. Core principles—honor, courage, commitment, and the sharing of hardship and risk—make for great military leaders.

In the wake of corporate scandals, society has been asking about what the right governance structure is to help create a successful business model. According to J. Collins, the right question to ask is, "Who should we choose to run our corporations?" (2003, 55). Extraordinary leaders do not create success by providing obscene rewards and making news, they build companies that prosper long after the leader is gone, and they make an impact on the industry and their community beyond the confines of the company's quarterly share price. The leaders we have profiled in this chapter united people with them, not behind them. They combine a technical desire to improve the product to meet customer needs with business common sense and a deep respect for employees. In short, they focus on the people and on the long view of the business.

Although there will always be particular challenges to efficiency in government, there is hope for both bringing principled people to government and incorporating practices that work in the private sector. Achieving real change in government is difficult to achieve and even harder to detect (Buckley et al. 1998). However, principles that create account-ability and tie budget to outcomes are being borrowed from business and introduced. Emerging implementation of a rational information technology policy and adoption of best practices from private industry help to drive new opportunities. The structures of government leads those professionals who work within it to seek stability. Those who are successful communicate a simple yet compelling vision for the future and focus on the personal side to achieve an agenda while building collaboration in the process. A belief in the principle of democracy, with all its built-in inefficiencies, is a necessary foundation.

SUMMARY

While people appear to succeed at key roles in the military, in business, and in politics and government organizations, few are truly effective leaders. Truly successful leaders make a lasting positive impact that changes the world around them and the people they lead. They are distinguished by their integrity and capacity to subordinate their own self-interest to higher principles and to their people. While people may fail in particular instances due to a shortfall in technical competence, it is character flaws that lead to disastrous failure—failure that hinders the good of one's country, employees, or democ-racy. What is the antidote to character flaws? While we would not propose that every military unit, business concern, or government bureaucracy needs its own philosopher, reference to the teaching of virtue on a larger scale would be advisable. If society is no longer prepared to teach heroic virtue in the home, then other institutions may need to assist in taking on that role, as the military has begun to do.

*   *   *

The views expressed in this chapter are solely those of the authors and do not represent the official views of the U.S. Department of Labor.

The authors thank the leaders who contributed to this chapter through their reflection and the time they generously devoted to the interviews. In alphabetical order they in-clude Arthur Amdurer, Commander Erik Anderson USNR, Sally Atwater, Commander Chip Beck USNR (Ret.), Major Christopher Breslin USMC (Ret.), Joseph H. Comer—former vice president at Halter Marine Group, Robert J. Crnkovich—National Tax Part-ner at Ernst and Young, Samuel W. Diehl, Captain James Dulin USN (Ret.), Daniel R. Foley, Martin D. Goldberg, Charles L. Grizzle, Ambassador Margaret Heckler, Captain

J. William Hines USN (Ret.), Nancy Mohr Kennedy, Commander Bryce E. Lefever USN, Dr. Ernest W. Lefever, Dr. Brian L. Maruffi at the Fordham University Graduate School of Business, Major General Terrence P. Murray USMC (Ret.), Lieutenant Colonel Darryl P. Olson USMC (Ret.), David D. Smith, and Brigadier General Leon Wilson USAF (Ret). William Mea, the senior author, would particularly like to thank General Terry Murray for being the yardstick by which he measures leadership, Colonel Bo Olson, who risked his own life to make the author's possible, and Nancy Kennedy and Charlie Grizzle for being his political mentors.

REFERENCES

Bandow, D., and D.L. Schindler. (2003). *Wealth, Poverty, and Human Destiny.* Wilmington, DE: ISI Books.

Bass, B.M. (1961). *Leadership, Psychology, and Organizational Behavior.* New York: Harper.

Buckley, M. Ronald, W.J. Mea, D. Weise, and S.M. Carraher. (1998). "Evaluating Change in Public Organizations: An Alpha, Beta, Gamma Change Perspective." In *Accountability and Radical Change in Public Organizations*, ed. R.R. Sims, 229–242. Westport, CT: Quorum Books.

Buckley, W.F. (2004). "Vote Vanities." Editorial, *Washington Times*, January 17: A11.

Carson, R.C., J.N. Butcher, and J.C. Coleman. (1988). *Abnormal Psychology and Modern Life.* Glenview, IL: Scott, Foresman.

Collins, J. (2003). "The Ten Greatest CEOs of All Time." *Fortune*, 148 (2) July 21: 54–68.

D'Souza, D. (2002) *What's So Great About America?* New York: Penguin Books.

Himsel, D. (2003). *Leadership Sopranos Style: How to Become a More Effective Leader.* Chicago: Dearborn Trade.

Lombardo, M., and R.W. Eichenger. (2002). *The Career Architect: A Development Planner.* Minneapolis, MN: Lominger Limited.

Mumford, E. (1909). *The Origins of Leadership.* Chicago: University of Chicago Press.

Nichloson, N. (1998). "How Hardwired Is Human Behavior?" *Harvard Business Review* (July–August): 135–147.

Rathus, S.A. (1990). *Psychology.* Ft. Worth, TX: Holt, Rinehart and Winston.

Roberts, W. (1989). *Leadership Secrets of Attila the Hun.* New York: Warner Books.

Rosenberg, N., and L.E. Birdzell. (1986). *How the West Became Rich: The Economic Transformation of the Industrial World.* New York: Basic Books.

Stogdill, R.M. (1974). *Handbook of Leadership: A Survey of Theory and Research.* New York: Free Press.

Sulowitz, K.J. (2004). "Worse than Enemies: The CEO's Destructive Confidant." *Harvard Business Review* (February): 64–71.

Tead, O. (1935). *The Art of Leadership.* New York: McGraw-Hill.

U.S. Naval Academy. (1992). Reef Points. Annapolis, MD: Naval Institute Press.

PART V

GLOBAL LEADERSHIP

CHAPTER 17

WORLDVIEW AND GLOBAL LEADERSHIP

JOHN R. VISSER

Although many have debated the degree to which leaders are "born" or "made," or articulated the importance of vision to leadership effectiveness, less attention has been given to the impact of a leader's worldview on his or her effectiveness. Worldviews are perceptual frameworks for seeing and understanding the self and the environment, guides used to determine how things ought to be and how people should conduct themselves. As Walsh and Middleton (1984, 35) note in *The Transforming Vision*, worldviews rest ultimately on the answers to life's most fundamental questions, questions such as "Who am I? Why am I here? What is the nature of reality? What's wrong? What should things be like?"

The worldview of a leader is especially relevant to people interested in leadership effectiveness in lower-income developing economies, where hundreds of millions of people often remain mired in poverty, awaiting skilled, visionary leaders with the kind of integral worldview that can lead an entire nation out of poverty. In such a setting, leaders need far more than charisma, goals, or contingency strategies; they need a worldview that is based on a clear picture of who they are and how things really are; they need to understand not only what people need, but the complex ways in which they work together to build "capital" that is essential for melding their efforts and talents into globally competitive productive activity.

It is no secret that hundreds of millions of dollars have been spent around the world trying to plant democracies in political and economic soils unenriched by the kind of civil society and political and economic leadership that grow out of a consistent integrated moral worldview. In addition to skills and vision, effective country leaders need the right kind of values, and worldviews that adequately address structural questions related to morality, equity, and justice. And they cannot afford to have large numbers of their citizens view these values as personal, relative, or subjective, because truly effective leadership is a communal process that demands as much from the followers as from the leader.

Unfortunately, a discussion of the topic of "country leadership" goes well beyond the (already interdisciplinary) leadership research into economic development, political studies, civil society, and history, to name the most obvious. Nevertheless, this broader research offers insight into the importance of a leader's worldview and also has the potential to enhance and integrate much of what we see in the leadership literature. As noted in Stogdill's *Handbook of Leadership* (1974), scholars have been writing about leadership for decades without agreeing on its definition. The second edition of this handbook also notes that a preoccupation with empirical measurement often restricts researchers from dealing with the most important (but difficult to quantify) aspects of leadership (Bass 1990, 6). A third quandary evident from the research is the refusal of some writers to refer to some people, such as Hitler or Stalin, as leaders because of the damage they inflicted on millions of people. Nevertheless, these and similar differences of opinion are inevitable given the varied worldviews of the writers, a component of which may be the assumption that the only good way to know something is through empirical verification. Differences represent an inability to admit that before good *leadership* can be defined, we need to wrestle with the meaning of *good*. This immediately takes the discussion back to the level of worldviews and "habits of the heart" (Bellah 1986).

This chapter proposes that organizations and nations need leaders who understand that they must nurture the development of seven different kinds of "capital" to spur real and sustainable progress: physical, economic, intellectual/emotional, spiritual/moral, environmental, governmental, and social capital. Leaders who have a clear picture in their minds of the essentiality, interdependence, and fragility of all seven of these forms of capital, and have the capability, by enriching and shaping the worldview of their citizens, to build up and meld them, have "the right stuff" to lead countries; those who do not are doomed to limited success at best and "regime change" or the ash heap of history at worst.

LEADERSHIP LITERATURE

Before describing our worldview model in detail, it is important to connect it to the large and significant body of related literature. Much of this literature comes from psychology and education, and, more recently, from organizational behavior, human resource management, and public administration. Northouse (2004) distinguishes a dozen approaches, theories, and offshoots in this literature, which he labels as the trait, skills, style, situational, and psychodynamic "approaches," contingency, path-goal, and leader-member exchange "theories," transformational leadership, team leadership, women in leadership, and leadership ethics.

As Stogdill (1974), Mann (1959), and a host of others have noted, in ancient times and still today, a massive amount of time and energy has been devoted to studying "great men," in the hope of discovering the traits of great leaders. Charisma is likely the most studied of these traits, but other more easily measured traits, such as confidence, drive, intelligence, empathy, self-control, and creativity, have come to form the backbone of modern personality tests (Myers and McCaulley 1985). The limitations of the traits approach are well documented, but, in addition, in failing to address underlying worldview questions, many of the most commonly quoted traits may not be particularly convincing to people who have a long history of suffering under poor country leaders. Most likely, the leaders who destroyed their countries were charismatic, confident, and ambitious.

And, given the ability of creative people to deceive, it may be impossible to tell which of those currently seeking to lead is truly empathetic or self-controlled.

On the other hand, proponents of situational approaches to leadership have pointed out that good leaders, regardless of their traits, need to use different approaches in different situations. Some, for example, Fiedler (1967), even went so far as to suggest that a leader might have to be removed if a situation changed because his or her traits might not be suited for the new situation. This led to the (continuing) discussion about "task vs. relationship orientation" and the skills that a leader needs (e.g., problem-solving ability), and an eventual consensus (with the help of Blake and Mouton's 1964 "Leadership Grid") that an effective leader did not necessarily have to sacrifice the accomplishment of tasks in order to build relationships. Meanwhile, proponents of the contingency approach (Fiedler 1964, 1967; Fiedler and Garcia 1987) further noted that the effectiveness of a leader also depended on variables such as leader-member relations, task structure, and power position.

It is hard to dispute that a country leader needs to be skilled at both the task at hand and relationship building, or that situation will affect strategy and style, but one must remember that not all country leaders come to power because of their ability to build relationships. The task of leading a country has not been well-defined in the leadership literature, let alone the degree to which it is structured or unstructured. And frankly, most people are more interested, for example, in the impact of Saddam Hussein's leadership on his people than the fact that his leader-member relationships were based on a kind of forced loyalty related to his position of power (especially his ability and willingness to punish). Even though some research shows that a task orientation is most effective in either smooth or crisis situations, while a relationship orientation is more effective in moderate situations, it is more important to understand why and how leaders like Saddam turn smooth situations into crises.

Returning to the major schools of thought, the path-goal (Evans 1970; House 1971) and leader-member exchange (Dansereau, Graen, and Haga 1975; Graen 1976) theories are perhaps more relevant to the subject of country leadership because of the special attention they place on leader-follower interaction. Discussed together, these theories point out the importance of focusing on follower needs and goals, recognizing that these goals and needs may be affected by the nature of the tasks at hand and different for individual followers. They also note that this dynamic is complicated by the presence of "in-groups" and "out-groups." Unfortunately for country leaders, the focus on the needs of subordinates for clarity, direction, or freedom within the context of simple, complex, or ambiguous tasks, or in-groups and out-groups, although useful for staff management strategy, is less suited to the complexities of influencing a populace. Likewise, the hope of choosing the right style (e.g., participative or directive) seems rather inconsequential when working with a parliament or millions of citizens. Psychodynamic approaches also seem relatively unhelpful when it comes to what makes country leaders effective. Although self-knowledge is always beneficial, and insight into the psychological makeup of cabinet members will undoubtedly be useful, it would be impossible to "know" millions of citizens in this way, and psychology is only one part of a very large puzzle. It is

much more critical to have insight into one's worldview, rather than just one's psychological makeup, and the dominant worldview components of the citizenry, rather than
their individual psychological tendencies.

It is probably the concept of transformational leadership (Downton 1973; Burns 1978;
Bass 1990), henceforth TL, that comes the closest to having the breadth and depth needed
to address worldview concerns, although it has also been criticized for its complexity.
Many popular business writers, such as Covey (1991) and Peters and Waterman (1982),
and a host of writers in the field of educational leadership (see Bergquist 1992; Bogue
1994; McDade and Lewis 1994; and Wilcox and Ebbs 1992) subscribe to the basis tenets
of TL. In addition to critical traits, such as confidence, TL also focuses on the leader's
vision and values, and the ability to articulate those values to effect change by serving as
a role model and catalyst in the process of transforming followers and organizations.
Among other things, Larson and LaFasto (1989) stress that transformational leaders are
principled people with lofty goals, able to achieve a unified team effort. Bennis and
Nanus (1985) say they have the ability to create "shared meaning" and devotion to duty,
and to display the kind of character (reliability and transparency) that engenders trust.
Tichy and DeVanna (1986, 1990) point out that they see clearly where change is needed,
and manage to institutionalize change. These kinds of tasks are no small accomplishment for leaders in countries with millions of citizens, but no less is needed for poverty-
stricken countries suffering from corruption, nepotism, strife, and thinking patterns that
have for too long tied them to their poverty. Some scholars (see Conger and Kanungo
1988; and Yukl 1989) have been tempted to reduce TL to charismatic leadership, but this
does not do justice to the importance of the worldviews of transformational leaders, nor
does it recognize that worldview can become institutionalized to some extent as visionary leaders manage to include their values and vision into their organizations (see Collins
and Porras 1994, 2001). Indeed, as cultural anthropologists know, countries and entire
cultures develop ways of seeing the world that are very unique. These ways of seeing are
passed from generation to generation through child-rearing practices, religious beliefs,
and educational systems, each of which is ultimately rooted in worldview.

A quick aside based on the author's impressions of the old Soviet Union illustrates
this point. By 1991, almost everything in the country had been touched by its predominant religion. We are not talking about Russian Orthodoxy here, but rather the (at least
initial) victor in the seventy-year-long religious war that had so ruthlessly sterilized Orthodoxy, namely, atheistic communism. Marxist-Leninist doctrine had left its mark everywhere. Single-family homes were nowhere to be seen. Apartment buildings, jammed
with pint-sized apartments and claustrophobic elevators stretched out as far as the eye
could see. Abortion helped keep families from outgrowing their apartments, and prices
were nicely controlled on everything. The architectural uniformity of state-owned buildings nicely complemented the one-color-fits-all overcoats filling the store racks inside.
All of this was in the name of attaining sanctifying equality and avoiding the carnal sin
of individuality. Statues of the saints (Lenin, Stalin, Dzerzhinsky, the Cosmonauts, and
the other heroes) stood everywhere, providing icon-like evidence of the core beliefs of
leaders intent on molding the worldview of the Soviet citizens into their image.

The beginning of this era can be traced to when Vladimir Lenin seized power with the official Declaration of the Separation of Church and State. At first "purely religious" sermons were allowed and registered churches were permitted to remain open, but by the time Stalin was finished interpreting the meaning of *separation*, 98 percent of the Russian Orthodox churches had been closed, Bible printing was prohibited, children were not permitted to attend worship services, attendees of unregistered church services were given twenty-five-year prison sentences, and tens of thousands of priests had been killed. Nikita Khrushchev extended this assault to evangelical Protestant churches when he took over in 1959. Soviet leaders operated for seven decades on the belief that wealth was created primarily by labor (thereby neglecting modern "values based" management techniques, marketing, and finance) until the economy finally imploded under the weight of lack of incentives, moral and political corruption, and widespread shortages. It was not until March 1985 that Mikhail Gorbachev severed the official link that had been forged between Marxist-Leninist political and economic philosophy and atheism. Interestingly, this turnaround, important to the eventual breakup of the country, was only lightly covered in the Western press, probably because the Western press lacked a good understanding of the importance of subtle shifts in the worldviews of country leaders.

In contrast to the example of the Soviet Union, countries thrive when their leaders see the big picture, and have the moral strength and consistency to change the tasks, relationships, and environmental factors that are hurting their people. This thought is consistent not only with TL but also with the literature on servant leadership and leadership ethics. As Robert Greenleaf (1970, 1977) has ably noted, leaders who are effective in seeing and focusing on followers' needs will be more effective. Along the same lines, Brady (1999) highlights the importance of an ethic of caring in building the kind of trust and cooperation that promotes change. Block (1993), Covey (1991), De Pree (1989), Gilligan (1982), and a host of others make nearly the same point—effective leadership requires a willingness to serve, which goes hand in hand with an emphasis on honesty and justice, respect for the dignity of the individual, and an emphasis on building community.

This focus on ethics and serving has given impetus to a recent flurry of books and papers on spiritual leadership. Three somewhat distinct groups have focused on the spirituality of leaders: those interested in the psychological aspects, new age (popular) writers, and those interested in the traditional religious aspects of spirituality (e.g., Christian or Buddhist). All of these, to one degree or another, focus the integration of leaders, followers, and work into a system that promotes self-awareness, modeling, integrity, community, high moral and ethical standards, service, growth, and self-governance. Various terms have been used to describe this, such as spiritual, inspirational, or transcendental leadership. Some (e.g., Sanders, Hopkins, and Geroy 2003) have attempted to identify dimensions of spirituality such as consciousness, moral character, and faith, and to link them with the progression from transactional to transformational to transcendental leadership. A growing number of books draw leadership lessons from biblical accounts (Blanchard, Hybels, and Hodges 1999; Jones 1995; Manz 1998). Others (Kelly, Nelson, and Bethge 2003) have attempted to draw leadership lessons from the lives of people like Bonhoeffer, Ghandi, or Mother Theresa, who made significant impacts through their "spiritual engagement" of the world. The logical conclusion of this heightened interest in spirituality is the coinage of the term "spiritual intelligence" (Emmons 1999, 2000) and the expectation that it will carve out a spot in the mainstream literature as "emotional intelligence" (Goleman 1995) did in the 1990s. But useful as all these perspectives are, they are not the same as a focus on worldviews, which will be described forthwith. Before doing that, however, we must address what people expect from a country leader.

THE TASK OF A COUNTRY LEADER

We can get some insight into the task of a country leader by reminding ourselves that Bill Clinton gained the presidency of the United States in 1992 in part because he was able to effectively remind himself, "It's the economy, stupid!" Likewise, more than one military leader has repeated the adage that ultimately "an army marches on its stomach." Citizens of countries desire a decent standard of living, and most also desire an environment where they can know what is happening, find out what is wrong, and be allowed to work together to improve things. Undoubtedly, this is why so many countries, including many headed by incompetent leaders, have signed onto the United Nations Declaration of Human Rights (Brownlie 1992). However, many leaders capable of signing onto this document lack the integral worldview needed to put the principles embodied in it into practice. We argue that the best explanation for this is not their inability to understand leadership theories, but their inability to see the world as it really is. We will return to this later.

One example of a worldview limitation fatal to a country leader is the tendency to think that the wealth of the world is basically fixed, so if one person ends up with more wealth, someone else will end up with less. Many people believe, for example, that a profit must be at the expense of employees' salary or wages, or that when a business buys goods from another country, the foreign country is being exploited. Of course, part of the reason for this is that sometimes one person's gain is another person's loss. This is most obvious in the case of outright stealing, or war and pillage. It is less obvious with slacking workers, corrupt governments, poorly run companies, or complex international contracts. Another reason for wealth confusion is that it is often so difficult to distinguish wealth creation from redistribution that entire nations have gone hundreds of years wrongly confusing the two. European powers established colonies on the assumption that exploiting resources and trading manufactured goods for raw materials would make them rich. Pre–World War II Japan believed the same, only to learn after the war (and beyond the shadow of a doubt) that a nation does not need to be endowed with great supplies of natural resources or to use imperialism to dominate another's natural resources in order to thrive. Many countries struggle in spite of abundant natural resources, while relatively natural-resource-poor islands like Hong Kong, the UK, and Taiwan thrive. Evidently, resource endowments can either help or hurt a nation, depending on the worldview of the people and their leaders. Many resource-rich African nations like Nigeria, Sierra Leone, and Angola have seen far more political upheaval than wealth accumulation from their oil, gold, or diamonds. In fact, recent research by Woolcock, Pritchett and Isham (2001) of the World Bank seems to make a good case that in the absence of certain moral and ethical beliefs, natural resource windfalls may hurt real progress by trapping nations in the lure of easy money, inviting corruption, and financing political conflict.

These findings have led some to assume that the most important component in a country leader's worldview is a belief in free markets and democracy. But it does not take long to realize that Asian nations like Korea, Thailand, Indonesia, and Malaysia experienced phenomenal wealth increases for decades even though their "markets" were distorted by tariffs and other import barriers, cartels, and government interference. Likewise, China has grown remarkably for nearly three decades despite a lack of democracy, whereas many countries in Africa, where hundreds of millions of dollars have been spent on democratization, have made little or no progress in the past twenty-five years. Experiences in Russia and other former Soviet bloc countries also hint that effective country leadership requires much more than an understanding of the potential benefits of freedom and democracy.

Clearly, worldview makes a difference. Beliefs that an economy is a zero-sum game, a Darwinian jungle where labor, business, and government fight each other, or a collection of co-conspirators who feather each others' nests at the expense of the average person, are all very different from the belief that progress is ultimately rooted in service, cooperation, and fairness. Only a worldview containing the latter belief will succeed in implementing, for example, an efficient voluntary tax system, a truly civil society, or pluralistic approaches to building consensus.

For decades, specialists in economic development focused on highly quantifiable measures like capital-output ratios, investment rates, and population growth to try to explain the varying degrees of progress among countries. Recently, scholars such as Lawrence Harrison (1985, 1992) and Joel Kotkin (1992) have shed this straitjacket via some careful comparative analyses of the historical development of countries and ethnic groups, which make it all but impossible to ignore the possibility that cultural variables are likely more helpful in understanding differences in country economic outcomes than is empirical data mining. Other scholars and organizations such as the World Bank, although reluctant to abandon their empiricism, have complemented or extended this work by showing via cross-cultural studies and surveys how incompetence in government and the absence of civil society are often the primary barriers to progress (see, e.g., *World Development Report* 1997). But historical analyses and studies of government or civil society take leadership analysis only so far. Sadly, country leadership has too often been a recurring story of people unable to "see" the source of their problems or learn from their mistakes. Effective leaders need worldviews open to asking what it means for their citizens to have good and meaningful lives, and where goodness and meaning come from, even if the answers are complex and counterintuitive or go against their preconceived notions. Likewise, citizens need to have beliefs that are consistent with development. Regardless of a leader's skill level, little development will take place where people fear the revenge of spirits or witches that oppose change, believe in the fundamental unworthiness of whole groups of people, see no reason to hope, refuse to move to where jobs are, do not trust each other, or choose revenge and retribution over cooperation and compromise.

COUNTRY LEADERSHIP, WEALTH, AND WELL-BEING

Bass (1990), in his development of the concept of *transformational leadership*, made it clear that effective leaders are successful in identifying people's needs and helping them meet those needs. As Abraham Maslow pointed out much earlier, these needs take many forms and may follow a hierarchical rank order in many people's lives. Economists as a group have pointed out that "wealth" is important in the process of meeting needs because little or nothing can be produced in the future without some accumulation of wealth in the present. The farmer depends on accumulating wealth in the form of seed, equipment, and money to sow next year's crop. The factory accumulates "retained earnings" to purchase new equipment or production facilities. The young couple accumulates a down payment in order to purchase their first house. A psychiatrist accumulates knowledge to properly diagnose his patients and meet their needs.

But what is wealth and how is it measured? Wealth has seven primary sources that collectively comprise a much broader conceptualization of wealth than is popularly held:

1. Our common endowment (land, mineral, water, etc.);
2. Savings handed down to us because previous generations limited their consumption and made wise investments with their surplus;
3. New wealth we create by limiting our own consumption to something less than the value of what we earn or produce;
4. Investment of our wealth prudently, regardless of its source, so that it increases our income or the productivity and the value of what we produce in the future;
5. Taking of appropriate steps to keep existing assets from unnecessary depreciation and depletion;
6. The existence of a moral, political, and economic atmosphere in which productive activity is encouraged and the (real) market values of assets rise; and
7. The beliefs of people.

Humanity has collectively been given the gift of an earth weighing approximately 6 sextillion tons, surrounded by an immensely useful atmosphere, receiving a steady supply of energy daily, filled with hundreds of different elements with millions of potential uses. Through the individual and collective work of ancestors, societies have been given living quarters, workplaces, places of worship, material objects, aesthetic creations, services, and perhaps most important, ideas, technologies, principles, and codes of conduct that create, preserve, and renew wealth.

It is fair to say at this point that country leaders, even though they may have never read Adam Smith, must nevertheless subscribe to his ideas about the importance of "world images," moral conduct, and responsible government in the creation of wealth. Smith spent a lot of time arguing that people needed to create institutions that encouraged citizens to act in morally and socially responsible ways. He considered the market to be one of the institutions that would do this, and wrote about how self-interest could serve the public good. However, he also noted that markets alone were not guaranteed to encourage responsible actions without other institutions that fostered respect for life, property, a concern for the common good, and virtues like self-control, prudence, and farsightedness.

Oddly, given the perception that many have of him today, Smith believed government would naturally get larger as civilization advanced, and wrote *The Wealth of Nations* in part to convince politicians and officials to recognize their responsibility to seek the public good and to create an atmosphere where people would have incentives to do what was in the best interest of *all* people. His desire for limited government reflected more than anything his belief that other institutions in society were better qualified to provide the moral and ethical training that undergird the creation of wealth, and his conviction that government officials were often neither in a good position to micromanage economic exchanges nor inclined to promote the public good. Markets, he believed, had the potential to pit selfish competitors against each other, forcing them to promote the public good and produce better products and services, resulting in greater wealth overall. Government, acting properly within its sphere of authority, would promote both justice and institutions that would focus on improving people's material being and moral decency, also enhancing the creation of wealth.

Smith clearly understood that ideas and beliefs were the foundation of an effective country. He was a student of the nature of man, who saw man as a "weak and imperfect creature," and mentioned frequently how character problems such as pride, avarice, or injustice hampered the creation of wealth. But he also believed a "benevolent Creator" had planted in people the ability and desire to see themselves as potentially praiseworthy. He wrote extensively about how government needed to create institutions that would channel people's natural inclinations toward self-interest, insecurity, passion, and power toward productive ends. In fact, a major theme of his first book, *The Theory of Moral Sentiments*, was the need for people to create institutions and structures that would transform their natural inclination toward self-love and self-interest into altruistic and benevolent behavior. He believed and promoted the idea that people and nations should pursue economic activity out of "the love of mankind" instead of attempting to obstruct the development of their neighbors. Oriented by a Calvinist religious heritage, Smith quietly gave away much of the wealth he had been instrumental in creating during his lifetime (Muller 1993). He also discussed that excessive attention to commerce could result in the neglect of other important aspects of culture, and that excessive dependence on reason had the potential to create a moral vacuum. He believed the very existence of society depended on virtues like politeness, truth, fidelity, chastity, dependability, and justice. Although opposed to religious monopoly and the idea that any one group of clerics could corner the "truth," he clearly felt that moral teaching, aimed at inculcating proper beliefs about what constituted moral behavior, was at the core of the creation of a good society. He supported laws, for example, discouraging divorce, since he understood innately what we know today through exhaustive empirical study: that the break-down of the family is bad for children, for moral behavior, and for economic well-being (Smith 1993).

WORLDVIEW, LEADERSHIP, AND SATISFACTION

Adam Smith, of course, is not the end of the story. As insightful as his writings were, an effective country leader also needs to "see" the true source of attributes like happiness, satisfaction, or fulfillment. Various scholars have noted that increased income has a much more pronounced effect on happiness, or "life satisfaction," in poor countries than in wealthy countries. Once income levels reach the point where people's basic needs are met, many other things rightfully deserve more attention. David Myers's (1992) research on happiness among wealthy North Americans supports these findings and concludes that hardly any of the things that we generally assume would be related to happiness, such as age, race, location, education, money, economic status, pleasure, possessions, or even physical abilities, are particularly useful in explaining differences in happiness or hopefulness. Hence, effective leadership requires far more than giving people what they want. This is especially true in poverty-stricken countries where people's expectations are low. For example, a woman who is treated more like property than a person, a child growing up in abject poverty or a violent home, and people living in a lawless country may have so little hope that their expectations differ very little from their reality. Although such people are "satisfied" in some sense, a moral leader should never accept their paltry goals and hopeless situation. The impoverished need the opportunity to find out how much more there can be in life, and what it takes to get there. This underscores the need for effective country leaders to have certain traits, the ability to be transformational, and an integral worldview.

AN INTEGRAL WORLDVIEW FOR COUNTRY LEADERSHIP

In addition to knowing people's needs and wants, visionary country leaders understand intuitively that the well-being of people and the usefulness of material (tangible) and nonmaterial (intangible) things are interdependent. A machine, for example, will not just increase in value when moved to a factory where it will be used more intensively. It will also increase in value when it is operated in a responsible manner, by a moral, wise, socially connected, and stable individual who is trusted and valued by a team of solid managers in a financially responsible company operating in a politically and economically stable country. Likewise, a person will command a higher wage, or capital a greater return, because they are more productive in that environment. Similarly, the value of the government will be greater when the natural environment in which it operates is not abused and depleted, where companies and individuals obey the laws (e.g., do not cheat on their taxes), where machines are being used effectively, and workers are more productive. The value of financial capital is multiplied in an appropriate intellectual and moral climate, and so on. Both wealth and well-being, then, flow out of communal activity that depends as much on knowledge and ethics as on machines and money.

This is best illustrated by the diagram shown in Figure 17.1, which is an extension of a diagram first introduced in the book, *Civil Society: A Foundation for Sustainable Economic Development* (Rose 1998). As the diagram indicates, economic development is a process, and it is useful to think of the productive process as a wheel, and development as the continuous movement of this wheel over time. Before a wheel can function properly, "material" must be gathered for the building process. As the diagram illustrates, there are seven types of resources or "wheel segments" that must be in place before the development wheel can be "rounded out" and function well. The word capital is used to describe these segments insofar as we are already accustomed to identifying land, machines, and financial investments as forms of capital. Here, the traditional understanding of capital is broadened to include communal and nonphysical things that must also be available before meaningful economic activity can take place. Clearly, healthy quantities of these things, such as infrastructure, systems, knowledge, trust, and the like, are as important as physical and financial capital for productive activity to take place (i.e., for the wheel to be "rounded out" and for peoples lives to improve).

Before proceeding, each of these forms of capital needs some explanation. Moving clockwise from the top of the wheel we provide the following descriptions:

- *Physical capital* refers to assets such as infrastructure (utilities, highways), buildings, machinery, and other forms of applied technology, and also tangible things that keep humans physically productive, such as nutritious food, health care, and housing.
- *Economic capital* includes traditional investments in stocks, bonds, and other financial assets, but also things like wise macroeconomic and microeconomic decisions, incentives to save and invest, predictability and fairness in economic policies, and efficiency in markets, including financial markets.
- *Intellectual/emotional capital* includes literacy, general knowledge, skills, intelligence, creativity, and also traits that have come to be known as emotional intelligence, such as self-awareness, empathy, motivation, or self-regulation. This represents an elaboration on what has traditionally been referred to as human capital, which, unfortunately, is still sometimes mistakenly reduced to the term "labor."
- *Spiritual/moral capital* includes honesty and integrity, the ability to distinguish right from wrong, moral behavior, limits to selfishness, respect/genuine concern for others, courage, and a host of other "positive values" that flow from people's basic belief and commitments and profoundly affect the structure, direction, and effectiveness of human activity. It is included in part because, increasingly, in a variety of fields of study, including leadership, spirituality is being recognized as an important force for shaping human thought and behavior *in addition to* intellectual and emotional variables, but also because a leader's effectiveness is multiplied many times over when the hearts of followers are set in the right direction and the "habits of the heart" have become well established.

Figure 17.1   **The Wheel of Development and Critical Capital Needs**

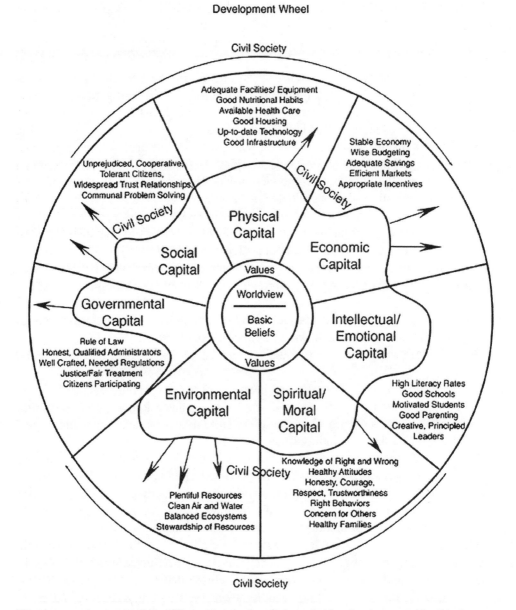

Wheel segments represent the different types of capital needed for development. The misshapen wheel illustrates capital impairment resulting from shortages of critical components of capital. Civil society enables countries to round out the wheel by acquiring or building essential forms of capital. The ultimate shape, structure, and strength of the wheel depends on the prevailing worldviews in the country.

Source: Based on Rose (1998).

- *Environmental capital* (often referred to as natural capital) includes things such as raw materials, clean air, pure water, good soil, adequate sunlight, species diversity, intact ecosystems, and so forth. Some of this capital is renewable (e.g., forests, fisheries) and some is not (e.g., oil, minerals).
- *Governmental capital* includes what is sometimes referred to as "political capital" (the resources available to political leaders to design and carry out policy) but also includes elements such as the "rule of law," fair elections, efficient and effective regulatory agencies, a widespread concern for justice, well-established conflict resolution procedures, widespread political participation, and the capability to deliver needed "public goods."
- *Social capital* may be defined as a widely shared commitment to the values of trust and mutual assistance demonstrated by the habits of cooperation. Social capital is best understood by observing the myriad of associations that people form in all areas of life, but especially the hundreds of thousands of voluntary associations such as advocacy groups, church committees, sports clubs, parent-teacher associations, ethnic celebrations, community service boards, and the like.

An integral view of human activity also notes that all seven of these asset categories, like traditionally defined assets, take time to accumulate (i.e., they represent some endowment or "savings" from the past), need to be developed (i.e., we can and should "invest" in them), and have the potential to be either overutilized (depleted) or undersupplied. Because a round wheel will cover far more distance and thus more development, wealth creation, or well-being with less resource waste than a misshapen wheel, this model presumes that an effective country leader needs an intuitive understanding of the importance of giving people incentives to build up, preserve, and replenish all seven of these forms of wealth/capital. A shortage in one or more of the needed inputs will result in something akin to the misshapen inner wheel in the diagram and reduce citizen satisfaction appreciably, either in the short run or the long run. He or she must also recognize that the intangible forms of capital may prove to be even more important to a smooth-functioning economy and citizen well-being than the traditional forms of capital.

Balance is the key. The value of a particular resource is highly influenced by the presence of the other resource categories. Everyone understands the benefits of bringing food to drought-stricken areas, or on-line library resources to educationally disadvantaged children, but the wheel analogy uses the term "needed resources" to refer to complex social arrangements, systems, institutions, and beliefs that are encompassed by terms such as social capital, governmental capital, and spiritual/moral capital. Indeed, the story of modern wealth creation is really the story of the discovery and accumulation of increasingly intangible forms of capital. In ancient times, people thought of wealth in terms of natural resources and hoarded things like gold and silver. Later, and especially at the time of the industrial revolution, they began to see the value of transforming these resources into machines and other forms of physical capital. Later still, the value of exchanging financial, intellectual, and governmental capital moved to the forefront. Many world leaders are just beginning to see the potential benefits from the exchange of social and spiritual/moral capital. And it is not only economic development specialists and leadership theorists that have discovered the importance of this. Groups as diverse as Russian Orthodox patriarchs such as the late Alexander Men and inner-city pastors in the United States (e.g., Eugene Rivers and Jeffrey Brown of the Ten-Point Coalition) have seen deficiencies in spiritual/moral capital damage nearly all other forms of capital, and, therefore, any meaningful progress in their communities.

Each form of capital can be rightly described as both an input and an output with respect to human productive activity. Healthy quantities of social capital (e.g., trust relationships) have the potential to build up economic capital and vice versa, but, once again, balance is the key. An overemphasis on the physical and economic segments leading to the overproduction of material things can result in the depletion of environmental capital. But just as overproduction can exhaust topsoil, or mining can deplete scarce mineral resources, so an overemphasis on profit can exhaust a workforce and damage other forms of capital as well. For example, an extreme emphasis on labor productivity can erode social, governmental, or spiritual/moral capital as "burned out" shift workers are too exhausted to interact with their children or neighbors, participate in the political process, or attend a church or synagogue.

Some social scientists would argue that some economically developed countries are in jeopardy of depleting various aspects of social and spiritual/moral capital almost beyond recovery in the same way that some natural ecosystems have been disturbed beyond the point of reestablishing the complex natural interactions necessary for their survival. This has provoked fear that—in the same way that pretending natural laws do not exist can irreparably damage an ecosystem—pretending that all spiritual, moral, or social principles are up for grabs can almost irreparably damage the social and moral fabric of a society. Nevertheless, it is by no means clear that less economically or educationally developed countries are in any better shape when it comes to capital impairment. They struggle with different kinds of capital impairment, but their problems are certainly not less severe. The truth is that this is an imperfect world; every society, community, organization, or individual life requires a unique effort to restore balance because of having greater or lesser problems in different sectors of the wheel. Successful country leaders will inspire citizens to work toward the vision of the ideal—to bring balance, wholeness, and well-being into every aspect of life—and lay the framework necessary for this. Many scholars have referred to this framework as a *civil society*.

AN INTRODUCTION TO CIVIL SOCIETY

What is civil society? The modern attention given to this subject can perhaps best be traced back to December 1948 when the General Assembly of the United Nations unanimously adopted the Universal Declaration of Human Rights (Brownlie 1992). Most of the thirty articles in the declaration focused on rights such as the right to life, liberty, freedom of religion, freedom from arbitrary arrest, presumed guilt, slavery or torture, equal protection under the law, impartial public hearings, privacy, freedom of movement, association, employment, and equal pay for equal work. The declaration also underscored the importance of marriage and family and property ownership. Thus, the document dealt more with the beliefs guiding a state's policies than with the thousands of institutions, laws, processes, and values needed to make it truly civil.

One comprehensive definition of civil society defines it as "a set of institutions, processes and attitudes that promote cooperation among individuals, private associations and government agencies to produce practical solutions to common problems." Today, the term is most commonly used to refer to mediating institutions that provide a buffer between the individual and the state, guided by a commitment to values such as transparency, participation, and peaceable change. Some writers have described civil society as the "third leg" of a three-legged stool upon which society rests. In this way they distinguish civil society from government and markets (the other two legs), while simultaneously acknowledging the dependence of government and markets on civil society. Remove any one of the three legs and the stool cannot stand.

Robert Bothwell's (1997, 249) summary of the approaches to the subject is helpful in this regard. He argues that the degree to which civil society exists in a country can be assessed in four fundamental ways.

1. Observing behaviors: i.e., do we see lots of evidence in the society of trust, openness, participation, public debate, etc.?
2. Inspecting societal foundations: i.e., are freedom of speech, religion, association, the rule of law, educational opportunity, capable government and political processes in place?
3. Examining broad outcomes: i.e., is income widely distributed, are literacy rates or life expectancy high?
4. Examining institutions: i.e., how many religious organizations, community-based organizations, clubs, voluntary groups, consumer groups, unions, professional associations, etc. are there?

Thus, by closely examining these components of civil society we can ascertain the relative level of "civility" of any observed civilization.

The Absence of Civil Society

George B.N. Ayittey (1998), in his book *Africa in Chaos*, describes how international organizations and Western countries spent hundreds of millions of dollars in Africa trying to establish democracy before finally recognizing that it might never take root unless the political and economic soil was first prepared and enriched by a civil society. Without leadership capable of ushering in a civil society, there simply was not enough incentive, for example, for central banks to refrain from creating money for politicians' pet projects, for judges to risk their jobs and financial security by insisting that the powerful and disenfranchised be subject to the law, or for autocrats to allow a free press or install qualified civil servants in their governments instead of unqualified friends and relatives. Ayittey notes that even in fairly large countries with solid natural resource endowments, for example, Nigeria, foreign investors exited through much of the 1990s, tired of bribes, extortion, permission fees, confiscatory exchange rates, petty and not-so-petty crime, and the threat of serious conflict. Much of Africa became a textbook illustration for making the point that in a "free market" global economy, countries with leaders unwilling or unable to nurture healthy civil societies would not be able to compete.

A brief foray into the problem of corruption will enlighten our understanding of the importance of the worldview of country leaders. Corruption is multifaceted, but often includes bribery, extortion, nepotism, favoritism, black market activities, patronage, conflicts of interest, official theft, falsification of records, and the widespread expectation of excessive and often illegal "service fees" to get things done. It is clear from the data of organizations like Transparency International, Political Risk Services, and Economist Intelligence Unit that there is a strong inverse relationship between the amount of corruption in a country and the health of its economy. There are many reasons for this, the most commonly cited of which are the following:

- Corruption makes economic activity less efficient because of delays associated with receiving permits, permissions, access, and so forth.
- Corruption reduces spontaneous cooperation with government because trust relationships are damaged as citizens come to see government not as a servant, but as a predator. This greatly reduces the ability of government to exercise its legitimate authority and carry out its objectives, increasing, for example, the nonpayment of taxes, rent seeking, theft, and other economically damaging behaviors among citizens.
- Corruption lowers the return on investment for government projects because there is a tendency for officials to choose infrastructure projects that benefit them personally or consolidate their power in some way. Such projects are almost always lower quality or provide lower return than others that have less tangible but widespread and public benefits (see Rose-Ackerman 1999).
- Corruption results in a society-wide focus on short-term gains because a corrupt environment is one in which the future is often unpredictable. This impedes the kind of long-term investing and risk taking that is associated with the development of whole new industries and the economy as a whole.
- Corrupt countries attract the least efficient and least reputable foreign companies (in that these companies would otherwise have trouble competing and therefore have the most to gain by paying bribes). Overall foreign investment is reduced because costs associated with corruption function as a tax. Likewise, capital tends to flee from uncertain environments (because people are concerned that their savings will be jeopardized by arbitrary actions), and less private/public foreign aid, and the like flows in, creating a depressing effect on the country's currency.
- Corruption slows the growth of small businesses (the engines of grassroots economic growth) via bureaucratic sclerosis and the imposition of unaffordable payments (de Soto 2000).
- Corruption causes talented people and ethical, efficient companies to become frustrated, and to seek to locate outside of the country (if they are able).

- Corruption results in inefficient resource allocation because arbitrary choices by government distort economic decisions throughout the society. Some public and private goods and services remain priced well above world prices and others well below, which leads to other inefficient decisions.

A current example is the damage done to the country of Zimbabwe by Robert Mugabe (Power 2003). By the end of 2003, life expectancy had slipped to thirty-five years from fifty-six years thirty years earlier, and humanitarian agencies were feeding or planning to feed nearly 6 million people, or approximately half of the population. Less than five years earlier the country was exporting copious amounts of grain to feed people outside their country. To be sure, drought was one culprit, HIV infected more than a quarter of the adults, and many trading partners imposed sanctions. But the "jewel of Africa" had and still has excellent soil, natural beauty, good infrastructure, and a literacy rate of nearly 90 percent. What Zimbabwe did not have was a leader who understood the interconnections between the seven forms of capital in our illustration, and it is this that is at the root of the implosion of the country. Under Mugabe's leadership, nearly 5,000 farms have been confiscated in the past several years and turned over to his political supporters. At the end of 2003, fewer than 3 percent of these were still functioning fully, unemployment was over 60 percent, and inflation had reached nearly 800 percent.

Mugabe's most obvious mistake was to take land away from the people who knew how to combine this resource with the other six forms of capital to make it productive. In doing so, he also impaired other forms of capital. He ran roughshod over justice (damaging government capital) insofar as two-thirds of these farmers had titles that had been issued not by some colonial repressor, but by Mugabe's government itself. Alarmed at the inflation rate caused by his own bungling, he fixed grain prices at a fraction of the market-clearing price, damaging economic capital. Farmers chose not to grow grain at a loss, further impairing both economic and physical capital. For example, corn production was down by two-thirds and wheat by nearly 90 percent when compared to 2000. If people tried to export to avoid a loss, he forced them to convert their foreign money to Zimbabwean dollars at an exchange rate that left them with pennies on the dollar, further impairing economic capital. Roving bands of thugs tore down fencing, and equipment was stolen, dismantled, or sold as scrap, impairing physical capital. Rejecting the humility and honesty that would characterize a servant leader, he tried to hide the truth about the shortages, rig the election, shut down opposition newspapers, and keep foreign journalists from exposing the truth, and he jailed and abused opponents, thus impairing spiritual/moral and intellectual/emotional capital. As his power slipped, he indoctrinated the youth of the country through his National Youth Service Training Program, and gave preferential treatment in civil service jobs and university admissions to loyal followers, further impairing these forms of capital. Amazingly, he "saw" the need for this beehive of unproductive government activity while being unable to "see" the significance of nearly 10 percent of the country's population having been orphaned because of his unwillingness to make it a priority to tackle the beliefs and attitudes at the root of his country's AIDs epidemic.

Time and money spent on damage control is time and money not spent solving more perplexing problems. The same argument extends to the care and maintenance of infra-structure, political processes, psychological health, moral values, ecosystems, and every other component of the seven segments of our wheel. Clearly, Mugabe's perceptions that accountability stops at the law (and *he* is the law), that authority is a license rather than an obligation to serve, that people are expendable rather than priceless, and that public property is his treasure trove rather than a sacred trust are the primary causes of his ineffective leadership. But these off-base foundational beliefs inevitably lead to other stultifying beliefs such as "the ends justify the means," "my needs and wants come first," or "it is only a problem if it is exposed," all of which tend to perpetuate corruption and inefficiency. Given this, it seems that his leadership techniques deserve less atten-tion than his misguided worldview.

The Benefits of Civil Society

Hundreds of benefits accrue to country leaders who are either wise enough to promote or fortunate enough to benefit from civil society, but the discussion is limited here to how participation, transparency, and a commitment to peaceable change build, preserve, re-plenish, and balance the kinds of capital that constitute and create wealth and well-being. Participation, for example, prepares people to serve and lead by giving them opportunities to learn and practice important managerial skills, such as planning, orga-nizing, leading, problem solving, conflict resolution, and communicating. Robert Putnam's (1993) research concluded that civil societies promote efficiency in business because the networking and trust relationships they nurtured fostered the sharing of useful informa-tion, services, and equipment, faster and sounder strategic alliances, and highly efficient "handshake" business deals. Civil societies also teach people to see high-trust environ-ments as normative rather than exceptional, enabling both government and business to devote fewer resources to supervision and internal control and more to innovation and production. Civil societies provide outlets for people to do good works, to be a needed part of a community, to increase their network of contacts and sources of information, and enhance their confidence. Civil societies enable people to learn ideas of justice, fairness, and the limits to self-interest, which strengthen interpersonal relationships, keep organizations functioning smoothly, and save countries and markets from becoming bloody battlegrounds.

Civil societies also function as a safety net for people, providing services free of charge and solving social problems. For example, churches and other voluntary groups minister to the "down and out," tutor struggling students, and promote positive values such as moderation, honesty, self-discipline, service, and respect. Both the suffrage movement and the battle against racial discrimination have their roots in civil society organizations. What is the value of all the contributions made by women or people of color because civil society organizations gave them opportunities that would have been unavailable elsewhere? How much better governed are countries that have been willing to tap the skills of talented women and minority group members than those who have limited themselves to a small subset of the talent available? And what of property rights and their massive impact on the creation of wealth? Are they not an extension of a belief in the importance of participation, unsustainable in the absence of a civil society? In short, civil society provides an atmosphere where moral and spiritual capital is formed and replenished, and in doing so, protects and builds all other forms of capital.

Transparency, too, has incalculable benefits. It lowers the cost of accessing information and ideas, makes markets more accessible, prices more accurate, and leads to better economic decisions. It improves government and organization efficiency and exposes corruption by allowing the sun to shine on procedures and decisions, so time, talents, and financial resources will be employed more productively. The overall size of government tends to stay smaller where civil society organizations are active, and people look to each other to solve problems first, and look to government only when it is the best means. Could the "rule of law" exist in the absence of the commitment to transparency that is part of an open civil society? Would businesses even seriously try to compete for government contracts if they could be kept out of markets or have their competitive bids rejected arbitrarily, with no opportunity to bring the injustice to the light?

Civil society organizations also promote peaceful change. Examples range from neighborhood associations and arbitration boards resolving conflicts at the local level to economic development arms of church denominations and organizations that send language teachers around the world to build healthy cross-cultural friendships at the international level. Collectively, they make a country leader's job much easier by substituting cooperation, honesty, and friendship for destructive competition, conflict, and war. But what causes civil society to develop?

WORLDVIEW: THE CORE OF EFFECTIVE COUNTRY LEADERSHIP

As much as civil society can do for development, its potential benefit and very existence depends on the values that undergird it. There are limits even to good things like transparency and participation. Without trust and integrity, transparency can degenerate into snooping and inefficiency, and without honesty and a sense of community, participation can lead to disinformation and chaos. The core of the wheel determines whether countries prosecute fraud, enforce labor laws, or try to outlaw or regulate activities such as telemarketing scams or the illicit drug trade. The core determines whether countries encourage charitable giving, volunteer activity, or family stability. The core determines whether a leader sees economic policy as inextricably tied to political and social policy, or not-for-profits as important to economic growth as for-profits. The core determines whether a leader focuses primarily on differences in gender, race, or ethnicity, or on the really important things such as justice, the promotion of good values, or the development of civil society organizations. Movement toward a civil society requires movement toward a consensus about the nature of man, his calling or task in the world, right and wrong, basic human rights, and so forth. For this to happen, a critical mass of the citizens in a country must see the world appropriately. The development wheel recognizes this

Table 17.1

Dimensions of Worldview

- Assumptions about the nature of the universe/reality
- Assumptions about the nature and perfectibility of people
- Values/ideas of right/wrong, good/bad, important/unimportant, praiseworthy/lamentable
- Assumptions about truth and how to ascertain it
- Concept of justice
- Beliefs about the nature of authority
- View of time (cyclical or straight line)
- Attitudes toward change/risk taking
- Assumptions about people
  - Egalitarian or elitist
  - Gender roles/relationships
  - Character ideals
- Sense of responsibility for/duty to others
  - Self-interest vs. concern for others
  - Extent of concern
    - Inner circle
    - Outside immediate family/friendship circles
    - Unborn/future generations
  - Motivators: guilt, shame, duty, and so forth
  - Respect for/role of government
  - Beliefs about the use of force
  - Attitudes toward wealth/property, material gain, limits to consumption
- Expectations of others
- Relative emphases/boundaries/ideas of balance
  - Wholeness/unity/community vs. distinctiveness/diversity/independence
  - Work vs. leisure or rest
  - Freedom vs. order
  - Incentive vs. security
  - Trust vs. accountability
  - Exploitation vs. preservation
  - Passion/impatience vs. self-control/patience
  - Optimism vs. pessimism

and places people's beliefs and values at the core of both civil society and the capital building process.

As noted earlier, one's worldview depends on who he or she is (personal characteristics and circumstances) and how he or she answers the most fundamental questions of life. But worldviews are not just individual. Cultural anthropologists and scholars of religion have uncovered a wealth of evidence that people who share a common culture, language, belief system, and educational system have far more similarities than differences in the way they see the world. Thus, we can speak of a *community's* worldview and identify what its members believe about themselves, the world, what should be, and what things can be made better. Table 17.1 outlines some of the most important dimensions of a worldview. This demonstrates that one's worldview colors his or her perception of almost everything and is therefore also at the core of the institutions that a society creates (educational, economic, social, political/legal, religious, etc.). It also implies that a country leader may need or orchestrate fundamental shifts in worldview to be effective.

Fundamental shifts in worldview are rooted in beliefs, as evidenced by the fact that people who subscribe to the same expression of a particular religion or nontheologically based belief system have great similarities in how they see and interpret the world, even when they have different cultural backgrounds. Beliefs (which often are by their very nature religious) are the great indirect force in the world, having an impact well beyond the obvious things such as work schedules, holidays, or charitable contributions. Appropriate beliefs are at the root of civil society since they are at the core of trust relationships (Fukuyama 1995), democracy (Glendon, and Blankenhorn 1995), effective governing (Braithwaite and Levi 1994), and the rule of law (Coats 1998), and a "good society" (Etzioni 1996) provides the social cohesion needed for a country to risk the kind of transparency and participation needed for civil society (Eberly 1998; Green 1993). Appropriate beliefs are critical to the economic success of countries (Landes 1998; Harrison 1992; Ayittey 1998) and at the root of the unusual accomplishment of communities and subcultures all over the world (Harrison 1992; Kotkin 1992).

Beliefs and values have been at the core of the rise and fall of nations, companies, and individuals. They spur us to start companies, set records, establish foundations, or win Nobel prizes, but they also cause us to defraud each other, and saddle us with abused and permanently damaged children, disease, and terrorism. Our laws reflect our religious beliefs. This is obvious in the case of the prohibition against murdering a fellow citizen and less obvious when creditors are expected to forgive debtors in bankruptcy. In the United States religious beliefs have influenced the rules government sets up for business activity, the enforcement of those rules, business structures and management practices (including the way accounting, finance, or marketing is done), and the personal economic decisions of individuals and families. They influence social organization, aesthetics, and education. Researchers long ago established links between even external and obviously imperfect proxies for what people believe (e.g., church attendance) and family stability (Bergin 1991), poverty (Freeman 1985), teen pregnancy, suicide (Larson, Larson and Gartner 1990), drug abuse (Daum and Lavenhar 1980), crime (Rohrbaugh and Jessor 1975), mental and physical health (Comstock and Partridge 1972), and longevity and happiness (Beit-Hallami 1974). And when *intrinsic* beliefs are distinguished from *extrinsic* behavior, the impact of beliefs becomes even more striking (Kahoe 1974; Wiebe and Fleck 1980).

It is our foundational beliefs that ultimately influence our ability to maintain unity in the midst of diversity, humility in the pursuit of wisdom, or motivation in the midst of security. They help us balance trust with accountability, or stewardship with productivity. They are at the core of the struggle to maintain order in the face of freedom, or responsibility in the face of compassion. Foundational beliefs determine our ability to pursue truth without denigration, promote courage without rashness, or maintain pluralism and privacy within community. Much more could be said, of course. But perhaps it is enough to say that very little in the Western world, from our limited liability corporations, to our financial institutions, to our efforts to eradicate productivity-sapping diseases, remain untouched by our core beliefs. The same is true elsewhere.

But just noting that all actions are ultimately rooted in beliefs is not enough, because all belief systems are not "created equal." The minds and hearts of people with differing religious beliefs are wired in very different ways, and the simple truth is that some beliefs lead to better outcomes than others. As some writers have put it (Himmelfarb 1995), "shared values" are sometimes "bad" values. And it should not be presumed, as is too often the case in academia, that shared "bad" values are necessarily religiously based. Religious beliefs, in spite of the fact that few attempts have been made to empirically verify their importance, often square completely with the way things really are or should be, while secular beliefs are sometimes off the mark (Ehrenberg 1999). However, taking the religious beliefs of a leader or his followers seriously requires that we be open to letting the concepts of faith and religion out of the little box into which they have gradually been crammed by many Western thinkers over the past few centuries. Religion is commonly thought of as primarily relating to the afterlife or acts of worship in large magnificent buildings. Many view religion as little more than a mysterious, mystical process unrelated to day-to-day living. Some find religion useful for helping uncover so-called moral principles, caring for the poor, performing acts of mercy, but little else.

Religious belief and practice do have something to say about the possibility of life after death, moral conduct, and acts of mercy, but to stop at this point with regard to any faith system is the intellectual equivalent of describing all Americans as "rich and selfish," or the earth as "big and green." The Christian faith, for example, is substantial and complex, and in many cases so thoroughly intertwined with Western culture as to be almost indistinguishable to the untrained eye. It is so pervasive that even people who have not darkened the door of a church for decades still breathe the air of their religious forebears. In the United States or Europe this means that even those who seldom open a Bible, assume as normal and right what the Bible teaches about justice, righteousness, obedience to authority, law, property, work, accountability, favoritism, integrity, respect, tolerance, human rights, or compassion. Unfortunately, our unwillingness to compare, contrast, and dissect religious beliefs has left gaping holes in our scholarship. And this does not just apply to beliefs commonly thought of as religious. Other belief systems, both religious and secular, are also complex, extensive, and pervasive. The power of belief is as pervasive for those who put their faith in freedom, money, or technology as it is for those who put their faith in Buddha, Allah, or Christ.

CONCLUSION

The approach to leadership presented here is closely related to the transformational approach, but explicitly recognizes the essentiality of balancing seven critical forms of capital to the transformation process. It draws from the holistic, stewardship, and "new paradigm" approaches that others have emphasized (Block 1993; Bennis, Parikh, and Lessem 1994) but calls more attention to the critical importance of how a leader *sees* the world. The worldview approach also has much in common with the "spirituality school" of leadership effectiveness, but with two important differences. We do not see spirituality as a kind of intelligence, such as emotional or traditional measures of intelligence, but rather as a lens through which we view the world, and which radically changes our answers to fundamental questions, assumptions, problem identification, and strategies for making things better. Additionally, we do not think of spirituality as either generic or necessarily good or beneficial. Its impact on leaders, countries, citizens, or employees can range from extremely positive to horrific, depending on the integrity of the beliefs. Trying to integrate a kind of generic and inoffensive spirituality into an organization could result in settling for the lowest common denominator, instead of reaching for the highest human possibilities.

Much has been gained in the study of the relationship between the values and actions of country leaders and the health of their countries. Research cited here makes it clear that historians, political theorists, and civil society proponents understand well that worldviews and beliefs are critical to the development of a civil society, and are thus at the core of the ebb and flow of countries and their leaders. Threads of this also run through the sociology, psychology, philosophy, and theology literature. Although they may not use the same language, the writers of many popular leadership books and the leaders they write about seem also to recognize the importance of these things in their discussion of spirituality, values, teamwork, and transparency. In spite of this, much of the scholarly research on leadership has too often sidestepped the importance of the worldviews of leaders and followers.

In contrast, we think the economic development experiences of countries point us in the direction of tackling the admittedly difficult tasks of defining major worldview groups and their components, parsing leaders into these groups, and studying their tendencies and effectiveness in different situations. A concerted effort is needed to study how the nonnegotiable issues that frame a leader's life, or the "habits [and desires] of his heart" interact with his traits and style, the tendencies of the followers, or the contingencies or dynamics of the team, relations, or situation. This has the potential to open the door to a fully integrated theory of leadership. It may just turn out that some kinds of leaders are more effective than others across cultures, organizations, and situations because they have worldviews that enable them to see problems as they are, passionately care about meeting universal human needs, and fill our hearts and minds with inspiration.

We have tried to illustrate here that there are a significant number of religiously based tensions woven into our lives like the threads and colors of a fabric. Attempts to define and distinguish worldviews and decipher key components (Sire 1988; Badly 1996; Walsh and Middleton 1984) are positive first steps and offer much potential for understanding leadership effectiveness, especially in the long run. A caution to those who would take this path is that this will be a messy task, to say the least. Discussions of worldviews and the beliefs that undergird them have been avoided in the past in part because of a long tradition in Western scholarship that has privatized beliefs in general, and especially religious beliefs. The predominant perspective in the leadership research seems to be that a little bit of religion is okay, as long as it does not challenge other religious and secular belief systems to the level of seriously examining their assumptions or implications. But the avoidance of the significant role that beliefs play has not necessarily been intentional. In an attempt to be inclusive and tolerant of all belief systems, leadership scholars stepped gingerly around them all, and in the process made them all but irrelevant by assumption.

The experiences of countries and their leaders are relevant for organizations of all kinds. People expect from their employers many of the same things they expect from their countries: to have their basic needs met, to feel secure, to have the opportunity to develop, to be part of a community, to reach important goals, to strive for the greater good, and so on. Because of this the task of an organization leader may not be as different from the task of a country leader as many think. Correspondingly, organizations, like countries, need a balanced supply of all seven forms of capital to reach peak effectiveness. For this to happen, leaders need an integral worldview and organizations need to be transformed over time into miniature civil societies. But civil societies cannot be ushered in at will. The prerequisites of a civil society (e.g., participation, transparency, and a commitment to peaceable change) are themselves values. All ethical and truly transformational leaders, from William Wilberforce and Martin Niemoller to Martin Luther King and Mother Theresa, drew their strength and courage from healthy beliefs and values, such as the rightness of peaceable change, patience, and self-sacrifice. Leadership effectiveness, then, like civil society, economic development, and much of the rest of what we consider important in life, is ultimately rooted in an integral worldview.

REFERENCES

Ayittey, G.B.N. (1998). *Africa in Chaos.* New York: St. Martin's Press.

Badly, K. (1996). *Worldviews:The Challenge of Choice.* Toronto: Irwin.

Bass, B.M. (1990). *Bass & Stogdill's Handbook of Leadership: Theory, Research, & Managerial Applications,* 3d ed. New York: Free Press–Macmillan.

Beit-Hallami, B. (1974). "Psychology of Religion 1880–1939: The Rise and Fall of a Psychological Movement." *Journal of the History of the Behavioral Sciences* 10: 84–90.

Bellah, R.N. (1986). *Habits of the Heart: Individualism and Commitment in American Life.* Berkeley: University of California Press.

Bennis, W.G., J. Parikh, and R. Lessem. (1994). *Beyond Leadership: Balancing Economics, Ethics, and Ecology.* Cambridge, MA: Blackwell Press.

Bennis, W.G., and B. Nanus. (1985). *Leaders: The Strategies for Taking Charge.* New York: Harper and Row.

Bergin, A.E. (1991). "Values and Religious Issues in Psychotherapy and Mental Health." *American Psychologist* 46: 394–403.

Bergquist, W.H. (1992). *The Four Cultures of the Academy: Insights and Strategies for Improving Leadership in Collegiate Organizations.* San Francisco: Jossey-Bass.

Blake, R.R., and J.S. Mouton. (1964). *The Managerial Grid.* Houston: Gulf.

Blanchard, K.H., B. Hybels, and P. Hodges. (1999). *Leadership by the Book: Tools to Transform Your Workplace.* Colorado Springs, CO: WaterBrook Press.

Block, P. (1993). *Stewardship: Choosing Service Over Self-Interest.* San Francisco: Berrett-Koehler.

Bogue, E.G. (1994). *Leadership by Design: Strengthening Integrity in Higher Education.* San Francisco: Jossey-Bass.

Bothwell, R. (1997). "Indicators of a Healthy Civil Society." In *Beyond Prince and Merchant: Citizen Participation and the Rise of Civil Society*, ed. J. Burbidge, 249–251. Brussels: Institute of Cultural Affairs International.

Brady, F.N. (1999). "A Systematic Approach to Teaching Ethics in Business." *Journal of Business Ethics* 19 (3): 309–319.

Braithwaite, V., and M. Levi. (1998). *Trust and Governance.* New York: Russell Sage Foundation.

Brownlie, I. (1992). *Basic Documents on Human Rights*, 3d ed. Oxford: Clarendon Press.

Burns, J.M. (1978). *Leadership.* New York: Harper and Row.

Coats, D.R., and J.W.Skillen, eds. (1998). *Mending Fences: Renewing Justice Between Government and Civil Society*, Grand Rapids, MI: Baker Books.

Collins, J. (2001). *Good to Great: Why Some Companies Make the Leap . . . and Others Don't.* New York: Harper Business.

Collins, J.C., and J.I. Porras. (1994). *Built to Last: Successful Habits of Visionary Companies.* New York: Harper Business.

Comstock, G.W., and K.B. Partridge. (1972). "Church Attendance and Health." *Journal of Chronic Disease* 25: 665–672.

Conger, J.A., and R.N. Kanungo, eds. (1988). *Charismatic Leadership.* San Francisco: Jossey-Bass.

Covey, S.R. (1991). *Principle-Centered Leadership.* New York: Summit Books.

Dansereau, F., G.G. Graen, and W. Haga. (1975). "A Vertical Dyad Linkage Approach to Leadership in Formal Organizations." *Organizational Behavior and Performance* 13: 46–78.

Daum, M., and M.A. Lavenhar. (1980). "Religiosity and Drug Use." National Institute of Drug Abuse DHEW Publication No. (ADM): 80–939.

De Pree, M. (1989). *Leadership Is an Art.* New York: Doubleday.

de Soto, H. (2000). *The Mystery of Capital: Why Capitalism Triumphs in the West and Fails Everywhere Else.* New York: Basic Books.

Downton, J.V. (1973). *Rebel Leadership: Commitment and Charisma in a Revolutionary Process.* New York: Free Press.

Eberly, D. (1998). *America's Promise: Civil Society and the Renewal of American Culture.* Lanham, MD: Rowman & Littlefield.

Ehrenberg, J. (1999). *Civil Society: The Critical History of an Idea.* New York: New York University Press.

Emmons, R. (1999). *The Psychology of Ultimate Concerns: Motivation and Spirituality in Personality.* New York: Guildford Press.

———. (2000). "Spirituality and Intelligence: Problems and Prospects." *International Journal for the Psychology of Religion* 10 (1): 57–64.

Etzioni, A. (1996). *The Golden Rule.* New York: Basic Books.

Evans, M.G. (1970). "The Effects of Supervisory Behavior on the Path-Goal Relationship." *Organizational Behavior and Human Performance* 5: 277–298.

Fiedler, F.E. (1964). "A Contingency Model of Leadership Effectiveness." In *Advances in Experimental Social Psychology,* ed. L. Berkowitz, 149–190. New York: Academic Press.

———. (1967). *A Theory of Leadership Effectiveness.* New York: McGraw-Hill.

Fiedler, F.E., and J.E. Garcia. (1987). *New Approaches to Leadership: Cognitive Resources and Organizational Performance.* New York: John Wiley.

Freeman, R.B. (1985). "Who Escapes? The Relation of Church-Going and Other Background Factors to the Socio-Economic Performance of Black Male Youths from Inner-City Poverty Tracts." Working Paper Series No. 1656. Cambridge, MA: National Bureau of Economic Research.

Fukuyama, F. (1995). *Trust: The Social Virtues and the Creation of Prosperity.* New York: Free Press.

Gilligan, C. (1982). *In a Different Voice: Psychological Theory and Women's Development.* Cambridge, MA: Harvard University Press.

Glendon, M.A., and D. Blankenhorn, eds. (1995). *Seedbeds of Virtue: Sources of Competence, Character, and Citizenship in American Society.* Lanham, MD: Madison Books.

Goleman, D. (1995). *Emotional Intelligence.* New York: Bantam Books.

Graen, G.G. (1976). "Role-making Processes Within Complex Organizations." In *Handbook of Industrial and Organizational Psychology,* ed. M.D. Dunnette, 1202–1245. Chicago: Rand McNally.

Green, D.G. (1993). *Reinventing Civil Society: The Rediscovery of Welfare Without Politics.* London: IEA Health and Welfare Unit.

Greenleaf, R.K. (1970). *The Servant as Leader.* Newton Centre, MA: Robert K. Greenleaf Center.

———. (1977). *Servant Leadership: A Journey into the Nature of Legitimate Power and Greatness.* New York: Paulist.

Harrison, L.E. (1985). *Underdevelopment Is a State of Mind.* Landham, MD: Madison Books.

———. (1992). *Who Prospers? How Cultural Values Shape Economic and Political Success.* New York: Basic Books.

Himmelfarb, G. (1995). *The De-moralization of Society: From Victorian Virtues to Modern Values.* New York: Knopf.

House, R.J. (1971). "A Path-Goal Theory of Leader Effectiveness." *Administrative Science Quarterly* 16: 321–328.

Jones, L.B. (1995). *Jesus CEO: Using Ancient Wisdom for Visionary Leadership.* New York: Hyperion.

Kahoe, R.D. (1974). "Personality and Achievement Correlates on Intrinsic and Extrinsic Religious Orientations." *Journal of Personality and Social Psychology* 29: 812–818.

Kelly, G.B., B.F. Nelson, and R. Bethge. (2003). *The Cost of Moral Leadership: The Spirituality of Dietrich Bonhoeffer.* Grand Rapids, MI: W.B. Eerdmans.

Kotkin, J. (1992). *Tribes: How Race, Religion, and Identity Determine Success in the New Global Economy.* New York: Random House.

Landes, D.S. (1998). *The Wealth and Poverty of Nations: Why Some Are So Rich and Some So Poor.* New York: Norton.

Larson, C.E., and F.M.J. La Fasto. (1989). *Teamwork: What Must Go Right/What Can Go Wrong.* Newbury Park, CA: Sage.

Larson, D.B., S.S. Larson, and J. Gartner. (1990). "Families, Relationships and Health." In *Behavior and Medicine,* ed. D. Wedding, 135–147. Baltimore: Mosby Year Book.

Mann, R.D. (1959). "A Review of the Relationship Between Personality and Performance in Small Groups. *Psychological Bulletin* 56: 241–270.

Manz, C.C. (1998). *Leadership Wisdom of Jesus: Practical Lessons for Today.* San Francisco: Berrett-Koehler.

McDade, S.A., and P.H. Lewis, eds. (1994). *Developing Administrative Excellence: Creating a Culture of Leadership.* San Francisco: Jossey-Bass.

Muller, J.Z. (1993). *Adam Smith: In His Time and Ours.* Princeton, NJ: Princeton University Press.

Myers, D.G. (1992). *The Pursuit of Happiness: Who Is Happy and Why.* New York: William Morrow.

Myers, I.B., and B.H. McCaulley. (1985). *Manual: A Guide to the Development and Use of the Myers-Briggs Type Indicator.* Palo Alto, CA: Consulting Psychologists Press.

Northouse, P. (2004). *Leadership: Theory and Practice*, 3rd ed. Thousand Oaks, CA: Sage.

Peters, T.J., and R.H. Waterman (1982). *In Search of Excellence: Lessons from America's Best-Run Companies.* New York: Harper and Row.

Power, S. (2003). "How to Kill A Country: Turning a Breadbasket into a Basket Case in Ten Easy Steps—the Robert Mugabe Way." *Atlantic Monthly* (December): 87–100.

Putnam, R.D. (1993). *Making Democracy Work: Civic Traditions in Modern Italy.* Princeton, NJ: Princeton University Press.

Rohrbaugh, J., and R. Jessor. (1975). "Religiosity in Youth: A Personal Control Against Deviant Behavior." *Journal of Personality* 43 (1): 136–155.

Rose-Ackerman, S. (1999). *Corruption and Government: Causes, Consequences, and Reform.* New York: Cambridge University Press.

Sanders III, J.E., W.E. Hopkins, and G.D. Geroy. (2003). "From Transactional to Transcendental: Toward an Integrated Theory of Leadership." *Journal of Leadership Studies* 9 (4): 21–31.

Sire, J.W. (1988). *The Universe Next Door: A Basic Worldview Catalog.* Downers Grove, IL: InterVarsity Press.

Smith, A. (1993). *An Inquiry Into the Nature and Causes of the Wealth of Nations.* Indianapolis, IN: Hackett.

Stogdill, R.M. (1974). *Handbook of Leadership: A Survey of Theory and Research.* New York: Free Press.

Tichy, N.W., and M.A. Devanna. (1986; reprint 1990). *The Transformational Leader,* 2d ed. New York: Wiley.

Walsh, B., and J. Middleton. (1984). *The Transforming Vision: Shaping a Christian World View.* Downers Grove, IL: InterVarsity Press.

Wiebe K.F., and J.R. Fleck. (1980). "Personality Correlates of Intrinsic, Extrinsic and Non-Religious Orientations." *Journal of Psychology* 105: 111–117.

Wilcox, J.R., and S.L. Ebbs. (1992). *The Leadership Compass: Values and Ethics in Higher Education.* Washington, DC: George Washington University's ERIC Clearinghouse on Higher Education.

Woolcock, M., L. Pritchett, and J. Isham. (2001). "The Social Foundations of Poor Economic Growth in Resource-Rich Countries." In *Resource Abundance and Economic Development,* ed. R. Auty, 76–92. New York: Oxford University Press.

World Development Report. (1997). New York: Oxford University Press.

Yukl, G. (1989). "Managerial Leadership: A Review of Theory and Research." *Journal of Management* 15 (Fall): 59–68.

Chapter 18

What Good Is This to Me?

Managerial Implications of Global Leadership Research

Marcus W. Dickson and Deanne N. Den Hartog

All over the world and throughout history there have been leaders. The ancient Egyptians, Hebrews, Chinese, and Greeks (among many others) all had systems for recognizing and choosing leaders, though those systems differed quite widely, as did the things that the leaders were expected to do and the ways they were expected to behave. Nonetheless, in all of those cases leadership involved disproportionate influence—leaders by definition are more influential than nonleaders—and at least to some degree, being a leader was associated with both power and status. The situation remains much the same today—there are significant differences between cultures in commonly accepted leadership styles, and these differences are of critical importance. However, not everything is different—there are also some core characteristics that seem to carry over from culture to culture.

A major difference today, though, is that we have the potential benefit of a substantial amount of research on leadership in different cultures. Unfortunately, empirical research on these topics is sometimes obscured behind academic jargon and available only in specialized academic journals targeted at other academics. Thus, findings from this research remain unknown to the very people who could most benefit from them. When these resources are not available, managers and executives may turn to sources that are more readily available at the local bookstore. Sadly, in many cases these books claim to offer much more than they actually deliver.

In this chapter, we have a few rather modest goals. First, we hope to demonstrate that country and culture really do matter when trying to determine what makes up that chimera called "effective leadership." Second, we hope to show that managers and executives who deal with cultural issues relating to leadership can meaningfully apply well-designed scholarly research on cross-cultural leadership. Finally, we hope to provide some concrete recommendations for managers and executives about the sorts of research-based information that they may find useful when wrestling with leadership and culture, and for how to go about finding that information. In short, the issue that we want to focus on is why managers and executives should pay attention to cross-cultural research on leadership—what can they actually *do* with these findings?

First, we will address the question of "universality of leadership," which some people and organizations adopt (to their peril, we believe) by advocating the position that "leadership is leadership the world over, and what works here will work elsewhere." We describe some different ways to think about universality, and compare it to the alternative of "cultural contingency," which is the idea that culture matters. We raise the possibility that both of these positions can be true, and provide some evidence from research to show how this can be the case. Next, we describe an approach to thinking about differences between cultures based on a series of dimensions of culture that can be measured and used to compare different societies. We then relate those dimensions to several different leadership outcomes. Along the way, we will describe several cross-cultural research studies, with a primary focus on the Global Leadership and Organizational Behavior Effectiveness (GLOBE) Project,[1] in which we have both been active for several years. (In short, GLOBE is a project in which over 180 social scientists from all over the world have gathered data about leadership and cultural values and practices from thousands of middle managers in 64 different cultures.)

At that point, we should have made a compelling argument that culture does matter for leadership. We will then conclude the chapter by identifying several specific topics of importance for managers and executives for which empirical research on culture and leadership would be useful, and presenting an initial strategy for incorporating research into the decision process.

A QUICK REMINDER ABOUT CROSS-CULTURAL RESEARCH AND STEREOTYPING

One of the biggest challenges for people attempting to apply the results of cross-cultural research is being able to find the balance between understanding that there are behaviors and values that are more common or typical in a given culture, and engaging in stereotyping. For example, it is true that the German culture is characterized by (among many other things) promptness, a focus on ensuring certainty and reducing ambiguity, and formality. It is *not* true that all Germans are going to arrive five minutes early for meetings and be uncomfortable when a situation is characterized by uncertainty. In other words, cross-cultural research on all topics can give guidance about the relative likelihood that members of groups of people will think, feel, and behave in certain ways, and in general, those tendencies will be borne out. However, a specific person's cultural background should certainly not be used as a primary means of predicting that person's performance, especially when other information about the individual is available.

"UNIVERSALITY," AND WHAT IT MEANS (AND DOES NOT MEAN)

When talking about leadership in a cross-cultural context, we often talk about things that are "universal," with the assumption that if something is not universal, then it must be "culturally contingent," or dependent on the culture in which the behavior occurs. However, the concept of "universality" is very rarely defined, or even given a lot of thought. This is unfortunate, as the following examples will make clear.

We have pointed out elsewhere (Den Hartog and Dickson 2004) that the concept of participation—often seen as something that good leaders encourage in their subordinates—means very different things in different countries. In "Western" cultures, people typically think of participation as referring to having some influence on a decision by taking part in the decision-making process. In Java, however, people feel that they have participated when they have engaged in a specific cooperative form of decision making. In Japan, participation implies that the decision was reached through a process of building consensus referred to as *ringi*. The point is that fundamentally, leadership and all of its components can mean different things in different societies, and one of the major benefits of cross-cultural research on leadership can be insight into what those differences are likely to be when we encounter a new cultural situation.

The situation that we are describing—in which a general leadership attribute is valued in all cultures, but where the behaviors related to the attribute are very different in different cultures—has been referred to as a "variform universal." We do not intend to throw a lot of jargon into this chapter, but this distinction seems to us to be an important one to make, and it is helpful to have a way to refer to it.

A second example of a variform universal is the idea of being "visionary." This is a trait that is seen as a positive leader attribute in most cultures, but what one needs to do to be seen as visionary varies from one culture to another. One of the main places where we see these differences is not in the content of the vision, but rather in the ways that a leader's vision for his or her organization is communicated to employees. In some cultures (including in the United States), a more "macho" style of vision communication—where the effort to achieve the vision is describe in terms of conflict, combat, and victory—is seen as effective. Fu and Yukl (2000), however, point out that in China, leaders would typically express an organizational vision in a nonaggressive manner, perhaps because of the prevalence of Confucian values (e.g., kindness, benevolence) in the society.

As a final example, we can consider risk taking. A certain amount of risk taking is generally seen in the United States as being an important part of effective leadership, but risk taking is not universally valued as contributing to outstanding leadership, and risk taking is closer to a variform universal, in that it means different things in different societies. An excellent example of this comes from Martinez and Dorfman (1998), who describe a Mexican entrepreneur who engaged in "risky" behavior by appointing a woman from the Mexican lower class to be a member of the administrative staff. The entrepreneur made this decision based on the woman's hard work, education, and expertise, and he did it over widespread stockholder opposition. For that entrepreneur in that country at that time, such a hire was considered to be evidence of high risk taking. In many other countries where social status is less important than it is in Mexico, this hiring decision would not have generated opposition at all, and in fact might have been seen as conservative (hiring a person with such strong credentials). In short, the same behavior can mean very different things in cultures that differ in their core shared values. We, as cross-cultural researchers and as consumers of cross-cultural research, must be very careful to take context into account where appropriate in interpreting the meanings of research.

Now, before we focus explicitly on cross-cultural research on leadership, it is important to understand the basic framework that underlies much cross-cultural research in general. We will first discuss the research approach of relying on cultural dimensions, and then talk about how societies that are similar can be clustered together. We will then turn to the question of leadership differences between cultures and between clusters of cultures, and conclude with specific areas in which research in this area can be meaningfully applied to promote success in the workplace.

CULTURAL DIMENSIONS

Geert Hofstede (1980, 2001) is widely credited with developing a framework for classifying countries based on the work-related values that predominate in those countries. Hofstede developed several "dimensions of culture" that can be measured and used to compare countries.

A good way to think about these dimensions is to compare them to the ways we think about personality. The best way to know someone's personality is to spend a lot of time with them, and to develop a deep and intimate knowledge of that person's preferences, values, beliefs, quirks, and so forth. However, it takes a lot of time to develop that type of a relationship, and we never develop that deep a relationship with a large number of people. Even when we do, we do not have any meaningful way to compare people to each other. A different approach is to use dimensions of personality—we can say that John is more extroverted than Joe, even if we do not know either person exceptionally well. That information can be useful if we want to make a decision about, for example, what jobs John and Joe might be good at. It would be less useful if we wanted to determine which of these two people to have as a close friend.

Similarly, the best way to know a country's culture is to live in that country, learn the language, spend time with people there, and learn the values and practices that are common and expected there. However, few people will ever develop that level of knowledge of more than two or three countries in their lifetimes. So Hofstede developed several dimensions that can be used to compare countries based on the work-related values that are prevalent in those countries. The dimensions can be useful when we need to compare countries on things such as the degree to which they can tolerate ambiguity (which could be useful for predicting comfort with new ventures, for example), but the dimensions are unlikely to be useful when deciding where we would like to live or spend an extended vacation.

The dimensions that Hofstede developed have become widely used in cross-cultural research in general, and in cross-cultural leadership research in particular. The dimensions are:

- *Uncertainty avoidance*, which reflects the extent to which members of a society actively work to reduce ambiguity, or accept and embrace ambiguity as acceptable or desirable. This can be reflected in small things such as punctuality, or in larger things such as level of comfort with taking on debt, and the extent to which deadlines are seen as hard or soft.

- *Power distance*, which reflects the extent to which members of a society believe that it is acceptable or desirable for those higher in the hierarchy to be treated with deference and respect, to be obeyed, and to have extra privileges—in short, to be seen as different and above others. This can be seen in such things as the willingness to question supervisors' directives, the acceptance of special perquisites for those of higher rank, or rituals and norms of behavior when interacting with superiors.

- *Individualism-collectivism*, which describes the extent to which a society is focused primarily on the individual and his or her well-being and advancement, or on the group or organization, and group harmony. The United States is often seen as the most (or at least one of the most) individualistic societies in the world today, and this can be clearly seen in the structure of the U.S. Constitution, which is designed to protect the individual from the majority (e.g., through protections for freedom of unpopular speech). It can also be seen in common sayings, such as "the squeaky wheel gets the grease," meaning that the person who demands attention for themselves will eventually get what they want. Contrast this to a common saying in Japan (a collectivistic society): "The nail that sticks up is hammered down," meaning that the person who stands out from the group will be brought back into line.

- *Future orientation*, which describes the extent to which a society has a long-term or a short-term focus in its business and other dealings. The United States is often criticized internationally because of the common practice in U.S. corporations of focusing on quarterly stock prices and sales (and rewarding executives who thus make shortsighted business decisions in an effort to bolster those quarterly prices and sales), rather than taking a longer view of the organization's future, as is more common in, among others, most European countries.

- *Masculinity-femininity*, which is probably the most controversial of Hofstede's dimensions. This dimension refers to the extent to which a society is characterized by aggressiveness, competition, achievement orientation, and other stereotypically masculine traits, or is characterized by a focus on nurturance, harmony, mutual advancement, and other stereotypically feminine traits. In Hofstede's conceptualization, it also includes the extent to which men and women are expected to fulfill different or similar roles in the society (though as we will note below, some other researchers have separated this component out into a separate dimension).

CULTURE CLUSTERS

To return to our earlier analogy about personality, just as it is obvious that each person has his or her own unique personality, each society has its own unique culture. However, just as there are people whose personalities are similar to each other, there are societies whose cultures are similar to each other. Several researchers have wrestled with this topic, and almost twenty years ago Ronen and Shenkar (1985) created a set of "culture clusters," or groupings of cultures that are similar to each other. Recently, several other researchers have also addressed the topic of clustering cultures together (e.g., Lewis 2000; Inglehart 1997), and the GLOBE Project researchers developed an updated set of clusters based on the cultural values of the countries in their study. These clusters have several implications for leadership and other business issues, but before getting to those, we need to describe the clusters themselves.

Using a statistical technique called cluster analysis, GLOBE identified ten clusters of countries. The countries within each cluster are similar to one another in many ways, and are generally different in important ways from the countries in the other clusters. It is important to note that even though the GLOBE study includes countries from every major language grouping, from every inhabited continent, and all of the G7 nations, there are many societies that are not included in the study. It is possible that other clusters would emerge if additional societies were included in the data set, though it also seems quite likely that many societies not included in the data set would fit cleanly into one of the ten clusters identified. The ten clusters are shown in Table 18.1.

The fact that countries are clustered together based on their similarities to one another is not at all to say that the countries in these clusters are identical to one another. We have routinely been reminded of this when we have presented these clusters at various conferences in the past couple of years, and audience members have come to talk with us afterward. Frequently, they will tell us that we got all of the clusters right, except for the cluster in which their home country is included. They will go on to identify all of the differences between their home country and the other countries in the cluster, but will then again affirm, "the rest of the clusters are really accurate." This led us to speculate about why this might be.

Our conclusion can be explained with an analogy. If you listen to a piece of music with which you are very familiar, you will notice if even one note is played differently, and objectively small changes in the playing of the piece can seem to be quite significant. However, if listening to music with which you are unfamiliar, there can be objectively large changes from time to time that are barely noticed (if they are noticed at all). Similarly, we concluded that people are typically most familiar with the countries with which their home country is most similar, probably due to the fact that culturally similar countries tend to be geographically close. Even objectively small differences between familiar cultures can seem quite large and meaningful because they are very evident (or salient), while the larger magnitude differences between less familiar cultures may be less noticeable.

Though the GLOBE Project identified a wide range of differences between the culture clusters, the ones of most relevance here are differences between the clusters in terms of leadership. Before describing those, we first need to explain the ways that leadership was assessed. We turn to that topic now.

LEADERSHIP BEHAVIORS AND ATTRIBUTES

In the past several years, leadership researchers have returned their attention to interpersonal and relational skills as being important for leadership effectiveness. For those interested in finding ways to select or identify people likely to be effective as leaders, the reason for this emphasis on personal characteristics is not hard to see (Aditya, House, and Kerr

Table 18.1

Clusters of Countries Identified in the GLOBE Project

Anglo	*Latin American*
Australia	Argentina
Canada	Bolivia
England	Brazil
Ireland	Colombia
New Zealand	Costa Rica
South Africa (White sample)	Ecuador
United States	El Salvador
	Guatemala
Latin European	Mexico
France	Venezuela
Israel	
Italy	*Sub-Saharan African*
Portugal	Namibia
Spain	Nigeria
Switzerland (French-speaking)	South Africa (Black sample)
	Zambia
Nordic European	Zimbabwe
Denmark	
Finland	*Southern Asian*
Sweden	India
	Indonesia
Germanic European	Iran
Austria	Malaysia
Germany (East and West)	Philippines
Netherlands	Thailand
Switzerland	
	Arab and Middle Eastern
Eastern European	Egypt
Albania	Kuwait
Georgia	Morocco
Greece	Qatar
Hungary	Turkey
Kazakhstan	
Poland	*Confucian Asian*
Russia	China
Slovenia	Hong Kong
	Japan
	Singapore
	South Korea
	Taiwan

2000). A major question is whether these personal characteristics that are associated with effective leadership within a single country are also useful in other cultural settings. The GLOBE Project is the largest project to date to attempt to address this question.

In addition to measuring the values and practices of the different cultures, the GLOBE study also gathered information about the common leadership preferences in those cultures. Specifically, GLOBE asked about the characteristics that are seen to most inhibit or facilitate a person's being an outstanding leader. First, we will describe the results based on some of the specific leader behaviors and attributes that GLOBE asked about. Afterward, we will describe some broader categories of leader behaviors and attributes, and describe how the "leadership dimensions" relate to the country clusters described above.

Universally Endorsed Leader Characteristics

As we alluded to above, in the GLOBE study, middle managers from over sixty different cultures were asked for their perceptions of over 200 different leader attributes and behaviors, with a specific focus on whether these attributes and behaviors inhibited or facilitated a person's being an outstanding leader. Of this wide range of leader characteristics, about twenty were seen as facilitating outstanding leadership in every country studied. Den Hartog et al. (1999) describe these, and point out that in all participating countries, outstanding leaders are expected to be: encouraging, intelligent, trustworthy, and excellence oriented, and are expected *not* to be ruthless, irritable, or dictatorial. On the face of it, these results do not seem surprising. However, it is important to remember when reviewing these results that these are what middle managers *describe* as being effective. It is possible that the attributes that people prefer, and the attributes that would actually lead to high levels of organizational performance, could differ and could differ by culture.

Culturally Contingent Leader Characteristics

Den Hartog et al. (1999) also report that in the vast majority of cases, the degree to which a particular attribute was seen as inhibiting or facilitating outstanding leadership varied by culture. (In presenting these results, we will describe them based on the scale that the middle managers in the study responded to. A high score on the seven-point scale means that the attribute is seen as facilitating outstanding leadership, and a low score means that the attribute is seen as impeding outstanding leadership.)

Two examples show the range of scores on these leadership attributes. We mentioned the idea of risk taking earlier in this chapter. When we asked specifically about the attribute "risk taking," the averages for the sixty-four cultures in the study ranged from 2.14 (meaning that it strongly inhibits outstanding leadership) to 5.96 (meaning that it substantially contributes to outstanding leadership). The range for the leader attribute of "sensitive" had even greater variability, with culture averages ranging from 1.96 to 6.35. Clearly, cultural differences play a major role here.

Fortunately, it is possible to look at these differences and see how they relate to broader patterns of cultural values. In other words, different cultures' responses to various leadership styles are typically in line with other work-related beliefs and values. Here, we can rely on the cultural dimensions described earlier to make sense of some of the cultural differences in responses to leader attributes. For example, the dimension of power distance can clearly be seen as the origin of several differences. "Elitist" and "domineering" are both leader attributes that differ widely in endorsement between cultures, and in each case, they are seen as contributing to outstanding leadership in cultures that are high on power distance, and are seen as inhibiting outstanding leadership in cultures low in power distance. Other research has shown that subordinates in high power distance societies are typically reluctant to challenge their supervisors or to express disagreement with them (Adsit et al. 1997), and that employees in these societies are typically more willing to accept and abide by formal rules and procedures set by top management for handling day to day events (Smith et al. 2002). In fact, some research has shown that employees in high power distance cultures do not perform as well in empowered workplaces as they do in disempowered workplaces, though the employees *prefer* the empowered situation (Eylon and Au 1999). These examples help to clarify that the cultural values that characterize a society aid in determining not only what leader behaviors are accepted but also what leader behaviors are expected.

Similarly, some of the leader attributes that varied in their endorsement between cultures can be explained by looking at the dimension of uncertainty avoidance, which, as we mentioned above, refers to the degree to which ambiguity is actively avoided or embraced in a society. Leader attributes such as being risk taking, habitual, procedural, able to anticipate, formal, cautious, and orderly are seen as inhibiting outstanding leadership in some countries and facilitating it in others. But the tolerance for ambiguity is also shown in the expectations that leaders have of their subordinates (Stewart et al. 1994). Managers in the UK, which is lower in uncertainty avoidance, wanted subordinates who were resourceful and could improvise in response to a crisis. German managers, on the other hand, wanted subordinates who were reliable and punctual, which is congruent with the higher levels of uncertainty avoidance found in Germany.

As a further point, these same researchers found that this cultural value affected the ways that future leaders are prepared to be leaders. In societies that are high in uncertainty avoidance, there is more value placed on career stability and the development of specialized expertise, and the expectation is that young managers will spend more time in a single job developing specific task-related expertise. Conversely, in countries lower on uncertainty avoidance, broader preparation and more generalized expertise is the norm, in line with values of career mobility and advancement. The influence of this dimension extends beyond leader training and preparation, however. Rauch, Frese, and Sonnentag (2000) showed that in a low uncertainty avoidance society (Ireland), long-term planning was devalued and seen as risky because of the expectation that customer preferences and demands can change rapidly and unexpectedly, while in a high uncertainty avoidance society (Germany), long-term planning is seen as a critical means of meeting customer expectations of quality and on-time delivery. Thus, the same distal goal (satisfying customer expectations) leads to different proximal strategies in ways that are clearly related to the societal comfort with ambiguity.

Finally, in the GLOBE study, the leader attributes of being autonomous, unique, and independent were all found to contribute to outstanding leadership in some cultures but to have the opposite effect in others. These attributes seem to reflect different cultural preferences for individualism or collectivism. There is a substantial amount of research showing other ways that cultural individualism impacts the leadership process, including research showing that employees in collectivistic societies more readily identify with their leaders' goals or with a shared vision for the organization (Jung, Bass, and

Sosik 1995), while those in individualistic societies may engage in the required behaviors without having a personal sense of identification with the vision. Those in collectivistic societies are also more likely to be willing (or even eager) to subordinate their own personal goals to the goals of the group (Triandis 1995).

Interpersonal Acumen

An aspect of effective leadership that was not originally considered for the GLOBE study is social intelligence, and particularly an aspect of social intelligence known as interpersonal acumen, or IA (Rosnow et al. 1994). In short, IA refers to the ability to decipher underlying motives in interpersonal behavior. Clearly, this has relevance to the leadership endeavor, as evident behaviors and underlying motives are not always the same—behaviors are not always what they appear to be. Leaders who are better able to identify discrepancies between apparent and actual motives are likely to be more effective in the long run than are those who are less able to accurately discern those discrepancies. This is especially true for such common leadership situations as negotiation and conflict resolution, as well as in other more routine aspects of managing a group of followers or employees.

Interestingly, though IA was not originally intended to be part of the GLOBE study, Ram Aditya and Bob House (2002) were able to construct a measure of IA using leadership trait and attribute items that were not used for other leadership dimensions. The leadership traits and attributes that are combined to measure the perceived importance of IA for outstanding leadership are:

- cunning, describing an individual as being sly, deceitful, and full of guile;
- indirect communication, describing a leader who does not go straight to the point, and uses metaphors and examples to communicate;
- evasive behaviors, describing a leader who refrains from making negative remarks in order to maintain good relationships; and
- sensitivity, characterizing a leader who is aware of even slight changes in others' moods, and moderates his or her own behavior accordingly.

There are large differences between societies in the extent to which IA and its component parts are seen as facilitating or inhibiting outstanding leadership. Just as one example, the leadership trait of being cunning was rated on average in Switzerland as 1.26 on a seven-point scale where 1 represents a trait that greatly inhibits outstanding leadership, but in Colombia, the same trait was rated on average as 6.37. Though much of this research on the importance of IA for leadership across cultures is still in its infancy, and cluster differences on this scale have not yet been tested, these initial results suggest that this is yet another leadership characteristic to which attention should be paid by managers and executives wrestling with cross-cultural leadership selection and placement.

Leadership Styles

In addition to looking at the 200-plus leader behaviors and attributes individually (and in small groupings like those for interpersonal acumen), the GLOBE researchers also looked at major styles of leadership, combining the behaviors and attributes into larger groupings of related items. Ultimately, GLOBE identified six major categories of leader behaviors and attributes, and there are several differences between the culture clusters on the degree to which these categories of leader characteristics are seen as being typical of outstanding leaders. Specifically, the six dimensions are:

- Charismatic/value-based leadership, for example, being visionary, inspirational, decisive, and having integrity;
- Team-oriented leadership, for example, acting collaboratively, integrating, and being diplomatic;
- Participative leadership, for example, being non-autocratic and allowing participation in decision making;
- Autonomous leadership, for example, being individualistic, independent, and unique;
- Humane leadership, for example, showing modesty, tolerance, and sensitivity; and
- Self-protective leadership, for example, being self-centered, status conscious, and a face-saver.

Just as we were interested in whether particular leadership attributes were universally endorsed or depended on the culture, we were also interested in whether there are styles of leadership that are likely to be well-received regardless of the culture in which they take place, or whether the acceptability of various leadership styles is dependent upon the culture. To look at this, we tested the relationships between the six leadership styles and the ten country clusters described earlier.

As before, we found that the universality and the cultural-contingency positions are both true, to some extent. Specifically, there were two dimensions of leadership that were strongly endorsed in all ten of the culture clusters. These are the *charismatic leadership* dimension—which focuses on things like setting a challenging vision for the organization and being inspirational—and the *team-oriented* leadership dimension—which focuses on things like collaboration and information sharing. Even though all clusters endorsed these leadership styles, the endorsement was strongest in the Anglo, Southern Asian, and Latin American clusters and was somewhat less strong in the Middle Eastern cluster. In light of what is known about these clusters in terms of their work-related values, this makes sense—the Middle Eastern cluster of countries tends to endorse the value of power distance, and this is somewhat discrepant from the notion of a leader's vision, which is often presented in terms of what *we* can accomplish.

The *humane leadership* dimension had a somewhat different pattern of endorsement, and overall it was not as strongly endorsed as the charismatic or the team-oriented leadership dimensions. For this dimension, the Southern Asia, Anglo, and Sub-Saharan Africa clusters more strongly endorsed this leadership style, while the Latin and Nordic Europe clusters endorsed it somewhat less strongly. While this may seem to be a somewhat unexpected pattern of results, we in GLOBE have come to recognize that this dimension has a flavor of benevolent paternalism to it—the leader behaviors described tend to reflect caring for others who are subordinate to the leader in an "I know what is best for you" manner, rather than reflecting what many Americans would think of as humane styles of leadership.

The dimension of *autonomous leadership*, which reflects the tendency to be independent and unique, was generally seen as neither facilitating nor inhibiting a leader from being effective. This is not overly surprising, as uniqueness in and of itself does not necessarily imply "effective." A person can be unlike anyone else and thus be highly creative in the face of crisis, or be unlike anyone else and thus be unable to communicate effectively because of a radically different perception of problems. Nonetheless, there were still clusters where autonomous leadership was seen as slightly positively related to being an outstanding leader (e.g., Eastern and Germanic Europe), and others where it was slightly negatively related (e.g., Latin Europe, Middle East).

For two of the leadership dimensions, there was substantial variability in the degree to which the country clusters endorsed them, and we see these as being particularly important for managers to attend to in making decisions such as expatriate assignments. For these two dimensions, the congruence between the typical behaviors of a particular organizational leader and the cultural preferences of the location to which the leader could be assigned seems likely to have more impact on the eventual success of that leader. The two dimensions are *self-protective leadership* and *participative leadership*.

In general, leadership that is focused on maintaining one's image or status, or focused on preserving "face," (i.e., the self-protective leadership dimensions) was perceived to inhibit the effectiveness of a leader (i.e., the means for all ten clusters were below the mid-point of the scale). However, this approach was seen as more inhibiting in the Nordic, Germanic, and Anglo clusters, and it was rejected to a lesser degree in the Middle Eastern, Confucian, and Southern Asian clusters. This makes sense, in that the latter three clusters (and especially the latter two) are those in which some form of the concept of "face" is critically important for the respect of both peers and others, but also for one's self-respect. In these cultures, a leader who does not attend to the maintenance of his or her own face, and that of the organization, is not likely to be successful. However, it appears that even in these clusters, behaviors that are solely focused on the maintenance of face are not seen as particularly desirable or effective.

The process of involving employees in the decision-making process (i.e., the participative leadership dimension) was seen as contributing to effective leadership for all culture clusters, though, again, there was a substantial amount of variation in the degree to which the clusters endorsed this. The GLOBE results suggest that the Germanic, Anglo, and Nordic clusters were particularly attuned to participative leadership, whereas the Middle Eastern, East European, Confucian, and Southern Asian clusters were not. Again, this is not surprising in that the clusters that were less enthralled with participative leadership tend to be those clusters that are lower on the cultural value of individualism and higher on the value of power distance—in both cases, these values would be supportive of a leader who claimed the authority to make decisions on his or her own for the benefit of the group.

Are There Differences Based on a Company's Industry?

Throughout this chapter, we have talked about differences in leadership preferences as if the only important factor were culture. Of course, that is not the case—there are a number of factors that will affect the leadership preferences of specific individuals, including individual personality, values and interests, the culture of the organization, and the degree to which the current situation seems to require more or less "leaderly" behavior. We have focused on societal culture because of its broad impact, and we have not attended to the range of factors that are likely to be idiosyncratic for individuals or small groups of individuals (e.g., personality, organizational culture, etc.).

However, it is important to recognize that there are potentially broad differences in leadership preferences based on the industry to which an organization belongs, and that these differences might have an impact across societies in the same way that societal culture appears to have an impact across industries. The GLOBE Project examined this, by examining organizations in three industries: telecommunications, food processing, and financial services. These industries were chosen because they are present in some form in virtually every society, and because they represent differing degrees of dynamism and change (i.e., telecommunications is highly dynamic, food processing relatively less dynamic, and financial services has traditionally been nondynamic but is facing rapid change with the advent of globalization and advancing technology).

In order to look at this question, we examined whether the practices that characterize the cultures in the various culture clusters are predictive of the practices that characterize organizations within those clusters. We then tested whether there were differences in the relationships between cultural practices and organizational practices that could be explained by the industry to which the organizations belonged. In brief, GLOBE found that the organizational practices of the financial industry are least affected by cultural practices, while the organizational practices of the food processing and telecommunications industries show greater sensitivity to culture cluster differences. In other words, organizations in some industries are more sensitive to the pressures and expectations present in their host countries, while organizations in other industries seem to be most influenced by the expectations and requirements of the industry itself. This presumably holds true for both the practices that characterize the organizations, and for the leadership traits and attributes that are seen as most effective.

IMPLICATIONS FOR LEADERS

Thus far in this chapter, we have presented the results of research showing the importance of country culture in determining the leadership traits and attributes that will be seen as effective, and the styles of leadership that are likely to be preferred in different cultural contexts. We hope we have convinced even the skeptical reader that, in short, culture matters. We would like to go a little further in the final section of the chapter, though, and speculate about specific topics for which culture matters. In other words, we want to return to the title of our chapter and answer the managerial/executive question of "what good is this to me?"

To answer this question, we first want to make the link back to the research we have already discussed. Hanges, Dickson, and Gupta (2002) have pointed out that there are two common reactions by organizations when they have to interact with employees in another culture. The first they refer to as the "brute force" model, in which companies impose the structures and practices of the home country on the employees or organization in the second country. This may be because of a belief in the primacy of structure (e.g., "This is the way we do things here, and it is the way we will do things there, too."), or it may be because of a lack of forethought about the possible implications of such implementation. Indeed, Earley and Gibson point out that "models of organizational behavior developed in the West do not take . . . cultural differences into consideration" (2000, 6), and we would argue that corporations are even less prone to consider culture than are organizational behavior researchers and theorists.

In this chapter we have pointed out several reasons why this brute force model may not always be a viable strategy, and why employees may resist it. Of course, in some cases companies will not be concerned with resistance—when a new factory is the only game in town and unemployment is high, employees will take those jobs and stay with those jobs because they have no other choice. However, we believe that this is not the optimal situation for organizational effectiveness.

The second approach that organizations may take in this situation is the "extreme cultural contingency" approach, in which organizations are *overly* sensitive to culture and assume that because the new worksite is in a different country, nothing from the home country will be applicable.

We believe that neither of these extreme positions is always right, but we also do not believe that either of these positions is always wrong. Fortunately, the research we have described thus far presents a specific avenue for making inferences about when some practices might be applicable, and when they might not be. Specifically, we believe that it is possible to identify cultures that are relatively similar to each other in terms of work-related values, and that leadership styles and organizational practices from one country are more likely to be effectively implemented in similar cultures than they are in dissimilar cultures. The range of research on culture clusters that has been described earlier thus seems to be of particular importance.

By understanding the relative similarity or dissimilarity of societies in terms of their work related values, practicing managers and executives are likely to be better able to make decisions about a wide range of important topics, including the development of human resource practices related to compensation, the structure of work, and employee selection; decisions about expatriate assignments; and at a more macro level, about international mergers and acquisitions. We will discuss each of these examples in turn.

Likely Range of Application of Human Resource Practices

One of the places where we often see culture being ignored is in the imposition of human resource practices onto people, facilities, or organizations in countries other than where those practices were developed. A common example of this is when U.S. companies have expanded by acquiring organizations in their same industry that are located in other countries.

Reward Systems

Reward systems are particularly ripe for cultural misfit—the ideas of individual achievement and pay for performance are so inherent in American thinking that it is often forgotten that these are not core values or expectations in other cultures. Zhou (2002) provided an excellent example of this when she described the imposition of a pay-for-performance system at a factory in China. Eventually, the women there (all of the employees were women) went to the American supervisor and requested a meeting. The first point to recognize in this situation occurs here—in a society that is characterized by high power distance and respect for authority, it is exceedingly rare for a group of employees to seek out a meeting with a superior for the purpose of requesting a change. Once the meeting occurred, the women asked that the old pay system be implemented—a system in which the older workers were paid more, because they had greater need for higher pay. The women argued that this change would be "more fair."

An important lesson to take from this (and many other similar events) is that people generally want to be treated fairly—they want "distributive justice," in which the outcomes of decisions about pay and other rewards are fair. However, the things that constitute fairness will differ substantially and predictably according to culture. Generally speaking, members of collectivist cultures prefer pay systems that do not differentiate between individuals in their performance (though differentiation based on other factors such as age and need are often acceptable), while members of individualistic cultures (e.g., in the United States or Australia) tend to prefer pay-for-performance systems, in which the people who do the most get the most. In each case, people perceive the reward system they prefer as being fundamentally more fair than the alternatives, and efforts at "rational persuasion" about the merits of the alternative system are unlikely to succeed.

Work Teams

When addressing the topic of teams, several issues emerge, including the extent to which work is organized into teams versus being individually oriented, the extent to which teams are ad hoc or long lasting, and the extent to which the teams themselves are multinational in composition. Each of these merits significant attention—more attention than space allows here.

Earley and Gibson (2002) have written extensively about the issue of multinational teams, and they convincingly argue that as business continues to globalize, it will become more and more common for teams to comprise individuals from several cultures. This could occur when team members have immigrated to a company's home country and now live and work in the same area, or it could occur when teams or project task forces are created with representatives from locations around the world. Computer-mediated communication can facilitate this latter form of multinational team, adding an additional level of complexity to already complex interactions.

Earley and Gibson (2002) point out several specific manifestations of differences in the cultural dimensions described earlier. For example, multinational team members from cultures where men and women are expected to behave differently and fulfill different societal roles (i.e., high masculinity cultures, in Hofstede's parlance) may find it difficult to interact effectively with team members from cultures where gender is less of a consideration (i.e., low masculinity countries). Similarly, members from high power distance cultures may be uncomfortable in a leaderless group, which is common for those in low power distance cultures. Those from high uncertainty avoidance cultures may prefer regularly scheduled meeting times (virtual or face to face) or firm deadlines for response to electronic mail messages, while those from low uncertainty avoidance cultures may find such practices constraining.

The implication for leaders seems to be that, given the increasing use of multinational teams, steps need to be taken to explicitly recognize the varying comfort levels of multinational team members with the group process, and to develop norms that work for that particular conglomeration of people and cultures. These norms need not be an "average" of the cultural expectations of the members—few female team members from low masculinity cultures would willingly reduce their input in order to accommodate the cultural norms of those from high masculinity cultures, for example. But once the origins of potential points of tension are identified and recognized, it becomes easier for team members to work outside their typical patterns.

Personnel Selection Systems

One of the primary tasks of leaders is to choose the people who will work for and with them. The processes by which this occurs vary widely from country to country, as does the extent to which these processes are regulated by law. The underlying values systems that guide personnel selection are likely to be more similar within a culture cluster, we believe, and thus it may be less difficult to export a selection system to a new company location in another culture if that culture is in the same cluster.

For example, in all of the countries in the Anglo cluster, the core expectation for personnel selection is that hiring will be based on ability and potential, rather than on personal relationship, and many organizations have internal rules against nepotism, or the hiring of relatives. In the Southern Asian cluster, however, the hiring of relatives and friends is clearly viewed with less disfavor and in many cases is seen as a desirable practice because it ensures that there is someone to "vouch" for the newly hired person.

Steiner and Gilliland (1996) point out that the "face validity," or the ease with which an applicant can understand why a selection tool is appropriate, was seen as the most important factor determining the acceptability of a selection tool in their study of France and the United States. They further showed that there were statistically significant but not insurmountable differences in the acceptability of various selection tools between the two countries (which do cross a cluster boundary in the GLOBE data). A key issue seems to be the degree to which applicants understand why and how selection tools are to be used, though this may require different levels of explanation and education across clusters, and where the core values of selection differ (as in the example above), it may be exceptionally difficult to gain widespread acceptance of a culturally incongruent selection system.

Thus, we suggest that the culture clusters can provide some guidance about the extent to which a given selection system and philosophy will be applicable and accepted in a different cultural context. Again, it may be possible to impose a system in a culture under certain circumstances, but there is a wealth of research suggesting that when a hiring system is seen as unfair (regardless of the "objective" fairness of the system), there is a lower rate of acceptance of offers, the companies reputation can suffer, turnover tends to be higher, and, in some countries, there is a greater chance of legal action against the company (Landy and Conte 2004).

Mergers, Acquisitions, and Joint Ventures

One of the decisions that managers and executives may face is how to implement a decision to merge with or acquire another company, or to establish a joint venture. These are never easy tasks to accomplish, and they are made more difficult when they are multinational. Unfortunately, to date there is very little solid empirical research on the influence of culture on the success of these endeavors, and so at this point we move (somewhat cautiously) beyond the data to speculate about the applicability of existing research to these situations.

Our basic expectation is simple, and similar to what we proposed regarding human resource systems—we would expect that mergers, acquisitions, and joint ventures that occur between two companies within the same culture cluster will be more likely to succeed than those that cross cluster boundaries. As one of us writes from Detroit, Michigan, the example of this that most readily springs to mind is the merger between the German automaker Daimler-Benz and the U.S. automaker Chrysler to form Daimler-Chrysler—a merger that has been far less successful than any of the involved parties might have hoped. (Indeed, major Chrysler shareholders have taken the whole matter to court, arguing that it was not a merger at all, but rather a takeover by Daimler-Benz.) Many reports during the early months of the merger and still today report on vast cultural difficulties that the two companies faced when attempting to integrate, including problems that should have been foreseeable such as radically different salary structures for executives and differing norms for vacation and time off. Underlying these difficulties, at core, are different values related to how work is done and what work means, and different expectations for what leadership is and how the leadership task is carried out.

This is not to suggest that within-cluster interactions are going to be without difficulty. Clearly, even within-country mergers, acquisitions, and joint ventures often fail. We would simply argue that the odds of success are higher when engaging with other organizations within the same cluster, because the patterns of work-related values are more likely to be reconcilable. When disputes do arise, they may reflect differences in the expected practices and behaviors, rather than radical differences in the core values, and conflict arising from differences in practices that reflect the same value may be more easily resolved than conflict reflecting differences in fundamental beliefs and values.

CONCLUSION

The primary lesson for managers and executives that we want to impart is that culture does matter for leaders, and that it matters in different ways in different places. Second, the information provided by cross-cultural leadership research can provide some useful guidance in the face of cultural uncertainty. Clearly, culture is not the only thing that matters—information about products and markets and talent pool and local business law and regulation and a host of other issues also come into play. But by knowing something about the values and practices that tend to characterize a society, and about the leadership styles and attributes that are seen as desirable and effective in a society, a manager or executive will clearly have a better likelihood of making good decisions than if that information is missing. An understanding of the dimensions that have been identified in extensive leadership research and where various societies fall on those dimensions, will provide leaders with at least a starting point for making sense of unexpected difficulties that arise when working across cultural boundaries, and for preventing those difficulties from arising in the first place.

NOTE

1. Except where otherwise noted, descriptions of findings from the GLOBE Project come from House et al. (2004) and Den Hartog et al. (1999).

REFERENCES

Aditya, R., and R.J. House. (2002). "Interpersonal Acumen and Leadership Across Cultures: Pointers from the GLOBE Study." In *Multiple Intelligences and Leadership*, ed. R.E. Riggio and S.E. Murphy, 215–240. Mahwah, NJ: Lawrence Erlbaum.

Aditya, R.N., R.J. House, and S. Kerr. (2000). "Theory and Practice of Leadership: Into the New Millennium." In *Industrial and Organizational Psychology: Linking Theory and Practice*, ed. C.L. Cooper and E.A. Locke, 130–164. New York: Blackwell.

Adsit, D.J., M. London, S. Crom, and D. Jones. (1997). "Cross-cultural Differences in Upward Ratings in a Multinational Company." *International Journal of Human Resource Management* 8: 385–401.

Den Hartog, D.N., and M.W. Dickson. (2004). "Leadership and Culture." In *The Nature of Leadership*," ed. J. Antonakis, A.T. Cianciolo, and R.J. Sternberg, 249–278. Thousand Oaks, CA: Sage.

Den Hartog, D.N., R.J. House, P.J. Hanges, S.A. Ruiz-Quintanilla, P.W. Dorfman, and GLOBE Associates. (1999). "Culture Specific and Cross-culturally Generalizable Implicit Leadership Theories: Are Attributes of Charismatic/transformational Leadership Universally Endorsed?" *Leadership Quarterly Special Issue: Charismatic and Transformational Leadership: Taking Stock of the Present and Future (Part I)* 10 (2): 219–256.

Earley, P.C., and C.B. Gibson. (2002). *Multinational Work Teams: A New Perspective.* Mahwah, NJ: Lawrence Erlbaum.

Eylon, D., and K.Y. Au. (1999). "Exploring Empowerment Cross-cultural Differences along the Power Distance Dimension." *International Journal of Intercultural Relations* 23 (3): 373–385.

Fu, P.P., and G. Yukl. (2000). "Perceived Effectiveness of Influence Tactics in the United States and China." *Leadership Quarterly* 11 (2): 251–266.

Hanges, P.J., M.W. Dickson, and V. Gupta. (2002). "Managerial Implications of Cultural Clusters: Generalizations from Project GLOBE." Paper presented at the combined CHRM/CIBER conference The Role of Cross-national Research in International HRM: Theory Development and Global Application in Chicago, September 19–20.

Hofstede, G. (1980). *Culture's Consequences: International Differences in Work-related Values.* Abridged ed. Newbury Park, CA: Sage.

———. (2001). *Culture's Consequences: Comparing Values, Behaviors, Institutions, and Organizations across Nations.* 2d ed. Newbury Park, CA: Sage.

House, R.J., P.J. Hanges, M. Javidan, P.W. Dorfman, and V. Gupta, eds. (2004). *Leadership, Culture, and Organizations: The GLOBE Study of 62 Societies.* Thousand Oaks, CA: Sage.

Inglehart, R. (1997). *Modernization and Postmodernization: Cultural, Economic and Political Change in 43 Societies.* Princeton, NJ: Princeton University Press.

Jung, D.I., B.M. Bass, and J.J. Sosik. (1995). "Bridging Leadership and Culture: A Theoretical Consideration of Transformational Leadership and Collectivistic Cultures." *Journal of Leadership Studies* 2: 3–18.

Landy, F.J., and J.M. Conte. (2004). *Work in the 21st Century: An Introduction to Industrial and Organizational Psychology.* Boston: McGraw-Hill.

Lewis, R.D. (2000). *When Cultures Collide: Managing Successfully Across Cultures.* London: Nicholas Brealey.

Martinez, S., and P.W. Dorfman. (1998). "The Mexican Entrepreneur: An Ethnographic Study of the Mexican Empressario." *International Studies of Management and Organizations* 28: 97–123.

Rauch, A., M. Frese, and S. Sonnentag. (2000). Cultural Differences in Planning/Success Relationships: A Comparison of Small Enterprises in Ireland, West Germany, and East Germany." *Journal of Small Business Management* 38: 28–41.

Ronen, S., and O. Shenkar. (1985). "Clustering Countries on Attitudinal Dimensions: A Review and Synthesis." *Academy of Management Review* 10: 435–454.

Rosnow, R.R., A.A. Skleder, M.A. Jaeger, and B. Rind. (1994). Intelligence and the Epistemics of Interpersonal Acumen: Testing Some Implications of Gardner's Theory. *Intelligence* 19: 93–116.

Smith, P.B., et al. (2002). "Cultural Values, Sources of Guidance, and Their Relevance to Managerial Behavior: A 47–Nation Study." *Journal of Cross-Cultural Psychology* 33 (2): 188–208.

Steiner, D.D., and S.W. Gilliland. (1996). "Fairness Reactions to Personnel Selection Techniques in France and the United States." *Journal of Applied Psychology* 81: 134–141.

Stewart, R., J.L. Barsoux, A. Kieser, H.D. Ganter, and P. Walgenbach. (1994). *Managing in Britain and Germany.* London: St. Martin's Press/Macmillan Press.

Triandis, H.C. (1995). *Individualism and Collectivism.* Boulder, CO: Westview Press.

Zhou, J. (2002). "Employee Creativity." Paper presented at the combined CHRM/CIBER conference The Role of Cross-national Research in International HRM: Theory Development and Global Application in Chicago, September 19–20.

CHAPTER 19

NEW RULES FOR A NEW CENTURY

Help for Management and Leadership in
This New Global Century

KENNETH L. MURRELL

At the end of the 1990s, many writers were attempting to forecast what good management practices might look like in the coming century. Now that we are fully into that new century it is clear that few, if any, of us could have predicted the dramatic events of this new 100-year cycle. The collapse of the high-tech market, the horrible events of September 11, 2001, with the wide array of violent repercussions, including a war in Iraq and much more, rocked the world very deeply. The impact of this new century's birth trauma will be felt for many decades. So what is the effect on organizational life and what can be offered as both hope and advice? That is the special focus of this chapter.

In an earlier series of papers, the author looked at changes that both managers and workers should be aware of and where appropriate should support. The common theme was "Twenty-One Rules for a New Century." This chapter will take each of those new rules and examine the evidence so far experienced about how crucial each rule will be to this new century. In particular, the emphasis is on the hope and optimism that this new century should still be able to generate. Through the toughest of times the human spirit has been able to emerge, and the form of organizational life has been on a steady evolutionary path since humanity fully recognized how crucial organizations are to our very existence. This new century offers much to look forward to as well as much to be cautious about. The rules are being rewritten daily, but in observance of these "new" rules there exist many opportunities for organizations to continue to evolve and develop. These new rules have challenged our past assumptions, and now is the time to see how we can best respond to each of them as managers and leaders of organizations.

In particular, those who can more clearly see the new conditions are those who can best help lead their organizations in this new era of human needs. Organizations driven by profit, service organizations of all types, and the still very important public sector organizations are all experiencing significant and severely disruptive changes. These new organizational realities reflect why humanity must continue to develop and learn to work together far more effectively. In learning to do this an organizational legacy will be created for the next generation. That legacy of new thinking and the creation of organizations that have learned to follow these new rules will create not just better organizations that can respond more effectively to today's environment, but, equally important, they will create templates for developing more ideal models of organizations and work communities that the next generation will inherit.

THE TWENTY-ONE RULES FOR FUTURE ORGANIZATIONS AND EMPLOYEES

The original rules are followed by italicized comments on what the situation is now in the midst of this new century.

Rule 1. Improve Quality and Lower Costs—*Yes, and Do It Even Faster!*

As the mantra of business today and for the past decade the globally competitive world promises no organization long-term survival unless it can continue to meet what was once an impossible standard. Our international high-tech firms are some of the best examples of organizations forcing this new reality onto everyone, and the pressure is only building. Who can deny that it is possible to buy a better and faster computer system each month at a lower and lower cost? Even the automobile industry is backing off annual price increases, and, without a doubt, in most cases, the quality of its products is also improving. So, naturally, the managers and leaders of the future must also be able to live up to these expectations. This creates two demands.

One demand is that every leader and manager must continue to learn. This could be called the *professional development imperative.* The second and equally important demand is that individuals have the ability to manage the stress and pressure this puts on them (Rule 18 will also touch on this later). Required of the new leader, and, as I point out later this means every person in the organization, will be a sense of professional responsibility in order to take utmost advantage of all the development opportunities possible, if necessary, even on one's own time and at one's own expense.

In a near zero inflationary period, particularly given the global source of labor, the pressure is on productivity—*yours.* Every day, concern about how to do more and do it better is expected. Rather than let this be a demoralizing demand, the leader can help reframe it as a way to live, a philosophy of learning something new each day in order to continually improve. This reinforces the need to help find the kind of workforce that truly cares about the work requirements of one's organization. If an individual cannot do this, then this improvement expectation is often perceived as too great an external demand and stressor. For those who care about their work deeply, the daily improvement in doing it can be satisfying. Helping others to carefully choose their careers takes on added importance when a leader recognizes that his or her organization cannot survive doing demanding work unless sufficient intrinsic satisfaction is involved.

Rule 2. Return Customer and Product to Center Stage—*and Keep Them There!*

Organizations have always been very dependent on both customer and product, but for many years following the last world war, the U.S. economy, in particular, was fortunate to have a very large market with much pent-up demand and very few global competitors. Two to three decades ago that began to change dramatically as both Japan and Germany began taking market share in many major industries. That change became the wake-up call to many organizations, and a return to customer and product concern led to renewed American competitiveness. The future presents a golden opportunity for organizations that are close to the customer and able to continually improve production processes. New leaders must understand this, and, in order to prosper, they must be able to offer goods and services directly to the customer as well as be knowledgeable about and integrated into the production process. All staff and most management positions are at risk during this restructuring period. The career tracks that can respond to Rule 1, by offering more for less, and that meet the requirements of Rule 2, by being close to the action, are those most needed in this new economy. Both represent a call to a new standard of service to the customer.

The future offers no guarantee that leadership roles will be the highest paying positions or even those with the most status, but, clearly this is where the needs are and will be for a long time. In leadership development it is apparent that continuous improvement is essential and that without organizational dedication to expanded horizontal and vertical leadership, organizations are at serious risk.

Rule 3. Organizational Power Is Created, Not Shared—*Everywhere!*

No matter how many times managers or leaders say they want to share power, one should be careful not to assume they really want to give up the one resource they will always bemoan not having enough of. Everyone in the organization who is trying to do a job wants more power, and there is nothing inherently wrong in that unless one assumes that power is a zero-sum game. In organizational life it is possible to increase levels of influence, that is, to have more power, by working together to achieve common goals rather than competing to direct others' actions. This is called "cooperation" and it is vital to the success of the larger organization. Power is not a zero-sum game in principle. We have learned to think of it that way only because so much of what we pay attention to is limited in nature. True, we cannot all be paid mega bucks, but if we share an increasingly larger pie, as at Microsoft, for example, many of us could retire as independently wealthy before we reach fifty. It is also possible to have a group of employees who are all above average and who help one another and themselves to improve each day, and this often accounts for the success of firms like Intel. Influence is infinite and so is power if it is used to respond to the world of needs and not just to battle over finite physical resources. Creativity is a natural gift and so are the productivity gains achieved through learning to work together. The role of employees is to demonstrate daily the laws of empowerment, where more is possible with less, and people learn to work better together. Managers in particular need help in this area because of the overly political world they often have to live in.

When productivity gains do occur, a test of the "empowerment principle," that is, of creating power or influence, has also occurred. The new employee may do well to keep teaching these lessons to those too far away from the real work to know that this is how progress is made. Too often, managers are frightened by true empowerment because they have less experience in working with others cooperatively, but, with experience, they can learn that not everything happening in the organization is a political struggle over limited resources.

Rule 4. Progress Is Subjective, Quality Is Not—*Sustainability Is Built from Quality!*

In a world of change, the very idea of progress is in a state of flux. The term "post-modern" reflects serious questions concerning what progress is all about and whether growth is always better. It is less debatable that each of us, as producers or consumers, knows and values what quality is. We all want the feel and sense of quality in what we do and what we buy, particularly if it is affordable. In this is the key to another expanded role for the leader and manager of tomorrow. The future will require more candid and timely feedback about the nature of work and the products produced in the organizations we are a part of. Our voices as employees and central stakeholders in the future of the firm require us not to hold back but to share our views. In fact we may have to take a much stronger stand in arguing for quality and to build higher expectations of what we can produce in order to assure that we have careers in the future. The role of whistle-blower and corporate conscience will be expanded, and smart companies will build in more protections for those who disagree with current actions that threaten future viability of the firm. As corporate loyalty wanes and fear of job loss increases, it will be necessary to structure in rewards and training to prevent employees from allowing shoddy products or inferior service to be maintained. It is in the best interests of all to help develop quality, and to a greater extent than even some managers or fickle stockholders will propose. Career success depends greatly on an organization's long-term success. Unless the commitment is made to help build long-term quality, the organization will not survive.

Rule 5. Global Thinking Really Leads Local Action—*And Any Thinking Less Than Global Thinking Is Dangerous!*

As organizations become increasingly global, it is necessary for everyone within the organization to pay attention to a larger world. If for no other reason than to better know their competitors every person should be aware of who out there represents benchmarks in the development of world standards of work in their field. This is being done around the world as other societies look to the United States as a model. We also have a lot to learn and should be equally concerned about how quality work is performed around the world. Technological breakthroughs make the competition far closer than it has ever been. The amount of offshore electronically assisted work and ease of travel have created a very different world than existed even just a decade ago. The movement of labor across country frontiers is a quickly emerging trend. Now is the time to learn about worldwide labor conditions while we still have the natural advantage of a well-trained labor force. That advantage is not predicted to last much longer, so tomorrow it may be too late to learn how and with whom to compete. It is equally important it to know with whom to partner and to ally as well as with whom to compete. Currently jobs such as call center staffing and technical assistance are flowing to India. Instead of competing with India for these entry-level jobs, it may be more appropriate to look at partnering with them in terms of sharing knowledge and systems so that both parties benefit. In short, it is crucial that we train our graduates to offer much more than just technical services. One of the areas where they can increase their skills is by learning to work effectively across cultures and thus be able to assist in developing effective partnerships to compete with others who cannot work across cultures as well.

The other part of this new rule is that if one is a highly trained professional there may be a large market for one's skills outside the United States. Selling one's knowledge and expertise overseas may be a very good way of learning more about world class expectations, and it may also provide options if the local market goes into a slump. If a company gains by exporting, professionals may also test the world value of what they have to offer.

Rule 6. Continuous Quality Improvement Seeds Global Development— *Which Is Necessary for a Long-term Existence!*

To go beyond where we are is a natural human quest and a path of development for both an organization and the society of which it is a part. For everyone in the organization this is a journey that can help make meaning out of each day's toil and effort. The commitment to quality and its continuous improvement is the definition of the principle of *kaizen* as developed by the Japanese following their defeat in World War II. The desire to rebuild their society and never again to suffer through a devastating war keeps them focused and driven as a nation. That same kind of development drive is inherent in all societies, and, when organized and used well, it not only changes that single society, it changes the world.

To be a part of that grander vision and to play even a small role in that transformation has kept many people growing and expanding in professional potential. This is the vital energy or spirit that makes it worthwhile to commit to an organization for a major part of one's week and eventually a large part of one's life. As the leaders and managers of tomorrow commit to that effort, to help organizations transform themselves, the end result will be a changed world. Organizations are vital actors in determining the state of the world in many ways well beyond just economic impact. Their family and local community are where the value of that commitment is most likely to show. Far more important than the politicians and chief executive officers (CEOs) of the world, it is this daily work of so many millions, and globally billions, of people that keeps the world going. Each person's special effort is necessary to support the whole, and only as each person reaches for the highest quality possible will the future prosperity and development of the planet be assured. This may seem like a heavy burden for each of us, but it has always been the case that the world survives only from the effort of the many and not the glory of a few. This reality is not what sells newspapers but as one travels around the world the one common experience is that this is a world full of basically good people getting up each day to take care of their families and to do their jobs. The world moves forward based on the positive involvement of the many and not the symbols or images of the few.

The best efforts of today's leaders and managers are vitally needed to answer the question of what they need to know about this process and how it will help us better prepare for a place in this new century. The improvement of the whole will come only from the efforts of the many, and the leader and manager's role needs to be seen more clearly for what it represents. Leaders and managers should take the time to honor and respect their own efforts and contributions and do likewise for all the other individuals they come in contact with. Leaders and managers must appreciate what they have offered and what they can continue to offer as they grow and develop in their jobs. This continuous process of improvement should be viewed as a blessing as it represents the potential for the evolution of our very fragile species. Leaders and managers should enjoy and appreciate each small step in that direction of development and schedule time to celebrate the contribution they and their organizations are making.

Rule 7. Short-term Thinking Destroys Quality and Delays Development— *Moving Faster Today Is Not the Only Answer!*

If we allow ourselves to get caught by the short-term disease of modern management, nonthinking, then the idea of sustainable organization is out of the question. Not only that but the chance of ever reaching the performance levels desired will be eliminated in all but the shortest of measures. Again, management has a difficult role to play in a position where much needed information is lacking. Management and executive reward systems also force much of this short-term thinking and it is more than Wall Street that is at fault. It is necessary for the employee of the future to know enough about business or the economic environment of the organization to be able to express the concerns required to reflect a longer-term view of the organization. Saturn Motors as well as other progressive organizations today insist on their workforces having an education that in many ways resembles that of those studying for a masters in business administration. These companies want employees to have a bigger picture not only so that they better understand the larger world, but also so that managers have a better view of the worlds in which they work. The only way to break down the walls between managers and workers is to help them to understand each others' language. Leaders in this new age will move naturally toward doing this, and it will often mean the difference between success and failure for their organization.

Everyone must better articulate and support the values of a longer-term perspective when it comes to business and other decisions. In the past this would have been frowned upon by many under the assumption that the workers could not possibly know enough to have a voice in determining how an organization should be run. Today that attitude is sadly outdated and the emergence of "open book" management methods, whereby all corporate data are shared, and the modern communication revolution, which makes that so much more feasible, is dramatically changing employees' expectations. As this occurs, leadership is being redefined as stewardship and service leadership—trends that will be with us for the rest of this new century.

Rule 8. Appreciation Precedes Problem Identification—*Problems Do Exist but What Works Best Is to Go Well Beyond the "Fixed" State!*

To find reasons to go to work creates a very different experience than to spend hours trying to justify calling in sick. It is not that there are no good reasons to stay away from work, it is just that the attitude you bring to work, more than anything else, will affect the kind of work experiences you have. Finding and valuing the intrinsic rewards and challenges of your work life will give you and those around you a much healthier outlook and create a reality in which you can find value. Based on the principle of first looking for the strength to be able to address limits and problems, a whole field of organizational change has emerged. This field, called "appreciative inquiry," or AI, has been practiced by numerous organizations with similar results. People are able to become excited again about why they wanted to work in the first place. The meaning of daily commitment to an organization has been rediscovered and from this has come the ability to help change situations. Responses to problem issues are not grounded in denial but instead emerge out of an appreciation of what in the organization is worthy of care and concern. People become much more able to work together and the spirit of cooperation increases when the blaming behavior of a problem-oriented attack is reduced.

For all of us the experience of working from strengths is much more affirming and empowering. It is not to deny problems and limits but to approach them from a position of hope and optimism rather than cynicism or despair. It is one of the hallmarks of being able to work well with others in difficult and demanding times. For the next century these traits will be essential in career development as they have proved to be in organization development.

Rule 9. Component Optimization May Destroy System Optimization—*Yes, the Parts Do Have to Work Together and Relational Infrastructure Is the New Answer!*

A most important lesson for the new century is that it is not always the star of the game who helps the team to win. While team effort is the expected norm for next-century organizations, this in no way diminishes the importance of the individual. The issue is context, and the rule is that it is impossible to compete effectively to reach world class performance levels if the actions of one detract from the success of the whole. The game is much more complicated than any sports analogy can express, and even the notion of war, where strategy and tactics were born, is thought of as more static and slower to adjust to world changes than business. The new realities demand change at all levels, and optimizing one part of an organization does not necessarily imply high performance of the whole. Employees must be able to recognize the organization as a larger team that extends beyond their own operational team. Organizations are very complex, and in order for a single employee or part of a team to add value it is often very important for them to understand the larger picture.

The emerging concept of relationships that form the most effective infrastructure for work organizations is being tested and improved every day. This is the heart and soul of what has been called "communities of practice and knowledge management." Relationships are what make these concepts come alive and help the organization perform at the level of world class competition. This also incorporates the notion of a continually learning organization since there is no indication at all that either the pace or the complexity of the global economy will decrease. An effective leader or manager must understand basic systems theory and the role of the parts in relationship to the whole of an organization. This is not an overly complicated concept, but it does take an ability to look well beyond one's individual role and to develop the whole system as a part of the relational structure and understand all of its elements.

Rule 10. Flatter Organization Design Can Enhance Power—*But It Is Also About How This Design Is Created That Is Important!*

As every good manager is learning, the key to twenty-first century high performance is empowerment and the delayering of organizations. What they may not know as well is that this can create power in the sense that the overall organization can be much more effective only when managers and employees both become more powerful. The new century demands enhanced power not distributed power; in other words, it is about creating influence not passing it around. The win-win of empowerment is as important for the workforce to teach management as vice versa. Both groups must be able to learn these lessons and to build on them for the success of the whole. For the employee the goal is to find the type of organization and corporate culture that allows them as well as their managers to be successful. In both cases, the organization builds success, and leaders must know how to make this happen and to recruit only those who can naturally understand the importance of this.

The key to success in this setting is not working up the proverbial chain of command but instead creating the commands, as in work teams, throughout the organization, which provides challenges and opportunities for career development via the route of high performance. Being part of a world-class team and doing the job as well as it is done anywhere in the world is the only source of security, outside of inheriting great wealth. It is an advantage to be able to deliver high performance, because in that arena it is a seller's market, and your success in one organization can easily lead to success in another if necessary. Your mobility and economic security are tied directly to your levels of performance in your current job. Doing well and building a world-class reputation along with having an ability to work with equally talented others will provide options. In the new economic reality there are no guarantees of lifelong employment but there are a variety of opportunities to develop skills and abilities. This attracts the best employees today and there is no reason to expect this to change in the future. Learn to go after the jobs in flattened structures with assured development opportunities. Create the career power that comes from ability and marketable skills. Consider all that you do carefully from this perspective and help your own children to learn this because it is a new world in which the old assumptions of the industrial paradigm no longer hold up. Your success depends directly on what you can do and how well you can do it working with others. Today those work relationships will be with peers and colleagues, and your experiences of joint success will be the factors that keep you employed and help you succeed.

Rule 11. Organizational Development Is Moving Horizontally and Bottom Up—*Making Change Leaders of Us All!*

The idea that everyone in the future will be far more responsible not only for the structure of an organization but also for encouraging everyone to be involved in setting its culture may sound a little far out for many today. However, the trend line is definitely in this direction and efforts to get all employees involved in the change process are occurring on many different fronts. Large-scale change efforts are being designed today under the labels of "Future Search Conference Design," "Real Time Strategic Change," and "Participatory Democracy," to name a few. Each of these change efforts is as concerned with moving the change process out and down as it is with getting top-level buy-in.

The goal is to mobilize employees in the change effort, and few things more positively impact one's career than a period of time serving a leadership role in one of these change programs. Underlying each of these models of change is an assumption of collaborative work skills and employees with a sense of the potential for positive change in the organization.

The employee of the next century should not only be open to change but even more so be able to help lead it. This is a fairly radical departure from the old notion of the employee as a set of hands. The emphasis now and increasingly in the future will be on the employee as a total person with leadership skills never before so in demand or so expected. The employees able to meet this challenge will be seen as very valuable to an organization that knows it must either change or risk its very survival. Every leader and manager would do well to learn these change skills and develop attitudes that are known to be helpful in developing change programs. There are numerous books and articles available on the subject as well as good training and educational opportunities all over the United States, but the decision to prepare for this dramatically different set of responsibilities lies with you. It can make a significant difference in one's career if one is able to lead change instead of just waiting to be changed, or even worse, out of ignorance, being positioned primarily to resist change.

Rule 12. Ambiguity Is a Catalyst for Development—*If It Is Such an Uncertain World, Why Do We Manage as if It Is Not?*

Many of the new roles for the leader and manager of the future are unknown at this point or at most are only being guessed at. This does not mean that one should sit around confused or wait to be told what to do in specific terms to prepare for tomorrow. One of the first things any professional has to learn is how to deal with increasing degrees of ambiguity and uncertainty, and that demand is now being placed on every one of us. The world is changing so fast that rules and roles are also undergoing constant change. This means that employees often have to be able to create their own best estimates of what is needed and how to go about getting it with the help of many others. In ambiguity two things are confused, the goals and the means to achieve them. Professional workers of the future must at least know why they are working, what their own goals are, and how to develop the skills (means) to accomplish their goals. This starts the process of clarifying ambiguity and thus helping the organization. This process starts with every individual, no matter where they are in the organization. It moves out from the individual to the team and to the total organization as questions are asked and leadership emerges to help guide the discussion of why and how people are supposed to work in this particular organization.

Ambiguity is thus not allowed to detract from the organization's ability to perform. Achieving that state of clarity is absolutely dependent upon individual employees knowing why they are working (goal), and how to continually develop their skills to help both themselves and their organization. In this way and using a process that forces everyone to answer these two essential questions, the threat of not acting in an ambiguous situation is reduced and the organization is able to move forward while checking its assumptions for success. That is why the questions raised are useful catalysts in determining both the vision and mission of the organization. As a valued member of the organization of the future it will demand that you be a leader of the organization and its change process no matter what other roles you also have.

Rule 13. Conflict and Diversity Are Natural Assets—*And in This Era of a New Global War We Had Better Learn How to Do Better with What Is Necessary for Our Survival!*

The idea that conflict can be an asset is not always easy to relate to, but for the organization of tomorrow it is a very important concept. In any organization, and in high-performance systems in particular, there are many natural disagreements. Employees with strong views are essential to organizations if their views are based on experience and knowledge. When inevitable differences emerge, it is critical that employees of the future not back away or give up their responsibility but instead present their views and different perspectives clearly. Conflicts over ideas and strategies are potential positive factors when leaders and employees are skilled at conflict management and dispute resolution. Creativity and new approaches come from differences if handled maturely, and, if not, better ideas may fail to be developed. Conflict in this case is not about personalities or petty politics but about substantive issues and important differences in the competing answers. Very often the final best answer is yet to be discovered and it cannot be found if all ideas and thoughts are not put on the table. This requires all those involved to be able to carefully articulate and explain their own or their team's thinking and to be persuasive in helping the organization to make the best decision. This valuable skill can enhance one's career if conflict skills are developed and practiced at the right time in the right way.

This potential for conflict and the development of creativity are assisted by the natural diversity that exists in any growing organization. In particular, the issue of cultural diversity is very important. Some argue that one of society's most important assets is its abundant diversity. Diversity is what gives us a multitude of options about how to see and how to act in ways that the world values. Taking differences as challenges to create better options, or what might be called third ways, is a very important asset of skill sets for the future. The leader and manager of the future must be comfortable with differences not only in age, gender, race, and ethnicity but also in political outlooks and spiritual practices. Beyond comfort with diversity, we all need to learn how to thrive and be creative in a multicultural and richly diverse world. In this setting where much can be achieved, there should be no incentives to take the easy route. Instead professional integrity should help each of us to work with others to develop better approaches and ways of meeting new-world challenges. The advantage of practicing these new skills is that they are exactly the ones required by the new global realities. There is great demand for those able to work with others who are very different from themselves but who care deeply about the organization and its potential. This potential is reached when a better way is forged out of many different ways through long and intense involvement and open sharing of views. In a word, trust across barriers must be developed by those who are confident in themselves and who have the ability to reach out to others for their mutual benefit and service to a greater cause.

Rule 14. Working Smarter Is Much Smarter—*And Equally Important Is Working with Heart as Well as Head!*

The old paradigm taught each of us to work hard and to do an honest day's work for an honest day's pay. That lesson was likely drilled into our heads every day as we grew up. We heard it from parents, teachers, media, and nearly everywhere we turned. We were told this as a sacred fact, and because the same message was given to the generation before and the generation before that many of us learned the lesson well. We internalized it and most likely are trying to instill the same message in the next generation.

But the truth is that this is only half the lesson we need for ourselves and to teach the next generation. Now we all must learn to work smarter as well. Now the operational slogan is to work smart and be more productive each day. The more productive we can become, often the more the pay, and quite often the more job satisfaction. This can occur as we learn to work not only hard but also much, much smarter.

New ways of working or working less through efficiencies that improve output are what is important. It is no longer good enough to give a good honest effort. It is now critical to find ways to work better and to stop doing it if it does not add value. Efforts that demonstrate thought, and not just repeated hard work, will be rewarded more and more. In fact the ultimate reward for many is to take their good ideas and mental contributions to someone else, or to set up a new organization that has the capacity to work smarter and not just harder. Entrepreneurship is where many of the work-smarter proponents are going—and going fast—in many industries where the barriers to entry are low. The old barriers of huge capital costs for plants and equipment are falling fast and the personal computer revolution, combined with the Internet, makes much more possible. The work-smarter professional is finding out that it is not necessary to remain employed in a company that is stuck in the age of work-hard-only thinking, or, more accurately, where there is a shortage of thinking. If one wants a good job then the skills necessary involve bringing to the organization both a work ethic and an ability to improve the organization. This is sometimes accomplished by emphasizing that performance quality is valued more than the quantity of work that is done.

Rule 15. Training/Education Is the Prime Infrastructure—*Every Successful Change Process Is Built from a Knowledge and Skill Base Built in from Day One!*

To teach managers the importance of continuous organizational learning is easier than to convince them of the need to see training as investing rather than spending the corporation's limited resources. The new leader/manager needs to be able to help the organization see the importance of training as an investment in the company's capacity to learn. This can be done in several ways, including documenting the cost savings and new ideas that come from training as well as making special efforts to demonstrate the values of cross training and shared training experiences. Employees of the future must also be able to see themselves as decision makers in terms of how to invest their own limited resources in continuous learning. Lifelong learning is much more than a saying, it is a philosophy and a way of staying ahead and employable in a rapidly changing world. Employees need to be able to contract and negotiate with their organization for the investments necessary to their development, or look elsewhere for the kind of environment where they are seen as worth investing in. Good leaders will make this happen. In the next century this will become even more critical as the terms of employment shift from long-term security to enhanced opportunity. Given opportunities, the new employees must have the skills and abilities for success of the organization as well as their own career success.

It is very important to view education and training as long-term skill building rather than shorter-term credentialing, as it is too often seen. Everyone in the future will be expected to have the skills and experiences necessary, and, yet, without help from the organization, this is not always possible. So in addition to becoming better learners, the new reality also requires us all to be better negotiators. This requires very different skills than the previous generation of employees had, as they could wait for a benevolent company or training office to figure out what they needed. Tomorrow's companies are not likely to act out of any motive that is not bottom-line oriented. Because it is very possible that the training office may have been replaced or outsourced, it is everyone's job to determine what they need and how to go about getting company support for it. And if company support is not there, employees of the future will ask whether they should go for the training anyway or look for another organization that values the learning process. Waiting to be told how one should develop is not an option for the employee of the future. Everyone must be proactive, educated about the options, and determined to get what they need, when they need it. Professional development should, of course, be supported by the company but cannot be relied upon. The risk to your own career development is too great to wait for some well-meaning person or office to finally recognize what you should have been able to see all along. You, like everyone else, and that includes those who would like to have your job, need continual learning and development. It is the investment in you that will pay off for years to come—learn to make it happen in one way or the other. In this there is no other choice.

Rule 16. Strong Individuals Build Strong Teams—*And Only When Strong Teams Help to Build and Work Well with Other Strong Teams Do Organizations Gain!*

In this rule it is important to understand that you need *not* give up your own unique talents and abilities to be part of a high-performing team. In fact, it is just the opposite. High-performance teams are never created by weak individuals. Nor are they created by those who hold back just to fit in. Equally true is that no team can perform well if it is not able to get the best from each individual. Each of us must learn these rules not just from theory books but from the experience of working on high-performance teams. This team experience can come from anywhere—sports or other outside team activities are two good possibilities—but each person needs the experience of success while part of a strong team. In this way it is possible to learn how much stronger one can be as part of a team of other strong and capable people. Many professional athletes understand this well and will even go so far as only to compete with other strong teams in order to keep improving their own personal skills and strengths.

Teamwork requires skills in addition to what you have as an individual but it should not require you to limit or sacrifice your talents and abilities. Team success takes much more from you in that you have to able to see the larger picture. This is very similar to many of the rules that expect everyone to accept additional, new responsibilities in the future. You will be expected not only to learn from others but also to help create shared leadership systems where everyone brings all their talents and abilities to the game. In the increasingly competitive world, our potential comparative advantage lies in two areas. First, as discussed in Rule 13, diversity is a unique strength that we in North America are blessed with in abundance. Second, when we work together as a team that brings out all of the unique strengths this diversity offers, we can put together organizations that are able to outperform any in the world. With these advantages, strong individuals will be able to offer their talents along with a team of capable others to create exciting careers in areas where we will be able to maintain a leadership role in a very competitive world.

Rule 17. Managers Are Not Necessary for Success but Management Is—
Management and Leadership in Every Part of the Organization Is the Only Answer!

One of the most difficult rules for management to accept is that their jobs are important but their titles are meaningless. Even worse is the assumption that employees cannot do this work, which is very wrong and often causes economic disaster. Increasingly, management is not about titles or special privileges for a few, but about shared leadership roles of the many. Layers of managers are not necessary when everyone is clear about how important the jobs are. This means that the new-century employee had better be able to step up to the responsibilities previously reserved for supervisors and managers and to manage in a team environment with others. New-century managers and leaders will by necessity be dedicated to helping this happen. If not, they will put the sustainability of the organization at severe risk.

Working in this way without a lot of close supervision is just one more example of the professionalization of all workers. Spending money for one group of people simply to look over, that is, supervise, another group of people is a serious waste of limited resources. The economics of this old industrial-management model paradigm is not working today and will be even more obsolete tomorrow. Organizations cannot afford two salaries for the work of one person. Self-management principles, after more than thirty years of being promoted as a more humane way of managing, are now also being accepted as good economic principles as well.

What this tells the new employee is to get an education in the basics of management and to help develop the kind of organization that will be able to succeed globally by relying on more multitalented and more self-managing employees. This does not mean that there will be no more managers but that their roles will continue to change dramatically, as the partnerships between managers and workers in developing the organization continue to grow. Managers should become allies and act as the coaches and resources needed to help develop the organization's capabilities. But the job now requires more partnering skills on the part of both management and the new employee. Self-management does not mean autonomy but instead an even greater ability to work with others. Those new employees able to learn this will be the ones with options and potential careers in organizations that are more likely to succeed in the future. This new reality plus the constant demand for better leadership is the only job security anyone can have.

Rule 18. Spiritual and Family Support Are Essential for High
Performance—*What Gives Life or Provides Spirit in Work Is More Than Any One Simple Bottom Line!*

Given all the new pressures on the employee and all the changes expected to be made, the need for considerable support is undeniable. Research on change tell us that change is managed better by organizations that have strong support systems. These are places and things in one's life that offer care, understanding, and help in formulating ways to adapt to high levels of stress. These are most often found in two places: home, that is, in family, and in a person's own unique spiritual practices and beliefs. In parts of the world where stress levels are the highest it has been noted that those who are most resilient and often most successful in getting jobs done are those who have these two support systems firmly developed. In organizations that seek high performance outcomes the notion of community often plays a very important role in stress management and in helping everyone deal with the tremendous changes they are engaged in.

All of us must learn not only to select organizations well in terms of this supportive community environment but also to be responsible for building our own personal support systems in ways that work best. All of this, again, places the responsibility on everyone to help develop the organization into a culture of high performance that also serves as a supportive community to enhance stress management. The need for new skills for the new manager and employee places a great deal of pressure on both, and for this reason a strong support base is essential. As with the issue of professional development, the new world of work will expect all of us to take advantage of corporate resources to help develop ourselves as well as to do what is necessary on our own in order to build our career foundation and stress management program. Both in the family and in the spiritual domain, issues of privacy are to be protected but the sharing of these values with others in one's work community, as long as it is not coerced, seems to be a natural and useful activity. The new organization places many demands on everyone, and each of us deserves the support necessary to help the organization achieve. Much of that support must be built, and, if it is not, the new demands can create pressures beyond our coping skills. If this occurs, all the other systems will fail. Then, what might in the past have seemed a private issue of family and spiritual support is now a priority concern that should be given due attention. In organizations of the future it will be expected that everyone is given help in building the support system needed for long-term performance as well as professional growth.

Rule 19. Leadership Is Learning Focused but Responsibility Is Built—
Building This Is One of the Biggest Areas of Demand and Only a Most Limited Skill Set Is Available!

No matter where you work in the organization, one of your most important jobs is to learn. This is as true for the senior executive as it is for the newest employee. And in this learning principle is also a new rule for management, namely, that it needs to learn how to develop leadership throughout the organization. If this is done, the organization will be strengthened for the globally competitive next century.

What this tells the organization to prepare for has been repeated in several earlier rules but this one emphasizes building the leadership skills that work best at the collegial or peer level, where influence often comes without formal authority. Several good and very popular books have been written on this subject, which is one of those obvious trends in management that we need to learn much more about. Now employees have the opportunity to start developing their leadership skills and taking on more and more responsibility. In this way they stand a good chance of setting themselves up as role models for others to emulate. Corporations wanting to practice this rule will be looking for employees who can operate in this manner and with whom they can create their shared leadership models. The demands of this rule are many, but it can work if it helps to create a sense of responsibility in everyone, motivating them to offer their own leadership capabilities and not to overly rely on just a few leaders in the organization. To learn how to do this effectively is a tremendous challenge to the organization and will require strong leadership at all levels.

Rule 20. Transformational Leadership May Be Invisible but the Results Are Not—*And Transformation Begins with the Person but Only in the Right Environment, Created for It to Flourish, Will It Last!*

The chances of successful development of organizations of the new century will be directly related to whether those working in them see the organizations' success as absolutely critical for success in their own careers. The employees of the future will seek a successful organization, and that is one where its leadership speaks in terms of results and not one that has just a good public relations department. As recent research indicates, the charismatic and heroic leadership examples are not what explains the success and staying power of what are called visionary companies. Those companies that have been the most successful over a long period of time have leadership that has evolved internally and built a core ideology in which everyone in the organization believes. In this new century, workplace top-level management is not seen as the reason for the firm's success but only as one part of a larger picture where dedication and skills at all levels are viewed as crucial. In this way, leadership is more diffuse and often far more shared than leadership represented by the model of a central figure of an all-powerful CEO or board chair. In these settings, everyone is encouraged to offer his or her best and to develop unique leadership talents to help form a long-term successful career, while making the maximum contribution to the organization.

Organizations that develop transformational leadership at all levels are developing the sustaining capacity to grow and develop over the long term and not just during the reign of a particularly charismatic executive. This offers the employee a special advantage in that the very skills demanded in these settings are going to be more and more sought after by other organizations in the future. Transforming leadership has the additional advantage of changing leaders as much as anyone else, and this helps to create lasting career strength. You stand to gain the most in terms of career development by working within organizations that make a commitment to help you also develop as a leader.

Rule 21. Interdependency Underlies the Transformation Process—*Yes, We Still Are in This Together, All of Us!*

As mentioned in the introduction, this final rule summarizes all the new skills and abilities everyone needs in the organizations of the new century. This means that all of us must be able to work with others in shared leadership roles to re-create the idea of what an organization is. In fact, a more accurate description for all of this is that the new employee must be able to work with others to create work communities. In these communities work will be achieved that everyone cares enough about to invest themselves in the process and to develop their professional talents as the organization evolves. Linkage with others and a culture of work that gives a person back the dignity and meaning of work will be rewards in themselves. The new employee will gain the pride of also being able to create with others something beyond just a job. In this way the nature of work itself will be transformed and the experience will be transforming not just to the individual employee but to all those who manage and lead in this model of what organizations must be to succeed.

It should be clear to everyone, as we move along in this startling new world of the twenty-first century, that there are some tremendous social problems that we must deal with more effectively. Our culture needs a transforming experience as it looks beyond the present and develops expectations for a better future. That future can be more easily developed by people with the transforming experiences that new organizations are capable of providing. The new employee model assumes the ability to change, to continue learning, and to be a part of the leadership process that makes transformation possible. The new century offers much in the way of opportunities and exciting challenges that go well beyond the narrow definition of a job. Good leaders and managers will still be in short supply but now the job will be viewed as even more important and not just the work of a few. The potential exists to work toward the improvement not only of the organization we choose to work within but also of the society we were born into or migrated to. Now we have a chance to help create what we feel is a much better world, not only in our work life but also in society at large.

SUMMARY AND CONCLUDING COMMENTS

Managers have been forewarned that many serious changes will have to occur if their organizations are to remain competitive. They also know there will be fewer managers designated by official title and their roles will be significantly different. For employees of the future the messages are similar, except there will be many more of them and their professional responsibilities will be greatly enlarged. Many books have been written for the new manager but only a few describe the new employees' roles. In order to correct this imbalance, this chapter has tried to focus on the roles of leaders and managers as well as on the role of the new employee. Some major points of concern are as follows:

- Doing more with less will be expected.
- Empowerment will be necessary and for everyone.
- Quality concerns will drive global competitiveness.
- Long-term development requires employee advocacy.
- Organization development and renewal needs everyone.

- Uncertainty, change, and diversity are the givens.
- Leadership and learning are what it is all about.

This summary list cannot reflect all twenty-one rules but the essence is there, especially in the last point about the importance of continual learning. The leadership/learning responsibility is the most important message of all. The organizations of the future, and in this society in particular, will be expected to have much greater leadership capacity throughout the system.

Employees will be expected to enlarge their professional responsibilities and even to take on leadership roles in organizational change. Their voices are needed if companies are to respond to their customers and to build toward long-term success. The empowerment of the workforce is not an option or something that can be mandated from above. Conditions and reward structures will have to change to reflect the needs of the future and not the paradigms of the past.

Organizations will survive only when they develop the strengths and abilities of all in the system and not just a few. And those are the organizations all of us should seek out. Before any employee can possibly succeed in this new century's work environment, he or she must develop the team and interpersonal skills to perform in a complex and fast-changing world. In this way, technical and other skills will have a chance to be used. The organizations of tomorrow will in many ways be expected to understand the larger picture and to aid and assist society and be more responsive to the changing environment. These in many ways are new roles for organizations and their leaders. The important lesson is not just to respond to these changes but to be very much aware that these new demands are only a few of what will be a very long list of growing responsibilities.

The key to success is captured in the above final point, keep learning, and, in particular, keep learning how to lead and assist in the continual change process. Technical competency is in many ways assumed to exist in each and every employee. The critical difference now is reflected in what else each of us can bring to the system and how he or she work can with others to see technical competence used well. Change is the name of the game in this increasingly global market place and no one predicts this will do anything but increase. As a successful employee or manager of the future, be prepared for the challenges you will be offered. In meeting them, there is also a good chance you will improve the quality of your work life and hence your life as a whole.

REFERENCES

Bellman, G.M. (1996). *Your Signature Path. Gaining New Perspectives on Life and Work.* San Francisco: Berrett-Koehler.

Cameron, K.S., J. Dutton, and R.E. Quinn, eds. (2003). *Positive Organizational Scholarship: Foundations of a New Discipline.* San Francisco: Berrett-Koehler.

Goleman, D., R. Boyatzis, and A. McKee. (2002). *Primal Leadership: Realizing the Power of Emotional Intelligence.* Boston: Harvard Business School Press.

Herman, S.M. (1994). *A Force of Ones. Reclaiming Individual Power in a Time of Teams, Work Groups, and Other Crowds.* San Francisco: Jossey-Bass.

James, J. (1996). *Thinking in the Future Tense. Leadership Skills for a New Age.* New York: Simon and Schuster.

Murrell, K.L. (1997). "Emergent Theories of Leadership for the Next Century. Towards Relational Concepts." *Organization Development Journal* 15 (Fall): 35–42.

Pinchot, G., and E. Pinchot. (1993). *The Intelligent Organization: Engaging the Talent & Initiative of Everyone in the Workplace.* San Francisco: Berrett-Koehler.

Quinn, R.E. (1996). *Deep Change. Discovering the Leader Within.* San Francisco: Jossey-Bass.

Seiling, J.G. (1997). *The Membership Organization. Achieving Top Performance Through the New Workplace Community.* Palo Alto: Davies-Black.

Stack, J., with B. Burlingham. (1992). *The Great Game of Business. Unlocking the Power and Profitability of Open-Book Management.* New York: Doubleday.

CHAPTER 20

RESTORING ETHICS CONSCIOUSNESS TO ORGANIZATIONS AND THE WORKPLACE

Every Contemporary Leader's Challenge

RONALD R. SIMS

Advances in technology, communication, and transportation have minimized the world's borders, creating a new global economy. More and more countries are attempting to industrialize and compete internationally. Because of these trends, more and more organizations are doing business outside their home countries. These transactions across national boundaries define global business that is having an impact on leaders in public, not-for-profit, and private sector organizations. Globalization brings together people with different cultures, values, laws, and ethical standards. Today's increasingly international or global organizations and their leaders must not only understand the values, culture, and ethical standards of her or his own country but also be sensitive to those of other countries while also recognizing how much they influence many aspects of organizational behavior including employees' acceptance of and adherence to organizational norms and values. Today's leaders must understand that along with strong ethical leadership, a strong organizational culture in support of ethical behavior will play a key role in guiding employees' behavior no matter where they may find themselves in this increasingly global world.

This chapter is concerned with "doing the right thing," and that means increasing our understanding of what leaders can do to increase the likelihood that their organizations will not stray from "doing the right thing." As introduced by other contributors in this book "doing the right thing" is critical to successful leadership regardless of whether one focuses on leaders in the profit, public, or not-for-profit sectors; small, medium, or large organization; or local, regional, national, or global arenas. Leaders who fail to deter their organizations from straying away from "doing the right thing" can expect to see behavior that leads to ethical, reputational, and financial fall, a fall that they very often will find themselves unable to recover from. Just like Humpty Dumpty, all the king's horses and all the king's men will be unable to help leaders and their organizations to get up from their fall.

Following a discussion of why ethics matters, the chapter discusses the role of strong ethical culture organizations, top management, boards of directors, middle managers, and the organization's value systems in restoring ethics consciousness to organizations or the workplace. The chapter then discusses the role of ethical leadership, creating a climate for whistle-blowing, and providing a forum for dialogue and moral conversation in restoring ethical consciousness to the workplace. The chapter concludes with a discussion of the need for leaders to continually take advantage of opportunities to institutionalize ethical behavior in organizations as a proactive approach for preventing the need to undertake an ethical turnaround or restore ethics consciousness to an organization.

A CRISIS OF ETHICS

Ethics in the twenty-first century has taken on a new importance and is seen as critical to the economic sustainability of organizations and countries. Leaders who want to successfully participate in the global arena and do not recognize this new reality face global scrutiny as evidenced in the recent business scandals in the United States. On the world stage, there are serious questions and concerns about the willingness of U.S. leaders and others who are part of international entities to act ethically. Given the world stage that leaders find themselves on, it is important that they pay increased attention to building and sustaining organizations with strong ethical cultures. And this means redoubling their efforts to restore ethical consciousness to organizations.

For the past year (and some would say decades), many executives, administrators, social scientists, and the public at large see unethical behavior as a cancer working on the fabric of society in too many of today's organizations and beyond. Many are also concerned that we face a crisis of ethics in the West that is undermining our competitive strength. This crisis involves national leaders, businesspeople, government officials, religious leaders, customers, and employees. Especially worrisome is unethical behavior among employees at all levels of the organization. For example, consider the notion that employees account for a higher percentage of retail thefts than do customers, or the suggestion that one in every fifteen employees steals from his or her employer.

In addition, we are all too familiar with what we continue to hear about illegal and unethical behavior on Wall Street, pension scandals in which disreputable executives gamble on risky business ventures with employees' retirement funds, organizations that expose their workers to hazardous working conditions, and blatant favoritism in hiring and promotion practices found in many parts of the world, or the wave of charges levied against various religious leaders. Recall, also, the questions raised about some charitable organizations and how they did or did not appropriately handle millions of dollars earmarked for relatives of those who perished during the Twin Towers terrorist attacks on September 11, 2001. Although such practices occur throughout the world, their presence nonetheless serves to remind us of the challenge facing leaders and their organizations as we move further into the twenty-first century.

This challenge is especially difficult because standards for what constitutes ethical behavior in different parts of the world (and even in different parts of some countries) lie in a "gray zone" where clear-cut right versus wrong answers may not always exist. Each nation has a distinctive culture and different beliefs about what organizational activities are acceptable or unethical. Cultural issues that create ethical issues in international business, for example, include differences in language, body language, time perception, and religion. According to cultural relativism, morality varies from one culture to another, and organizational practices are defined as right or wrong by the particular culture in which they occur. As a result, sometimes a case can be made that unethical behavior is forced on organizations by the environment in which it exists and laws such as the Foreign Corrupt Practices Act (FCPA). For example, if you were a sales representative for an American company abroad and your foreign competitors used bribes to get business, what would you do? In the United States such behavior is illegal, yet it is perfectly acceptable in other countries. What is ethical here? Similarly, in many countries women are systematically discriminated against in the workplace; it is felt that their place is in the home. In the United States, again, this practice is illegal. If you ran an American company in one of these countries, would you hire women in important positions? If you did, your company might be isolated in the larger business community, and you might lose business. If you did not, you might be violating what most Americans believe to be fair business practices. The Omnibus Trade and Competitiveness Act reduced the force of the FCPA and has made the prosecution and applicability of the FCPA in global business settings nonthreatening.

Globally, organizations have begun working together to minimize the negative effects of pollution and support environmentally responsibility. Joint agreements and international cooperatives have successfully policed and prosecuted offenders of reasonable emission standards.

Advances in telecommunications have intensified such ethical issues as privacy protection and fraud as well as patent, copyright, and trademark infringement. They have also made it easier to carry out questionable financial activities, notably, money laundering, which involves transferring illegally received money or using it in financial transactions so as to conceal the source of ownership or to facilitate an illegal activity.

Numerous attempts have been made to establish a set of global or universal ethical standards. Although many cultures share certain values, differences surface when these values are explained from the perspective of a specific culture. Consider the fact that although U.S. laws prohibit American companies from discrimination in employment, discrimination in other countries is often justified on the basis of cultural norms and values. Multinational corporations should strive to understand the human rights issues of each country in which they conduct business.

Engaging in gray-zone ethical behaviors or what some would call "clear" unethical behaviors is ultimately self-defeating. Leaders of today's organizations, whether for-profit or not-for-profit, should always strive to operate profitably. However, gray-zone ethical behaviors can curtail profitability. Maybe not today, maybe not until the market has redefined itself, but sometime in the future, it will happen.

The effective leadership and management of ethical issues today in an increasingly global world require leaders to ensure that members of their organizations do not commit unethical acts and are familiar with how to deal with ethical issues in their everyday work lives. These charges are especially important today as it appears that the American and global society of the first decade of the 2000s is clamoring for a renewed emphasis on values, morals, and ethics, and that the business debate of this period is but a subset of this larger societal concern. Whether today's leaders will be able to respond and ratchet their organization's reputation to a new plateau remains to be seen. One thing is sure: There is a renewed interest in global ethics in general and business ethics in particular that is not likely to dissipate in the near term.

Today's leaders must be willing to live with the consequences of ethical missteps, yet, the real challenge is for leaders to prevent the occurrence of such missteps in the first place. Prevention means leaders take the time to create organizations committed to "doing the right thing" and being proactive in developing strong ethical culture organizations (SECOs) with definitive courses of action that organizational members are expected to take regardless of the choices that may confront them. A SECO begins when leaders accept the fact that ethics and "doing the right thing" matter.

WHY ETHICS MATTERS

Ethical behavior by employees is important to the viability of all organizations. "Doing what's right" matters to leaders and their organizations, their employees, stakeholders, and the public at large. To leaders and members of their organizations, acting ethically and legally means saving billions of dollars each year in theft, lawsuits, and settlements. A number of organizations have paid significant financial penalties for acting unethically (Frooman 1997). And many of them will undoubtedly never fully recover from their ethical misdeeds. Studies have estimated that workplace theft costs U.S. businesses $40 billion each year and that employees account for a higher percentage of retail thefts than do customers (Zemke 1986; Silverstein 1989). Costs to businesses also include ineffective information flow throughout the organization; deterioration of relationships; declining productivity, creativity, and loyalty; and absenteeism and turnover. Organizations that have a strong reputation for unethical and uncaring behavior toward employees also have a difficult time recruiting and retaining valued professionals (Weiss 1989).

For today's business leaders and managers, leading and managing ethically also means managing with integrity (succeeding and being ethical at the same time). Integrity cascades throughout an organization. It shapes, influences, and maintains the values, tone, climate, or culture of the organization; communications among all its members; and the commitment and realism of everyone in the organization. Ethics matters in business because all the internal and external stakeholders stand to gain when organizations, groups, and individuals seek to do what is right, as well as to do things the right way.

Employees care about ethics because they are attracted to ethically and socially responsible companies (Levering and Milton 2000). A list of the 100 best companies to work for is regularly published in *Fortune* magazine (www.fortune.com). While the list continues to change, it is instructive to observe some of the characteristics of good employers that surveyed employees repeatedly cite. The most frequently mentioned characteristics include profit sharing, bonuses, and monetary awards. The list also contains policies and benefits that balance work and personal life and those that encourage social responsibility, all of which are part of the new social contract. Consider these policies and benefits described by employees:

- "When it comes to flextime requests, managers are encouraged to 'do what is right and human.'"
- "An employee hotline to report violations of company values."
- "Will fire clients who don't respect its security officers."
- "Employees donated more than 28,000 hours of volunteer labor last year."

There are moral benefits of paying attention to ethics as well as other types of benefits. The following paragraphs describe various types of benefits, for example, from managing ethics in the workplace.

Attention to organizational ethics has substantially improved society in the United States and around the world. For example, some decades ago workers' limbs were torn off and disabled workers were condemned to poverty and often to starvation. Children in our country worked sixteen-hour days. Trusts controlled some markets to the extent that prices were fixed and small businesses choked out. Price fixing crippled normal market forces. Employees were terminated based on personalities. Influence was applied through intimidation and harassment. Then society reacted and demanded that businesses place high value on fairness and equal rights. Antitrust laws were instituted. Government agencies were established. Unions were organized. Laws and regulations were established.

Ethics programs help maintain a moral course in turbulent times. Attention to organizational ethics is critical during times of fundamental change—times much like those faced now by businesses, both not-for-profit and for-profit (and government organizations beginning with the reinvention of government movement in the 1990s). During times of change, there is often no clear moral compass to guide leaders through complex conflicts about what is right or wrong. However, continuing attention to ethics in the workplace sensitizes leaders and staff to how they want to act—consistently.

A commitment to ethics cultivates strong teamwork and productivity, two very important characteristics for today's successful organizations. Ethics programs align employee behaviors with the most important ethical values preferred by leaders of the organization. Ongoing attention and dialogue regarding values in the workplace build openness, integrity, and community—critical ingredients of strong teams in the workplace. Employees feel strong alignment between their values and those of the organization. They react with strong motivation and performance.

Ethics programs support employee growth and meaning. Attention to ethics in the workplace helps employees face reality—both good and bad—in the organization and themselves. Employees feel full confidence that they can admit and deal with whatever comes their way.

Ethical climates and ethical consciousness or institutionalized organizational ethics are an insurance policy—they help ensure that policies are legal. There are an increasing number of lawsuits in regard to human resources management (HRM) matters and to the effects of an organization's services or products on stakeholders. Ethical principles are often state-of-the-art legal matters. These principles are often applied to current, major ethical issues to become legislation. Attention to ethics ensures highly ethical policies and procedures in the workplace. It is far better to incur the cost of mechanisms to ensure ethical practices now than to incur costs of litigation later. A major intent of well-designed HRM policies or HR-minded leadership, as suggested by Scott Quatro in chapter 15, is to ensure ethical treatment of employees, for example, in matters of hiring, evaluating, disciplining, firing, and so forth. For example, some have noted that "an employer can be subject to suit for breach of contract for failure to comply with any promise it made, so the gap between stated corporate culture and actual practice has significant legal, as well as ethical implications" (Drake and Drake 1988, 119).

Attention to organizational ethics helps to avoid criminal acts "of omission" and can lower fines. Ethics programs tend to detect ethical issues and violations early on so they can be reported or addressed. In some cases, when organizational leaders are aware of an actual or potential violation and do not report it to the appropriate authorities, this can be considered a criminal act in the United States, for example, in business dealings with certain government agencies, such as the Defense Department. The Federal Sentencing Guidelines specify major penalties for various types of major ethics violations. However, the guidelines potentially lower fines if an organization has clearly made an effort to operate ethically.

Ethics programs identify preferred values and ensure that organizational behaviors are aligned with those values. This effort includes recording the values, developing policies and procedures to align behaviors with preferred values, and then training all personnel about the policies and procedures. This overall effort is very useful for several other programs in today's workplace that requires behaviors to be aligned with values, including quality management, strategic planning, and diversity management. For example, successful team performance in a "Six Sigma" quality organization includes high priority on certain operating values, for example, trust among stakeholders, performance, reliability, measurement, and feedback. Many of these organizations use ethics tools in their quality programs to ensure integrity in their relationships with stakeholders. Ethics management techniques are also highly useful for managing strategic values, such as expanding market share or reducing costs. Ethics management programs are also useful in managing diversity. Diversity programs require recognizing and applying diverse values and perspectives—these activities are the basis of an organization committed to sound ethics.

As noted earlier, a commitment to ethics promotes a strong public image or reputation. Attention to ethics is strong public relations—admittedly, managing ethics should not be done primarily for reasons of public relations. But, frankly, the fact that an organization regularly gives attention to its ethics can portray a strong positive to the public. People see those organizations as valuing people more than profit, as striving to operate with the utmost of integrity and honor. Aligning behavior with values is critical to effective marketing and public relations programs. Consider how Johnson & Johnson handled the Tylenol crisis (as introduced by Bilimora and Godwin in chapter 14) versus how Exxon handled the oil spill in Alaska. Ethical values, consistently applied, are the cor-

nerstones for today's leaders in building a competitive, successful, and socially responsible business, local jurisdiction, church, or any type of organization.

A commitment to ethical values in the workplace legitimizes leadership or managerial actions, strengthens the coherence and balance of the organization's culture, improves trust in relationships between individuals and groups, supports greater consistency
in standards and qualities of products, and cultivates greater sensitivity to the impact of
the organization's values and messages.

Last—and most important—an unwavering commitment to ethics in the organization
or workplace is the right thing to do.

As suggested in the first part of this section there is evidence that paying attention to
ethical issues pays off for organizations. In the early 1990s, James Burke, then the chief
executive officer (CEO) of Johnson & Johnson, put together a list of companies that
devoted a great deal of attention to ethics. The group included Johnson & Johnson, Coca-
Cola, Gerber, Kodak, 3M, and Pitney Bowes. Over a forty-year period, the market value
of these organizations grew at an annual rate of 11.3 percent, as compared to the 6.2
percent for the Dow Jones industrials as a whole (Nelson and Quick 2003). Other evidence has also demonstrated that ethics and financial performance are linked. In a recent
study of the 500 largest U.S. public corporations, those that claim a commitment to
ethical behavior toward their stakeholders have better financial performance than those
firms that do not (Verschoor 1998). While these results do not demonstrate a causal
relationship between ethics and performance, the findings hint at the presence of a relationship between the two. Doing the right thing can have a positive effect on an
organization's performance.

RESTORING ETHICAL CONSCIOUSNESS TO
ORGANIZATIONS AND THE WORKPLACE

As evidenced by the ongoing news headlines of numerous leaders and their organizations
not doing the right thing, it is definitely a tough time to be a leader. Navigating through the
uncertain waters of the current economy, many for-profit organizations are buffeted by
corporate scandals and tossed about by wild fluctuations in the stock market. As soon as
the wave of mismanagement and deceit seems to subside, someone comes out with a revised earnings statement that $3 billion reported in profits was actually a loss and we begin
to sink again. It is clearly a tough time to be at the helm. Tyco, WorldCom, Global Crossing, Arthur Andersen, and Enron have run aground, and in each case, poor leadership has
cost the company and the crew their livelihoods. Leaders in these and other organizations
pursued profits at the expense of everything else and doomed the organization.

In this unstable climate, it is not surprising that some individuals have chosen an
unethical path. In recent years, long-term investors have been looking for a minimum 10
percent annual growth rate even as the market contracts, and more recent investors keep
thinking that the enormous profits of the dot-com glory days are the norm. The profit
motive has been so strong that it seems to have overwhelmed all other concerns. From
the most senior leader to the accounting department, down to the district manager and

department head, the focus in many organizations seems to have shifted from what the business produces to the wealth it can create.

The problem appears to lie in a misunderstanding of the very essence of business. Business is all about creating unique products and services for customers. Businesses that succeed have leaders and employees who are focused on being experts at their crafts and producing the most sophisticated products and services in the marketplace. It is not surprising that when businesses focus on their people and products, profits follow. Yet when profit motive becomes the sole focal point, businesses get into trouble and the end result can be business failure.

As investor confidence tumbles and markets contract, the Bush administration has tried to solve the current crisis, demanding that CEOs sign off on their financial statements and adopt transparent accounting practices. The government is prosecuting white-collar crime and making lofty statements. They are preaching the gospel of full disclosure. While all these intentions are honorable, they will not be enough. Government regulation cannot stop a crime before it starts. Regulators can only provide guidelines and punish noncompliance. They cannot foster virtue or ethical consciousness. Unless leaders at all levels in the organization are acting out of a sense of moral responsibility, the current crisis will not pass. True ethical behavior must be internally driven. External agents can only force compliance, not encourage choice, and ultimately, virtuous behavior is a choice.

Restoring ethical consciousness to organizations and the workplace begins by establishing a culture based on always "doing the ethical right thing," whether the actor is an individual employee, team, or a whole organization. When leaders pay attention to developing and maintaining such a culture they will be less likely to find their organizations confronted with a soiled reputation at best.

Leaders committed to restoring ethical consciousness must recognize the importance of developing a strong organizational culture founded on ethical principles and moral values. Such a culture is a vital driving force behind countering unethical behavior, institutionalizing ethics, and continuing overall reputational success. An organization's culture can be strong and cohesive in the sense that the organization conducts its operations according to a clear and explicit set of principles and moral values, that leaders devote considerable time to communicating these principles and values to organization members and explaining how they relate to its organizational environment, and that the values are shared widely across the organization—by senior leaders, middle managers, and rank-and-file employees alike.

STRONG ETHICAL CULTURE ORGANIZATIONS

Strong ethical culture organizations typically have creeds or values statements, and leaders at all levels of the organization regularly stress the importance of using these values and principles as the basis for decisions and actions taken throughout the organization. In SECOs, values and behavioral norms are so deeply rooted that they do not change much when new leaders take over—although they can erode over time if leaders cease to nurture them. And they may not change much as an organization evolves and the organization acts to make organizational adjustments, either because the new organizational direction or focus is compatible with the present culture or because the dominant traits of the culture are organizational direction neutral and can be used to support any number of plausible organizational strategies.

Some factors that contribute to the development of SECOs are (1) a founder or strong leader who establishes values, principles, and practices that are consistent and sensible in light of customer needs, competitive conditions, and organizational requirements; (2) a sincere, long-standing leadership commitment to operating the organization according to these established traditions, thereby creating an internal environment that supports ethical decision making and organizational strategies based on shared cultural norms; and (3) a genuine concern for the well-being of the organization's three biggest stakeholders—employees, customers, and stockholders (or those from the broader community).

Strong ethical culture organizations are built on the premise that leaders must constantly find ways to ensure that unhealthy or unethical cultural characteristics are identified and eliminated. For example, one unhealthy trait that can contribute to unethical behavior is a politicized internal environment that allows influential leaders or managers to operate autonomous "fiefdoms" and resist staying true to the organization's accepted values, principles, and practices. In politically dominated cultures, many issues and decisions get resolved and made on the basis of turf, vocal support or opposition by powerful executives, personal lobbying by a key executive, and conditions among individuals or departments with a vested interest in a particular outcome. What is best for the organization plays second fiddle to personal aggrandizement. One need only remember how leaders and others at Salomon Brothers, Tyco, WorldCom, and Enron lost sight of what was in the best interest of the organization because they were in powerful positions and the decision-making process was driven by a politically dominated culture that saw numerous leaders' vested interests in particular outcomes supersede the right thing to do for the larger organization, community, or society.

MANAGEMENT'S ROLE IN INSTITUTIONALIZING ETHICS IN THE ORGANIZATION OR THE WORKPLACE

As noted earlier, a SECO founded on ethical organizational principles and moral values is important to organizational success. Leaders must ensure that organizational members care about how the organization operates; otherwise the organization's reputation, and ultimately its performance, is put at risk. Organizational ethics and values programs are not window dressing; they are typically undertaken to communicate and create an environment of strongly held values and convictions and to make ethical conduct a way of life. Moral values and high ethical standards nurture the organization culture in a very positive way—they connote integrity, "doing the right thing," and genuine concern for all stakeholders. Value statements serve as a cornerstone for culture building; a code of ethics serves as a cornerstone for developing an organizational conscience. Table 20.1 indicates the kinds of topics such statements cover.

Table 20.1

Topics Frequently Covered in Value Statements and Codes of Ethics

Topics covered in values statements	Topics covered in codes of ethics
• Importance of customers and customer service • Commitment to quality • Commitment to innovation • Respect for the individual employee and the duty the organization has to employees • Importance of honesty, integrity, and ethical standards • Duty to stockholders • Duty to suppliers • Corporate citizenship • Importance of protecting the environment	• Honesty and observance of the law • Conflicts of interest • Fairness in selling and marketing practices • Using inside information and securities trading • Supplier relationships and procurement practices • Payments to obtain business/ Foreign Corrupt Practices Act • Acquiring and using information about others • Political activities • Use of company assets, resources, and property • Protection of proprietary information • Pricing, contracting, and billing

Leaders help organizations establish values and ethical standards in a number of different ways, which, if used properly, lead to the institutionalization of ethics and avoid the need to have to restore ethics consciousness to the organization. Tradition-steeped organizations with a rich folklore rely heavily on ethical leadership word-of-mouth indoctrination and the power of tradition to instill (or institutionalize) values and enforce ethical conduct. But many leaders today too often convey their organization's values and codes of ethics to stakeholders and interested parties in their annual reports, on their Web sites, and in documents provided to all employees. In these situations, efforts to institutionalize or build ethics into the organization's culture are quite obvious as the values and codes of ethics are hammered in at orientation courses for new employees and in refresher courses for leaders, managers, and employees. Leaders who make stakeholders aware of an organization's commitment to ethical organizational conduct are also important to developing SECOs or the institutionalization of ethics. The trend in recent years of making stakeholders more aware of the organization's commitment to ethical organizational conduct is partly attributable to greater leadership understanding of the role these statements play in culture building and partly attributable to a growing trend by consumers to search out "ethical" products, a greater emphasis on corporate social responsibility by large investors, and increasing political and legal pressures on organizations to behave ethically.

Top Management's Role

Leaders and organizations that are committed to being SECOs recognize that there is considerable difference between saying the right things (having a well-articulated organizational value statement or code of ethics) and truly leading an organization in an ethical and socially responsible way. Leaders who are truly committed to ethical conduct make ethical behavior a fundamental component of their every action. They put a stake in the ground, explicitly stating what the organization intends and expects. Value statements and codes of ethical conduct are used as a benchmark for judging both organization policies and every individual's conduct. They do not forget that trust, integrity, and fairness do matter, and they are crucial to other leaders in the organization. Consider Springfield ReManufacturing Corporation's Jack Stack.

In the late 1980s, Stack's Springfield ReManufacturing Corporation emerged as a model of how management and labor could successfully work together in a culture of trust and ownership. Leaders like Stack were known for taking concepts like ethics and fairness seriously. As the dot-com era took hold in the late 1990s, Stack and others never forgot that trust, integrity, and fairness were important to the bottom line. Stack made sure his organization was transparent—not only for investors but also for employees, customers, and suppliers. The interests of shareholders, employees, customers, and Springfield ReManufacturing's surrounding community all continued to be treated as equals in the organization's eyes. While the pressure from Wall Street and the dot-com mania of the 1990s were leading to corporate excess, Stack stuck with the "open book management" culture that had made him something of a celebrity years earlier as many gathered to hear him during his annual trek to the Massachusetts Institute of Technology's Sloan School of Management for its Birthing of Giants program for new CEOs. By sharing all of the company's financial information with all employees and giving them an ownership stake in the company, Stack had built a level of mutual trust and respect unusual in business.

Other organizations such as Southwest Airlines (as discussed by other authors in this book) and Harley-Davidson held similar beliefs and maintained strong ethical leadership and comparable organizational cultures. Organizational cultures that have not veered out of control over the past two decades nor fallen victim to the "bottom line" or "profit at any cost" mentality quite evident in too many of today's leaders and organizations. As with other beliefs and attitudes espoused by organizations and their members, top leaders set the tone. The values they espouse, the incentives they put in place, and their own behavior provide the cues for the rest of the organization. This is because all others in an organization look to top management for their cues as to what is acceptable practice. A former executive of a major steel company stated it well: "Starting at the top, management has to set an example for all the others to follow" (Foy 1975, 2). Top management, through its capacity to set a personal example and to shape policy, is in the ideal position to provide a highly visible role model. The authority and ability to shape policy, both formal and implied, forms one of the vital aspects of the job of any leader in any organization. This "role modeling through visible action" is an important aspect of becoming a moral manager who recognizes that managers live in a fishbowl and that employees are watching them for cues about what is important (Trevino, Hartman, and Brown 2000, 134).

In the private sector, John Gutfreund, Dennis Kozlowski, Ken Lay, and Jeffrey Skilling are examples of weak leadership (or role modeling): their behaviors sent cues to employees that unacceptable practices were okay. Such role modeling by an organization's leaders is guaranteed to increase the likelihood that unethical practices become a part of the organizational fiber. An example of positive ethical leadership may be seen in the case of an organization that was manufacturing vacuum tubes. One day the plant manager called a hurried meeting to announce that a sample of the tubes had failed a critical safety test. This meant that the batch of 10,000 tubes was of highly questionable safety and performance and standards. The plant manager wondered out loud, "What are we going to do now?" The vice president for technical operations looked around the room at each person and then declared in a low voice, "Scrap them!" According to a person who worked for this vice president, that act set the tone for the corporation for years, because every person present knew of situations in which faulty products had been shipped under pressures of time and budget (Gittler 1986, 16). The vice president clearly exhibited the kind of leadership (role modeling) that is necessary to build SECOs and restore ethical consciousness to the workplace or organizations.

Too many public, private, and not-for-profit, and some global leaders highlighted for "doing the wrong thing" in recent years provide vivid examples of how a leader's actions and behaviors communicated important messages to others in the organization. In the absence of knowing what to do, most members of an organization look to the behavior of leaders for their cues as to what conduct is acceptable. In the case of the vice president of operations, another point is illustrated. When we speak of leaders providing ethical leadership, it is not just restricted to top management. Vice presidents, plant managers, frontline managers, and, indeed, all managerial personnel carry the responsibility for role modeling ethical leadership.

In a period in which the importance of restoring ethical consciousness to the workplace and organizations is strongly being advocated, leaders must stress the primacy of integrity and morality as vital components of the organization's culture. There are many different ways and situations in which organizational leaders need to do this. In general, leaders need to create a climate of moral or ethical consciousness. In everything they do, leaders must stress the importance of sound ethical principles and practices. A former president and chief operating officer for Caterpillar Tractor Company suggested four specific actions for accomplishing this (Morgan 1977, 60):

1. Create clear and concise policies that define the company's business ethics and conduct.
2. Select for employment and partnerships only those people and organizations whose characters and ethics appear to be in keeping with corporate standards.
3. Promote people on the basis of their performance and ethical conduct and beliefs.
4. Company employees must feel safe enough to meet the obligation and the opportunity to report perceived irregularities in ethics or in accounting transactions.

The leader must infuse the organization's climate with values and ethical consciousness, not just run a one-person show. This point is made vividly clear by the following observation: "Ethics programs which are seen as part of one manager's management system, and not as a part of the general organizational process, will be less likely to have a lasting role in the organization" (Brenner 1990, 7).

Top management commitment is crucial but not sufficient. Champions are also needed at lower organizational levels, especially lower level managers or supervisors. Many organizations are addressing the leadership requirement by the formation of task or advisory committees on ethics, often headed by a senior manager. Some organizations also have a standing committee that oversees ethical behavior company-wide. Citicorp has developed ethical principles to guide the company and create open communications. In order to promote communication at different levels of the organization, Citicorp has instituted a committee on good corporate practice whose aim is to institutionalize ethical standards and eliminate conflict of interest.

The Board of Directors' Role

Traditionally, directors in for-profit organizations have functioned as guardians of the financial interest of stockholders, with a specific concern for earnings and dividends. Even this role has been performed in a largely passive manner. Now, in the aftermath of major business scandals, the system of corporate governance and the role of directors have become subjects of special interest.

To help counter unethical behavior, help in the institutionalization of ethics process, or restore ethical consciousness to organizations, boards must take on a more active leadership role in organizations and extend their oversight beyond traditional matters of profits or passive oversight to areas of ethics. A concern for ethical performance is not necessarily consistent with stockholder interest, of course, but directors should recognize that there is a connection between ethics and profits.

The board of directors should demand moral leadership, because as directors they presumably have power to require ethical performance by management. The overall institutional impact of a board that demands ethical performance is greater than that of a president or vice president who does the same.

Recognition of the growing responsibility and accountability of directors as a result of the Tycos, WorldComs, and Enrons of the world by the courts and the Securities and Exchange Commission (SEC) has begun to serve as an impetus to increasing directors' involvement in ensuring that leaders and their organizations "do the right thing." In holding board members responsible, for example, the SEC has taken the position that anyone in a position to know what is going on and to do something about it will be held liable. Overt action or direct participation in a fraud is not necessary for a judgment of liability. Directors presumably have access to the facts, or they should probe sufficiently to get the facts. Boards of directors must recognize that they have a responsibility for playing a significant role in an organization's efforts either to do the right thing or to return ethical consciousness to the workplace and organizations.

Middle Management's Role

In order for an organization to develop SECOs or institutionalize ethics, middle managers must also assume responsibility for convincing employees and for influencing their concern for moral values and ethical practice. Middle management must make certain that every department and employee fosters compliance with corporate ethical standards. They must ensure that ethical policies are followed in their department, focusing on things that are likely to crop up as moral or ethical dilemmas in connection with the activities of their departments. They must see that their people clearly and explicitly understand what is expected of them in the way of ethical behavior. They must tell employees not only what to do and what not to do but also how violations will be dealt with. They must encourage employees to spot and report potential ethical problems. They must develop a radar system that keeps them in touch with the ethical climate of their department and the organization (for example, ensuring that climate and attitude or ethical audit surveys are conducted).

The following analogy illustrates this requirement. In talking of the international environmental situation, one can conceive of the world as a ship commanded by fifteen different captains, all of whom speak different languages, and all of whom, being near-sighted, can see only five feet in front of the ship. Yet the ship must have ten feet of clearance in order to maneuver. This dilemma can easily face middle managers. By the time they have identified potential ethical problems they are upon them. They need something comparable to radar to inform them of potential ethical obstacles. If they fail to anticipate them, they will surely bump into them. They must be willing to get as much help and input as possible—ask their people for recommendations for changes in policies and procedures. And they must ensure that the organization has a hotline for anonymously reporting unethical behavior.

THE ORGANIZATION'S VALUE SYSTEM

Both top and middle management have responsibility for developing the organization's value system, which is a cornerstone to SECOs or restoring ethical consciousness to organizations. According to the president of a consulting firm that specializes in individual and organizational performance, "Our experience with scores of clients correlates excellence most closely with consistent, clear and serious management value systems" (Weiss 1989, 40). One company with a clearly defined value system is Merck & Co., a pharmaceutical firm. The effectiveness of its value system is reflected in Merck's consistently high-quality performance. For three successive years, Merck was voted America's most admired company in *Fortune* magazine's polls of chief executive officers.

In many organizations over the years, managers and employees have tended to be self-serving, more concerned with protecting themselves and their interests than with any kind of ethics—not so at Merck. For example, the company's field marketing representatives try to determine what is right for the doctor and the patient instead of how a particular sale might affect total sales volume. Such a focus is unusual in a highly competitive field such as pharmaceuticals.

Merck's example shows that a positive approach is one key to success. When management compromises on quality, worker morale suffers and production slows down. And it is easy for management to pay a great deal of lip service to ethics and values, but what is more important is to put them into action and to act as examples.

Leaders should keep in mind the following guidelines for establishing values that can help build and sustain SECOs:

- Values cannot be taught, they must be lived. Employees do what they have seen done, not what they are told. If their superiors engage in unethical behavior, they will become lax in their own work habits.
- Values must be simple and easy to articulate. Leaders should ask themselves whether the values are realistic and whether they apply to daily decision making.
- Values apply to internal as well as external operations. In other words, leaders cannot expect workers to treat customers well if they in turn do not treat their workers well in terms of honesty, frankness, and performance-based rewards.
- Values are first communicated in the selection process. It is easier to hire people who share the corporate values than it is to train someone who does not identify with them to begin with. One executive recruiter said, "The best run organizations place a premium on the candidate's approach to issues of ethics and judgment. Anyone can read a balance sheet, but not everyone can handle a product quality or conflict of interest problem" (Weiss 1989, 41).

Leaders have an obligation to constantly monitor their organization's value system and make efforts to revise it when appropriate. Such a revision would be necessary from time to time, especially when:

- Downsizing, layoffs, decline in performance, attrition, or redeployment of the workforce are necessary.
- Significantly different groups are combined.
- Traditional values are inappropriate for the new climate.
- There has been a transgression of ethics, morals, or the law.
- There has been a significant strategic redirection.

ETHICAL TURNAROUNDS: RESTORING ETHICS CONSCIOUSNESS TO THE ORGANIZATION

Today's organizational leaders must be committed to returning ethics consciousness to the workplace. And they can do this by changing the organization's culture, creating a climate for whistle-blowing, and providing a forum for dialogue and good moral conversation.

An ethical turnaround begins with ethical leadership. And, restoring ethics consciousness to an organization ultimately means that organizational leaders actively reinforce a SECO. The five most important elements in changing or reinforcing a SECO are: (1) what leaders pay attention to; (2) how leaders react to crises; (3) how leaders behave; (4) how leaders allocate rewards; and (5) how leaders hire and fire individuals.

Attention. Leaders in an organization communicate their priorities, values, and beliefs through the themes that consistently emerge from what they focus on. These themes are reflected in what they notice, comment on, measure, and control. If leaders are consistent in what they pay attention to, measure, and control, employees receive clear signals about what is important in the organization. If, however, leaders are inconsistent, employees spend a lot of time trying to decipher and find meaning in the inconsistent signals. Returning ethics consciousness to the workplace means that leaders focus attention on improving the ethical fiber of the organization by not disregarding the long-term implications of employees' actions in favor of the most recent bottom-line profits or headlines.

Reaction to Crises. The way leaders deal with crises communicates a powerful message about culture. Returning ethics consciousness to the workplace means that leaders swiftly react to any ethical crisis facing the organization by complying with authorities and firing ethical wrongdoers. The organization's leaders must not lie or cover up ethical and legal transgressions, and they must avoid preserving ethical wrongdoers at any cost.

Role Modeling. Through role modeling, teaching, and coaching, leaders can reinforce values that support an ethical organizational culture. As noted several times in this chapter, employees often emulate leaders' behavior and look to the leaders for cues to the appropriate behavior. Returning ethics consciousness to the workplace will occur when leaders convey the image of the moral manager. This means that leaders proactively set the example of honesty and integrity for the rest of the organization.

Allocation of Rewards. To ensure that values are accepted, leaders must reward behavior that is consistent with values and doing the right thing. Using rewards and discipline effectively may be the most powerful way for leaders to send signals about desirable and undesirable conduct. Returning ethics consciousness to the workplace means rewarding those who accomplish their goals by behaving in ways that are consistent with stated values and conveying that a lack of commitment to ethical principles will ensure that employees will not be promoted.

Criteria for Selection and Dismissal. A powerful way that leaders reinforce culture is through the selection of newcomers to the organization and through the way it fires employees and the rationale behind the firing. Organizations must have clear policies that employees understand on the criteria for selection and dismissal. Having to reprimand an employee who displays unethical behavior that is against the organization may be viewed as a failure to reinforce the values within the organization. Returning ethics consciousness to the workplace means that leaders must bring into the organization only employees who are committed to ethical principles and must usher out all employees connected to ethical misconduct.

Create a Climate for Whistle-blowing

Creating a culture or climate where whistle-blowing is encouraged and whistle-blowers are safe is important to returning ethics consciousness to the workplace (an organization). This means that the organization:

1. Takes the time to manage whistle-blowing by communicating the conditions that are appropriate for the disclosure of wrongdoing.

2. Clearly delineates wrongful behavior and the appropriate ways to respond to or disclose wrongdoing.
3. Recognizes that to silence a whistle-blower or to muzzle a watchdog is very likely to result in further compounding of problems.
4. Creates a culture in which employees feel safe and do not have to conceal and distort information.
5. Takes employees' complaints and whistle-blowers' information seriously.
6. Sets up channels and other mechanisms that not only allow but also promote healthy, open communication.
7. Conducts organizational audits or assessment to look at existing ethical standards (i.e., level of commitment from top management, the nature of training programs, communication tools such as help and hot lines, and the magnitude of organizational risks in matters ranging from internal harassment to product safety).
8. Integrates standards and ethical values into everything—from hiring to firing, training, compensation, and so on.

Whistle-blowers should be perceived as heroes rather than "vile wretches." Leaders have a responsibility to listen to and respond to their employees, especially regarding observations and reporting of illegal and immoral acts. Mechanisms such as "ethics offices" are part of an organization's responsibility to provide due process for employees to report personal grievances, to obtain effective and just resolution of them, and to report the wrongdoings of others, including the employers.

Provide a Forum for Dialogue and Good Moral Conversation

Providing a forum for dialogue is one of the most proactive gestures leaders can use to return ethics consciousness to the workplace. Dialogue encourages give and take and provides organization-sponsored opportunities for employees to discuss ethical expectations, individual and organizational actions, and ethically charged situations or gray areas. Dialogue leads to good moral conversation that in the long run promotes deeper commitment to the ethical employee-employer relationships or contracts and ethical practices in an organization.

Dialogue is good conversation and serves many purposes. It facilitates self-awareness and awareness of others. It is a source of learning. It is liberating, ensures that there is room for all voices, and lends itself to the creation of psychological safety, which opens the door for good moral conversations among different levels of employees in the organization.

Good conversation is a way for employees to develop "clear and compelling ethical views or positions" in and out of the workplace. Good conversation can have three main effects. First, it can legitimize ethical concern as an important dimension of life. Second, it is one way an employee can seek guidance and gain clarity about what to do in a particular situation. Finally, it is out of public discussion and agreement that feelings of ethical obligation ultimately arise. Thus, the essence of learning about and living within ethical boundaries in an organization is to be in dialogue with co-workers about the ethical "rules of the road."

The primary purpose of engaging in moral conversation in organizations is to test, expand, enrich, and deepen employee understanding of business ethics so that each employee can better apply principles, rules, virtues, structures, moral ideals, and background beliefs to problems encountered in business.

Recognize an Unethical Organization

Organizational leaders who want to hire and retain employees who wish to be a part of an ethical organization have to be aware of the organization's ethical character (or culture). Employees can be aware of the ethical character of a current or potential employer as they can of its economic health. For example, if an organization emphasizes short-term revenues over long-term results, it may be creating an unethical atmosphere. If an organization links its ethical behavior to a code of ethics but will not address the complexity of ethical dilemmas, then the code may merely be window dressing. Proactive leaders and organizations approach establishing a code of ethics as more than adopting a document. Establishing board-level committees to monitor the ethical behavior of the organization helps leaders be on the lookout for danger signs that indicate when employees or leaders themselves may be drifting away from doing the right thing. Ethics training programs in organizations also demonstrate a commitment to ethics in the workplace. However, leaders must ensure that such training initiatives are proactive rather than reactive, as has been the case for many organizations in teaching ethics in the post-Enron business world (Salant 2002).

A leader who encourages unethical behavior or discourages ethical behavior because of the financial implications will not be one for whom many people want to work. Ethical problems are not legal problems. A leader who fails to realize this distinction is at risk, as is one who sees ethical problems only as a public relations issue.

The treatment of employees can indicate the ethical nature of an organization. If employees are not treated as well as customers or if performance-appraisal standards are unfair or arbitrary, the company may be unethical. Additionally, an absence of procedures for handling ethical issues, or the lack of a whistle-blowing mechanism, or even the lack of a basic communication avenue between employees and supervisors can indicate an organization that is ethically at risk. Finally, leaders who fail to recognize their organization's obligations to the public as well as to its shareholders and expect employees to leave their private ethics at home is an organization at risk for unethical behavior (Cooke 1991).

Relentlessly Pursue Institutionalizing Ethical Behavior

In the end, the only way leaders and organizations can avoid ethical falls is by constantly communicating their desire for employees at all levels to behave ethically and responsibly. This means that organizational leaders use every opportunity to communicate what the organization stands for and against.

Establish the value. First and foremost in any organization's attempt to institutionalize ethical behavior, it must establish ethical considerations as an organizational value. An organization's mission statement often details its goal of providing the highest quality product at the least cost. It recognizes the commitment to all stakeholders. In addition, it needs to add a commitment to an ethical standard.

Communicate the value. An organization must communicate its commitment to ethical values to employees and external stakeholders. Codes of conduct or ethics can be adopted. Distribution of such codes should not stop with upper and middle managers; consequently, all employees should be apprised of the corporate code of behavior. Communication cannot be limited to distribution, however, because actions speak louder than words (Giacalone and Ashworth 1988). Leaders and the organization are able to foster employee commitment to the organization's goal of ethical behavior in the same way that they foster employee commitment to its other goals.

An employee has a commitment to an organization in direct relationship to that employee's involvement with the organization. A leader or manager can influence that commitment by making sure adherence to the ethical goal is rewarded with *visibility*; being explicit in its expectations regarding ethical or unethical behavior; making clear that ethical or unethical actions result in *irreversible* results, consistent punishment, or rewards; and finally, that employees take actions of their own *volition* to act ethically or unethically and be responsible for the outcomes (Sims 2002).

Select and train employees with ethical behavior in mind. Organizations can, during their recruitment process, include in their criteria the principles they look for in an employee as a moral actor. Several methods can be used to elicit this kind of information; honesty tests, background checks, along with a signed commitment by the person to the Corporate Code of Ethics. Pizza Hut, Inc.'s top management looks for *integrity* when hiring and promoting employees in the organization. Integrity includes an internal allegiance to excellence, honesty, a sense of teamwork, and a balanced perspective on long-term goals and short-term profits (Reinemund 1992).

Early in the employment process, a *social contract* is formed between the employer and employee. Social contracts typically cover the inducement of the employer and the contribution of the employee. The degree to which both parties satisfy the expectations established by this contract affects the success of the relationship. It is important for organizations and employees to understand the expectations of the social contract as well. It is important for leaders and managers to understand that if the two do not or cannot agree on this aspect, then the relationship will suffer.

Because ethical behavior cannot be reduced to simple "dos and don'ts," both parties have ever-changing expectations, and thus there must be opportunity and structure to address an evolving set of expectations.

Training employees to make an ethical analysis as part of their decision-making processes is critical. Training can be formal, focused on the organization's goals and objectives and on techniques of decision making. Training can also be achieved through the normal socialization during orientation of a new employee. If leaders are operating ethically then the role models that employees emulate will exhibit the proper ethical behavior. The system of rewards and punishment will confirm and reinforce ethical behavior.

While the points highlighted in this section will not guarantee that ethical missteps will not occur in an organization, they do increase the likelihood that the organization will avoid taking an ethical fall causing a need to undertake an ethical turnaround as has happened in many organizations in recent years.

CONCLUSION: COMMITMENT TO ETHICAL ACTION

The importance of ethics in the increasingly global twenty-first century will continue to be critical to leader and organizational success. Leaders and organizations engaging in unethical behaviors are ultimately self-defeating. Businesses, whether for-profit or not-for-profit, should always strive to operate profitably. However, unethical behaviors can curtail profitability. Maybe not today, maybe not until the market has redefined itself, but sometime in the future, it will happen.

Ethical behavior is what is morally accepted as "good" and "right" as opposed to "bad" or "wrong" in a particular setting. For the leader, this means acting in ways consistent with one's personal values and the commonly held values of the organization and society. Is it ethical, for example, to pay a bribe to obtain a business contract in a foreign country? Is it ethical to allow your company to withhold information that might discourage a job candidate from joining your organization? Is it ethical to ask someone to take a job you know will not be good for their career progress? Is it ethical to do personal business on company time?

The list of questions could go on and on. Despite one's initial inclinations in response to these questions, the major point of it all is to remind leaders that the public at large is demanding that government officials, business leaders and managers, workers in general, and the organizations they represent all act according to high ethical and moral standards. There is every indication that the future will bring a renewed concern with maintaining high standards of ethical behavior in organizational transactions and in the workplace.

In concluding this chapter the views of one writer on the ethical organization provides the following four principles for highly ethical organizations (Pastin 1986, 14):

- They are at ease interacting with diverse internal and external stakeholder groups. The ground rules of these firms make the good of these stakeholder groups part of the organizations' own good.
- They are obsessed with fairness. Their ground rules emphasize that the other person's interests count as much as their own.
- Responsibility is individual rather than collective, with individuals assuming personal responsibility for actions of the organization. These organizations' ground rules mandate that individuals are responsible to themselves.
- They see their activities in terms of purpose. This purpose is a way of operating that

members of the organization highly value. And purpose ties the organization to its environment.

Additionally, we offer the following characteristics of a high-integrity organization:

- There exists a clear vision and picture of integrity throughout the organization.
- The vision is owned and embodied by top management, over time.
- The reward system is aligned with the vision of integrity.
- Policies and practices of the organization are aligned with the vision; there are no mixed messages.
- It is understood that every significant leadership decision has ethical value dimensions.
- Everyone is expected to work through conflicting-stakeholder value perspectives.

It may be a tough time to be in business, but an ethical orientation can help organizations weather the storm. Organizations can withstand the lean years, but the only organizations that will do so are those whose organizational culture encourages right action and rewards ethical behavior. This breeds long-term trust from employees and customers and reassures investors. It is not enough to sign a paper that says your company is behaving ethically. It is not enough to give money to worthy causes and be "socially responsible," although it is a nice start.

Leaders and their organizations must reorient themselves to the practice of business. Another way to put this is: "If the next generation of managers is not trained to recognize that a competitive edge is no longer solely based on market share, then these companies—no matter how committed their leadership is to implementing an ethical approach to business—will fail to reach their desired state" (Sims 2002, 19).

Leaders must focus on "doing the right things" the ethical things that helped them succeed from the first, and must not be hypnotized by the bottom line or gray-zone ethical practices. They must seek virtue for the good of the economy, their communities, the organization, the employees, and the global community. They must return and restore ethical consciousness to the workplace and organizations. Nothing less is acceptable!

REFERENCES

Brenner, S.N. (1990). *Influences on Corporate Ethics Programs.* San Diego, CA: International Association for Business and Society.

Cooke, R.A. (1991). "Danger Signs of Unethical Behavior: How to Determine If Your Firm Is at Ethical Risk." *Journal of Business Ethics* 10: 249–253.

Drake, B.H., and E. Drake. (1988). "Ethical and Legal Aspects of Managing Corporate Cultures." *California Management Review* 16: 107–123.

Fortune Magazine. www.fortune.com.

Foy, L.W. (1975). "Business Ethics: A Reappraisal." Distinguished Lecture Series, Columbia Graduate School of Business (January 30): 2.

Frooman, J. (1997). "Socially Irresponsible and Illegal Behavior and Shareholder Wealth." *Business & Society* 36 (3): 221–229.

Giacalone, R.A., and D.N. Ashworth. (1988). "From Lip Service to Community Service." *Business and Society Review* 66: 31–33.

Gittler, H. (1986). "Listen to the Whistle-Blowers Before It's Too Late." *Wall Street Journal* (March 10): 16.

Levering, R., and M. Milton. (2000). "The 100 Best Companies to Work For." *Fortune Magazine* (January 10): 82–114.

Morgan, L.L. (1977). "Business Ethics Starts with the Individual." *Management Accounting* (March): 14, 60.

Nelson, D.L., and J.C. Quick. (2003). *Organizational Behavior: Foundations, Realities, and Challenges* 4th ed. Mason, OH: South-Western.

Pastin, M. (1986). *The Hard Problems of Management: Gaining the Ethics Edge.* San Francisco: Jossey-Bass.

Reinemund, S.R. (1992). "Today's Ethics and Tomorrow's Work Place." *Business Forum* 17 (2): 6–9.

Salant, J.D. (2002). "After Enron, More Firms Teach Ethics." *Virginia Daily Press* (November 3): E1, E3.

Silverstein, S. (1989). "One in 15 Employees in Study Caught Stealing." *Los Angeles Times* (December 2): D-1.

Sims, R.R. (2002). "Enron: How a Failure of Leadership, Culture and Unethical Behavior Brought a Giant to Its Knees." *William and Mary Business* (Fall/Winter): 18–19.

Trevino, L.K., L.P. Hartman, and M. Brown. (2000). "Moral Person and Moral Manager: How Executives Develop a Reputation for Ethical Leadership," *California Management Review* 42 (4): 128–142.

Verschoor, C.C. (1998). "A Study of the Link Between a Corporation's Financial Performance and Its Commitment to Ethics." *Journal of Business Ethics* 17 (13): 1509–1516.

Weiss, A. (1989). "The Value System." *Personnel Administrator* 34 (July): 40–41.

Zemke, R. (1986). "Employee Theft: How to Cut Your Losses." *Training* (May): 74–78.

ABOUT THE AUTHORS

Andrea B. Bear currently serves as deputy director for development, marketing, and community relations at the Chrysler Museum of Art, a nonprofit institution in Norfolk, Virginia. She is co-founder and president of Full Potential Organizations, LLC, a management consulting firm specializing in leadership development and team building. She has more than twenty years of leadership experience gleaned from a wide variety of positions, including more than a decade in television news. She holds an MBA from the College of William and Mary and a BA from the University of Virginia.

Diana Bilimoria is associate professor of organizational behavior in the Department of Organizational Behavior, Weatherhead School of Management, Case Western Reserve University. She received her PhD from the University of Michigan. She has served as editor of the *Journal of Management Education.* Dr. Bilimoria's research focuses on corporate and nonprofit governance and leadership; women leaders, directors, and entrepreneurs; and management education. She has published in journals such as the *Academy of Management Journal, Human Relations, Group and Organization Management*, and *Journal of Management Education*, and volumes such as *Women in Management: Current Research Issues, Women on Corporate Boards of Directors*, and *Advances in Strategic Management.*

Herrington J. Bryce is currently Life of Virginia Professor of Business Administration at the College of William and Mary, where he teaches both corporate and nonprofit finance. His most recent of nine books is *Financial and Strategic Management for Nonprofit Organizations*, 3d ed. (Jossey-Bass, John Wiley 2000), which is on the recommended list of the American Bar Association and the American Association of Corporate Secretaries, among others. Bryce was a fellow at the Institute of Politics at Harvard, a Brookings Economic Policy Fellow, a NATO fellow, and a faculty member at MIT (regional planning), Clark University (Massachusetts), and the University of Maryland, College Park, where he headed the graduate program in budgetary and legal studies. He has served on many state and local government committees including the Treasury Board, which issues all state-related debt for the Commonwealth of Virginia. Bryce currently serves on the advisory committees for Guidestar (the major compiler of nonprofit tax data) and the National Center on Nonprofit Enterprise and was the editor and principal writer for Harcourt Brace's monthly newsletter on financial strategies aimed at CFOs, CEOs, CPAs, and attorneys specializing in nonprofit work. Bryce was also the special editor for the public sector and nonprofit management section of the *American Management Association Handbook* (1994). He has lectured in several countries including Russia, China, Estonia, the Republic of Georgia, and Cyprus. In addition to academic journals, Bryce has written lengthy editorials on nonprofits in the *Washington Post*, *Wall Street Journal*, *Nonprofit Times*, *Nonprofit World*, and *Director's Monthly* (for corporate directors), among others. Bryce holds a PhD in economics from the Maxwell School at Syracuse University, a BS from Mankato State University, and a CLU and ChFC from the American College.

Shawn M. Carraher, PhD, is professor of management and global entrepreneurship at Texas A & M University Commerce and director of the International Family Business Center and the Small Business Institute. He also serves on the graduate faculties of Tec de Monterrey in Mexico City and Nova Southeastern University. Since completing his doctorate at the University of Oklahoma, he has taught at the University of Wisconsin-Milwaukee, California State University-Chico, Indiana State University, and Indiana University working on projects that combine human resource management, organizational behavior, and strategic management in cross-cultural entrepreneurial settings. He has authored more than 60 research articles, made more than 100 academic research presentations, conducted more than 500 mission-based goal-setting seminars, and taught with the Fulbright program in Ukraine and Thailand. He is also the program chair for the Small Business Institute, Competitive Papers chair and vice president of marketing for the U.S. Association for Small Business & Entrepreneurship, president elect of the SouthWest Academy of Management, and Division Chair of Division 1 of the Academy of Management. He lives in Greenville, Texas, with his wife of three years and a son—and is expecting another child to be born before the publication of the book.

Richard F. Cullins, EdD, is a program manager for Air Traffic Training in the Federal Aviation Administration in Washington, DC. His academic interests include public administration, organizational learning and development, learning style, and management theory and practice. He has worked in training and development in the public and private sectors for over twenty-five years.

Deanne N. Den Hartog holds a master of science and a doctoral degree in organizational psychology from the Free University in Amsterdam, the Netherlands. She is currently a full professor of Organizational Psychology at the School of Economics and Business of the Erasmus University in Rotterdam, the Netherlands. Her research has focused on cross-cultural and transformational leadership processes. Other research interests include team reflexivity and effectiveness as well as human resource management. She has published on these topics in a variety of journals (e.g., *The Leadership Quarterly*, *Journal of Organizational Behavior*) as well as in international volumes and two Dutch books.

Marcus W. Dickson is associate professor of psychology and area head of the Industrial/Organizational Psychology program at Wayne State University in Detroit, Michigan. He is a partner with Personnel and Human Resource Innovations, LLC (The PHI Group), and also a senior research advisor with the Gallup Organization's consulting and research branches. He was a charter member of the Global Leadership and Organizational Behavior Effectiveness (GLOBE) Research Project, a member of the GLOBE Coordinating Team for six years, and served as Co-Principal Investigator on that project for two years. Dr. Dickson received his PhD in industrial/organizational psychology from the University of Maryland in 1997. His areas of research and consulting expertise include organizational leadership, cross-cultural organizational culture analysis, organizational performance evaluation and assessment, and computer-mediated communication in organizations. He currently serves as a member of the editorial board of the *Journal of Organizational Behavior*, and his work has appeared in *Journal of Applied Psychology*, *The Leadership Quarterly*, *Applied Psychology: An International Review*, and *The Handbook of Organizational Culture and Climate*, among others. He formerly worked for William M. Mercer, Inc., an international human resources consulting firm, in Washington, DC.

Tom R. Eucker has been with Intel Corporation for twenty years as a training manager, organization and leadership development consultant, and, more recently, knowledge management and business process improvement specialist. Eucker's consulting and research interests focus on learning and knowledge systems design, corporate culture, change management, knowledge management, and business process improvement. He has authored several articles and chapters and has served for over a decade on the editorial board of the *Performance Improvement Quarterly*, the research journal for the International Society for Performance and Instruction. Eucker received a BA in psychology from Linfield College, and holds a PhD in instructional psychology from the University of Southern California. He lives in Higley, Arizona, with his wife, Ruthann, and one of their three adult children.

Michael A. Fitzgibbon (d. 2004) operated Lafayette River Consulting, LLC, which specialized in management assessment and development and organization development. He had over twenty-five years of experience as an internal and external change agent, helping organizations maximize their human capital. He held leadership positions in organization and management development at Philip Morris, Brown & Root, and American Airlines. He presented papers at the national meetings of the American Society for Training and Development (ASTD) and the American Compensation Association, and at the International Congress for Assessment Center Technology. He authored over a dozen articles on a variety of topics. Michael served on the executive committee of the board of directors of the Elizabeth River Project in Hampton Roads and was a director of the Southeastern Virginia chapter of ASTD.

Ann Gilley is associate professor of management at the School of Business of Pfeiffer University in Charlotte, North Carolina. She is also a vice president for Trilogy Consulting Group, a performance consulting firm. Ann has spent approximately fourteen years working in a variety of managerial capacities for financial and insurance institutions. She has co-authored eight books, including *The Manager as Change Agent*, *The*

Performance Challenge, Beyond the Learning Organization, Strategically Integrated HRD, and *Organizational Learning, Performance, and Change*, which won the Academy of Human Resource Development (AHRD) book of the year award for 2000. She serves on the editorial board of the book series *New Perspectives in Organizational Learning, Performance, and Change* for Perseus Publishing, now part of Basic Books. Ann earned her BS in business administration from Michigan Technological University, an MBA from Grand Valley State University, and a PhD in organizational and human resource development from Iowa State University. She lives near Ludington, Michigan, with her husband, Jerry.

Jerry W. Gilley is professor and program chair of the Human Resource Studies Program at Colorado State University. For six years, he served as principal (senior partner) and director of organizational development for Mercer Human Resource Consulting (formerly known as William M. Mercer, Inc.), the world's largest compensation, benefits, and human resource consulting firm. His publication record consists of fifteen books, forty-six refereed journal articles, four monographs, and sixteen book chapters. His book *Organizational Learning, Performance, and Change: An Introduction to Strategic HRD* was selected by the Academy of Human Resource Development (AHRD) as their 2000 book of the year. His other books include: *Principles of HRD* (2002), *The Manager as Change Agent* (2001), *Philosophy and Practice of Organizational Learning, Performance, and Change* (2001), *Beyond the Learning Organization* (2000), *The Performance Challenge* (1999), and *Stop Managing, and Start Coaching* (1996) which was selected as one of the thirty best business books for 1996 by Soundview Executive Book Summaries. In 2003, he was appointed editor of the *Manager As . . .* book series for Praeger Publishing Business Books Division. The series focuses on practice-oriented books for managers regarding their roles and responsibilities. In 2001, he was appointed editor of the *New Perspectives in Organizational Learning Performance and Change* book series for Basis Books Business Division, which publishes professional books for human resource and managerial professionals. In 2003, he was elected president elect of the AHRD. He has been director of the HRD Professors Network American Society for Training and Development (ASTD) and a board of directors member of International Board of Standards for Training, Performance, and Improvement and the AHRD. He has made several national presentations at the International Conference for the ASTD, AHRD, and Linkage Conferences (Global Human Resource Institute, Mentoring and Coaching Conference, and Consulting Skills Conference).

Lindsey Godwin is a PhD student in organizational behavior at the Weatherhead School of Management, Case Western Reserve University. She holds an MS in conflict analysis and resolution from George Mason University and a BA in psychology and sociology from Ohio Wesleyan University. She has worked as director of the University Dispute Resolution Project at George Mason and interned with the National Institutes of Health Office of the Ombudsmen and the DC Superior Court's Conflict Resolution Division. Her current research interests include exploring organizational practices that improve organizations' impact on both their workforce and their external environment, including the antecedents and outcomes of organizations that implement a triple-bottom-line approach in their business strategy. Specifically, she is interested in exploring women's leadership, women in entrepreneurship, and the dynamics of using new communicative technologies for building interorganizational coalitions and the promotion of socially responsible business practices.

Erik Hoekstra is chief development officer for Harbor Consulting Group and the Interstates Companies. An experienced organizational and people-development professional, Hoekstra has served leadership roles in wholesale distribution, retail management, and was chairperson of the Business Department at Dordt College, a four-year liberal arts college in Iowa. His consulting and research work focuses on corporate culture and performance, leadership development, strategic planning, and balanced-scorecard implementation. Erik regularly works with senior managers to diagnose, analyze, and provide solutions for organizational challenges across various enterprises, using primarily a "systems thinking" approach to problem solving. He leads seminars in the areas of negotiation, constructive confrontation, performance coaching, delegation, team building, and change-process leadership. Hoekstra holds bachelors degrees in history and philosophy from Trinity Christian College, a master's degree in international management from the Rotterdam School of Management in the Netherlands, and a PhD in organizational learning from Iowa State University. He lives in Sioux Center, Iowa, with his wife, Barb, and their four children.

Rev. Michael W. Honeycutt is senior pastor of Southwood Presbyterian Church (PCA) in Huntsville, Alabama. Before entering the ministry, Honeycutt owned a real estate development firm in Myrtle Beach, South Carolina. Since then, he has served two churches and taught courses in Greek, homiletics, and ecclesiastical history in the United States, Scotland, and Ukraine. He has also authored biographies of nineteenth-century Scottish theologian William Cunningham and seventeenth-century Dutch theologian Herman Witsius, and contributed book reviews to various journals in the United States and Scotland. In addition, he serves as ministerial adviser for Twin Lakes Fellowship, a ministry to strengthen the church, and chairs the Examination Committee for his presbytery. Honeycutt received a BS in building science and an MS in management from Clemson University, an MDiv in theology from Covenant Theological Seminary, and a PhD in ecclesiastical history from the University of Edinburgh. He lives in Huntsville, Alabama, with his wife, Judy, and their three children, Wade, Wesley, and Mary Katherine.

R. Kevin McClean is assistant professor of marketing in the Ken Blanchard College of Business at Grand Canyon University, and brings over thirty years of industry experience to his teaching and writing activities. With expertise in services marketing, performance measurement, electric energy deregulation, and cost analysis, McClean has held progressively responsible assignments in customer service, accounting, financial controls, business planning, and marketing for one of the nation's largest investor-owned utilities. He was a corporate representative to the Edison Electric Institute's (EEI) budgeting and financial forecasting committee and is a past chairman of that committee. He has spoken extensively at the local, state, and national level on issues relating to the deregulation of the electric energy market, has been interviewed by print, radio, and television media concerning electric energy deregulation, and served as an expert witness in this regard in proceedings before a state's regulatory commission staff. He has taught at industry conferences and seminars, including that co-sponsored by the University of Wisconsin-Madison and EEI, on varied subjects including marketing management, planning, business ethics, and budgeting and financial controls. McClean received a BA from King's College, in Pennsylvania; an MBA from St. John's University, in New York; and a Doctor of Professional Studies from Pace University, in New York. He lives in Phoenix, Arizona, with his wife, Mary.

William J. Mea, PhD, is deputy to the chief financial officer at the U.S. Department of Labor and also a commander in the U.S. Naval Reserves. Following completion of graduate studies at Auburn University, he served as a clinical psychologist on active duty in a number of worldwide locations—including in the Persian Gulf during Operation Desert Storm and the U.S. Naval Academy where he taught leadership. Following active military service he worked on reengineering projects and was a manager at KPMG Peat Marwick (now BearingPoint), where his work focused on major information technology initiatives in manufacturing organizations. He has been an appointee in the Bush administration since October 2001 and was recalled to active duty during Operation Iraqi Freedom. His research interests focus on the areas of information technology, manufacturing process, and strategy. He lives in Arlington, Virginia, with his wife of ten years and four young children.

Kenneth L. Murrell is professor of management and MIS at the University of West Florida in Pensacola, Florida. He lives there most of the year with his wife and three children, the rest of the year he spends time in the woods of New Mexico or traveling. He travels and works to support educational programs at three other universities, Pepperdine and its doctoral program in organizational change, Antioch University and its new masters program in Whole Systems Design in Chicago, and the University of Monterrey in Mexico and its wonderful organization development (OD) students and faculty. Ken has a number of organizational clients interested in his OD and empowerment work, and many years ago he was an internal consultant for a large multinational corporation. His passion is centered around using education and organizational development to help advance the work of organizations around the world, and for ten years he worked closely with the United Nations Development Programme in Europe and Africa.

Craig Osten is vice president of Ministry Resources for the Alliance Defense Fund in Scottsdale, Arizona, where he is responsible for the organization's radio, video, and print communications. Osten has over twenty years of managerial experience working for religious nonprofit organizations, including thirteen years at one of the largest religious nonprofit organizations in the world, where he served as the assistant to the organization's founder and president. In this role he provided research and editorial assistance for a number of best-selling books, as well as for monthly publications and a daily radio broadcast. In addition, he has an extensive background in young adult ministries and has served as a political reporter for the CBS affiliate in Sacramento, California. Osten has authored or co-authored several books and book chapters for a number of major publishers, including Tyndale House and Thomas Nelson Publishers. He is married, has one daughter, and lives in northeast Phoenix.

Scott R. Peterson is president of Harbor Group, a holding company for the Interstates Companies and related concerns. An experienced accounting and management professional, Peterson has spent fifteen years both running and building businesses. He has expertise in developing and growing client, vendor, and business partner relationships. He also has a great passion for developing, coaching, and mentoring servant leaders and great business team members. Peterson believes in the importance of offering guidance and providing accountability to team members and business units, and in developing and casting a compelling envisioned future. Peterson is a member of the Construction Financial Management Association, the Institute of Internal Auditors, and the National Association of Corporate Directors. He is also a licensed certified public accountant and certified internal auditor. Peterson received a BS in accounting and an MBA from the University of South Dakota. He lives in Sioux Center, Iowa, with his wife, Jana, and their three children.

Scott A. Quatro is assistant professor of management in the Ken Blanchard College of Business at Grand Canyon University in Phoenix, Arizona. An experienced human resource management and organizational development professional, Quatro has been a senior consultant with a major management consulting firm and a corporate human resource manager for a Fortune 500 retail company. His consulting and research work focuses on strategic human resource management and organizational spirituality. He has authored and co-authored several articles, chapters, and books, including *The Manager as Change Agent* (2001). He serves on the editorial board of the book series *New Perspectives in Organizational Learning, Performance, and Change* from Perseus Publishing as well as the peer review board of the *Journal of Business Ethics.* Quatro received a BA in English from Pepperdine University, an MBA from the College of William and Mary, and a PhD in organizational learning and human resource development from Iowa State University. He lives in Paradise Valley, Arizona, with his wife, Jamie, and their four children.

Lane D. Sauser, DPA, is chief financial officer for the College of Agriculture and the Alabama Agricultural Experiment Station at Auburn University. She earned her BBA degree in marketing and MBA degree in finance from Georgia State University and a doctorate in public administration from the University of Alabama. She is a licensed certified public accountant, as well as a certified government finance officer and certified government financial manager. As chief financial officer, she has primary responsibility for incorporating financial forecasting, budgeting, planning, and reporting, human resources administration, and financial administration of state and federal appropriations for the Alabama Agricultural Experiment Station and College of Agriculture. Previously she was assistant director of the Center for Governmental Services at Auburn University, where she managed and delivered training and financial management consulting services to state and local governments throughout Alabama. She has conducted many workshops on budgeting, financial reporting, financial administration, and performance measurement. She has provided consultation to cities and counties throughout the state on revenue and expenditure analysis, fixed asset management, business licensing administration, and fiscal policy and procedures.

William I. Sauser, Jr., PhD, is associate dean of Business and Engineering Outreach and professor of management at Auburn University. He earned his BS in management and MS and PhD in industrial/organizational psychology at the Georgia Institute of Technology. His interests include organizational development, strategic planning, human relations in the workplace, business ethics, and continuing professional education. He is a Fellow of the American Council on Education and the Society for Advancement of Management, a former president of the Alabama Psychological Association and the Society for Advancement of Management, and a former chair of the Alabama Board of Examiners in Psychology. Sauser was awarded the 2003 Frederick W. Taylor Key by the Society for Advancement of Management in recognition of his career achievements.

Ronald R. Sims is Floyd Dewey Gottwalld Senior Professor in the Graduate School of Business at the College of William and Mary, where he teaches organization behavior, leadership, business ethics, change management, and human resource management. He received his PhD in organizational behavior from Case Western Reserve University. Sims is the author or co-author of twenty books and more than seventy-five articles that have appeared in a wide variety of scholarly and practitioner journals. His most recent books are: *School System Change: Charting a Course for Renewal* (with Serbrenia J. Sims) (2004); *Ethics and Corporate Social Responsibility: Why Giants Fall* (2003); *Teaching Business Ethics for Effective Learning* (2002); *Organizational Success through Effective Human Resources Management* (2002); *Changing the Way We Manage Change* (2002); and *Managing Organizational Behavior* (2002). His research focuses on a variety of topics including leadership and change management, human resources management, employee training and management development, learning styles, experiential learning, and business ethics. Sims has provided consultation in the areas of change management, human resources management, and employee and leadership development to organizations in the private, public, and not-for-profit sectors over the past twenty-one years.

Serbrenia J. Sims is a private consultant and former director of Accountability Assessment and Grants Writing for Williamsburg-James City County Public Schools in Williamsburg, Virginia. She received her doctorate in higher education administration from the College of William and Mary and a masters of public administration from Auburn University at Montgomery. She has taught K-12 and has an endorsement in educational administration from the state of Virginia. She has published several articles, books, and chapters in books in the areas of testing and accountability, total quality management, human resource management, and diversity awareness. Her research interests include curriculum development, strategic planning, program evaluation, and integrating technology in the classroom. She has served as a clinical faculty member for Williamsburg-James City County Schools and the School of Education at the College of William and Mary.

Rev. Clay Smith serves as assistant pastor at Covenant Community Church, Scottsdale, Arizona, a member congregation of the Presbyterian Church in America. Prior to joining the church staff, Smith worked with a relief and development organization operating throughout the third world. He also held administrative and teaching-assistant positions at a graduate theological school. Rev. Smith received a BS in biochemistry and molecular biology from Mississippi State University and MDiv from Covenant Theological Seminary. He resides in Scottsdale, Arizona, with his wife, Missy, and their daughter.

Joe A. Sumners, PhD, is director of the Economic Development Institute (EDI) at Auburn University. Prior to his appointment to this position in 2002, he served for two years as associate director of EDI. Before coming to EDI, he served as training and research coordinator for Auburn University's Center for Governmental Services. He also served on the political science faculty at the University of Alabama at Birmingham and Stephen F. Austin State University in Nacodoches, Texas. Sumners received his BS and MA degrees from Auburn University and his PhD from the University of Georgia. A member of the board of directors of Alabama Communities of Excellence, he has conducted over 150 workshops and courses for Alabama county and municipal officers over the past ten years. He has directed strategic planning efforts in the Alabama cities of Northport, Sylacauga, Brewton, Gadsden, Uniontown, and Eufala; helped prepare an economic development plan for Shelby County; and currently is directing strategic planning projects for Pickens County, Hale County, and the City of Monroe.

Christopher Taylor is a director at Blackwater USA, a private military company and homeland security consulting firm. He spent thirteen years in the Marine Corps as an Infantryman and Force Recon Marine. As a marine, he was the Distinguished Honor Graduate at Non-commissioned Officer's Leadership Course, received the Leadership Award at Amphibious Reconnaissance School, and again received the Leadership Award at the U.S. Marine Combatant Diver Course. After leaving the Marine Corps as a staff sergeant, Chris attended graduate school at William and Mary, where he earned his MBA in 2002 and received the Dean's Award for Leadership and Service at graduation. Prior to becoming a director at Blackwater USA, Chris taught visit, board, search, and seizure (VBSS) and force protection tactics to sailors at the Antiterrorism Warfare Development Group at Blackwater.

John R. Visser is professor of business administration and chair of the department of business and economics at Dordt College in Sioux Center, Iowa. His writing is informed by experience in banking, importing and exporting, consulting, and a quarter century of teaching experience in the United States, Africa, Asia, and Eastern and Western Europe. Visser's research and writing has shifted over time from the highly specialized and quantitative world of mathematically modeling bank stock prices to the interdisciplinary roots of value creation, that is, the role of culture, civil society, and religious beliefs and practices in economic development, the creation of wealth, and the well-being of societies. His writings have ranged from an article in the *Financial Analyst's Journal*, to co-authoring a chapter in *Civil Society: A Foundation for Economic Development*, to a background paper for the Russian Unity Party's platform, to articles in religious periodicals. Visser received his BS in industrial engineering from the University of Illinois, an MBA from De Paul University, and a PhD in business administration (finance) from the University of Alabama. He lives in Sioux Center, Iowa, with his wife, Linda.

L. Keith Whitney is an associate professor of business law and finance and chair of the business administration division at Seaver College, Pepperdine University, Malibu, California. An experienced attorney who practiced law in Illinois, Whitney has authored several articles on various aspects of corporate law and finance. He also worked as a tax accountant with Arthur Andersen & Company in St. Louis, Missouri. His current interest relates to leadership theory and practice. He is a consultant in leadership development with a focus on servant leadership. Whitney is also an ordained minister and co-author of a religious book, *Living with God: Devotions to Strengthen Your Christian Walk* (1997). Whitney received a BS in finance and an MBA from Eastern Illinois University and a Juris Doctorate from Texas Tech University. He lives in Newbury Park, California, with his wife, Karen. He is the proud father of two daughters, Kirsten and Kari.

Michael D. Yonker is executive vice president and chief financial officer of InFocus Corporation (NASDAQ: INFS), the worldwide leader in digital projection technologies located in Wilsonville, Oregon. A former certified public accountant, Yonker also has served as CFO of Wieden + Kennedy in Portland, Oregon, from 1998 to 2001. He also served as CFO of InFocus from 1993 through 1998. Prior to that, he was a partner with Arthur Andersen & Company, where he worked from 1980 through 1992. His specialties have included high-tech initial public offerings and organizational development. Yonker received his bachelors degree in accounting and finance from Linfield College. He and his wife, Robin, have been married for twenty-four years. They have three children—two sons at Pepperdine University and a daughter in high school.

INDEX